Knowing God
PERSONALLY

The following four principles will help you discover how to know God personally and experience the abundant life he promised.

1 *God loves you and created you to know him personally.*

(references should be read in context wherever possible.)

God's Love
"God loved the people of this world so much that he gave his only Son, so that everyone who has faith in him will have eternal life and never really die." *(John 3.16)*

God's Plan
"Eternal life is to know you, the only true God, and to know Jesus Christ, the one you sent." *(John 17.3)*

⋯⟩ *What prevents us from knowing God personally?*

2 *Man is sinful and separated from God, so we cannot know him personally or experience his love.*

Man is Sinful
"All of us have sinned and fallen short of God's glory." *(Romans 3.23)*

Man was created to have fellowship with God; but, because of his stubborn self-will, he chose to go his own independent way and fellowship with God was broken. This self-will, characterized by an attitude of active rebellion or passive indifference, is evidence of what the Bible calls sin.

Man is Separated
"Sin pays off with death." [spiritual separation from God] *(Romans 6.23)*

This diagram illustrates that God is holy and people are sinful. A great gulf separates the two. The arrows illustrate that people are continually trying to reach God and establish a personal relationship with Him through our own efforts, such as a good life, philosophy, or religion, but we inevitably fail.

┄┅▷ *The third principle explains the only way to bridge this gulf...*

3 Jesus Christ is God's only provision for man's sin. Through him alone we can know God personally and experience God's love.

He Died in Our Place
"But God showed how much he loved us by having Christ die for us, even though we were sinful." *(Romans 5.8)*

He Rose From the Dead
"Christ died for our sins . . . He was buried, and three days later he was raised to life, as the Scriptures say. Christ appeared to Peter, then to the twelve. After this, He appeared to more than five hundred other followers." *(1 Corinthians 15.3–6a)*

He is the Only Way to God
"'I am the way, the truth, and the life!' Jesus answered. 'Without me, no one can go to the Father.'" *(John 14.6)*

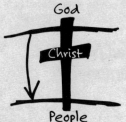

This diagram illustrates that God has bridged the gulf that separates us from him by sending his Son, Jesus Christ, to die on the cross in our place to pay the penalty for our sins.

┄┅▷ *It is not enough just to know these truths...*

We must individually receive Jesus Christ as Savior and Lord; then we can know God personally and experience His love.

We Must Receive Christ
"Yet some people accepted him, and put their faith in him. So he gave them the right to be the children of God." *(John 1.12)*

We Receive Christ Through Faith
"You were saved by faith in God, who treats us much better than we deserve [grace]. This is God's gift to you, and not anything you have done on your own. It isn't something you have earned, so there is nothing you can brag about." *(Ephesians 2.8,9)*

When We Receive Christ, We Experience a New Birth
(Read John 3.1–8.)

Self-Directed Life
S *Self is on the throne*
† *Christ is outside the life*
• *Interests are directed by self, often resulting in discord and frustration*

Christ-Directed Life
† *Christ is in the life and on the throne*
S *Self is yielding to Christ*
• *Interests are directed by Christ, resulting in harmony with God's plan*

We Receive Christ by Personal Invitation
[Christ speaking] "Listen! I am standing and knocking at your door. If you hear my voice and open the door, I will come in and we will eat together." *(Revelation 3.20)*

Receiving Christ involves turning to God from self (repentance) and trusting Christ to come into our lives to forgive us of our sins and to make us what he wants us to be. Just to agree intellectually that Jesus Christ is the son of God and that he died on the cross for our sins is not enough. Nor is it enough to have an emotional experience. We receive Jesus Christ by faith, as an act of the will.

These two circles represent two kinds of lives:

Which circle best describes your life? Which circle would you like to have represent your life?

···❖ *The following explains how you can receive Christ:*

You can receive Christ right now by faith through prayer

(Prayer is talking with God)

God knows your heart and is not concerned with your words as he is with the attitude of your heart. The following is a suggested prayer:

"Lord Jesus, I want to know you personally. Thank you for dying on the cross for my sins. I open the door of my life and receive you as my Savior and Lord. Thank you for forgiving me of my sins and giving me eternal life. Take control of the throne of my life. Make me the kind of person you want me to be."

Does this prayer express the desire of your heart?

If it does, pray this prayer right now, and Christ will come into your life, as he promised.

If you just prayed that prayer we would like to help you grow in your new faith in Christ. Send us an e-mail at our website (http://www.thecampusministry.com) and we'll try to put you in touch with people near you who can help you understand the Bible more and introduce you to other people who have a relationship with God. The following material will help you understand more about what you've just done.

How to know that Christ is in your life

Did you receive Christ into your life?

According to his promise in Revelation 3.20, where is Christ right now in relation to you? Christ said that he would come into your life and be your friend so you can know him personally. Would he mislead you? On what authority do you know that God has answered your prayer? (The trustworthiness of God himself and his Word.)

The Bible Promises Eternal Life to All Who Receive Christ
"God has also said that he gave us eternal life, and that this life comes to us from his Son. And so, if we have God's Son, we have this life. But if we don't have the Son, we don't have this life." *(1 John 5.11–13)*

Thank God often that Christ is in your life and that he will never leave you (Hebrews 13.5). You can know on the basis of His promise that Christ lives in you and that you have eternal life from the very moment you invite him in. He will not deceive you.

⋯⟡ *An important reminder...*

Do not depend on feelings

The promise of God's Word, the Bible—not our feelings—is our authority. The Christian lives by faith (trust) in the trustworthiness of God himself and his Word. This train diagram illustrates the relationship among fact (God and his Word), faith (our trust in God and his Word), and feeling (the result of our faith and obedience) (John 14.21).

The train will run with or without a caboose. However, it would be useless to attempt to pull the train by the caboose. In the same way, we as Christians do not depend on feelings or emotions, but we place our faith (trust) in the trustworthiness of God and the promises of his Word.

Now that you have entered into a personal relationship with Christ

The moment you received Christ by faith, as an act of your will, many things happened, including the following:

1   Christ came into your life (Revelation 3.20 and Colossians 1.27).
2   Your sins were forgiven (Colossians 1.14).
3   You became a child of God (John 1.12).
4   You received eternal life (John 5.24).
5   You began the great adventure for which God created you (John 10.10; 2 Corinthians 5.17 and 1 Thessalonians 5.18).

Can you think of anything more wonderful that could happen to you than entering into a personal relationship with Jesus Christ? Would you like to thank God in prayer right now for what he has done for you? By thanking God, you demonstrate your faith.

····⁕ *To enjoy your new relationship with God...*

Suggestions for Christian growth

Spiritual growth results from trusting Jesus Christ. "The people God accepts because of their faith will live" (Galatians 3.11). A life of faith will enable you to trust God increasingly with every detail of your life, and to practice the following:

G   Go to God in prayer daily (John 15.7).

R   Read God's Word daily (Acts 17.11)—begin with John's Gospel.

O   Obey God moment by moment (John 14.21).

W   Witness for Christ by your life and words (Matthew 4.19; John 15.8).

T   Trust God for every detail of your life (1 Peter 5.7).

H   Holy Spirit—Allow him to control and empower your daily life and witness (Galatians 5.16,17; Acts 1.8).

Fellowship in a good church

God's Word admonishes us not to forsake "the the habit of meeting for worship…" (Hebrews 10.25). Several logs burn brightly together; but put one aside on the cold hearth and the fire goes out. So it is with your relationship with other Christians. If you do not belong to a church, do not wait to be invited. Take the initiative; call the pastor of a nearby church where Christ is honored and his Word is preached. Start this week, and make plans to attend regularly.

If you would like additional information, visit us online at **http://www.uscm.org** or write us at:

Campus Crusade for Christ
U.S. Campus Ministry
100 Lake Hart Drive 2500
Orlando, FL 32832-0100

Answers

to the Top 5 Questions College Students Would Ask God

If you could ask God any question, what would you ask him? That is what we asked hundreds of college students recently. Most were a bit tongue-tied at first, but eventually came up with some good questions. And really, wouldn't we all like to know the answers to these questions about God that have stumped us all our lives? According to our survey of more than 600 students, these are the top five questions you would like God to answer:

1. Why is there so much evil and suffering in the world?
2. Will God really forgive all of my sins?
3. What does the future hold for me?
4. What does God want from me?
5. Aren't all religions the same?

Not all questions we got were that great. Here are some of the questions we saved to answer at another time:

Why the '70s?

Who killed JFK?

Why am I going bald?

Why is the grass green and the sky blue?

Do we amuse you?

Is there a Bermuda Triangle?

Why are there exams?

Why ask why?

Good questions require good answers. That's why we pooled together a few of our keenest minds to come up with some respectable, reasoned answers. We don't claim to know everything, but it's a start. Try this as an experiment: ponder these first five questions on your own and then compare your responses with ours. If you like what you read, then there's a whole lot more for you to discover as you read the rest of this most incredible Book (because that's where we really got the answers).

1

Why is there so much evil and suffering in the world?

Our biggest question with evil is, "Why doesn't God prevent it from happening?" If he really is this all-good, all-powerful being, doesn't he have the resources to prevent all this suffering?

The best response Christian theologians give is that if God prevented the opportunity for doing evil things then we would be mere robots. If this were true, God could not allow anyone to think or act freely.

For us to be truly free, God gives us the opportunity to make our own choices, even if one of the choices brings harm to others. But it is a fallacy to say that God is unconcerned about all the evil going on around us. Like a loving parent, he is compassionate and caring.

The question we really need to ask: "Is there any purpose behind our suffering?" From the Bible we see some reasons for suffering:

To develop character

In the fifth chapter of the letter to the Romans, the apostle Paul writes that suffering produces endurance, and endurance produces character, and out of character comes hope. This is the hope inside our hearts that God is with us and will give us the strength and faith to sustain us in adversity.

To get our attention

Does suffering equal eternal judgment or punishment? No. Rather suffering is sometimes the loving discipline of a father who has our best interests at heart.

The purpose of God's discipline in our lives is not vindictiveness, but instead that we become more like him. "It is never fun to be corrected. In fact, at the time it is always painful. But if we learn to obey by being corrected, we will do right and live at peace" (Hebrews 12.11). He is removing everything that inhibits us from becoming like him. Perhaps there is an area of our lives that we've been unwilling to turn over to him. God may choose to use suffering in that area as his tool to get our attention and listen to him.

To bring praise to God

Most of the time what we really want is an end to the pain that comes from the suffering. It may be that our perspective is skewed. We think everything is a cause-and-effect relationship. Sometimes things happen just to show that God is in control and that he is able to work in people's lives. (See John 9.1–3.)

The English author C.S. Lewis said that 80 percent of suffering comes because of the moral evilness of humankind. If we believe what he said, what are we to do with the other 20 percent? Answer: There are just some things we are never going to fully understand here on Earth.

We do know that God is good, he is in control, and he is not the author of sin. If any of these three points were not true, he would not be the all-powerful, benevolent God of the Bible. This is sometimes hard to believe when we've just experienced a personal tragedy or hardship. And if it is true that God is all-good, all-powerful and is concerned, then we now have a moral grid to help us see God's plan through our suffering.

Jesus seemed drawn like a magnet to human grief, sorrow, and suffering. Often in the Gospels Jesus' statements and actions are preceded by these words, "He felt sorry for them..."

So, God allows suffering and feels the emotions of hurt and pity when we suffer. He also does something active to deal with it. He comforts us in the middle of our suffering when we allow him. He also helps us in our healing process. Finally, he gives us the greatest Healer of all—his Son, Jesus, who endured the greatest suffering (on the cross) so that we would not have to suffer forever for our sins.

Sure, it hurts to embrace the pain of others (or of ourselves) but always remember, God is right there with us to help make sense of it all even when it seems senseless. Since there really is a God of the kind we have described, then guilty people who seem to get away with their crimes here on Earth will all have their day of reckoning eventually.

And that's why we need to be connected with God in order to understand why we suffer. Even if we never understand the exact "whys" behind our suffering, we can still receive comfort and strength from a God who genuinely understands and cares about us.

Thank you to Dave Carlson, Tom Cox, Tim Downs, Su Hecht, Mark Hurt, Greg Kriefall, Bruce McCluggage and Dave Patchin.

Will God really forgive all of my sins?

Experiencing guilt is like being a live rabbit in the mouth of an enthusiastic dog. It grabs us by the neck and shakes us around. We feel totally helpless until released from its grip.

This is how it feels when we don't feel forgiven. Whether we feel bad for hurting another person or doing something we know God wouldn't want us to do, guilt grabs us by the neck and shakes us about.

We respond in different ways to this guilt. We beat ourselves up for being such a bad person. Or we try to justify our actions. None of this truly gets rid of the guilt. What we need is forgiveness, whether from the other person or God.

To experience the forgiveness of God we need to accept what God says about payment for sin. God has declared that people have turned away from him and needed to be punished. Because of his great love and justice, God sent his son, Jesus Christ, to pay the penalty for our sin. Our response is to accept that forgiveness. If you have never done this, you can look at the supplemental section called *Knowing God Personally*. If you have received his forgiveness through Jesus Christ, then let's look at what the Bible says about forgiveness.

God has an infinite capacity and ability to forgive.

If Christ is a complete provision for our sin, then we must have complete forgiveness of our sins, from the past, present and future. The forgiveness issue rests on the adequacy of Christ's provision and our response to that provision. The reason Christ's sacrifice for sins completely satisfies the justice of God is that, unlike us, Jesus was perfect. That is why his death was acceptable to God and paid for our sin, once for all. God has an infinite capacity and ability to forgive. We often experience a limit to forgiveness in our human relationships, therefore we translate that experience to our relationship with God. But we ought not think of God in the same category. Unlike humans, God's forgiveness is not limited.

But guilt can be tenacious. Ever had a flashback—something bad from your past that continually comes back to your mind to haunt you? We need to remember that God has genuinely forgiven all our sins. We need to trust God and his promise to us that he has truly forgiven us when we've placed our trust in Christ's death as payment for our sin.

Here's what you can do to experience God's forgiveness:

Confess your sin

Confession means to agree with God. When we confess our sins, we are simply agreeing with God that we have sinned against him. It is an admission of guilt. If you want your relationship with God to be restored completely, then you must confess your sins to God. Admit to him that you have sinned. Unconfessed sin can block us from enjoying our relationship with God. Confession is the way to restore our relationship to God the way he intended it to be. We never lose our relationship with God, but when we have unconfessed sin in our lives, we do lose that warm friendship with him.

It's like a relationship with your mother. If you do something to hurt her, she will still be your mother but you won't have a friendship with her. But if you admit your wrong to her and she forgives you then your friendship has been restored. The same is true with God. Our sin will inhibit our friendship with him. We need to do something about it and that is confession.

> But if we confess our sins to God, he can always be trusted to forgive us and take our sins away. (1 John 1.9)

Agree we've been forgiven

This is where faith comes in. We need to trust God that he has already forgiven us and he will no longer punish us for our sins.

Turn away from your sin

To repent means to turn away from sin, to change one's mind. It expresses sorrow for sin. Repenting from a sin is expressing the desire to quit doing what you just confessed. This is not always an easy process. When we sin, we naturally want to run away from God, not to him. It takes perseverance to keep coming back to God to confess one's sin.

Making amends is another part of repentance. If you've stolen something, you need to return it. If you broke something, you need to pay for it. If you've hurt someone's feelings, you need to apologize and restore your relationship with that person. And you need to forgive those who have hurt you.

> "If you forgive others for the wrongs they do to you, your Father in heaven will forgive you. But if you don't forgive others, your father will not forgive your sins." (Matthew 6.14,15)

> Instead, be kind and merciful, and forgive others, just as God forgave you because of Christ. (Ephesians 4.32)

This is the forgiveness God intends for you. The result is experiencing authentic joy and freedom that comes from knowing God. He no longer views you as guilty. You are free to relate to your Creator not as an offended judge but as a gentle Father (Romans 8.15). The guilt you carry can be removed. When you seek forgiveness through Christ, you move from being alienated from God to being the object of his delight!

Thank you to Dave Carlson, Su Hecht, Greg Kriefall, Dawson McAllister, Bruce McCluggage, Gary Purdy, and John Studebaker.

What does the future hold for me?

When we consider God, it seems only natural to ask him about our future. Deep down we somehow know that God is big and awesome and all-knowing. "So why doesn't he let us in on some of what he knows?" we ask. He does, if we know where to look. Many of us don't bother, however, so we go looking somewhere else.

And a-searching we will go—palm readers, fortune tellers, horoscopes, psychic hotlines and fortune cookies. Book and movie sales usually do well when a futuristic scene of what the world could be like is involved. Some of us sit up and notice when a new prophet or wise man is discovered by the current media whose predictions have rung somewhat true through the ages.

Trying to figure out what academic degree to pursue? Now even YOU have become a part of the 'fortune-telling' crowd if you are one of those concerned about your starting salary and the economic laws of supply and demand when it comes to professions.

However, none of these dimly lit pursuits of prediction seem to satisfy our cravings for knowledge of the future. We probably don't realize WHY we want to know the future to begin with. If we first ask,"Why know the future?", then we can get at what we really desire out of this life.

So, for what do we really long? Do we realize the deep internal needs behind our pursuit of things in the world?

A co-ed sleeps around with some guys from a fraternity hoping to eventually bag one of them as a boyfriend. What she really needs is to feel love and acceptance. A stud athlete works out every day to eventually make the football team. What he really needs is to feel respect. An intellectual giant spends endless nights in the science lab hoping to validate his latest theory. What he really needs to feel is

> *We probably don't realize WHY we want to know the future to begin with.*

significance. A business degree student "works over" her peers hoping to garner an office in the entrepreneur club. What she really needs to feel is worth.

Our question about our futures should not be over what boyfriend or girlfriend or job or accolades may come our way, but how will our ultimate needs of love, security, recognition, and significance be met. Could it be that we have been looking in the wrong places for the answers to what our futures may hold?

Any question of the future can best be answered by recognizing the origin of the question. If we have a future then by necessity we also have a present and finally a past. How far back could we go? To the origin of it all. And here we have a choice. Either we are here as a result of chance chemical reactions occurring with no design or order over a period of billions of years, or we have ultimately come into existence as a result of an Intelligent Designer who created from nothing the universe and everything in it.

If there really is a God and he has created you, then two important questions follow: 1) Where will you spend eternity? and 2) What is your purpose for existing here on earth? These two questions help focus on the more important aspects of one's future. They cover the two time frames that make up everyone's life—the time one lives here on earth and the eternity after death.

The answers to these two overarching life realities lay the foundation of how you view every future decision you make. In fact, one can easily see that once the question of where one spends eternity is answered, then this will profoundly affect how one answers the second one about life here on earth.

> *Because of God's eternal nature and never-ending love toward his children, this security need never be shaken.*

Therefore, the question "What does the future hold for me?" really dissolves into "Where will I spend eternity and how can I know for sure?" Now we must humbly come to the Maker of the galaxies and inquire of him. And what is his response? Plenty. God has sent prophets and messengers throughout history to tell of God and his character. These have all been recorded in the Bible, God's Word to us. You now hold a special portion of that in your very hands.

In the letter to the Romans in the New Testament, we are told that God has given us minds to help us reason about truth. He has also made us with consciences to help us determine what is right and what is wrong, what pleases God and what does not. God also became flesh and lived here on earth. His son, Jesus, came not just as another prophet or wise man, he came to be the world's savior by dying as a sacrifice for all of the world's sin.

As we place our faith and trust in Jesus we become "a new person" (2 Corinthians 5.17). From that point on, we can be sure of God's promise to us that we will spend eternity in heaven with him. This is a result of God making us spiritually alive as we place our faith in Jesus. This means we admit our sins before God and then place them upon Christ who came to pay the just penalty upon the cross. For more information on this read the section titled, *Knowing God Personally.*

The Christian's certainty in his future now becomes based upon God and his unchanging promises for his life. It is no longer based on circumstances which can flux or be destroyed in a moment's notice. Even the ultimate threat of losing our very lives does not change any aspects of our relationship with God. We will spend eternity with him and it all begins not when we die but the moment we respond to God's love for us by placing our faith and trust in him and his Word.

God changes our hearts and attitudes and causes us to want to love and serve him and others in ways that we could not do before we knew him. We experience a peace that literally goes beyond understanding even in the midst of trying circumstances that may have devastated us before. God gives us the stable qualities of joy and expectancy as we live out our lives on a day-to-day basis, constantly growing stronger in our character, as we learn more about God and what he wants to do in and through our lives.

These qualities of love, peace, and joy are but a few of the things in store for our futures as Christians. They are the real needs and desires that we all long for.

Not only are these incredible traits reflected more and more in the Christian's life but with them comes a tremendous security. This security is based upon God's unchanging forgiveness of the believer who has trusted in Christ. Because of God's eternal nature and never-ending love toward his children, this security need never be shaken.

Since many students do not understand this deep need for security, they often feel worried or even discouraged when they ponder their futures. Some don't even want to think about next semester in light of all their present-day problems. Others live in the past of their hurts and pain and subsequent bitterness.

On the other hand, some students may have a bright overly optimistic view of their future because they have yet to encounter one of life's harsher realities, but when they do...crash, boom, smash. The class they wanted is already filled, their girlfriend or boyfriend dumps them off at the curb, they lose a job, a good friend betrays them, they start failing their first class, school funds dry up, their best friend dies in an accident—these are just a few. Their security was based on a false premise that all the wonderful things that have carried their lives in the past would automatically continue in the future. This hardly ever happens!

Whether overly idealistic or pessimistic, God never intended us to live this way. We need something outside of ourselves, outside of the temporary, external things in the world to give us the meaning and the constancy that our hearts long to feel...we want a love that will never die.

What does the future hold for me? You really don't want a list of 100 predictions, you want to know that everything is going to be all right. And with God, it will be ultimately. Why? Because he made you. While you may not know what the future holds, you can know that God is the one who holds the future and that he is good and in control (Jeremiah 29.11,12).

Look at all the things around you that were designed and invented by humans to make your life a little easier. All of them were made for an intended purpose or function. And they all operate best when used according to the original designer's plans. Are you not worth much more than these inanimate objects? Even though you may have a wonderful family that loves you and friends that have the best in mind for you, can that compare with the God of the universe? He knows exactly what you need and desires for you to live out the best life you can live.

By Bruce McCluggage

4 What does God want from me?

Whenever we think about God, it seems inevitable that we'll ask him (or others) what in the world does he really want from us.

However, we run into an internal conflict right away when we ponder who God is compared to who we are. God is perfect. He does not sin or do evil things. He is perfect and totally just in all his ways. This is what is meant when God says he is holy. The "problem" is when we realize that this is also what God requires of us. He states quite clearly in the Bible, "Be holy as I am holy."

We actually need God to be perfect. If not, then what would our lives be like if, whenever God spoke to his creation, all his decrees would now be open for revision and updates? All his commandments would be reduced to nothing more than really good advice.

Here's our problem: If God really is good, then he has no option but to exercise his wrath and judgment of our sin. Remember, if God is holy and pure then he cannot stand to be in the presence of evil.

So, God's perfection and his ensuing expectation of perfection in us does three things. First, it tells us what God is like and that we can actually trust God to even greater degrees because we know he will always act consistently and truthfully with us.

Second, God's standard of perfection actually benefits all of us, for without rules and order in the world, we would probably self-destruct in a short amount of time. Total anarchy and chaos would reign. God's laws written on our hearts compel us to at least want to do the right thing even though we may not even acknowledge God at times.

Third, God is the only one who can provide a solution for the problem of our falling short of God's perfect standard. Remember, we can't take a shortcut by asking God to lower his standard either.

What does God want from us? Answer: He wants us to quit trying to "fix" ourselves.

Our sin and its destructive consequences hurts and damages people. But we don't really understand the impact of sin until we recognize that it hurts God most of all. In fact, the Bible describes God as grieving over his lost and sinful creation. Not just in general either, but for each and every time one of us turns his back on him.

Once we fully grasp what God has saved us from, the attitude of thankfulness and service to God will be a natural outflowing. We don't have to work at thanking folks for things they do for us, we simply open our mouths and the words come; we see a need, and our hands and feet go into motion. We don't have to think about it or plan for it or psych ourselves up to do it. This same thing happens with our relationship with God.

God offers us a purpose and a plan for our lives, and never quits initiating with us even when we have turned our backs on him or have just plain forgotten about his love. We simply open our hand and receive what we somehow knew all along we needed—forgiveness.

We cannot earn God's approval.

What does God want from us? Answer: Receive what he has already done to solve the problem of our imperfection, and then thank him for it. Specifially, we need to acknowledge that Jesus Christ died on the cross in our place to pay the penalty for our sins.

Now we can understand those initial answers to the question of what God wants from us. He desires perfection because He himself is perfect. And since we are made in God's image we too can understand moral rights and wrongs, and choose between what is perfect and what is imperfect. God also desires perfection because it is the best way for us to live.

However, we all fail in this endeavor. Even our good works point to our sinful natures, thinking we can help God forgive or accept us more. We cannot earn God's approval. This brings us to utter despair and gloom, which is exactly where God wants us in order to fully understand and appreciate all of what he did on his part to restore our broken relationship with him. All we need do is humbly receive what God has already done through Jesus' sacrificial death on the cross, paying the penalty for our sin. As a result, we freely show our gratitude through word and deed back to God and his world.

As you begin to more fully embrace what it is that God has already done for you, can you see that the original question of "What does God want from me?" becomes "What do I get to do for God?" As you live out the answers to that question, you will be thrilled to know that God has something far better in store than what you could have ever imagined.

By Bruce McCluggage

Aren't all religions the same?

We'll take a look at a few major world faith systems—Hinduism, New Age, Buddhism, Islam, Christianity. Each of these religions has sects with differing beliefs. The description given here focuses on the heart of that religion. Here you will find a brief description of each, the distinguishing characteristics of each spiritual belief system, and how Christianity is unique in comparison.

Hinduism

Most Hindus worship a multitude of gods and goddesses, some 300,000 of them. These various gods all converge into a universal spirit called the Ultimate Reality or Brahman. Brahman is not a god but more of a term for ultimate oneness.

Hindus see their position in life as based on their actions in a previous life. If their behavior was evil, they might experience tremendous hardships in this life. A Hindu's goal is to become free from the law of karma ... to be free from continuous reincarnations.

There are three possible ways to end this cycle of karma:
1. Be lovingly devoted to any of the Hindu gods or goddesses;
2. Grow in knowledge through the meditation of Brahman (oneness)—to realize that circumstances in life are not real, that selfhood is an illusion and only Brahman is real;
3. Be dedicated to various religious ceremonies and rites.

New Age

New Age promotes the development of the person's own power or divinity. When referring to god, a follower of New Age is not talking about a transcendent, personal God who created the universe, but is referring to a higher consciousness within themselves. A person in New Age would see themselves as god, the cosmos, the universe. In fact, everything that the person sees, hears, feels or imagines is to be considered divine.

Highly eclectic, New Age presents itself as a collection of ancient spiritual traditions. It acknowledges many gods and goddesses, as in Hinduism. The Earth is viewed as the source of all spirituality and has its own intelligence, emotions and deity. But superceding all is self. Self is the originator, controller and god of all. There is no reality outside of what the person determines.

New Age teaches a wide array of eastern mysticism and spiritual, metaphysical and psychic techniques—such as breathing exercises, chanting, drumming, meditating—to develop an altered consciousness and one's own divinity.

Buddhism

Buddhists do not worship any gods or God. People outside of Buddhism often think that Buddhists worship the Buddha. However, Buddha (Siddhartha Gautama) never claimed to be divine, and Buddhists reject the notion of any supernatural power. The Buddhists see the universe as operating by natural law. Life is seen as consisting of pain: pain in birth, sickness, death, and continuous sorrow and despair.

Most Buddhists believe a person has hundreds or thousands of reincarnations, all bringing misery. And it is the desire for happiness that causes a person's reincarnation. Therefore, the goal of a Buddhist is to purify one's heart and to let go of all desires. A person must abandon all sensuous pleasures, all evil, all joy and all sorrow.

To do so, Buddhists are to follow a list of religious principles and intense meditation. When a Buddhist meditates it is not the same as praying or focusing on a god, it is more of a self-discipline. Through dedicated meditation a person may reach Nirvana—"the blowing out" of the flame of desire.

Islam

A follower of Islam is called a Muslim. Muslims believe there is the one almighty God, named Allah, who is infinitely superior and distant from humankind. Allah is viewed as the creator of the universe and the source of all good and all evil. Everything that happens is Allah's will. He is a powerful and strict judge, too great to be approached by people. So it is impossible for individuals to have a relationship with Allah or know much about him.

Though a Muslim honors several prophets, Muhammad is considered the last or most recent prophet, therefore his words and lifestyle are the Muslim's authority. To be a Muslim, one has to follow five religious duties, called the Five Pillars of Islam:

1. Repeat a creed about Allah and Muhammad;
2. Recite certain prayers in Arabic five times a day while facing Mecca;
3. Give to the needy;
4. Observe Ramadan: one month each year, fast from food, drink, sex and smoking from sunrise to sunset;
5. Pilgrimage once in one's lifetime to worship at a shrine in Mecca.

At death—based on one's faithfulness to these duties—a Muslim hopes to enter Paradise, a place of sensual pleasure. If not, they will be eternally punished in hell.

Christianity

Christians believe in a God of justice and love who has revealed himself and can be personally known in this life. In Christianity the believer's focus is not on religious rituals or performing good works, but on enjoying a loving relationship with God and growing in their knowledge of him.

Faith in Jesus Christ himself, not just in his teachings, is how the Christian experiences joy and a meaningful life. In his life on earth Jesus did not identify himself as a prophet pointing to God or as a teacher of enlightenment. Rather, Jesus claimed to be God in human form. He performed miracles, forgave people of their sin and said that anyone who believed in him would have eternal life. He made statements like, "I am the light for the world! Follow me, and you won't be walking in the dark. You will have the light that gives life" (John 8.12).

Christians regard the Bible as God's written message to humankind. In addition to it being an historical record of Jesus' life and miracles, the Bible reveals God's personality, his love and truth, and how one can have a relationship with him.

What is the difference?

In looking at these major belief systems and their views of God, we find tremendous diversity:

Hindus believe in 300,000 gods.
Buddhists say there is no deity.
New Age followers believe they are god.
Muslims believe in a powerful but detached god.
Christians believe in a God who is loving and approachable.

Obviously, it is not logical to affirm that all of these claims are equally valid. They cannot all be true, for they affirm contrary claims.

The world's major faiths (Hinduism, New Age, Buddhism, Islam, Christianity) are each quite unique. Christianity affirms that there is a personal, loving God who can be known in this life. Christianity speaks of a God who welcomes us into a relationship with him and comes along side us as a comforter, counselor and powerful God who loves us.

You can begin a relationship with God right now. It is as simple as asking God for his forgiveness of your sin and inviting him to enter your life. You can do so right now, simply by telling him your heart's desire: "God, I ask you to forgive me and invite you to enter my heart right now. Thank you Jesus for dying for my sins. Thank you for coming into my life as you said you would."

In other religions a person has a relationship with teachings, ideas, paths, rituals. In Christianity a person can have a relationship with the loving and powerful God. You can talk with him and he will guide you in this life now. He doesn't just point you to a path, a philosophy. He welcomes you to know him, to experience joy, and to have confidence in a loving God in the midst of life's challenges. "Think how much the Father loves us. He loves us so much that he lets us be called his children, as we truly are" (1 John 3.1).

By Marilyn Adamson

The
NEW
TESTAMENT

with
Psalms and Proverbs

Contemporary English Version

PUBLISHED
for
CAMPUS CRUSADE FOR CHRIST
by

AMERICAN BIBLE SOCIETY
NEW YORK

The NEW TESTAMENT

Contemporary English Version

Quotation Rights For The Contemporary English Version

The American Bible Society is glad to grant authors and publishers the right to use up to one thousand (1,000) verses from the *Contemporary English Version* text in church, religious and other publications without the need to seek and receive written permission. However, the extent of quotation must not comprise a complete book nor should it amount to more than 50% of the work. The proper copyright notice must appear on the title or copyright page.

When quotations from *CEV* are used in a non-saleable media, such as church bulletins, orders of service, poster, transparencies or similar media, a complete copyright notice is not required, but the initials *(CEV)* must appear at the end of each quotation.

Requests for quotations in excess of one thousand (1,000) verses in any publication must be directed to, and written approval received from, the American Bible Society, 1865 Broadway, New York, NY 10023.

Cover design and auxiliary material at the front provided by
The Campus Media Team, Campus Crusade for Christ

Text: Copyright © 1995, American Bible Society
Maps: Copyright © 1976, 1978, United Bible Societies
ISBN 1-57334-054-5

Printed in the United States of America
Eng. Bible CEV 250-110022
ABS-7/00-200,000-MW1

WELCOME TO THE
Contemporary English
Version

L anguages are spoken before they are written. And far more communication is done through the spoken word than through the written word. In fact, more people *hear* the Bible read than read it for themselves. Traditional translations of the Bible count on the *reader's* ability to understand a *written* text. But the *Contemporary English Version* differs from all other English Bibles—past and present—in that it takes into account the needs of the *hearer,* as well as those of the reader, who may not be familiar with traditional biblical language.

The *Contemporary English Version* has been described as a "user-friendly" and a "mission-driven" translation that can be *read* aloud without stumbling, *heard* without misunderstanding, and *listened to* with enjoyment and appreciation, because the language is contemporary and the style is lucid and lyrical.

The *Contemporary English Version* invites you to *read,* to *hear,* to *understand* and to *share*

*the Word of God now
as never before!*

In order to assure a text that is faithful to the meaning of the original, the *Contemporary English Version* New Testament was translated directly from the Greek text published by the United Bible Societies (third edition corrected and compared with the fourth revised edition). The drafts in their earliest stages were sent for review and comment to a number of biblical scholars, theologians, and educators representing a wide variety of church traditions. In addition, drafts were sent for review and comment to all English-speaking Bible Societies and to more than forty United Bible Societies' translation consultants around the world. Final approval of the text was given by the American Bible Society Board of Trustees on the recommendation of its Translations Subcommittee.

CONTENTS
(with book abbreviations)

ABOUT THE
NEW TESTAMENT

The New Testament is a collection of 27 books and letters written in Greek. They are arranged in four groups:

(1) Gospels and Acts. This group contains the four Gospels, which are Matthew, Mark, Luke, and John. The term "gospel" means "good news," and these four Gospels tell the good news about Jesus Christ. The group also contains the book of Acts, which tells how the good news spread in the years after Jesus died and was raised from death.

(2) Letters of Paul. This group is made up of Romans, 1 and 2 Corinthians, Galatians, Ephesians, Philippians, Colossians, 1 and 2 Thessalonians, 1 and 2 Timothy, Titus, and Philemon. These letters have traditionally been called "epistles," and each one is named for the group or person that it was written to.

(3) Other Letters. This group contains letters written by people other than Paul. It contains Hebrews, James, 1 and 2 Peter, 1, 2, and 3 John, and Jude. The Letter to the Hebrews doesn't give its author's name, but each of the other letters is named for the person who wrote it.

(4) Revelation. This book is quite different from the other New Testament books, because it is a book of visions and prophecies.

MATTHEW

ABOUT THIS BOOK

The Sermon on the Mount (5.1—7.28), the Lord's Prayer (6.9-13), and the Golden Rule (7.12: "Treat others as you want them to treat you") are all in this book. It is perhaps the best known and the most quoted of all the books that have ever been written about Jesus. That is one reason why Matthew was placed first among the four books about Jesus called Gospels.

One of the most important ideas found here is that God expects his people to obey him, and this is what is meant by the Greek word that appears in many translations as *righteousness*. It is used seven times by Matthew, but only once by Luke, and not at all by Mark. So it is an important clue to much of what Matthew wants his readers to understand about the teaching of Jesus.

Jesus first uses this word at his own baptism, when he tells John the Baptist, "We must do all that God wants us to do" (3.15). Then, during his Sermon on the Mount, he speaks five more times of what God's people must do to obey him (5.6, 10, 20; 6.1, 33). And finally, he reminds the chief priests and leaders of the people, "John the Baptist showed you how to do right" (21.32).

Matthew wanted to provide for the people of his time a record of Jesus' message and ministry. It is clear that the Old Testament Scriptures were very important to these people. And Matthew never fails to show when these texts point to the coming of Jesus as the Messiah sent from God. Matthew wrote this book to make sure Christians knew that their faith in Jesus as the Messiah was well anchored in the Old Testament Scriptures, and to help them grow in faith.

Matthew ends his story with the words of Jesus to his followers, which tell what they are to do after he leaves them:

> *I have been given all authority in heaven and on earth! Go to the people of all nations and make them my disciples. Baptize them in the name of the Father, the Son, and the Holy Spirit, and teach them to do everything I have told you. I will be with you always, even until the end of the world.*　　　　　*(28.18b-20)*

A QUICK LOOK AT THIS BOOK

The Ancestors and Birth of Jesus (1.1—2.23)
The Message of John the Baptist (3.1-12)
The Baptism and Temptation of Jesus (3.13—4.11)
Jesus in Galilee (4.12—18.35)
Jesus Goes from Galilee to Jerusalem (19.1—20.34)
Jesus' Last Week: His Trial and Death (21.1—27.66)
Jesus Is Alive (28.1-20)

The Ancestors of Jesus
(Luke 3.23-38)

1 Jesus Christ came from the family of King David and also from the family of Abraham. And this is a list of his ancestors. 2-6aFrom Abraham to King David, his ancestors were:

Abraham, Isaac, Jacob, Judah and his brothers (Judah's sons were Perez and Zerah, and their mother was Tamar), Hezron;

Ram, Amminadab, Nahshon, Salmon, Boaz (his mother was Rahab), Obed (his mother was Ruth), Jesse, and King David.

6b-11From David to the time of the exile in Babylonia, the ancestors of Jesus were:

David, Solomon (his mother had been Uriah's wife), Rehoboam, Abijah, Asa, Jehoshaphat, Jehoram;

Uzziah, Jotham, Ahaz, Hezekiah, Manasseh, Amon, Josiah, and Jehoiachin and his brothers.

12-16From the exile to the birth of Jesus, his ancestors were:

Jehoiachin, Shealtiel, Zerubbabel, Abiud, Eliakim, Azor, Zadok, Achim;

Eliud, Eleazar, Matthan, Jacob, and Joseph, the husband of Mary, the mother of Jesus, who is called the Messiah.

17There were fourteen generations from Abraham to David. There were also fourteen from David to the exile in Babylonia and fourteen more to the birth of the Messiah.

The Birth of Jesus
(Luke 2.1-7)

18This is how Jesus Christ was born. A young woman named Mary was engaged to Joseph from King David's family. But before they were married, she learned that she was going to have a baby by God's Holy Spirit. 19Joseph was a good man*a* and did not want to embarrass Mary in front of everyone. So he decided to quietly call off the wedding.

20While Joseph was thinking about this, an angel from the Lord came to him in a dream. The angel said, "Joseph, the baby that Mary will have is from the Holy Spirit. Go ahead and marry her. 21Then after her baby is born, name him Jesus,*b* because he will save his people from their sins."

22So the Lord's promise came true, just as the prophet had said, 23"A virgin will have a baby boy, and he will be called Immanuel," which means "God is with us."

24After Joseph woke up, he and Mary were soon married, just as the Lord's angel had told him to do. 25But they did not sleep together before her baby was born. Then Joseph named him Jesus.

The Wise Men

2 When Jesus was born in the village of Bethlehem in Judea, Herod was king. During this time some wise men*c* from the east came to Jerusalem 2and said, "Where is the child born to be king of the Jews? We saw his star in the east*d* and have come to worship him."

3When King Herod heard about this, he was worried, and so was everyone else in Jerusalem. 4Herod brought together the chief priests and the teachers of the Law of Moses and asked them, "Where will the Messiah be born?" 5They told him, "He will be born in Bethlehem, just as the prophet wrote,

6 'Bethlehem in the land
    of Judea,
you are very important
    among the towns of Judea.
From your town
    will come a leader,
who will be like a shepherd
    for my people Israel.' "

7Herod secretly called in the wise men and asked them when they had first seen the star. 8He told them, "Go to Bethlehem and search carefully for the child. As soon as you find him, let me know. I want to go and worship him too."

9The wise men listened to what the king said and then left. And the star they had seen in the east went on ahead of them until it stopped over the place where the child was. 10They were thrilled and excited to see the star.

11When the men went into the house and saw the child with Mary, his mother, they knelt down and worshiped him. They took out their gifts of gold, frankincense, and myrrh*e* and gave them to him. 12Later they were warned in a dream not to return to Herod, and they went back home by another road.

The Escape to Egypt

13After the wise men had gone, an angel from the Lord appeared to Joseph in a dream and said, "Get up! Hurry and take the child and his mother to Egypt! Stay there until I tell you to return, because Herod is looking for the child and wants to kill him."

14That night, Joseph got up and took his wife and the child to Egypt, 15where they stayed until Herod died. So the Lord's promise came true, just as the prophet had said, "I called my son out of Egypt."

The Killing of the Children

16When Herod found out that the wise men from the east had tricked him, he was very angry. He gave orders for his men to kill all the boys who lived in or near Bethlehem and were two years old

---

*a*1.19 *good man*: Or "kind man," or "man who always did the right thing."   *b*1.21 *name him Jesus*: In Hebrew the name "Jesus" means "the Lord saves."   *c*2.1 *wise men*: People famous for studying the stars.   *d*2.2 *his star in the east*: Or "his star rise."   *e*2.11 *frankincense, and myrrh*: Frankincense was a valuable powder that was burned to make a sweet smell. Myrrh was a valuable sweet-smelling powder often used in perfume.

and younger. This was based on what he had learned from the wise men.

[17]So the Lord's promise came true, just as the prophet Jeremiah had said,

[18] "In Ramah a voice was heard
    crying and weeping loudly.
Rachel was mourning
    for her children,
and she refused
to be comforted,
    because they were dead."

The Return from Egypt

[19]After King Herod died, an angel from the Lord appeared in a dream to Joseph while he was still in Egypt. [20]The angel said, "Get up and take the child and his mother back to Israel. The people who wanted to kill him are now dead."

[21]Joseph got up and left with them for Israel. [22]But when he heard that Herod's son Archelaus was now ruler of Judea, he was afraid to go there. Then in a dream he was told to go to Galilee, [23]and they went to live there in the town of Nazareth. So the Lord's promise came true, just as the prophet had said, "He will be called a Nazarene."[f]

The Preaching of John the Baptist
(Mark 1.1-8; Luke 3.1-18; John 1.19-28)

3 Years later, John the Baptist started preaching in the desert of Judea. [2]He said, "Turn back to God! The kingdom of heaven[g] will soon be here."[h]

[3]John was the one the prophet Isaiah was talking about, when he said,

"In the desert someone
    is shouting,
'Get the road ready
    for the Lord!
Make a straight path
    for him.' "

[4]John wore clothes made of camel's hair. He had a leather strap around his waist and ate grasshoppers and wild honey.

[5]From Jerusalem and all Judea and from the Jordan River Valley crowds of people went to John. [6]They told how sorry they were for their sins, and he baptized them in the river.

[7]Many Pharisees and Sadducees also came to be baptized. But John said to them:

You bunch of snakes! Who warned you to run from the coming judgment? [8]Do something to show that you have really given up your sins. [9]And don't start telling yourselves that you belong to Abraham's family. I tell you that God can turn these stones into children for Abraham. [10]An ax is ready to cut the trees down at their roots. Any tree that doesn't produce good fruit will be chopped down and thrown into a fire.

[11]I baptize you with water so that you will give up your sins.[i] But someone more powerful is going to come, and I am not good enough even to carry his sandals.[j] He will baptize you with the Holy Spirit and with fire. [12]His threshing fork is in his hand, and he is ready to separate the wheat from the husks.[k] He will store the wheat in a barn and burn the husks in a fire that never goes out.

The Baptism of Jesus
(Mark 1.9-11; Luke 3.21, 22)

[13]Jesus left Galilee and went to the Jordan River to be baptized by John. [14]But John kept objecting and said, "I ought to be baptized by you. Why have you come to me?"

[15]Jesus answered, "For now this is how it should be, because we must do all that God wants us to do." Then John agreed.

[16]So Jesus was baptized. And as soon as he came out of the water, the sky opened, and he saw the Spirit of God coming down on him like a dove. [17]Then a voice from heaven said, "This is my own dear Son, and I am pleased with him."

Jesus and the Devil
(Mark 1.12, 13; Luke 4.1-13)

4 The Holy Spirit led Jesus into the desert, so that the devil could test him. [2]After Jesus had gone without eating[l] for forty days and nights, he was very hungry. [3]Then the devil came to him and said, "If you are God's Son, tell these stones to turn into bread."

---

[f]**2.23** *He will be called a Nazarene:* The prophet who said this is not known.   [g]**3.2** *kingdom of heaven:* In the Gospel of Matthew "kingdom of heaven" is used with the same meaning as "God's kingdom" in Mark and Luke.   [h]**3.2** *will soon be here:* Or "is already here."
[i]**3.11** *so that you will give up your sins:* Or "because you have given up your sins."
[j]**3.11** *carry his sandals:* This was one of the duties of a slave.   [k]**3.12** *His threshing fork is in his hand, and he is ready to separate the wheat from the husks:* After Jewish farmers had trampled out the grain, they used a large fork to pitch the grain and the husks into the air. Wind would blow away the light husks, and the grain would fall back to the ground, where it could be gathered up.   [l]**4.2** *without eating:* The Jewish people sometimes went without eating (also called "fasting") to show their love for God or to show sorrow for their sins.

[4]Jesus answered, "The Scriptures say:

'No one can live only on food.
People need every word
    that God has spoken.' "

[5]Next, the devil took Jesus to the holy city and had him stand on the highest part of the temple. [6]The devil said, "If you are God's Son, jump off. The Scriptures say:

'God will give his angels
    orders about you.
They will catch you
    in their arms,
and you won't hurt
    your feet on the stones.' "

[7]Jesus answered, "The Scriptures also say, 'Don't try to test the Lord your God!' "

[8]Finally, the devil took Jesus up on a very high mountain and showed him all the kingdoms on earth and their power. [9]The devil said to him, "I will give all this to you, if you will bow down and worship me."

[10]Jesus answered, "Go away Satan! The Scriptures say:

'Worship the Lord your God
    and serve only him.' "

[11]Then the devil left Jesus, and angels came to help him.

Jesus Begins His Work
(Mark 1.14, 15; Luke 4.14, 15)

[12]When Jesus heard that John had been put in prison, he went to Galilee. [13]But instead of staying in Nazareth, Jesus moved to Capernaum. This town was beside Lake Galilee in the territory of Zebulun and Naphtali.[m] [14]So God's promise came true, just as the prophet Isaiah had said,

[15] "Listen, lands of Zebulun
        and Naphtali,
    lands along the road
    to the sea and east
        of the Jordan!
    Listen Galilee,
        land of the Gentiles!
[16] Although your people
        live in darkness,
    they will see
        a bright light.
    Although they live
        in the shadow of death,

a light will shine
    on them."

[17]Then Jesus started preaching, "Turn back to God! The kingdom of heaven will soon be here."[n]

Jesus Chooses Four Fishermen
(Mark 1.16-20; Luke 5.1-11)

[18]While Jesus was walking along the shore of Lake Galilee, he saw two brothers. One was Simon, also known as Peter, and the other was Andrew. They were fishermen, and they were casting their net into the lake. [19]Jesus said to them, "Come with me! I will teach you how to bring in people instead of fish." [20]Right then the two brothers dropped their nets and went with him.

[21]Jesus walked on until he saw James and John, the sons of Zebedee. They were in a boat with their father, mending their nets. Jesus asked them to come with him too. [22]Right away they left the boat and their father and went with Jesus.

Jesus Teaches, Preaches, and Heals
(Luke 6.17-19)

[23]Jesus went all over Galilee, teaching in the Jewish meeting places and preaching the good news about God's kingdom. He also healed every kind of disease and sickness. [24]News about him spread all over Syria, and people with every kind of sickness or disease were brought to him. Some of them had a lot of demons in them, others were thought to be crazy,[o] and still others could not walk. But Jesus healed them all.

[25]Large crowds followed Jesus from Galilee and the region around the ten cities known as Decapolis.[p] They also came from Jerusalem, Judea, and from across the Jordan River.

The Sermon on the Mount

5 When Jesus saw the crowds, he went up on the side of a mountain and sat down.[q]

Blessings
(Luke 6.20-23)

Jesus' disciples gathered around him, [2]and he taught them:

[3] God blesses those people
        who depend only on him.
    They belong to the kingdom
        of heaven![r]

---

[m]**4.13** *Zebulun and Naphtali*: In Old Testament times these tribes were in northern Palestine, and in New Testament times many Gentiles lived where these tribes had once been.
[n]**4.17** *The kingdom of heaven will soon be here*: See the two notes at 3.2.   [o]**4.24** *thought to be crazy*: In ancient times people with epilepsy were thought to be crazy.   [p]**4.25** *the ten cities known as Decapolis*: A group of ten cities east of Samaria and Galilee, where the people followed the Greek way of life.   [q]**5.1** *sat down*: Teachers in the ancient world, including Jewish teachers, usually sat down when they taught.   [r]**5.3** *They belong to the kingdom of heaven*: Or "The kingdom of heaven belongs to them."

⁴ God blesses those people
who grieve.
    They will find comfort!
⁵ God blesses those people
who are humble.
The earth will belong
to them!
⁶ God blesses those people
who want to obey him *s*
    more than to eat or drink.
They will be given
what they want!
⁷ God blesses those people
who are merciful.
They will be treated
with mercy!
⁸ God blesses those people
whose hearts are pure.
They will see him!
⁹ God blesses those people
who make peace.
They will be called
his children!
¹⁰ God blesses those people
who are treated badly
    for doing right.
They belong to the kingdom
    of heaven.*t*

¹¹God will bless you when people insult you, mistreat you, and tell all kinds of evil lies about you because of me. ¹²Be happy and excited! You will have a great reward in heaven. People did these same things to the prophets who lived long ago.

Salt and Light
(Mark 9.50; Luke 14.34, 35)

¹³You are like salt for everyone on earth. But if salt no longer tastes like salt, how can it make food salty? All it is good for is to be thrown out and walked on.

¹⁴You are like light for the whole world. A city built on top of a hill cannot be hidden, ¹⁵and no one would light a lamp and put it under a clay pot. A lamp is placed on a lampstand, where it can give light to everyone in the house. ¹⁶Make your light shine, so that others will see the good that you do and will praise your Father in heaven.

The Law of Moses

¹⁷Don't suppose that I came to do away with the Law and the Prophets.*u* I did not come to do away with them, but to give them their full meaning. ¹⁸Heaven and earth may disappear. But I promise you that not even a period or comma will ever disappear from the Law. Everything written in it must happen.

¹⁹If you reject even the least important command in the Law and teach others to do the same, you will be the least important person in the kingdom of heaven. But if you obey and teach others its commands, you will have an important place in the kingdom. ²⁰You must obey God's commands better than the Pharisees and the teachers of the Law obey them. If you don't, I promise you that you will never get into the kingdom of heaven.

Anger

²¹You know that our ancestors were told, "Do not murder" and "A murderer must be brought to trial." ²²But I promise you that if you are angry with someone,*v* you will have to stand trial. If you call someone a fool, you will be taken to court. And if you say that someone is worthless, you will be in danger of the fires of hell.

²³So if you are about to place your gift on the altar and remember that someone is angry with you, ²⁴leave your gift there in front of the altar. Make peace with that person, then come back and offer your gift to God.

²⁵Before you are dragged into court, make friends with the person who has accused you of doing wrong. If you don't, you will be handed over to the judge and then to the officer who will put you in jail. ²⁶I promise you that you will not get out until you have paid the last cent you owe.

Marriage

²⁷You know the commandment which says, "Be faithful in marriage." ²⁸But I tell you that if you look at another woman and want her, you are already unfaithful in your thoughts. ²⁹If your right eye causes you to sin, poke it out and throw it away. It is better to lose one part of your body, than for your whole body to end up in hell. ³⁰If your right hand causes you to sin, chop it off and throw it away! It is better to lose one part of your body, than for your whole body to be thrown into hell.

---

*s***5.6** *who want to obey him*: Or "who want to do right" or "who want everyone to be treated right." *t***5.10** *They belong to the kingdom of heaven*: See the note at 5.3. *u***5.17** *the Law and the Prophets*: The Jewish Scriptures, that is, the Old Testament. *v***5.22** *someone*: In verses 22-24 the Greek text has "brother," which may refer to people in general or to other followers.

Divorce
(Matthew 19.9; Mark 10.11, 12; Luke 16.18)

31You have been taught that a man who divorces his wife must write out divorce papers for her.*w* **32**But I tell you not to divorce your wife unless she has committed some terrible sexual sin.*x* If you divorce her, you will cause her to be unfaithful, just as any man who marries her is guilty of taking another man's wife.

Promises

33You know that our ancestors were told, "Don't use the Lord's name to make a promise unless you are going to keep it." **34**But I tell you not to swear by anything when you make a promise! Heaven is God's throne, so don't swear by heaven. **35**The earth is God's footstool, so don't swear by the earth. Jerusalem is the city of the great king, so don't swear by it. **36**Don't swear by your own head. You cannot make one hair white or black. **37**When you make a promise, say only "Yes" or "No." Anything else comes from the devil.

Revenge
(Luke 6.29, 30)

38You know that you have been taught, "An eye for an eye and a tooth for a tooth." **39**But I tell you not to try to get even with a person who has done something to you. When someone slaps your right cheek,*y* turn and let that person slap your other cheek. **40**If someone sues you for your shirt, give up your coat as well. **41**If a soldier forces you to carry his pack one mile, carry it two miles.*z* **42**When people ask you for something, give it to them. When they want to borrow money, lend it to them.

Love
(Luke 6.27, 28, 32-36)

43You have heard people say, "Love your neighbors and hate your enemies." **44**But I tell you to love your enemies and pray for anyone who mistreats you. **45**Then you will be acting like your Father in heaven. He makes the sun rise on both good and bad people. And he sends rain for the ones who do right and for the ones who do wrong. **46**If you love only those people who love you, will God reward you for that? Even tax collectors*a* love their friends. **47**If you greet only your friends, what's so great about that? Don't even unbelievers do that? **48**But you must always act like your Father in heaven.

Giving

6 When you do good deeds, don't try to show off. If you do, you won't get a reward from your Father in heaven. **2**When you give to the poor, don't blow a loud horn. That's what showoffs do in the meeting places and on the street corners, because they are always looking for praise. I can assure you that they already have their reward.

3When you give to the poor, don't let anyone know about it.*b* **4**Then your gift will be given in secret. Your Father knows what is done in secret, and he will reward you.

Prayer
(Luke 11.2-4)

5When you pray, don't be like those show-offs who love to stand up and pray in the meeting places and on the street corners. They do this just to look good. I can assure you that they already have their reward.

6When you pray, go into a room alone and close the door. Pray to your Father in private. He knows what is done in private, and he will reward you.

7When you pray, don't talk on and on as people do who don't know God. They think God likes to hear long prayers. **8**Don't be like them. Your Father knows what you need before you ask.

9You should pray like this:

Our Father in heaven,
 help us to honor
  your name.
10 Come and set up
  your kingdom,
 so that everyone on earth
  will obey you,

---

*w***5.31** *write out divorce papers for her*: Jewish men could divorce their wives, but the women could not divorce their husbands. The purpose of writing these papers was to make it harder for a man to divorce his wife. Before this law was made, all a man had to do was to send his wife away and say that she was no longer his wife. *x***5.32** *some terrible sexual sin*: This probably refers to the laws about the wrong kinds of marriages that are forbidden in Leviticus 18.6-18 or to some serious sexual sin. *y***5.39** *right cheek*: A slap on the right cheek was a bad insult. *z***5.41** *two miles*: A Roman soldier had the right to force a person to carry his pack as far as one mile. *a***5.46** *tax collectors*: These were usually Jewish people who paid the Romans for the right to collect taxes. They were hated by other Jews who thought of them as traitors to their country and to their religion. *b***6.3** *don't let anyone know about it*: The Greek text has, "Don't let your left hand know what your right hand is doing."

as you are obeyed
in heaven.
[11] Give us our food for today.[c]
[12] Forgive us for doing wrong,
as we forgive others.
[13] Keep us from being tempted
and protect us from evil.[d]

[14]If you forgive others for the
wrongs they do to you, your Father
in heaven will forgive you. [15]But if
you don't forgive others, your Father
will not forgive your sins.

Worshiping God by Going without Eating

[16]When you go without eating,[e]
don't try to look gloomy as those
show-offs do when they go without
eating. I can assure you that they already have their reward. [17]Instead,
comb your hair and wash your face.
[18]Then others won't know that you
are going without eating. But your
Father sees what is done in private,
and he will reward you.

Treasures in Heaven
(Luke 12.33, 34)

[19]Don't store up treasures on
earth! Moths and rust can destroy
them, and thieves can break in and
steal them. [20]Instead, store up your
treasures in heaven, where moths
and rust cannot destroy them, and
thieves cannot break in and steal
them. [21]Your heart will always be
where your treasure is.

Light
(Luke 11.34-36)

[22]Your eyes are like a window for
your body. When they are good, you
have all the light you need. [23]But
when your eyes are bad, everything
is dark. If the light inside you is
dark, you surely are in the dark.

Money
(Luke 16.13)

[24]You cannot be the slave of two
masters! You will like one more than
the other or be more loyal to one
than the other. You cannot serve
both God and money.

Worry
(Luke 12.22-31)

[25]I tell you not to worry about your
life. Don't worry about having something to eat, drink, or wear. Isn't life
more than food or clothing? [26]Look

at the birds in the sky! They don't
plant or harvest. They don't even
store grain in barns. Yet your Father
in heaven takes care of them. Aren't
you worth more than birds?
[27]Can worry make you live
longer?[f] [28]Why worry about clothes?
Look how the wild flowers grow.
They don't work hard to make their
clothes. [29]But I tell you that Solomon
with all his wealth[g] wasn't as well
clothed as one of them. [30]God gives
such beauty to everything that grows
in the fields, even though it is here
today and thrown into a fire tomorrow. He will surely do even more for
you! Why do you have such little faith?
[31]Don't worry and ask yourselves,
"Will we have anything to eat? Will
we have anything to drink? Will we
have any clothes to wear?" [32]Only
people who don't know God are always worrying about such things.
Your Father in heaven knows that
you need all of these. [33]But more
than anything else, put God's work
first and do what he wants. Then the
other things will be yours as well.
[34]Don't worry about tomorrow. It
will take care of itself. You have
enough to worry about today.

Judging Others
(Luke 6.37, 38, 41, 42)

7 Don't condemn others, and God
won't condemn you. [2]God will be as
hard on you as you are on others! He
will treat you exactly as you treat
them.
[3]You can see the speck in your
friend's eye, but you don't notice the
log in your own eye. [4]How can you
say, "My friend, let me take the
speck out of your eye," when you
don't see the log in your own eye?
[5]You're nothing but show-offs! First,
take the log out of your own eye.
Then you can see how to take the
speck out of your friend's eye.
[6]Don't give to dogs what belongs
to God. They will only turn and attack you. Don't throw pearls down
in front of pigs. They will trample all
over them.

Ask, Search, Knock
(Luke 11.9-13)

[7]Ask, and you will receive. Search,
and you will find. Knock, and the
door will be opened for you. [8]Every-
one who asks will receive. Everyone
who searches will find. And the door

---

[c]**6.11** *our food for today*: Or "the food that we need" or "our food for the coming day."
[d]**6.13** *evil*: Or "the evil one," that is, the devil. Some manuscripts add, "The kingdom, the power,
and the glory are yours forever. Amen." [e]**6.16** *without eating*: See the note at 4.2.
[f]**6.27** *live longer*: Or "grow taller." [g]**6.29** *Solomon with all his wealth*: The Jewish people
thought that Solomon was the richest person who had ever lived.

will be opened for everyone who knocks. 9Would any of you give your hungry child a stone, if the child asked for some bread? 10Would you give your child a snake if the child asked for a fish? 11As bad as you are, you still know how to give good gifts to your children. But your heavenly Father is even more ready to give good things to people who ask.

12Treat others as you want them to treat you. This is what the Law and the Prophets[h] are all about.

The Narrow Gate
(Luke 13.24)

13Go in through the narrow gate. The gate to destruction is wide, and the road that leads there is easy to follow. A lot of people go through that gate. 14But the gate to life is very narrow. The road that leads there is so hard to follow that only a few people find it.

A Tree and Its Fruit
(Luke 6.43-45)

15Watch out for false prophets! They dress up like sheep, but inside they are wolves who have come to attack you. 16You can tell what they are by what they do. No one picks grapes or figs from thornbushes. 17A good tree produces good fruit, and a bad tree produces bad fruit. 18A good tree cannot produce bad fruit, and a bad tree cannot produce good fruit. 19Every tree that produces bad fruit will be chopped down and burned. 20You can tell who the false prophets are by their deeds.

A Warning
(Luke 13.26, 27)

21Not everyone who calls me their Lord will get into the kingdom of heaven. Only the ones who obey my Father in heaven will get in. 22On the day of judgment many will call me their Lord. They will say, "We preached in your name, and in your name we forced out demons and worked many miracles." 23But I will tell them, "I will have nothing to do with you! Get out of my sight, you evil people!"

Two Builders
(Luke 6.47-49)

24Anyone who hears and obeys these teachings of mine is like a wise person who built a house on solid rock. 25Rain poured down, rivers flooded, and winds beat against that house. But it did not fall, because it was built on solid rock.

26Anyone who hears my teachings and doesn't obey them is like a foolish person who built a house on sand. 27The rain poured down, the rivers flooded, and the winds blew and beat against that house. Finally, it fell with a crash.

28When Jesus finished speaking, the crowds were surprised at his teaching. 29He taught them like someone with authority, and not like their teachers of the Law of Moses.

Jesus Heals a Man
(Mark 1.40-45; Luke 5.12-16)

8 As Jesus came down the mountain, he was followed by large crowds. 2Suddenly a man with leprosy[i] came and knelt in front of Jesus. He said, "Lord, you have the power to make me well, if only you wanted to."

3Jesus put his hand on the man and said, "I want to! Now you are well." At once the man's leprosy disappeared. 4Jesus told him, "Don't tell anyone about this, but go and show the priest that you are well. Then take a gift to the temple just as Moses commanded, and everyone will know that you have been healed."[j]

Jesus Heals an Army Officer's Servant
(Luke 7.1-10; John 4.43-54)

5When Jesus was going into the town of Capernaum, an army officer came up to him and said, 6"Lord, my servant is at home in such terrible pain that he can't even move."

7"I will go and heal him," Jesus replied.

8But the officer said, "Lord, I'm not good enough for you to come into my house. Just give the order, and my servant will get well. 9I have officers who give orders to me, and I have soldiers who take orders from me. I can say to one of them, 'Go!' and he goes. I can say to another, 'Come!' and he comes. I can say to my servant, 'Do this!' and he will do it."

10When Jesus heard this, he was so surprised that he turned and said to the crowd following him, "I tell you that in all of Israel I've never found anyone

---

h 7.12 *the Law and the Prophets*: See the note at 5.17.   i 8.2 *leprosy*: In biblical times the word "leprosy" was used for many different kinds of skin diseases.   j 8.4 *everyone will know that you have been healed*: People with leprosy had to be examined by a priest and told that they were well (that is "clean") before they could once again live a normal life in the Jewish community. The gift that Moses commanded was the sacrifice of some lambs together with flour mixed with olive oil.

with this much faith! [11]Many people will come from everywhere to enjoy the feast in the kingdom of heaven with Abraham, Isaac, and Jacob. [12]But the ones who should have been in the kingdom will be thrown out into the dark. They will cry and grit their teeth in pain."

[13]Then Jesus said to the officer, "You may go home now. Your faith has made it happen."

Right then his servant was healed.

Jesus Heals Many People
(Mark 1.29-34; Luke 4.38-41)

[14]Jesus went to the home of Peter, where he found that Peter's mother-in-law was sick in bed with fever. [15]He took her by the hand, and the fever left her. Then she got up and served Jesus a meal.

[16]That evening many people with demons in them were brought to Jesus. And with only a word he forced out the evil spirits and healed everyone who was sick. [17]So God's promise came true, just as the prophet Isaiah had said,

"He healed our diseases
and made us well."

Some Who Wanted To Go with Jesus
(Luke 9.57-62)

[18]When Jesus saw the crowd,[k] he went across Lake Galilee. [19]A teacher of the Law of Moses came up to him and said, "Teacher, I'll go anywhere with you!"

[20]Jesus replied, "Foxes have dens, and birds have nests. But the Son of Man doesn't have a place to call his own."

[21]Another disciple said to Jesus, "Lord, let me wait till I bury my father."

[22]Jesus answered, "Come with me, and let the dead bury their dead." [l]

A Storm
(Mark 4.35-41; Luke 8.22-25)

[23]After Jesus left in a boat with his disciples, [24]a terrible storm suddenly struck the lake, and waves started splashing into their boat.

Jesus was sound asleep, [25]so the disciples went over to him and woke him up. They said, "Lord, save us! We're going to drown!"

[26]But Jesus replied, "Why are you so afraid? You surely don't have much faith." Then he got up and ordered the wind and the waves to calm down. And everything was calm.

[27]The men in the boat were amazed and said, "Who is this? Even the wind and the waves obey him."

Two Men with Demons in Them
(Mark 5.1-20; Luke 8.26-39)

[28]After Jesus had crossed the lake, he came to shore near the town of Gadara[m] and started down the road. Two men with demons in them came to him from the tombs.[n] They were so fierce that no one could travel that way. [29]Suddenly they shouted, "Jesus, Son of God, what do you want with us? Have you come to punish us before our time?"

[30]Not far from there a large herd of pigs was feeding. [31]So the demons begged Jesus, "If you force us out, please send us into those pigs!" [32]Jesus told them to go, and they went out of the men and into the pigs. All at once the pigs rushed down the steep bank into the lake and drowned.

[33]The people taking care of the pigs ran to the town and told everything, especially what had happened to the two men. [34]Everyone in town came out to meet Jesus. When they saw him, they begged him to leave their part of the country.

Jesus Heals a Crippled Man
(Mark 2.1-12; Luke 5.17-26)

9 Jesus got into a boat and crossed back over to the town where he lived.[o] [2]Some people soon brought to him a crippled man lying on a mat. When Jesus saw how much faith they had, he said to the crippled man, "My friend, don't worry! Your sins are forgiven."

[3]Some teachers of the Law of Moses said to themselves, "Jesus must think he is God!"

[4]But Jesus knew what was in their minds, and he said, "Why are you thinking such evil things? [5]Is it easier for me to tell this crippled man that his sins are forgiven or to tell him to get up and walk? [6]But I will show you that the Son of Man has the right to forgive sins here on earth." So Jesus said to the man, "Get up! Pick up your mat and go on home." [7]The man got up and went home. [8]When the crowds saw this, they were afraid[p] and praised God for giving such authority to people.

[k]**8.18** *saw the crowd*: Some manuscripts have "large crowd." Others have "large crowds."
[l]**8.22** *let the dead bury their dead*: For the Jewish people a proper burial of their dead was a very important duty. But Jesus teaches that following him is even more important.
[m]**8.28** *Gadara*: Some manuscripts have "Gergesa." Others have "Gerasa." [n]**8.28** *tombs*: It was thought that demons and evil spirits lived in tombs and in caves that were used for burying the dead. [o]**9.1** *where he lived*: Capernaum (see 4.13). [p]**9.8** *afraid*: Some manuscripts have "amazed."

Jesus Chooses Matthew
(Mark 2.13-17; Luke 5.27-32)

9As Jesus was leaving, he saw a tax collector*q* named Matthew sitting at the place for paying taxes. Jesus said to him, "Come with me." Matthew got up and went with him.

10Later, Jesus and his disciples were having dinner at Matthew's house.*r* Many tax collectors and other sinners were also there. 11Some Pharisees asked Jesus' disciples, "Why does your teacher eat with tax collectors and other sinners?"

12Jesus heard them and answered, "Healthy people don't need a doctor, but sick people do. 13Go and learn what the Scriptures mean when they say, 'Instead of offering sacrifices to me, I want you to be merciful to others.' I didn't come to invite good people to be my followers. I came to invite sinners."

People Ask about Going without Eating
(Mark 2.18-22; Luke 5.33-39)

14One day some followers of John the Baptist came and asked Jesus, "Why do we and the Pharisees often go without eating,*s* while your disciples never do?"

15Jesus answered:

The friends of a bridegroom don't go without eating while he is still with them. But the time will come when he will be taken from them. Then they will go without eating.

16No one uses a new piece of cloth to patch old clothes. The patch would shrink and tear a bigger hole.

17No one pours new wine into old wineskins. The wine would swell and burst the old skins.*t* Then the wine would be lost, and the skins would be ruined. New wine must be put into new wineskins. Both the skins and the wine will then be safe.

A Dying Girl and a Sick Woman
(Mark 5.21-43; Luke 8.40-56)

18While Jesus was still speaking, an official came and knelt in front of him. The man said, "My daughter has just now died! Please come and place your hand on her. Then she will live again."

19Jesus and his disciples got up and went with the man. 20A woman who had been bleeding for twelve years came up behind Jesus and barely touched his clothes. 21She had said to herself, "If I can just touch his clothes, I will get well."

22Jesus turned. He saw the woman and said, "Don't worry! You are now well because of your faith." At that moment she was healed.

23When Jesus went into the home of the official and saw the musicians and the crowd of mourners,*u* 24he said, "Get out of here! The little girl isn't dead. She is just asleep." Everyone started laughing at Jesus. 25But after the crowd had been sent out of the house, Jesus went to the girl's bedside. He took her by the hand and helped her up.

26News about this spread all over that part of the country.

Jesus Heals Two Blind Men

27As Jesus was walking along, two blind men began following him and shouting, "Son of David,*v* have pity on us!"

28After Jesus had gone indoors, the two blind men came up to him. He asked them, "Do you believe I can make you well?"

"Yes, Lord," they answered.

29Jesus touched their eyes and said, "Because of your faith, you will be healed." 30They were able to see, and Jesus strictly warned them not to tell anyone about him. 31But they left and talked about him to everyone in that part of the country.

Jesus Heals a Man Who Could Not Talk

32As Jesus and his disciples were on their way, some people brought to him a man who could not talk because a demon was in him. 33After Jesus had forced the demon out, the man started talking. The crowds were so amazed that they began saying, "Nothing like this has ever happened in Israel!"

34But the Pharisees said, "The leader of the demons gives him the power to force out demons."

Jesus Has Pity on People

35Jesus went to every town and village. He taught in their meeting places and preached the good news about God's kingdom. Jesus also healed every kind of disease and sickness. 36When he saw the crowds, he felt sorry for them. They were confused and helpless, like sheep without a shepherd. 37He said to his disciples, "A large crop is in the fields, but there are only a few workers.

*q***9.9** *tax collector*: See the note at 5.46.   *r***9.10** *Matthew's house*: Or "Jesus' house."
*s***9.14** *without eating*: See the note at 4.2.   *t***9.17** *swell and burst the old skins*: While the juice from grapes was becoming wine, it would swell and stretch the skins in which it had been stored. If the skins were old and stiff, they would burst.   *u***9.23** *the crowd of mourners*: The Jewish people often hired mourners for funerals.   *v***9.27** *Son of David*: The Jewish people expected the Messiah to be from the family of King David, and for this reason the Messiah was often called the "Son of David."

38Ask the Lord in charge of the harvest to send out workers to bring it in."

Jesus Chooses His Twelve Apostles
(Mark 3.13-19; Luke 6.12-16)

10 Jesus called together his twelve disciples. He gave them the power to force out evil spirits and to heal every kind of disease and sickness. 2The first of the twelve apostles was Simon, better known as Peter. His brother Andrew was an apostle, and so were James and John, the two sons of Zebedee. 3Philip, Bartholomew, Thomas, Matthew the tax collector,w James the son of Alphaeus, and Thaddaeus were also apostles. 4The others were Simon, known as the Eager One,x and Judas Iscariot,y who later betrayed Jesus.

Instructions for the Twelve Apostles
(Mark 6.7-13; Luke 9.1-6)

5Jesus sent out the twelve apostles with these instructions:

Stay away from the Gentiles and don't go to any Samaritan town. 6Go only to the people of Israel, because they are like a flock of lost sheep. 7As you go, announce that the kingdom of heaven will soon be here.z 8Heal the sick, raise the dead to life, heal people who have leprosy,a and force out demons. You received without paying, now give without being paid. 9Don't take along any gold, silver, or copper coins. 10And don't carryb a traveling bag or an extra shirt or sandals or a walking stick. Workers deserve their food. 11So when you go to a town or a village, find someone worthy enough to have you as their guest and stay with them until you leave. 12When you go to a home, give it your blessing of peace. 13If the home is deserving, let your blessing remain with them. But if the home isn't deserving, take back your blessing of peace. 14If someone won't welcome you or listen to your message, leave their home or town. And shake the dust from your feet at them.c 15I promise you that the day of judgment will be easier for the towns of Sodom and Gomorrahd than for that town.

Warning about Trouble
(Mark 13.9-13; Luke 21.12-17)

16I am sending you like lambs into a pack of wolves. So be as wise as snakes and as innocent as doves. 17Watch out for people who will take you to court and have you beaten in their meeting places. 18Because of me, you will be dragged before rulers and kings to tell them and the Gentiles about your faith. 19But when someone arrests you, don't worry about what you will say or how you will say it. At that time you will be given the words to say. 20But you will not really be the one speaking. The Spirit from your Father will tell you what to say.

21Brothers and sisters will betray one another and have each other put to death. Parents will betray their own children, and children will turn against their parents and have them killed. 22Everyone will hate you because of me. But if you remain faithful until the end, you will be saved. 23When people mistreat you in one town, hurry to another one. I promise you that before you have gone to all the towns of Israel, the Son of Man will come.

24Disciples are not better than their teacher, and slaves are not better than their master. 25It is enough for disciples to be like their teacher and for slaves to be like their master. If people call the head of the family Satan, what will they say about the rest of the family?

The One To Fear
(Luke 12.2-7)

26Don't be afraid of anyone! Everything that is hidden will be found out, and every secret will be known. 27Whatever I say to you in the dark, you must tell in the light. And you must announce from the housetops whatever I have whispered to you. 28Don't be afraid of people. They can kill you, but they cannot harm your soul. Instead, you should fear God who can destroy both your body and your soul in hell. 29Aren't two sparrows sold for only a penny? But your Father

---

w**10.3** *tax collector*: See the note at 5.46.   x**10.4** *Eager One*: The Greek text has "Zealot," a name later given to the members of a Jewish group that resisted and fought against the Romans.   y**10.4** *Iscariot*: This may mean "a man from Kerioth" (a place in Judea). But more probably it means "a man who was a liar" or "a man who was a betrayer."   z**10.7** *will soon be here*: Or "is already here."   a**10.8** *leprosy*: See the note at 8.2.   b**10.9,10** *Don't take along . . . don't carry*: Or "Don't accept . . . don't accept."   c**10.14** *shake the dust from your feet at them*: This was a way of showing rejection (see Acts 13.51).   d**10.15** *Sodom and Gomorrah*: During the time of Abraham the Lord destroyed these towns because the people there were so evil.

knows when any one of them falls to the ground. ³⁰Even the hairs on your head are counted. ³¹So don't be afraid! You are worth much more than many sparrows.

Telling Others about Christ
(Luke 12.8, 9)

³²If you tell others that you belong to me, I will tell my Father in heaven that you are my followers. ³³But if you reject me, I will tell my Father in heaven that you don't belong to me.

Not Peace, but Trouble
(Luke 12.51-53; 14.26, 27)

³⁴Don't think that I came to bring peace to the earth! I came to bring trouble, not peace. ³⁵I came to turn sons against their fathers, daughters against their mothers, and daughters-in-law against their mothers-in-law. ³⁶Your worst enemies will be in your own family.

³⁷If you love your father or mother or even your sons and daughters more than me, you are not fit to be my disciples. ³⁸And unless you are willing to take up your cross and come with me, you are not fit to be my disciples. ³⁹If you try to save your life, you will lose it. But if you give it up for me, you will surely find it.

Rewards
(Mark 9.41)

⁴⁰Anyone who welcomes you welcomes me. And anyone who welcomes me also welcomes the one who sent me. ⁴¹Anyone who welcomes a prophet, just because that person is a prophet, will be given the same reward as a prophet. Anyone who welcomes a good person, just because that person is good, will be given the same reward as a good person. ⁴²And anyone who gives one of my most humble followers a cup of cool water, just because that person is my follower, will surely be rewarded.

John the Baptist
(Luke 7.18-35)

11 After Jesus had finished instructing his twelve disciples, he left and began teaching and preaching in the towns.ᵉ

²John was in prison when he heard what Christ was doing. So John sent some of his followers ³to ask Jesus, "Are you the one we should be looking for? Or must we wait for someone else?"

⁴Jesus answered, "Go and tell John what you have heard and seen. ⁵The blind are now able to see, and the lame can walk. People with leprosyᶠ are being healed, and the deaf can hear. The dead are raised to life, and the poor are hearing the good news. ⁶God will bless everyone who doesn't reject me because of what I do."

⁷As John's followers were going away, Jesus spoke to the crowds about John:

What sort of person did you go out into the desert to see? Was he like tall grass blown about by the wind? ⁸What kind of man did you go out to see? Was he someone dressed in fine clothes? People who dress like that live in the king's palace. ⁹What did you really go out to see? Was he a prophet? He certainly was. I tell you that he was more than a prophet. ¹⁰In the Scriptures God says about him, "I am sending my messenger ahead of you to get things ready for you." ¹¹I tell you that no one ever born on this earth is greater than John the Baptist. But whoever is least in the kingdom of heaven is greater than John.

¹²From the time of John the Baptist until now, violent people have been trying to take over the kingdom of heaven by force. ¹³All the Books of the Prophets and the Law of Mosesᵍ told what was going to happen up to the time of John. ¹⁴And if you believe them, John is Elijah, the prophet you are waiting for. ¹⁵If you have ears, pay attention!

¹⁶You people are like children sitting in the market and shouting to each other,

¹⁷ "We played the flute,
　　but you would not dance!
We sang a funeral song,
　　but you would not mourn!"

¹⁸John the Baptist did not go around eating and drinking, and you said, "That man has a demon in him!" ¹⁹But the Son of Man goes around eating and drinking, and you say, "That man eats and drinks too much! He is even a friend of tax collectorsʰ and sinners." Yet Wisdom is shown to be right by what it does.

The Unbelieving Towns
(Luke 10.13-15)

²⁰In the towns where Jesus had worked most of his miracles, the people

---

ᵉ**11.1** *the towns:* The Greek text has "their towns," which may refer to the towns of Galilee or to the towns where Jesus' disciples had lived.　ᶠ**11.5** *leprosy:* See the note at 8.2.
ᵍ**11.13** *the Books of the Prophets and the Law of Moses:* The Jewish Scriptures, that is, the Old Testament.　ʰ**11.19** *tax collectors:* See the note at 5.46.

refused to turn to God. So Jesus was upset with them and said:

²¹You people of Chorazin are in for trouble! You people of Bethsaida are in for trouble too! If the miracles that took place in your towns had happened in Tyre and Sidon, the people there would have turned to God long ago. They would have dressed in sackcloth and put ashes on their heads.*ⁱ* ²²I tell you that on the day of judgment the people of Tyre and Sidon will get off easier than you will.

²³People of Capernaum, do you think you will be honored in heaven? You will go down to hell! If the miracles that took place in your town had happened in Sodom, that town would still be standing. ²⁴So I tell you that on the day of judgment the people of Sodom will get off easier than you.

Come to Me and Rest
(Luke 10.21, 22)

²⁵At that moment Jesus said:

My Father, Lord of heaven and earth, I am grateful that you hid all this from wise and educated people and showed it to ordinary people. ²⁶Yes, Father, that is what pleased you.

²⁷My Father has given me everything, and he is the only one who knows the Son. The only one who truly knows the Father is the Son. But the Son wants to tell others about the Father, so that they can know him too.

²⁸If you are tired from carrying heavy burdens, come to me and I will give you rest. ²⁹Take the yoke*ʲ* I give you. Put it on your shoulders and learn from me. I am gentle and humble, and you will find rest. ³⁰This yoke is easy to bear, and this burden is light.

A Question about the Sabbath
(Mark 2.23-28; Luke 6.1-5)

12 One Sabbath, Jesus and his disciples were walking through some wheat fields.*ᵏ* His disciples were hungry and began picking and eating grains of wheat. ²Some Pharisees noticed this and said to Jesus, "Why are your disciples picking grain on the Sabbath? They are not supposed to do that!"

³Jesus answered:

You surely must have read what David did when he and his followers were hungry. ⁴He went into the house of God, and then they ate the sacred loaves of bread that only priests are supposed to eat. ⁵Haven't you read in the Law of Moses that the priests are allowed to work in the temple on the Sabbath? But no one says that they are guilty of breaking the law of the Sabbath. ⁶I tell you that there is something here greater than the temple. ⁷Don't you know what the Scriptures mean when they say, "Instead of offering sacrifices to me, I want you to be merciful to others?" If you knew what this means, you would not condemn these innocent disciples of mine. ⁸So the Son of Man is Lord over the Sabbath.

A Man with a Crippled Hand
(Mark 3.1-6; Luke 6.6-11)

⁹Jesus left and went into one of the Jewish meeting places, ¹⁰where there was a man whose hand was crippled. Some Pharisees wanted to accuse Jesus of doing something wrong, and they asked him, "Is it right to heal someone on the Sabbath?"

¹¹Jesus answered, "If you had a sheep that fell into a ditch on the Sabbath, wouldn't you lift it out? ¹²People are worth much more than sheep, and so it is right to do good on the Sabbath." ¹³Then Jesus told the man, "Hold out your hand." The man did, and it became as healthy as the other one.

¹⁴The Pharisees left and started making plans to kill Jesus.

God's Chosen Servant

¹⁵When Jesus found out what was happening, he left there and large crowds followed him. He healed all of their sick, ¹⁶but warned them not to tell anyone about him. ¹⁷So God's promise came true, just as Isaiah the prophet had said,

¹⁸ "Here is my chosen servant!
   I love him,
      and he pleases me.
   I will give him my Spirit,
      and he will bring justice
         to the nations.
¹⁹ He won't shout or yell
      or call out in the streets.
²⁰ He won't break off a bent reed
      or put out a dying flame,
   but he will make sure
      that justice is done.

---

*ⁱ***11.21** *sackcloth . . . ashes on their heads:* This was one way that people showed how sorry they were for their sins.   *ʲ***11.29** *yoke:* Yokes were put on the necks of animals, so that they could pull a plow or wagon. A yoke was a symbol of obedience and hard work.   *ᵏ***12.1** *walking through some wheat fields:* It was the custom to let hungry travelers pick grains of wheat.

21 All nations will place
their hope in him."

Jesus and the Ruler of the Demons
(Mark 3.20-30; Luke 11.14-23; 12.10)

22Some people brought to Jesus a man who was blind and could not talk because he had a demon in him. Jesus healed the man, and then he was able to talk and see. 23The crowds were so amazed that they asked, "Could Jesus be the Son of David?"*l*
24When the Pharisees heard this, they said, "He forces out demons by the power of Beelzebul, the ruler of the demons!"
25Jesus knew what they were thinking, and he said to them:

Any kingdom where people fight each other will end up ruined. And a town or family that fights will soon destroy itself. 26So if Satan fights against himself, how can his kingdom last? 27If I use the power of Beelzebul to force out demons, whose power do your own followers use to force them out? Your followers are the ones who will judge you. 28But when I force out demons by the power of God's Spirit, it proves that God's kingdom has already come to you. 29How can anyone break into a strong man's house and steal his things, unless he first ties up the strong man? Then he can take everything.
30If you are not on my side, you are against me. If you don't gather in the harvest with me, you scatter it. 31-32I tell you that any sinful thing you do or say can be forgiven. Even if you speak against the Son of Man, you can be forgiven. But if you speak against the Holy Spirit, you can never be forgiven, either in this life or in the life to come.

A Tree and Its Fruit
(Luke 6.43-45)

33A good tree produces only good fruit, and a bad tree produces bad fruit. You can tell what a tree is like by the fruit it produces. 34You are a bunch of evil snakes, so how can you say anything good? Your words show what is in your hearts. 35Good people bring good things out of their hearts, but evil people bring evil things out of their hearts. 36I promise you that on the day of judgment, everyone will have to account for every careless word they have spoken. 37On that day they will be told that they are either innocent or guilty because of the things they have said.

A Sign from Heaven
(Mark 8.11, 12; Luke 11.29-32)

38Some Pharisees and teachers of the Law of Moses said, "Teacher, we want you to show us a sign from heaven."
39But Jesus replied:
You want a sign because you are evil and won't believe! But the only sign you will get is the sign of the prophet Jonah. 40He was in the stomach of a big fish for three days and nights, just as the Son of Man will be deep in the earth for three days and nights. 41On the day of judgment the people of Nineveh*m* will stand there with you and condemn you. They turned to God when Jonah preached, and yet here is something far greater than Jonah. 42The Queen of the South*n* will also stand there with you and condemn you. She traveled a long way to hear Solomon's wisdom, and yet here is something much greater than Solomon.

Return of an Evil Spirit
(Luke 11.24-26)

43When an evil spirit leaves a person, it travels through the desert, looking for a place to rest. But when the demon doesn't find a place, 44it says, "I will go back to the home I left." When it gets there and finds the place empty, clean, and fixed up, 45it goes off and finds seven other evil spirits even worse than itself. They all come and make their home there, and the person ends up in worse shape than before. That's how it will be with you evil people of today.

Jesus' Mother and Brothers
(Mark 3.31-35; Luke 8.19-21)

46While Jesus was still speaking to the crowds, his mother and brothers came and stood outside because they wanted to talk with him. 47Someone told Jesus, "Your mother and brothers are standing outside and want to talk with you."*o*
48Jesus answered, "Who is my mother and who are my brothers?" 49Then he pointed to his disciples and said, "These are my mother and my brothers! 50Any-

---

*l***12.23** *Could Jesus be the Son of David*: Or "Does Jesus think he is the Son of David?" See the note at 9.27. *m***12.41** *Nineveh*: During the time of Jonah this city was the capital of the Assyrian Empire, which was Israel's worst enemy. But Jonah was sent there to preach, so that the people would turn to the Lord and be saved. *n***12.42** *Queen of the South*: Sheba, probably a country in southern Arabia. *o***12.47** *with you*: Some manuscripts do not have verse 47.

one who obeys my Father in heaven is my brother or sister or mother."

A Story about a Farmer
(Mark 4.1-9; Luke 8.4-8)

13 That same day Jesus left the house and went out beside Lake Galilee, where he sat down to teach.[p] ²Such large crowds gathered around him that he had to sit in a boat, while the people stood on the shore. ³Then he taught them many things by using stories. He said:

A farmer went out to scatter seed in a field. ⁴While the farmer was scattering the seed, some of it fell along the road and was eaten by birds. ⁵Other seeds fell on thin, rocky ground and quickly started growing because the soil wasn't very deep. ⁶But when the sun came up, the plants were scorched and dried up, because they did not have enough roots. ⁷Some other seeds fell where thornbushes grew up and choked the plants. ⁸But a few seeds did fall on good ground where the plants produced a hundred or sixty or thirty times as much as was scattered. ⁹If you have ears, pay attention!

Why Jesus Used Stories
(Mark 4.10-12; Luke 8.9, 10)

¹⁰Jesus' disciples came to him and asked, "Why do you use nothing but stories when you speak to the people?"
¹¹Jesus answered:

I have explained the secrets about the kingdom of heaven to you, but not to others. ¹²Everyone who has something will be given more. But people who don't have anything will lose even what little they have. ¹³I use stories when I speak to them because when they look, they cannot see, and when they listen, they cannot hear or understand. ¹⁴So God's promise came true, just as the prophet Isaiah had said,

"These people will listen
and listen,
    but never understand.
They will look and look,
    but never see.
¹⁵ All of them have
    stubborn minds!
Their ears are stopped up,
    and their eyes are covered.
They cannot see or hear
    or understand.
If they could,
they would turn to me,
    and I would heal them."

¹⁶But God has blessed you, because your eyes can see and your ears can hear! ¹⁷Many prophets and good people were eager to see what you see and to hear what you hear. But I tell you that they did not see or hear.

Jesus Explains the Story about the Farmer
(Mark 4.13-20; Luke 8.11-15)

¹⁸Now listen to the meaning of the story about the farmer:
¹⁹The seeds that fell along the road are the people who hear the message about the kingdom, but don't understand it. Then the evil one comes and snatches the message from their hearts. ²⁰The seeds that fell on rocky ground are the people who gladly hear the message and accept it right away. ²¹But they don't have deep roots, and they don't last very long. As soon as life gets hard or the message gets them in trouble, they give up.
²²The seeds that fell among the thornbushes are also people who hear the message. But they start worrying about the needs of this life and are fooled by the desire to get rich. So the message gets choked out, and they never produce anything. ²³The seeds that fell on good ground are the people who hear and understand the message. They produce as much as a hundred or sixty or thirty times what was planted.

Weeds among the Wheat

²⁴Jesus then told them this story:
The kingdom of heaven is like what happened when a farmer scattered good seed in a field. ²⁵But while everyone was sleeping, an enemy came and scattered weed seeds in the field and then left.
²⁶When the plants came up and began to ripen, the farmer's servants could see the weeds. ²⁷The servants came and asked, "Sir, didn't you scatter good seed in your field? Where did these weeds come from?"
²⁸"An enemy did this," he replied.
His servants then asked, "Do you want us to go out and pull up the weeds?"
²⁹"No!" he answered. "You might also pull up the wheat. ³⁰Leave the weeds alone until harvest time. Then I'll tell my workers to gather the weeds and tie them up and burn them. But I'll have them store the wheat in my barn."

---

[p]**13.1** *sat down to teach:* Teachers in the ancient world, including Jewish teachers, usually sat down when they taught.

Stories about a Mustard Seed and Yeast
(Mark 4.30-32; Luke 13.18-21)

³¹Jesus told them another story:

The kingdom of heaven is like what happens when a farmer plants a mustard seed in a field. ³²Although it is the smallest of all seeds, it grows larger than any garden plant and becomes a tree. Birds even come and nest on its branches.

³³Jesus also said:

The kingdom of heaven is like what happens when a woman mixes a little yeast into three big batches of flour. Finally, all the dough rises.

The Reason for Teaching with Stories
(Mark 4.33, 34)

³⁴Jesus used stories when he spoke to the people. In fact, he did not tell them anything without using stories. ³⁵So God's promise came true, just as the prophet*q* had said,

"I will use stories
    to speak my message
and to explain things
    that have been hidden
since the creation
    of the world."

Jesus Explains the Story about the Weeds

³⁶After Jesus left the crowd and went inside,*r* his disciples came to him and said, "Explain to us the story about the weeds in the wheat field."

³⁷Jesus answered:

The one who scattered the good seed is the Son of Man. ³⁸The field is the world, and the good seeds are the people who belong to the kingdom. The weed seeds are those who belong to the evil one, ³⁹and the one who scattered them is the devil. The harvest is the end of time, and angels are the ones who bring in the harvest.

⁴⁰Weeds are gathered and burned. That's how it will be at the end of time. ⁴¹The Son of Man will send out his angels, and they will gather from his kingdom everyone who does wrong or causes others to sin. ⁴²Then he will throw them into a flaming furnace, where people will cry and grit their teeth in pain. ⁴³But everyone who has done right will shine like the sun in their Father's kingdom. If you have ears, pay attention!

A Hidden Treasure

⁴⁴The kingdom of heaven is like what happens when someone finds treasure hidden in a field and buries it again. A person like that is happy and goes and sells everything in order to buy that field.

A Valuable Pearl

⁴⁵The kingdom of heaven is like what happens when a shop owner is looking for fine pearls. ⁴⁶After finding a very valuable one, the owner goes and sells everything in order to buy that pearl.

A Fish Net

⁴⁷The kingdom of heaven is like what happens when a net is thrown into a lake and catches all kinds of fish. ⁴⁸When the net is full, it is dragged to the shore, and the fishermen sit down to separate the fish. They keep the good ones, but throw the bad ones away. ⁴⁹That's how it will be at the end of time. Angels will come and separate the evil people from the ones who have done right. ⁵⁰Then those evil people will be thrown into a flaming furnace, where they will cry and grit their teeth in pain.

New and Old Treasures

⁵¹Jesus asked his disciples if they understood all these things. They said, "Yes, we do."

⁵²So he told them, "Every student of the Scriptures who becomes a disciple in the kingdom of heaven is like someone who brings out new and old treasures from the storeroom."

The People of Nazareth Turn against Jesus
(Mark 6.1-6; Luke 4.16-30)

⁵³When Jesus had finished telling these stories, he left ⁵⁴and went to his hometown. He taught in their meeting place, and the people were so amazed that they asked, "Where does he get all this wisdom and the power to work these miracles? ⁵⁵Isn't he the son of the carpenter? Isn't Mary his mother, and aren't James, Joseph, Simon, and Judas his brothers? ⁵⁶Don't his sisters still live here in our town? How can he do all this?" ⁵⁷So the people were very unhappy because of what he was doing.

But Jesus said, "Prophets are honored by everyone, except the people of their hometown and their own family." ⁵⁸And because the people did not have any faith, Jesus did not work many miracles there.

---

*q***13.35** *the prophet:* Some manuscripts have "the prophet Isaiah."   *r***13.36** *went inside:* Or "went home."

The Death of John the Baptist
(Mark 6.14-29; Luke 9.7-9)

14 About this time Herod the ruler[s] heard the news about Jesus [2]and told his officials, "This is John the Baptist! He has come back from death, and that's why he has the power to work these miracles."

[3-4]Herod had earlier arrested John and had him chained and put in prison. He did this because John had told him, "It isn't right for you to take Herodias, the wife of your brother Philip." [5]Herod wanted to kill John. But the people thought John was a prophet, and Herod was afraid of what they might do.

[6]When Herod's birthday came, the daughter of Herodias danced for the guests. She pleased Herod [7]so much that he swore to give her whatever she wanted. [8]But the girl's mother told her to say, "Here on a platter I want the head of John the Baptist!"

[9]The king was sorry for what he had said. But he did not want to break the promise he had made in front of his guests. So he ordered a guard [10]to go to the prison and cut off John's head. [11]It was taken on a platter to the girl, and she gave it to her mother. [12]John's followers took his body and buried it. Then they told Jesus what had happened.

Jesus Feeds Five Thousand
(Mark 6.30-44; Luke 9.10-17; John 6.1-14)

[13]After Jesus heard about John, he crossed Lake Galilee[t] to go to some place where he could be alone. But the crowds found out and followed him on foot from the towns. [14]When Jesus got out of the boat, he saw the large crowd. He felt sorry for them and healed everyone who was sick.

[15]That evening the disciples came to Jesus and said, "This place is like a desert, and it is already late. Let the crowds leave, so they can go to the villages and buy some food."

[16]Jesus replied, "They don't have to leave. Why don't you give them something to eat?"

[17]But they said, "We have only five small loaves of bread[u] and two fish." [18]Jesus asked his disciples to bring the food to him, [19]and he told the crowd to sit down on the grass. Jesus took the five loaves and the two fish. He looked up toward heaven and blessed the food. Then he broke the bread and handed it to his disciples, and they gave it to the people.

[20]After everyone had eaten all they wanted, Jesus' disciples picked up twelve large baskets of leftovers.

[21]There were about five thousand men who ate, not counting the women and children.

Jesus Walks on the Water
(Mark 6.45-52; John 6.15-21)

[22]Right away, Jesus made his disciples get into a boat and start back across the lake.[v] But he stayed until he had sent the crowds away. [23]Then he went up on a mountain where he could be alone and pray. Later that evening, he was still there.

[24]By this time the boat was a long way from the shore. It was going against the wind and was being tossed around by the waves. [25]A little while before morning, Jesus came walking on the water toward his disciples. [26]When they saw him, they thought he was a ghost. They were terrified and started screaming.

[27]At once, Jesus said to them, "Don't worry! I am Jesus. Don't be afraid."

[28]Peter replied, "Lord, if it is really you, tell me to come to you on the water."

[29]"Come on!" Jesus said. Peter then got out of the boat and started walking on the water toward him.

[30]But when Peter saw how strong the wind was, he was afraid and started sinking. "Save me, Lord!" he shouted.

[31]Right away, Jesus reached out his hand. He helped Peter up and said, "You surely don't have much faith. Why do you doubt?"

[32]When Jesus and Peter got into the boat, the wind died down. [33]The men in the boat worshiped Jesus and said, "You really are the Son of God!"

Jesus Heals Sick People in Gennesaret
(Mark 6.53-56)

[34]Jesus and his disciples crossed the lake and came to shore near the town of Gennesaret. [35]The people found out that he was there, and they sent word to everyone who lived in that part of the country. So they brought all the sick people to Jesus. [36]They begged him just to let them touch his clothes, and everyone who did was healed.

The Teaching of the Ancestors
(Mark 7.1-13)

15 About this time some Pharisees and teachers of the Law of Moses came from Jerusalem. They asked Jesus, [2]"Why don't your disciples obey what our ancestors taught us to do?

---

[s]**14.1** *Herod the ruler*: Herod Antipas, the son of Herod the Great (see 2.1). [t]**14.13** *crossed Lake Galilee*: To the east side. [u]**14.17** *small loaves of bread*: These would have been flat and round or in the shape of a bun. [v]**14.22** *back across the lake*: To the west side.

They don't even wash their hands[w] before they eat."

3Jesus answered:

Why do you disobey God and follow your own teaching? 4Didn't God command you to respect your father and mother? Didn't he tell you to put to death all who curse their parents? 5But you let people get by without helping their parents when they should. You let them say that what they have has been offered to God.[x] 6Is this any way to show respect to your parents? You ignore God's commands in order to follow your own teaching. 7And you are nothing but show-offs! Isaiah the prophet was right when he wrote that God had said,

8 "All of you praise me
with your words,
but you never really
think about me.
9 It is useless for you
to worship me,
when you teach rules
made up by humans."

What Really Makes People Unclean
(Mark 7.14-23)

10Jesus called the crowd together and said, "Pay attention and try to understand what I mean. 11The food that you put into your mouth doesn't make you unclean and unfit to worship God. The bad words that come out of your mouth are what make you unclean."

12Then his disciples came over to him and asked, "Do you know that you insulted the Pharisees by what you said?"

13Jesus answered, "Every plant that my Father in heaven did not plant will be pulled up by the roots. 14Stay away from those Pharisees! They are like blind people leading other blind people, and all of them will fall into a ditch."

15Peter replied, "What did you mean when you talked about the things that make people unclean?"

16Jesus then said:

Don't any of you know what I am talking about by now? 17Don't you know that the food you put into your mouth goes into your stomach and then out of your body? 18But the words that come out of your mouth come from your heart. And they are what make you unfit to worship God. 19Out of your heart come evil thoughts, murder, unfaithfulness in marriage, vulgar deeds, stealing, telling lies, and insulting others. 20These are what make you unclean. Eating without washing your hands will not make you unfit to worship God.

A Woman's Faith
(Mark 7.24-30)

21Jesus left and went to the territory near the cities of Tyre and Sidon. 22Suddenly a Canaanite woman[y] from there came out shouting, "Lord and Son of David,[z] have pity on me! My daughter is full of demons." 23Jesus did not say a word. But the woman kept following along and shouting, so his disciples came up and asked him to send her away.

24Jesus said, "I was sent only to the people of Israel! They are like a flock of lost sheep."

25The woman came closer. Then she knelt down and begged, "Please help me, Lord!"

26Jesus replied, "It isn't right to take food away from children and feed it to dogs."[a]

27"Lord, that's true," the woman said, "but even dogs get the crumbs that fall from their owner's table."

28Jesus answered, "Dear woman, you really do have a lot of faith, and you will be given what you want." At that moment her daughter was healed.

Jesus Heals Many People

29From there, Jesus went along Lake Galilee. Then he climbed a hill and sat down. 30Large crowds came and brought many people who were crippled or blind or lame or unable to talk. They placed them, and many others, in front of Jesus, and he healed them all. 31Everyone was amazed at what they saw and heard. People who had never spoken could now speak. The lame were healed, the crippled could walk, and the blind were able to see. Everyone was praising the God of Israel.

Jesus Feeds Four Thousand
(Mark 8.1-10)

32Jesus called his disciples together and told them, "I feel sorry for these people. They have been with me for three days, and they don't have anything to eat. I don't want to send them away hungry. They might faint on their way home."

---

[w]**15.2** *wash their hands*: The Jewish people had strict laws about washing their hands before eating, especially if they had been out in public. [x]**15.5** *has been offered to God*: According to Jewish custom, when people said something was offered to God, it belonged to him and could not be used for anyone else, not even for their own parents. [y]**15.22** *Canaanite woman*: This woman was not Jewish. [z]**15.22** *Son of David*: See the note at 9.27.
[a]**15.26** *feed it to dogs*: The Jewish people sometimes referred to Gentiles as dogs.

[33]His disciples said, "This place is like a desert. Where can we find enough food to feed such a crowd?"

[34]Jesus asked them how much food they had. They replied, "Seven small loaves of bread[b] and a few little fish."

[35]After Jesus had told the people to sit down, [36]he took the seven loaves of bread and the fish and gave thanks. He then broke them and handed them to his disciples, who passed them around to the crowds.

[37]Everyone ate all they wanted, and the leftovers filled seven large baskets.

[38]There were four thousand men who ate, not counting the women and children.

[39]After Jesus had sent the crowds away, he got into a boat and sailed across the lake. He came to shore near the town of Magadan.[c]

A Demand for a Sign from Heaven
(Mark 8.11-13; Luke 12.54-56)

16 The Pharisees and Sadducees came to Jesus and tried to test him by asking for a sign from heaven. [2]He told them:

If the sky is red in the evening, you say the weather will be good. [3]But if the sky is red and gloomy in the morning, you say it is going to rain. You can tell what the weather will be like by looking at the sky. But you don't understand what is happening now.[d] [4]You want a sign because you are evil and won't believe! But the only sign you will be given is what happened to Jonah.[e]
Then Jesus left.

The Yeast of the Pharisees and Sadducees
(Mark 8.14-21)

[5]The disciples had forgotten to bring any bread when they crossed the lake.[f] [6]Jesus then warned them, "Watch out! Guard against the yeast of the Pharisees and Sadducees."

[7]The disciples talked this over and said to each other, "He must be saying this because we didn't bring along any bread."

[8]Jesus knew what they were thinking and said:

You surely don't have much faith! Why are you talking about not having any bread? [9]Don't you understand? Have you forgotten about the five thousand people and all those baskets of leftovers from just five loaves of bread? [10]And what about the four thousand people and all those baskets of leftovers from only seven loaves of bread? [11]Don't you know by now that I am not talking to you about bread? Watch out for the yeast of the Pharisees and Sadducees!

[12]Finally, the disciples understood that Jesus wasn't talking about the yeast used to make bread, but about the teaching of the Pharisees and Sadducees.

Who Is Jesus?
(Mark 8.27-30; Luke 9.18-21)

[13]When Jesus and his disciples were near the town of Caesarea Philippi, he asked them, "What do people say about the Son of Man?"

[14]The disciples answered, "Some people say you are John the Baptist or maybe Elijah[g] or Jeremiah or some other prophet."

[15]Then Jesus asked them, "But who do you say I am?"

[16]Simon Peter spoke up, "You are the Messiah, the Son of the living God."

[17]Jesus told him:

Simon, son of Jonah, you are blessed! You didn't discover this on your own. It was shown to you by my Father in heaven. [18]So I will call you Peter, which means "a rock." On this rock I will build my church, and death itself will not have any power over it. [19]I will give you the keys to the kingdom of heaven, and God in heaven will allow whatever you allow on earth. But he will not allow anything that you don't allow.

[20]Jesus told his disciples not to tell anyone that he was the Messiah.

Jesus Speaks about His Suffering and Death
(Mark 8.31—9.1; Luke 9.22-27)

[21]From then on, Jesus began telling his disciples what would happen to him. He said, "I must go to Jerusalem. There the nation's leaders, the chief priests, and the teachers of the Law of Moses will make me suffer terribly. I will be killed, but three days later I will rise to life."

[22]Peter took Jesus aside and told him to stop talking like that. He said, "God would never let this happen to you, Lord!"

[23]Jesus turned to Peter and said, "Satan, get away from me! You're in my way

---

[b]**15.34** *small loaves of bread*: See the note at 14.17.   [c]**15.39** *Magadan*: The location is unknown.   [d]**16.2, 3** *If the sky is red . . . what is happening now*: The words of Jesus in verses 2 and 3 are not in some manuscripts.   [e]**16.4** *what happened to Jonah*: Jonah was in the stomach of a big fish for three days and nights (see 12.40).   [f]**16.5** *crossed the lake*: To the east side.   [g]**16.14** *Elijah*: Many of the Jewish people expected the prophet Elijah to come and prepare the way for the Messiah.

because you think like everyone else and not like God."

24Then Jesus said to his disciples:

If any of you want to be my followers, you must forget about yourself. You must take up your cross and follow me. 25If you want to save your life,*h* you will destroy it. But if you give up your life for me, you will find it. 26What will you gain, if you own the whole world but destroy yourself? What would you give to get back your soul?

27The Son of Man will soon come in the glory of his Father and with his angels to reward all people for what they have done. 28I promise you that some of those standing here will not die before they see the Son of Man coming with his kingdom.

The True Glory of Jesus
(Mark 9.2-13; Luke 9.28-36)

17 Six days later Jesus took Peter and the brothers James and John with him. They went up on a very high mountain where they could be alone. 2There in front of the disciples, Jesus was completely changed. His face was shining like the sun, and his clothes became white as light.

3All at once Moses and Elijah were there talking with Jesus. 4So Peter said to him, "Lord, it is good for us to be here! Let us make three shelters, one for you, one for Moses, and one for Elijah."

5While Peter was still speaking, the shadow of a bright cloud passed over them. From the cloud a voice said, "This is my own dear Son, and I am pleased with him. Listen to what he says!" 6When the disciples heard the voice, they were so afraid that they fell flat on the ground. 7But Jesus came over and touched them. He said, "Get up and don't be afraid!" 8When they opened their eyes, they saw only Jesus.

9On their way down from the mountain, Jesus warned his disciples not to tell anyone what they had seen until after the Son of Man had been raised from death.

10The disciples asked Jesus, "Don't the teachers of the Law of Moses say that Elijah must come before the Messiah does?"

11Jesus told them, "Elijah certainly will come and get everything ready. 12In fact, he has already come. But the people did not recognize him and treated him just as they wanted to. They will

soon make the Son of Man suffer in the same way." 13Then the disciples understood that Jesus was talking to them about John the Baptist.

Jesus Heals a Boy
(Mark 9.14-29; Luke 9.37-43a)

14Jesus and his disciples returned to the crowd. A man knelt in front of him 15and said, "Lord, have pity on my son! He has a bad case of epilepsy and often falls into a fire or into water. 16I brought him to your disciples, but none of them could heal him."

17Jesus said, "You people are too stubborn to have any faith! How much longer must I be with you? Why do I have to put up with you? Bring the boy here." 18Then Jesus spoke sternly to the demon. It went out of the boy, and right then he was healed.

19Later the disciples went to Jesus in private and asked him, "Why couldn't we force out the demon?"

20-21Jesus replied:

It is because you don't have enough faith! But I can promise you this. If you had faith no larger than a mustard seed, you could tell this mountain to move from here to there. And it would. Everything would be possible for you.*i*

Jesus Again Speaks about His Death
(Mark 9.30-32; Luke 9.43b-45)

22While Jesus and his disciples were going from place to place in Galilee, he told them, "The Son of Man will be handed over to people 23who will kill him. But three days later he will rise to life." All of this made the disciples very sad.

Paying the Temple Tax

24When Jesus and the others arrived in Capernaum, the collectors for the temple tax came to Peter and asked, "Does your teacher pay the temple tax?"

25"Yes, he does," Peter answered.

After they had returned home, Jesus went up to Peter and asked him, "Simon, what do you think? Do the kings of this earth collect taxes and fees from their own people or from foreigners?"*j*

26Peter answered, "From foreigners."

Jesus replied, "Then their own people*k* don't have to pay. 27But we don't want to cause trouble. So go cast a line into the lake and pull out the first fish you hook. Open its mouth, and you will find a coin. Use it to pay your taxes and mine."

---

h **16.25** *life:* In verses 25 and 26 the same Greek word is translated "life," "yourself," and "soul."
i **17.20,21** *for you:* Some manuscripts add, "But the only way to force out that kind of demon is by praying and going without eating."   *j* **17.25** *from their own people or from foreigners:* Or "from their children or from others."   *k* **17.26** *From foreigners . . . their own people:* Or "From other people . . . their children."

Who Is the Greatest?
(Mark 9.33-37; Luke 9.46-48)

18 About this time the disciples came to Jesus and asked him who would be the greatest in the kingdom of heaven. [2]Jesus called a child over and had the child stand near him. [3]Then he said:

I promise you this. If you don't change and become like a child, you will never get into the kingdom of heaven. [4]But if you are as humble as this child, you are the greatest in the kingdom of heaven. [5]And when you welcome one of these children because of me, you welcome me.

Temptations To Sin
(Mark 9.42-48; Luke 17.1, 2)

[6]It will be terrible for people who cause even one of my little followers to sin. Those people would be better off thrown into the deepest part of the ocean with a heavy stone tied around their necks! [7]The world is in for trouble because of the way it causes people to sin. There will always be something to cause people to sin, but anyone who does this will be in for trouble.

[8]If your hand or foot causes you to sin, chop it off and throw it away! You would be better off to go into life crippled or lame than to have two hands or two feet and be thrown into the fire that never goes out. [9]If your eye causes you to sin, poke it out and get rid of it. You would be better off to go into life with only one eye than to have two eyes and be thrown into the fires of hell.

The Lost Sheep
(Luke 15.3-7)

[10-11]Don't be cruel to any of these little ones! I promise you that their angels are always with my Father in heaven.[l] [12]Let me ask you this. What would you do if you had a hundred sheep and one of them wandered off? Wouldn't you leave the ninety-nine on the hillside and go look for the one that had wandered away? [13]I am sure that finding it would make you happier than having the ninety-nine that never wandered off. [14]That's how it is with your Father in heaven. He doesn't want any of these little ones to be lost.

When Someone Sins
(Luke 17.3)

[15]If one of my followers[m] sins against you, go and point out what was wrong. But do it in private, just between the two of you. If that person listens, you have won back a follower. [16]But if that one refuses to listen, take along one or two others. The Scriptures teach that every complaint must be proven true by two or more witnesses. [17]If the follower refuses to listen to them, report the matter to the church. Anyone who refuses to listen to the church must be treated like an unbeliever or a tax collector.[n]

Allowing and Not Allowing

[18]I promise you that God in heaven will allow whatever you allow on earth, but he will not allow anything you don't allow. [19]I promise that when any two of you on earth agree about something you are praying for, my Father in heaven will do it for you. [20]Whenever two or three of you come together in my name,[o] I am there with you.

An Official Who Refused To Forgive

[21]Peter came up to the Lord and asked, "How many times should I forgive someone[p] who does something wrong to me? Is seven times enough?" [22]Jesus answered:

Not just seven times, but seventy-seven times![q] [23]This story will show you what the kingdom of heaven is like:

One day a king decided to call in his officials and ask them to give an account of what they owed him. [24]As he was doing this, one official was brought in who owed him fifty million silver coins. [25]But he didn't have any money to pay what he owed. The king ordered him to be sold, along with his wife and children and all he owned, in order to pay the debt.

[26]The official got down on his knees and began begging, "Have pity on me, and I will pay you every cent I owe!" [27]The king felt sorry for him and let him go free. He even told the official that he did not have to pay back the money.

[28]As the official was leaving, he happened to meet another official,

---

[l]**18.10,11** *in heaven*: Some manuscripts add, "The Son of Man came to save people who are lost." [m]**18.15** *followers*: The Greek text has "brother," which is used here and elsewhere in this chapter to refer to a follower of Christ. [n]**18.17** *tax collector*: See the note at 5.46. [o]**18.20** *in my name*: Or "as my followers." [p]**18.21** *someone*: Or "a follower." See the note at 18.15. [q]**18.22** *seventy-seven times*: Or "seventy times seven." The large number means that one follower should never stop forgiving another.

who owed him a hundred silver coins. So he grabbed the man by the throat. He started choking him and said, "Pay me what you owe!"

29The man got down on his knees and began begging, "Have pity on me, and I will pay you back." 30But the first official refused to have pity. Instead, he went and had the other official put in jail until he could pay what he owed.

31When some other officials found out what had happened, they felt sorry for the man who had been put in jail. Then they told the king what had happened. 32The king called the first official back in and said, "You're an evil man! When you begged for mercy, I said you did not have to pay back a cent. 33Don't you think you should show pity to someone else, as I did to you?" 34The king was so angry that he ordered the official to be tortured until he could pay back everything he owed. 35That is how my Father in heaven will treat you, if you don't forgive each of my followers with all your heart.

Teaching about Divorce
(Mark 10.1-12)

19 When Jesus finished teaching, he left Galilee and went to the part of Judea that is east of the Jordan River. 2Large crowds followed him, and he healed their sick people.

3Some Pharisees wanted to test Jesus. They came up to him and asked, "Is it right for a man to divorce his wife for just any reason?"

4Jesus answered, "Don't you know that in the beginning the Creator made a man and a woman? 5That's why a man leaves his father and mother and gets married. He becomes like one person with his wife. 6Then they are no longer two people, but one. And no one should separate a couple that God has joined together."

7The Pharisees asked Jesus, "Why did Moses say that a man could write out divorce papers and send his wife away?"

8Jesus replied, "You are so heartless! That's why Moses allowed you to divorce your wife. But from the beginning God did not intend it to be that way. 9I say that if your wife has not committed some terrible sexual sin,*r* you must not divorce her to marry someone else. If you do, you are unfaithful."

10The disciples said, "If that's how it is between a man and a woman, it's better not to get married."

11Jesus told them, "Only those people

who have been given the gift of staying single can accept this teaching. 12Some people are unable to marry because of birth defects or because of what someone has done to their bodies. Others stay single for the sake of the kingdom of heaven. Anyone who can accept this teaching should do so."

Jesus Blesses Little Children
(Mark 10.13-16; Luke 18.15-17)

13Some people brought their children to Jesus, so that he could place his hands on them and pray for them. His disciples told the people to stop bothering him. 14But Jesus said, "Let the children come to me, and don't try to stop them! People who are like these children belong to God's kingdom."*s* 15After Jesus had placed his hands on the children, he left.

A Rich Young Man
(Mark 10.17-31; Luke 18.18-30)

16A man came to Jesus and asked, "Teacher, what good thing must I do to have eternal life?"

17Jesus said to him, "Why do you ask me about what is good? Only God is good. If you want to have eternal life, you must obey his commandments."

18"Which ones?" the man asked.

Jesus answered, "Do not murder. Be faithful in marriage. Do not steal. Do not tell lies about others. 19Respect your father and mother. And love others as much as you love yourself." 20The young man said, "I have obeyed all of these. What else must I do?"

21Jesus replied, "If you want to be perfect, go sell everything you own! Give the money to the poor, and you will have riches in heaven. Then come and be my follower." 22When the young man heard this, he was sad, because he was very rich.

23Jesus said to his disciples, "It's terribly hard for rich people to get into the kingdom of heaven! 24In fact, it's easier for a camel to go through the eye of a needle than for a rich person to get into God's kingdom."

25When the disciples heard this, they were greatly surprised and asked, "How can anyone ever be saved?"

26Jesus looked straight at them and said, "There are some things that people cannot do, but God can do anything."

27Peter replied, "Remember, we have left everything to be your followers! What will we get?"

28Jesus answered:

Yes, all of you have become my

---

*r*19.9 *some terrible sexual sin*: See the note at 5.32.   *s*19.14 *People who are like these children belong to God's kingdom*: Or "God's kingdom belongs to people who are like these children."

followers. And so in the future world, when the Son of Man sits on his glorious throne, I promise that you will sit on twelve thrones to judge the twelve tribes of Israel. ²⁹All who have given up home or brothers and sisters or father and mother or children or land for me will be given a hundred times as much. They will also have eternal life. ³⁰But many who are now first will be last, and many who are last will be first.

Workers in a Vineyard

20 As Jesus was telling what the kingdom of heaven would be like, he said:

Early one morning a man went out to hire some workers for his vineyard. ²After he had agreed to pay them the usual amount for a day's work, he sent them off to his vineyard.

³About nine that morning, the man saw some other people standing in the market with nothing to do. ⁴He said he would pay them what was fair, if they would work in his vineyard. ⁵So they went.

At noon and again about three in the afternoon he returned to the market. And each time he made the same agreement with others who were loafing around with nothing to do.

⁶Finally, about five in the afternoon the man went back and found some others standing there. He asked them, "Why have you been standing here all day long doing nothing?"

⁷"Because no one has hired us," they answered. Then he told them to go work in his vineyard.

⁸That evening the owner of the vineyard told the man in charge of the workers to call them in and give them their money. He also told the man to begin with the ones who were hired last. ⁹When the workers arrived, the ones who had been hired at five in the afternoon were given a full day's pay.

¹⁰The workers who had been hired first thought they would be given more than the others. But when they were given the same, ¹¹they began complaining to the owner of the vineyard. ¹²They said, "The ones who were hired last worked for only one hour. But you paid them the same that you did us. And we worked in the hot sun all day long!"

¹³The owner answered one of them, "Friend, I didn't cheat you. I paid you exactly what we agreed on. ¹⁴Take your money now and go! What business is it of yours if I want to pay them the same that I paid you? ¹⁵Don't I have the right to do what I want with my own money? Why should you be jealous, if I want to be generous?"

¹⁶Jesus then said, "So it is. Everyone who is now first will be last, and everyone who is last will be first."

Jesus Again Tells about His Death
(Mark 10.32-34; Luke 18.31-34)

¹⁷As Jesus was on his way to Jerusalem, he took his twelve disciples aside and told them in private:

¹⁸We are now on our way to Jerusalem, where the Son of Man will be handed over to the chief priests and the teachers of the Law of Moses. They will sentence him to death, ¹⁹and then they will hand him over to foreigners^t who will make fun of him. They will beat him and nail him to a cross. But on the third day he will rise from death.

A Mother's Request
(Mark 10.35-45)

²⁰The mother of James and John^u came to Jesus with her two sons. She knelt down and started begging him to do something for her. ²¹Jesus asked her what she wanted, and she said, "When you come into your kingdom, please let one of my sons sit at your right side and the other at your left."^v

²²Jesus answered, "Not one of you knows what you are asking. Are you able to drink from the cup^w that I must soon drink from?"

James and John said, "Yes, we are!"

²³Jesus replied, "You certainly will drink from my cup! But it isn't for me to say who will sit at my right side and at my left. That is for my Father to say."

²⁴When the ten other disciples heard this, they were angry with the two brothers. ²⁵But Jesus called the disciples together and said:

You know that foreign rulers like to order their people around. And their great leaders have full power over everyone they rule. ²⁶But don't act like them. If you want to be great, you must be the servant of all the others. ²⁷And if you want to be

---

^t**20.19** *foreigners*: The Romans, who ruled Judea at this time.   ^u**20.20** *mother of James and John*: The Greek text has "mother of the sons of Zebedee" (see 26.37).   ^v**20.21** *right side . . . left*: The most powerful people in a kingdom sat at the right and left side of the king. ^w**20.22** *drink from the cup*: In the Scriptures a cup is sometimes used as a symbol of suffering. To "drink from the cup" is to suffer.

first, you must be the slave of the rest. [28]The Son of Man did not come to be a slave master, but a slave who will give his life to rescue[x] many people.

Jesus Heals Two Blind Men
(Mark 10.46-52; Luke 18.35-43)

[29]Jesus was followed by a large crowd as he and his disciples were leaving Jericho. [30]Two blind men were sitting beside the road. And when they heard that Jesus was coming their way, they shouted, "Lord and Son of David,[y] have pity on us!"

[31]The crowd told them to be quiet, but they shouted even louder, "Lord and Son of David, have pity on us!"

[32]When Jesus heard them, he stopped and asked, "What do you want me to do for you?"

[33]They answered, "Lord, we want to see!"

[34]Jesus felt sorry for them and touched their eyes. Right away they could see, and they became his followers.

Jesus Enters Jerusalem
(Mark 11.1-11; Luke 19.28-38; John 12.12-19)

21 When Jesus and his disciples came near Jerusalem, he went to Bethphage on the Mount of Olives and sent two of them on ahead. [2]He told them, "Go into the next village, where you will at once find a donkey and her colt. Untie the two donkeys and bring them to me. [3]If anyone asks why you are doing that, just say, 'The Lord[z] needs them.' Right away he will let you have the donkeys."

[4]So God's promise came true, just as the prophet had said,

[5] "Announce to the people
    of Jerusalem:
'Your king is coming to you!
He is humble
    and rides on a donkey.
He comes on the colt
    of a donkey.' "

[6]The disciples left and did what Jesus had told them to do. [7]They brought the donkey and its colt and laid some clothes on their backs. Then Jesus got on.

[8]Many people spread clothes in the road, while others put down branches[a] which they had cut from trees. [9]Some people walked ahead of Jesus and oth-

ers followed behind. They were all shouting,

"Hooray[b] for the Son of David![c]
God bless the one who comes
    in the name of the Lord.
Hooray for God
    in heaven above!"

[10]When Jesus came to Jerusalem, everyone in the city was excited and asked, "Who can this be?"

[11]The crowd answered, "This is Jesus, the prophet from Nazareth in Galilee."

Jesus in the Temple
(Mark 11.15-19; Luke 19.45-48; John 2.13-22)

[12]Jesus went into the temple and chased out everyone who was selling or buying. He turned over the tables of the moneychangers and the benches of the ones who were selling doves. [13]He told them, "The Scriptures say, 'My house should be called a place of worship.' But you have turned it into a place where robbers hide."

[14]Blind and lame people came to Jesus in the temple, and he healed them. [15]But the chief priests and the teachers of the Law of Moses were angry when they saw his miracles and heard the children shouting praises to the Son of David.[c] [16]The men said to Jesus, "Don't you hear what those children are saying?"

"Yes, I do!" Jesus answered. "Don't you know that the Scriptures say, 'Children and infants will sing praises'?" [17]Then Jesus left the city and went out to the village of Bethany, where he spent the night.

Jesus Puts a Curse on a Fig Tree
(Mark 11.12-14, 20-24)

[18]When Jesus got up the next morning, he was hungry. He started out for the city, [19]and along the way he saw a fig tree. But when he came to it, he found only leaves and no figs. So he told the tree, "You will never again grow any fruit!" Right then the fig tree dried up.

[20]The disciples were shocked when they saw how quickly the tree had dried up. [21]But Jesus said to them, "If you have faith and don't doubt, I promise that you can do what I did to this tree. And you will be able to do even more. You can tell this mountain to get up and jump into the sea, and it will. [22]If you

---

[x]**20.28** *rescue*: The Greek word often, though not always, means the payment of a price to free a slave or a prisoner.   [y]**20.30** *Son of David*: See the note at 9.27.   [z]**21.3** *The Lord*: Or "The master of the donkeys."   [a]**21.8** *spread clothes . . . put down branches*: This was one way that the Jewish people welcomed a famous person.   [b]**21.9** *Horray*: This translates a word that can mean "please save us." But it is most often used as a shout of praise to God. [c]**21.9,15** *Son of David*: See the note at 9.27.

have faith when you pray, you will be given whatever you ask for."

A Question about Jesus' Authority
(Mark 11.27-33; Luke 20.1-8)

23Jesus had gone into the temple and was teaching when the chief priests and the leaders of the people came up to him. They asked, "What right do you have to do these things? Who gave you this authority?"

24Jesus answered, "I have just one question to ask you. If you answer it, I will tell you where I got the right to do these things. 25Who gave John the right to baptize? Was it God in heaven or merely some human being?"

They thought it over and said to each other, "We can't say that God gave John this right. Jesus will ask us why we didn't believe John. 26On the other hand, these people think that John was a prophet, and we are afraid of what they might do to us. That's why we can't say that it was merely some human who gave John the right to baptize." 27So they told Jesus, "We don't know."

Jesus said, "Then I won't tell you who gave me the right to do what I do."

A Story about Two Sons

28Jesus said:

I will tell you a story about a man who had two sons. Then you can tell me what you think. The father went to the older son and said, "Go work in the vineyard today!" 29His son told him that he would not do it, but later he changed his mind and went. 30The man then told his younger son to go work in the vineyard. The boy said he would, but he didn't go. 31Which one of the sons obeyed his father?

"The older one," the chief priests and leaders answered.

Then Jesus told them:

You can be sure that tax collectors*d* and prostitutes will get into the kingdom of God before you ever will! 32When John the Baptist showed you how to do right, you would not believe him. But these evil people did believe. And even when you saw what they did, you still would not change your minds and believe.

Renters of a Vineyard
(Mark 12.1-12; Luke 20.9-19)

33Jesus told the chief priests and leaders to listen to this story:

A land owner once planted a vineyard. He built a wall around it and dug a pit to crush the grapes in. He also built a lookout tower. Then he rented out his vineyard and left the country. 34When it was harvest time, the owner sent some servants to get his share of the grapes. 35But the renters grabbed those servants. They beat up one, killed one, and stoned one of them to death. 36He then sent more servants than he did the first time. But the renters treated them in the same way.

37Finally, the owner sent his own son to the renters, because he thought they would respect him. 38But when they saw the man's son, they said, "Someday he will own the vineyard. Let's kill him! Then we can have it all for ourselves." 39So they grabbed him, threw him out of the vineyard, and killed him.

40Jesus asked, "When the owner of that vineyard comes, what do you suppose he will do to those renters?"

41The chief priests and leaders answered, "He will kill them in some horrible way. Then he will rent out his vineyard to people who will give him his share of grapes at harvest time."

42Jesus replied, "You surely know that the Scriptures say,

'The stone that the builders
   tossed aside
is now the most important
   stone of all.
This is something
the Lord has done,
   and it is amazing to us.'

43I tell you that God's kingdom will be taken from you and given to people who will do what he demands. 44Anyone who stumbles over this stone will be crushed, and anyone it falls on will be smashed to pieces."*e*

45When the chief priests and the Pharisees heard these stories, they knew that Jesus was talking about them. 46So they looked for a way to arrest Jesus. But they were afraid to, because the people thought he was a prophet.

The Great Banquet
(Luke 14.15-24)

22 Once again Jesus used stories to teach the people: 2The kingdom of heaven is like what happened when a king gave a wedding banquet for his son. 3The king sent some servants to tell the invited guests to come to the banquet, but the guests refused. 4He sent other servants to say to the

---

*d*21.31 *tax collectors*: See the note at 5.46. manuscripts.

*e*21.44 *pieces*: Verse 44 is not in some

guests, "The banquet is ready! My cattle and prize calves have all been prepared. Everything is ready. Come to the banquet!"

⁵But the guests did not pay any attention. Some of them left for their farms, and some went to their places of business. ⁶Others grabbed the servants, then beat them up and killed them.

⁷This made the king so furious that he sent an army to kill those murderers and burn down their city. ⁸Then he said to the servants, "It is time for the wedding banquet, and the invited guests don't deserve to come. ⁹Go out to the street corners and tell everyone you meet to come to the banquet." ¹⁰They went out on the streets and brought in everyone they could find, good and bad alike. And the banquet room was filled with guests.

¹¹When the king went in to meet the guests, he found that one of them wasn't wearing the right kind of clothes for the wedding. ¹²The king asked, "Friend, why didn't you wear proper clothes for the wedding?" But the guest had no excuse. ¹³So the king gave orders for that person to be tied hand and foot and to be thrown outside into the dark. That's where people will cry and grit their teeth in pain. ¹⁴Many are invited, but only a few are chosen.

Paying Taxes
(Mark 12.13-17; Luke 20.20-26)

¹⁵The Pharisees got together and planned how they could trick Jesus into saying something wrong. ¹⁶They sent some of their followers and some of Herod's followers*f* to say to him, "Teacher, we know that you are honest. You teach the truth about what God wants people to do. And you treat everyone with the same respect, no matter who they are. ¹⁷Tell us what you think! Should we pay taxes to the Emperor or not?"

¹⁸Jesus knew their evil thoughts and said, "Why are you trying to test me? You show-offs! ¹⁹Let me see one of the coins used for paying taxes." They brought him a silver coin, ²⁰and he asked, "Whose picture and name are on it?"

²¹"The Emperor's," they answered.

Then Jesus told them, "Give the Emperor what belongs to him and give God what belongs to God." ²²His answer surprised them so much that they walked away.

Life in the Future World
(Mark 12.18-27; Luke 20.27-40)

²³The Sadducees did not believe that people would rise to life after death. So that same day some of the Sadducees came to Jesus and said:

²⁴Teacher, Moses wrote that if a married man dies and has no children, his brother should marry the widow. Their first son would then be thought of as the son of the dead brother.

²⁵Once there were seven brothers who lived here. The first one married, but died without having any children. So his wife was left to his brother. ²⁶The same thing happened to the second and third brothers and finally to all seven of them. ²⁷At last the woman died. ²⁸When God raises people from death, whose wife will this woman be? She had been married to all seven brothers.

²⁹Jesus answered:

You are completely wrong! You don't know what the Scriptures teach. And you don't know anything about the power of God. ³⁰When God raises people to life, they won't marry. They will be like the angels in heaven. ³¹And as for people being raised to life, God was speaking to you when he said, ³²"I am the God worshiped by Abraham, Isaac, and Jacob."*g* He isn't the God of the dead, but of the living.

³³The crowds were surprised to hear what Jesus was teaching.

The Most Important Commandment
(Mark 12.28-34; Luke 10.25-28)

³⁴After Jesus had made the Sadducees look foolish, the Pharisees heard about it and got together. ³⁵One of them was an expert in the Jewish Law. So he tried to test Jesus by asking, ³⁶"Teacher, what is the most important commandment in the Law?"

³⁷Jesus answered:

Love the Lord your God with all your heart, soul, and mind. ³⁸This is the first and most important commandment. ³⁹The second most important commandment is like this one. And it is, "Love others as much as you love yourself." ⁴⁰All the Law of Moses and the Books of the

---

*f*22.16 *Herod's followers*: People who were political followers of the family of Herod the Great (see 2.1) and his son Herod Antipas (see 14.1), and who wanted Herod to be king in Jerusalem.
*g*22.32 *I am the God worshiped by Abraham, Isaac, and Jacob*: Jesus argues that if God is worshiped by these three, they must still be alive, because he is the God of the living.

Prophets[h] are based on these two commandments.

About David's Son
(Mark 12.35-37; Luke 20.41-44)

[41]While the Pharisees were still there, Jesus asked them, [42]"What do you think about the Messiah? Whose family will he come from?"

They answered, "He will be a son of King David."[i]

[43]Jesus replied, "How then could the Spirit lead David to call the Messiah his Lord? David said,

[44] 'The Lord said to my Lord:
Sit at my right side[j]
until I make your enemies
into a footstool for you.'

[45]If David called the Messiah his Lord, how can the Messiah be a son of King David?" [46]No one was able to give Jesus an answer, and from that day on, no one dared ask him any more questions.

Jesus Condemns the Pharisees and the Teachers of the Law of Moses
(Mark 12.38-40; Luke 11.37-52; 20.45-47)

23 Jesus said to the crowds and to his disciples:

[2]The Pharisees and the teachers of the Law are experts in the Law of Moses. [3]So obey everything they teach you, but don't do as they do. After all, they say one thing and do something else.

[4]They pile heavy burdens on people's shoulders and won't lift a finger to help. [5]Everything they do is just to show off in front of others. They even make a big show of wearing Scripture verses on their foreheads and arms, and they wear big tassels[k] for everyone to see. [6]They love the best seats at banquets and the front seats in the meeting places. [7]And when they are in the market, they like to have people greet them as their teachers.

[8]But none of you should be called a teacher. You have only one teacher, and all of you are like brothers and sisters. [9]Don't call anyone on earth your father. All of you have the same Father in heaven. [10]None of you should be called the leader. The Messiah is your only leader. [11]Whoever is the greatest should be the servant of the others. [12]If you put yourself above others, you will be put down. But if you humble yourself, you will be honored.

[13-14]You Pharisees and teachers of the Law of Moses are in for trouble! You're nothing but show-offs. You lock people out of the kingdom of heaven. You won't go in yourselves, and you keep others from going in.[l]

[15]You Pharisees and teachers of the Law of Moses are in for trouble! You're nothing but show-offs. You travel over land and sea to win one follower. And when you have done so, you make that person twice as fit for hell as you are.

[16]You are in for trouble! You are supposed to lead others, but you are blind. You teach that it doesn't matter if a person swears by the temple. But you say that it does matter if someone swears by the gold in the temple. [17]You blind fools! Which is greater, the gold or the temple that makes the gold sacred? [18]You also teach that it doesn't matter if a person swears by the altar. But you say that it does matter if someone swears by the gift on the altar. [19]Are you blind? Which is more important, the gift or the altar that makes the gift sacred? [20]Anyone who swears by the altar also swears by everything on it. [21]And anyone who swears by the temple also swears by God, who lives there. [22]To swear by heaven is the same as swearing by God's throne and by the one who sits on that throne.

[23]You Pharisees and teachers are show-offs, and you're in for trouble! You give God a tenth of the spices from your garden, such as mint, dill, and cumin. Yet you neglect the more important matters of the Law, such as justice, mercy, and faithfulness. These are the important things you should have done, though you should not have left the others undone either. [24]You blind leaders! You strain out a small fly but swallow a camel.

[25]You Pharisees and teachers are show-offs, and you're in for trouble!

[h]**22.40** *the Law of Moses and the Books of the Prophets*: The Jewish Scriptures, that is, the Old Testament. [i]**22.42** *son of King David*: See the note at 9.27. [j]**22.44** *right side*: The place of power and honor. [k]**23.5** *wearing Scripture verses on their foreheads and arms . . . tassels*: As a sign of their love for the Lord and his teachings, the Jewish people had started wearing Scripture verses in small leather boxes. But the Pharisees tried to show off by making the boxes bigger than necessary. The Jewish people were also taught to wear tassels on the four corners of their robes to show their love for God. [l]**23.13,14** *from going in*: Some manuscripts add, "You Pharisees and teachers are in for trouble! And you're nothing but show-offs! You cheat widows out of their homes and then pray long prayers just to show off. So you will be punished most of all."

You wash the outside of your cups and dishes, while inside there is nothing but greed and selfishness. [26]You blind Pharisee! First clean the inside of a cup, and then the outside will also be clean.

[27]You Pharisees and teachers are in for trouble! You're nothing but show-offs. You're like tombs that have been whitewashed.[m] On the outside they are beautiful, but inside they are full of bones and filth. [28]That's what you are like. Outside you look good, but inside you are evil and only pretend to be good.

[29]You Pharisees and teachers are nothing but show-offs, and you're in for trouble! You build monuments for the prophets and decorate the tombs of good people. [30]And you claim that you would not have taken part with your ancestors in killing the prophets. [31]But you really prove that you really are the relatives of the ones who killed the prophets. [32]So keep on doing everything they did. [33]You are nothing but snakes and the children of snakes! How can you escape going to hell?

[34]I will send prophets and wise people and experts in the Law of Moses to you. But you will kill them or nail them to a cross or beat them in your meeting places or chase them from town to town. [35]That's why you will be held guilty for the murder of every good person, beginning with the good man Abel. This also includes Barachiah's son Zechariah,[n] the man you murdered between the temple and the altar. [36]I can promise that you people living today will be punished for all these things!

Jesus Loves Jerusalem
(Luke 13.34, 35)

[37]Jerusalem, Jerusalem! Your people have killed the prophets and have stoned the messengers who were sent to you. I have often wanted to gather your people, as a hen gathers her chicks under her wings. But you wouldn't let me. [38]And now your temple will be deserted. [39]You won't see me again until you say,

"Blessed is the one who comes in the name of the Lord."

The Temple Will Be Destroyed
(Mark 13.1, 2; Luke 21.5, 6)

24 After Jesus left the temple, his disciples came over and said, "Look at all these buildings!"

[2]Jesus replied, "Do you see these buildings? They will certainly be torn down! Not one stone will be left in place."

Warning about Trouble
(Mark 13.3-13; Luke 21.7-19)

[3]Later, as Jesus was sitting on the Mount of Olives, his disciples came to him in private and asked, "When will this happen? What will be the sign of your coming and of the end of the world?"

[4]Jesus answered:

Don't let anyone fool you. [5]Many will come and claim to be me. They will say that they are the Messiah, and they will fool many people.

[6]You will soon hear about wars and threats of wars, but don't be afraid. These things will have to happen first, but that isn't the end. [7]Nations and kingdoms will go to war against each other. People will starve to death, and in some places there will be earthquakes. [8]But this is just the beginning of troubles.

[9]You will be arrested, punished, and even killed. Because of me, you will be hated by people of all nations. [10]Many will give up and will betray and hate each other. [11]Many false prophets will come and fool a lot of people. [12]Evil will spread and cause many people to stop loving others. [13]But if you keep on being faithful right to the end, you will be saved. [14]When the good news about the kingdom has been preached all over the world and told to all nations, the end will come.

The Horrible Thing
(Mark 13.14-23; Luke 21.20-24)

[15]Someday you will see that "Horrible Thing" in the holy place, just as the prophet Daniel said. Everyone who reads this must try to understand! [16]If you are living in Judea at that time, run to the mountains. [17]If you are on the roof[o] of your house, don't go inside to get anything. [18]If you are out in the field, don't go back for your coat. [19]It will be a ter-

---

[m]**23.27** *whitewashed*: Tombs were whitewashed to keep anyone from accidentally touching them. A person who touched a dead body or a tomb was considered unclean and could not worship with the rest of the Jewish people.   [n]**23.35** *Zechariah*: Genesis is the first book in the Jewish Scriptures, and it tells that Abel was the first person to be murdered. Second Chronicles is the last book in the Jewish Scriptures, and the last murder that it tells about is that of Zechariah.   [o]**24.17** *roof*: In Palestine the houses usually had a flat roof. Stairs on the outside led up to the roof, which was made of beams and boards covered with packed earth.

rible time for women who are expecting babies or nursing young children. 20And pray that you won't have to escape in winter or on a Sabbath.*p* 21This will be the worst time of suffering since the beginning of the world, and nothing this terrible will ever happen again. 22If God doesn't make the time shorter, no one will be left alive. But because of God's chosen ones, he will make the time shorter.

23Someone may say, "Here is the Messiah!" or "There he is!" But don't believe it. 24False messiahs and false prophets will come and work great miracles and signs. They will even try to fool God's chosen ones. 25But I have warned you ahead of time. 26If you are told that the Messiah is out in the desert, don't go there! And if you are told that he is in some secret place, don't believe it! 27The coming of the Son of Man will be like lightning that can be seen from east to west. 28Where there is a corpse, there will always be buzzards.*q*

When the Son of Man Appears
(Mark 13.24-27; Luke 21.25-28)

29Right after those days of suffering,

"The sun will become dark,
and the moon
will no longer shine.
The stars will fall,
and the powers in the sky*r*
will be shaken."

30Then a sign will appear in the sky. And there will be the Son of Man.*s* All nations on earth will weep when they see the Son of Man coming on the clouds of heaven with power and great glory. 31At the sound of a loud trumpet, he will send his angels to bring his chosen ones together from all over the earth.

A Lesson from a Fig Tree
(Mark 13.28-31; Luke 21.29-33)

32Learn a lesson from a fig tree. When its branches sprout and start putting out leaves, you know that summer is near. 33So when you see all these things happening, you will know that the time has almost come.*t* 34I can promise you that some of the people of this generation will still be alive when all this happens. 35The sky and the earth won't last forever, but my words will.

No One Knows the Day or Time
(Mark 13.32-37; Luke 17.26-30, 34-36)

36No one knows the day or hour. The angels in heaven don't know, and the Son himself doesn't know.*u* Only the Father knows. 37When the Son of Man appears, things will be just as they were when Noah lived. 38People were eating, drinking, and getting married right up to the day that the flood came and Noah went into the big boat. 39They didn't know anything was happening until the flood came and swept them all away. That is how it will be when the Son of Man appears.

40Two men will be in the same field, but only one will be taken. The other will be left. 41Two women will be together grinding grain, but only one will be taken. The other will be left. 42So be on your guard! You don't know when your Lord will come. 43Homeowners never know when a thief is coming, and they are always on guard to keep one from breaking in. 44Always be ready! You don't know when the Son of Man will come.

Faithful and Unfaithful Servants
(Luke 12.35-48)

45Who are faithful and wise servants? Who are the ones the master will put in charge of giving the other servants their food supplies at the proper time? 46Servants are fortunate if their master comes and finds them doing their job. 47You may be sure that a servant who is always faithful will be put in charge of everything the master owns. 48But suppose one of the servants thinks that the master won't return until late. 49Suppose that evil servant

---

*p***24.20** *in winter or on a Sabbath*: In Palestine the winters are cold and rainy and make travel difficult. The Jewish people were not allowed to travel much more than half a mile on the Sabbath. For these reasons it was hard for them to escape from their enemies in the winter or on a Sabbath.   *q***24.28** *Where there is a corpse, there will always be buzzards*: This saying may mean that when anything important happens, people soon know about it. Or the saying may mean that whenever something bad happens, curious people gather around and stare. But the word translated "buzzard" also means "eagle" and may refer to the Roman army, which had an eagle as its symbol.   *r***24.29** *the powers in the sky*: In ancient times people thought that the stars were spiritual powers.   *s***24.30** *And there will be the Son of Man*: Or "And it will be the Son of Man."   *t***24.33** *the time has almost come*: Or "he (that is, the Son of Man) will soon be here."   *u***24.36** *and the Son himself doesn't know*: These words are not in some manuscripts.

starts beating the other servants and eats and drinks with people who are drunk. [50]If that happens, the master will surely come on a day and at a time when the servant least expects him. [51]That servant will then be punished and thrown out with the ones who only pretended to serve their master. There they will cry and grit their teeth in pain.

A Story about Ten Girls

25 The kingdom of heaven is like what happened one night when ten girls took their oil lamps and went to a wedding to meet the groom.[v] [2]Five of the girls were foolish and five were wise. [3]The foolish ones took their lamps, but no extra oil. [4]The ones who were wise took along extra oil for their lamps.

[5]The groom was late arriving, and the girls became drowsy and fell asleep. [6]Then in the middle of the night someone shouted, "Here's the groom! Come to meet him!"

[7]When the girls got up and started getting their lamps ready, [8]the foolish ones said to the others, "Let us have some of your oil! Our lamps are going out."

[9]The girls who were wise answered, "There's not enough oil for all of us! Go and buy some for yourselves."

[10]While the foolish girls were on their way to get some oil, the groom arrived. The girls who were ready went into the wedding, and the doors were closed. [11]Later the other girls returned and shouted, "Sir, sir! Open the door for us!"

[12]But the groom replied, "I don't even know you!"

[13]So, my disciples, always be ready! You don't know the day or the time when all this will happen.

A Story about Three Servants
(Luke 19.11-27)

[14]The kingdom is also like what happened when a man went away and put his three servants in charge of all he owned. [15]The man knew what each servant could do. So he handed five thousand coins to the first servant, two thousand to the second, and one thousand to the third. Then he left the country.

[16]As soon as the man had gone, the servant with the five thousand coins used them to earn five thousand more. [17]The servant who had two thousand coins did the same with his money and earned two thousand more. [18]But the servant with one thousand coins dug a hole and hid his master's money in the ground.

[19]Some time later the master of those servants returned. He called them in and asked what they had done with his money. [20]The servant who had been given five thousand coins brought them in with the five thousand that he had earned. He said, "Sir, you gave me five thousand coins, and I have earned five thousand more."

[21]"Wonderful!" his master replied. "You are a good and faithful servant. I left you in charge of only a little, but now I will put you in charge of much more. Come and share in my happiness!"

[22]Next, the servant who had been given two thousand coins came in and said, "Sir, you gave me two thousand coins, and I have earned two thousand more."

[23]"Wonderful!" his master replied. "You are a good and faithful servant. I left you in charge of only a little, but now I will put you in charge of much more. Come and share in my happiness!"

[24]The servant who had been given one thousand coins then came in and said, "Sir, I know that you are hard to get along with. You harvest what you don't plant and gather crops where you haven't scattered seed. [25]I was frightened and went out and hid your money in the ground. Here is every single coin!"

[26]The master of the servant told him, "You are lazy and good-for-nothing! You know that I harvest what I don't plant and gather crops where I haven't scattered seed. [27]You could have at least put my money in the bank, so that I could have earned interest on it."

[28]Then the master said, "Now your money will be taken away and given to the servant with ten thousand coins! [29]Everyone who has something will be given more, and they will have more than enough. But everything will be taken from those who don't have anything. [30]You are a worthless servant, and you will be thrown out into the dark where people will cry and grit their teeth in pain."

---

[v]**25.1** *to meet the groom*: Some manuscripts add "and the bride." It was the custom for the groom to go to the home of the bride's parents to get his bride. Young girls and other guests would then go with them to the home of the groom's parents, where the wedding feast would take place.

The Final Judgment

³¹When the Son of Man comes in his glory with all of his angels, he will sit on his royal throne. ³²The people of all nations will be brought before him, and he will separate them, as shepherds separate their sheep from their goats.

³³He will place the sheep on his right and the goats on his left. ³⁴Then the king will say to those on his right, "My father has blessed you! Come and receive the kingdom that was prepared for you before the world was created. ³⁵When I was hungry, you gave me something to eat, and when I was thirsty, you gave me something to drink. When I was a stranger, you welcomed me, ³⁶and when I was naked, you gave me clothes to wear. When I was sick, you took care of me, and when I was in jail, you visited me."

³⁷Then the ones who pleased the Lord will ask, "When did we give you something to eat or drink? ³⁸When did we welcome you as a stranger or give you clothes to wear ³⁹or visit you while you were sick or in jail?"

⁴⁰The king will answer, "Whenever you did it for any of my people, no matter how unimportant they seemed, you did it for me."

⁴¹Then the king will say to those on his left, "Get away from me! You are under God's curse. Go into the everlasting fire prepared for the devil and his angels! ⁴²I was hungry, but you did not give me anything to eat, and I was thirsty, but you did not give me anything to drink. ⁴³I was a stranger, but you did not welcome me, and I was naked, but you did not give me any clothes to wear. I was sick and in jail, but you did not take care of me."

⁴⁴Then the people will ask, "Lord, when did we fail to help you when you were hungry or thirsty or a stranger or naked or sick or in jail?"

⁴⁵The king will say to them, "Whenever you failed to help any of my people, no matter how unimportant they seemed, you failed to do it for me."

⁴⁶Then Jesus said, "Those people will be punished forever. But the ones who pleased God will have eternal life."

The Plot To Kill Jesus
(Mark 14.1, 2; Luke 22.1, 2; John 11.45-53)

26 When Jesus had finished teaching, he told his disciples, ²"You know that two days from now will be Passover. That is when the Son of Man will be handed over to his enemies and nailed to a cross."

³At that time the chief priests and the nation's leaders were meeting at the home of Caiaphas the high priest. ⁴They planned how they could sneak around and have Jesus arrested and put to death. ⁵But they said, "We must not do it during Passover, because the people will riot."

At Bethany
(Mark 14.3-9; John 12.1-8)

⁶Jesus was in the town of Bethany, eating at the home of Simon, who had leprosy.ʷ ⁷A woman came in with a bottle of expensive perfume and poured it on Jesus' head. ⁸But when his disciples saw this, they became angry and complained, "Why such a waste? ⁹We could have sold this perfume for a lot of money and given it to the poor."

¹⁰Jesus knew what they were thinking, and he said:

Why are you bothering this woman? She has done a beautiful thing for me. ¹¹You will always have the poor with you, but you won't always have me. ¹²She has poured perfume on my body to prepare it for burial.ˣ ¹³You may be sure that wherever the good news is told all over the world, people will remember what she has done. And they will tell others.

Judas and the Chief Priests
(Mark 14.10, 11; Luke 22.3-6)

¹⁴Judas Iscariotʸ was one of the twelve disciples. He went to the chief priests ¹⁵and asked, "How much will you give me if I help you arrest Jesus?" They paid Judas thirty silver coins, ¹⁶and from then on he started looking for a good chance to betray Jesus.

Jesus Eats the Passover Meal with His Disciples
(Mark 14.12-21; Luke 22.7-13; John 13.21-30)

¹⁷On the first day of the Festival of Thin Bread, Jesus' disciples came to him and asked, "Where do you want us to prepare the Passover meal?"

¹⁸Jesus told them to go to a certain man in the city and tell him, "Our teacher says, 'My time has come! I want to eat the Passover meal with my disciples in your home.' " ¹⁹They did as Jesus told them and prepared the meal.

²⁰⁻²¹When Jesus was eating with his twelve disciples that evening, he said, "One of you will surely hand me over to my enemies."

ʷ**26.6** *leprosy:* See the note at 8.2.   ˣ**26.12** *poured perfume on my body to prepare it for burial:* The Jewish people taught that giving someone a proper burial was even more important than helping the poor.   ʸ**26.14** *Iscariot:* See the note at 10.4.

²²The disciples were very sad, and each one said to Jesus, "Lord, you can't mean me!"

²³He answered, "One of you men who has eaten with me from this dish will betray me. ²⁴The Son of Man will die, as the Scriptures say. But it's going to be terrible for the one who betrays me! That man would be better off if he had never been born."

²⁵Judas said, "Teacher, you surely don't mean me!"

"That's what you say!" Jesus replied. But later, Judas did betray him.

The Lord's Supper
(Mark 14.22-26; Luke 22.14-23;
1 Corinthians 11.23-25)

²⁶During the meal Jesus took some bread in his hands. He blessed the bread and broke it. Then he gave it to his disciples and said, "Take this and eat it. This is my body."

²⁷Jesus picked up a cup of wine and gave thanks to God. He then gave it to his disciples and said, "Take this and drink it. ²⁸This is my blood, and with it God makes his agreement with you. It will be poured out, so that many people will have their sins forgiven. ²⁹From now on I am not going to drink any wine, until I drink new wine with you in my Father's kingdom." ³⁰Then they sang a hymn and went out to the Mount of Olives.

Peter's Promise
(Mark 14.27-31; Luke 22.31-34; John 13.36-38)

³¹Jesus said to his disciples, "During this very night, all of you will reject me, as the Scriptures say,

'I will strike down
    the shepherd,
and the sheep
    will be scattered.'

³²But after I am raised to life, I will go to Galilee ahead of you."

³³Peter spoke up, "Even if all the others reject you, I never will!"

³⁴Jesus replied, "I promise you that before a rooster crows tonight, you will say three times that you don't know me." ³⁵But Peter said, "Even if I have to die with you, I will never say I don't know you."

All the others said the same thing.

Jesus Prays
(Mark 14.32-42; Luke 22.39-46)

³⁶Jesus went with his disciples to a place called Gethsemane. When they got

there, he told them, "Sit here while I go over there and pray."

³⁷Jesus took along Peter and the two brothers, James and John.ᶻ He was very sad and troubled, ³⁸and he said to them, "I am so sad that I feel as if I am dying. Stay here and keep awake with me."

³⁹Jesus walked on a little way. Then he knelt with his face to the ground and prayed, "My Father, if it is possible, don't make me suffer by having me drink from this cup.ᵃ But do what you want, and not what I want."

⁴⁰He came back and found his disciples sleeping. So he said to Peter, "Can't any of you stay awake with me for just one hour? ⁴¹Stay awake and pray that you won't be tested. You want to do what is right, but you are weak."

⁴²Again Jesus went to pray and said, "My Father, if there is no other way, and I must suffer, I will still do what you want."

⁴³Jesus came back and found them sleeping again. They simply could not keep their eyes open. ⁴⁴He left them and prayed the same prayer once more.

⁴⁵Finally, Jesus returned to his disciples and said, "Are you still sleeping and resting?ᵇ The time has come for the Son of Man to be handed over to sinners. ⁴⁶Get up! Let's go. The one who will betray me is already here."

Jesus Is Arrested
(Mark 14.43-50; Luke 22.47-53; John 18.3-12)

⁴⁷Jesus was still speaking, when Judas the betrayer came up. He was one of the twelve disciples, and a large mob armed with swords and clubs was with him. They had been sent by the chief priests and the nation's leaders. ⁴⁸Judas had told them ahead of time, "Arrest the man I greet with a kiss."ᶜ

⁴⁹Judas walked right up to Jesus and said, "Hello, teacher." Then Judas kissed him.

⁵⁰Jesus replied, "My friend, why are you here?"ᵈ

The men grabbed Jesus and arrested him. ⁵¹One of Jesus' followers pulled out a sword. He struck the servant of the high priest and cut off his ear.

⁵²But Jesus told him, "Put your sword away. Anyone who lives by fighting will die by fighting. ⁵³Don't you know that I could ask my Father, and right away he would send me more than twelve armies of angels? ⁵⁴But then, how could the words of the Scriptures come true, which say that this must happen?"

ᶻ**26.37** *the two brothers, James and John*: The Greek text has "the two sons of Zebedee" (see 27.56). ᵃ**26.39** *having me drink from this cup*: In the Scriptures "to drink from a cup" sometimes means to suffer (see the note at 20.22). ᵇ**26.45** *Are you still sleeping and resting?*: Or "You may as well keep on sleeping and resting." ᶜ**26.48** *the man I greet with a kiss*: It was the custom for people to greet each other with a kiss on the cheek. ᵈ**26.50** *why are you here?*: Or "do what you came for."

55Jesus said to the mob, "Why do you come with swords and clubs to arrest me like a criminal? Day after day I sat and taught in the temple, and you didn't arrest me. 56But all this happened, so that what the prophets wrote would come true."

All of Jesus' disciples left him and ran away.

Jesus Is Questioned by the Council
(Mark 14.53-65; Luke 22.54, 55, 63-71;
John 18.13, 14, 19-24)

57After Jesus had been arrested, he was led off to the house of Caiaphas the high priest. The nation's leaders and the teachers of the Law of Moses were meeting there. 58But Peter followed along at a distance and came to the courtyard of the high priest's palace. He went in and sat down with the guards to see what was going to happen.

59The chief priests and the whole council wanted to put Jesus to death. So they tried to find some people who would tell lies about him in court.e 60But they could not find any, even though many did come and tell lies. At last, two men came forward 61and said, "This man claimed that he would tear down God's temple and build it again in three days."

62The high priest stood up and asked Jesus, "Why don't you say something in your own defense? Don't you hear the charges they are making against you?" 63But Jesus did not answer. So the high priest said, "With the living God looking on, you must tell the truth. Tell us, are you the Messiah, the Son of God?"f

64"That is what you say!" Jesus answered. "But I tell all of you,

'Soon you will see
    the Son of Man
sitting at the right sideg
    of God All-Powerful
and coming on the clouds
    of heaven.' "

65The high priest then tore his robe and said, "This man claims to be God! We don't need any more witnesses! You have heard what he said. 66What do you think?"

They answered, "He is guilty and deserves to die!" 67Then they spit in his face and hit him with their fists. Others slapped him 68and said, "You think you are the Messiah! So tell us who hit you!"

Peter Says He Doesn't Know Jesus
(Mark 14.66-72; Luke 22.56-62;
John 18.15-18, 25-27)

69While Peter was sitting out in the courtyard, a servant girl came up to him and said, "You were with Jesus from Galilee."

70But in front of everyone Peter said, "That isn't so! I don't know what you are talking about!"

71When Peter had gone out to the gate, another servant girl saw him and said to some people there, "This man was with Jesus from Nazareth."

72Again Peter denied it, and this time he swore, "I don't even know that man!"

73A little while later some people standing there walked over to Peter and said, "We know that you are one of them. We can tell it because you talk like someone from Galilee."

74Peter began to curse and swear, "I don't know that man!"

Right then a rooster crowed, 75and Peter remembered that Jesus had said, "Before a rooster crows, you will say three times that you don't know me." Then Peter went out and cried hard.

Jesus Is Taken to Pilate
(Mark 15.1; Luke 23.1, 2; John 18.28-32)

27 Early the next morning all the chief priests and the nation's leaders met and decided that Jesus should be put to death. 2They tied him up and led him away to Pilate the governor.

The Death of Judas
(Acts 1.18, 19)

3Judas had betrayed Jesus, but when he learned that Jesus had been sentenced to death, he was sorry for what he had done. He returned the thirty silver coins to the chief priests and leaders 4and said, "I have sinned by betraying a man who has never done anything wrong."

"So what? That's your problem," they replied. 5Judas threw the money into the temple and then went out and hanged himself.

6The chief priests picked up the money and said, "This money was paid to have a man killed. We can't put it in the temple treasury." 7Then they had a meeting and decided to buy a field that belonged to someone who made clay pots. They wanted to use it as a graveyard for foreigners. 8That's why people still call that place "Field of Blood." 9So the words of the prophet Jeremiah came true,

"They took
    the thirty silver coins,
the price of a person
    among the people of Israel.

e**26.59** *some people who would tell lies about him in court:* The Law of Moses taught that two witnesses were necessary before a person could be put to death (see verse 60).   f**26.63** *Son of God:* One of the titles used for the kings of Israel.   g**26.64** *right side:* See the note at 22.44.

¹⁰ They paid it
    for a potter's field,^h
as the Lord
    had commanded me."

Pilate Questions Jesus
(Mark 15.2-5; Luke 23.3-5; John 18.33-38)

¹¹Jesus was brought before Pilate the governor, who asked him, "Are you the king of the Jews?"

"Those are your words!" Jesus answered. ¹²And when the chief priests and leaders brought their charges against him, he did not say a thing.

¹³Pilate asked him, "Don't you hear what crimes they say you have done?" ¹⁴But Jesus did not say anything, and the governor was greatly amazed.

The Death Sentence
(Mark 15.6-15; Luke 23.13-26; John 18.39—19.16)

¹⁵During Passover the governor always freed a prisoner chosen by the people. ¹⁶At that time a well-known terrorist named Jesus Barabbasⁱ was in jail. ¹⁷So when the crowd came together, Pilate asked them, "Which prisoner do you want me to set free? Do you want Jesus Barabbas or Jesus who is called the Messiah?" ¹⁸Pilate knew that the leaders had brought Jesus to him because they were jealous.

¹⁹While Pilate was judging the case, his wife sent him a message. It said, "Don't have anything to do with that innocent man. I have had nightmares because of him."

²⁰But the chief priests and the leaders convinced the crowds to ask for Barabbas to be set free and for Jesus to be killed. ²¹Pilate asked the crowd again, "Which of these two men do you want me to set free?"

"Barabbas!" they replied.

²²Pilate asked them, "What am I to do with Jesus, who is called the Messiah?"

They all yelled, "Nail him to a cross!"

²³Pilate answered, "But what crime has he done?"

"Nail him to a cross!" they yelled even louder.

²⁴Pilate saw that there was nothing he could do and that the people were starting to riot. So he took some water and washed his hands^j in front of them and said, "I won't have anything to do with killing this man. You are the ones doing it!"

²⁵Everyone answered, "We and our own families will take the blame for his death!"

²⁶Pilate set Barabbas free. Then he ordered his soldiers to beat Jesus with a whip and nail him to a cross.

Soldiers Make Fun of Jesus
(Mark 15.16-21; John 19.2, 3)

²⁷The governor's soldiers led Jesus into the fortress^k and brought together the rest of the troops. ²⁸They stripped off Jesus' clothes and put a scarlet robe^l on him. ²⁹They made a crown out of thorn branches and placed it on his head, and they put a stick in his right hand. The soldiers knelt down and pretended to worship him. They made fun of him and shouted, "Hey, you king of the Jews!" ³⁰Then they spit on him. They took the stick from him and beat him on the head with it.

Jesus Is Nailed to a Cross
(Mark 15.22-32; Luke 23.27-43; John 19.17-27)

³¹When the soldiers had finished making fun of Jesus, they took off the robe. They put his own clothes back on him and led him off to be nailed to a cross. ³²On the way they met a man from Cyrene named Simon, and they forced him to carry Jesus' cross.

³³They came to a place named Golgotha, which means "Place of a Skull."^m ³⁴There they gave Jesus some wine mixed with a drug to ease the pain. But when Jesus tasted what it was, he refused to drink it.

³⁵The soldiers nailed Jesus to a cross and gambled to see who would get his clothes. ³⁶Then they sat down to guard him. ³⁷Above his head they put a sign that told why he was nailed there. It read, "This is Jesus, the King of the Jews." ³⁸The soldiers also nailed two criminals on crosses, one to the right of Jesus and the other to his left.

³⁹People who passed by said terrible things about Jesus. They shook their heads and ⁴⁰shouted, "So you're the one who claimed you could tear down the temple and build it again in three days! If you are God's Son, save yourself and come down from the cross!"

⁴¹The chief priests, the leaders, and the teachers of the Law of Moses also

---

^h**27.10** *a potter's field*: Perhaps a field owned by someone who made clay pots. But it may have been a field where potters came to get clay or to make pots or to throw away their broken pieces of pottery. ⁱ**27.16** *Jesus Barabbas*: Here and in verse 17 many manuscripts have "Barabbas." ^j**27.24** *washed his hands*: To show that he was innocent. ^k**27.27** *fortress*: The place where the Roman governor stayed. It was probably at Herod's palace west of Jerusalem, though it may have been Fortress Antonia north of the temple, where the Roman troops were stationed. ^l**27.28** *scarlet robe*: This was probably a Roman soldier's robe. ^m**27.33** *Place of a Skull*: The place was probably given this name because it was near a large rock in the shape of a human skull.

made fun of Jesus. They said, [42]"He saved others, but he can't save himself. If he is the king of Israel, he should come down from the cross! Then we will believe him. [43]He trusted God, so let God save him, if he wants to. He even said he was God's Son." [44]The two criminals also said cruel things to Jesus.

The Death of Jesus
(Mark 15.33-41; Luke 23.44-49; John 19.28-30)

[45]At noon the sky turned dark and stayed that way until three o'clock. [46]Then about that time Jesus shouted, "Eli, Eli, lema sabachthani?" [n] which means, "My God, my God, why have you deserted me?"

[47]Some of the people standing there heard Jesus and said, "He's calling for Elijah." [o] [48]One of them at once ran and grabbed a sponge. He soaked it in wine, then put it on a stick and held it up to Jesus.

[49]Others said, "Wait! Let's see if Elijah will come[p] and save him." [50]Once again Jesus shouted, and then he died.

[51]At once the curtain in the temple[q] was torn in two from top to bottom. The earth shook, and rocks split apart. [52]Graves opened, and many of God's people were raised to life. [53]Then after Jesus had risen to life, they came out of their graves and went into the holy city, where they were seen by many people.

[54]The officer and the soldiers guarding Jesus felt the earthquake and saw everything else that happened. They were frightened and said, "This man really was God's Son!"

[55]Many women had come with Jesus from Galilee to be of help to him, and they were there, looking on at a distance. [56]Mary Magdalene, Mary the mother of James and Joseph, and the mother of James and John[r] were some of these women.

Jesus Is Buried
(Mark 15.42-47; Luke 23.50-56; John 19.38-42)

[57]That evening a rich disciple named Joseph from the town of Arimathea [58]went and asked for Jesus' body. Pilate gave orders for it to be given to Joseph, [59]who took the body and wrapped it in a clean linen cloth. [60]Then Joseph put the body in his own tomb that had been cut into solid rock[s] and had never been used. He rolled a big stone against the entrance to the tomb and went away.

[61]All this time Mary Magdalene and the other Mary were sitting across from the tomb.

[62]On the next day, which was a Sabbath, the chief priests and the Pharisees went together to Pilate. [63]They said, "Sir, we remember what that liar said while he was still alive. He claimed that in three days he would come back from death. [64]So please order the tomb to be carefully guarded for three days. If you don't, his disciples may come and steal his body. They will tell the people that he has been raised to life, and this last lie will be worse than the first one." [t]

[65]Pilate said to them, "All right, take some of your soldiers and guard the tomb as well as you know how." [66]So they sealed it tight and placed soldiers there to guard it.

Jesus Is Alive
(Mark 16.1-8; Luke 24.1-12; John 20.1-10)

28 The Sabbath was over, and it was almost daybreak on Sunday when Mary Magdalene and the other Mary went to see the tomb. [2]Suddenly a strong earthquake struck, and the Lord's angel came down from heaven. He rolled away the stone and sat on it. [3]The angel looked as bright as lightning, and his clothes were white as snow. [4]The guards shook from fear and fell down, as though they were dead.

[5]The angel said to the women, "Don't be afraid! I know you are looking for Jesus, who was nailed to a cross. [6]He isn't here! God has raised him to life, just as Jesus said he would. Come, see the place where his body was lying. [7]Now hurry! Tell his disciples that he has been raised to life and is on his way to Galilee. Go there, and you will see him. That is what I came to tell you."

[8]The women were frightened and yet very happy, as they hurried from the tomb and ran to tell his disciples. [9]Suddenly Jesus met them and greeted them. They went near him, held on to his feet, and worshiped him. [10]Then Jesus said, "Don't be afraid! Tell my

---

[n]**27.46** *Eli . . . sabachthani:* These words are in Hebrew.   [o]**27.47** *Elijah:* In Aramaic the name "Elijah" sounds like "Eli," which means "my God."   [p]**27.49** *Elijah will come:* See the note at 16.14.   [q]**27.51** *curtain in the temple:* There were two curtains in the temple. One was at the entrance, and the other separated the holy place from the most holy place that the Jewish people thought of as God's home on earth. The second curtain is probably the one that is meant.   [r]**27.56** *of James and John:* The Greek text has "of Zebedee's sons" (see 26.37).   [s]**27.60** *tomb . . . solid rock:* Some of the Jewish people buried their dead in rooms carved into solid rock. A heavy stone was rolled against the entrance.   [t]**27.64** *the first one:* Probably the belief that Jesus is the Messiah.

followers to go to Galilee. They will see me there."

Report of the Guard

[11]While the women were on their way, some soldiers who had been guarding the tomb went into the city. They told the chief priests everything that had happened. [12]So the chief priests met with the leaders and decided to bribe the soldiers with a lot of money. [13]They said to the soldiers, "Tell everyone that Jesus' disciples came during the night and stole his body while you were asleep. [14]If the governor[u] hears about this, we will talk to him. You won't have anything to worry about." [15]The soldiers took the money and did what they were told. The people of Judea still tell each other this story.

[u]**28.14** *governor*: Pontius Pilate.

What Jesus' Followers Must Do
(Mark 16.14-18; Luke 24.36-49; John 20.19-23; Acts 1.6-8)

[16]Jesus' eleven disciples went to a mountain in Galilee, where Jesus had told them to meet him. [17]They saw him and worshiped him, but some of them doubted.

[18]Jesus came to them and said:

I have been given all authority in heaven and on earth! [19]Go to the people of all nations and make them my disciples. Baptize them in the name of the Father, the Son, and the Holy Spirit, [20]and teach them to do everything I have told you. I will be with you always, even until the end of the world.

MARK

ABOUT THIS BOOK

This is the shortest of the four New Testament books that tell about the life and teachings of Jesus, but it is also the most action-packed. From the very beginning of his ministry, Jesus worked mighty wonders. After choosing four followers (1.16-20), he immediately performed many miracles of healing. Among those healed were a man with an evil spirit in him (1.21-28), Simon's mother-in-law (1.30, 31), crowds of sick people (1.32-34), and a man with leprosy (1.40-45). Over and over Mark tells how Jesus healed people, but always in such a way as to show that he did these miracles by the power of God.

The religious leaders refused to accept Jesus. This led to conflicts (2.2—3.6) that finally made them start looking for a way to kill him (11.18). But the demons saw the power of Jesus, and they knew that he was the Son of God, although Jesus would not let them tell anyone.

This book is full of miracles that amazed the crowds and Jesus' followers. But, according to Mark, the most powerful miracle of Jesus is his suffering and death. The first person to understand this miracle was the Roman soldier who saw Jesus die on the cross and said, "This man really was the Son of God!" (15.39).

This Gospel is widely thought to be the first one written. The many explanations of Aramaic words and Jewish customs in Mark suggest that Mark wrote to Gentile or non-Jewish Christians. He wants to tell about Jesus and to encourage readers to believe in the power of Jesus to rescue them from sickness, demons, and death. He also wants to remind them that the new life of faith is not an easy life, and that they must follow Jesus by serving others and being ready to suffer as he did.

The first followers of Jesus to discover the empty tomb were three women, and the angel told them:

> *Don't be alarmed! You are looking for Jesus from Nazareth, who was nailed to a cross. God has raised him to life, and he isn't here.* (16.6)

A QUICK LOOK AT THIS BOOK

The Message of John the Baptist (1.1-8)
The Baptism and Temptation of Jesus (1.9-13)
Jesus in Galilee (1.14—9.50)
Jesus Goes from Galilee to Jerusalem (10.1-52)
Jesus' Last Week: His Trial and Death (11.1—15.47)
Jesus Is Alive (16.1-8)
Jesus Appears to His Followers (16.9-20)

The Preaching of John the Baptist
(Matthew 3.1-12; Luke 3.1-18; John 1.19-28)

1 This is the good news about Jesus Christ, the Son of God.ᵃ ²It began just as God had said in the book written by Isaiah the prophet,

"I am sending my messenger
to get the way ready
    for you.
³ In the desert
    someone is shouting,
'Get the road ready
    for the Lord!

ᵃ**1.1** *the Son of God*: These words are not in some manuscripts.

Make a straight path
for him.' "

⁴So John the Baptist showed up in the
desert and told everyone, "Turn back to
God and be baptized! Then your sins
will be forgiven."

⁵From all Judea and Jerusalem
crowds of people went to John. They
told how sorry they were for their sins,
and he baptized them in the Jordan
River.

⁶John wore clothes made of camel's
hair. He had a leather strap around his
waist and ate grasshoppers and wild
honey.

⁷John also told the people, "Someone
more powerful is going to come. And I
am not good enough even to stoop down
and untie his sandals.*b* ⁸I baptize you
with water, but he will baptize you with
the Holy Spirit!"

The Baptism of Jesus
(Matthew 3.13-17; Luke 3.21, 22)

⁹About that time Jesus came from
Nazareth in Galilee, and John baptized
him in the Jordan River. ¹⁰As soon as Jesus came out of the water, he saw the
sky open and the Holy Spirit coming
down to him like a dove. ¹¹A voice from
heaven said, "You are my own dear Son,
and I am pleased with you."

Jesus and Satan
(Matthew 4.1-11; Luke 4.1-13)

¹²Right away God's Spirit made Jesus
go into the desert. ¹³He stayed there for
forty days while Satan tested him. Jesus
was with the wild animals, but angels
took care of him.

Jesus Begins His Work
(Matthew 4.12-17; Luke 4.14, 15)

¹⁴After John was arrested, Jesus went
to Galilee and told the good news that
comes from God.*c* ¹⁵He said, "The time
has come! God's kingdom will soon be
here.*d* Turn back to God and believe the
good news!"

Jesus Chooses Four Fishermen
(Matthew 4.18-22; Luke 5.1-11)

¹⁶As Jesus was walking along the
shore of Lake Galilee, he saw Simon
and his brother Andrew. They were fishermen and were casting their nets into
the lake. ¹⁷Jesus said to them, "Come
with me! I will teach you how to bring
in people instead of fish." ¹⁸Right then
the two brothers dropped their nets and
went with him.

¹⁹Jesus walked on and soon saw
James and John, the sons of Zebedee.
They were in a boat, mending their nets.
²⁰At once Jesus asked them to come
with him. They left their father in the
boat with the hired workers and went
with him.

A Man with an Evil Spirit
(Luke 4.31-37)

²¹Jesus and his disciples went to the
town of Capernaum. Then on the next
Sabbath he went into the Jewish meeting place and started teaching. ²²Every-
one was amazed at his teaching. He
taught with authority, and not like the
teachers of the Law of Moses. ²³Sud-
denly a man with an evil spirit*e* in him
entered the meeting place and yelled,
²⁴"Jesus from Nazareth, what do you
want with us? Have you come to destroy
us? I know who you are! You are God's
Holy One."

²⁵Jesus told the evil spirit, "Be quiet
and come out of the man!" ²⁶The spirit
shook him. Then it gave a loud shout
and left.

²⁷Everyone was completely surprised
and kept saying to each other, "What is
this? It must be some new kind of powerful teaching! Even the evil spirits obey
him." ²⁸News about Jesus quickly
spread all over Galilee.

Jesus Heals Many People
(Matthew 8.14-17; Luke 4.38-41)

²⁹As soon as Jesus left the meeting
place with James and John, they went
home with Simon and Andrew. ³⁰When
they got there, Jesus was told that Simon's mother-in-law was sick in bed
with fever. ³¹Jesus went to her. He took
hold of her hand and helped her up. The
fever left her, and she served them a
meal.

³²That evening after sunset,*f* all who
were sick or had demons in them were
brought to Jesus. ³³In fact, the whole
town gathered around the door of the
house. ³⁴Jesus healed all kinds of terrible diseases and forced out a lot of
demons. But the demons knew who he
was, and he did not let them speak.

³⁵Very early the next morning, Jesus
got up and went to a place where he
could be alone and pray. ³⁶Simon and
the others started looking for him.
³⁷And when they found him, they said,
"Everyone is looking for you!"

³⁸Jesus replied, "We must go to the
nearby towns, so that I can tell the good
news to those people. This is why I have

---

*b***1.7** *untie his sandals*: This was the duty of a slave.   *c***1.14** *that comes from God*: Or "that is
about God."   *d***1.15** *will soon be here*: Or "is already here."   *e***1.23** *evil spirit*: A Jewish
person who had an evil spirit was considered "unclean" and was not allowed to eat or worship
with other Jewish people.   *f***1.32** *after sunset*: The Sabbath was over, and a new day began
at sunset.

come." [39]Then Jesus went to Jewish meeting places everywhere in Galilee, where he preached and forced out demons.

Jesus Heals a Man
(Matthew 8.1-4; Luke 5.12-16)

[40]A man with leprosy[g] came to Jesus and knelt down.[h] He begged, "You have the power to make me well, if only you wanted to."

[41]Jesus felt sorry for[i] the man. So he put his hand on him and said, "I want to! Now you are well." [42]At once the man's leprosy disappeared, and he was well.

[43]After Jesus strictly warned the man, he sent him on his way. [44]He said, "Don't tell anyone about this. Just go and show the priest that you are well. Then take a gift to the temple as Moses commanded, and everyone will know that you have been healed."[j]

[45]The man talked about it so much and told so many people, that Jesus could no longer go openly into a town. He had to stay away from the towns, but people still came to him from everywhere.

Jesus Heals a Crippled Man
(Matthew 9.1-8; Luke 5.17-26)

2 Jesus went back to Capernaum, and a few days later people heard that he was at home.[k] [2]Then so many of them came to the house that there wasn't even standing room left in front of the door.

Jesus was still teaching [3]when four people came up, carrying a crippled man on a mat. [4]But because of the crowd, they could not get him to Jesus. So they made a hole in the roof[l] above him and let the man down in front of everyone.

[5]When Jesus saw how much faith they had, he said to the crippled man, "My friend, your sins are forgiven."

[6]Some of the teachers of the Law of Moses were sitting there. They started wondering, [7]"Why would he say such a thing? He must think he is God! Only God can forgive sins."

[8]Right away, Jesus knew what they were thinking, and he said, "Why are you thinking such things? [9]Is it easier for me to tell this crippled man that his sins are forgiven or to tell him to get up and pick up his mat and go on home? [10]I will show you that the Son of Man has the right to forgive sins here on earth." So Jesus said to the man, [11]"Get up! Pick up your mat and go on home."

[12]The man got right up. He picked up his mat and went out while everyone watched in amazement. They praised God and said, "We have never seen anything like this!"

Jesus Chooses Levi
(Matthew 9.9-13; Luke 5.27-32)

[13]Once again, Jesus went to the shore of Lake Galilee. A large crowd gathered around him, and he taught them. [14]As he walked along, he saw Levi, the son of Alphaeus. Levi was sitting at the place for paying taxes, and Jesus said to him, "Come with me!" So he got up and went with Jesus.

[15]Later, Jesus and his disciples were having dinner at Levi's house.[m] Many tax collectors[n] and other sinners had become followers of Jesus, and they were also guests at the dinner.

[16]Some of the teachers of the Law of Moses were Pharisees, and they saw that Jesus was eating with sinners and tax collectors. So they asked his disciples, "Why does he eat with tax collectors and sinners?"

[17]Jesus heard them and answered, "Healthy people don't need a doctor, but sick people do. I didn't come to invite good people to be my followers. I came to invite sinners."

People Ask about Going without Eating
(Matthew 9.14-17; Luke 5.33-39)

[18]The followers of John the Baptist and the Pharisees often went without eating.[o] Some people came and asked Jesus, "Why do the followers of John and those of the Pharisees often go without eating, while your disciples never do?"

[19]Jesus answered:

---

[g]**1.40** *leprosy:* In biblical times the word "leprosy" was used for many different kinds of skin diseases. [h]**1.40** *and knelt down:* These words are not in some manuscripts. [i]**1.41** *felt sorry for:* Some manuscripts have "was angry with." [j]**1.44** *everyone will know that you have been healed:* People with leprosy had to be examined by a priest and told that they were well (that is, "clean") before they could once again live a normal life in the Jewish community. The gift that Moses commanded was the sacrifice of some lambs together with flour mixed with olive oil. [k]**2.1** *at home:* Or "in the house" (perhaps Simon Peter's home). [l]**2.4** *roof:* In Palestine the houses usually had a flat roof. Stairs on the outside led up to the roof that was made of beams and boards covered with packed earth. [m]**2.15** *Levi's house:* Or "Jesus' house." [n]**2.15** *tax collectors:* These were usually Jewish people who paid the Romans for the right to collect taxes. They were hated by other Jews who thought of them as traitors to their country and to their religion. [o]**2.18** *without eating:* The Jewish people sometimes went without eating (also called "fasting") to show their love for God or to show sorrow for their sins.

The friends of a bridegroom don't go without eating while he is still with them. [20]But the time will come when he will be taken from them. Then they will go without eating.

[21]No one patches old clothes by sewing on a piece of new cloth. The new piece would shrink and tear a bigger hole.

[22]No one pours new wine into old wineskins. The wine would swell and burst the old skins.[p] Then the wine would be lost, and the skins would be ruined. New wine must be put into new wineskins.

A Question about the Sabbath
(Matthew 12.1-8; Luke 6.1-5)

[23]One Sabbath Jesus and his disciples were walking through some wheat fields. His disciples were picking grains of wheat as they went along.[q] [24]Some Pharisees asked Jesus, "Why are your disciples picking grain on the Sabbath? They are not supposed to do that!"

[25]Jesus answered, "Haven't you read what David did when he and his followers were hungry and in need? [26]It was during the time of Abiathar the high priest. David went into the house of God and ate the sacred loaves of bread that only priests are allowed to eat. He also gave some to his followers."

[27]Jesus finished by saying, "People were not made for the good of the Sabbath. The Sabbath was made for the good of people. [28]So the Son of Man is Lord over the Sabbath."

A Man with a Crippled Hand
(Matthew 12.9-14; Luke 6.6-11)

3 The next time that Jesus went into the meeting place, a man with a crippled hand was there. [2]The Pharisees[r] wanted to accuse Jesus of doing something wrong, and they kept watching to see if Jesus would heal him on the Sabbath.

[3]Jesus told the man to stand up where everyone could see him. [4]Then he asked, "On the Sabbath should we do good deeds or evil deeds? Should we save someone's life or destroy it?" But no one said a word.

[5]Jesus was angry as he looked around at the people. Yet he felt sorry for them because they were so stubborn. Then he told the man, "Stretch out your hand." He did, and his bad hand was healed.

[6]The Pharisees left. And right away they started making plans with Herod's followers[s] to kill Jesus.

Large Crowds Come to Jesus

[7]Jesus led his disciples down to the shore of the lake. Large crowds followed him from Galilee, Judea, [8]and Jerusalem. People came from Idumea, as well as other places east of the Jordan River. They also came from the region around the cities of Tyre and Sidon. All of these crowds came because they had heard what Jesus was doing. [9]He even had to tell his disciples to get a boat ready to keep him from being crushed by the crowds.

[10]After Jesus had healed many people, the other sick people begged him to let them touch him. [11]And whenever any evil spirits saw Jesus, they would fall to the ground and shout, "You are the Son of God!" [12]But Jesus warned the spirits not to tell who he was.

Jesus Chooses His Twelve Apostles
(Matthew 10.1-4; Luke 6.12-16)

[13]Jesus decided to ask some of his disciples to go up on a mountain with him, and they went. [14]Then he chose twelve of them to be his apostles,[t] so that they could be with him. He also wanted to send them out to preach [15]and to force out demons. [16]Simon was one of the twelve, and Jesus named him Peter. [17]There were also James and John, the two sons of Zebedee. Jesus called them Boanerges, which means "Thunderbolts." [18]Andrew, Philip, Bartholomew, Matthew, Thomas, James son of Alphaeus, and Thaddaeus were also apostles. The others were Simon, known as the Eager One,[u] [19]and Judas Iscariot,[v] who later betrayed Jesus.

Jesus and the Ruler of Demons
(Matthew 12.22-32; Luke 11.14-23; 12.10)

[20]Jesus went back home,[w] and once again such a large crowd gathered that

---

[p]**2.22** *swell and burst the old skins*: While the juice from grapes was becoming wine, it would swell and stretch the skins in which it had been stored. If the skins were old and stiff, they would burst.   [q]**2.23** *went along*: It was the custom to let hungry travelers pick grains of wheat.   [r]**3.2** *Pharisees*: The Greek text has "they" (but see verse 6).   [s]**3.6** *Herod's followers*: People who were political followers of the family of Herod the Great and his son Herod Antipas.   [t]**3.14** *to be his apostles*: These words are not in some manuscripts.   [u]**3.18.** *Eager One*: The Greek text has "Zealot," a name later given to the members of a Jewish group that resisted and fought against the Romans.   [v]**3.19** *Iscariot*: This may mean "a man from Kerioth" (a place in Judea). But more probably it means "a man who was a liar" or "a man who was a betrayer."   [w]**3.20** *went back home*: Or "entered a house" (perhaps the home of Simon Peter).

there was no chance even to eat. [21]When Jesus' family heard what he was doing, they thought he was crazy and went to get him under control.

[22]Some teachers of the Law of Moses came from Jerusalem and said, "This man is under the power of Beelzebul, the ruler of demons! He is even forcing out demons with the help of Beelzebul."

[23]Jesus told the people to gather around him. Then he spoke to them in riddles and said:

How can Satan force himself out? [24]A nation whose people fight each other won't last very long. [25]And a family that fights won't last long either. [26]So if Satan fights against himself, that will be the end of him.

[27]How can anyone break into the house of a strong man and steal his things, unless he first ties up the strong man? Then he can take everything.

[28]I promise you that any of the sinful things you say or do can be forgiven, no matter how terrible those things are. [29]But if you speak against the Holy Spirit, you can never be forgiven. That sin will be held against you forever.

[30]Jesus said this because the people were saying that he had an evil spirit in him.

Jesus' Mother and Brothers
(Matthew 12.46-50; Luke 8.19-21)

[31]Jesus' mother and brothers came and stood outside. Then they sent someone with a message for him to come out to them. [32]The crowd that was sitting around Jesus told him, "Your mother and your brothers and sisters[x] are outside and want to see you."

[33]Jesus asked, "Who is my mother and who are my brothers?" [34]Then he looked at the people sitting around him and said, "Here are my mother and my brothers. [35]Anyone who obeys God is my brother or sister or mother."

A Story about a Farmer
(Matthew 13.1-9; Luke 8.4-8)

4 The next time Jesus taught beside Lake Galilee, a big crowd gathered. It was so large that he had to sit in a boat out on the lake, while the people stood on the shore. [2]He used stories to teach them many things, and this is part of what he taught:

[3]Now listen! A farmer went out to scatter seed in a field. [4]While the farmer was scattering the seed, some of it fell along the road and was eaten by birds. [5]Other seeds fell on thin, rocky ground and quickly started growing because the soil wasn't very deep. [6]But when the sun came up, the plants were scorched and dried up, because they did not have enough roots. [7]Some other seeds fell where thornbushes grew up and choked out the plants. So they did not produce any grain. [8]But a few seeds did fall on good ground where the plants grew and produced thirty or sixty or even a hundred times as much as was scattered.

[9]Then Jesus said, "If you have ears, pay attention."

Why Jesus Used Stories
(Matthew 13.10-17; Luke 8.9, 10)

[10]When Jesus was alone with the twelve apostles and some others, they asked him about these stories. [11]He answered:

I have explained the secret about God's kingdom to you, but for others I can use only stories. [12]The reason is,

"These people will look
    and look, but never see.
They will listen and listen,
    but never understand.
If they did,
they would turn to God,
    and he would forgive them."

Jesus Explains the Story about the Farmer
(Matthew 13.18-23; Luke 8.11-15)

[13]Jesus told them:
If you don't understand this story, you won't understand any others. [14]What the farmer is spreading is really the message about the kingdom. [15]The seeds that fell along the road are the people who hear the message. But Satan soon comes and snatches it away from them. [16]The seeds that fell on rocky ground are the people who gladly hear the message and accept it right away. [17]But they don't have any roots, and they don't last very long. As soon as life gets hard or the message gets them in trouble, they give up.

[18]The seeds that fell among the thornbushes are also people who hear the message. [19]But they start worrying about the needs of this life. They are fooled by the desire to get rich and to have all kinds of other things. So the message gets choked out, and they never produce anything. [20]The seeds that fell on good ground are the people who hear and welcome the message. They produce thirty or sixty or even a hundred times as much as was planted.

---

[x]**3.32** *and sisters*: These words are not in some manuscripts.

Light
(Luke 8.16-18)

21Jesus also said:

You don't light a lamp and put it under a clay pot or under a bed. Don't you put a lamp on a lampstand? 22There is nothing hidden that will not be made public. There is no secret that will not be well known. 23If you have ears, pay attention!

24Listen carefully to what you hear! The way you treat others will be the way you will be treated—and even worse. 25Everyone who has something will be given more. But people who don't have anything will lose what little they have.

Another Story about Seeds

26Again Jesus said:

God's kingdom is like what happens when a farmer scatters seed in a field. 27The farmer sleeps at night and is up and around during the day. Yet the seeds keep sprouting and growing, and he doesn't understand how. 28It is the ground that makes the seeds sprout and grow into plants that produce grain. 29Then when harvest season comes and the grain is ripe, the farmer cuts it with a sickle.*y*

A Mustard Seed
(Matthew 13.31, 32; Luke 13.18, 19)

30Finally, Jesus said:

What is God's kingdom like? What story can I use to explain it? 31It is like what happens when a mustard seed is planted in the ground. It is the smallest seed in all the world. 32But once it is planted, it grows larger than any garden plant. It even puts out branches that are big enough for birds to nest in its shade.

The Reason for Teaching with Stories
(Matthew 13.34, 35)

33Jesus used many other stories when he spoke to the people, and he taught them as much as they could understand. 34He did not tell them anything without using stories. But when he was alone with his disciples, he explained everything to them.

A Storm
(Matthew 8.23-27; Luke 8.22-25)

35That evening, Jesus said to his disciples, "Let's cross to the east side." 36So they left the crowd, and his disciples started across the lake with him in the boat. Some other boats followed along.

37Suddenly a windstorm struck the lake. Waves started splashing into the boat, and it was about to sink.

38Jesus was in the back of the boat with his head on a pillow, and he was asleep. His disciples woke him and said, "Teacher, don't you care that we're about to drown?"

39Jesus got up and ordered the wind and the waves to be quiet. The wind stopped, and everything was calm.

40Jesus asked his disciples, "Why were you afraid? Don't you have any faith?"

41Now they were more afraid than ever and said to each other, "Who is this? Even the wind and the waves obey him!"

A Man with Evil Spirits
(Matthew 8.28-34; Luke 8.26-39)

5 Jesus and his disciples crossed Lake Galilee and came to shore near the town of Gerasa.*z* 2When he was getting out of the boat, a man with an evil spirit quickly ran to him 3from the graveyard*a* where he had been living. No one was able to tie the man up anymore, not even with a chain. 4He had often been put in chains and leg irons, but he broke the chains and smashed the leg irons. No one could control him. 5Night and day he was in the graveyard or on the hills, yelling and cutting himself with stones.

6When the man saw Jesus in the distance, he ran up to him and knelt down. 7He shouted, "Jesus, Son of God in heaven, what do you want with me? Promise me in God's name that you won't torture me!" 8The man said this because Jesus had already told the evil spirit to come out of him.

9Jesus asked, "What is your name?"

The man answered, "My name is Lots, because I have 'lots' of evil spirits." 10He then begged Jesus not to send them away.

11Over on the hillside a large herd of pigs was feeding. 12So the evil spirits begged Jesus, "Send us into those pigs! Let us go into them." 13Jesus let them go, and they went out of the man and into the pigs. The whole herd of about two thousand pigs rushed down the steep bank into the lake and drowned.

14The men taking care of the pigs ran to the town and the farms to spread the news. Then the people came out to see what had happened. 15When they came to Jesus, they saw the man who had once been full of demons. He was sitting there with his clothes on and in his right mind, and they were terrified.

---

*y***4.29** *sickle:* A knife with a long curved blade, used to cut grain and other crops.
*z***5.1** *Gerasa:* Some manuscripts have "Gadara," and others have "Gergesa." *a***5.3** *graveyard:* It was thought that demons and evil spirits lived in graveyards.

¹⁶Everyone who had seen what had happened told about the man and the pigs. ¹⁷Then the people started begging Jesus to leave their part of the country.

¹⁸When Jesus was getting into the boat, the man begged to go with him. ¹⁹But Jesus would not let him. Instead, he said, "Go home to your family and tell them how much the Lord has done for you and how good he has been to you."

²⁰The man went away into the region near the ten cities known as Decapolis^b and began telling everyone how much Jesus had done for him. Everyone who heard what had happened was amazed.

A Dying Girl and a Sick Woman
(Matthew 9.18-26; Luke 8.40-56)

²¹Once again Jesus got into the boat and crossed Lake Galilee.^c Then as he stood on the shore, a large crowd gathered around him. ²²The person in charge of the Jewish meeting place was also there. His name was Jairus, and when he saw Jesus, he went over to him. He knelt at Jesus' feet ²³and started begging him for help. He said, "My daughter is about to die! Please come and touch her, so she will get well and live." ²⁴Jesus went with Jairus. Many people followed along and kept crowding around.

²⁵In the crowd was a woman who had been bleeding for twelve years. ²⁶She had gone to many doctors, and they had not done anything except cause her a lot of pain. She had paid them all the money she had. But instead of getting better, she only got worse.

²⁷The woman had heard about Jesus, so she came up behind him in the crowd and barely touched his clothes. ²⁸She had said to herself, "If I can just touch his clothes, I will get well." ²⁹As soon as she touched them, her bleeding stopped, and she knew she was well.

³⁰At that moment Jesus felt power go out from him. He turned to the crowd and asked, "Who touched my clothes?" ³¹His disciples said to him, "Look at all these people crowding around you! How can you ask who touched you?" ³²But Jesus turned to see who had touched him.

³³The woman knew what had happened to her. She came shaking with fear and knelt down in front of Jesus. Then she told him the whole story. ³⁴Jesus said to the woman, "You are now well because of your faith. May

God give you peace! You are healed, and you will no longer be in pain."

³⁵While Jesus was still speaking, some men came from Jairus' home and said, "Your daughter has died! Why bother the teacher anymore?"

³⁶Jesus heard^d what they said, and he said to Jairus, "Don't worry. Just have faith!"

³⁷Jesus did not let anyone go with him except Peter and the two brothers, James and John. ³⁸They went home with Jairus and saw the people crying and making a lot of noise.^e ³⁹Then Jesus went inside and said to them, "Why are you crying and carrying on like this? The child isn't dead. She is just asleep." ⁴⁰But the people laughed at him.

After Jesus had sent them all out of the house, he took the girl's father and mother and his three disciples and went to where she was. ⁴¹⁻⁴²He took the twelve-year-old girl by the hand and said, "Talitha, koum!"^f which means, "Little girl, get up!" The girl got right up and started walking around.

Everyone was greatly surprised. ⁴³But Jesus ordered them not to tell anyone what had happened. Then he said, "Give her something to eat."

The People of Nazareth Turn against Jesus
(Matthew 13.53-58; Luke 4.16-30)

6 Jesus left and returned to his hometown^g with his disciples. ²The next Sabbath he taught in the Jewish meeting place. Many of the people who heard him were amazed and asked, "How can he do all this? Where did he get such wisdom and the power to work these miracles? ³Isn't he the carpenter,^h the son of Mary? Aren't James, Joseph, Judas, and Simon his brothers? Don't his sisters still live here in our town?" The people were very unhappy because of what he was doing.

⁴But Jesus said, "Prophets are honored by everyone, except the people of their hometown and their relatives and their own family." ⁵Jesus could not work any miracles there, except to heal a few sick people by placing his hands on them. ⁶He was surprised that the people did not have any faith.

Instructions for the Twelve Apostles
(Matthew 10.5-15; Luke 9.1-6)

Jesus taught in all the neighboring villages. ⁷Then he called together his

---

^b**5.20** *the ten cities known as Decapolis*: A group of ten cities east of Samaria and Galilee, where the people followed the Greek way of life. ^c**5.21** *crossed Lake Galilee*: To the west side. ^d**5.36** *heard*: Or "ignored." ^e**5.38** *crying and making a lot of noise*: The Jewish people often hired mourners for funerals. ^f**5.41,42** *Talitha, koum*: These words are in Aramaic, a language spoken in Palestine during the time of Jesus. ^g**6.1** *hometown*: Nazareth. ^h**6.3** *carpenter*: The Greek word may also mean someone who builds or works with stone or brick.

twelve apostles and sent them out two by two with power over evil spirits. [8]He told them, "You may take along a walking stick. But don't carry food or a traveling bag or any money. [9]It's all right to wear sandals, but don't take along a change of clothes. [10]When you are welcomed into a home, stay there until you leave that town. [11]If any place won't welcome you or listen to your message, leave and shake the dust from your feet[i] as a warning to them."

[12]The apostles left and started telling everyone to turn to God. [13]They forced out many demons and healed a lot of sick people by putting olive oil[j] on them.

The Death of John the Baptist
(Matthew 14.1-12; Luke 9.7-9)

[14]Jesus became so well-known that Herod the ruler[k] heard about him. Some people thought he was John the Baptist, who had come back to life with the power to work miracles. [15]Others thought he was Elijah[l] or some other prophet who had lived long ago. [16]But when Herod heard about Jesus, he said, "This must be John! I had his head cut off, and now he has come back to life."

[17-18]Herod had earlier married Herodias, the wife of his brother Philip. But John had told him, "It isn't right for you to take your brother's wife!" So, in order to please Herodias, Herod arrested John and put him in prison.

[19]Herodias had a grudge against John and wanted to kill him. But she could not do it [20]because Herod was afraid of John and protected him. He knew that John was a good and holy man. Even though Herod was confused by what John said,[m] he was glad to listen to him. And he often did.

[21]Finally, Herodias got her chance when Herod gave a great birthday celebration for himself and invited his officials, his army officers, and the leaders of Galilee. [22]The daughter of Herodias[n] came in and danced for Herod and his guests. She pleased them so much that Herod said, "Ask for anything, and it's yours! [23]I swear that I will give you as much as half of my kingdom, if you want it."

[24]The girl left and asked her mother, "What do you think I should ask for?"

Her mother answered, "The head of John the Baptist!"

[25]The girl hurried back and told Herod, "Right now on a platter I want the head of John the Baptist!"

[26]The king was very sorry for what he had said. But he did not want to break the promise he had made in front of his guests. [27]At once he ordered a guard to cut off John's head there in prison. [28]The guard put the head on a platter and took it to the girl. Then she gave it to her mother.

[29]When John's followers learned that he had been killed, they took his body and put it in a tomb.

Jesus Feeds Five Thousand
(Matthew 14.13-21; Luke 9.10-17; John 6.1-14)

[30]After the apostles returned to Jesus,[o] they told him everything they had done and taught. [31]But so many people were coming and going that Jesus and the apostles did not even have a chance to eat. Then Jesus said, "Let's go to a place[p] where we can be alone and get some rest." [32]They left in a boat for a place where they could be alone. [33]But many people saw them leave and figured out where they were going. So people from every town ran on ahead and got there first.

[34]When Jesus got out of the boat, he saw the large crowd that was like sheep without a shepherd. He felt sorry for the people and started teaching them many things.

[35]That evening the disciples came to Jesus and said, "This place is like a desert, and it is already late. [36]Let the crowds leave, so they can go to the farms and villages near here and buy something to eat."

[37]Jesus replied, "You give them something to eat."

But they asked him, "Don't you know that it would take almost a year's wages[q] to buy all of these people something to eat?"

[38]Then Jesus said, "How much bread do you have? Go and see!"

They found out and answered, "We have five small loaves of bread[r] and two fish." [39]Jesus told his disciples to have the people sit down on the green grass.

[i]**6.11** *shake the dust from your feet*: This was a way of showing rejection. [j]**6.13** *olive oil*: The Jewish people used olive oil as a way of healing people. Sometimes olive oil is a symbol for healing by means of a miracle (see James 5.14). [k]**6.14** *Herod the ruler*: Herod Antipas, the son of Herod the Great. [l]**6.15** *Elijah*: Many of the Jewish people expected the prophet Elijah to come and prepare the way for the Messiah. [m]**6.20** *was confused by what John said*: Some manuscripts have "did many things because of what John said." [n]**6.22** *Herodias*: Some manuscripts have "Herod." [o]**6.30** *the apostles returned to Jesus*: From the mission on which he had sent them (see 6.7, 12, 13). [p]**6.31** *a place*: This was probably northeast of Lake Galilee (see verse 45). [q]**6.37** *almost a year's wages*: The Greek text has "two hundred silver coins." Each coin was the average day's wage for a worker. [r]**6.38** *small loaves of bread*: These would have been flat and round or in the shape of a bun.

⁴⁰They sat down in groups of a hundred and groups of fifty.

⁴¹Jesus took the five loaves and the two fish. He looked up toward heaven and blessed the food. Then he broke the bread and handed it to his disciples to give to the people. He also divided the two fish, so that everyone could have some.

⁴²After everyone had eaten all they wanted, ⁴³Jesus' disciples picked up twelve large baskets of leftover bread and fish.

⁴⁴There were five thousand men who ate the food.

Jesus Walks on the Water
(Matthew 14.22-33; John 6.15-21)

⁴⁵Right away, Jesus made his disciples get into the boat and start back across to Bethsaida. But he stayed until he had sent the crowds away. ⁴⁶Then he told them good-by and went up on the side of a mountain to pray.

⁴⁷Later that evening he was still there by himself, and the boat was somewhere in the middle of the lake. ⁴⁸He could see that the disciples were struggling hard, because they were rowing against the wind. Not long before morning, Jesus came toward them. He was walking on the water and was about to pass the boat.

⁴⁹When the disciples saw Jesus walking on the water, they thought he was a ghost, and they started screaming. ⁵⁰All of them saw him and were terrified. But at that same time he said, "Don't worry! I am Jesus. Don't be afraid." ⁵¹He then got into the boat with them, and the wind died down. The disciples were completely confused. ⁵²Their minds were closed, and they could not understand the true meaning of the loaves of bread.

Jesus Heals Sick People in Gennesaret
(Matthew 14.34-36)

⁵³Jesus and his disciples crossed the lake and brought the boat to shore near the town of Gennesaret. ⁵⁴As soon as they got out of the boat, the people recognized Jesus. ⁵⁵So they ran all over that part of the country to bring their sick people to him on mats. They brought them each time they heard where he was. ⁵⁶In every village or farm or marketplace where Jesus went, the people brought their sick to him. They begged him to let them just touch his clothes, and everyone who did was healed.

The Teaching of the Ancestors
(Matthew 15.1-9)

7 Some Pharisees and several teachers of the Law of Moses from Jerusalem came and gathered around Jesus. ²They noticed that some of his disciples ate without first washing their hands.ˢ

³The Pharisees and many other Jewish people obey the teachings of their ancestors. They always wash their hands in the proper wayᵗ before eating. ⁴None of them will eat anything they buy in the market until it is washed. They also follow a lot of other teachings, such as washing cups, pitchers, and bowls.ᵘ

⁵The Pharisees and teachers asked Jesus, "Why don't your disciples obey what our ancestors taught us to do? Why do they eat without washing their hands?"

⁶Jesus replied:
You are nothing but show-offs!
The prophet Isaiah was right when he wrote that God had said,

"All of you praise me
   with your words,
but you never really
   think about me.
⁷ It is useless for you
   to worship me,
when you teach rules
   made up by humans."

⁸You disobey God's commands in order to obey what humans have taught. ⁹You are good at rejecting God's commands so that you can follow your own teachings! ¹⁰Didn't Moses command you to respect your father and mother? Didn't he tell you to put to death all who curse their parents? ¹¹But you let people get by without helping their parents when they should. You let them say that what they own has been offered to God.ᵛ ¹²You won't let those people help their parents. ¹³And you ignore God's commands in order to follow your own teaching. You do a lot of other things that are just as bad.

What Really Makes People Unclean
(Matthew 15.10-20)

¹⁴Jesus called the crowd together again and said, "Pay attention and try to understand what I mean. ¹⁵⁻¹⁶The food that you put into your mouth doesn't

---

ˢ**7.2** _without first washing their hands_: The Jewish people had strict laws about washing their hands before eating, especially if they had been out in public.   ᵗ**7.3** _in the proper way_: The Greek text has "with the fist," but the exact meaning is not clear. It could mean "to the wrist" or "to the elbow."   ᵘ**7.4** _bowls_: Some manuscripts add "and sleeping mats."   ᵛ**7.11** _has been offered to God_: According to Jewish custom, when anything was offered to God, it could not be used for anyone else, not even for a person's parents.

make you unclean and unfit to worship God. The bad words that come out of your mouth are what make you unclean."[w]

[17]After Jesus and his disciples had left the crowd and had gone into the house, they asked him what these sayings meant. [18]He answered, "Don't you know what I am talking about by now? You surely know that the food you put into your mouth cannot make you unclean. [19]It doesn't go into your heart, but into your stomach, and then out of your body." By saying this, Jesus meant that all foods were fit to eat.

[20]Then Jesus said:

What comes from your heart is what makes you unclean. [21]Out of your heart come evil thoughts, vulgar deeds, stealing, murder, [22]unfaithfulness in marriage, greed, meanness, deceit, indecency, envy, insults, pride, and foolishness. [23]All of these come from your heart, and they are what make you unfit to worship God.

A Woman's Faith
(Matthew 15.21-28)

[24]Jesus left and went to the region near the city of Tyre, where he stayed in someone's home. He did not want people to know he was there, but they found out anyway. [25]A woman whose daughter had an evil spirit in her heard where Jesus was. And right away she came and knelt down at his feet. [26]The woman was Greek and had been born in the part of Syria known as Phoenicia. She begged Jesus to force the demon out of her daughter. [27]But Jesus said, "The children must first be fed! It isn't right to take away their food and feed it to dogs."[x]

[28]The woman replied, "Lord, even dogs eat the crumbs that children drop from the table."

[29]Jesus answered, "That's true! You may go now. The demon has left your daughter." [30]When the woman got back home, she found her child lying on the bed. The demon had gone.

Jesus Heals a Man Who Was Deaf and Could Hardly Talk

[31]Jesus left the region around Tyre and went by way of Sidon toward Lake Galilee. He went through the land near the ten cities known as Decapolis.[y] [32]Some people brought to him a man who was deaf and could hardly talk. They begged Jesus just to touch him.

[33]After Jesus had taken him aside from the crowd, he stuck his fingers in the man's ears. Then he spit and put it on the man's tongue. [34]Jesus looked up toward heaven, and with a groan he said, "Effatha!"[z] which means "Open up!" [35]At once the man could hear, and he had no more trouble talking clearly.

[36]Jesus told the people not to say anything about what he had done. But the more he told them, the more they talked about it. [37]They were completely amazed and said, "Everything he does is good! He even heals people who cannot hear or talk."

Jesus Feeds Four Thousand
(Matthew 15.32-39)

8 One day another large crowd gathered around Jesus. They had not brought along anything to eat. So Jesus called his disciples together and said, [2]"I feel sorry for these people. They have been with me for three days, and they don't have anything to eat. [3]Some of them live a long way from here. If I send them away hungry, they might faint on their way home."

[4]The disciples said, "This place is like a desert. Where can we find enough food to feed such a crowd?"

[5]Jesus asked them how much food they had. They replied, "Seven small loaves of bread."[a]

[6]After Jesus told the crowd to sit down, he took the seven loaves and blessed them. He then broke the loaves and handed them to his disciples, who passed them out to the crowd. [7]They also had a few little fish, and after Jesus had blessed these, he told the disciples to pass them around.

[8-9]The crowd of about four thousand people ate all they wanted, and the leftovers filled seven large baskets.

As soon as Jesus had sent the people away, [10]he got into the boat with the disciples and crossed to the territory near Dalmanutha.[b]

A Sign from Heaven
(Matthew 16.1-4)

[11]The Pharisees came out and started an argument with Jesus. They wanted to test him by asking for a sign from heaven. [12]Jesus groaned and said, "Why are you always looking for a sign? I can promise you that you will not be given one!" [13]Then he left them. He again got into a boat and crossed over to the other side of the lake.

[w]**7.15,16** *unclean*: Some manuscripts add, "If you have ears, pay attention." [x]**7.27** *feed it to dogs*: The Jewish people often referred to Gentiles as dogs. [y]**7.31** *the ten cities known as Decapolis*: See the note at 5.20. [z]**7.34** *Effatha*: This word is in Aramaic, a language spoken in Palestine during the time of Jesus. [a]**8.5** *small loaves of bread*: See the note at 6.38. [b]**8.10** *Dalmanutha*: The place is unknown.

The Yeast of the Pharisees and of Herod
(Matthew 16.5-12)

[14]The disciples had forgotten to bring any bread, and they had only one loaf with them in the boat. [15]Jesus warned them, "Watch out! Guard against the yeast of the Pharisees and of Herod."[c] [16]The disciples talked this over and said to each other, "He must be saying this because we don't have any bread." [17]Jesus knew what they were thinking and asked, "Why are you talking about not having any bread? Don't you understand? Are your minds still closed? [18]Are your eyes blind and your ears deaf? Don't you remember [19]how many baskets of leftovers you picked up when I fed those five thousand people with only five small loaves of bread?"

"Yes," the disciples answered. "There were twelve baskets."

[20]Jesus then asked, "And how many baskets of leftovers did you pick up when I broke seven small loaves of bread for those four thousand people?"

"Seven," they answered.

[21]"Don't you know what I am talking about by now?" Jesus asked.

Jesus Heals a Blind Man at Bethsaida

[22]As Jesus and his disciples were going into Bethsaida, some people brought a blind man to him and begged him to touch the man. [23]Jesus took him by the hand and led him out of the village, where he spit into the man's eyes. He placed his hands on the blind man and asked him if he could see anything. [24]The man looked up and said, "I see people, but they look like trees walking around."

[25]Once again Jesus placed his hands on the man's eyes, and this time the man stared. His eyes were healed, and he saw everything clearly. [26]Jesus said to him, "You may return home now, but don't go into the village."

Who Is Jesus?
(Matthew 16.13-20; Luke 9.18-21)

[27]Jesus and his disciples went to the villages near the town of Caesarea Philippi. As they were walking along, he asked them, "What do people say about me?"

[28]The disciples answered, "Some say you are John the Baptist or maybe Elijah.[d] Others say you are one of the prophets."

[29]Then Jesus asked them, "But who do you say I am?"

"You are the Messiah!" Peter replied.

[30]Jesus warned the disciples not to tell anyone about him.

Jesus Speaks about His Suffering and Death
(Matthew 16.21-28; Luke 9.22-27)

[31]Jesus began telling his disciples what would happen to him. He said, "The nation's leaders, the chief priests, and the teachers of the Law of Moses will make the Son of Man suffer terribly. He will be rejected and killed, but three days later he will rise to life." [32]Then Jesus explained clearly what he meant.

Peter took Jesus aside and told him to stop talking like that. [33]But when Jesus turned and saw the disciples, he corrected Peter. He said to him, "Satan, get away from me! You are thinking like everyone else and not like God."

[34]Jesus then told the crowd and the disciples to come closer, and he said:

If any of you want to be my followers, you must forget about yourself. You must take up your cross and follow me. [35]If you want to save your life,[e] you will destroy it. But if you give up your life for me and for the good news, you will save it. [36]What will you gain, if you own the whole world but destroy yourself? [37]What could you give to get back your soul?

[38]Don't be ashamed of me and my message among these unfaithful and sinful people! If you are, the Son of Man will be ashamed of you when he comes in the glory of his Father with the holy angels.

9 I can assure you that some of the people standing here will not die before they see God's kingdom come with power.

The True Glory of Jesus
(Matthew 17.1-13; Luke 9.28-36)

[2]Six days later Jesus took Peter, James, and John with him. They went up on a high mountain, where they could be alone. There in front of the disciples, Jesus was completely changed. [3]And his clothes became much whiter than any bleach on earth could make them. [4]Then Moses and Elijah were there talking with Jesus.

[5]Peter said to Jesus, "Teacher, it is good for us to be here! Let us make three shelters, one for you, one for Moses, and one for Elijah." [6]But Peter and the others were terribly frightened, and he did not know what he was talking about.

[7]The shadow of a cloud passed over and covered them. From the cloud a voice said, "This is my Son, and I love him. Listen to what he says!" [8]At once

---

[c]**8.15** *Herod*: Herod Antipas, the son of Herod the Great.   [d]**8.28** *Elijah*: See the note at 6.15.

[e]**8.35** *life*: In verses 35-37 the same Greek word is translated "life," "yourself," and "soul."

the disciples looked around, but they saw only Jesus.

9As Jesus and his disciples were coming down the mountain, he told them not to say a word about what they had seen, until the Son of Man had been raised from death. 10So they kept it to themselves. But they wondered what he meant by the words "raised from death."

11The disciples asked Jesus, "Don't the teachers of the Law of Moses say that Elijah must come before the Messiah does?"

12Jesus answered:

Elijah certainly will come[f] to get everything ready. But don't the Scriptures also say that the Son of Man must suffer terribly and be rejected? 13I can assure you that Elijah has already come. And people treated him just as they wanted to, as the Scriptures say they would.

Jesus Heals a Boy
(Matthew 17.14-20; Luke 9.37-43a)

14When Jesus and his three disciples came back down, they saw a large crowd around the other disciples. The teachers of the Law of Moses were arguing with them.

15The crowd was really surprised to see Jesus, and everyone hurried over to greet him.

16Jesus asked, "What are you arguing about?"

17Someone from the crowd answered, "Teacher, I brought my son to you. A demon keeps him from talking. 18Whenever the demon attacks my son, it throws him to the ground and makes him foam at the mouth and grit his teeth in pain. Then he becomes stiff. I asked your disciples to force out the demon, but they couldn't do it."

19Jesus said, "You people don't have any faith! How much longer must I be with you? Why do I have to put up with you? Bring the boy to me."

20They brought the boy, and as soon as the demon saw Jesus, it made the boy shake all over. He fell down and began rolling on the ground and foaming at the mouth.

21Jesus asked the boy's father, "How long has he been like this?"

The man answered, "Ever since he was a child. 22The demon has often tried to kill him by throwing him into a fire or into water. Please have pity and help us if you can!"

23Jesus replied, "Why do you say 'if you can'? Anything is possible for someone who has faith!"

24Right away the boy's father shouted, "I do have faith! Please help me to have even more."

25When Jesus saw that a crowd was gathering fast, he spoke sternly to the evil spirit that had kept the boy from speaking or hearing. He said, "I order you to come out of the boy! Don't ever bother him again."

26The spirit screamed and made the boy shake all over. Then it went out of him. The boy looked dead, and almost everyone said he was. 27But Jesus took hold of his hand and helped him stand up.

28After Jesus and the disciples had gone back home and were alone, they asked him, "Why couldn't we force out that demon?"

29Jesus answered, "Only prayer can force out that kind of demon."

Jesus Again Speaks about His Death
(Matthew 17.22, 23; Luke 9.43b-45)

30Jesus left with his disciples and started through Galilee. He did not want anyone to know about it, 31because he was teaching the disciples that the Son of Man would be handed over to people who would kill him. But three days later he would rise to life. 32The disciples did not understand what Jesus meant, and they were afraid to ask.

Who Is the Greatest?
(Matthew 18.1-5; Luke 9.46-48)

33Jesus and his disciples went to his home in Capernaum. After they were inside the house, Jesus asked them, "What were you arguing about along the way?" 34They had been arguing about which one of them was the greatest, and so they did not answer.

35After Jesus sat down and told the twelve disciples to gather around him, he said, "If you want the place of honor, you must become a slave and serve others!"

36Then Jesus had a child stand near him. He put his arm around the child and said, 37"When you welcome even a child because of me, you welcome me. And when you welcome me, you welcome the one who sent me."

For or against Jesus
(Luke 9.49, 50)

38John said, "Teacher, we saw a man using your name to force demons out of people. But he wasn't one of us, and we told him to stop."

39Jesus said to his disciples:

Don't stop him! No one who works miracles in my name will soon turn and say something bad about me. 40Anyone who isn't against us is for us. 41And anyone who gives you a cup of water in my

[f]9.12 *Elijah certainly will come*: See the note at 6.15.

name, just because you belong to me, will surely be rewarded.

Temptations To Sin
(Matthew 18.6-9; Luke 17.1, 2)

⁴²It will be terrible for people who cause even one of my little followers to sin. Those people would be better off thrown into the ocean with a heavy stone tied around their necks. ⁴³⁻⁴⁴So if your hand causes you to sin, cut it off! You would be better off to go into life crippled than to have two hands and be thrown into the fires of hell that never go out.*ᵍ* ⁴⁵⁻⁴⁶If your foot causes you to sin, chop it off. You would be better off to go into life lame than to have two feet and be thrown into hell.*ʰ* ⁴⁷If your eye causes you to sin, get rid of it. You would be better off to go into God's kingdom with only one eye than to have two eyes and be thrown into hell. ⁴⁸The worms there never die, and the fire never stops burning.

⁴⁹Everyone must be salted with fire.*ⁱ*

⁵⁰Salt is good. But if it no longer tastes like salt, how can it be made salty again? Have salt among you and live at peace with each other.*ʲ*

Teaching about Divorce
(Matthew 19.1-12; Luke 16.18)

10 After Jesus left, he went to Judea and then on to the other side of the Jordan River. Once again large crowds came to him, and as usual, he taught them.

²Some Pharisees wanted to test Jesus. So they came up to him and asked if it was right for a man to divorce his wife. ³Jesus asked them, "What does the Law of Moses say about that?"

⁴They answered, "Moses allows a man to write out divorce papers and send his wife away."

⁵Jesus replied, "Moses gave you this law because you are so heartless. ⁶But in the beginning God made a man and a woman. ⁷That's why a man leaves his father and mother and gets married. ⁸He becomes like one person with his wife. Then they are no longer two people, but one. ⁹And no one should separate a couple that God has joined together."

¹⁰When Jesus and his disciples were back in the house, they asked him about what he had said. ¹¹He told them, "A man who divorces his wife and marries someone else is unfaithful to his wife. ¹²A woman who divorces her husband*ᵏ* and marries again is also unfaithful."

Jesus Blesses Little Children
(Matthew 19.13-15; Luke 18.15-17)

¹³Some people brought their children to Jesus so that he could bless them by placing his hands on them. But his disciples told the people to stop bothering him.

¹⁴When Jesus saw this, he became angry and said, "Let the children come to me! Don't try to stop them. People who are like these little children belong to the kingdom of God.*ˡ* ¹⁵I promise you that you cannot get into God's kingdom, unless you accept it the way a child does." ¹⁶Then Jesus took the children in his arms and blessed them by placing his hands on them.

A Rich Man
(Matthew 19.16-30; Luke 18.18-30)

¹⁷As Jesus was walking down a road, a man ran up to him. He knelt down, and asked, "Good teacher, what can I do to have eternal life?"

¹⁸Jesus replied, "Why do you call me good? Only God is good. ¹⁹You know the commandments. 'Do not murder. Be faithful in marriage. Do not steal. Do not tell lies about others. Do not cheat. Respect your father and mother.' "

²⁰The man answered, "Teacher, I have obeyed all these commandments since I was a young man."

²¹Jesus looked closely at the man. He liked him and said, "There's one thing you still need to do. Go sell everything you own. Give the money to the poor, and you will have riches in heaven. Then come with me."

²²When the man heard Jesus say this, he went away gloomy and sad because he was very rich.

²³Jesus looked around and said to his disciples, "It's hard for rich people to get into God's kingdom!" ²⁴The disciples were shocked to hear this. So Jesus told them again, "It's terribly hard*ᵐ* to get

---

*ᵍ***9.43,44** *never go out:* Some manuscripts add, "The worms there never die, and the fire never stops burning." *ʰ***9.45,46** *thrown into hell:* Some manuscripts add, "The worms there never die, and the fire never stops burning." *ⁱ***9.49** *salted with fire:* Some manuscripts add "and every sacrifice will be seasoned with salt." The verse may mean that Christ's followers must suffer because of their faith. *ʲ***9.50** *Have salt among you and live at peace with each other:* This may mean that when Christ's followers have to suffer because of their faith, they must still try to live at peace with each other. *ᵏ***10.12** *A woman who divorces her husband:* Roman law let a woman divorce her husband, but Jewish law did not let a woman do this. *ˡ***10.14** *People who are like these little children belong to the kingdom of God:* Or "The kingdom of God belongs to people who are like these little children." *ᵐ***10.24** *hard:* Some manuscripts add "for people who trust in their wealth." Others add "for the rich."

into God's kingdom! [25]In fact, it's easier for a camel to go through the eye of a needle than for a rich person to get into God's kingdom."

[26]Jesus' disciples were even more amazed. They asked each other, "How can anyone ever be saved?"

[27]Jesus looked at them and said, "There are some things that people cannot do, but God can do anything."

[28]Peter replied, "Remember, we left everything to be your followers!"

[29]Jesus told him:

You can be sure that anyone who gives up home or brothers or sisters or mother or father or children or land for me and for the good news [30]will be rewarded. In this world they will be given a hundred times as many houses and brothers and sisters and mothers and children and pieces of land, though they will also be mistreated. And in the world to come, they will have eternal life. [31]But many who are now first will be last, and many who are now last will be first.

Jesus Again Tells about His Death
(Matthew 20.17-19; Luke 18.31-34)

[32]The disciples were confused as Jesus led them toward Jerusalem, and his other followers were afraid. Once again, Jesus took the twelve disciples aside and told them what was going to happen to him. He said:

[33]We are now on our way to Jerusalem where the Son of Man will be handed over to the chief priests and the teachers of the Law of Moses. They will sentence him to death and hand him over to foreigners,[n] [34]who will make fun of him and spit on him. They will beat him and kill him. But three days later he will rise to life.

The Request of James and John
(Matthew 20.20-28)

[35]James and John, the sons of Zebedee, came up to Jesus and asked, "Teacher, will you do us a favor?"

[36]Jesus asked them what they wanted, [37]and they answered, "When you come into your glory, please let one of us sit at your right side and the other at your left."[o]

[38]Jesus told them, "You don't really know what you're asking! Are you able to drink from the cup[p] that I must soon drink from or be baptized as I must be baptized?"[q]

[39]"Yes, we are!" James and John answered.

Then Jesus replied, "You certainly will drink from the cup from which I must drink. And you will be baptized just as I must! [40]But it isn't for me to say who will sit at my right side and at my left. That is for God to decide."

[41]When the ten other disciples heard this, they were angry with James and John. [42]But Jesus called the disciples together and said:

You know that those foreigners who call themselves kings like to order their people around. And their great leaders have full power over the people they rule. [43]But don't act like them. If you want to be great, you must be the servant of all the others. [44]And if you want to be first, you must be everyone's slave. [45]The Son of Man did not come to be a slave master, but a slave who will give his life to rescue[r] many people.

Jesus Heals Blind Bartimaeus
(Matthew 20.29-34; Luke 18.35-43)

[46]Jesus and his disciples went to Jericho. And as they were leaving, they were followed by a large crowd. A blind beggar by the name of Bartimaeus son of Timaeus was sitting beside the road. [47]When he heard that it was Jesus from Nazareth, he shouted, "Jesus, Son of David,[s] have pity on me!" [48]Many people told the man to stop, but he shouted even louder, "Son of David, have pity on me!"

[49]Jesus stopped and said, "Call him over!"

They called out to the blind man and said, "Don't be afraid! Come on! He is calling for you." [50]The man threw off his coat as he jumped up and ran to Jesus.

[51]Jesus asked, "What do you want me to do for you?"

The blind man answered, "Master,[t] I want to see!"

[52]Jesus told him, "You may go. Your eyes are healed because of your faith."

Right away the man could see, and he went down the road with Jesus.

---

[n]**10.33** *foreigners*: The Romans who ruled Judea at this time.   [o]**10.37** *right side . . . left*: The most powerful people in a kingdom sat at the right and left side of the king.   [p]**10.38** *drink from the cup*: In the Scriptures a "cup" is sometimes used as a symbol of suffering. To "drink from the cup" would be to suffer.   [q]**10.38** *as I must be baptized*: Baptism is used with the same meaning that "cup" has in this verse.   [r]**10.45** *rescue*: The Greek word often, though not always, means the payment of a price to free a slave or a prisoner.   [s]**10.47** *Son of David*: The Jewish people expected the Messiah to be from the family of King David, and for this reason the Messiah was often called the "Son of David."   [t]**10.51** *Master*: A Hebrew word that may also mean "Teacher."

Jesus Enters Jerusalem
(Matthew 21.1-11; Luke 19.28-40;
John 12.12-19)

11 Jesus and his disciples reached Bethphage and Bethany near the Mount of Olives. When they were getting close to Jerusalem, Jesus sent two of them on ahead. [2]He told them, "Go into the next village. As soon as you enter it, you will find a young donkey that has never been ridden. Untie the donkey and bring it here. [3]If anyone asks why you are doing that, say, 'The Lord[u] needs it and will soon bring it back.' "

[4]The disciples left and found the donkey tied near a door that faced the street. While they were untying it, [5]some of the people standing there asked, "Why are you untying the donkey?" [6]They told them what Jesus had said, and the people let them take it.

[7]The disciples led the donkey to Jesus. They put some of their clothes on its back, and Jesus got on. [8]Many people spread clothes on the road, while others went to cut branches from the fields.[v]

[9]In front of Jesus and behind him, people went along shouting,

"Hooray![w]
God bless the one who comes
 in the name of the Lord!
[10] God bless the coming kingdom
 of our ancestor David.
Hooray for God
 in heaven above!"

[11]After Jesus had gone to Jerusalem, he went into the temple and looked around at everything. But since it was already late in the day, he went back to Bethany with the twelve disciples.

Jesus Puts a Curse on a Fig Tree
(Matthew 21.18, 19)

[12]When Jesus and his disciples left Bethany the next morning, he was hungry. [13]From a distance Jesus saw a fig tree covered with leaves, and he went to see if there were any figs on the tree. But there were not any, because it wasn't the season for figs. [14]So Jesus said to the tree, "Never again will anyone eat fruit from this tree!" The disciples heard him say this.

Jesus in the Temple
(Matthew 21.12-17; Luke 19.45-48;
John 2.13-22)

[15]After Jesus and his disciples reached Jerusalem, he went into the temple and began chasing out everyone who was selling and buying. He turned over the tables of the moneychangers and the benches of those who were selling doves. [16]Jesus would not let anyone carry things through the temple. [17]Then he taught the people and said, "The Scriptures say, 'My house should be called a place of worship for all nations.' But you have made it a place where robbers hide!"

[18]The chief priests and the teachers of the Law of Moses heard what Jesus said, and they started looking for a way to kill him. They were afraid of him, because the crowds were completely amazed at his teaching.

[19]That evening, Jesus and the disciples went outside the city.

A Lesson from the Fig Tree
(Matthew 21.20-22)

[20]As the disciples walked past the fig tree the next morning, they noticed that it was completely dried up, roots and all. [21]Peter remembered what Jesus had said to the tree. Then Peter said, "Teacher, look! The tree you put a curse on has dried up."

[22]Jesus told his disciples:
 Have faith in God! [23]If you have faith in God and don't doubt, you can tell this mountain to get up and jump into the sea, and it will. [24]Everything you ask for in prayer will be yours, if you only have faith. [25-26]Whenever you stand up to pray, you must forgive what others have done to you. Then your Father in heaven will forgive your sins.[x]

A Question about Jesus' Authority
(Matthew 21.23-27; Luke 20.1-8)

[27]Jesus and his disciples returned to Jerusalem. And as he was walking through the temple, the chief priests, the nation's leaders, and the teachers of the Law of Moses came over to him. [28]They asked, "What right do you have to do these things? Who gave you this authority?"

[29]Jesus answered, "I have just one question to ask you. If you answer it, I will tell you where I got the right to do these things. [30]Who gave John the right to baptize? Was it God in heaven or merely some human being?"

[31]They thought it over and said to each other, "We can't say that God gave John this right. Jesus will ask us why we didn't believe John. [32]On the other hand, these people think that John was a prophet. So we can't say that it was

---

[u]**11.3** *The Lord:* Or "The master of the donkey." This was one way that the Jewish people welcomed a famous person. [v]**11.8** *spread . . . branches from the fields:* [w]**11.9** *Hooray:* This translates a word that can mean "please save us." But it is most often used as a shout of praise to God. [x]**11.25,26** *your sins:* Some manuscripts add, "But if you do not forgive others, God will not forgive you."

merely some human who gave John the right to baptize."

They were afraid of the crowd [33]and told Jesus, "We don't know."

Jesus replied, "Then I won't tell you who gave me the right to do what I do."

Renters of a Vineyard
(Matthew 21.33-46; Luke 20.9-19)

12 Jesus then told them this story: A farmer once planted a vineyard. He built a wall around it and dug a pit to crush the grapes in. He also built a lookout tower. Then he rented out his vineyard and left the country.

[2]When it was harvest time, he sent a servant to get his share of the grapes. [3]The renters grabbed the servant. They beat him up and sent him away without a thing.

[4]The owner sent another servant, but the renters beat him on the head and insulted him terribly. [5]Then the man sent another servant, and they killed him. He kept sending servant after servant. They beat some of them and killed others.

[6]The owner had a son he loved very much. Finally, he sent his son to the renters because he thought they would respect him. [7]But they said to themselves, "Someday he will own this vineyard. Let's kill him! That way we can have it all for ourselves." [8]So they grabbed the owner's son and killed him. Then they threw his body out of the vineyard.

[9]Jesus asked, "What do you think the owner of the vineyard will do? He will come and kill those renters and let someone else have his vineyard. [10]You surely know that the Scriptures say,

'The stone that the builders
    tossed aside
is now the most important
    stone of all.
[11] This is something
the Lord has done,
    and it is amazing to us.' "

[12]The leaders knew that Jesus was really talking about them, and they wanted to arrest him. But because they were afraid of the crowd, they let him alone and left.

Paying Taxes
(Matthew 22.15-22; Luke 20.20-26)

[13]The Pharisees got together with Herod's followers.[y] Then they sent some men to trick Jesus into saying something wrong. [14]They went to him and said, "Teacher, we know that you are honest. You treat everyone with the same respect, no matter who they are. And you teach the truth about what God wants people to do. Tell us, should we pay taxes to the Emperor or not?"

[15]Jesus knew what they were up to, and he said, "Why are you trying to test me? Show me a coin!"

[16]They brought him a silver coin, and he asked, "Whose picture and name are on it?"

"The Emperor's," they answered.

[17]Then Jesus told them, "Give the Emperor what belongs to him and give God what belongs to God." The men were amazed at Jesus.

Life in the Future World
(Matthew 22.23-33; Luke 20.27-40)

[18]The Sadducees did not believe that people would rise to life after death. So some of them came to Jesus and said:

[19]Teacher, Moses wrote that if a married man dies and has no children, his brother should marry the widow. Their first son would then be thought of as the son of the dead brother. [20]There were once seven brothers. The first one married, but died without having any children. [21]The second brother married his brother's widow, and he also died without having children. The same thing happened to the third brother, [22]and finally to all seven brothers. At last the woman died. [23]When God raises people from death, whose wife will this woman be? After all, she had been married to all seven brothers.

[24]Jesus answered:

You are completely wrong! You don't know what the Scriptures teach. And you don't know anything about the power of God. [25]When God raises people to life, they won't marry. They will be like the angels in heaven. [26]You surely know about people being raised to life. You know that in the story about Moses and the burning bush, God said, "I am the God worshiped by Abraham, Isaac, and Jacob."[z] [27]He isn't the God of the dead, but of the living. You Sadducees are all wrong.

The Most Important Commandment
(Matthew 22.34-40; Luke 10.25-28)

[28]One of the teachers of the Law of Moses came up while Jesus and the Sadducees were arguing. When he heard

---

[y]**12.13** *Herod's followers*: People who were political followers of the family of Herod the Great and his son Herod Antipas. [z]**12.26** *"I am the God worshiped by Abraham, Isaac, and Jacob"*: Jesus argues that if God is worshiped by these three, they must still be alive, because he is the God of the living.

Jesus give a good answer, he asked him, "What is the most important commandment?"

²⁹Jesus answered, "The most important one says: 'People of Israel, you have only one Lord and God. ³⁰You must love him with all your heart, soul, mind, and strength.' ³¹The second most important commandment says: 'Love others as much as you love yourself.' No other commandment is more important than these."

³²The man replied, "Teacher, you are certainly right to say there is only one God. ³³It is also true that we must love God with all our heart, mind, and strength, and that we must love others as much as we love ourselves. These commandments are more important than all the sacrifices and offerings that we could possibly make."

³⁴When Jesus saw that the man had given a sensible answer, he told him, "You are not far from God's kingdom." After this, no one dared ask Jesus any more questions.

About David's Son
(Matthew 22.41-46; Luke 20.41-44)

³⁵As Jesus was teaching in the temple, he said, "How can the teachers of the Law of Moses say that the Messiah will come from the family of King David? ³⁶The Holy Spirit led David to say,

'The Lord said to my Lord:
    Sit at my right side*ᵃ*
until I make your enemies
    into a footstool for you.'

³⁷If David called the Messiah his Lord, how can the Messiah be his son?"*ᵇ* The large crowd enjoyed listening to Jesus teach.

Jesus Condemns the Pharisees and the Teachers of the Law of Moses
(Matthew 23.1-36; Luke 20.45-47)

³⁸As Jesus was teaching, he said: Guard against the teachers of the Law of Moses! They love to walk around in long robes and be greeted in the market. ³⁹They like the front seats in the meeting places and the best seats at banquets. ⁴⁰But they cheat widows out of their homes and pray long prayers just to show off. They will be punished most of all.

A Widow's Offering
(Luke 21.1-4)

⁴¹Jesus was sitting in the temple near the offering box and watching people put in their gifts. He noticed that many rich people were giving a lot of money. ⁴²Finally, a poor widow came up and put

in two coins that were worth only a few pennies. ⁴³Jesus told his disciples to gather around him. Then he said:

I tell you that this poor widow has put in more than all the others. ⁴⁴Everyone else gave what they didn't need. But she is very poor and gave everything she had. Now she doesn't have a cent to live on.

The Temple Will Be Destroyed
(Matthew 24.1, 2; Luke 21.5, 6)

13 As Jesus was leaving the temple, one of his disciples said to him, "Teacher, look at these beautiful stones and wonderful buildings!"

²Jesus replied, "Do you see these huge buildings? They will certainly be torn down! Not one stone will be left in place."

Warning about Trouble
(Matthew 24.3-14; Luke 21.7-19)

³Later, as Jesus was sitting on the Mount of Olives across from the temple, Peter, James, John, and Andrew came to him in private. ⁴They asked, "When will these things happen? What will be the sign that they are about to take place?"

⁵Jesus answered:

Watch out and don't let anyone fool you! ⁶Many will come and claim to be me. They will use my name and fool many people.

⁷When you hear about wars and threats of wars, don't be afraid. These things will have to happen first, but that isn't the end. ⁸Nations and kingdoms will go to war against each other. There will be earthquakes in many places, and people will starve to death. But this is just the beginning of troubles.

⁹Be on your guard! You will be taken to courts and beaten with whips in their meeting places. And because of me, you will have to stand before rulers and kings to tell about your faith. ¹⁰But before the end comes, the good news must be preached to all nations.

¹¹When you are arrested, don't worry about what you will say. You will be given the right words when the time comes. But you will not really be the ones speaking. Your words will come from the Holy Spirit.

¹²Brothers and sisters will betray each other and have each other put to death. Parents will betray their own children, and children will turn against their parents and have them killed. ¹³Everyone will hate you because of me. But if you keep on

---

*ᵃ***12.36** *right side*: The place of power and honor. at 10.47.

*ᵇ***12.37** *David . . . his son*: See the note

being faithful right to the end, you will be saved.

The Horrible Thing
(Matthew 24.15-21; Luke 21.20-24)

[14]Someday you will see that "Horrible Thing" where it should not be.[c] Everyone who reads this must try to understand! If you are living in Judea at that time, run to the mountains. [15]If you are on the roof[d] of your house, don't go inside to get anything. [16]If you are out in the field, don't go back for your coat. [17]It will be an awful time for women who are expecting babies or nursing young children. [18]Pray that it won't happen in winter.[e] [19]This will be the worst time of suffering since God created the world, and nothing this terrible will ever happen again. [20]If the Lord doesn't make the time shorter, no one will be left alive. But because of his chosen and special ones, he will make the time shorter.

[21]If someone should say, "Here is the Messiah!" or "There he is!" don't believe it. [22]False messiahs and false prophets will come and work miracles and signs. They will even try to fool God's chosen ones. [23]But be on your guard! That's why I am telling you these things now.

When the Son of Man Appears
(Matthew 24.29-31; Luke 21.25-28)

[24]In those days, right after that time of suffering,

"The sun will become dark,
  and the moon
    will no longer shine.
[25] The stars will fall,
  and the powers in the sky[f]
    will be shaken."

[26]Then the Son of Man will be seen coming in the clouds with great power and glory. [27]He will send his angels to gather his chosen ones from all over the earth.

A Lesson from a Fig Tree
(Matthew 24.32-35; Luke 21.29-33)

[28]Learn a lesson from a fig tree. When its branches sprout and start putting out leaves, you know summer is near. [29]So when you see all these things happening, you will know that the time has almost come.[g] [30]You can be sure that some

of the people of this generation will still be alive when all this happens. [31]The sky and the earth will not last forever, but my words will.

No One Knows the Day or Time
(Matthew 24.36-44)

[32]No one knows the day or the time. The angels in heaven don't know, and the Son himself doesn't know. Only the Father knows. [33]So watch out and be ready! You don't know when the time will come. [34]It is like what happens when a man goes away for a while and places his servants in charge of everything. He tells each of them what to do, and he orders the guard to keep alert. [35]So be alert! You don't know when the master of the house will come back. It could be in the evening or at midnight or before dawn or in the morning. [36]But if he comes suddenly, don't let him find you asleep. [37]I tell everyone just what I have told you. Be alert!

A Plot To Kill Jesus
(Matthew 26.1-5; Luke 22.1, 2; John 11.45-53)

14 It was now two days before Passover and the Festival of Thin Bread. The chief priests and the teachers of the Law of Moses were planning how they could sneak around and have Jesus arrested and put to death. [2]They were saying, "We must not do it during the festival, because the people will riot."

At Bethany
(Matthew 26.6-13; John 12.1-8)

[3]Jesus was eating in Bethany at the home of Simon, who once had leprosy,[h] when a woman came in with a very expensive bottle of sweet-smelling perfume.[i] After breaking it open, she poured the perfume on Jesus' head. [4]This made some of the guests angry, and they complained, "Why such a waste? [5]We could have sold this perfume for more than three hundred silver coins and given the money to the poor!" So they started saying cruel things to the woman.

[6]But Jesus said:

Leave her alone! Why are you bothering her? She has done a beautiful thing for me. [7]You will always have the poor with you. And whenever you want to, you can give to

---

[c]**13.14** *where it should not be*: Probably the holy place in the temple.   [d]**13.15** *roof*: See the note at 2.4.   [e]**13.18** *in winter*: In Palestine the winters are cold and rainy and make travel difficult.   [f]**13.25** *the powers in the sky*: In ancient times people thought that the stars were spiritual powers.   [g]**13.29** *the time has almost come*: Or "he (that is, the Son of Man) will soon be here."   [h]**14.3** *leprosy*: In biblical times the word "leprosy" was used for many different skin diseases.   [i]**14.3** *sweet-smelling perfume*: The Greek text has "perfume made of pure spikenard," a plant used to make perfume.

them. But you won't always have me here with you. [8]She has done all she could by pouring perfume on my body to prepare it for burial. [9]You may be sure that wherever the good news is told all over the world, people will remember what she has done. And they will tell others.

Judas and the Chief Priests
(Matthew 26.14-16; Luke 22.3-6)

[10]Judas Iscariot[j] was one of the twelve disciples. He went to the chief priests and offered to help them arrest Jesus. [11]They were glad to hear this, and they promised to pay him. So Judas started looking for a good chance to betray Jesus.

Jesus Eats with His Disciples
(Matthew 26.17-25; Luke 22.7-14, 21-23; John 13.21-30)

[12]It was the first day of the Festival of Thin Bread, and the Passover lambs were being killed. Jesus' disciples asked him, "Where do you want us to prepare the Passover meal?"

[13]Jesus said to two of the disciples, "Go into the city, where you will meet a man carrying a jar of water.[k] Follow him, [14]and when he goes into a house, say to the owner, 'Our teacher wants to know if you have a room where he can eat the Passover meal with his disciples.' [15]The owner will take you upstairs and show you a large room furnished and ready for you to use. Prepare the meal there."

[16]The two disciples went into the city and found everything just as Jesus had told them. So they prepared the Passover meal.

[17-18]While Jesus and the twelve disciples were eating together that evening, he said, "The one who will betray me is now eating with me."

[19]This made the disciples sad, and one after another they said to Jesus, "You surely don't mean me!"

[20]He answered, "It is one of you twelve men who is eating from this dish with me. [21]The Son of Man will die, just as the Scriptures say. But it is going to be terrible for the one who betrays me. That man would be better off if he had never been born."

The Lord's Supper
(Matthew 26.26-30; Luke 22.14-23; 1 Corinthians 11.23-25)

[22]During the meal Jesus took some bread in his hands. He blessed the bread and broke it. Then he gave it to his disci-

ples and said, "Take this. It is my body."

[23]Jesus picked up a cup of wine and gave thanks to God. He gave it to his disciples, and they all drank some. [24]Then he said, "This is my blood, which is poured out for many people, and with it God makes his agreement. [25]From now on I will not drink any wine, until I drink new wine in God's kingdom." [26]Then they sang a hymn and went out to the Mount of Olives.

Peter's Promise
(Matthew 26.31-35; Luke 22.31-34; John 13.36-38)

[27]Jesus said to his disciples, "All of you will reject me, as the Scriptures say,

'I will strike down
    the shepherd,
and the sheep
    will be scattered.'

[28]But after I am raised to life, I will go ahead of you to Galilee."

[29]Peter spoke up, "Even if all the others reject you, I never will!"

[30]Jesus replied, "This very night before a rooster crows twice, you will say three times that you don't know me."

[31]But Peter was so sure of himself that he said, "Even if I have to die with you, I will never say that I don't know you!"

All the others said the same thing.

Jesus Prays
(Matthew 26.36-46; Luke 22.39-46)

[32]Jesus went with his disciples to a place called Gethsemane, and he told them, "Sit here while I pray."

[33]Jesus took along Peter, James, and John. He was sad and troubled and [34]told them, "I am so sad that I feel as if I am dying. Stay here and keep awake with me."

[35-36]Jesus walked on a little way. Then he knelt down on the ground and prayed, "Father,[l] if it is possible, don't let this happen to me! Father, you can do anything. Don't make me suffer by having me drink from this cup.[m] But do what you want, and not what I want."

[37]When Jesus came back and found the disciples sleeping, he said to Simon Peter, "Are you asleep? Can't you stay awake for just one hour? [38]Stay awake and pray that you won't be tested. You want to do what is right, but you are weak."

[39]Jesus went back and prayed the same prayer. [40]But when he returned to the disciples, he found them sleeping again. They simply could not keep their

---

[j]14.10 *Iscariot:* See the note at 3.19.   **[k]14.13** *a man carrying a jar of water:* A male slave carrying water could mean that the family was rich.   **[l]14.35,36** *Father:* The Greek text has "Abba," which is an Aramaic word meaning "father."   **[m]14.35,36** *by having me drink from this cup:* See the note at 10.38.

eyes open, and they did not know what to say.

[41]When Jesus returned to the disciples the third time, he said, "Are you still sleeping and resting?[n] Enough of that! The time has come for the Son of Man to be handed over to sinners. [42]Get up! Let's go. The one who will betray me is already here."

Jesus Is Arrested
(Matthew 26.47-56; Luke 22.47-53; John 18.3-12)

[43]Jesus was still speaking, when Judas the betrayer came up. He was one of the twelve disciples, and a mob of men armed with swords and clubs were with him. They had been sent by the chief priests, the nation's leaders, and the teachers of the Law of Moses. [44]Judas had told them ahead of time, "Arrest the man I greet with a kiss.[o] Tie him up tight and lead him away."

[45]Judas walked right up to Jesus and said, "Teacher!" Then Judas kissed him, [46]and the men grabbed Jesus and arrested him.

[47]Someone standing there pulled out a sword. He struck the servant of the high priest and cut off his ear.

[48]Jesus said to the mob, "Why do you come with swords and clubs to arrest me like a criminal? [49]Day after day I was with you and taught in the temple, and you didn't arrest me. But what the Scriptures say must come true."

[50]All of Jesus' disciples ran off and left him. [51]One of them was a young man who was wearing only a linen cloth. And when the men grabbed him, [52]he left the cloth behind and ran away naked.

Jesus Is Questioned by the Council
(Matthew 26.57-68; Luke 22.54, 55, 63-71; John 18.13, 14, 19-24)

[53]Jesus was led off to the high priest. Then the chief priests, the nation's leaders, and the teachers of the Law of Moses all met together. [54]Peter had followed at a distance. And when he reached the courtyard of the high priest's house, he sat down with the guards to warm himself beside a fire.

[55]The chief priests and the whole council tried to find someone to accuse Jesus of a crime, so they could put him to death. But they could not find anyone to accuse him. [56]Many people did tell lies against Jesus, but they did not agree on what they said. [57]Finally, some men stood up and lied about him. They said,

[58]"We heard him say he would tear down this temple that we built. He also claimed that in three days he would build another one without any help." [59]But even then they did not agree on what they said.

[60]The high priest stood up in the council and asked Jesus, "Why don't you say something in your own defense? Don't you hear the charges they are making against you?" [61]But Jesus kept quiet and did not say a word. The high priest asked him another question, "Are you the Messiah, the Son of the glorious God?"[p]

[62]"Yes, I am!" Jesus answered.

"Soon you will see
    the Son of Man
sitting at the right side[q]
    of God All-Powerful,
and coming with the clouds
    of heaven."

[63]At once the high priest ripped his robe apart and shouted, "Why do we need more witnesses? [64]You heard him claim to be God! What is your decision?" They all agreed that he should be put to death.

[65]Some of the people started spitting on Jesus. They blindfolded him, hit him with their fists, and said, "Tell us who hit you!" Then the guards took charge of Jesus and beat him.

Peter Says He Doesn't Know Jesus
(Matthew 26.69-75; Luke 22.56-62; John 18.15-18, 25-27)

[66]While Peter was still in the courtyard, a servant girl of the high priest came up [67]and saw Peter warming himself by the fire. She stared at him and said, "You were with Jesus from Nazareth!"

[68]Peter replied, "That isn't true! I don't know what you're talking about. I don't have any idea what you mean." He went out to the gate, and a rooster crowed.[r]

[69]The servant girl saw Peter again and said to the people standing there, "This man is one of them!"

[70]"No, I'm not!" Peter replied.

A little while later some of the people said to Peter, "You certainly are one of them. You're a Galilean!"

[71]This time Peter began to curse and swear, "I don't even know the man you're talking about!"

[72]Right away the rooster crowed a second time. Then Peter remembered that Jesus had told him, "Before a rooster crows twice, you will say three

---

[n]**14.41** *Are you still sleeping and resting?*: Or "You may as well keep on sleeping and resting."
[o]**14.44** *greet with a kiss*: It was the custom for people to greet each other with a kiss on the cheek. [p]**14.61** *Son of the glorious God*: "Son of God" was one of the titles used for the kings of Israel. [q]**14.62** *right side*: See the note at 12.36. [r]**14.68** *a rooster crowed*: These words are not in some manuscripts.

times that you don't know me." So Peter started crying.

Pilate Questions Jesus
(Matthew 27.1, 2, 11-14; Luke 23.1-5;
John 18.28-38)

15 Early the next morning the chief priests, the nation's leaders, and the teachers of the Law of Moses met together with the whole Jewish council. They tied up Jesus and led him off to Pilate. ²He asked Jesus, "Are you the king of the Jews?"

"Those are your words," Jesus answered. ³The chief priests brought many charges against Jesus. ⁴Then Pilate questioned him again, "Don't you have anything to say? Don't you hear what crimes they say you have done?" ⁵But Jesus did not answer, and Pilate was amazed.

The Death Sentence
(Matthew 27.15-26; Luke 23.13-25;
John 18.39—19.16)

⁶During Passover, Pilate always freed one prisoner chosen by the people. ⁷And at that time there was a prisoner named Barabbas. He and some others had been arrested for murder during a riot. ⁸The crowd now came and asked Pilate to set a prisoner free, just as he usually did. ⁹Pilate asked them, "Do you want me to free the king of the Jews?" ¹⁰Pilate knew that the chief priests had brought Jesus to him because they were jealous. ¹¹But the chief priests told the crowd to ask Pilate to free Barabbas. ¹²Then Pilate asked the crowd, "What do you want me to do with this man you say is*ˢ* the king of the Jews?" ¹³They yelled, "Nail him to a cross!" ¹⁴Pilate asked, "But what crime has he done?"

"Nail him to a cross!" they yelled even louder. ¹⁵Pilate wanted to please the crowd. So he set Barabbas free. Then he ordered his soldiers to beat Jesus with a whip and nail him to a cross.

Soldiers Make Fun of Jesus
(Matthew 27.27-30; John 19.2, 3)

¹⁶The soldiers led Jesus inside the courtyard of the fortress*ᵗ* and called together the rest of the troops. ¹⁷They put a purple robe*ᵘ* on him, and on his head they placed a crown that they had made out of thorn branches. ¹⁸They made fun of Jesus and shouted, "Hey, you king of the Jews!" ¹⁹Then they beat him on the head with a stick. They spit on him and knelt down and pretended to worship him.

²⁰When the soldiers had finished making fun of Jesus, they took off the purple robe. They put his own clothes back on him and led him off to be nailed to a cross. ²¹Simon from Cyrene happened to be coming in from a farm, and they forced him to carry Jesus' cross. Simon was the father of Alexander and Rufus.

Jesus Is Nailed to a Cross
(Matthew 27.31-44; Luke 23.27-43;
John 19.17-27)

²²The soldiers took Jesus to Golgotha, which means "Place of a Skull."*ᵛ* ²³There they gave him some wine mixed with a drug to ease the pain, but he refused to drink it.

²⁴They nailed Jesus to a cross and gambled to see who would get his clothes. ²⁵It was about nine o'clock in the morning when they nailed him to the cross. ²⁶On it was a sign that told why he was nailed there. It read, "This is the King of the Jews." ²⁷⁻²⁸The soldiers also nailed two criminals on crosses, one to the right of Jesus and the other to his left.*ʷ*

²⁹People who passed by said terrible things about Jesus. They shook their heads and shouted, "Ha! So you're the one who claimed you could tear down the temple and build it again in three days. ³⁰Save yourself and come down from the cross!"

³¹The chief priests and the teachers of the Law of Moses also made fun of Jesus. They said to each other, "He saved others, but he can't save himself. ³²If he is the Messiah, the king of Israel, let him come down from the cross! Then we will see and believe." The two criminals also said cruel things to Jesus.

The Death of Jesus
(Matthew 27.45-56; Luke 23.44-49;
John 19.28-30)

³³About noon the sky turned dark and stayed that way until around three o'clock. ³⁴Then about that time Jesus shouted, "Eloi, Eloi, lema sabachthani?"*ˣ* which means, "My God, my God, why have you deserted me?"

---

*ˢ***15.12** *this man you say is:* These words are not in some manuscripts.   *ᵗ***15.16** *fortress:* The place where the Roman governor stayed. It was probably at Herod's palace west of Jerusalem, though it may have been Fortress Antonia, north of the temple, where the Roman troops were stationed.   *ᵘ***15.17** *purple robe:* This was probably a Roman soldier's robe.   *ᵛ***15.22** *Place of a Skull:* The place was probably given this name because it was near a large rock in the shape of a human skull.   *ʷ***15.27-28** *left:* Some manuscripts add, "So the Scriptures came true which say, 'He was accused of being a criminal.'"   *ˣ***15.34** *Eloi . . . sabachthani:* These words are in Aramaic, a language spoken in Palestine during the time of Jesus.

[35]Some of the people standing there heard Jesus and said, "He is calling for Elijah."[y] [36]One of them ran and grabbed a sponge. After he had soaked it in wine, he put it on a stick and held it up to Jesus. He said, "Let's wait and see if Elijah will come[z] and take him down!" [37]Jesus shouted and then died.

[38]At once the curtain in the temple[a] tore in two from top to bottom.

[39]A Roman army officer was standing in front of Jesus. When the officer saw how Jesus died, he said, "This man really was the Son of God!"

[40-41]Some women were looking on from a distance. They had come with Jesus to Jerusalem. But even before this they had been his followers and had helped him while he was in Galilee. Mary Magdalene and Mary the mother of the younger James and of Joseph were two of these women. Salome was also one of them.

Jesus Is Buried
(Matthew 27.57-61; Luke 23.50-56; John 19.38-42)

[42]It was now the evening before the Sabbath, and the Jewish people were getting ready for that sacred day. [43]A man named Joseph from Arimathea was brave enough to ask Pilate for the body of Jesus. Joseph was a highly respected member of the Jewish council, and he was also waiting for God's kingdom to come.

[44]Pilate was surprised to hear that Jesus was already dead, and he called in the army officer to find out if Jesus had been dead very long. [45]After the officer told him, Pilate let Joseph have Jesus' body.

[46]Joseph bought a linen cloth and took the body down from the cross. He had it wrapped in the cloth, and he put it in a tomb that had been cut into solid rock. Then he rolled a big stone against the entrance to the tomb.

[47]Mary Magdalene and Mary the mother of Joseph were watching and saw where the body was placed.

Jesus Is Alive
(Matthew 28.1-8; Luke 24.1-12; John 20.1-10)

16 After the Sabbath, Mary Magdalene, Salome, and Mary the mother of James bought some spices to put on Jesus' body. [2]Very early on Sunday morning, just as the sun was coming up, they went to the tomb. [3]On their way, they were asking one another, "Who will roll the stone away from the entrance for us?" [4]But when they looked, they saw that the stone had already been rolled away. And it was a huge stone!

[5]The women went into the tomb, and on the right side they saw a young man in a white robe sitting there. They were alarmed.

[6]The man said, "Don't be alarmed! You are looking for Jesus from Nazareth, who was nailed to a cross. God has raised him to life, and he isn't here. You can see the place where they put his body. [7]Now go and tell his disciples, and especially Peter, that he will go ahead of you to Galilee. You will see him there, just as he told you."

[8]When the women ran from the tomb, they were confused and shaking all over. They were too afraid to tell anyone what had happened.

ONE OLD ENDING
TO MARK'S GOSPEL[b]

Jesus Appears to Mary Magdalene
(Matthew 28.9, 10; John 20.11-18)

[9]Very early on the first day of the week, after Jesus had risen to life, he appeared to Mary Magdalene. Earlier he had forced seven demons out of her. [10]She left and told his friends, who were crying and mourning. [11]Even though they heard that Jesus was alive and that Mary had seen him, they would not believe it.

Jesus Appears to Two Disciples
(Luke 24.13-35)

[12]Later, Jesus appeared in another form to two disciples, as they were on their way out of the city. [13]But when these disciples told what had happened, the others would not believe.

What Jesus' Followers Must Do
(Matthew 28.16-20; Luke 24.36-49; John 20.19-23; Acts 1.6-8)

[14]Afterwards, Jesus appeared to his eleven disciples as they were eating. He scolded them because they were too stubborn to believe the ones who had seen him after he had been raised to life. [15]Then he told them:

Go and preach the good news to everyone in the world. [16]Anyone who believes me and is baptized will be saved. But anyone who refuses to believe me will be condemned.

[17]Everyone who believes me will be

---

[y]**15.35** *Elijah:* The name "Elijah" sounds something like "Eloi," which means "my God."
[z]**15.36** *see if Elijah will come:* See the note at 6.15.   [a]**15.38** *curtain in the temple:* There were two curtains in the temple. One was at the entrance, and the other separated the holy place from the most holy place that the Jewish people thought of as God's home on earth. The second curtain is probably the one which is meant.   [b]**16.9** *One Old Ending to Mark's Gospel:* Verses 9-20 are not in some manuscripts.

able to do wonderful things. By using my name they will force out demons, and they will speak new languages. [18]They will handle snakes and will drink poison and not be hurt. They will also heal sick people by placing their hands on them.

Jesus Returns to Heaven
(Luke 24.50-53; Acts 1.9-11)

[19]After the Lord Jesus had said these things to the disciples, he was taken back up to heaven where he sat down at the right side[c] of God. [20]Then the disciples left and preached everywhere. The Lord was with them, and the miracles they worked proved that their message was true.

ANOTHER OLD ENDING TO MARK'S GOSPEL[d]

[9-10]The women quickly told Peter and his friends what had happened. Later, Jesus sent the disciples to the east and to the west with his sacred and everlasting message of how people can be saved forever.

[c]**16.19** *right side*: See the note at 12.36. [d]**16.9,10** *Another Old Ending to Mark's Gospel*: Some manuscripts and early translations have both this shorter ending and the longer one (verses 9-20).

LUKE

ABOUT THIS BOOK

God's love is for everyone! Jesus came into the world to be the Savior of all people! These are two of the main thoughts in this book. Several of the best known stories that Jesus used for teaching about God's love are found only in Luke's Gospel: The Good Samaritan (10.25-37), A Lost Sheep (15.1-7), and A Lost Son (15.11-32). Only Luke tells how Jesus visited in the home of a hated tax collector (19.1-10) and promised life in paradise to a dying criminal (23.39-43).

Luke mentions God's Spirit more than any of the other New Testament writers. For example, the power of the Spirit was with John the Baptist from the time he was born (1.15). And the angel promised Mary, "The Holy Spirit will come down to you . . . So your child will be called the holy Son of God" (1.35). Jesus followed the Spirit (4.1, 14, 18; 10.21) and taught that the Spirit is God's greatest gift (11.13).

Luke shows how important prayer was to Jesus. Jesus prayed often: after being baptized (3.21), before choosing the disciples (6.12), before asking his disciples who they thought he was (9.18), and before giving up his life on the cross (23.34, 46). From Luke we learn of three stories that Jesus told to teach about prayer (11.5-9; 18.1-8, 9-14).

An important part of Luke's story is the way in which he shows the concern of Jesus for the poor: the good news is preached to them (4.18; 7.22), they receive God's blessings (6.20), they are invited to the great feast (14.13, 21), the poor man Lazarus is taken to heaven by angels (16.20, 22), and Jesus commands his disciples to sell what they have and give the money to the poor (12.33).

To make sure that readers would understand that Jesus was raised physically from death, Luke reports that the risen Jesus ate a piece of fish (24.42, 43). There could be no mistake about the risen Jesus: he was not a ghost. His being raised from death was real and not someone's imagination. Luke also wrote another book—the Acts of the Apostles—to show what happened to Jesus' followers after he was raised from death and taken up to heaven. No other Gospel has a second volume that continues the story.

Luke closes this first book that he wrote by telling that Jesus returned to heaven. But right before Jesus leaves, he tells his disciples:

> *The Scriptures say that the Messiah must suffer, then three days later he will rise from death. They also say that all people of every nation must be told in my name to turn to God, in order to be forgiven. So beginning in Jerusalem, you must tell everything that has happened.*   (24.46-48)

A QUICK LOOK AT THIS BOOK

1 Many people have tried to tell the story of what God has done among us. [2]They wrote what we had been told by the ones who were there in the beginning and saw what happened. [3]So I made a careful study[a] of everything and then decided to write and tell you exactly what took place. Honorable Theophilus, [4]I have done this to let you know the truth about what you have heard.

An Angel Tells about the Birth of John

[5]When Herod was king of Judea, there was a priest by the name of Zechariah from the priestly group of Abijah. His wife Elizabeth was from the family of Aaron.[b] [6]Both of them were good people and pleased the Lord God by obeying all that he had commanded. [7]But they did not have children. Elizabeth could not have any, and both Zechariah and Elizabeth were already old.

[8]One day Zechariah's group of priests were on duty, and he was serving God as a priest. [9]According to the custom of the priests, he had been chosen to go into the Lord's temple that day and to burn incense,[c] [10]while the people stood outside praying.

[11]All at once an angel from the Lord appeared to Zechariah at the right side of the altar. [12]Zechariah was confused and afraid when he saw the angel. [13]But the angel told him:

Don't be afraid, Zechariah! God has heard your prayers. Your wife Elizabeth will have a son, and you must name him John. [14]His birth will make you very happy, and many people will be glad. [15]Your son will be a great servant of the Lord. He must never drink wine or beer, and the power of the Holy Spirit will be with him from the time he is born.

[16]John will lead many people in Israel to turn back to the Lord their God. [17]He will go ahead of the Lord with the same power and spirit that Elijah[d] had. And because of John, parents will be more thoughtful of their children. And people who now disobey God will begin to think as they ought to. That is how John will get people ready for the Lord.

[18]Zechariah said to the angel, "How will I know this is going to happen? My wife and I are both very old."

[19]The angel answered, "I am Gabriel, God's servant, and I was sent to tell you this good news. [20]You have not believed what I have said. So you will not be able to say a thing until all this happens. But everything will take place when it is supposed to."

[21]The crowd was waiting for Zechariah and kept wondering why he was staying so long in the temple. [22]When he did come out, he could not speak, and they knew he had seen a vision. He motioned to them with his hands, but did not say a thing.

[23]When Zechariah's time of service in the temple was over, he went home. [24]Soon after that, his wife was expecting a baby, and for five months she did not leave the house. She said to herself, [25]"What the Lord has done for me will keep people from looking down on me."[e]

An Angel Tells about the Birth of Jesus

[26]One month later God sent the angel Gabriel to the town of Nazareth in Galilee [27]with a message for a virgin named Mary. She was engaged to Joseph from the family of King David. [28]The angel greeted Mary and said, "You are truly blessed! The Lord is with you."

[29]Mary was confused by the angel's words and wondered what they meant. [30]Then the angel told Mary, "Don't be afraid! God is pleased with you, [31]and you will have a son. His name will be Jesus. [32]He will be great and will be called the Son of God Most High. The Lord God will make him king, as his ancestor David was. [33]He will rule the people of Israel forever, and his kingdom will never end."

[34]Mary asked the angel, "How can this happen? I am not married!"

[35]The angel answered, "The Holy Spirit will come down to you, and God's power will come over you. So your child will be called the holy Son of God. [36]Your relative Elizabeth is also going to have a son, even though she is old. No one thought she could ever have a baby, but in three months she will have a son. [37]Nothing is impossible for God!"

[38]Mary said, "I am the Lord's servant! Let it happen as you have said." And the angel left her.

Mary Visits Elizabeth

[39]A short time later Mary hurried to a town in the hill country of Judea. [40]She went into Zechariah's home, where she greeted Elizabeth. [41]When Elizabeth heard Mary's greeting, her baby moved within her.

The Holy Spirit came upon Elizabeth. [42]Then in a loud voice she said to Mary:

---

[a]**1.3** *a careful study*: Or "a study from the beginning." [b]**1.5** *Aaron*: The brother of Moses and the first priest. [c]**1.9** *burn incense*: This was done twice a day, once in the morning and again in the late afternoon. [d]**1.17** *Elijah*: The prophet Elijah was known for his power to work miracles. [e]**1.25** *keep people from looking down on me*: When a married woman could not have children, it was thought that the Lord was punishing her.

God has blessed you more than any other woman! He has also blessed the child you will have. ⁴³Why should the mother of my Lord come to me? ⁴⁴As soon as I heard your greeting, my baby became happy and moved within me. ⁴⁵The Lord has blessed you because you believed that he will keep his promise.

Mary's Song of Praise

⁴⁶Mary said:

With all my heart
I praise the Lord,
⁴⁷and I am glad
because of God my Savior.
⁴⁸ He cares for me,
his humble servant.
From now on,
all people will say
God has blessed me.
⁴⁹ God All-Powerful has done
great things for me,
and his name is holy.
⁵⁰ He always shows mercy
to everyone
who worships him.
⁵¹ The Lord has used
his powerful arm
to scatter those
who are proud.
⁵² He drags strong rulers
from their thrones
and puts humble people
in places of power.
⁵³ God gives the hungry
good things to eat,
and sends the rich away
with nothing.
⁵⁴ He helps his servant Israel
and is always merciful
to his people.
⁵⁵ The Lord made this promise
to our ancestors,
to Abraham and his family
forever!

⁵⁶Mary stayed with Elizabeth about three months. Then she went back home.

The Birth of John the Baptist

⁵⁷When Elizabeth's son was born, ⁵⁸her neighbors and relatives heard how kind the Lord had been to her, and they too were glad.

⁵⁹Eight days later they did for the child what the Law of Moses commands.ᶠ They were going to name him Zechariah, after his father. ⁶⁰But Elizabeth said, "No! His name is John."

⁶¹The people argued, "No one in your family has ever been named John." ⁶²So they motioned to Zechariah to find out what he wanted to name his son.

⁶³Zechariah asked for a writing tablet. Then he wrote, "His name is John." Everyone was amazed. ⁶⁴Right away, Zechariah started speaking and praising God.

⁶⁵All the neighbors were frightened because of what had happened, and everywhere in the hill country people kept talking about these things. ⁶⁶Everyone who heard about this wondered what this child would grow up to be. They knew that the Lord was with him.

Zechariah Praises the Lord

⁶⁷The Holy Spirit came upon Zechariah, and he began to speak:

⁶⁸ Praise the Lord,
the God of Israel!
He has come
to save his people.
⁶⁹ Our God has given us
a mighty Saviorᵍ
from the family
of David his servant.
⁷⁰ Long ago the Lord promised
by the words
of his holy prophets
⁷¹ to save us from our enemies
and from everyone
who hates us.
⁷² God said he would be kind
to our people and keep
his sacred promise.
⁷³ He told our ancestor Abraham
⁷⁴ that he would rescue us
from our enemies.
Then we could serve him
without fear,
⁷⁵ by being holy and good
as long as we live.

⁷⁶ You, my son, will be called
a prophet of God
in heaven above.
You will go ahead of the Lord
to get everything ready
for him.
⁷⁷ You will tell his people
that they can be saved
when their sins
are forgiven.
⁷⁸ God's love and kindness
will shine upon us
like the sun that rises
in the sky.ʰ
⁷⁹ On us who live
in the dark shadow
of death

ᶠ1.59 *what the Law of Moses commands*: This refers to circumcision. It is the cutting off of skin from the private part of Jewish boys eight days after birth to show that they belong to the Lord. ᵍ1.69 *a mighty Savior*: The Greek text has "a horn of salvation." In the Scriptures animal horns are often a symbol of great strength. ʰ1.78 *like the sun that rises in the sky*: Or "like the Messiah coming from heaven."

this light will shine
to guide us
into a life of peace.

80As John grew up, God's Spirit gave
him great power. John lived in the
desert until the time he was sent to the
people of Israel.

The Birth of Jesus
(Matthew 1.18-25)

2 About that time Emperor Augustus
gave orders for the names of all the
people to be listed in record books.*i*
2These first records were made when
Quirinius was governor of Syria.*j*

3Everyone had to go to their own
hometown to be listed. **4**So Joseph had
to leave Nazareth in Galilee and go to
Bethlehem in Judea. Long ago Bethlehem had been King David's hometown,
and Joseph went there because he was
from David's family.

5Mary was engaged to Joseph and
traveled with him to Bethlehem. She
was soon going to have a baby, **6**and
while they were there, **7**she gave birth to
her first-born*k* son. She dressed him in
baby clothes*l* and laid him on a bed of
hay, because there was no room for
them in the inn.

The Shepherds

8That night in the fields near Bethlehem some shepherds were guarding
their sheep. **9**All at once an angel came
down to them from the Lord, and the
brightness of the Lord's glory flashed
around them. The shepherds were
frightened. **10**But the angel said, "Don't
be afraid! I have good news for you,
which will make everyone happy. **11**This
very day in King David's hometown a
Savior was born for you. He is Christ
the Lord. **12**You will know who he is, because you will find him dressed in baby
clothes and lying on a bed of hay."

13Suddenly many other angels came
down from heaven and joined in praising God. They said:

14 "Praise God in heaven!
   Peace on earth to everyone
      who pleases God."

15After the angels had left and gone
back to heaven, the shepherds said to
each other, "Let's go to Bethlehem and
see what the Lord has told us about."

16They hurried off and found Mary and
Joseph, and they saw the baby lying on
a bed of hay.

17When the shepherds saw Jesus, they
told his parents what the angel had said
about him. **18**Everyone listened and was
surprised. **19**But Mary kept thinking
about all this and wondering what it
meant.

20As the shepherds returned to their
sheep, they were praising God and saying wonderful things about him. Everything they had seen and heard was just
as the angel had said.

21Eight days later Jesus' parents did
for him what the Law of Moses commands.*m* And they named him Jesus,
just as the angel had told Mary when he
promised she would have a baby.

Simeon Praises the Lord

22The time came for Mary and Joseph
to do what the Law of Moses says a
mother is supposed to do after her baby
is born.*n*

They took Jesus to the temple in Jerusalem and presented him to the Lord,
23just as the Law of the Lord says, "Each
first-born*o* baby boy belongs to the
Lord." **24**The Law of the Lord also says
that parents have to offer a sacrifice,
giving at least a pair of doves or two
young pigeons. So that is what Mary
and Joseph did.

25At this time a man named Simeon
was living in Jerusalem. Simeon was a
good man. He loved God and was waiting for God to save the people of Israel.
God's Spirit came to him **26**and told him
that he would not die until he had seen
Christ the Lord.

27When Mary and Joseph brought Jesus to the temple to do what the Law of
Moses says should be done for a new
baby, the Spirit told Simeon to go into
the temple. **28**Simeon took the baby Jesus in his arms and praised God,

29 "Lord, I am your servant,
      and now I can die in peace,
   because you have kept
      your promise to me.
30 With my own eyes I have seen
   what you have done
      to save your people,
31 and foreign nations
   will also see this.

---

*i***2.1** *names . . . listed in record books*: This was done so that everyone could be made to pay
taxes to the Emperor.   *j***2.2** *Quirinius was governor of Syria*: It is known that Quirinius made
a record of the people in A.D. 6 or 7. But the exact date of the record taking that Luke mentions
is not known.   *k***2.7** *first-born*: The Jewish people said that the first-born son in each of their
families belonged to the Lord.   *l***2.7** *dressed him in baby clothes*: The Greek text has
"wrapped him in wide strips of cloth," which was how young babies were dressed.
*m***2.21** *what the Law of Moses commands*: See the note at 1.59.   *n***2.22** *after her baby is
born*: After a Jewish mother gave birth to a son, she was considered "unclean" and had to stay
home until he was circumcised (see the note at 1.59). Then she had to stay home for another 33
days, before offering a sacrifice to the Lord.   *o***2.23** *first-born*: See the note at 2.7.

[32] Your mighty power is a light
　for all nations,
and it will bring honor
　to your people Israel."

[33] Jesus' parents were surprised at what Simeon had said. [34] Then he blessed them and told Mary, "This child of yours will cause many people in Israel to fall and others to stand. The child will be like a warning sign. Many people will reject him, [35] and you, Mary, will suffer as though you had been stabbed by a dagger. But all this will show what people are really thinking."

Anna Speaks about the Child Jesus

[36] The prophet Anna was also there in the temple. She was the daughter of Phanuel from the tribe of Asher, and she was very old. In her youth she had been married for seven years, but her husband died. [37] And now she was eighty-four years old.[p] Night and day she served God in the temple by praying and often going without eating.[q]

[38] At that time Anna came in and praised God. She spoke about the child Jesus to everyone who hoped for Jerusalem to be set free.

The Return to Nazareth

[39] After Joseph and Mary had done everything that the Law of the Lord commands, they returned home to Nazareth in Galilee. [40] The child Jesus grew. He became strong and wise, and God blessed him.

The Boy Jesus in the Temple

[41] Every year Jesus' parents went to Jerusalem for Passover. [42] And when Jesus was twelve years old, they all went there as usual for the celebration. [43] After Passover his parents left, but they did not know that Jesus had stayed on in the city. [44] They thought he was traveling with some other people, and they went a whole day before they started looking for him. [45] When they could not find him with their relatives and friends, they went back to Jerusalem and started looking for him there.

[46] Three days later they found Jesus sitting in the temple, listening to the teachers and asking them questions. [47] Everyone who heard him was surprised at how much he knew and at the answers he gave.

[48] When his parents found him, they were amazed. His mother said, "Son, why have you done this to us? Your father and I have been very worried, and we have been searching for you!"

[49] Jesus answered, "Why did you have to look for me? Didn't you know that I would be in my Father's house?"[r] [50] But they did not understand what he meant.

[51] Jesus went back to Nazareth with his parents and obeyed them. His mother kept on thinking about all that had happened.

[52] Jesus became wise, and he grew strong. God was pleased with him and so were the people.

The Preaching of John the Baptist
(Matthew 3.1-12; Mark 1.1-8; John 1.19-28)

3 For fifteen years[s] Emperor Tiberius had ruled that part of the world. Pontius Pilate was governor of Judea, and Herod[t] was the ruler of Galilee. Herod's brother, Philip, was the ruler in the countries of Iturea and Trachonitis, and Lysanias was the ruler of Abilene. [2] Annas and Caiaphas were the Jewish high priests.[u]

At that time God spoke to Zechariah's son John, who was living in the desert. [3] So John went along the Jordan Valley, telling the people, "Turn back to God and be baptized! Then your sins will be forgiven." [4] Isaiah the prophet wrote about John when he said,

"In the desert
　someone is shouting,
'Get the road ready
　for the Lord!
Make a straight path
　for him.
[5] Fill up every valley
and level every mountain
　and hill.
Straighten the crooked paths
and smooth out
　the rough roads.
[6] Then everyone will see
　the saving power of God.' "

[7] Crowds of people came out to be baptized, but John said to them, "You bunch of snakes! Who warned you to run from the coming judgment? [8] Do something to show that you really have given up your sins. Don't start saying that you belong to Abraham's family. God can turn these stones into children for Abraham.[v] [9] An ax is ready to cut the

---

[p]**2.37** *And now she was eighty-four years old*: Or "And now she had been a widow for eighty-four years." 　[q]**2.37** *without eating*: The Jewish people sometimes went without eating (also called "fasting") to show their love for God or to show sorrow for their sins. 　[r]**2.49** *in my Father's house*: Or "doing my Father's work." 　[s]**3.1** *For fifteen years*: This was either A.D. 28 or 29, and Jesus was about thirty years old (see 3.23). 　[t]**3.1** *Herod*: Herod Antipas, the son of Herod the Great. 　[u]**3.2** *Annas and Caiaphas . . . high priests*: Annas was high priest from A.D. 6 until 15. His son-in-law Caiaphas was high priest from A.D. 18 until 37. 　[v]**3.8** *children for Abraham*: The Jewish people thought they were God's chosen people because of God's promises to their ancestor Abraham.

trees down at their roots. Any tree that doesn't produce good fruit will be cut down and thrown into a fire."

¹⁰The crowds asked John, "What should we do?"

¹¹John told them, "If you have two coats, give one to someone who doesn't have any. If you have food, share it with someone else."

¹²When tax collectors*ʷ* came to be baptized, they asked John, "Teacher, what should we do?"

¹³John told them, "Don't make people pay more than they owe."

¹⁴Some soldiers asked him, "And what about us? What do we have to do?"

John told them, "Don't force people to pay money to make you leave them alone. Be satisfied with your pay."

¹⁵Everyone became excited and wondered, "Could John be the Messiah?"

¹⁶John said, "I am just baptizing with water. But someone more powerful is going to come, and I am not good enough even to untie his sandals.*ˣ* He will baptize you with the Holy Spirit and with fire. ¹⁷His threshing fork*ʸ* is in his hand, and he is ready to separate the wheat from the husks. He will store the wheat in his barn and burn the husks with a fire that never goes out."

¹⁸In many different ways John preached the good news to the people. ¹⁹But to Herod the ruler, he said, "It was wrong for you to take Herodias, your brother's wife." John also said that Herod had done many other bad things. ²⁰Finally, Herod put John in jail, and this was the worst thing he had done.

The Baptism of Jesus
(Matthew 3.13-17; Mark 1.9-11)

²¹While everyone else was being baptized, Jesus himself was baptized. Then as he prayed, the sky opened up, ²²and the Holy Spirit came down upon him in the form of a dove. A voice from heaven said, "You are my own dear Son, and I am pleased with you."

The Ancestors of Jesus
(Matthew 1.1-17)

²³When Jesus began to preach, he was about thirty years old. Everyone thought he was the son of Joseph. But his family went back through Heli, ²⁴Matthat, Levi, Melchi, Jannai, Joseph, ²⁵Mattathias, Amos, Nahum, Esli, Naggai, ²⁶Maath, Mattathias, Semein, Josech, Joda; ²⁷Joanan, Rhesa, Zerubbabel, She-

altiel, Neri, ²⁸Melchi, Addi, Cosam, Elmadam, Er, ²⁹Joshua, Eliezer, Jorim, Matthat, Levi;

³⁰Simeon, Judah, Joseph, Jonam, Eliakim, ³¹Melea, Menna, Mattatha, Nathan, David, ³²Jesse, Obed, Boaz, Salmon, Nahshon;

³³Amminadab, Admin, Arni, Hezron, Perez, Judah, ³⁴Jacob, Isaac, Abraham, Terah, Nahor, ³⁵Serug, Reu, Peleg, Eber, Shelah;

³⁶Cainan, Arphaxad, Shem, Noah, Lamech, ³⁷Methuselah, Enoch, Jared, Mahalaleel, Kenan, ³⁸Enosh, and Seth.

The family of Jesus went all the way back to Adam and then to God.

Jesus and the Devil
(Matthew 4.1-11; Mark 1.12, 13)

4 When Jesus returned from the Jordan River, the power of the Holy Spirit was with him, and the Spirit led him into the desert. ²For forty days Jesus was tested by the devil, and during that time he went without eating.*ᶻ* When it was all over, he was hungry.

³The devil said to Jesus, "If you are God's Son, tell this stone to turn into bread."

⁴Jesus answered, "The Scriptures say, 'No one can live only on food.' "

⁵Then the devil led Jesus up to a high place and quickly showed him all the nations on earth. ⁶The devil said, "I will give all this power and glory to you. It has been given to me, and I can give it to anyone I want to. ⁷Just worship me, and you can have it all."

⁸Jesus answered, "The Scriptures say:

'Worship the Lord your God
   and serve only him!' "

⁹Finally, the devil took Jesus to Jerusalem and had him stand on top of the temple. The devil said, "If you are God's Son, jump off. ¹⁰⁻¹¹The Scriptures say:

'God will tell his angels
   to take care of you.
They will catch you
   in their arms,
and you will not hurt
   your feet on the stones.' "

¹²Jesus answered, "The Scriptures also say, 'Don't try to test the Lord your God!' "

¹³After the devil had finished testing Jesus in every way possible, he left him for a while.

---

*ʷ***3.12** *tax collectors*: These were usually Jewish people who paid the Romans for the right to collect taxes. They were hated by other Jews who thought of them as traitors to their country and to their religion. *ˣ***3.16** *untie his sandals*: This was the duty of a slave. *ʸ***3.17** *threshing fork*: After Jewish farmers had trampled out the grain, they used a large fork to pitch the grain and the husks into the air. Wind would blow away the light husks, and the grain would fall back to the ground, where it could be gathered up. *ᶻ***4.2** *went without eating*: See the note at 2.37.

Jesus Begins His Work
(Matthew 4.12-17; Mark 1.14, 15)

14Jesus returned to Galilee with the power of the Spirit. News about him spread everywhere. **15**He taught in the Jewish meeting places, and everyone praised him.

The People of Nazareth Turn against Jesus
(Matthew 13.53-58; Mark 6.1-6)

16Jesus went back to Nazareth, where he had been brought up, and as usual he went to the meeting place on the Sabbath. When he stood up to read from the Scriptures, **17**he was given the book of Isaiah the prophet. He opened it and read,

18 "The Lord's Spirit
    has come to me,
because he has chosen me
to tell the good news
    to the poor.
The Lord has sent me
to announce freedom
    for prisoners,
to give sight to the blind,
to free everyone
    who suffers,
19 and to say, 'This is the year
    the Lord has chosen.' "

20Jesus closed the book, then handed it back to the man in charge and sat down. Everyone in the meeting place looked straight at Jesus. **21**Then Jesus said to them, "What you have just heard me read has come true today."

22All the people started talking about Jesus and were amazed at the wonderful things he said. They kept on asking, "Isn't he Joseph's son?"

23Jesus answered:

You will certainly want to tell me this saying, "Doctor, first make yourself well." You will tell me to do the same things here in my own hometown that you heard I did in Capernaum. **24**But you can be sure that no prophets are liked by the people of their own hometown.

25Once during the time of Elijah there was no rain for three and a half years, and people everywhere were starving. There were many widows in Israel, **26**but Elijah was sent only to a widow in the town of Zarephath near the city of Sidon. **27**During the time of the prophet Elisha, many men in Israel had leprosy.[a] But no one was healed, except Naaman who lived in Syria.

28When the people in the meeting place heard Jesus say this, they became so angry **29**that they got up and threw him out of town. They dragged him to the edge of the cliff on which the town was built, because they wanted to throw him down from there. **30**But Jesus slipped through the crowd and got away.

A Man with an Evil Spirit
(Mark 1.21-28)

31Jesus went to the town of Capernaum in Galilee and taught the people on the Sabbath. **32**His teaching amazed them because he spoke with power. **33**There in the Jewish meeting place was a man with an evil spirit. He yelled out, **34**"Hey, Jesus of Nazareth, what do you want with us? Are you here to get rid of us? I know who you are! You are God's Holy One."

35Jesus ordered the evil spirit to be quiet and come out. The demon threw the man to the ground in front of everyone and left without harming him.

36They all were amazed and kept saying to each other, "What kind of teaching is this? He has power to order evil spirits out of people!" **37**News about Jesus spread all over that part of the country.

Jesus Heals Many People
(Matthew 8.14-17; Mark 1.29-34)

38Jesus left the meeting place and went to Simon's home. When Jesus got there, he was told that Simon's mother-in-law was sick with a high fever. **39**So Jesus went over to her and ordered the fever to go away. Right then she was able to get up and serve them a meal.

40After the sun had set, people with all kinds of diseases were brought to Jesus. He put his hands on each one of them and healed them. **41**Demons went out of many people and shouted, "You are the Son of God!" But Jesus ordered the demons not to speak because they knew he was the Messiah.

42The next morning Jesus went out to a place where he could be alone, and crowds came looking for him. When they found him, they tried to stop him from leaving. **43**But Jesus said, "People in other towns must hear the good news about God's kingdom. That's why I was sent." **44**So he kept on preaching in the Jewish meeting places in Judea.[b]

Jesus Chooses His First Disciples
(Matthew 4.18-22; Mark 1.16-20)

5 Jesus was standing on the shore of Lake Gennesaret,[c] teaching the people as they crowded around him to hear

---

[a]**4.27** *leprosy*: In biblical times the word "leprosy" was used for many different kinds of skin diseases. [b]**4.44** *Judea*: Some manuscripts have "Galilee." [c]**5.1** *Lake Gennesaret*: Another name for Lake Galilee.

God's message. ²Near the shore he saw two boats left there by some fishermen who had gone to wash their nets. ³Jesus got into the boat that belonged to Simon and asked him to row it out a little way from the shore. Then Jesus sat down*d* in the boat to teach the crowd.

⁴When Jesus had finished speaking, he told Simon, "Row the boat out into the deep water and let your nets down to catch some fish."

⁵"Master," Simon answered, "we have worked hard all night long and have not caught a thing. But if you tell me to, I will let the nets down." ⁶They did it and caught so many fish that their nets began ripping apart. ⁷Then they signaled for their partners in the other boat to come and help them. The men came, and together they filled the two boats so full that they both began to sink.

⁸When Simon Peter saw this happen, he knelt down in front of Jesus and said, "Lord, don't come near me! I am a sinner." ⁹Peter and everyone with him were completely surprised at all the fish they had caught. ¹⁰His partners James and John, the sons of Zebedee, were surprised too.

Jesus told Simon, "Don't be afraid! From now on you will bring in people instead of fish." ¹¹The men pulled their boats up on the shore. Then they left everything and went with Jesus.

Jesus Heals a Man
(Matthew 8.1-4; Mark 1.40-45)

¹²Jesus came to a town where there was a man who had leprosy.*e* When the man saw Jesus, he knelt down to the ground in front of Jesus and begged, "Lord, you have the power to make me well, if only you wanted to."

¹³Jesus put his hand on him and said, "I want to! Now you are well." At once the man's leprosy disappeared. ¹⁴Jesus told him, "Don't tell anyone about this, but go and show yourself to the priest. Offer a gift to the priest, just as Moses commanded, and everyone will know that you have been healed."*f*

¹⁵News about Jesus kept spreading. Large crowds came to listen to him teach and to be healed of their diseases. ¹⁶But Jesus would often go to some place where he could be alone and pray.

Jesus Heals a Crippled Man
(Matthew 9.1-8; Mark 2.1-12)

¹⁷One day some Pharisees and experts in the Law of Moses sat listening to Jesus teach. They had come from every village in Galilee and Judea and from Jerusalem.

God had given Jesus the power to heal the sick, ¹⁸and some people came carrying a crippled man on a mat. They tried to take him inside the house and put him in front of Jesus. ¹⁹But because of the crowd, they could not get him to Jesus. So they went up on the roof,*g* where they removed some tiles and let the mat down in the middle of the room.

²⁰When Jesus saw how much faith they had, he said to the crippled man, "My friend, your sins are forgiven."

²¹The Pharisees and the experts began arguing, "Jesus must think he is God! Only God can forgive sins."

²²Jesus knew what they were thinking, and he said, "Why are you thinking that? ²³Is it easier for me to tell this crippled man that his sins are forgiven or to tell him to get up and walk? ²⁴But now you will see that the Son of Man has the right to forgive sins here on earth." Jesus then said to the man, "Get up! Pick up your mat and walk home."

²⁵At once the man stood up in front of everyone. He picked up his mat and went home, giving thanks to God. ²⁶Everyone was amazed and praised God. What they saw surprised them, and they said, "We have seen a great miracle today!"

Jesus Chooses Levi
(Matthew 9.9-13; Mark 2.13-17)

²⁷Later, Jesus went out and saw a tax collector*h* named Levi sitting at the place for paying taxes. Jesus said to him, "Come with me." ²⁸Levi left everything and went with Jesus.

²⁹In his home Levi gave a big dinner for Jesus. Many tax collectors and other guests were also there.

³⁰The Pharisees and some of their teachers of the Law of Moses grumbled to Jesus' disciples, "Why do you eat and drink with those tax collectors and other sinners?"

³¹Jesus answered, "Healthy people don't need a doctor, but sick people do.

---

*d***5.3** *sat down:* Teachers in the ancient world, including Jewish teachers, usually sat down when they taught. *e***5.12** *leprosy:* See the note at 4.27. *f***5.14** *everyone will know that you have been healed:* People with leprosy had to be examined by a priest and told that they were well (that is, "clean") before they could once again live a normal life in the Jewish community. The gift that Moses commanded was the sacrifice of some lambs together with flour mixed with olive oil. *g***5.19** *roof:* In Palestine the houses usually had a flat roof. Stairs on the outside led up to the roof, which was made of beams and boards covered with packed earth. Luke says that the roof was made of (clay) tiles, which were also used for making roofs in New Testament times. *h***5.27** *tax collector:* See the note at 3.12.

[32]I didn't come to invite good people to turn to God. I came to invite sinners."

People Ask about Going without Eating
(Matthew 9.14-17; Mark 2.18-22)

[33]Some people said to Jesus, "John's followers often pray and go without eating,[i] and so do the followers of the Pharisees. But your disciples never go without eating or drinking."

[34]Jesus told them, "The friends of a bridegroom don't go without eating while he is still with them. [35]But the time will come when he will be taken from them. Then they will go without eating."

[36]Jesus then told them these sayings:
No one uses a new piece of cloth to patch old clothes. The patch would shrink and make the hole even bigger.

[37]No one pours new wine into old wineskins. The new wine would swell and burst the old skins.[j] Then the wine would be lost, and the skins would be ruined. [38]New wine must be put only into new wineskins.

[39]No one wants new wine after drinking old wine. They say, "The old wine is better."

A Question about the Sabbath
(Matthew 12.1-8; Mark 2.23-28)

6 One Sabbath when Jesus and his disciples were walking through some wheat fields,[k] the disciples picked some wheat. They rubbed the husks off with their hands and started eating the grain. [2]Some Pharisees said, "Why are you picking grain on the Sabbath? You're not supposed to do that!"

[3]Jesus answered, "You surely have read what David did when he and his followers were hungry. [4]He went into the house of God and took the sacred loaves of bread that only priests were supposed to eat. He not only ate some himself, but even gave some to his followers."

[5]Jesus finished by saying, "The Son of Man is Lord over the Sabbath."

A Man with a Crippled Hand
(Matthew 12.9-14; Mark 3.1-6)

[6]On another Sabbath[l] Jesus was teaching in a Jewish meeting place, and a man with a crippled right hand was there. [7]Some Pharisees and teachers of the Law of Moses kept watching Jesus to see if he would heal the man. They did this because they wanted to accuse Jesus of doing something wrong.

[8]Jesus knew what they were thinking. So he told the man to stand up where everyone could see him. And the man stood up. [9]Then Jesus asked, "On the Sabbath should we do good deeds or evil deeds? Should we save someone's life or destroy it?"

[10]After he had looked around at everyone, he told the man, "Stretch out your hand." He did, and his bad hand became completely well.

[11]The teachers and the Pharisees were furious and started saying to each other, "What can we do about Jesus?"

Jesus Chooses His Twelve Apostles
(Matthew 10.1-4; Mark 3.13-19)

[12]About that time Jesus went off to a mountain to pray, and he spent the whole night there. [13]The next morning he called his disciples together and chose twelve of them to be his apostles. [14]One was Simon, and Jesus named him Peter. Another was Andrew, Peter's brother. There were also James, John, Philip, Bartholomew, [15]Matthew, Thomas, and James the son of Alphaeus. The rest of the apostles were Simon, known as the Eager One,[m] [16]Jude, who was the son of James, and Judas Iscariot,[n] who later betrayed Jesus.

Jesus Teaches, Preaches, and Heals
(Matthew 4.23-25)

[17]Jesus and his apostles went down from the mountain and came to some flat, level ground. Many other disciples were there to meet him. Large crowds of people from all over Judea, Jerusalem, and the coastal cities of Tyre and Sidon were there too. [18]These people had come to listen to Jesus and to be healed of their diseases. All who were troubled by evil spirits were also healed. [19]Everyone was trying to touch Jesus, because power was going out from him and healing them all.

Blessings and Troubles
(Matthew 5.1-12)

[20]Jesus looked at his disciples and said:

---

[i]**5.33** *without eating*: See the note at 2.37.   [j]**5.37** *swell and burst the old skins*: While the juice from grapes was becoming wine, it would swell and stretch the skins in which it had been stored. If the skins were old and stiff, they would burst.   [k]**6.1** *walking through some wheat fields*: It was the custom to let hungry travelers pick grains of wheat.   [l]**6.6** *On another Sabbath*: Some manuscripts have a reading which may mean "the Sabbath after the next."   [m]**6.15** *known as the Eager One*: The word "eager" translates the Greek word "zealot," which was a name later given to the members of a Jewish group that resisted and fought against the Romans.   [n]**6.16** *Iscariot*: This may mean "a man from Kerioth" (a place in Judea). But more probably it means "a man who was a liar" or "a man who was a betrayer."

God will bless you people
who are poor.
His kingdom belongs to you!
21 God will bless
you hungry people.
You will have plenty
to eat!
God will bless you people
who are crying.
You will laugh!

22God will bless you when others
hate you and won't have anything to
do with you. God will bless you
when people insult you and say
cruel things about you, all because
you are a follower of the Son of
Man. 23Long ago your own people
did these same things to the
prophets. So when this happens to
you, be happy and jump for joy! You
will have a great reward in heaven.

24 But you rich people
are in for trouble.
You have already had
an easy life!
25 You well-fed people
are in for trouble.
You will go hungry!
You people
who are laughing now
are in for trouble.
You are going to cry
and weep!

26You are in for trouble when
everyone says good things about
you. That is what your own people
said about those prophets who told
lies.

Love for Enemies
(Matthew 5.38-48; 7.12a)

27This is what I say to all who will
listen to me:
Love your enemies, and be good to
everyone who hates you. 28Ask God
to bless anyone who curses you, and
pray for everyone who is cruel to
you. 29If someone slaps you on one
cheek, don't stop that person from
slapping you on the other cheek. If
someone wants to take your coat,
don't try to keep back your shirt.
30Give to everyone who asks and
don't ask people to return what they
have taken from you. 31Treat others
just as you want to be treated.
32If you love only someone who
loves you, will God praise you for
that? Even sinners love people who
love them. 33If you are kind only to
someone who is kind to you, will
God be pleased with you for that?
Even sinners are kind to people who

are kind to them. 34If you lend
money only to someone you think
will pay you back, will God be
pleased with you for that? Even sinners lend to sinners because they
think they will get it all back.

35But love your enemies and be
good to them. Lend without expecting to be paid back.º Then you will
get a great reward, and you will be
the true children of God in heaven.
He is good even to people who are
unthankful and cruel. 36Have pity on
others, just as your Father has pity
on you.

Judging Others
(Matthew 7.1-5)

37Jesus said:
Don't judge others, and God won't
judge you. Don't be hard on others,
and God won't be hard on you. Forgive others, and God will forgive
you. 38If you give to others, you will
be given a full amount in return. It
will be packed down, shaken together, and spilling over into your
lap. The way you treat others is the
way you will be treated.
39Jesus also used some sayings as he
spoke to the people. He said:
Can one blind person lead another
blind person? Won't they both fall
into a ditch? 40Are students better
than their teacher? But when they
are fully trained, they will be like
their teacher.
41You can see the speck in your
friend's eye. But you don't notice the
log in your own eye. 42How can you
say, "My friend, let me take the
speck out of your eye," when you
don't see the log in your own eye?
You show-offs! First, get the log out
of your own eye. Then you can see
how to take the speck out of your
friend's eye.

A Tree and Its Fruit
(Matthew 7.17-20; 12.34b, 35)

43A good tree cannot produce bad
fruit, and a bad tree cannot produce
good fruit. 44You can tell what a tree
is like by the fruit it produces. You
cannot pick figs or grapes from
thornbushes. 45Good people do good
things because of the good in their
hearts. Bad people do bad things because of the evil in their hearts. Your
words show what is in your heart.

Two Builders
(Matthew 7.24-27)

46Why do you keep on saying that
I am your Lord, when you refuse to

º6.35 *without expecting to be paid back*: Some manuscripts have "without giving up on
anyone."

do what I say? ⁴⁷Anyone who comes and listens to me and obeys me ⁴⁸is like someone who dug down deep and built a house on solid rock. When the flood came and the river rushed against the house, it was built so well that it didn't even shake. ⁴⁹But anyone who hears what I say and doesn't obey me is like someone whose house wasn't built on solid rock. As soon as the river rushed against that house, it was smashed to pieces!

Jesus Heals an Army Officer's Servant
(Matthew 8.5-13; John 4.43-54)

7 After Jesus had finished teaching the people, he went to Capernaum. ²In that town an army officer's servant was sick and about to die. The officer liked this servant very much. ³And when he heard about Jesus, he sent some Jewish leaders to ask him to come and heal the servant.

⁴The leaders went to Jesus and begged him to do something. They said, "This man deserves your help! ⁵He loves our nation and even built us a meeting place." ⁶So Jesus went with them.

When Jesus wasn't far from the house, the officer sent some friends to tell him, "Lord, don't go to any trouble for me! I am not good enough for you to come into my house. ⁷And I am certainly not worthy to come to you. Just say the word, and my servant will get well. ⁸I have officers who give orders to me, and I have soldiers who take orders from me. I can say to one of them, 'Go!' and he goes. I can say to another, 'Come!' and he comes. I can say to my servant, 'Do this!' and he will do it."

⁹When Jesus heard this, he was so surprised that he turned and said to the crowd following him, "In all of Israel I've never found anyone with this much faith!"

¹⁰The officer's friends returned and found the servant well.

A Widow's Son
¹¹Soon Jesus and his disciples were on their way to the town of Nain, and a big crowd was going along with them. ¹²As they came near the gate of the town, they saw people carrying out the body of a widow's only son. Many people from the town were walking along with her.

¹³When the Lord saw the woman, he felt sorry for her and said, "Don't cry!"

¹⁴Jesus went over and touched the stretcher on which the people were carrying the dead boy. They stopped, and Jesus said, "Young man, get up!" ¹⁵The

boy sat up and began to speak. Jesus then gave him back to his mother.

¹⁶Everyone was frightened and praised God. They said, "A great prophet is here with us! God has come to his people."

¹⁷News about Jesus spread all over Judea and everywhere else in that part of the country.

John the Baptist
(Matthew 11.1-19)

¹⁸⁻¹⁹John's followers told John everything that was being said about Jesus. So he sent two of them to ask the Lord, "Are you the one we should be looking for? Or must we wait for someone else?"

²⁰When these messengers came to Jesus, they said, "John the Baptist sent us to ask, 'Are you the one we should be looking for? Or are we supposed to wait for someone else?' "

²¹At that time Jesus was healing many people who were sick or in pain or were troubled by evil spirits, and he was giving sight to a lot of blind people. ²²Jesus said to the messengers sent by John, "Go and tell John what you have seen and heard. Blind people are now able to see, and the lame can walk. People who have leprosy[p] are being healed, and the deaf can now hear. The dead are raised to life, and the poor are hearing the good news. ²³God will bless everyone who doesn't reject me because of what I do."

²⁴After John's messengers had gone, Jesus began speaking to the crowds about John:

What kind of person did you go out to the desert to see? Was he like tall grass blown about by the wind? ²⁵What kind of man did you really go out to see? Was he someone dressed in fine clothes? People who wear expensive clothes and live in luxury are in the king's palace. ²⁶What then did you go out to see? Was he a prophet? He certainly was! I tell you that he was more than a prophet. ²⁷In the Scriptures, God calls John his messenger and says, "I am sending my messenger ahead of you to get things ready for you." ²⁸No one ever born on this earth is greater than John. But whoever is least important in God's kingdom is greater than John. ²⁹Everyone had been listening to John. Even the tax collectors[q] had obeyed God and had done what was right by letting John baptize them. ³⁰But the Pharisees and the experts in the Law of Moses refused to obey God and be baptized by John.

³¹Jesus went on to say:

---

*p***7.22** *leprosy:* See the note at 4.27.   *q***7.29** *tax collectors:* See the note at 3.12.

What are you people like? What kind of people are you? [32]You are like children sitting in the market and shouting to each other,

"We played the flute,
but you would not dance!
We sang a funeral song,
but you would not cry!"

[33]John the Baptist did not go around eating and drinking, and you said, "John has a demon in him!" [34]But because the Son of Man goes around eating and drinking, you say, "Jesus eats and drinks too much! He is even a friend of tax collectors and sinners." [35]Yet Wisdom is shown to be right by what its followers do.

Simon the Pharisee

[36]A Pharisee invited Jesus to have dinner with him. So Jesus went to the Pharisee's home and got ready to eat.[r] [37]When a sinful woman in that town found out that Jesus was there, she bought an expensive bottle of perfume. [38]Then she came and stood behind Jesus. She cried and started washing his feet with her tears and drying them with her hair. The woman kissed his feet and poured the perfume on them. [39]The Pharisee who had invited Jesus saw this and said to himself, "If this man really were a prophet, he would know what kind of woman is touching him! He would know that she is a sinner."

[40]Jesus said to the Pharisee, "Simon, I have something to say to you."

"Teacher, what is it?" Simon replied.

[41]Jesus told him, "Two people were in debt to a moneylender. One of them owed him five hundred silver coins, and the other owed him fifty. [42]Since neither of them could pay him back, the moneylender said that they didn't have to pay him anything. Which one of them will like him more?"

[43]Simon answered, "I suppose it would be the one who had owed more and didn't have to pay it back."

"You are right," Jesus said.

[44]He turned toward the woman and said to Simon, "Have you noticed this woman? When I came into your home, you didn't give me any water so I could wash my feet. But she has washed my feet with her tears and dried them with her hair. [45]You didn't greet me with a kiss, but from the time I came in, she has not stopped kissing my feet. [46]You didn't even pour olive oil on my head,[s] but she has poured expensive perfume on my feet. [47]So I tell you that all her sins are forgiven, and that is why she has shown great love. But anyone who has been forgiven for only a little will show only a little love."

[48]Then Jesus said to the woman, "Your sins are forgiven."

[49]Some other guests started saying to one another, "Who is this who dares to forgive sins?"

[50]But Jesus told the woman, "Because of your faith, you are now saved.[t] May God give you peace!"

Women Who Helped Jesus

8 Soon after this, Jesus was going through towns and villages, telling the good news about God's kingdom. His twelve apostles were with him, [2]and so were some women who had been healed of evil spirits and all sorts of diseases. One of the women was Mary Magdalene,[u] who once had seven demons in her. [3]Joanna, Susanna, and many others had also used what they owned to help Jesus[v] and his disciples. Joanna's husband Chuza was one of Herod's officials.[w]

A Story about a Farmer
(Matthew 13.1-9; Mark 4.1-9)

[4]When a large crowd from several towns had gathered around Jesus, he told them this story:

[5]A farmer went out to scatter seed in a field. While the farmer was doing it, some of the seeds fell along the road and were stepped on or eaten by birds. [6]Other seeds fell on rocky ground and started growing. But the plants did not have enough water and soon dried up. [7]Some other seeds fell where thornbushes grew up and choked the plants. [8]The rest of the seeds fell on good ground where they grew and produced a hundred times as many seeds.

---

[r]**7.36** *got ready to eat*: On special occasions the Jewish people often followed the Greek and Roman custom of lying down on their left side and leaning on their left elbow, while eating with their right hand. This is how the woman could come up behind Jesus and wash his feet (see verse 38). [s]**7.44-46** *washed my feet . . . greet me with a kiss . . . pour olive oil on my head*: Guests in a home were usually offered water so they could wash their feet, because most people either went barefoot or wore sandals and would come in the house with very dusty feet. Guests were also greeted with a kiss on the cheek, and special ones often had sweet-smelling olive oil poured on their head. [t]**7.50** *saved*: Or "healed." The Greek word may have either meaning. [u]**8.2** *Magdalene*: Meaning "from Magdala," a small town on the western shore of Lake Galilee. There is no hint that she is the sinful woman in 7.36-50. [v]**8.3** *used what they owned to help Jesus*: Women often helped Jewish teachers by giving them money. [w]**8.3** *Herod's officials*: Herod Antipas, the son of Herod the Great.

When Jesus had finished speaking, he said, "If you have ears, pay attention!"

Why Jesus Used Stories
(Matthew 13.10-17; Mark 4.10-12)

⁹Jesus' disciples asked him what the story meant. ¹⁰So he answered:

I have explained the secrets about God's kingdom to you, but for others I can only use stories. These people look, but they don't see, and they hear, but they don't understand.

Jesus Explains the Story about a Farmer
(Matthew 13.18-23; Mark 4.13-20)

¹¹This is what the story means: The seed is God's message, ¹²and the seeds that fell along the road are the people who hear the message. But the devil comes and snatches the message out of their hearts, so that they will not believe and be saved. ¹³The seeds that fell on rocky ground are the people who gladly hear the message and accept it. But they don't have deep roots, and they believe only for a little while. As soon as life gets hard, they give up.

¹⁴The seeds that fell among the thornbushes are also people who hear the message. But they are so eager for riches and pleasures that they never produce anything. ¹⁵Those seeds that fell on good ground are the people who listen to the message and keep it in good and honest hearts. They last and produce a harvest.

Light
(Mark 4.21-25)

¹⁶No one lights a lamp and puts it under a bowl or under a bed. A lamp is always put on a lampstand, so that people who come into a house will see the light. ¹⁷There is nothing hidden that will not be found. There is no secret that will not be well known. ¹⁸Pay attention to how you listen! Everyone who has something will be given more, but people who have nothing will lose what little they think they have.

Jesus' Mother and Brothers
(Matthew 12.46-50; Mark 3.31-35)

¹⁹Jesus' mother and brothers went to see him, but because of the crowd they could not get near him. ²⁰Someone told Jesus, "Your mother and brothers are standing outside and want to see you."

²¹Jesus answered, "My mother and my brothers are those people who hear and obey God's message."

A Storm
(Matthew 8.23-27; Mark 4.35-41)

²²One day, Jesus and his disciples got into a boat, and he said, "Let's cross the lake."ˣ They started out, ²³and while they were sailing across, he went to sleep.

Suddenly a windstorm struck the lake, and the boat started sinking. They were in danger. ²⁴So they went to Jesus and woke him up, "Master, Master! We are about to drown!"

Jesus got up and ordered the wind and waves to stop. They obeyed, and everything was calm. ²⁵Then Jesus asked the disciples, "Don't you have any faith?"

But they were frightened and amazed. They said to each other, "Who is this? He can give orders to the wind and the waves, and they obey him!"

A Man with Demons in Him
(Matthew 8.28-34; Mark 5.1-20)

²⁶Jesus and his disciples sailed across Lake Galilee and came to shore near the town of Gerasa.ʸ ²⁷As Jesus was getting out of the boat, he was met by a man from that town. The man had demons in him. He had gone naked for a long time and no longer lived in a house, but in the graveyard.ᶻ

²⁸The man saw Jesus and screamed. He knelt down in front of him and shouted, "Jesus, Son of God in heaven, what do you want with me? I beg you not to torture me!" ²⁹He said this because Jesus had already told the evil spirit to go out of him.

The man had often been attacked by the demon. And even though he had been bound with chains and leg irons and kept under guard, he smashed whatever bound him. Then the demon would force him out into lonely places.

³⁰Jesus asked the man, "What is your name?"

He answered, "My name is Lots." He said this because there were 'lots' of demons in him. ³¹They begged Jesus not to send them to the deep pit,ᵃ where they would be punished.

³²A large herd of pigs was feeding there on the hillside. So the demons begged Jesus to let them go into the pigs, and Jesus let them go. ³³Then the demons left the man and went into the pigs. The whole herd rushed down the steep bank into the lake and drowned.

ˣ**8.22** *cross the lake*: To the eastern shore of Lake Galilee, where most of the people were not Jewish. ʸ**8.26** *Gerasa*: Some manuscripts have "Gergesa." ᶻ**8.27** *graveyard*: It was thought that demons and evil spirits lived in graveyards. ᵃ**8.31** *deep pit*: The place where evil spirits are kept and punished.

34When the men taking care of the pigs saw this, they ran to spread the news in the town and on the farms. 35The people went out to see what had happened, and when they came to Jesus, they also found the man. The demons had gone out of him, and he was sitting there at the feet of Jesus. He had clothes on and was in his right mind. But the people were terrified. 36Then all who had seen the man healed told about it. 37Everyone from around Gerasa*b* begged Jesus to leave, because they were so frightened.

When Jesus got into the boat to start back, 38the man who had been healed begged to go with him. But Jesus sent him off and said, 39"Go back home and tell everyone how much God has done for you." The man then went all over town, telling everything that Jesus had done for him.

A Dying Girl and a Sick Woman
(Matthew 9.18-26; Mark 5.21-43)

40Everyone had been waiting for Jesus, and when he came back, a crowd was there to welcome him. 41Just then the man in charge of the Jewish meeting place came and knelt down in front of Jesus. His name was Jairus, and he begged Jesus to come to his home 42because his twelve-year-old child was dying. She was his only daughter.

While Jesus was on his way, people were crowding all around him. 43In the crowd was a woman who had been bleeding for twelve years. She had spent everything she had on doctors,*c* but none of them could make her well. 44As soon as she came up behind Jesus and barely touched his clothes, her bleeding stopped.

45"Who touched me?" Jesus asked.

While everyone was denying it, Peter said, "Master, people are crowding all around and pushing you from every side."*d*

46But Jesus answered, "Someone touched me, because I felt power going out from me." 47The woman knew that she could not hide, so she came trembling and knelt down in front of Jesus. She told everyone why she had touched him and that she had been healed right away.

48Jesus said to the woman, "You are now well because of your faith. May God give you peace!"

49While Jesus was speaking, someone came from Jairus' home and said, "Your daughter has died! Why bother the teacher anymore?"

50When Jesus heard this, he told Jairus, "Don't worry! Have faith, and your daughter will get well."

51Jesus went into the house, but he did not let anyone else go with him, except Peter, John, James, and the girl's father and mother. 52Everyone was crying and weeping for the girl. But Jesus said, "The child isn't dead. She is just asleep." 53The people laughed at him because they knew she was dead.

54Jesus took hold of the girl's hand and said, "Child, get up!" 55She came back to life and got right up. Jesus told them to give her something to eat. 56Her parents were surprised, but Jesus ordered them not to tell anyone what had happened.

Instructions for the Twelve Apostles
(Matthew 10.5-15; Mark 6.7-13)

9 Jesus called together his twelve apostles and gave them complete power over all demons and diseases. 2Then he sent them to tell about God's kingdom and to heal the sick. 3He told them, "Don't take anything with you! Don't take a walking stick or a traveling bag or food or money or even a change of clothes. 4When you are welcomed into a home, stay there until you leave that town. 5If people won't welcome you, leave the town and shake the dust from your feet*e* as a warning to them."

6The apostles left and went from village to village, telling the good news and healing people everywhere.

Herod Is Worried
(Matthew 14.1-12; Mark 6.14-29)

7Herod*f* the ruler heard about all that was happening, and he was worried. Some people were saying that John the Baptist had come back to life. 8Others were saying that Elijah had come*g* or that one of the prophets from long ago had come back to life. 9But Herod said, "I had John's head cut off! Who is this I hear so much about?" Herod was eager to meet Jesus.

Jesus Feeds Five Thousand
(Matthew 14.13-21; Mark 6.30-44; John 6.1-14)

10The apostles came back and told Jesus everything they had done. He then took them with him to the village of Bethsaida, where they could be alone. 11But a lot of people found out about

---

*b***8.37** *Gerasa:* See the note at 8.26. *c***8.43** *She had spent everything she had on doctors:* Some manuscripts do not have these words. *d***8.45** *from every side:* Some manuscripts add "and you ask, 'Who touched me?' " *e***9.5** *shake the dust from your feet:* This was a way of showing rejection. *f***9.7** *Herod:* Herod Antipas, the son of Herod the Great. *g***9.8** *Elijah had come:* Many of the Jewish people expected the prophet Elijah to come and prepare the way for the Messiah.

this and followed him. Jesus welcomed them. He spoke to them about God's kingdom and healed everyone who was sick.

¹²Late in the afternoon the twelve apostles came to Jesus and said, "Send the crowd to the villages and farms around here. They need to find a place to stay and something to eat. There is nothing in this place. It is like a desert!"

¹³Jesus answered, "You give them something to eat."

But they replied, "We have only five small loaves of bread*ʰ* and two fish. If we are going to feed all these people, we will have to go and buy food." ¹⁴There were about five thousand men in the crowd.

Jesus said to his disciples, "Have the people sit in groups of fifty." ¹⁵They did this, and all the people sat down. ¹⁶Jesus took the five loaves and the two fish. He looked up toward heaven and blessed the food. Then he broke the bread and fish and handed them to his disciples to give to the people.

¹⁷Everyone ate all they wanted. What was left over filled twelve baskets.

Who Is Jesus?
(Matthew 16.13-19; Mark 8.27-29)

¹⁸When Jesus was alone praying, his disciples came to him, and he asked them, "What do people say about me?"

¹⁹They answered, "Some say that you are John the Baptist or Elijah*ⁱ* or a prophet from long ago who has come back to life."

²⁰Jesus then asked them, "But who do you say I am?"

Peter answered, "You are the Messiah sent from God."

²¹Jesus strictly warned his disciples not to tell anyone about this.

Jesus Speaks about His Suffering and Death
(Matthew 16.20-28; Mark 8.30—9.1)

²²Jesus told his disciples, "The nation's leaders, the chief priests, and the teachers of the Law of Moses will make the Son of Man suffer terribly. They will reject him and kill him, but three days later he will rise to life."

²³Then Jesus said to all the people:

If any of you want to be my followers, you must forget about yourself. You must take up your cross each day and follow me. ²⁴If you want to save your life,*ʲ* you will destroy it. But if you give up your life for me, you will save it. ²⁵What will you gain, if you own the whole world but destroy yourself or waste your life? ²⁶If you are ashamed of me and my message, the Son of Man will be ashamed of you when he comes in his glory and in the glory of his Father and the holy angels. ²⁷You can be sure that some of the people standing here will not die before they see God's kingdom.

The True Glory of Jesus
(Matthew 17.1-8; Mark 9.2-8)

²⁸About eight days later Jesus took Peter, John, and James with him and went up on a mountain to pray. ²⁹While he was praying, his face changed, and his clothes became shining white. ³⁰Suddenly Moses and Elijah were there speaking with him. ³¹They appeared in heavenly glory and talked about all that Jesus' death*ᵏ* in Jerusalem would mean.

³²Peter and the other two disciples had been sound asleep. All at once they woke up and saw how glorious Jesus was. They also saw the two men who were with him.

³³Moses and Elijah were about to leave, when Peter said to Jesus, "Master, it is good for us to be here! Let us make three shelters, one for you, one for Moses, and one for Elijah." But Peter did not know what he was talking about.

³⁴While Peter was still speaking, a shadow from a cloud passed over them, and they were frightened as the cloud covered them. ³⁵From the cloud a voice spoke, "This is my chosen Son. Listen to what he says!"

³⁶After the voice had spoken, Peter, John, and James saw only Jesus. For some time they kept quiet and did not say anything about what they had seen.

Jesus Heals a Boy
(Matthew 17.14-18; Mark 9.14-27)

³⁷The next day Jesus and his three disciples came down from the mountain and were met by a large crowd. ³⁸Just then someone in the crowd shouted, "Teacher, please do something for my son! He is my only child! ³⁹A demon often attacks him and makes him scream. It shakes him until he foams at the mouth, and it won't leave him until it has completely worn the boy out. ⁴⁰I begged your disciples to force out the demon, but they couldn't do it."

⁴¹Jesus said to them, "You people are stubborn and don't have any faith! How much longer must I be with you? Why do I have to put up with you?"

Then Jesus said to the man, "Bring your son to me." ⁴²While the boy was

---

*ʰ***9.13** *small loaves of bread*: These would have been flat and round or in the shape of a bun.
*ⁱ***9.19** *Elijah*: See the note at 9.8.   *ʲ***9.24** *life*: In verses 24, 25 a Greek word which often means "soul" is translated "life" and "yourself."   *ᵏ***9.31** *Jesus' death*: In Greek this is "his departure," which probably includes his rising to life and his return to heaven.

being brought, the demon attacked him and made him shake all over. Jesus ordered the demon to stop. Then he healed the boy and gave him back to his father. [43]Everyone was amazed at God's great power.

Jesus Again Speaks about His Death
(Matthew 17.22, 23; Mark 9.30-32)

While everyone was still amazed at what Jesus was doing, he said to his disciples, [44]"Pay close attention to what I am telling you! The Son of Man will be handed over to his enemies." [45]But the disciples did not know what he meant. The meaning was hidden from them. They could not understand it, and they were afraid to ask.

Who Is the Greatest?
(Matthew 18.1-5; Mark 9.33-37)

[46]Jesus' disciples were arguing about which one of them was the greatest. [47]Jesus knew what they were thinking, and he had a child stand there beside him. [48]Then he said to his disciples, "When you welcome even a child because of me, you welcome me. And when you welcome me, you welcome the one who sent me. Whichever one of you is the most humble is the greatest."

For or against Jesus
(Mark 9.38-40)

[49]John said, "Master, we saw a man using your name to force demons out of people. But we told him to stop, because he isn't one of us."

[50]"Don't stop him!" Jesus said. "Anyone who isn't against you is for you."

A Samaritan Village Refuses To Receive Jesus

[51]Not long before it was time for Jesus to be taken up to heaven, he made up his mind to go to Jerusalem. [52]He sent some messengers on ahead to a Samaritan village to get things ready for him. [53]But he was on his way to Jerusalem, so the people there refused to welcome him. [54]When the disciples James and John saw what was happening, they asked, "Lord, do you want us to call down fire from heaven to destroy these people?"[l]

[55]But Jesus turned and corrected them for what they had said.[m] [56]Then they all went on to another village.

Three People Who Wanted To Be Followers
(Matthew 8.19-22)

[57]Along the way someone said to Jesus, "I'll go anywhere with you!"

[58]Jesus said, "Foxes have dens, and birds have nests, but the Son of Man doesn't have a place to call his own."

[59]Jesus told someone else to come with him. But the man said, "Lord, let me wait until I bury my father."[n]

[60]Jesus answered, "Let the dead take care of the dead, while you go and tell about God's kingdom."

[61]Then someone said to Jesus, "I want to go with you, Lord, but first let me go back and take care of things at home."

[62]Jesus answered, "Anyone who starts plowing and keeps looking back isn't worth a thing to God's kingdom!"

The Work of the Seventy-Two Followers

10 Later the Lord chose seventy-two[o] other followers and sent them out two by two to every town and village where he was about to go. [2]He said to them:

A large crop is in the fields, but there are only a few workers. Ask the Lord in charge of the harvest to send out workers to bring it in. [3]Now go, but remember, I am sending you like lambs into a pack of wolves. [4]Don't take along a moneybag or a traveling bag or sandals. And don't waste time greeting people on the road.[p] [5]As soon as you enter a home, say, "God bless this home with peace." [6]If the people living there are peace-loving, your prayer for peace will bless them. But if they are not peace-loving, your prayer will return to you. [7]Stay with the same family, eating and drinking whatever they give you, because workers are worth what they earn. Don't move around from house to house.

[8]If the people of a town welcome you, eat whatever they offer. [9]Heal their sick and say, "God's kingdom will soon be here!"[q]

[10]But if the people of a town refuse to welcome you, go out into the

[l]9.54 *to destroy these people*: Some manuscripts add "as Elijah did." [m]9.55 *what they had said*: Some manuscripts add, "and said, 'Don't you know what spirit you belong to? The Son of Man did not come to destroy people's lives, but to save them.' " [n]9.59 *bury my father*: The Jewish people taught that giving someone a proper burial was even more important than helping the poor. [o]10.1 *seventy-two*: Some manuscripts have "seventy." According to Jewish tradition, there were seventy nations on earth. But the ancient Greek translation of the Old Testament has "seventy-two" in place of "seventy." Jesus probably chose this number of followers to show that his message was for everyone in the world. [p]10.4 *waste time greeting people on the road*: In those days a polite greeting could take a long time. [q]10.9 *will soon be here*: Or "is already here."

street and say, [11]"We are shaking the dust from our feet[r] as a warning to you. And you can be sure that God's kingdom will soon be here!"[s] [12]I tell you that on the day of judgment the people of Sodom will get off easier than the people of that town!

The Unbelieving Towns
(Matthew 11.20-24)

[13]You people of Chorazin are in for trouble! You people of Bethsaida are also in for trouble! If the miracles that took place in your towns had happened in Tyre and Sidon, the people there would have turned to God long ago. They would have dressed in sackcloth and put ashes on their heads.[t] [14]On the day of judgment the people of Tyre and Sidon will get off easier than you will. [15]People of Capernaum, do you think you will be honored in heaven? Well, you will go down to hell!

[16]My followers, whoever listens to you is listening to me. Anyone who says "No" to you is saying "No" to me. And anyone who says "No" to me is really saying "No" to the one who sent me.

The Return of the Seventy-Two

[17]When the seventy-two[u] followers returned, they were excited and said, "Lord, even the demons obeyed when we spoke in your name!"

[18]Jesus told them:

I saw Satan fall from heaven like a flash of lightning. [19]I have given you the power to trample on snakes and scorpions and to defeat the power of your enemy Satan. Nothing can harm you. [20]But don't be happy because evil spirits obey you. Be happy that your names are written in heaven!

Jesus Thanks His Father
(Matthew 11.25-27; 13.16, 17)

[21]At that same time, Jesus felt the joy that comes from the Holy Spirit,[v] and he said:

My Father, Lord of heaven and earth, I am grateful that you hid all this from wise and educated people and showed it to ordinary people. Yes, Father, that is what pleased you. [22]My Father has given me everything, and he is the only one who

knows the Son. The only one who really knows the Father is the Son. But the Son wants to tell others about the Father, so that they can know him too.

[23]Jesus then turned to his disciples and said to them in private, "You are really blessed to see what you see! [24]Many prophets and kings were eager to see what you see and to hear what you hear. But I tell you that they did not see or hear."

The Good Samaritan

[25]An expert in the Law of Moses stood up and asked Jesus a question to see what he would say. "Teacher," he asked, "what must I do to have eternal life?"

[26]Jesus answered, "What is written in the Scriptures? How do you understand them?"

[27]The man replied, "The Scriptures say, 'Love the Lord your God with all your heart, soul, strength, and mind.' They also say, 'Love your neighbors as much as you love yourself.'"

[28]Jesus said, "You have given the right answer. If you do this, you will have eternal life."

[29]But the man wanted to show that he knew what he was talking about. So he asked Jesus, "Who are my neighbors?"

[30]Jesus replied:

As a man was going down from Jerusalem to Jericho, robbers attacked him and grabbed everything he had. They beat him up and ran off, leaving him half dead. [31]A priest happened to be going down the same road. But when he saw the man, he walked by on the other side. [32]Later a temple helper[w] came to the same place. But when he saw the man who had been beaten up, he also went by on the other side.

[33]A man from Samaria then came traveling along that road. When he saw the man, he felt sorry for him [34]and went over to him. He treated his wounds with olive oil and wine[x] and bandaged them. Then he put him on his own donkey and took him to an inn, where he took care of him. [35]The next morning he gave the innkeeper two silver coins and said, "Please take care of the man. If you spend more than this on him, I will pay you when I return."

[36]Then Jesus asked, "Which one of

[r]**10.11** _shaking the dust from our feet_: This was a way of showing rejection.   [s]**10.11** _will soon be here_: Or "is already here."   [t]**10.13** _dressed in sackcloth . . . ashes on their heads_: This was one way that people showed how sorry they were for their sins.   [u]**10.17** _seventy-two_: See the note at 10.1.   [v]**10.21** _the Holy Spirit_: Some manuscripts have "his spirit."   [w]**10.32** _temple helper_: A man from the tribe of Levi, whose job it was to work around the temple.   [x]**10.34** _olive oil and wine_: In New Testament times these were used as medicine. Sometimes olive oil is a symbol for healing by means of a miracle (see James 5.14).

these three people was a real neighbor to the man who was beaten up by robbers?"

37The teacher answered, "The one who showed pity."

Jesus said, "Go and do the same!"

Martha and Mary

38The Lord and his disciples were traveling along and came to a village. When they got there, a woman named Martha welcomed him into her home. 39She had a sister named Mary, who sat down in front of the Lord and was listening to what he said. 40Martha was worried about all that had to be done. Finally, she went to Jesus and said, "Lord, doesn't it bother you that my sister has left me to do all the work by myself? Tell her to come and help me!"

41The Lord answered, "Martha, Martha! You are worried and upset about so many things, 42but only one thing is necessary. Mary has chosen what is best, and it will not be taken away from her."

Prayer
(Matthew 6.9-13; 7.7-11)

11 When Jesus had finished praying, one of his disciples said to him, "Lord, teach us to pray, just as John taught his followers to pray."

2So Jesus told them, "Pray in this way:

'Father, help us
    to honor your name.
Come and set up
    your kingdom.
3 Give us each day
    the food we need.y
4 Forgive our sins,
    as we forgive everyone
    who has done wrong to us.
And keep us
    from being tempted.' "

5Then Jesus went on to say:

Suppose one of you goes to a friend in the middle of the night and says, "Let me borrow three loaves of bread. 6A friend of mine has dropped in, and I don't have a thing for him to eat." 7And suppose your friend answers, "Don't bother me! The door is bolted, and my children and I are in bed. I cannot get up to give you something."

8He may not get up and give you the bread, just because you are his friend. But he will get up and give you as much as you need, simply because you are not ashamed to keep on asking.

9So I tell you to ask and you will receive, search and you will find, knock and the door will be opened for you. 10Everyone who asks will receive, everyone who searches will find, and the door will be opened for everyone who knocks. 11Which one of you fathers would give your hungry child a snake if the child asked for a fish? 12Which one of you would give your child a scorpion if the child asked for an egg? 13As bad as you are, you still know how to give good gifts to your children. But your heavenly Father is even more ready to give the Holy Spirit to anyone who asks.

Jesus and the Ruler of Demons
(Matthew 12.22-30; Mark 3.20-27)

14Jesus forced a demon out of a man who could not talk. And after the demon had gone out, the man started speaking, and the crowds were amazed. 15But some people said, "He forces out demons by the power of Beelzebul, the ruler of the demons!"

16Others wanted to put Jesus to the test. So they asked him to show them a sign from God. 17Jesus knew what they were thinking, and he said:

A kingdom where people fight each other will end up in ruin. And a family that fights will break up. 18If Satan fights against himself, how can his kingdom last? Yet you say that I force out demons by the power of Beelzebul. 19If I use his power to force out demons, whose power do your own followers use to force them out? They are the ones who will judge you. 20But if I use God's power to force out demons, it proves that God's kingdom has already come to you.

21When a strong man arms himself and guards his home, everything he owns is safe. 22But if a stronger man comes and defeats him, he will carry off the weapons in which the strong man trusted. Then he will divide with others what he has taken. 23If you are not on my side, you are against me. If you don't gather in the crop with me, you scatter it.

Return of an Evil Spirit
(Matthew 12.43-45)

24When an evil spirit leaves a person, it travels through the desert, looking for a place to rest. But when it doesn't find a place, it says, "I will go back to the home I left." 25When it gets there and finds the place

y11.3 *the food we need:* Or "food for today" or "food for the coming day."

clean and fixed up, 26it goes off and finds seven other evil spirits even worse than itself. They all come and make their home there, and that person ends up in worse shape than before.

Being Really Blessed

27While Jesus was still talking, a woman in the crowd spoke up, "The woman who gave birth to you and nursed you is blessed!"

28Jesus replied, "That's true, but the people who are really blessed are the ones who hear and obey God's message!"z

A Sign from God
(Matthew 12.38-42; Mark 8.12)

29As crowds were gathering around Jesus, he said:

You people of today are evil! You keep looking for a sign from God. But what happened to Jonaha is the only sign you will be given. 30Just as Jonah was a sign to the people of Nineveh, the Son of Man will be a sign to the people of today. 31When the judgment comes, the Queen of the Southb will stand there with you and condemn you. She traveled a long way to hear Solomon's wisdom, and yet here is something far greater than Solomon. 32The people of Nineveh will also stand there with you and condemn you. They turned to God when Jonah preached, and yet here is something far greater than Jonah.

Light
(Matthew 5.15; 6.22, 23)

33No one lights a lamp and then hides it or puts it under a clay pot. A lamp is put on a lampstand, so that everyone who comes into the house can see the light. 34Your eyes are the lamp for your body. When your eyes are good, you have all the light you need. But when your eyes are bad, everything is dark. 35So be sure that your light isn't darkness. 36If you have light, and nothing is dark, then light will be everywhere, as when a lamp shines brightly on you.

Jesus Condemns the Pharisees and Teachers of the Law of Moses
(Matthew 23.1-36; Mark 12.38-40; Luke 20.45-47)

37When Jesus finished speaking, a Pharisee invited him home for a meal. Jesus went and sat down to eat.c 38The Pharisee was surprised that he did not wash his handsd before eating. 39So the Lord said to him:

You Pharisees clean the outside of cups and dishes, but on the inside you are greedy and evil. 40You fools! Didn't God make both the outside and the inside?e 41If you would only give what you have to the poor, everything you do would please God.

42You Pharisees are in for trouble! You give God a tenth of the spices from your gardens, such as mint and rue. But you cheat people, and you don't love God. You should be fair and kind to others and still give a tenth to God.

43You Pharisees are in for trouble! You love the front seats in the meeting places, and you like to be greeted with honor in the market. 44But you are in for trouble! You are like unmarked gravesf that people walk on without even knowing it.

45A teacher of the Law of Moses spoke up, "Teacher, you said cruel things about us."

46Jesus replied:

You teachers are also in for trouble! You load people down with heavy burdens, but you won't lift a finger to help them carry the loads. 47Yes, you are really in for trouble. You build monuments to honor the prophets your own people murdered long ago. 48You must think that was the right thing for your people to do, or else you would not have built monuments for the prophets they murdered.

49Because of your evil deeds, the Wisdom of God said, "I will send prophets and apostles to you. But you will murder some and mistreat others." 50You people living today will be punished for all the prophets who have been murdered since the beginning of the world. 51This includes every prophet from the time

---

z11.28 "That's true, but the people who are really blessed . . . message": Or " 'That's not true, the people who are blessed . . . message.' " a11.29 what happened to Jonah: Jonah was in the stomach of a big fish for three days and nights (see Matthew 12.40). b11.31 Queen of the South: Sheba, probably a country in southern Arabia. c11.37 sat down to eat: See the note at 7.36. d11.38 did not wash his hands: The Jewish people had strict laws about washing their hands before eating, especially if they had been out in public. e11.40 Didn't God make both the outside and the inside?: Or "Doesn't the person who washes the outside always wash the inside too?" f11.44 unmarked graves: Tombs were whitewashed to keep anyone from accidentally touching them. A person who touched a dead body or a tomb was considered unclean and could not worship with other Jewish people.

of Abel to the time of Zechariah,^{g} who was murdered between the altar and the temple. You people will certainly be punished for all of this.

^{52}You teachers of the Law of Moses are really in for trouble! You carry the keys to the door of knowledge about God. But you never go in, and you keep others from going in.

^{53}Jesus was about to leave, but the teachers and the Pharisees wanted to get even with him. They tried to make him say what he thought about other things, ^{54}so that they could catch him saying something wrong.

Warnings

12 As thousands of people crowded around Jesus and were stepping on each other, he told his disciples:

Be sure to guard against the dishonest teaching^h of the Pharisees! It is their way of fooling people. ^{2}Everything that is hidden will be found out, and every secret will be known. ^{3}Whatever you say in the dark will be heard when it is day. Whatever you whisper in a closed room will be shouted from the housetops.

The One To Fear
(Matthew 10.28-31)

^{4}My friends, don't be afraid of people. They can kill you, but after that, there is nothing else they can do. ^{5}God is the one you must fear. Not only can he take your life, but he can throw you into hell. God is certainly the one you should fear! ^{6}Five sparrows are sold for just two pennies, but God doesn't forget a one of them. ^{7}Even the hairs on your head are counted. So don't be afraid! You are worth much more than many sparrows.

Telling Others about Christ
(Matthew 10.32, 33; 12.32; 10.19, 20)

^{8}If you tell others that you belong to me, the Son of Man will tell God's angels that you are my followers. ^{9}But if you reject me, you will be rejected in front of them. ^{10}If you speak against the Son of Man, you can be forgiven, but if you speak against the Holy Spirit, you cannot be forgiven.

^{11}When you are brought to trial in the Jewish meeting places or before rulers or officials, don't worry about how you will defend yourselves or what you will say. ^{12}At that time the Holy Spirit will tell you what to say.

A Rich Fool

^{13}A man in a crowd said to Jesus, "Teacher, tell my brother to give me my share of what our father left us when he died."

^{14}Jesus answered, "Who gave me the right to settle arguments between you and your brother?"

^{15}Then he said to the crowd, "Don't be greedy! Owning a lot of things won't make your life safe."

^{16}So Jesus told them this story:

A rich man's farm produced a big crop, ^{17}and he said to himself, "What can I do? I don't have a place large enough to store everything."

^{18}Later, he said, "Now I know what I'll do. I'll tear down my barns and build bigger ones, where I can store all my grain and other goods. ^{19}Then I'll say to myself, 'You have stored up enough good things to last for years to come. Live it up! Eat, drink, and enjoy yourself.' "

^{20}But God said to him, "You fool! Tonight you will die. Then who will get what you have stored up?"

^{21}"This is what happens to people who store up everything for themselves, but are poor in the sight of God."

Worry
(Matthew 6.25-34)

^{22}Jesus said to his disciples:

I tell you not to worry about your life! Don't worry about having something to eat or wear. ^{23}Life is more than food or clothing. ^{24}Look at the crows! They don't plant or harvest, and they don't have storehouses or barns. But God takes care of them. You are much more important than any birds. ^{25}Can worry make you live longer?^{i} ^{26}If you don't have power over small things, why worry about everything else?

^{27}Look how the wild flowers grow! They don't work hard to make their clothes. But I tell you that Solomon with all his wealth^j wasn't as well clothed as one of these flowers. ^{28}God gives such beauty to everything that grows in the fields, even though it is here today and thrown

---

^{g}**11.51** _from the time of Abel . . . Zechariah:_ Genesis is the first book in the Jewish Scriptures, and it tells that Abel was the first person to be murdered. Second Chronicles is the last book in the Jewish Scriptures, and the last murder that it tells about is that of Zechariah. ^{h}**12.1** _dishonest teaching:_ The Greek text has "yeast," which is used here of a teaching that is not true (see Matthew 16.6, 12). ^{i}**12.25** _live longer:_ Or "grow taller." ^{j}**12.27** _Solomon with all his wealth:_ The Jewish people thought that Solomon was the richest person who had ever lived.

into a fire tomorrow. Won't he do even more for you? You have such little faith!

²⁹Don't keep worrying about having something to eat or drink. ³⁰Only people who don't know God are always worrying about such things. Your Father knows what you need. ³¹But put God's work first, and these things will be yours as well.

Treasures in Heaven
(Matthew 6.19-21)

³²My little group of disciples, don't be afraid! Your Father wants to give you the kingdom. ³³Sell what you have and give the money to the poor. Make yourselves moneybags that never wear out. Make sure your treasure is safe in heaven, where thieves cannot steal it and moths cannot destroy it. ³⁴Your heart will always be where your treasure is.

Faithful and Unfaithful Servants
(Matthew 24.45-51)

³⁵Be ready and keep your lamps burning ³⁶just like those servants who wait up for their master to return from a wedding feast. As soon as he comes and knocks, they open the door for him. ³⁷Servants are fortunate if their master finds them awake and ready when he comes! I promise you that he will get ready and have his servants sit down so he can serve them. ³⁸Those servants are really fortunate if their master finds them ready, even though he comes late at night or early in the morning. ³⁹You would surely not let a thief break into your home, if you knew when the thief was coming. ⁴⁰So always be ready! You don't know when the Son of Man will come.

⁴¹Peter asked Jesus, "Did you say this just for us or for everyone?"

⁴²The Lord answered:

Who are faithful and wise servants? Who are the ones the master will put in charge of giving the other servants their food supplies at the proper time? ⁴³Servants are fortunate if their master comes and finds them doing their job. ⁴⁴A servant who is always faithful will surely be put in charge of everything the master owns.

⁴⁵But suppose one of the servants thinks that the master won't return until late. Suppose that servant starts beating all the other servants and eats and drinks and gets drunk. ⁴⁶If that happens, the master will come on a day and at a time when the servant least expects him. That servant will then be punished and

thrown out with the servants who cannot be trusted.

⁴⁷If servants are not ready or willing to do what their master wants them to do, they will be beaten hard. ⁴⁸But servants who don't know what their master wants them to do will not be beaten so hard for doing wrong. If God has been generous with you, he will expect you to serve him well. But if he has been more than generous, he will expect you to serve him even better.

Not Peace, but Trouble
(Matthew 10.34-36)

⁴⁹I came to set fire to the earth, and I wish it were already on fire! ⁵⁰I am going to be put to a hard test. And I will have to suffer a lot of pain until it is over. ⁵¹Do you think that I came to bring peace to earth? No indeed! I came to make people choose sides. ⁵²A family of five will be divided, with two of them against the other three. ⁵³Fathers and sons will turn against one another, and mothers and daughters will do the same. Mothers-in-law and daughters-in-law will also turn against each other.

Knowing What To Do
(Matthew 16.2, 3; 5.25, 26)

⁵⁴Jesus said to all the people:

As soon as you see a cloud coming up in the west, you say, "It's going to rain," and it does. ⁵⁵When the south wind blows, you say, "It's going to get hot," and it does. ⁵⁶Are you trying to fool someone? You can predict the weather by looking at the earth and sky, but you don't really know what's going on right now. ⁵⁷Why don't you understand the right thing to do? ⁵⁸When someone accuses you of something, try to settle things before you are taken to court. If you don't, you will be dragged before the judge. Then the judge will hand you over to the jailer, and you will be locked up. ⁵⁹You won't get out until you have paid the last cent you owe.

Turn Back to God

13 About this same time Jesus was told that Pilate had given orders for some people from Galilee to be killed while they were offering sacrifices. ²Jesus replied:

Do you think that these people were worse sinners than everyone else in Galilee just because of what happened to them? ³Not at all! But you can be sure that if you don't turn back to God, every one of you will also be killed. ⁴What about those eighteen people who died when the tower in Siloam fell on them? Do you think they were worse than everyone else in Jerusalem? [5]Not at all! But you can be sure that if you don't turn back to God, every one of you will also die.

A Story about a Fig Tree

[6]Jesus then told them this story:

A man had a fig tree growing in his vineyard. One day he went out to pick some figs, but he didn't find any. [7]So he said to the gardener, "For three years I have come looking for figs on this tree, and I haven't found any yet. Chop it down! Why should it take up space?"

[8]The gardener answered, "Master, leave it for another year. I'll dig around it and put some manure on it to make it grow. [9]Maybe it will have figs on it next year. If it doesn't, you can have it cut down."

Healing a Woman on the Sabbath

[10]One Sabbath, Jesus was teaching in a Jewish meeting place, [11]and a woman was there who had been crippled by an evil spirit for eighteen years. She was completely bent over and could not straighten up. [12]When Jesus saw the woman, he called her over and said, "You are now well." [13]He placed his hands on her, and right away she stood up straight and praised God.

[14]The man in charge of the meeting place was angry because Jesus had healed someone on the Sabbath. So he said to the people, "Each week has six days when we can work. Come and be healed on one of those days, but not on the Sabbath."

[15]The Lord replied, "Are you trying to fool someone? Won't any one of you untie your ox or donkey and lead it out to drink on a Sabbath? [16]This woman belongs to the family of Abraham, but Satan has kept her bound for eighteen years. Isn't it right to set her free on the Sabbath?" [17]Jesus' words made his enemies ashamed. But everyone else in the crowd was happy about the wonderful things he was doing.

A Mustard Seed and Yeast
(Matthew 13.31-33; Mark 4.30-32)

[18]Jesus said, "What is God's kingdom like? What can I compare it with? [19]It is like what happens when someone plants a mustard seed in a garden. The seed grows as big as a tree, and birds nest in its branches."

[20]Then Jesus said, "What can I compare God's kingdom with? [21]It is like what happens when a woman mixes yeast into three batches of flour. Finally, all the dough rises."

The Narrow Door
(Matthew 7.13, 14, 21-23)

[22]As Jesus was on his way to Jerusalem, he taught the people in the towns and villages. [23]Someone asked him, "Lord, are only a few people going to be saved?"

Jesus answered:

[24]Do all you can to go in by the narrow door! A lot of people will try to get in, but will not be able to. [25]Once the owner of the house gets up and locks the door, you will be left standing outside. You will knock on the door and say, "Sir, open the door for us!"

But the owner will answer, "I don't know a thing about you!"

[26]Then you will start saying, "We dined with you, and you taught in our streets."

[27]But he will say, "I really don't know who you are! Get away from me, you evil people!"

[28]Then when you have been thrown outside, you will weep and grit your teeth because you will see Abraham, Isaac, Jacob, and all the prophets in God's kingdom. [29]People will come from all directions and sit down to feast in God's kingdom. [30]There are the ones who are now least important will be the most important, and those who are now most important will be least important.

Jesus and Herod

[31]At that time some Pharisees came to Jesus and said, "You had better get away from here! Herod[k] wants to kill you."

[32]Jesus said to them:

Go tell that fox, "I am going to force out demons and heal people today and tomorrow, and three days later I'll be through." [33]But I am going on my way today and tomorrow and the next day. After all, Jerusalem is the place where prophets are killed.

Jesus Loves Jerusalem
(Matthew 23.37-39)

[34]Jerusalem, Jerusalem! Your people have killed the prophets and have stoned the messengers who were sent to you. I have often wanted to gather your people, as a hen gathers her chicks under her wings. But you wouldn't let me. [35]Now your temple will be deserted.

---

[k]**13.31** *Herod*: Herod Antipas, the son of Herod the Great.

You won't see me again until the time when you say,

"Blessed is the one who comes in the name of the Lord."

Jesus Heals a Sick Man

14 One Sabbath, Jesus was having dinner in the home of an important Pharisee, and everyone was carefully watching Jesus. [2]All of a sudden a man with swollen legs stood up in front of him. [3]Jesus turned and asked the Pharisees and the teachers of the Law of Moses, "Is it right to heal on the Sabbath?" [4]But they did not say a word.

Jesus took hold of the man. Then he healed him and sent him away. [5]Afterwards, Jesus asked the people, "If your son or ox falls into a well, wouldn't you pull him out right away, even on the Sabbath?" [6]There was nothing they could say.

How To Be a Guest

[7]Jesus saw how the guests had tried to take the best seats. So he told them:

[8]When you are invited to a wedding feast, don't sit in the best place. Someone more important may have been invited. [9]Then the one who invited you will come and say, "Give your place to this other guest!" You will be embarrassed and will have to sit in the worst place.

[10]When you are invited to be a guest, go and sit in the worst place. Then the one who invited you may come and say, "My friend, take a better seat!" You will then be honored in front of all the other guests. [11]If you put yourself above others, you will be put down. But if you humble yourself, you will be honored.

[12]Then Jesus said to the man who had invited him:

When you give a dinner or a banquet, don't invite your friends and family and relatives and rich neighbors. If you do, they will invite you in return, and you will be paid back. [13]When you give a feast, invite the poor, the crippled, the lame, and the blind. [14]They cannot pay you back. But God will bless you and reward you when his people rise from death.

The Great Banquet
(Matthew 22.1-10)

[15]After Jesus had finished speaking, one of the guests said, "The greatest blessing of all is to be at the banquet in God's kingdom!"

[16]Jesus told him:

A man once gave a great banquet and invited a lot of guests. [17]When the banquet was ready, he sent a servant to tell the guests, "Everything is ready! Please come."

[18]One guest after another started making excuses. The first one said, "I bought some land, and I've got to look it over. Please excuse me."

[19]Another guest said, "I bought five teams of oxen, and I need to try them out. Please excuse me."

[20]Still another guest said, "I have just gotten married, and I can't be there."

[21]The servant told his master what happened, and the master became so angry that he said, "Go as fast as you can to every street and alley in town! Bring in everyone who is poor or crippled or blind or lame."

[22]When the servant returned, he said, "Master, I've done what you told me, and there is still plenty of room for more people."

[23]His master then told him, "Go out along the back roads and fence rows and make people come in, so that my house will be full. [24]Not one of the guests I first invited will get even a bite of my food!"

Being a Disciple
(Matthew 10.37, 38)

[25]Large crowds were walking along with Jesus, when he turned and said:

[26]You cannot be my disciple, unless you love me more than you love your father and mother, your wife and children, and your brothers and sisters. You cannot come with me unless you love me more than you love your own life.

[27]You cannot be my disciple unless you carry your own cross and come with me.

[28]Suppose one of you wants to build a tower. What is the first thing you will do? Won't you sit down and figure out how much it will cost and if you have enough money to pay for it? [29]Otherwise, you will start building the tower, but not be able to finish. Then everyone who sees what is happening will laugh at you. [30]They will say, "You started building, but could not finish the job."

[31]What will a king do if he has only ten thousand soldiers to defend himself against a king who is about to attack him with twenty thousand soldiers? Before he goes out to battle, won't he first sit down and decide if he can win? [32]If he thinks he won't be able to defend himself, he will send messengers and ask for peace while the other king is still a long way off. [33]So then, you cannot be my disciple unless you give away everything you own.

Salt and Light
(Matthew 5.13; Mark 9.50)

[34]Salt is good, but if it no longer tastes like salt, how can it be made to taste salty again? [35]It is no longer good for the soil or even for the manure pile. People simply throw it out. If you have ears, pay attention!

One Sheep
(Matthew 18.12-14)

15 Tax collectors[l] and sinners were all crowding around to listen to Jesus. [2]So the Pharisees and the teachers of the Law of Moses started grumbling, "This man is friendly with sinners. He even eats with them."

[3]Then Jesus told them this story: [4]If any of you has a hundred sheep, and one of them gets lost, what will you do? Won't you leave the ninety-nine in the field and go look for the lost sheep until you find it? [5]And when you find it, you will be so glad that you will put it on your shoulder [6]and carry it home. Then you will call in your friends and neighbors and say, "Let's celebrate! I've found my lost sheep."

[7]Jesus said, "In the same way there is more happiness in heaven because of one sinner who turns to God than over ninety-nine good people who don't need to."

One Coin

[8]Jesus told the people another story:
What will a woman do if she has ten silver coins and loses one of them? Won't she light a lamp, sweep the floor, and look carefully until she finds it? [9]Then she will call in her friends and neighbors and say, "Let's celebrate! I've found the coin I lost."

[10]Jesus said, "In the same way God's angels are happy when even one person turns to him."

Two Sons

[11]Jesus also told them another story:
Once a man had two sons. [12]The younger son said to his father, "Give me my share of the property." So the father divided his property between his two sons.

[13]Not long after that, the younger son packed up everything he owned and left for a foreign country, where he wasted all his money in wild living. [14]He had spent everything, when a bad famine spread through that whole land. Soon he had nothing to eat.

[15]He went to work for a man in that country, and the man sent him out to take care of his pigs.[m] [16]He would have been glad to eat what the pigs were eating,[n] but no one gave him a thing.

[17]Finally, he came to his senses and said, "My father's workers have plenty to eat, and here I am, starving to death! [18]I will go to my father and say to him, 'Father, I have sinned against God in heaven and against you. [19]I am no longer good enough to be called your son. Treat me like one of your workers.'"

[20]The younger son got up and started back to his father. But when he was still a long way off, his father saw him and felt sorry for him. He ran to his son and hugged and kissed him.

[21]The son said, "Father, I have sinned against God in heaven and against you. I am no longer good enough to be called your son."

[22]But his father said to the servants, "Hurry and bring the best clothes and put them on him. Give him a ring for his finger and sandals[o] for his feet. [23]Get the best calf and prepare it, so we can eat and celebrate. [24]This son of mine was dead, but has now come back to life. He was lost and has now been found." And they began to celebrate.

[25]The older son had been out in the field. But when he came near the house, he heard the music and dancing. [26]So he called one of the servants over and asked, "What's going on here?"

[27]The servant answered, "Your brother has come home safe and sound, and your father ordered us to kill the best calf." [28]The older brother got so angry that he would not even go into the house.

His father came out and begged him to go in. [29]But he said to his father, "For years I have worked for you like a slave and have always obeyed you. But you have never even given me a little goat, so that I could give a dinner for my friends. [30]This other son of yours wasted

---

[l]**15.1** *Tax collectors*: See the note at 3.12.   [m]**15.15** *pigs*: The Jewish religion taught that pigs were not fit to eat or even to touch. A Jewish man would have felt terribly insulted if he had to feed pigs, much less eat with them.   [n]**15.16** *what the pigs were eating*: The Greek text has "(bean) pods," which came from a tree in Palestine. These were used to feed animals. Poor people sometimes ate them too.   [o]**15.22** *ring . . . sandals*: These show that the young man's father fully accepted him as his son. A ring was a sign of high position in the family. Sandals showed that he was a son instead of a slave, since slaves did not usually wear sandals.

your money on prostitutes. And now
that he has come home, you ordered
the best calf to be killed for a feast."
31His father replied, "My son, you
are always with me, and everything I
have is yours. 32But we should be
glad and celebrate! Your brother was
dead, but he is now alive. He was
lost and has now been found."

A Dishonest Manager

16 Jesus said to his disciples:
A rich man once had a man-
ager to take care of his business. But
he was told that his manager was
wasting money. 2So the rich man
called him in and said, "What is this
I hear about you? Tell me what you
have done! You are no longer going
to work for me."
3The manager said to himself,
"What shall I do now that my master
is going to fire me? I can't dig
ditches, and I'm ashamed to beg. 4I
know what I'll do, so that people will
welcome me into their homes after
I've lost my job."
5Then one by one he called in the
people who were in debt to his master. He asked the first one, "How
much do you owe my master?"
6"A hundred barrels of olive oil,"
the man answered.
So the manager said, "Take your
bill and sit down and quickly write
'fifty'."
7The manager asked someone else
who was in debt to his master, "How
much do you owe?"
"A thousand bushels[p] of wheat,"
the man replied.
The manager said, "Take your bill
and write 'eight hundred'."
8The master praised his dishonest
manager for looking out for himself
so well. That's how it is! The people
of this world look out for themselves
better than the people who belong to
the light.
9My disciples, I tell you to use
wicked wealth to make friends for
yourselves. Then when it is gone,
you will be welcomed into an eternal
home. 10Anyone who can be trusted
in little matters can also be trusted
in important matters. But anyone
who is dishonest in little matters will
be dishonest in important matters.
11If you cannot be trusted with this
wicked wealth, who will trust you
with true wealth? 12And if you cannot be trusted with what belongs to
someone else, who will give you
something that will be your own?
13You cannot be the slave of two
masters. You will like one more than
the other or be more loyal to one
than to the other. You cannot serve
God and money.

Some Sayings of Jesus

(Matthew 11.12, 13; 5.31, 32; Mark 10.11, 12)

14The Pharisees really loved money.
So when they heard what Jesus said,
they made fun of him. 15But Jesus told
them:
You are always making yourselves
look good, but God sees what is in
your heart. The things that most
people think are important are
worthless as far as God is concerned.
16Until the time of John the Baptist, people had to obey the Law of
Moses and the Books of the
Prophets.[q] But since God's kingdom
has been preached, everyone is trying hard to get in. 17Heaven and
earth will disappear before the
smallest letter of the Law does.
18It is a terrible sin[r] for a man to
divorce his wife and marry another
woman. It is also a terrible sin for a
man to marry a divorced woman.

Lazarus and the Rich Man

19There was once a rich man who
wore expensive clothes and every
day ate the best food. 20But a poor
beggar named Lazarus was brought
to the gate of the rich man's house.
21He was happy just to eat the scraps
that fell from the rich man's table.
His body was covered with sores,
and dogs kept coming up to lick
them. 22The poor man died, and angels took him to the place of honor
next to Abraham.[s]
The rich man also died and was
buried. 23He went to hell[t] and was
suffering terribly. When he looked
up and saw Abraham far off and
Lazarus at his side, 24he said to
Abraham, "Have pity on me! Send
Lazarus to dip his finger in water
and touch my tongue. I'm suffering
terribly in this fire."
25Abraham answered, "My friend,

[p] **16.7** *A thousand bushels*: The Greek text has "A hundred measures," and each measure is about ten or twelve bushels. [q] **16.16** *the Law of Moses and the Books of the Prophets*: The Jewish Scriptures, that is, the Old Testament. [r] **16.18** *a terrible sin*: The Greek text uses a word that means the sin of being unfaithful in marriage. [s] **16.22** *the place of honor next to Abraham*: The Jewish people thought that heaven would be a banquet that God would give for them. Abraham would be the most important person there, and the guest of honor would sit next to him. [t] **16.23** *hell*: The Greek text has "hades," which the Jewish people often thought of as the place where the dead wait for the final judgment.

remember that while you lived, you had everything good, and Lazarus had everything bad. Now he is happy, and you are in pain. [26]And besides, there is a deep ditch between us, and no one from either side can cross over."

[27]But the rich man said, "Abraham, then please send Lazarus to my father's home. [28]Let him warn my five brothers, so they won't come to this horrible place."

[29]Abraham answered, "Your brothers can read what Moses and the prophets[u] wrote. They should pay attention to that."

[30]Then the rich man said, "No, that's not enough! If only someone from the dead would go to them, they would listen and turn to God."

[31]So Abraham said, "If they won't pay attention to Moses and the prophets, they won't listen even to someone who comes back from the dead."

Faith and Service
(Matthew 18.6, 7, 21, 22; Mark 9.42)

17 Jesus said to his disciples:
There will always be something that causes people to sin. But anyone who causes them to sin is in for trouble. A person who causes even one of my little followers to sin [2]would be better off thrown into the ocean with a heavy stone tied around their neck. [3]So be careful what you do.

Correct any followers[v] of mine who sin, and forgive the ones who say they are sorry. [4]Even if one of them mistreats you seven times in one day and says, "I am sorry," you should still forgive that person. [5]The apostles said to the Lord, "Make our faith stronger!"

[6]Jesus replied:
If you had faith no bigger than a tiny mustard seed, you could tell this mulberry tree to pull itself up, roots and all, and to plant itself in the ocean. And it would!

[7]If your servant comes in from plowing or from taking care of the sheep, would you say, "Welcome! Come on in and have something to eat"? [8]No, you wouldn't say that. You would say, "Fix me something to eat. Get ready to serve me, so I can have my meal. Then later on you can eat

and drink." [9]Servants don't deserve special thanks for doing what they are supposed to do. [10]And that's how it should be with you. When you've done all you should, then say, "We are merely servants, and we have simply done our duty."

Ten Men with Leprosy

[11]On his way to Jerusalem, Jesus went along the border between Samaria and Galilee. [12]As he was going into a village, ten men with leprosy[w] came toward him. They stood at a distance [13]and shouted, "Jesus, Master, have pity on us!"

[14]Jesus looked at them and said, "Go show yourselves to the priests."[x] On their way they were healed. [15]When one of them discovered that he was healed, he came back, shouting praises to God. [16]He bowed down at the feet of Jesus and thanked him. The man was from the country of Samaria.

[17]Jesus asked, "Weren't ten men healed? Where are the other nine? [18]Why was this foreigner the only one who came back to thank God?" [19]Then Jesus told the man, "You may get up and go. Your faith has made you well."

God's Kingdom
(Matthew 24.23-28, 37-41)

[20]Some Pharisees asked Jesus when God's kingdom would come. He answered, "God's kingdom isn't something you can see. [21]There is no use saying, 'Look! Here it is' or 'Look! There it is.' God's kingdom is here with you."[y]

[22]Jesus said to his disciples:
The time will come when you will long to see one of the days of the Son of Man, but you will not. [23]When people say to you, "Look there," or "Look here," don't go looking for him. [24]The day of the Son of Man will be like lightning flashing across the sky. [25]But first he must suffer terribly and be rejected by the people of today. [26]When the Son of Man comes, things will be just as they were when Noah lived. [27]People were eating, drinking, and getting married right up to the day when Noah went into the big boat. Then the flood came and drowned everyone on earth. [28]When Lot[z] lived, people were also eating and drinking. They were buying, selling, planting, and

---

[u]**16.29** *Moses and the prophets*: The Jewish Scriptures, that is, the Old Testament.
[v]**17.3** *followers*: The Greek text has "brothers," which is often used in the New Testament for followers of Jesus. [w]**17.12** *leprosy*: See the note at 4.27. [x]**17.14** *show yourselves to the priests*: See the note at 5.14. [y]**17.21** *here with you*: Or "in your hearts." [z]**17.27,28** *Noah . . . Lot*: When God destroyed the earth by a flood, he saved Noah and his family. And when God destroyed the cities of Sodom and Gomorrah and the evil people who lived there, he rescued Lot and his family (see Genesis 19.1-29).

building. [29]But on the very day Lot left Sodom, fiery flames poured down from the sky and killed everyone. [30]The same will happen on the day when the Son of Man appears.

[31]At that time no one on a rooftop[a] should go down into the house to get anything. No one in a field should go back to the house for anything. [32]Remember what happened to Lot's wife.[b]

[33]People who try to save their lives will lose them, and those who lose their lives will save them. [34]On that night two people will be sleeping in the same bed, but only one will be taken. The other will be left. [35-36]Two women will be together grinding wheat, but only one will be taken. The other will be left.[c]

[37]Then Jesus' disciples spoke up, "But where will this happen, Lord?"

Jesus said, "Where there is a corpse, there will always be buzzards."[d]

A Widow and a Judge

18 Jesus told his disciples a story about how they should keep on praying and never give up:

[2]In a town there was once a judge who didn't fear God or care about people. [3]In that same town there was a widow who kept going to the judge and saying, "Make sure that I get fair treatment in court."

[4]For a while the judge refused to do anything. Finally, he said to himself, "Even though I don't fear God or care about people, [5]I will help this widow because she keeps on bothering me. If I don't help her, she will wear me out."

[6]The Lord said:

Think about what that crooked judge said. [7]Won't God protect his chosen ones who pray to him day and night? Won't he be concerned for them? [8]He will surely hurry and help them. But when the Son of Man comes, will he find on this earth anyone with faith?

A Pharisee and a Tax Collector

[9]Jesus told a story to some people who thought they were better than others and who looked down on everyone else:

[10]Two men went into the temple to pray.[e] One was a Pharisee and the other a tax collector.[f] [11]The Pharisee stood over by himself and prayed,[g] "God, I thank you that I am not greedy, dishonest, and unfaithful in marriage like other people. And I am really glad that I am not like that tax collector over there. [12]I go without eating[h] for two days a week, and I give you one tenth of all I earn."

[13]The tax collector stood off at a distance and did not think he was good enough even to look up toward heaven. He was so sorry for what he had done that he pounded his chest and prayed, "God, have pity on me! I am such a sinner."

[14]Then Jesus said, "When the two men went home, it was the tax collector and not the Pharisee who was pleasing to God. If you put yourself above others, you will be put down. But if you humble yourself, you will be honored."

Jesus Blesses Little Children
(Matthew 19.13-15; Mark 10.13-16)

[15]Some people brought their little children for Jesus to bless. But when his disciples saw them doing this, they told the people to stop bothering him. [16]So Jesus called the children over to him and said, "Let the children come to me! Don't try to stop them. People who are like these children belong to God's kingdom.[i] [17]You will never get into God's kingdom unless you enter it like a child!"

A Rich and Important Man
(Matthew 19.16-30; Mark 10.17-31)

[18]An important man asked Jesus, "Good Teacher, what must I do to have eternal life?"

[19]Jesus said, "Why do you call me good? Only God is good. [20]You know the commandments: 'Be faithful in marriage. Do not murder. Do not steal. Do not tell lies about others. Respect your father and mother.' "

[21]He told Jesus, "I have obeyed all these commandments since I was a young man."

---

[a]**17.31** *rooftop*: See the note at 5.19.   [b]**17.32** *what happened to Lot's wife*: She turned into a block of salt when she disobeyed God (see Genesis 19.26).   [c]**17.35,36** *will be left*: Some manuscripts add, "Two men will be in the same field, but only one will be taken. The other will be left."   [d]**17.37** *Where there is a corpse, there will always be buzzards*: This saying may mean that when anything important happens, people soon know about it. Or the saying may mean that whenever something bad happens, curious people gather around and stare. But the word translated "buzzard" also means "eagle" and may refer to the Roman army, which had an eagle as its symbol.   [e]**18.10** *into the temple to pray*: Jewish people usually prayed there early in the morning and late in the afternoon.   [f]**18.10** *tax collector*: See the note at 3.12.   [g]**18.11** *stood over by himself and prayed*: Some manuscripts have "stood up and prayed to himself."   [h]**18.12** *without eating*: See the note at 2.37.   [i]**18.16** *People who are like these children belong to God's kingdom*: Or "God's kingdom belongs to people who are like these children."

[22]When Jesus heard this, he said, "There is one thing you still need to do. Go and sell everything you own! Give the money to the poor, and you will have riches in heaven. Then come and be my follower." [23]When the man heard this, he was sad, because he was very rich.

[24]Jesus saw how sad the man was. So he said, "It's terribly hard for rich people to get into God's kingdom! [25]In fact, it's easier for a camel to go through the eye of a needle than for a rich person to get into God's kingdom."

[26]When the crowd heard this, they asked, "How can anyone ever be saved?"

[27]Jesus replied, "There are some things that people cannot do, but God can do anything."

[28]Peter said, "Remember, we left everything to be your followers!"

[29]Jesus answered, "You can be sure that anyone who gives up home or wife or brothers or family or children because of God's kingdom [30]will be given much more in this life. And in the future world they will have eternal life."

Jesus Again Tells about His Death
(Matthew 20.17-19; Mark 10.32-34)

[31]Jesus took the twelve apostles aside and said:

We are now on our way to Jerusalem. Everything that the prophets wrote about the Son of Man will happen there. [32]He will be handed over to foreigners,[j] who will make fun of him, mistreat him, and spit on him. [33]They will beat him and kill him, but three days later he will rise to life.

[34]The apostles did not understand what Jesus was talking about. They could not understand, because the meaning of what he said was hidden from them.

Jesus Heals a Blind Beggar
(Matthew 20.29-34; Mark 10.46-52)

[35]When Jesus was coming close to Jericho, a blind man sat begging beside the road. [36]The man heard the crowd walking by and asked what was happening. [37]Some people told him that Jesus from Nazareth was passing by. [38]So the blind man shouted, "Jesus, Son of David,[k] have pity on me!" [39]The people

who were going along with Jesus told the man to be quiet. But he shouted even louder, "Son of David, have pity on me!"

[40]Jesus stopped and told some people to bring the blind man over to him. When the blind man was getting near, Jesus asked, [41]"What do you want me to do for you?"

"Lord, I want to see!" he answered.

[42]Jesus replied, "Look and you will see! Your eyes are healed because of your faith." [43]Right away the man could see, and he went with Jesus and started thanking God. When the crowds saw what happened, they praised God.

Zacchaeus

19 Jesus was going through Jericho, [2]where a man named Zacchaeus lived. He was in charge of collecting taxes[l] and was very rich. [3-4]Jesus was heading his way, and Zacchaeus wanted to see what he was like. But Zacchaeus was a short man and could not see over the crowd. So he ran ahead and climbed up into a sycamore tree.

[5]When Jesus got there, he looked up and said, "Zacchaeus, hurry down! I want to stay with you today." [6]Zacchaeus hurried down and gladly welcomed Jesus.

[7]Everyone who saw this started grumbling, "This man Zacchaeus is a sinner! And Jesus is going home to eat with him."

[8]Later that day Zacchaeus stood up and said to the Lord, "I will give half of my property to the poor. And I will now pay back four times as much[m] to everyone I have ever cheated."

[9]Jesus said to Zacchaeus, "Today you and your family have been saved,[n] because you are a true son of Abraham.[o] [10]The Son of Man came to look for and to save people who are lost."

A Story about Ten Servants
(Matthew 25.14-30)

[11]The crowd was still listening to Jesus as he was getting close to Jerusalem. Many of them thought that God's kingdom would soon appear, [12]and Jesus told them this story:

A prince once went to a foreign country to be crowned king and then to return. [13]But before leaving, he called in ten servants and gave

---

[j]**18.32** *foreigners*: The Romans, who ruled Judea at this time.   [k]**18.38** *Son of David*: The Jewish people expected the Messiah to be from the family of King David, and for this reason the Messiah was often called the "Son of David."   [l]**19.2** *in charge of collecting taxes*: See the note at 3.12.   [m]**19.8** *pay back four times as much*: Both Jewish and Roman law said that a person must pay back four times the amount that was taken.   [n]**19.9** *saved*: Zacchaeus was Jewish, but it is only now that he is rescued from sin and placed under God's care.   [o]**19.9** *son of Abraham*: As used in this verse, the words mean that Zacchaeus is truly one of God's special people.

each of them some money. He told them, "Use this to earn more money until I get back."

[14]But the people of his country hated him, and they sent messengers to the foreign country to say, "We don't want this man to be our king."

[15]After the prince had been made king, he returned and called in his servants. He asked them how much they had earned with the money they had been given.

[16]The first servant came and said, "Sir, with the money you gave me I have earned ten times as much."

[17]"That's fine, my good servant!" the king said. "Since you have shown that you can be trusted with a small amount, you will be given ten cities to rule."

[18]The second one came and said, "Sir, with the money you gave me, I have earned five times as much."

[19]The king said, "You will be given five cities."

[20]Another servant came and said, "Sir, here is your money. I kept it safe in a handkerchief. [21]You are a hard man, and I was afraid of you. You take what isn't yours, and you harvest crops you didn't plant."

[22]"You worthless servant!" the king told him. "You have condemned yourself by what you have just said. You knew that I am a hard man, taking what isn't mine and harvesting what I've not planted. [23]Why didn't you put my money in the bank? On my return, I could have had the money together with interest."

[24]Then he said to some other servants standing there, "Take the money away from him and give it to the servant who earned ten times as much."

[25]But they said, "Sir, he already has ten times as much!"

[26]The king replied, "Those who have something will be given more. But everything will be taken away from those who don't have anything. [27]Now bring me the enemies who didn't want me to be their king. Kill them while I watch!"

Jesus Enters Jerusalem
(Matthew 21.1-11; Mark 11.1-11; John 12.12-19)

[28]When Jesus had finished saying all this, he went on toward Jerusalem. [29]As he was getting near Bethphage and Bethany on the Mount of Olives, he sent two of his disciples on ahead. [30]He told them, "Go into the next village, where you will find a young donkey that has never been ridden. Untie the donkey and bring it here. [31]If anyone asks why you are doing that, just say, 'The Lord[p] needs it.' "

[32]They went off and found everything just as Jesus had said. [33]While they were untying the donkey, its owners asked, "Why are you doing that?"

[34]They answered, "The Lord[p] needs it."

[35]Then they led the donkey to Jesus. They put some of their clothes on its back and helped Jesus get on. [36]And as he rode along, the people spread clothes on the road[q] in front of him. [37]When Jesus was starting down the Mount of Olives, his large crowd of disciples were happy and praised God because of all the miracles they had seen. [38]They shouted,

"Blessed is the king who comes
    in the name of the Lord!
Peace in heaven
    and glory to God."

[39]Some Pharisees in the crowd said to Jesus, "Teacher, make your disciples stop shouting!"

[40]But Jesus answered, "If they keep quiet, these stones will start shouting."

[41]When Jesus came closer and could see Jerusalem, he cried [42]and said:

It is too bad that today your people don't know what will bring them peace! Now it is hidden from them. [43]Jerusalem, the time will come when your enemies will build walls around you to attack you. Armies will surround you and close in on you from every side. [44]They will level you to the ground and kill your people. Not one stone in your buildings will be left on top of another. This will happen because you did not see that God had come to save you.[r]

Jesus in the Temple
(Matthew 21.12-17; Mark 11.15-19; John 2.13-22)

[45]When Jesus entered the temple, he started chasing out the people who were selling things. [46]He told them, "The Scriptures say, 'My house should be a place of worship.' But you have made it a place where robbers hide!"

[47]Each day, Jesus kept on teaching in the temple. So the chief priests, the teachers of the Law of Moses, and some

---

[p]**19.31,34** *The Lord*: Or "The master of the donkey." This was one way that Jewish people welcomed a famous person. [q]**19.36** *spread clothes on the road*: [r]**19.44** *that God had come to save you*: The Jewish people looked for the time when God would come and rescue them from their enemies. But when Jesus came, many of them refused to obey him.

other important people tried to have him killed. [48]But they could not find a way to do it, because everyone else was eager to listen to him.

A Question about Jesus' Authority
(Matthew 21.23-27; Mark 11.27-33)

20 One day, Jesus was teaching in the temple and telling the good news. So the chief priests, the teachers, and the nation's leaders [2]asked him, "What right do you have to do these things? Who gave you this authority?"

[3]Jesus replied, "I want to ask you a question. [4]Who gave John the right to baptize? Was it God in heaven or merely some human being?"

[5]They talked this over and said to each other, "We can't say that God gave John this right. Jesus will ask us why we didn't believe John. [6]And we can't say that it was merely some human who gave John the right to baptize. The crowd will stone us to death, because they think John was a prophet."

[7]So they told Jesus, "We don't know who gave John the right to baptize."

[8]Jesus replied, "Then I won't tell you who gave me the right to do what I do."

Renters of a Vineyard
(Matthew 21.33-46; Mark 12.1-12)

[9]Jesus told the people this story:

A man once planted a vineyard and rented it out. Then he left the country for a long time. [10]When it was time to harvest the crop, he sent a servant to ask the renters for his share of the grapes. But they beat up the servant and sent him away without anything. [11]So the owner sent another servant. The renters also beat him up. They insulted him terribly and sent him away without a thing. [12]The owner sent a third servant. He was also beaten terribly and thrown out of the vineyard.

[13]The owner then said to himself, "What am I going to do? I know what. I'll send my son, the one I love so much. They will surely respect him!"

[14]When the renters saw the owner's son, they said to one another, "Someday he will own the vineyard. Let's kill him! Then we can have it all for ourselves." [15]So they threw him out of the vineyard and killed him.

Jesus asked, "What do you think the owner of the vineyard will do? [16]I'll tell you what. He will come and kill those renters and let someone else have his vineyard."

When the people heard this, they said, "This must never happen!"

[17]But Jesus looked straight at them and said, "Then what do the Scriptures mean when they say, 'The stone that the builders tossed aside is now the most important stone of all'? [18]Anyone who stumbles over this stone will get hurt, and anyone it falls on will be smashed to pieces."

[19]The chief priests and the teachers of the Law of Moses knew that Jesus was talking about them when he was telling this story. They wanted to arrest him right then, but they were afraid of the people.

Paying Taxes
(Matthew 22.15-22; Mark 12.13-17)

[20]Jesus' enemies kept watching him closely, because they wanted to hand him over to the Roman governor. So they sent some men who pretended to be good. But they were really spies trying to catch Jesus saying something wrong. [21]The spies said to him, "Teacher, we know that you teach the truth about what God wants people to do. And you treat everyone with the same respect, no matter who they are. [22]Tell us, should we pay taxes to the Emperor or not?"

[23]Jesus knew that they were trying to trick him. So he told them, [24]"Show me a coin." Then he asked, "Whose picture and name are on it?"

"The Emperor's," they answered.

[25]Then he told them, "Give the Emperor what belongs to him and give God what belongs to God." [26]Jesus' enemies could not catch him saying anything wrong there in front of the people. They were amazed at his answer and kept quiet.

Life in the Future World
(Matthew 22.23-33; Mark 12.18-27)

[27]The Sadducees did not believe that people would rise to life after death. So some of them came to Jesus [28]and said:

Teacher, Moses wrote that if a married man dies and has no children, his brother should marry the widow. Their first son would then be thought of as the son of the dead brother.

[29]There were once seven brothers. The first one married, but died without having any children. [30]The second one married his brother's widow, and he also died without having any children. [31]The same thing happened to the third one. Finally, all seven brothers married that woman and died without having any children. [32]At last the woman died. [33]When God raises people from death, whose wife will this woman be? All seven brothers had married her.

³⁴Jesus answered:

The people in this world get married. ³⁵But in the future world no one who is worthy to rise from death will either marry ³⁶or die. They will be like the angels and will be God's children, because they have been raised to life.

³⁷In the story about the burning bush, Moses clearly shows that people will live again. He said, "The Lord is the God worshiped by Abraham, Isaac, and Jacob."ˢ ³⁸So the Lord isn't the God of the dead, but of the living. This means that everyone is alive as far as God is concerned.

³⁹Some of the teachers of the Law of Moses said, "Teacher, you have given a good answer!" ⁴⁰From then on, no one dared to ask Jesus any questions.

About David's Son
(Matthew 22.41-46; Mark 12.35-37)

⁴¹Jesus asked, "Why do people say that the Messiah will be the son of King David?ᵗ ⁴²In the book of Psalms, David himself says,

'The Lord said to my Lord,
    Sit at my right sideᵘ
⁴³ until I make your enemies
    into a footstool for you.'

⁴⁴David spoke of the Messiah as his Lord, so how can the Messiah be his son?"

Jesus and the Teachers of the Law of Moses
(Matthew 23.1-36; Mark 12.38-40; Luke 11.37-54)

⁴⁵While everyone was listening to Jesus, he said to his disciples:

⁴⁶Guard against the teachers of the Law of Moses! They love to walk around in long robes, and they like to be greeted in the market. They want the front seats in the meeting places and the best seats at banquets. ⁴⁷But they cheat widows out of their homes and then pray long prayers just to show off. These teachers will be punished most of all.

A Widow's Offering
(Mark 12.41-44)

21 Jesus looked up and saw some rich people tossing their gifts into the offering box. ²He also saw a poor widow putting in two pennies. ³And he said, "I tell you that this poor woman has put in more than all the others. ⁴Everyone else gave what they didn't

need. But she is very poor and gave everything she had."

The Temple Will Be Destroyed
(Matthew 24.1, 2; Mark 13.1, 2)

⁵Some people were talking about the beautiful stones used to build the temple and about the gifts that had been placed in it. Jesus said, ⁶"Do you see these stones? The time is coming when not one of them will be left in place. They will all be knocked down."

Warning about Trouble
(Matthew 24.3-14; Mark 13.3-13)

⁷Some people asked, "Teacher, when will all this happen? How can we know when these things are about to take place?"

⁸Jesus replied:

Don't be fooled by those who will come and claim to be me. They will say, "I am Christ!" and "Now is the time!" But don't follow them. ⁹When you hear about wars and riots, don't be afraid. These things will have to happen first, but that isn't the end.

¹⁰Nations will go to war against one another, and kingdoms will attack each other. ¹¹There will be great earthquakes, and in many places people will starve to death and suffer terrible diseases. All sorts of frightening things will be seen in the sky.

¹²Before all this happens, you will be arrested and punished. You will be tried in your meeting places and put in jail. Because of me you will be placed on trial before kings and governors. ¹³But this will be your chance to tell about your faith.

¹⁴Don't worry about what you will say to defend yourselves. ¹⁵I will give you the wisdom to know what to say. None of your enemies will be able to oppose you or to say that you are wrong. ¹⁶You will be betrayed by your own parents, brothers, family, and friends. Some of you will even be killed. ¹⁷Because of me, you will be hated by everyone. ¹⁸But don't worry!ᵛ ¹⁹You will be saved by being faithful to me.

Jerusalem Will Be Destroyed
(Matthew 24.15-21; Mark 13.14-19)

²⁰When you see Jerusalem surrounded by soldiers, you will know that it will soon be destroyed. ²¹If you are living in Judea at that time, run to the mountains. If you are in

---

ˢ**20.37** *"The Lord is the God worshiped by Abraham, Isaac, and Jacob"*: Jesus argues that if God is worshiped by these three, they must be alive, because he is the God of the living. ᵗ**20.41** *the son of King David*: See the note at 18.38. ᵘ**20.42** *right side*: The place of power and honor. ᵛ**21.18** *But don't worry*: The Greek text has "Not a hair of your head will be lost," which means, "There's no need to worry."

the city, leave it. And if you are out in the country, don't go back into the city. ²²This time of punishment is what is written about in the Scriptures. ²³It will be an awful time for women who are expecting babies or nursing young children! Everywhere in the land people will suffer horribly and be punished. ²⁴Some of them will be killed by swords. Others will be carried off to foreign countries. Jerusalem will be overrun by foreign nations until their time comes to an end.

When the Son of Man Appears
(Matthew 24.29-31; Mark 13.24-27)

²⁵Strange things will happen to the sun, moon, and stars. The nations on earth will be afraid of the roaring sea and tides, and they won't know what to do. ²⁶People will be so frightened that they will faint because of what is happening to the world. Every power in the sky will be shaken.ʷ ²⁷Then the Son of Man will be seen, coming in a cloud with great power and glory. ²⁸When all of this starts happening, stand up straight and be brave. You will soon be set free.

A Lesson from a Fig Tree
(Matthew 24.32-35; Mark 13.28-31)

²⁹Then Jesus told them a story:
When you see a fig tree or any other tree ³⁰putting out leaves, you know that summer will soon come. ³¹So, when you see these things happening, you know that God's kingdom will soon be here. ³²You can be sure that some of the people of this generation will still be alive when all of this takes place. ³³The sky and the earth won't last forever, but my words will.

A Warning

³⁴Don't spend all of your time thinking about eating or drinking or worrying about life. If you do, the final day will suddenly catch you ³⁵like a trap. That day will surprise everyone on earth. ³⁶Watch out and keep praying that you can escape all that is going to happen and that the Son of Man will be pleased with you.
³⁷Jesus taught in the temple each day, and he spent each night on the Mount of Olives. ³⁸Everyone got up early and came to the temple to hear him teach.

A Plot To Kill Jesus
(Matthew 26.1-5, 14, 16; Mark 14.1, 2, 10, 11; John 11.45-53)

22 The Festival of Thin Bread, also called Passover, was near. ²The chief priests and the teachers of the Law of Moses were looking for a way to get rid of Jesus, because they were afraid of what the people might do. ³Then Satan entered the heart of Judas Iscariot,ˣ who was one of the twelve apostles.
⁴Judas went to talk with the chief priests and the officers of the temple police about how he could help them arrest Jesus. ⁵They were very pleased and offered to pay Judas some money. ⁶He agreed and started looking for a good chance to betray Jesus when the crowds were not around.

Jesus Eats with His Disciples
(Matthew 26.17-25; Mark 14.12-21; John 13.21-30)

⁷The day had come for the Festival of Thin Bread, and it was time to kill the Passover lambs. ⁸So Jesus said to Peter and John, "Go and prepare the Passover meal for us to eat."
⁹But they asked, "Where do you want us to prepare it?"
¹⁰Jesus told them, "As you go into the city, you will meet a man carrying a jar of water.ʸ Follow him into the house ¹¹and say to the owner, 'Our teacher wants to know where he can eat the Passover meal with his disciples.' ¹²The owner will take you upstairs and show you a large room ready for you to use. Prepare the meal there."
¹³Peter and John left. They found everything just as Jesus had told them, and they prepared the Passover meal.

The Lord's Supper
(Matthew 26.26-30; Mark 14.22-26; 1 Corinthians 11.23-25)

¹⁴When the time came for Jesus and the apostles to eat, ¹⁵he said to them, "I have very much wanted to eat this Passover meal with you before I suffer. ¹⁶I tell you that I will not eat another Passover meal until it is finally eaten in God's kingdom."
¹⁷Jesus took a cup of wine in his hands and gave thanks to God. Then he told the apostles, "Take this wine and share it with each other. ¹⁸I tell you that I will not drink any more wine until God's kingdom comes."
¹⁹Jesus took some bread in his hands and gave thanks for it. He broke the

---

ʷ**21.26** *Every power in the sky will be shaken*: In ancient times people thought that the stars were spiritual powers. ˣ**22.3** *Iscariot*: See the note at 6.16. ʸ**22.10** *a man carrying a jar of water*: A male slave carrying water would probably mean that the family was rich.

bread and handed it to his apostles. Then he said, "This is my body, which is given for you. Eat this as a way of remembering me!"

²⁰After the meal he took another cup of wine in his hands. Then he said, "This is my blood. It is poured out for you, and with it God makes his new agreement. ²¹The one who will betray me is here at the table with me! ²²The Son of Man will die in the way that has been decided for him, but it will be terrible for the one who betrays him!"

²³Then the apostles started arguing about who would ever do such a thing.

An Argument about Greatness

²⁴The apostles got into an argument about which one of them was the greatest. ²⁵So Jesus told them:

Foreign kings order their people around, and powerful rulers call themselves everyone's friends.ᶻ ²⁶But don't be like them. The most important one of you should be like the least important, and your leader should be like a servant. ²⁷Who do people think is the greatest, a person who is served or one who serves? Isn't it the one who is served? But I have been with you as a servant.

²⁸You have stayed with me in all my troubles. ²⁹So I will give you the right to rule as kings, just as my Father has given me the right to rule as a king. ³⁰You will eat and drink with me in my kingdom, and you will each sit on a throne to judge the twelve tribes of Israel.

Jesus' Disciples Will Be Tested
(Matthew 26.31-35; Mark 14.27-31; John 13.36-38)

³¹Jesus said, "Simon, listen to me! Satan has demanded the right to test each one of you, as a farmer does when he separates wheat from the husks.ᵃ ³²But Simon, I have prayed that your faith will be strong. And when you have come back to me, help the others."

³³Peter said, "Lord, I am ready to go with you to jail and even to die with you."

³⁴Jesus replied, "Peter, I tell you that before a rooster crows tomorrow morning, you will say three times that you don't know me."

Moneybags, Traveling Bags, and Swords

³⁵Jesus asked his disciples, "When I sent you out without a moneybag or a traveling bag or sandals, did you need anything?"

"No!" they answered.

³⁶Jesus told them, "But now, if you have a moneybag, take it with you. Also take a traveling bag, and if you don't have a sword,ᵇ sell some of your clothes and buy one. ³⁷Do this because the Scriptures say, 'He was considered a criminal.' This was written about me, and it will soon come true."

³⁸The disciples said, "Lord, here are two swords!"

"Enough of that!" Jesus replied.

Jesus Prays
(Matthew 26.36-46; Mark 14.32-42)

³⁹Jesus went out to the Mount of Olives, as he often did, and his disciples went with him. ⁴⁰When they got there, he told them, "Pray that you won't be tested."

⁴¹Jesus walked on a little way before he knelt down and prayed, ⁴²"Father, if you will, please don't make me suffer by having me drink from this cup.ᶜ But do what you want, and not what I want."

⁴³Then an angel from heaven came to help him. ⁴⁴Jesus was in great pain and prayed so sincerely that his sweat fell to the ground like drops of blood.ᵈ

⁴⁵Jesus got up from praying and went over to his disciples. They were asleep and worn out from being so sad. ⁴⁶He said to them, "Why are you asleep? Wake up and pray that you won't be tested."

Jesus Is Arrested
(Matthew 26.47-56; Mark 14.43-50; John 18.3-11)

⁴⁷While Jesus was still speaking, a crowd came up. It was led by Judas, one of the twelve apostles. He went over to Jesus and greeted him with a kiss.ᵉ ⁴⁸Jesus asked Judas, "Are you betraying the Son of Man with a kiss?"

⁴⁹When Jesus' disciples saw what was about to happen, they asked, "Lord, should we attack them with a sword?" ⁵⁰One of the disciples even struck at the high priest's servant with his sword and cut off the servant's right ear.

⁵¹"Enough of that!" Jesus said. Then

ᶻ**22.25** *everyone's friends*: This translates a Greek word that rulers sometimes used as a title for themselves or for special friends.   ᵃ**22.31** *separates wheat from the husks*: See the note at 3.17.   ᵇ**22.36** *moneybag . . . traveling bag . . . sword*: These were things that someone would take on a dangerous journey. Jesus was telling his disciples to be ready for anything that might happen. They seem to have understood what he meant (see 22.49-51).   ᶜ**22.42** *having me drink from this cup*: In the Scriptures "to drink from a cup" sometimes means to suffer. ᵈ**22.43, 44** *Then an angel . . . like drops of blood*: Verses 43, 44 are not in some manuscripts. ᵉ**22.47** *greeted him with a kiss*: It was the custom for people to greet each other with a kiss on the cheek.

he touched the servant's ear and healed it.

⁵²Jesus spoke to the chief priests, the temple police, and the leaders who had come to arrest him. He said, "Why do you come out with swords and clubs and treat me like a criminal? ⁵³I was with you every day in the temple, and you didn't arrest me. But this is your time, and darkness*ᶠ* is in control."

Peter Says He Doesn't Know Jesus
(Matthew 26.57, 58, 67-75; Mark 14.53, 54, 66-72; John 18.12-18, 25-27)

⁵⁴Jesus was arrested and led away to the house of the high priest, while Peter followed at a distance. ⁵⁵Some people built a fire in the middle of the court-yard and were sitting around it. Peter sat there with them, ⁵⁶and a servant girl saw him. Then after she had looked at him carefully, she said, "This man was with Jesus!"

⁵⁷Peter said, "Woman, I don't even know that man!"

⁵⁸A little later someone else saw Peter and said, "You are one of them!"

"No, I'm not!" Peter replied.

⁵⁹About an hour later another man insisted, "This man must have been with Jesus. They both come from Galilee."

⁶⁰Peter replied, "I don't know what you are talking about!" Right then, while Peter was still speaking, a rooster crowed.

⁶¹The Lord turned and looked at Peter. And Peter remembered that the Lord had said, "Before a rooster crows tomorrow morning, you will say three times that you don't know me." ⁶²Then Peter went out and cried hard.

⁶³The men who were guarding Jesus made fun of him and beat him. ⁶⁴They put a blindfold on him and said, "Tell us who struck you!" ⁶⁵They kept on insulting Jesus in many other ways.

Jesus Is Questioned by the Council
(Matthew 26.59-66; Mark 14.55-64; John 18.19-24)

⁶⁶At daybreak the nation's leaders, the chief priests, and the teachers of the Law of Moses got together and brought Jesus before their council. ⁶⁷They said, "Tell us! Are you the Messiah?"

Jesus replied, "If I said so, you wouldn't believe me. ⁶⁸And if I asked you a question, you wouldn't answer. ⁶⁹But from now on, the Son of Man will be seated at the right side of God All-Powerful."

⁷⁰Then they asked, "Are you the Son of God?"*ᵍ*

Jesus answered, "You say I am!"*ʰ*

⁷¹They replied, "Why do we need more witnesses? He said it himself!"

Pilate Questions Jesus
(Matthew 27.1, 2, 11-14; Mark 15.1-5; John 18.28-38)

23 Everyone in the council got up and led Jesus off to Pilate. ²They started accusing him and said, "We caught this man trying to get our people to riot and to stop paying taxes to the Emperor. He also claims that he is the Messiah, our king."

³Pilate asked Jesus, "Are you the king of the Jews?"

"Those are your words," Jesus answered.

⁴Pilate told the chief priests and the crowd, "I don't find him guilty of anything."

⁵But they all kept on saying, "He has been teaching and causing trouble all over Judea. He started in Galilee and has now come all the way here."

Jesus Is Brought before Herod

⁶When Pilate heard this, he asked, "Is this man from Galilee?" ⁷After Pilate learned that Jesus came from the region ruled by Herod,*ⁱ* he sent him to Herod, who was in Jerusalem at that time.

⁸For a long time Herod had wanted to see Jesus and was very happy because he finally had this chance. He had heard many things about Jesus and hoped to see him work a miracle. ⁹Herod asked him a lot of questions, but Jesus did not answer. ¹⁰Then the chief priests and the teachers of the Law of Moses stood up and accused him of all kinds of bad things. ¹¹Herod and his soldiers made fun of Jesus and insulted him. They put a fine robe on him and sent him back to Pilate. ¹²That same day Herod and Pilate became friends, even though they had been enemies before this.

The Death Sentence
(Matthew 27.15-26; Mark 15.6-15; John 18.39—19.16)

¹³Pilate called together the chief priests, the leaders, and the people. ¹⁴He told them, "You brought Jesus to me and said he was a troublemaker. But I have questioned him here in front of you, and I have not found him guilty of anything that you say he has done. ¹⁵Herod didn't find him guilty either and sent him back. This man doesn't deserve to be put to death! ¹⁶-¹⁷I will just

---

ᶠ22.53 darkness: Darkness stands for the power of the devil.   *ᵍ22.70 Son of God:* This was one of the titles used for the kings of Israel.   *ʰ22.70 You say I am:* Or "That's what you say." *ⁱ23.7 Herod:* Herod Antipas, the son of Herod the Great.

have him beaten with a whip and set free."[j]

[18]But the whole crowd shouted, "Kill Jesus! Give us Barabbas!" [19]Now Barabbas was in jail because he had started a riot in the city and had murdered someone.

[20]Pilate wanted to set Jesus free, so he spoke again to the crowds. [21]But they kept shouting, "Nail him to a cross! Nail him to a cross!"

[22]Pilate spoke to them a third time, "But what crime has he done? I have not found him guilty of anything for which he should be put to death. I will have him beaten with a whip and set free."

[23]The people kept on shouting as loud as they could for Jesus to be put to death. [24]Finally, Pilate gave in. [25]He freed the man who was in jail for rioting and murder, because he was the one the crowd wanted to be set free. Then Pilate handed Jesus over for them to do what they wanted with him.

Jesus Is Nailed to a Cross
(Matthew 27.31-44; Mark 15.21-32;
John 19.17-27)

[26]As Jesus was being led away, some soldiers grabbed hold of a man from Cyrene named Simon. He was coming in from the fields, but they put the cross on him and made him carry it behind Jesus.

[27]A large crowd was following Jesus, and in the crowd a lot of women were crying and weeping for him. [28]Jesus turned to the women and said:

Women of Jerusalem, don't cry for me! Cry for yourselves and for your children. [29]Someday people will say, "Women who never had children are really fortunate!" [30]At that time everyone will say to the mountains, "Fall on us!" They will say to the hills, "Hide us!" [31]If this can happen when the wood is green, what do you think will happen when it is dry?[k]

[32]Two criminals were led out to be put to death with Jesus. [33]When the soldiers came to the place called "The Skull,"[l]

they nailed Jesus to a cross. They also nailed the two criminals to crosses, one on each side of Jesus.

[34-35]Jesus said, "Father, forgive these people! They don't know what they're doing."[m] While the crowd stood there watching Jesus, the soldiers gambled for his clothes. The leaders insulted him by saying, "He saved others. Now he should save himself, if he really is God's chosen Messiah!"

[36]The soldiers made fun of Jesus and brought him some wine. [37]They said, "If you are the king of the Jews, save yourself!"

[38]Above him was a sign that said, "This is the King of the Jews."

[39]One of the criminals hanging there also insulted Jesus by saying, "Aren't you the Messiah? Save yourself and save us!"

[40]But the other criminal told the first one off, "Don't you fear God? Aren't you getting the same punishment as this man? [41]We got what was coming to us, but he didn't do anything wrong." [42]Then he said to Jesus, "Remember me when you come into power!"

[43]Jesus replied, "I promise that today you will be with me in paradise."[n]

The Death of Jesus
(Matthew 27.45-56; Mark 15.33-41;
John 19.28-30)

[44]Around noon the sky turned dark and stayed that way until the middle of the afternoon. [45]The sun stopped shining, and the curtain in the temple[o] split down the middle. [46]Jesus shouted, "Father, I put myself in your hands!" Then he died.

[47]When the Roman officer saw what had happened, he praised God and said, "Jesus must really have been a good man!"

[48]A crowd had gathered to see the terrible sight. Then after they had seen it, they felt brokenhearted and went home. [49]All of Jesus' close friends and the women who had come with him from Galilee stood at a distance and watched.

---

[j]23.16,17 *set free*: Some manuscripts add, "Pilate said this, because at every Passover he was supposed to set one prisoner free for the Jewish people." [k]23.31 *If this can happen when the wood is green, what do you think will happen when it is dry?*: This saying probably means, "If this can happen to an innocent person, what do you think will happen to one who is guilty?" [l]23.33 *"The Skull"*: The place was probably given this name because it was near a large rock in the shape of a human skull. [m]23.34,35 *Jesus said, "Father, forgive these people! They don't know what they're doing."*: These words are not in some manuscripts. [n]23.43 *paradise*: In the Greek translation of the Old Testament, this word is used for the Garden of Eden. In New Testament times it was sometimes used for the place where God's people are happy and at rest, as they wait for the final judgment. [o]23.45 *curtain in the temple*: There were two curtains in the temple. One was at the entrance, and the other separated the holy place from the most holy place that the Jewish people thought of as God's home on earth. The second curtain is probably the one which is meant.

Jesus Is Buried

(Matthew 27.57-61; Mark 15.42-47; John 19.38-42)

50-51 There was a man named Joseph, who was from Arimathea in Judea. Joseph was a good and honest man, and he was eager for God's kingdom to come. He was also a member of the council, but he did not agree with what they had decided.

52 Joseph went to Pilate and asked for Jesus' body. 53 He took the body down from the cross and wrapped it in fine cloth. Then he put it in a tomb that had been cut out of solid rock and had never been used. 54 It was Friday, and the Sabbath was about to begin.[p]

55 The women who had come with Jesus from Galilee followed Joseph and watched how Jesus' body was placed in the tomb. 56 Then they went to prepare some sweet-smelling spices for his burial. But on the Sabbath they rested, as the Law of Moses commands.

Jesus Is Alive

(Matthew 28.1-10; Mark 16.1-8; John 20.1-10)

24 Very early on Sunday morning the women went to the tomb, carrying the spices that they had prepared. 2 When they found the stone rolled away from the entrance, 3 they went in. But they did not find the body of the Lord[q] Jesus, 4 and they did not know what to think.

Suddenly two men in shining white clothes stood beside them. 5 The women were afraid and bowed to the ground. But the men said, "Why are you looking in the place of the dead for someone who is alive? 6 Jesus isn't here! He has been raised from death. Remember that while he was still in Galilee, he told you, 7 'The Son of Man will be handed over to sinners who will nail him to a cross. But three days later he will rise to life.' " 8 Then they remembered what Jesus had said.

9-10 Mary Magdalene, Joanna, Mary the mother of James, and some other women were the ones who had gone to the tomb. When they returned, they told the eleven apostles and the others what had happened. 11 The apostles thought it was all nonsense, and they would not believe.

12 But Peter ran to the tomb. And when he stooped down and looked in, he saw only the burial clothes. Then he returned, wondering what had happened.[r]

Jesus Appears to Two Disciples

(Mark 16.12, 13)

13 That same day two of Jesus' disciples were going to the village of Emmaus, which was about seven miles from Jerusalem. 14 As they were talking and thinking about what had happened, 15 Jesus came near and started walking along beside them. 16 But they did not know who he was.

17 Jesus asked them, "What were you talking about as you walked along?"

The two of them stood there looking sad and gloomy. 18 Then the one named Cleopas asked Jesus, "Are you the only person from Jerusalem who didn't know what was happening there these last few days?"

19 "What do you mean?" Jesus asked.

They answered:

> Those things that happened to Jesus from Nazareth. By what he did and said he showed that he was a powerful prophet, who pleased God and all the people. 20 Then the chief priests and our leaders had him arrested and sentenced to die on a cross. 21 We had hoped that he would be the one to set Israel free! But it has already been three days since all this happened.
>
> 22 Some women in our group surprised us. They had gone to the tomb early in the morning, 23 but did not find the body of Jesus. They came back, saying that they had seen a vision of angels who told them that he is alive. 24 Some men from our group went to the tomb and found it just as the women had said. But they didn't see Jesus either.

25 Then Jesus asked the two disciples, "Why can't you understand? How can you be so slow to believe all that the prophets said? 26 Didn't you know that the Messiah would have to suffer before he was given his glory?" 27 Jesus then explained everything written about himself in the Scriptures, beginning with the Law of Moses and the Books of the Prophets.[s]

28 When the two of them came near the village where they were going, Jesus seemed to be going farther. 29 They begged him, "Stay with us! It's already late, and the sun is going down." So Jesus went into the house to stay with them.

30 After Jesus sat down to eat, he took some bread. He blessed it and broke it. Then he gave it to them. 31 At once they knew who he was, but he disappeared.

[p] **23.54** *the Sabbath was about to begin*: The Sabbath begins at sunset on Friday.
[q] **24.3** *the Lord*: These words are not in some manuscripts. [r] **24.12** *what had happened*: Verse 12 is not in some manuscripts. [s] **24.27** *the Law of Moses and the Books of the Prophets*: See the note at 16.16.

³²They said to each other, "When he talked with us along the road and explained the Scriptures to us, didn't it warm our hearts?" ³³So they got right up and returned to Jerusalem.

The two disciples found the eleven apostles and the others gathered together. ³⁴And they learned from the group that the Lord was really alive and had appeared to Peter. ³⁵Then the disciples from Emmaus told what happened on the road and how they knew he was the Lord when he broke the bread.

What Jesus' Followers Must Do
(Matthew 28.16-20; Mark 16.14-18; John 20.19-23; Acts 1.6-8)

³⁶While Jesus' disciples were talking about what had happened, Jesus appeared and greeted them. ³⁷They were frightened and terrified because they thought they were seeing a ghost. ³⁸But Jesus said, "Why are you so frightened? Why do you doubt? ³⁹Look at my hands and my feet and see who I am! Touch me and find out for yourselves. Ghosts don't have flesh and bones as you see I have."

⁴⁰After Jesus said this, he showed them his hands and his feet. ⁴¹The disciples were so glad and amazed that they could not believe it. Jesus then asked them, "Do you have something to eat?" ⁴²They gave him a piece of baked fish. ⁴³He took it and ate it as they watched.

⁴⁴Jesus said to them, "While I was still with you, I told you that everything written about me in the Law of Moses, the Books of the Prophets, and in the Psalms ᵗ had to happen."

⁴⁵Then he helped them understand the Scriptures. ⁴⁶He told them:

The Scriptures say that the Messiah must suffer, then three days later he will rise from death. ⁴⁷They also say that all people of every nation must be told in my name to turn to God, in order to be forgiven. So beginning in Jerusalem, ⁴⁸you must tell everything that has happened. ⁴⁹I will send you the one my Father has promised, ᵘ but you must stay in the city until you are given power from heaven.

Jesus Returns to Heaven
(Mark 16.19, 20; Acts 1.9-11)

⁵⁰Jesus led his disciples out to Bethany, where he raised his hands and blessed them. ⁵¹As he was doing this, he left and was taken up to heaven. ᵛ ⁵²After his disciples had worshiped him, ʷ they returned to Jerusalem and were very happy. ⁵³They spent their time in the temple, praising God.

ᵗ**24.44** *Psalms*: The Jewish Scriptures were made up of three parts: (1) the Law of Moses, (2) the Books of the Prophets, (3) and the Writings, which included the Psalms. Sometimes the Scriptures were just called the Law or the Law (of Moses) and the Books of the Prophets. ᵘ**24.49** *the one my Father has promised*: Jesus means the Holy Spirit. ᵛ**24.51** *and was taken up to heaven*: These words are not in some manuscripts. ʷ**24.52** *After his disciples had worshiped him*: These words are not in some manuscripts.

JOHN

✝

ABOUT THIS BOOK

Who is Jesus Christ? John answers this question in the first chapter of his Gospel. Using the words of an early Christian hymn, he calls Jesus the "Word" by which God created everything and by which he gave life to everyone (1.3, 4). He shows how John the Baptist announced Jesus' coming, "Here is the Lamb of God who takes away the sin of the world" (1.29). When Philip met Jesus he knew Jesus was "the one that Moses and the Prophets wrote about" (1.45). And, in the words of Nathanael, Jesus is "the Son of God and the King of Israel" (1.49).

In John's Gospel we learn a lot about who Jesus is by observing what he said and did when he was with other people. These include a Samaritan woman who received Jesus' offer of life-giving water, a woman who had been caught in sin, his friend Lazarus who was brought back to life by Jesus, and his follower Thomas who doubted that Jesus was raised from death. Jesus also refers to himself as "I am", a phrase which translates the most holy name for God in the Hebrew Scriptures. He uses this name for himself when he makes his claim to be the life-giving bread, the light of the world, the good shepherd, and the true vine.

Jesus performs seven miracles that are more than miracles. Each of them is a "sign" that tells us something about Jesus as the Son of God. For example, by healing a lame man (5.1-8), Jesus shows that he is just like his Father, who never stops working (5.17). This sign also teaches that the Son does only what he sees his Father doing (5.19), and that like the Father "the Son gives life to anyone he wants to" (5.21).

The way John tells the story of Jesus is quite different from the other three Gospels. Here, Jesus has long conversations with people about who he is and what God sent him to do. In these conversations he teaches many important things—for example, that he is the way, the truth and the life.

Why did John write? John himself tells us, "So that you will put your faith in Jesus as the Messiah and the Son of God" (20.31). How is this possible? Jesus answers that question in his words to Nicodemus:

God loved the people of this world so much that he gave his only Son, so that everyone who has faith in him will have eternal life and never really die.   *(3.16)*

A QUICK LOOK AT THIS BOOK

The Word of Life

1 In the beginning was the one
who is called the Word.
The Word was with God
and was truly God.
2 From the very beginning
the Word was with God.

3 And with this Word,
God created all things.
Nothing was made
without the Word.
Everything that was created
4 received its life from him,
and his life gave light
to everyone.
5 The light keeps shining
in the dark,
and darkness has never
put it out.*a*
6 God sent a man named John,
7 who came to tell
about the light
and to lead all people
to have faith.
8 John wasn't that light.
He came only to tell
about the light.

9 The true light that shines
on everyone
was coming into the world.
10 The Word was in the world,
but no one knew him,
though God had made the world
with his Word.
11 He came into his own world,
but his own nation
did not welcome him.
12 Yet some people accepted him
and put their faith in him.
So he gave them the right
to be the children of God.
13 They were not God's children
by nature or because
of any human desires.
God himself was the one
who made them his children.

14 The Word became
a human being
and lived here with us.
We saw his true glory,
the glory of the only Son
of the Father.
From him all the kindness
and all the truth of God
have come down to us.

15 John spoke about him and shouted,
"This is the one I told you would come!

He is greater than I am, because he was
alive before I was born."
16 Because of all that the Son is, we
have been given one blessing after another.*b* 17 The Law was given by Moses,
but Jesus Christ brought us undeserved
kindness and truth. 18 No one has ever
seen God. The only Son, who is truly
God and is closest to the Father, has
shown us what God is like.

John the Baptist Tells about Jesus
(Matthew 3.1-12; Mark 1.1-8; Luke 3.15-17)

19-20 The Jewish leaders in Jerusalem
sent priests and temple helpers to ask
John who he was. He told them plainly,
"I am not the Messiah." 21 Then when
they asked him if he were Elijah, he
said, "No, I am not!" And when they
asked if he were the Prophet,*c* he also
said "No!"
22 Finally, they said, "Who are you
then? We have to give an answer to the
ones who sent us. Tell us who you are!"
23 John answered in the words of the
prophet Isaiah, "I am only someone
shouting in the desert, 'Get the road
ready for the Lord!' "
24 Some Pharisees had also been sent
to John. 25 They asked him, "Why are
you baptizing people, if you are not the
Messiah or Elijah or the Prophet?"
26 John told them, "I use water to baptize people. But here with you is someone you don't know. 27 Even though I
came first, I am not good enough to untie his sandals." 28 John said this as he
was baptizing east of the Jordan River
in Bethany.*d*

The Lamb of God

29 The next day, John saw Jesus coming toward him and said:
Here is the Lamb of God who
takes away the sin of the world! 30 He
is the one I told you about when I
said, "Someone else will come. He is
greater than I am, because he was
alive before I was born." 31 I didn't
know who he was. But I came to
baptize you with water, so that
everyone in Israel would see him.
32 I was there and saw the Spirit
come down on him like a dove from
heaven. And the Spirit stayed on
him. 33 Before this I didn't know who
he was. But the one who sent me to
baptize with water had told me,
"You will see the Spirit come down
and stay on someone. Then you will

---

*a*1.5 *put it out:* Or "understood it."   *b*1.16 *one blessing after another:* Or "one blessing in
place of another."   *c*1.21 *the Prophet:* Many of the Jewish people expected God to send
them a prophet who would be like Moses, but with even greater power (see Deuteronomy
18.15, 18).   *d*1.28 *Bethany:* An unknown village east of the Jordan with the same name as
the village near Jerusalem.

know that he is the one who will baptize with the Holy Spirit." 34I saw this happen, and I tell you that he is the Son of God.

The First Disciples of Jesus

35The next day, John was there again, and two of his followers were with him. 36When he saw Jesus walking by, he said, "Here is the Lamb of God!" 37John's two followers heard him, and they went with Jesus.

38When Jesus turned and saw them, he asked, "What do you want?"

They answered, "Rabbi, where do you live?" The Hebrew word "Rabbi" means "Teacher."

39Jesus replied, "Come and see!" It was already about four o'clock in the afternoon when they went with him and saw where he lived. So they stayed on for the rest of the day.

40One of the two men who had heard John and had gone with Jesus was Andrew, the brother of Simon Peter. 41The first thing Andrew did was to find his brother and tell him, "We have found the Messiah!" The Hebrew word "Messiah" means the same as the Greek word "Christ."

42Andrew brought his brother to Jesus. And when Jesus saw him, he said, "Simon son of John, you will be called Cephas." This name can be translated as "Peter."e

Jesus Chooses Philip and Nathanael

43-44The next day Jesus decided to go to Galilee. There he met Philip, who was from Bethsaida, the hometown of Andrew and Peter. Jesus said to Philip, "Come with me."

45Philip then found Nathanael and said, "We have found the one that Moses and the Prophetsf wrote about. He is Jesus, the son of Joseph from Nazareth."

46Nathanael asked, "Can anything good come from Nazareth?"

Philip answered, "Come and see."

47When Jesus saw Nathanael coming toward him, he said, "Here is a true descendant of our ancestor Israel. And he isn't deceitful."g

48"How do you know me?" Nathanael asked.

Jesus answered, "Before Philip called you, I saw you under the fig tree."

49Nathanael said, "Rabbi, you are the Son of God and the King of Israel!"

50Jesus answered, "Did you believe me just because I said that I saw you under the fig tree? You will see something even greater. 51I tell you for certain that you will see heaven open and God's angels going up and coming down on the Son of Man."h

Jesus at a Wedding in Cana

2 Three days later Mary, the mother of Jesus, was at a wedding feast in the village of Cana in Galilee. 2Jesus and his disciples had also been invited and were there.

3When the wine was all gone, Mary said to Jesus, "They don't have any more wine."

4Jesus replied, "Mother, my time hasn't yet come!i You must not tell me what to do."

5Mary then said to the servants, "Do whatever Jesus tells you to do."

6At the feast there were six stone water jars that were used by the people for washing themselves in the way that their religion said they must. Each jar held about twenty or thirty gallons. 7Jesus told the servants to fill them to the top with water. Then after the jars had been filled, 8he said, "Now take some water and give it to the man in charge of the feast."

The servants did as Jesus told them, 9and the man in charge drank some of the water that had now turned into wine. He did not know where the wine had come from, but the servants did. He called the bridegroom over 10and said, "The best wine is always served first. Then after the guests have had plenty, the other wine is served. But you have kept the best until last!"

11This was Jesus' first miracle,j and he did it in the village of Cana in Galilee. There Jesus showed his glory, and his disciples put their faith in him. 12After this, he went with his mother, his brothers, and his disciples to the town of Capernaum, where they stayed for a few days.

---

e1.42 *Peter*: The Aramaic name "Cephas" and the Greek name "Peter" each mean "rock."
f1.45 *Moses and the Prophets*: The Jewish Scriptures, that is, the Old Testament.
g1.47 *Israel . . . isn't deceitful*: Israel (meaning "a man who wrestled with God" or "a prince of God") was the name that the Lord gave to Jacob (meaning "cheater" or "deceiver"), the famous ancestor of the Jewish people. h1.51 *going up and coming down on the Son of Man*: When Jacob (see the note at verse 47) was running from his brother Esau, he had a dream in which he saw angels going up and down on a ladder from earth to heaven (see Genesis 32.22-32). i2.4 *my time hasn't yet come!*: The time when the true glory of Jesus would be seen, and he would be recognized as God's Son (see 12.23). j2.11,18,23 *miracle*: The Greek text has "sign." In the Gospel of John the word "sign" is used for the miracle itself and as a way of pointing to Jesus as the Son of God.

Jesus in the Temple
(Matthew 21.12, 13; Mark 11.15-17;
Luke 19.45, 46)

[13]Not long before the Jewish festival of Passover, Jesus went to Jerusalem. [14]There he found people selling cattle, sheep, and doves in the temple. He also saw moneychangers sitting at their tables. [15]So he took some rope and made a whip. Then he chased everyone out of the temple, together with their sheep and cattle. He turned over the tables of the moneychangers and scattered their coins.

[16]Jesus said to the people who had been selling doves, "Get those doves out of here! Don't make my Father's house a marketplace."

[17]The disciples then remembered that the Scriptures say, "My love for your house burns in me like a fire."

[18]The Jewish leaders asked Jesus, "What miracle[j] will you work to show us why you have done this?"

[19]"Destroy this temple," Jesus answered, "and in three days I will build it again!"

[20]The leaders replied, "It took forty-six years to build this temple. What makes you think you can rebuild it in three days?"

[21]But Jesus was talking about his body as a temple. [22]And when he was raised from death, his disciples remembered what he had told them. Then they believed the Scriptures and the words of Jesus.

Jesus Knows What People Are Like

[23]In Jerusalem during Passover many people put their faith in Jesus, because they saw him work miracles.[j] [24]But Jesus knew what was in their hearts, and he would not let them have power over him. [25]No one had to tell him what people were like. He already knew.

Jesus and Nicodemus

3 There was a man named Nicodemus who was a Pharisee and a Jewish leader. [2]One night he went to Jesus and said, "Sir, we know that God has sent you to teach us. You could not work these miracles, unless God were with you."

[3]Jesus replied, "I tell you for certain that you must be born from above[k] before you can see God's kingdom!"

[4]Nicodemus asked, "How can a grown man ever be born a second time?"

[5]Jesus answered:

I tell you for certain that before you can get into God's kingdom, you must be born not only by water, but by the Spirit. [6]Humans give life to their children. Yet only God's Spirit can change you into a child of God. [7]Don't be surprised when I say that you must be born from above. [8]Only God's Spirit gives new life. The Spirit is like the wind that blows wherever it wants to. You can hear the wind, but you don't know where it comes from or where it is going. [9]"How can this be?" Nicodemus asked.

[10]Jesus replied:

How can you be a teacher of Israel and not know these things? [11]I tell you for certain that we know what we are talking about because we have seen it ourselves. But none of you will accept what we say. [12]If you don't believe when I talk to you about things on earth, how can you possibly believe if I talk to you about things in heaven?

[13]No one has gone up to heaven except the Son of Man, who came down from there. [14]And the Son of Man must be lifted up, just as that metal snake was lifted up by Moses in the desert.[l] [15]Then everyone who has faith in the Son of Man will have eternal life.

[16]God loved the people of this world so much that he gave his only Son, so that everyone who has faith in him will have eternal life and never really die. [17]God did not send his Son into the world to condemn its people. He sent him to save them! [18]No one who has faith in God's Son will be condemned. But everyone who doesn't have faith in him has already been condemned for not having faith in God's only Son.

[19]The light has come into the world, and people who do evil things are judged guilty because they love the dark more than the light. [20]People who do evil hate the light and won't come to the light, because it clearly shows what they have done. [21]But everyone who lives by the truth will come to the light, because they want others to know that God is really the one doing what they do.

Jesus and John the Baptist

[22]Later, Jesus and his disciples went to Judea, where he stayed with them for a while and was baptizing people.

[23-24]John had not yet been put in jail.

---

[j]**2.11,18,23** *miracle:* The Greek text has "sign." In the Gospel of John the word "sign" is used for the miracle itself and as a way of pointing to Jesus as the Son of God. [k]**3.3** *from above:* Or "in a new way." The same Greek word is used in verses 7, 31. [l]**3.14** *just as that metal snake was lifted up by Moses in the desert:* When the Lord punished the people of Israel by sending snakes to bite them, he told Moses to hold a metal snake up on a pole. Everyone who looked at the snake was cured of the snake bites (see Numbers 21.4-9).

He was at Aenon near Salim, where there was a lot of water, and people were coming there for John to baptize them.

[25]John's followers got into an argument with a Jewish man[m] about a ceremony of washing.[n] [26]They went to John and said, "Rabbi, you spoke about a man when you were with him east of the Jordan. He is now baptizing people, and everyone is going to him."

[27]John replied:

No one can do anything unless God in heaven allows it. [28]You surely remember how I told you that I am not the Messiah. I am only the one sent ahead of him.

[29]At a wedding the groom is the one who gets married. The best man is glad just to be there and to hear the groom's voice. That's why I am so glad. [30]Jesus must become more important, while I become less important.

The One Who Comes from Heaven

[31]God's Son comes from heaven and is above all others. Everyone who comes from the earth belongs to the earth and speaks about earthly things. The one who comes from heaven is above all others. [32]He speaks about what he has seen and heard, and yet no one believes him. [33]But everyone who does believe him has shown that God is truthful. [34]The Son was sent to speak God's message, and he has been given the full power of God's Spirit. [35]The Father loves the Son and has given him everything. [36]Everyone who has faith in the Son has eternal life. But no one who rejects him will ever share in that life, and God will be angry with them forever.

4 Jesus knew that the Pharisees had heard that he was winning and baptizing more followers than John was. [2]But Jesus' disciples were really the ones doing the baptizing, and not Jesus himself.

Jesus and the Samaritan Woman

[3]Jesus left Judea and started for Galilee again. [4]This time he had to go through Samaria, [5]and on his way he came to the town of Sychar. It was near the field that Jacob had long ago given to his son Joseph. [6-8]The well that Jacob had dug was still there, and Jesus sat down beside it because he was tired from traveling. It was noon, and after Jesus' disciples had gone into town to buy some food, a Samaritan woman came to draw water from the well.

Jesus asked her, "Would you please give me a drink of water?"

[9]"You are a Jew," she replied, "and I am a Samaritan woman. How can you ask me for a drink of water when Jews and Samaritans won't have anything to do with each other?"[o]

[10]Jesus answered, "You don't know what God wants to give you, and you don't know who is asking you for a drink. If you did, you would ask me for the water that gives life."

[11]"Sir," the woman said, "you don't even have a bucket, and the well is deep. Where are you going to get this life-giving water? [12]Our ancestor Jacob dug this well for us, and his family and animals got water from it. Are you greater than Jacob?"

[13]Jesus answered, "Everyone who drinks this water will get thirsty again. [14]But no one who drinks the water I give will ever be thirsty again. The water I give is like a flowing fountain that gives eternal life."

[15]The woman replied, "Sir, please give me a drink of that water! Then I won't get thirsty and have to come to this well again."

[16]Jesus told her, "Go and bring your husband."

[17-18]The woman answered, "I don't have a husband."

"That's right," Jesus replied, "you're telling the truth. You don't have a husband. You have already been married five times, and the man you are now living with isn't your husband."

[19]The woman said, "Sir, I can see that you are a prophet. [20]My ancestors worshiped on this mountain,[p] but you Jews say Jerusalem is the only place to worship."

[21]Jesus said to her:

Believe me, the time is coming when you won't worship the Father either on this mountain or in Jerusalem. [22]You Samaritans don't really know the one you worship. But we Jews do know the God we worship, and by using us, God will save the world. [23]But a time is coming, and it is already here! Even now the true worshipers are being led by the Spirit to worship the Father

---

[m]**3.25** *a Jewish man*: Some manuscripts have "some Jewish men."   [n]**3.25** *about a ceremony of washing*: The Jewish people had many rules about washing themselves and their dishes, in order to make themselves fit to worship God.   [o]**4.9** *won't have anything to do with each other*: Or "won't use the same cups." The Samaritans lived in the land between Judea and Galilee. They worshiped God differently from the Jews and did not get along with them.   [p]**4.20** *this mountain*: Mount Gerizim, near the city of Shechem.

according to the truth. These are the ones the Father is seeking to worship him. ²⁴God is Spirit, and those who worship God must be led by the Spirit to worship him according to the truth.

²⁵The woman said, "I know that the Messiah will come. He is the one we call Christ. When he comes, he will explain everything to us."

²⁶"I am that one," Jesus told her, "and I am speaking to you now."

²⁷The disciples returned about this time and were surprised to find Jesus talking with a woman. But none of them asked him what he wanted or why he was talking with her.

²⁸The woman left her water jar and ran back into town. She said to the people, ²⁹"Come and see a man who told me everything I have ever done! Could he be the Messiah?" ³⁰Everyone in town went out to see Jesus.

³¹While this was happening, Jesus' disciples were saying to him, "Teacher, please eat something."

³²But Jesus told them, "I have food that you don't know anything about."

³³His disciples started asking each other, "Has someone brought him something to eat?"

³⁴Jesus said:

My food is to do what God wants! He is the one who sent me, and I must finish the work that he gave me to do. ³⁵You may say that there are still four months until harvest time. But I tell you to look, and you will see that the fields are ripe and ready to harvest.

³⁶Even now the harvest workers are receiving their reward by gathering a harvest that brings eternal life. Then everyone who planted the seed and everyone who harvests the crop will celebrate together. ³⁷So the saying proves true, "Some plant the seed, and others harvest the crop." ³⁸I am sending you to harvest crops in fields where others have done all the hard work.

³⁹A lot of Samaritans in that town put their faith in Jesus because the woman had said, "This man told me everything I have ever done." ⁴⁰They came and asked him to stay in their town, and he stayed on for two days.

⁴¹Many more Samaritans put their faith in Jesus because of what they heard him say. ⁴²They told the woman, "We no longer have faith in Jesus just because of what you told us. We have heard him ourselves, and we are certain that he is the Savior of the world!"

Jesus Heals an Official's Son
(Matthew 8.5-13; Luke 7.1-10)

⁴³⁻⁴⁴Jesus had said, "Prophets are honored everywhere, except in their own country." Then two days later he left ⁴⁵and went to Galilee. The people there welcomed him, because they had gone to the festival in Jerusalem and had seen everything he had done.

⁴⁶While Jesus was in Galilee, he returned to the village of Cana, where he had turned the water into wine. There was an official in Capernaum whose son was sick. ⁴⁷And when the man heard that Jesus had come from Judea, he went and begged him to keep his son from dying.

⁴⁸Jesus told the official, "You won't have faith unless you see miracles and wonders!"

⁴⁹The man replied, "Lord, please come before my son dies!"

⁵⁰Jesus then said, "Your son will live. Go on home to him." The man believed Jesus and started back home.

⁵¹Some of the official's servants met him along the road and told him, "Your son is better!" ⁵²He asked them when the boy got better, and they answered, "The fever left him yesterday at one o'clock."

⁵³The boy's father realized that at one o'clock the day before, Jesus had told him, "Your son will live!" So the man and everyone in his family put their faith in Jesus.

⁵⁴This was the second miracle*q* that Jesus worked after he left Judea and went to Galilee.

Jesus Heals a Sick Man

5 Later, Jesus went to Jerusalem for another Jewish festival.*r* ²In the city near the sheep gate was a pool with five porches, and its name in Hebrew was Bethzatha.*s*

³⁻⁴Many sick, blind, lame, and crippled people were lying close to the pool.*t*

⁵Beside the pool was a man who had been sick for thirty-eight years. ⁶When Jesus saw the man and realized that he had been crippled for a long time, he asked him, "Do you want to be healed?"

⁷The man answered, "Lord, I don't have anyone to put me in the pool when the water is stirred up. I try to get in, but someone else always gets there first."

⁸Jesus told him, "Pick up your mat

---

*q*4.54 *miracle*: See the note at 2.11.   *r*5.1 *another Jewish festival*: Either the Festival of Shelters or Passover.   *s*5.2 *Bethzatha*: Some manuscripts have "Bethesda" and others have "Bethsaida."   *t*5.3,4 *pool*: Some manuscripts add, "They were waiting for the water to be stirred, because an angel from the Lord would sometimes come down and stir it. The first person to get into the pool after that would be healed."

and walk!" ⁹Right then the man was healed. He picked up his mat and started walking around. The day on which this happened was a Sabbath.

¹⁰When the Jewish leaders saw the man carrying his mat, they said to him, "This is the Sabbath! No one is allowed to carry a mat on the Sabbath."

¹¹But he replied, "The man who healed me told me to pick up my mat and walk."

¹²They asked him, "Who is this man that told you to pick up your mat and walk?" ¹³But he did not know who Jesus was, and Jesus had left because of the crowd.

¹⁴Later, Jesus met the man in the temple and told him, "You are now well. But don't sin anymore or something worse might happen to you." ¹⁵The man left and told the leaders that Jesus was the one who had healed him. ¹⁶They started making a lot of trouble for Jesus because he did things like this on the Sabbath.

¹⁷But Jesus said, "My Father has never stopped working, and that is why I keep on working." ¹⁸Now the leaders wanted to kill Jesus for two reasons. First, he had broken the law of the Sabbath. But even worse, he had said that God was his Father, which made him equal with God.

The Son's Authority

¹⁹Jesus told the people:

I tell you for certain that the Son cannot do anything on his own. He can do only what he sees the Father doing, and he does exactly what he sees the Father do. ²⁰The Father loves the Son and has shown him everything he does. The Father will show him even greater things, and you will be amazed. ²¹Just as the Father raises the dead and gives life, so the Son gives life to anyone he wants to.

²²The Father doesn't judge anyone, but he has made his Son the judge of everyone. ²³The Father wants all people to honor the Son as much as they honor him. When anyone refuses to honor the Son, that is the same as refusing to honor the Father who sent him. ²⁴I tell you for certain that everyone who hears my message and has faith in the one who sent me has eternal life and will never be condemned. They have already gone from death to life.

²⁵I tell you for certain that the time will come, and it is already here, when all of the dead will hear the voice of the Son of God. And those who listen to it will live! ²⁶The Father has the power to give life,

and he has given that same power to the Son. ²⁷And he has given his Son the right to judge everyone, because he is the Son of Man.

²⁸Don't be surprised! The time will come when all of the dead will hear the voice of the Son of Man, ²⁹and they will come out of their graves. Everyone who has done good things will rise to life, but everyone who has done evil things will rise and be condemned.

³⁰I cannot do anything on my own. The Father sent me, and he is the one who told me how to judge. I judge with fairness, because I obey him, and I don't just try to please myself.

Witnesses to Jesus

³¹If I speak for myself, there is no way to prove I am telling the truth. ³²But there is someone else who speaks for me, and I know what he says is true. ³³You sent messengers to John, and he told them the truth. ³⁴I don't depend on what people say about me, but I tell you these things so that you may be saved. ³⁵John was a lamp that gave a lot of light, and you were glad to enjoy his light for a while.

³⁶But something more important than John speaks for me. I mean the things that the Father has given me to do! All of these speak for me and prove that the Father sent me.

³⁷The Father who sent me also speaks for me, but you have never heard his voice or seen him face to face. ³⁸You have not believed his message, because you refused to have faith in the one he sent.

³⁹You search the Scriptures, because you think you will find eternal life in them. The Scriptures tell about me, ⁴⁰but you refuse to come to me for eternal life.

⁴¹I don't care about human praise, ⁴²but I do know that none of you love God. ⁴³I have come with my Father's authority, and you have not welcomed me. But you will welcome people who come on their own. ⁴⁴How could you possibly believe? You like to have your friends praise you, and you don't care about praise that the only God can give!

⁴⁵Don't think that I will be the one to accuse you to the Father. You have put your hope in Moses, yet he is the very one who will accuse you. ⁴⁶Moses wrote about me, and if you had believed Moses, you would have believed me. ⁴⁷But if you don't believe what Moses wrote, how can you believe what I say?

Feeding Five Thousand
(Matthew 14.13-21; Mark 6.30-44;
Luke 9.10-17)

6 Jesus crossed Lake Galilee, which was also known as Lake Tiberias. [2]A large crowd had seen him work miracles to heal the sick, and those people went with him. [3-4]It was almost time for the Jewish festival of Passover, and Jesus went up on a mountain with his disciples and sat down.[u]

[5]When Jesus saw the large crowd coming toward him, he asked Philip, "Where will we get enough food to feed all these people?" [6]He said this to test Philip, since he already knew what he was going to do.

[7]Philip answered, "Don't you know that it would take almost a year's wages[v] just to buy only a little bread for each of these people?"

[8]Andrew, the brother of Simon Peter, was one of the disciples. He spoke up and said, [9]"There is a boy here who has five small loaves[w] of barley bread and two fish. But what good is that with all these people?"

[10]The ground was covered with grass, and Jesus told his disciples to have everyone sit down. About five thousand men were in the crowd. [11]Jesus took the bread in his hands and gave thanks to God. Then he passed the bread to the people, and he did the same with the fish, until everyone had plenty to eat.

[12]The people ate all they wanted, and Jesus told his disciples to gather up the leftovers, so that nothing would be wasted. [13]The disciples gathered them up and filled twelve large baskets with what was left over from the five barley loaves.

[14]After the people had seen Jesus work this miracle,[x] they began saying, "This must be the Prophet[y] who is to come into the world!" [15]Jesus realized that they would try to force him to be their king. So he went up on a mountain, where he could be alone.

Jesus Walks on the Water
(Matthew 14.22-27; Mark 6.45-52)

[16]That evening, Jesus' disciples went down to the lake. [17]They got into a boat and started across for Capernaum. Later that evening Jesus had still not come to them, [18]and a strong wind was making the water rough.

[19]When the disciples had rowed for three or four miles, they saw Jesus walking on the water. He kept coming closer to the boat, and they were terrified. [20]But he said, "I am Jesus![z] Don't be afraid!" [21]The disciples wanted to take him into the boat, but suddenly the boat reached the shore where they were headed.

The Bread That Gives Life

[22]The people who had stayed on the east side of the lake knew that only one boat had been there. They also knew that Jesus had not left in it with his disciples. But the next day [23]some boats from Tiberias sailed near the place where the crowd had eaten the bread for which the Lord had given thanks. [24]They saw that Jesus and his disciples had left. Then they got into the boats and went to Capernaum to look for Jesus. [25]They found him on the west side of the lake and asked, "Rabbi, when did you get here?"

[26]Jesus answered, "I tell you for certain that you are not looking for me because you saw the miracles,[a] but because you ate all the food you wanted. [27]Don't work for food that spoils. Work for food that gives eternal life. The Son of Man will give you this food, because God the Father has given him the right to do so."

[28]"What exactly does God want us to do?" the people asked.

[29]Jesus answered, "God wants you to have faith in the one he sent."

[30]They replied, "What miracle will you work, so that we can have faith in you? What will you do? [31]For example, when our ancestors were in the desert, they were given manna[b] to eat. It happened just as the Scriptures say, 'God gave them bread from heaven to eat.'"

[32]Jesus then told them, "I tell you for certain that Moses wasn't the one who gave you bread from heaven. My Father is the one who gives you the true bread from heaven. [33]And the bread that God gives is the one who came down from heaven to give life to the world."

[34]The people said, "Lord, give us this bread and don't ever stop!"

[35]Jesus replied:

I am the bread that gives life! No one who comes to me will ever be hungry. No one who has faith in me

[u]**6.3,4** *sat down*: Possibly to teach. Teachers in the ancient world, including Jewish teachers, usually sat down to teach. [v]**6.7** *almost a year's wages*: The Greek text has "two hundred silver coins." Each coin was worth the average day's wages for a worker. [w]**6.9** *small loaves*: These would have been flat and round or in the shape of a bun. [x]**6.14** *miracle*: See the note at 2.11. [y]**6.14** *the Prophet*: See the note at 1.21. [z]**6.20** *I am Jesus*: The Greek text has "I am" (see the note at 8.24). [a]**6.26** *miracles*: The Greek text has "signs" here and "sign" in verse 30 (see the note at 2.11). [b]**6.31** *manna*: When the people of Israel were wandering through the desert, the Lord gave them a special kind of food to eat. It tasted like a wafer and was called "manna," which in Hebrew means, "What is this?"

will ever be thirsty. [36]I have told you already that you have seen me and still do not have faith in me. [37]Everything and everyone that the Father has given me will come to me, and I won't turn any of them away.

[38]I didn't come from heaven to do what I want! I came to do what the Father wants me to do. He sent me, [39]and he wants to make certain that none of the ones he has given me will be lost. Instead, he wants me to raise them to life on the last day.[c] [40]My Father wants everyone who sees the Son to have faith in him and to have eternal life. Then I will raise them to life on the last day.

[41]The people started grumbling because Jesus had said he was the bread that had come down from heaven. [42]They were asking each other, "Isn't he Jesus, the son of Joseph? Don't we know his father and mother? How can he say that he has come down from heaven?"

[43]Jesus told them:

Stop grumbling! [44]No one can come to me, unless the Father who sent me makes them want to come. But if they do come, I will raise them to life on the last day. [45]One of the prophets wrote, "God will teach all of them." And so everyone who listens to the Father and learns from him will come to me.

[46]The only one who has seen the Father is the one who has come from him. No one else has ever seen the Father. [47]I tell you for certain that everyone who has faith in me has eternal life.

[48]I am the bread that gives life! [49]Your ancestors ate manna[d] in the desert, and later they died. [50]But the bread from heaven has come down, so that no one who eats it will ever die. [51]I am that bread from heaven! Everyone who eats it will live forever. My flesh is the life-giving bread that I give to the people of this world.

[52]They started arguing with each other and asked, "How can he give us his flesh to eat?"

[53]Jesus answered:

I tell you for certain that you won't live unless you eat the flesh and drink the blood of the Son of Man. [54]But if you do eat my flesh and drink my blood, you will have eternal life, and I will raise you to life on the last day. [55]My flesh is the true food, and my blood is the true drink.

[56]If you eat my flesh and drink my blood, you are one with me, and I am one with you.

[57]The living Father sent me, and I have life because of him. Now everyone who eats my flesh will live because of me. [58]The bread that comes down from heaven isn't like what your ancestors ate. They died, but whoever eats this bread will live forever.

[59]Jesus was teaching in a Jewish place of worship in Capernaum when he said these things.

The Words of Eternal Life

[60]Many of Jesus' disciples heard him and said, "This is too hard for anyone to understand."

[61]Jesus knew that his disciples were grumbling. So he asked, "Does this bother you? [62]What if you should see the Son of Man go up to heaven where he came from? [63]The Spirit is the one who gives life! Human strength can do nothing. The words that I have spoken to you are from that life-giving Spirit. [64]But some of you refuse to have faith in me." Jesus said this, because from the beginning he knew who would have faith in him. He also knew which one would betray him.

[65]Then Jesus said, "You cannot come to me, unless the Father makes you want to come. That is why I have told these things to all of you."

[66]Because of what Jesus said, many of his disciples turned their backs on him and stopped following him. [67]Jesus then asked his twelve disciples if they were going to leave him. [68]Simon Peter answered, "Lord, there is no one else that we can go to! Your words give eternal life. [69]We have faith in you, and we are sure that you are God's Holy One."

[70]Jesus told his disciples, "I chose all twelve of you, but one of you is a demon!" [71]Jesus was talking about Judas, the son of Simon Iscariot.[e] He would later betray Jesus, even though he was one of the twelve disciples.

Jesus' Brothers Don't Have Faith in Him

7 Jesus decided to leave Judea and to start going through Galilee because the Jewish leaders wanted to kill him. [2]It was almost time for the Festival of Shelters, [3]and Jesus' brothers said to him, "Why don't you go to Judea? Then your disciples can see what you are doing. [4]No one does anything in secret, if they want others to know about them. So let the world know what you are

---

[c]**6.39** *the last day*: When God will judge all people.   [d]**6.49** *manna*: See the note at 6.31.
[e]**6.71** *Iscariot*: This may mean "a man from Kerioth" (a place in Judea). But more probably it means "a man who was a liar" or "a man who was a betrayer."

doing!" [5]Even Jesus' own brothers had not yet become his followers.

[6]Jesus answered, "My time hasn't yet come,*f* but your time is always here. [7]The people of this world cannot hate you. They hate me, because I tell them that they do evil things. [8]Go on to the festival. My time hasn't yet come, and I am not going." [9]Jesus said this and stayed on in Galilee.

Jesus at the Festival of Shelters

[10]After Jesus' brothers had gone to the festival, he went secretly, without telling anyone. [11]During the festival the Jewish leaders looked for Jesus and asked, "Where is he?" [12]The crowds even got into an argument about him. Some were saying, "Jesus is a good man," while others were saying, "He is lying to everyone." [13]But the people were afraid of their leaders, and none of them talked in public about him.

[14]When the festival was about half over, Jesus went into the temple and started teaching. [15]The leaders were surprised and said, "How does this man know so much? He has never been taught!"

[16]Jesus replied:

I am not teaching something that I thought up. What I teach comes from the one who sent me. [17]If you really want to obey God, you will know if what I teach comes from God or from me. [18]If I wanted to bring honor to myself, I would speak for myself. But I want to honor the one who sent me. That is why I tell the truth and not a lie. [19]Didn't Moses give you the Law? Yet none of you obey it! So why do you want to kill me?

[20]The crowd replied, "You're crazy! What makes you think someone wants to kill you?"

[21]Jesus answered:

I worked one miracle,*g* and it amazed you. [22]Moses commanded you to circumcise your sons. But it wasn't really Moses who gave you this command. It was your ancestors, and even on the Sabbath you circumcise your sons [23]in order to obey the Law of Moses. Why are you angry with me for making someone completely well on the Sabbath? [24]Don't judge by appearances. Judge by what is right.

[25]Some of the people from Jerusalem were saying, "Isn't this the man they want to kill? [26]Yet here he is, speaking for everyone to hear. And no one is arguing with him. Do you suppose the authorities know that he is the Messiah? [27]But how could that be? No one knows where the Messiah will come from, but we know where this man comes from."

[28]As Jesus was teaching in the temple, he shouted, "Do you really think you know me and where I came from? I didn't come on my own! The one who sent me is truthful, and you don't know him. [29]But I know the one who sent me, because I came from him."

[30]Some of the people wanted to arrest Jesus right then. But no one even laid a hand on him, because his time had not yet come.*h* [31]A lot of people in the crowd put their faith in him and said, "When the Messiah comes, he surely won't perform more miracles*i* than this man has done!"

Officers Sent To Arrest Jesus

[32]When the Pharisees heard the crowd arguing about Jesus, they got together with the chief priests and sent some temple police to arrest him. [33]But Jesus told them, "I will be with you a little while longer, and then I will return to the one who sent me. [34]You will look for me, but you won't find me. You cannot go where I am going."

[35]The Jewish leaders asked each other, "Where can he go to keep us from finding him? Is he going to some foreign country where our people live? Is he going there to teach the Greeks?*j* [36]What did he mean by saying that we will look for him, but won't find him? Why can't we go where he is going?"

Streams of Life-Giving Water

[37]On the last and most important day of the festival, Jesus stood up and shouted, "If you are thirsty, come to me and drink! [38]Have faith in me, and you will have life-giving water flowing from deep inside you, just as the Scriptures say." [39]Jesus was talking about the Holy Spirit, who would be given to everyone that had faith in him. The Spirit had not yet been given to anyone, since Jesus had not yet been given his full glory.*k*

The People Take Sides

[40]When the crowd heard Jesus say this, some of them said, "He must be the Prophet!"*l* [41]Others said, "He is the Messiah!" Others even said, "Can the Mes-

*f*7.6 *My time hasn't yet come*: See the note at 2.4. lame man (5.1-18; see also the note at 2.11). at 2.4. *i*7.31 *miracles*: See the note at 2.11. followed Greek customs. *k*7.39 *had not yet been given his full glory*: In the Gospel of John, Jesus is given his full glory both when he is nailed to the cross and when he is raised from death to sit beside his Father in heaven. *g*7.21 *one miracle*: The healing of the *h*7.30 *his time had not yet come*: See the note *j*7.35 *Greeks*: Perhaps Gentiles or Jews who *l*7.40 *the Prophet*: See the note at 1.21.

siah come from Galilee? [42]The Scriptures say that the Messiah will come from the family of King David. Doesn't this mean that he will be born in David's hometown of Bethlehem?" [43]The people started taking sides against each other because of Jesus. [44]Some of them wanted to arrest him, but no one laid a hand on him.

The Leaders Refuse To Have Faith in Jesus

[45]When the temple police returned to the chief priests and Pharisees, they were asked, "Why didn't you bring Jesus here?"

[46]They answered, "No one has ever spoken like that man!"

[47]The Pharisees said to them, "Have you also been fooled? [48]Not one of the chief priests or the Pharisees has faith in him. [49]And these people who don't know the Law are under God's curse anyway."

[50]Nicodemus was there at the time. He was a member of the council, and was the same one who had earlier come to see Jesus.[m] He said, [51]"Our Law doesn't let us condemn people before we hear what they have to say. We cannot judge them before we know what they have done."

[52]Then they said, "Nicodemus, you must be from Galilee! Read the Scriptures, and you will find that no prophet is to come from Galilee."

A Woman Caught in Sin

8 [53]Everyone else went home, [1]but Jesus walked out to the Mount of Olives. [2]Then early the next morning he went to the temple. The people came to him, and he sat down[n] and started teaching them.

[3]The Pharisees and the teachers of the Law of Moses brought in a woman who had been caught in bed with a man who wasn't her husband. They made her stand in the middle of the crowd. [4]Then they said, "Teacher, this woman was caught sleeping with a man who isn't her husband. [5]The Law of Moses teaches that a woman like this should be stoned to death! What do you say?"

[6]They asked Jesus this question, because they wanted to test him and bring some charge against him. But Jesus simply bent over and started writing on the ground with his finger.

[7]They kept on asking Jesus about the woman. Finally, he stood up and said, "If any of you have never sinned, then go ahead and throw the first stone at her!" [8]Once again he bent over and began writing on the ground. [9]The people left one by one, beginning with the oldest. Finally, Jesus and the woman were there alone.

[10]Jesus stood up and asked her, "Where is everyone? Isn't there anyone left to accuse you?"

[11]"No sir," the woman answered.

Then Jesus told her, "I am not going to accuse you either. You may go now, but don't sin anymore."[o]

Jesus Is the Light for the World

[12]Once again Jesus spoke to the people. This time he said, "I am the light for the world! Follow me, and you won't be walking in the dark. You will have the light that gives life."

[13]The Pharisees objected, "You are the only one speaking for yourself, and what you say isn't true!"

[14]Jesus replied:

Even if I do speak for myself, what I say is true! I know where I came from and where I am going. But you don't know where I am from or where I am going. [15]You judge in the same way that everyone else does, but I don't judge anyone. [16]If I did judge, I would judge fairly, because I would not be doing it alone. The Father who sent me is here with me. [17]Your Law requires two witnesses to prove that something is true. [18]I am one of my witnesses, and the Father who sent me is the other one.

[19]"Where is your Father?" they asked.

"You don't know me or my Father!" Jesus answered. "If you knew me, you would know my Father."

[20]Jesus said this while he was still teaching in the place where the temple treasures were stored. But no one arrested him, because his time had not yet come.[p]

You Cannot Go Where I Am Going

[21]Jesus also told them, "I am going away, and you will look for me. But you cannot go where I am going, and you will die with your sins unforgiven."

[22]The Jewish leaders asked, "Does he intend to kill himself? Is that what he means by saying we cannot go where he is going?"

[23]Jesus answered, "You are from below, but I am from above. You belong to this world, but I don't. [24]That is why I said you will die with your sins unforgiven. If you don't have faith in me for

---

[m]**7.50** *who had earlier come to see Jesus*: See 3.1-21. [n]**8.2** *sat down*: See the note at 6.3, 4.
[o]**8.11** *don't sin anymore*: Verses 1-11 are not in some manuscripts. In other manuscripts these verses are placed after 7.36 or after 21.25 or after Luke 21.38, with some differences in the text.
[p]**8.20** *his time had not yet come*: See the note at 2.4.

who I am,*q* you will die, and your sins will not be forgiven."

25"Who are you?" they asked Jesus.

Jesus answered, "I am exactly who I told you at the beginning. 26There is a lot more I could say to condemn you. But the one who sent me is truthful, and I tell the people of this world only what I have heard from him."

27No one understood that Jesus was talking to them about the Father.

28Jesus went on to say, "When you have lifted up the Son of Man,*r* you will know who I am. You will also know that I don't do anything on my own. I say only what my Father taught me. 29The one who sent me is with me. I always do what pleases him, and he will never leave me."

30After Jesus said this, many of the people put their faith in him.

The Truth Will Set You Free

31Jesus told the people who had faith in him, "If you keep on obeying what I have said, you truly are my disciples. 32You will know the truth, and the truth will set you free."

33They answered, "We are Abraham's children! We have never been anyone's slaves. How can you say we will be set free?"

34Jesus replied:

I tell you for certain that anyone who sins is a slave of sin! 35And slaves don't stay in the family forever, though the Son will always remain in the family. 36If the Son gives you freedom, you are free! 37I know that you are from Abraham's family. Yet you want to kill me, because my message isn't really in your hearts. 38I am telling you what my Father has shown me, just as you are doing what your father has taught you.

Your Father Is the Devil

39The people said to Jesus, "Abraham is our father!"

Jesus replied, "If you were Abraham's children, you would do what Abraham did. 40Instead, you want to kill me for telling you the truth that God gave me. Abraham never did anything like that. 41But you are doing exactly what your father does."

"Don't accuse us of having someone else as our father!" they said. "We just have one father, and he is God."

42Jesus answered:

If God were your Father, you would love me, because I came from God and only from him. He sent me.

I did not come on my own. 43Why can't you understand what I am talking about? Can't you stand to hear what I am saying? 44Your father is the devil, and you do exactly what he wants. He has always been a murderer and a liar. There is nothing truthful about him. He speaks on his own, and everything he says is a lie. Not only is he a liar himself, but he is also the father of all lies.

45Everything I have told you is true, and you still refuse to have faith in me. 46Can any of you accuse me of sin? If you cannot, why won't you have faith in me? After all, I am telling you the truth. 47Anyone who belongs to God will listen to his message. But you refuse to listen, because you don't belong to God.

Jesus and Abraham

48The people told Jesus, "We were right to say that you are a Samaritan*s* and that you have a demon in you!"

49Jesus answered, "I don't have a demon in me. I honor my Father, and you refuse to honor me. 50I don't want honor for myself. But there is one who wants me to be honored, and he is also the one who judges. 51I tell you for certain that if you obey my words, you will never die."

52Then the people said, "Now we are sure that you have a demon. Abraham is dead, and so are the prophets. How can you say that no one who obeys your words will ever die? 53Are you greater than our father Abraham? He died, and so did the prophets. Who do you think you are?"

54Jesus replied, "If I honored myself, it would mean nothing. My Father is the one who honors me. You claim that he is your God, 55even though you don't really know him. If I said I didn't know him, I would be a liar, just like all of you. But I know him, and I do what he says. 56Your father Abraham was really glad to see me."

57"You are not even fifty years old!" they said. "How could you have seen Abraham?"

58Jesus answered, "I tell you for certain that even before Abraham was, I was, and I am."*t* 59The people picked up stones to kill Jesus, but he hid and left the temple.

Jesus Heals a Man Born Blind

9 As Jesus walked along, he saw a man who had been blind since birth. 2Jesus' disciples asked, "Teacher, why

---

*q*8.24 *I am:* For the Jewish people the most holy name of God is "Yahweh," which may be translated "I am." In the Gospel of John "I am" is sometimes used by Jesus to show that he is that one. *r*8.28 *lifted up the Son of Man:* See the note at 7.39. *s*8.48 *Samaritan:* See 4.9 and the note there. *t*8.58 *I am:* See the note at 8.24.

was this man born blind? Was it because he or his parents sinned?"

³"No, it wasn't!" Jesus answered. "But because of his blindness, you will see God work a miracle for him. ⁴As long as it is day, we must do what the one who sent me wants me to do. When night comes, no one can work. ⁵While I am in the world, I am the light for the world."

⁶After Jesus said this, he spit on the ground. He made some mud and smeared it on the man's eyes. ⁷Then he said, "Go and wash off the mud in Siloam Pool." The man went and washed in Siloam, which means "One Who Is Sent." When he had washed off the mud, he could see.

⁸The man's neighbors and the people who had seen him begging wondered if he really could be the same man. ⁹Some of them said he was the same beggar, while others said he only looked like him. But he told them, "I am that man."

¹⁰"Then how can you see?" they asked.

¹¹He answered, "Someone named Jesus made some mud and smeared it on my eyes. He told me to go and wash it off in Siloam Pool. When I did, I could see."

¹²"Where is he now?" they asked.

"I don't know," he answered.

The Pharisees Try To Find Out What Happened

¹³⁻¹⁴The day when Jesus made the mud and healed the man was a Sabbath. So the people took the man to the Pharisees. ¹⁵They asked him how he was able to see, and he answered, "Jesus made some mud and smeared it on my eyes. Then after I washed it off, I could see."

¹⁶Some of the Pharisees said, "This man Jesus doesn't come from God. If he did, he would not break the law of the Sabbath."

Others asked, "How could someone who is a sinner work such a miracle?"ᵘ

Since the Pharisees could not agree among themselves, ¹⁷they asked the man, "What do you say about this one who healed your eyes?"

"He is a prophet!" the man told them.

¹⁸But the Jewish leaders would not believe that the man had once been blind. They sent for his parents ¹⁹and asked them, "Is this the son that you said was born blind? How can he now see?"

²⁰The man's parents answered, "We are certain that he is our son, and we know that he was born blind. ²¹But we don't know how he got his sight or who gave it to him. Ask him! He is old enough to speak for himself."

²²⁻²³The man's parents said this because they were afraid of the Jewish leaders. The leaders had already agreed that no one was to have anything to do with anyone who said Jesus was the Messiah.

²⁴The leaders called the man back and said, "Swear by God to tell the truth! We know that Jesus is a sinner."

²⁵The man replied, "I don't know if he is a sinner or not. All I know is that I used to be blind, but now I can see!"

²⁶"What did he do to you?" the Jewish leaders asked. "How did he heal your eyes?"

²⁷The man answered, "I have already told you once, and you refused to listen. Why do you want me to tell you again? Do you also want to become his disciples?"

²⁸The leaders insulted the man and said, "You are his follower! We are followers of Moses. ²⁹We are sure that God spoke to Moses, but we don't even know where Jesus comes from."

³⁰"How strange!" the man replied. "He healed my eyes, and yet you don't know where he comes from. ³¹We know that God listens only to people who love and obey him. God doesn't listen to sinners. ³²And this is the first time in history that anyone has ever given sight to someone born blind. ³³Jesus could not do anything unless he came from God."

³⁴The leaders told the man, "You have been a sinner since the day you were born! Do you think you can teach us anything?" Then they said, "You can never come back into any of our meeting places!"

³⁵When Jesus heard what had happened, he went and found the man. Then Jesus asked, "Do you have faith in the Son of Man?"

³⁶He replied, "Sir, if you will tell me who he is, I will put my faith in him."

³⁷"You have already seen him," Jesus answered, "and right now he is talking with you."

³⁸The man said, "Lord, I put my faith in you!" Then he worshiped Jesus.

³⁹Jesus told him, "I came to judge the people of this world. I am here to give sight to the blind and to make blind everyone who can see."

⁴⁰When the Pharisees heard Jesus say this, they asked, "Are we blind?"

⁴¹Jesus answered, "If you were blind, you would not be guilty. But now that you claim to see, you will keep on being guilty."

A Story about Sheep

10 Jesus said:
I tell you for certain that only thieves and robbers climb over the fence instead of going in through the gate to the sheep pen. ²⁻³But the gatekeeper opens the gate for the

---

ᵘ**9.16** *miracle:* See the note at 2.11.

shepherd, and he goes in through it. The sheep know their shepherd's voice. He calls each of them by name and leads them out.

⁴When he has led out all of his sheep, he walks in front of them, and they follow, because they know his voice. ⁵The sheep will not follow strangers. They don't recognize a stranger's voice, and they run away. ⁶Jesus told the people this story. But they did not understand what he was talking about.

Jesus Is the Good Shepherd

⁷Jesus said:

I tell you for certain that I am the gate for the sheep. ⁸Everyone who came before me was a thief or a robber, and the sheep did not listen to any of them. ⁹I am the gate. All who come in through me will be saved. Through me they will come and go and find pasture.

¹⁰A thief comes only to rob, kill, and destroy. I came so that everyone would have life, and have it in its fullest. ¹¹I am the good shepherd, and the good shepherd gives up his life for his sheep. ¹²Hired workers are not like the shepherd. They don't own the sheep, and when they see a wolf coming, they run off and leave the sheep. Then the wolf attacks and scatters the flock. ¹³Hired workers run away because they don't care about the sheep.

¹⁴I am the good shepherd. I know my sheep, and they know me. ¹⁵Just as the Father knows me, I know the Father, and I give up my life for my sheep. ¹⁶I have other sheep that are not in this sheep pen. I must bring them together too, when they hear my voice. Then there will be one flock of sheep and one shepherd.

¹⁷The Father loves me, because I give up my life, so that I may receive it back again. ¹⁸No one takes my life from me. I give it up willingly! I have the power to give it up and the power to receive it back again, just as my Father commanded me to do.

¹⁹The people took sides because of what Jesus had told them. ²⁰Many of them said, "He has a demon in him! He is crazy! Why listen to him?"

²¹But others said, "How could anyone with a demon in him say these things? No one like that could give sight to a blind person!"

Jesus Is Rejected

²²That winter, Jesus was in Jerusalem for the Temple Festival. ²³One day he was walking in that part of the temple known as Solomon's Porch,ᵛ ²⁴and the people gathered all around him. They said, "How long are you going to keep us guessing? If you are the Messiah, tell us plainly!"

²⁵Jesus answered:

I have told you, and you refused to believe me. The things I do by my Father's authority show who I am. ²⁶But since you are not my sheep, you don't believe me. ²⁷My sheep know my voice, and I know them. They follow me, ²⁸and I give them eternal life, so that they will never be lost. No one can snatch them out of my hand. ²⁹My Father gave them to me, and he is greater than all others.ʷ No one can snatch them from his hands, ³⁰and I am one with the Father.

³¹Once again the people picked up stones in order to kill Jesus. ³²But he said, "I have shown you many good things that my Father sent me to do. Which one are you going to stone me for?"

³³They answered, "We are not stoning you because of any good thing you did. We are stoning you because you did a terrible thing. You are just a man, and here you are claiming to be God!"

³⁴Jesus replied:

In your Scriptures doesn't God say, "You are gods"? ³⁵You can't argue with the Scriptures, and God spoke to those people and called them gods. ³⁶So why do you accuse me of a terrible sin for saying that I am the Son of God? After all, it is the Father who prepared me for this work. He is also the one who sent me into the world. ³⁷If I don't do as my Father does, you should not believe me. ³⁸But if I do what my Father does, you should believe because of that, even if you don't have faith in me. Then you will know for certain that the Father is one with me, and I am one with the Father.

³⁹Again they wanted to arrest Jesus. But he escaped ⁴⁰and crossed the Jordan to the place where John had earlier been baptizing. While Jesus was there, ⁴¹many people came to him. They were saying, "John didn't work any miracles, but everything he said about Jesus is true." ⁴²A lot of those people also put their faith in Jesus.

The Death of Lazarus

11 ¹⁻²A man by the name of Lazarus was sick in the village of Bethany. He had two sisters, Mary and Martha. This was the same Mary who later

---

ᵛ **10.23** *Solomon's Porch*: A public place with tall columns along the east side of the temple.
ʷ **10.29** *he is greater than all others*: Some manuscripts have "they are greater than all others."

poured perfume on the Lord's head and wiped his feet with her hair. ³The sisters sent a message to the Lord and told him that his good friend Lazarus was sick.

⁴When Jesus heard this, he said, "His sickness won't end in death. It will bring glory to God and his Son."

⁵Jesus loved Martha and her sister and brother. ⁶But he stayed where he was for two more days. ⁷Then he said to his disciples, "Now we will go back to Judea."

⁸"Teacher," they said, "the people there want to stone you to death! Why do you want to go back?"

⁹Jesus answered, "Aren't there twelve hours in each day? If you walk during the day, you will have light from the sun, and you won't stumble. ¹⁰But if you walk during the night, you will stumble, because you don't have any light."

¹¹Then he told them, "Our friend Lazarus is asleep, and I am going there to wake him up."

¹²They replied, "Lord, if he is asleep, he will get better." ¹³Jesus really meant that Lazarus was dead, but they thought he was talking only about sleep.

¹⁴Then Jesus told them plainly, "Lazarus is dead! ¹⁵I am glad that I wasn't there, because now you will have a chance to put your faith in me. Let's go to him."

¹⁶Thomas, whose nickname was "Twin," said to the other disciples, "Come on. Let's go, so we can die with him."

Jesus Brings Lazarus to Life

¹⁷When Jesus got to Bethany, he found that Lazarus had already been in the tomb four days. ¹⁸Bethany was only about two miles from Jerusalem, ¹⁹and many people had come from the city to comfort Martha and Mary because their brother had died.

²⁰When Martha heard that Jesus had arrived, she went out to meet him, but Mary stayed in the house. ²¹Martha said to Jesus, "Lord, if you had been here, my brother would not have died. ²²Yet even now I know that God will do anything you ask."

²³Jesus told her, "Your brother will live again!"

²⁴Martha answered, "I know that he will be raised to life on the last day,ˣ when all the dead are raised."

²⁵Jesus then said, "I am the one who raises the dead to life! Everyone who has faith in me will live, even if they die. ²⁶And everyone who lives because of faith in me will never really die. Do you believe this?"

²⁷"Yes, Lord!" she replied. "I believe that you are Christ, the Son of God. You are the one we hoped would come into the world."

²⁸After Martha said this, she went and privately said to her sister Mary, "The Teacher is here, and he wants to see you." ²⁹As soon as Mary heard this, she got up and went out to Jesus. ³⁰He was still outside the village where Martha had gone to meet him. ³¹Many people had come to comfort Mary, and when they saw her quickly leave the house, they thought she was going out to the tomb to cry. So they followed her.

³²Mary went to where Jesus was. Then as soon as she saw him, she knelt at his feet and said, "Lord, if you had been here, my brother would not have died."

³³When Jesus saw that Mary and the people with her were crying, he was terribly upset ³⁴and asked, "Where have you put his body?"

They replied, "Lord, come and you will see."

³⁵Jesus started crying, ³⁶and the people said, "See how much he loved Lazarus."

³⁷Some of them said, "He gives sight to the blind. Why couldn't he have kept Lazarus from dying?"

³⁸Jesus was still terribly upset. So he went to the tomb, which was a cave with a stone rolled against the entrance. ³⁹Then he told the people to roll the stone away. But Martha said, "Lord, you know that Lazarus has been dead four days, and there will be a bad smell."

⁴⁰Jesus replied, "Didn't I tell you that if you had faith, you would see the glory of God?"

⁴¹After the stone had been rolled aside, Jesus looked up toward heaven and prayed, "Father, I thank you for answering my prayer. ⁴²I know that you always answer my prayers. But I said this, so that the people here would believe that you sent me."

⁴³When Jesus had finished praying, he shouted, "Lazarus, come out!" ⁴⁴The man who had been dead came out. His hands and feet were wrapped with strips of burial cloth, and a cloth covered his face.

Jesus then told the people, "Untie him and let him go."

The Plot To Kill Jesus
(Matthew 26.1-5; Mark 14.1, 2; Luke 22.1, 2)

⁴⁵Many of the people who had come to visit Mary saw the things that Jesus did, and they put their faith in him. ⁴⁶Others went to the Pharisees and told what Jesus had done. ⁴⁷Then the chief priests and the Pharisees called the council together and said, "What should we do? This man is working a lot of miracles.ʸ ⁴⁸If we don't stop him now,

---

ˣ**11.24** *the last day*: When God will judge all people.   ʸ**11.47** *miracles*: See the note at 2.11.

everyone will put their faith in him. Then the Romans will come and destroy our temple and our nation."[z]

[49]One of the council members was Caiaphas, who was also high priest that year. He spoke up and said, "You people don't have any sense at all! [50]Don't you know it is better for one person to die for the people than for the whole nation to be destroyed?" [51]Caiaphas did not say this on his own. As high priest that year, he was prophesying that Jesus would die for the nation. [52]Yet Jesus would not die just for the Jewish nation. He would die to bring together all of God's scattered people. [53]From that day on, the council started making plans to put Jesus to death.

[54]Because of this plot against him, Jesus stopped going around in public. He went to the town of Ephraim, which was near the desert, and he stayed there with his disciples.

[55]It was almost time for Passover. Many of the Jewish people who lived out in the country had come to Jerusalem to get themselves ready[a] for the festival. [56]They looked around for Jesus. Then when they were in the temple, they asked each other, "You don't think he will come here for Passover, do you?" [57]The chief priests and the Pharisees told the people to let them know if any of them saw Jesus. That is how they hoped to arrest him.

At Bethany
(Matthew 26.6-13; Mark 14.3-9)

12 Six days before Passover Jesus went back to Bethany, where he had raised Lazarus from death. [2]A meal had been prepared for Jesus. Martha was doing the serving, and Lazarus himself was there.

[3]Mary took a very expensive bottle of perfume[b] and poured it on Jesus' feet. She wiped them with her hair, and the sweet smell of the perfume filled the house.

[4]A disciple named Judas Iscariot[c] was there. He was the one who was going to betray Jesus, and he asked, [5]"Why wasn't this perfume sold for three hundred silver coins and the money given to the poor?" [6]Judas did not really care about the poor. He asked this because

he carried the moneybag and sometimes would steal from it. [7]Jesus replied, "Leave her alone! She has kept this perfume for the day of my burial. [8]You will always have the poor with you, but you won't always have me."

A Plot To Kill Lazarus

[9]A lot of people came when they heard that Jesus was there. They also wanted to see Lazarus, because Jesus had raised him from death. [10]So the chief priests made plans to kill Lazarus. [11]He was the reason that many of the Jewish people were turning from them and putting their faith in Jesus.

Jesus Enters Jerusalem
(Matthew 21.1-11; Mark 11.1-11; Luke 19.28-40)

[12]The next day a large crowd was in Jerusalem for Passover. When they heard that Jesus was coming for the festival, [13]they took palm branches and went out to greet him.[d] They shouted,

"Hooray![e]
God bless the one who comes
    in the name of the Lord!
God bless the King
    of Israel!"

[14]Jesus found a donkey and rode on it, just as the Scriptures say,

[15] "People of Jerusalem,
    don't be afraid!
Your King is now coming,
and he is riding
    on a donkey."

[16]At first, Jesus' disciples did not understand. But after he had been given his glory,[f] they remembered all this. Everything had happened exactly as the Scriptures said it would.

[17-18]A crowd had come to meet Jesus because they had seen him call Lazarus out of the tomb. They kept talking about him and this miracle.[g] [19]But the Pharisees said to each other, "There is nothing that can be done! Everyone in the world is following Jesus."

Some Greeks Want To Meet Jesus

[20]Some Greeks[h] had gone to Jerusalem to worship during Passover.

[z]11.48 *destroy our temple and our nation*: The Jewish leaders were afraid that Jesus would lead his followers to rebel against Rome and that the Roman army would then destroy their nation.   [a]11.55 *get themselves ready*: The Jewish people had to do certain things to prepare themselves to worship God.   [b]12.3 *very expensive bottle of perfume*: The Greek text has "expensive perfume made of pure spikenard," a plant used to make perfume.
[c]12.4 *Iscariot*: See the note at 6.71.   [d]12.13 *took palm branches and went out to greet him*: This was one way that the Jewish people welcomed a famous person.   [e]12.13 *Hooray*: This translates a word that can mean "please save us." But it is most often used as a shout of praise to God.   [f]12.16 *had been given his glory*: See the note at 7.39.   [g]12.17,18 *miracle*: See the note at 2.11.   [h]12.20 *Greeks*: Perhaps Gentiles who worshiped with the Jews. See the note at 7.35.

[21]Philip from Bethsaida in Galilee was there too. So they went to him and said, "Sir, we would like to meet Jesus." [22]Philip told Andrew. Then the two of them went to Jesus and told him.

The Son of Man Must Be Lifted Up

[23]Jesus said:

The time has come for the Son of Man to be given his glory.[i] [24]I tell you for certain that a grain of wheat that falls on the ground will never be more than one grain unless it dies. But if it dies, it will produce lots of wheat. [25]If you love your life, you will lose it. If you give it up in this world, you will be given eternal life. [26]If you serve me, you must go with me. My servants will be with me wherever I am. If you serve me, my Father will honor you.

[27]Now I am deeply troubled, and I don't know what to say. But I must not ask my Father to keep me from this time of suffering. In fact, I came into the world to suffer. [28]So Father, bring glory to yourself.

A voice from heaven then said, "I have already brought glory to myself, and I will do it again!" [29]When the crowd heard the voice, some of them thought it was thunder. Others thought an angel had spoken to Jesus.

[30]Then Jesus told the crowd, "That voice spoke to help you, not me. [31]This world's people are now being judged, and the ruler of this world[j] is already being thrown out! [32]If I am lifted up above the earth, I will make everyone want to come to me." [33]Jesus was talking about the way he would be put to death.

[34]The crowd said to Jesus, "The Scriptures teach that the Messiah will live forever. How can you say that the Son of Man must be lifted up? Who is this Son of Man?"

[35]Jesus answered, "The light will be with you for only a little longer. Walk in the light while you can. Then you won't be caught walking blindly in the dark. [36]Have faith in the light while it is with you, and you will be children of the light."

The People Refuse To Have Faith in Jesus

After Jesus had said these things, he left and went into hiding. [37]He had worked a lot of miracles[k] among the people, but they were still not willing to have faith in him. [38]This happened so that what the prophet Isaiah had said would come true,

"Lord, who has believed
     our message?
And who has seen
     your mighty strength?"

[39]The people could not have faith in Jesus, because Isaiah had also said,

[40] "The Lord has blinded
     the eyes of the people,
and he has made
     the people stubborn.
He did this so that they
could not see
     or understand,
and so that they
would not turn to the Lord
     and be healed."

[41]Isaiah said this, because he saw the glory of Jesus and spoke about him.[l] [42]Even then, many of the leaders put their faith in Jesus, but they did not tell anyone about it. The Pharisees had already given orders for the people not to have anything to do with anyone who had faith in Jesus. [43]And besides, the leaders liked praise from others more than they liked praise from God.

Jesus Came To Save the World

[44]In a loud voice Jesus said:

Everyone who has faith in me also has faith in the one who sent me. [45]And everyone who has seen me has seen the one who sent me. [46]I am the light that has come into the world. No one who has faith in me will stay in the dark.

[47]I am not the one who will judge those who refuse to obey my teachings. I came to save the people of this world, not to be their judge. [48]But everyone who rejects me and my teachings will be judged on the last day[m] by what I have said. [49]I don't speak on my own. I say only what the Father who sent me has told me to say. [50]I know that his commands will bring eternal life. That is why I tell you exactly what the Father has told me.

Jesus Washes the Feet of His Disciples

13 It was before Passover, and Jesus knew that the time had come for him to leave this world and to return to the Father. He had always loved his followers in this world, and he loved them to the very end.

[i]**12.23** *be given his glory*: See the note at 7.39. [j]**12.31** *world*: In the Gospel of John "world" sometimes refers to the people who live in this world and to the evil forces that control their lives. [k]**12.37** *miracles*: See the note at 2.11. [l]**12.41** *he saw the glory of Jesus and spoke about him*: Or "he saw the glory of God and spoke about Jesus." [m]**12.48** *the last day*: See the note at 6.39.

[2]Even before the evening meal started, the devil had made Judas, the son of Simon Iscariot,[n] decide to betray Jesus.

[3]Jesus knew that he had come from God and would go back to God. He also knew that the Father had given him complete power. [4]So during the meal Jesus got up, removed his outer garment, and wrapped a towel around his waist. [5]He put some water into a large bowl. Then he began washing his disciples' feet and drying them with the towel he was wearing.

[6]But when he came to Simon Peter, that disciple asked, "Lord, are you going to wash my feet?"

[7]Jesus answered, "You don't really know what I am doing, but later you will understand."

[8]"You will never wash my feet!" Peter replied.

"If I don't wash you," Jesus told him, "you don't really belong to me."

[9]Peter said, "Lord, don't wash just my feet. Wash my hands and my head."

[10]Jesus answered, "People who have bathed and are clean all over need to wash just their feet. And you, my disciples, are clean, except for one of you." [11]Jesus knew who would betray him. That is why he said, "except for one of you."

[12]After Jesus had washed his disciples' feet and had put his outer garment back on, he sat down again.[o] Then he said:

Do you understand what I have done? [13]You call me your teacher and Lord, and you should, because that is who I am. [14]And if your Lord and teacher has washed your feet, you should do the same for each other. [15]I have set the example, and you should do for each other exactly what I have done for you. [16]I tell you for certain that servants are not greater than their master, and messengers are not greater than the one who sent them. [17]You know these things, and God will bless you, if you do them.

[18]I am not talking about all of you. I know the ones I have chosen. But what the Scriptures say must come true. And they say, "The man who ate with me has turned against me!" [19]I am telling you this before it all happens. Then when it does happen, you will believe who I am.[p] [20]I tell you for certain that anyone who welcomes my messengers also welcomes me, and anyone who welcomes me welcomes the one who sent me.

Jesus Tells What Will Happen to Him

(Matthew 26.20-25; Mark 14.17-21; Luke 22.21-23)

[21]After Jesus had said these things, he was deeply troubled and told his disciples, "I tell you for certain that one of you will betray me." [22]They were confused about what he meant. And they just stared at each other.

[23]Jesus' favorite disciple was sitting next to him at the meal, [24]and Simon motioned for that disciple to find out which one Jesus meant. [25]So the disciple leaned toward Jesus and asked, "Lord, which one of us are you talking about?"

[26]Jesus answered, "I will dip this piece of bread in the sauce and give it to the one I was talking about."

Then Jesus dipped the bread and gave it to Judas, the son of Simon Iscariot.[q] [27]Right then Satan took control of Judas.

Jesus said, "Judas, go quickly and do what you have to do." [28]No one at the meal understood what Jesus meant. [29]But because Judas was in charge of the money, some of them thought that Jesus had told him to buy something they needed for the festival. Others thought that Jesus had told him to give some money to the poor. [30]Judas took the piece of bread and went out.

It was already night.

The New Command

[31]After Judas had gone, Jesus said:

Now the Son of Man will be given glory, and he will bring glory to God. [32]Then, after God is given glory because of him, God will bring glory to him, and God will do it very soon.

[33]My children, I will be with you for a little while longer. Then you will look for me, but you won't find me. I tell you just as I told the people, "You cannot go where I am going." [34]But I am giving you a new command. You must love each other, just as I have loved you. [35]If you love each other, everyone will know that you are my disciples.

Peter's Promise

(Matthew 26.31-35; Mark 14.27-31; Luke 22.31-34)

[36]Simon Peter asked, "Lord, where are you going?"

Jesus answered, "You can't go with me now, but later on you will."

[n]**13.2** *Iscariot*: See the note at 6.71. [o]**13.12** *sat down again*: On special occasions the Jewish people followed the Greek and Roman custom of lying down on their left side and leaning on their left elbow, while eating with their right hand. [p]**13.19** *I am*: See the note at 8.24. [q]**13.26** *Iscariot*: See the note at 6.71.

³⁷Peter asked, "Lord, why can't I go with you now? I would die for you!"

³⁸"Would you really die for me?" Jesus asked. "I tell you for certain that before a rooster crows, you will say three times that you don't even know me."

Jesus Is the Way to the Father

14 Jesus said to his disciples, "Don't be worried! Have faith in God and have faith in me.ʳ ²There are many rooms in my Father's house. I wouldn't tell you this, unless it was true. I am going there to prepare a place for each of you. ³After I have done this, I will come back and take you with me. Then we will be together. ⁴You know the way to where I am going."

⁵Thomas said, "Lord, we don't even know where you are going! How can we know the way?"

⁶"I am the way, the truth, and the life!" Jesus answered. "Without me, no one can go to the Father. ⁷If you had known me, you would have known the Father. But from now on, you do know him, and you have seen him."

⁸Philip said, "Lord, show us the Father. That is all we need."

⁹Jesus replied:

Philip, I have been with you for a long time. Don't you know who I am? If you have seen me, you have seen the Father. How can you ask me to show you the Father? ¹⁰Don't you believe that I am one with the Father and that the Father is one with me? What I say isn't said on my own. The Father who lives in me does these things.

¹¹Have faith in me when I say that the Father is one with me and that I am one with the Father. Or else have faith in me simply because of the things I do. ¹²I tell you for certain that if you have faith in me, you will do the same things that I am doing. You will do even greater things, now that I am going back to the Father. ¹³Ask me, and I will do whatever you ask. This way the Son will bring honor to the Father. ¹⁴I will do whatever you ask me to do.

The Holy Spirit Is Promised

¹⁵Jesus said to his disciples:

If you love me, you will do as I command. ¹⁶Then I will ask the Father to send you the Holy Spirit who will helpˢ you and always be with you. ¹⁷The Spirit will show you what is true. The people of this world cannot accept the Spirit, because they don't see or know him. But you know the Spirit, who is with you and will keep on living in you.

¹⁸I won't leave you like orphans. I will come back to you. ¹⁹In a little while the people of this world won't be able to see me, but you will see me. And because I live, you will live. ²⁰Then you will know that I am one with the Father. You will know that you are one with me, and I am one with you. ²¹If you love me, you will do what I have said, and my Father will love you. I will also love you and show you what I am like.

²²The other Judas, not Judas Iscariot,ᵗ then spoke up and asked, "Lord, what do you mean by saying that you will show us what you are like, but you will not show the people of this world?"

²³Jesus replied:

If anyone loves me, they will obey me. Then my Father will love them, and we will come to them and live in them. ²⁴But anyone who doesn't love me, won't obey me. What they have heard me say doesn't really come from me, but from the Father who sent me.

²⁵I have told you these things while I am still with you. ²⁶But the Holy Spirit will come and helpᵘ you, because the Father will send the Spirit to take my place. The Spirit will teach you everything and will remind you of what I said while I was with you.

²⁷I give you peace, the kind of peace that only I can give. It isn't like the peace that this world can give. So don't be worried or afraid.

²⁸You have already heard me say that I am going and that I will also come back to you. If you really love me, you should be glad that I am going back to the Father, because he is greater than I am.

²⁹I am telling you this before I leave, so that when it does happen, you will have faith in me. ³⁰I cannot speak with you much longer, because the ruler of this world is coming. But he has no power over me. ³¹I obey my Father, so that everyone in the world might know that I love him.

It is time for us to go now.

Jesus Is the True Vine

15 Jesus said to his disciples:
I am the true vine, and my Father is the gardener. ²He cuts away every branch of mine that

---

ʳ**14.1** *Have faith in God and have faith in me:* Or "You have faith in God, so have faith in me."
ˢ**14.16** *help:* The Greek word may mean "comfort," "encourage," or "defend."
ᵗ**14.22** *Iscariot:* See the note at 6.71. ᵘ**14.26** *help:* See the note at 14.16.

doesn't produce fruit. But he trims clean every branch that does produce fruit, so that it will produce even more fruit. ³You are already clean because of what I have said to you. *προελων. προνισας*

⁴Stay joined to me, and I will stay joined to you. Just as a branch cannot produce fruit unless it stays joined to the vine, you cannot produce fruit unless you stay joined to me. ⁵I am the vine, and you are the branches. If you stay joined to me, and I stay joined to you, then you will produce lots of fruit. But you cannot do anything without me. ⁶If you don't stay joined to me, you will be thrown away. You will be like dry branches that are gathered up and burned in a fire.

⁷Stay joined to me and let my teachings become part of you. Then you can pray for whatever you want, and your prayer will be answered. ⁸When you become fruitful disciples of mine, my Father will be honored. ⁹I have loved you, just as my Father has loved me. So remain faithful to my love for you. ¹⁰If you obey me, I will keep loving you, just as my Father keeps loving me, because I have obeyed him.

¹¹I have told you this to make you as completely happy as I am. ¹²Now I tell you to love each other, as I have loved you. ¹³The greatest way to show love for friends is to die for them. ¹⁴And you are my friends, if you obey me. ¹⁵Servants don't know what their master is doing, and so I don't speak to you as my servants. I speak to you as my friends, and I have told you everything that my Father has told me.

¹⁶You did not choose me. I chose you and sent you out to produce fruit, the kind of fruit that will last. Then my Father will give you whatever you ask for in my name.ᵛ ¹⁷So I command you to love each other.

The World's Hatred

¹⁸If the people of this worldʷ hate you, just remember that they hated me first. ¹⁹If you belonged to the world, its people would love you. But you don't belong to the world. I have chosen you to leave the world behind, and that is why its people hate you. ²⁰Remember how I told you that servants are not greater than their master. So if people mistreat me, they will mistreat you. If they do what I say, they will do what you say.

²¹People will do to you exactly what they did to me. They will do it because you belong to me, and they don't know the one who sent me. ²²If I had not come and spoken to them, they would not be guilty of sin. But now they have no excuse for their sin.

²³Everyone who hates me also hates my Father. ²⁴I have done things that no one else has ever done. If they had not seen me do these things, they would not be guilty. But they did see me do these things, and they still hate me and my Father too. ²⁵That is why the Scriptures are true when they say, "People hated me for no reason."

²⁶I will send you the Spirit who comes from the Father and shows what is true. The Spirit will helpˣ you and will tell you about me. ²⁷Then you will also tell others about me, because you have been with me from the beginning.

16 I am telling you this to keep you from being afraid. ²You will be chased out of the Jewish meeting places. And the time will come when people will kill you and think they are doing God a favor. ³They will do these things because they don't know either the Father or me. ⁴I am saying this to you now, so that when the time comes, you will remember what I have said.

The Work of the Holy Spirit

I was with you at the first, and so I didn't tell you these things. ⁵But now I am going back to the Father who sent me, and none of you asks me where I am going. ⁶You are very sad from hearing all of this. ⁷But I tell you that I am going to do what is best for you. That is why I am going away. The Holy Spirit cannot come to helpˣ you until I leave. But after I am gone, I will send the Spirit to you.

⁸The Spirit will come and show the people of this world the truth about sin and God's justice and the judgment. ⁹The Spirit will show them that they are wrong about sin, because they didn't have faith in me. ¹⁰They are wrong about God's justice, because I am going to the Father, and you won't see me again. ¹¹And they are wrong about the judgment, because God has already judged the ruler of this world.

¹²I have much more to say to you,

---

but right now it would be more than you could understand. [13]The Spirit shows what is true and will come and guide you into the full truth. The Spirit doesn't speak on his own. He will tell you only what he has heard from me, and he will let you know what is going to happen. [14]The Spirit will bring glory to me by taking my message and telling it to you. [15]Everything that the Father has is mine. That is why I have said that the Spirit takes my message and tells it to you.

Sorrow Will Turn into Joy

[16]Jesus told his disciples, "For a little while you won't see me, but after a while you will see me."

[17]They said to each other, "What does Jesus mean by saying that for a little while we won't see him, but after a while we will see him? What does he mean by saying that he is going to the Father? [18]What is this 'little while' that he is talking about? We don't know what he means."

[19]Jesus knew that they had some questions, so he said:

You are wondering what I meant when I said that for a little while you won't see me, but after a while you will see me. [20]I tell you for certain that you will cry and be sad, but the world will be happy. You will be sad, but later you will be happy.

[21]When a woman is about to give birth, she is in great pain. But after it is all over, she forgets the pain and is happy, because she has brought a child into the world. [22]You are now very sad. But later I will see you, and you will be so happy that no one will be able to change the way you feel. [23]When that time comes, you won't have to ask me about anything. I tell you for certain that the Father will give you whatever you ask for in my name. [24]You have not asked for anything in this way before, but now you must ask in my name.[y] Then it will be given to you, so that you will be completely happy.

[25]I have used examples to explain to you what I have been talking about. But the time will come when I will speak to you plainly about the Father and will no longer use examples like these. [26]You will ask the Father in my name,[z] and I won't have to ask him for you. [27]God the Father loves you because you love

me, and you believe that I have come from him. [28]I came from the Father into the world, but I am leaving the world and returning to the Father.

[29]The disciples said, "Now you are speaking plainly to us! You are not using examples. [30]At last we know that you understand everything, and we don't have any more questions. Now we believe that you truly have come from God."

[31]Jesus replied:

Do you really believe me? [32]The time will come and is already here when all of you will be scattered. Each of you will go back home and leave me by myself. But the Father will be with me, and I won't be alone. [33]I have told you this, so that you might have peace in your hearts because of me. While you are in the world, you will have to suffer. But cheer up! I have defeated the world.[a]

Jesus Prays

17 After Jesus had finished speaking to his disciples, he looked up toward heaven and prayed:

Father, the time has come for you to bring glory to your Son, in order that he may bring glory to you. [2]And you gave him power over all people, so that he would give eternal life to everyone you give him. [3]Eternal life is to know you, the only true God, and to know Jesus Christ, the one you sent. [4]I have brought glory to you here on earth by doing everything you gave me to do. [5]Now, Father, give me back the glory that I had with you before the world was created.

[6]You have given me some followers from this world, and I have shown them what you are like. They were yours, but you gave them to me, and they have obeyed you. [7]They know that you gave me everything I have. [8]I told my followers what you told me, and they accepted it. They know that I came from you, and they believe that you are the one who sent me. [9]I am praying for them, but not for those who belong to this world.[a] My followers belong to you, and I am praying for them. [10]All that I have is yours, and all that you have is mine, and they will bring glory to me.

[11]Holy Father, I am no longer in the world. I am coming to you, but my followers are still in the world.

So keep them safe by the power of the name that you have given me. Then they will be one with each other, just as you and I are one. [12]While I was with them, I kept them safe by the power you have given me. I guarded them, and not one of them was lost, except the one who had to be lost. This happened so that what the Scriptures say would come true.

[13]I am on my way to you. But I say these things while I am still in the world, so that my followers will have the same complete joy that I do. [14]I have told them your message. But the people of this world hate them, because they don't belong to this world, just as I don't.

[15]Father, I don't ask you to take my followers out of the world, but keep them safe from the evil one. [16]They don't belong to this world, and neither do I. [17]Your word is the truth. So let this truth make them completely yours. [18]I am sending them into the world, just as you sent me. [19]I have given myself completely for their sake, so that they may belong completely to the truth.

[20]I am not praying just for these followers. I am also praying for everyone else who will have faith because of what my followers will say about me. [21]I want all of them to be one with each other, just as I am one with you and you are one with me. I also want them to be one with us. Then the people of this world will believe that you sent me.

[22]I have honored my followers in the same way that you honored me, in order that they may be one with each other, just as we are one. [23]I am one with them, and you are one with me, so that they may become completely one. Then this world's people will know that you sent me. They will know that you love my followers as much as you love me.

[24]Father, I want everyone you have given me to be with me, wherever I am. Then they will see the glory that you have given me, because you loved me before the world was created. [25]Good Father, the people of this world don't know you. But I know you, and my followers know that you sent me. [26]I told them what you are like, and I will tell them even more. Then the love that you have for me will become part of them, and I will be one with them.

Jesus Is Betrayed and Arrested
(Matthew 26.47-56; Mark 14.43-50; Luke 22.47-53)

18 When Jesus had finished praying, he and his disciples crossed the Kidron Valley and went into a garden.[b] [2]Jesus had often met there with his disciples, and Judas knew where the place was.

[3-5]Judas had promised to betray Jesus. So he went to the garden with some Roman soldiers and temple police, who had been sent by the chief priests and the Pharisees. They carried torches, lanterns, and weapons. Jesus already knew everything that was going to happen, but he asked, "Who are you looking for?"

They answered, "We are looking for Jesus from Nazareth!"

Jesus told them, "I am Jesus!"[c] [6]At once they all backed away and fell to the ground.

[7]Jesus again asked, "Who are you looking for?"

"We are looking for Jesus from Nazareth," they answered.

[8]This time Jesus replied, "I have already told you that I am Jesus. If I am the one you are looking for, let these others go. [9]Then everything will happen, just as I said, 'I did not lose anyone you gave me.' "

[10]Simon Peter had brought along a sword. He now pulled it out and struck at the servant of the high priest. The servant's name was Malchus, and Peter cut off his right ear. [11]Jesus told Peter, "Put your sword away. I must drink from the cup[d] that the Father has given me."

Jesus Is Brought to Annas
(Matthew 26.57, 58; Mark 14.53, 54; Luke 22.54)

[12]The Roman officer and his men, together with the temple police, arrested Jesus and tied him up. [13]They took him first to Annas, who was the father-in-law of Caiaphas, the high priest that year. [14]This was the same Caiaphas who had told the Jewish leaders, "It is better if one person dies for the people."

Peter Says He Doesn't Know Jesus
(Matthew 26.69, 70; Mark 14.66-68; Luke 22.55-57)

[15]Simon Peter and another disciple followed Jesus. That disciple knew the high priest, and he followed Jesus into the courtyard of the high priest's house. [16]Peter stayed outside near the gate. But the other disciple came back out and

---

[b]**18.1** *garden*: The Greek word is usually translated "garden," but probably referred to an olive orchard.   [c]**18.3-5** *I am Jesus*: The Greek text has "I am" (see the note at 8.24).
[d]**18.11** *drink from the cup*: In the Scriptures a cup is sometimes used as a symbol of suffering. To "drink from the cup" is to suffer.

spoke to the girl at the gate. She let Peter go in, [17]but asked him, "Aren't you one of that man's followers?"

"No, I am not!" Peter answered.

[18]It was cold, and the servants and temple police had made a charcoal fire. They were warming themselves around it, when Peter went over and stood near the fire to warm himself.

Jesus Is Questioned by the High Priest
(Matthew 26.59-66; Mark 14.55-64; Luke 22.66-71)

[19]The high priest questioned Jesus about his followers and his teaching. [20]But Jesus told him, "I have spoken freely in front of everyone. And I have always taught in our meeting places and in the temple, where all of our people come together. I have not said anything in secret. [21]Why are you questioning me? Why don't you ask the people who heard me? They know what I have said."

[22]As soon as Jesus said this, one of the temple police hit him and said, "That's no way to talk to the high priest!"

[23]Jesus answered, "If I have done something wrong, say so. But if not, why did you hit me?" [24]Jesus was still tied up, and Annas sent him to Caiaphas the high priest.

Peter Again Denies that He Knows Jesus
(Matthew 26.71-75; Mark 14.69-72; Luke 22.58-62)

[25]While Simon Peter was standing there warming himself, someone asked him, "Aren't you one of Jesus' followers?"

Again Peter denied it and said, "No, I am not!"

[26]One of the high priest's servants was there. He was a relative of the servant whose ear Peter had cut off, and he asked, "Didn't I see you in the garden with that man?"

[27]Once more Peter denied it, and right then a rooster crowed.

Jesus Is Tried by Pilate
(Matthew 27.1, 2, 11-14; Mark 15.1-5; Luke 23.1-5)

[28]It was early in the morning when Jesus was taken from Caiaphas to the building where the Roman governor stayed. But the crowd waited outside. Any of them who had gone inside would have become unclean and would not be allowed to eat the Passover meal.[e]

[29]Pilate came out and asked, "What charges are you bringing against this man?"

[30]They answered, "He is a criminal! That's why we brought him to you."

[31]Pilate told them, "Take him and judge him by your own laws."

The crowd replied, "We are not allowed to put anyone to death." [32]And so what Jesus said about his death[f] would soon come true.

[33]Pilate then went back inside. He called Jesus over and asked, "Are you the king of the Jews?"

[34]Jesus answered, "Are you asking this on your own or did someone tell you about me?"

[35]"You know I'm not a Jew!" Pilate said. "Your own people and the chief priests brought you to me. What have you done?"

[36]Jesus answered, "My kingdom doesn't belong to this world. If it did, my followers would have fought to keep me from being handed over to the Jewish leaders. No, my kingdom doesn't belong to this world."

[37]"So you are a king," Pilate replied.

"You are saying that I am a king," Jesus told him. "I was born into this world to tell about the truth. And everyone who belongs to the truth knows my voice."

[38]Pilate asked Jesus, "What is truth?"

Jesus Is Sentenced to Death
(Matthew 27.15-31; Mark 15.6-20; Luke 23.13-25)

Pilate went back out and said, "I don't find this man guilty of anything! [39]And since I usually set a prisoner free for you at Passover, would you like for me to set free the king of the Jews?"

[40]They shouted, "No, not him! We want Barabbas." Now Barabbas was a terrorist.[g]

19 Pilate gave orders for Jesus to be beaten with a whip. [2]The soldiers made a crown out of thorn branches and put it on Jesus. Then they put a purple robe on him. [3]They came up to him and said, "Hey, you king of the Jews!" They also hit him with their fists.

[4]Once again Pilate went out. This time he said, "I will have Jesus brought out to you again. Then you can see for yourselves that I have not found him guilty."

[5]Jesus came out, wearing the crown of thorns and the purple robe. Pilate said, "Here is the man!"[h]

---

[e]**18.28** *would have become unclean and would not be allowed to eat the Passover meal*: Jewish people who came in close contact with foreigners right before Passover were not allowed to eat the Passover meal. [f]**18.32** *about his death*: Jesus had said that he would die by being "lifted up," which meant that he would die on a cross. The Romans killed criminals by nailing them on a cross, but they did not let the Jews kill anyone in this way. [g]**18.40** *terrorist*: Someone who stirred up trouble against the Romans in the hope of gaining freedom for the Jewish people. [h]**19.5** *"Here is the man!"*: Or "Look at the man!"

[6]When the chief priests and the temple police saw him, they yelled, "Nail him to a cross! Nail him to a cross!"

Pilate told them, "You take him and nail him to a cross! I don't find him guilty of anything."

[7]The crowd replied, "He claimed to be the Son of God! Our Jewish Law says that he must be put to death."

[8]When Pilate heard this, he was terrified. [9]He went back inside and asked Jesus, "Where are you from?" But Jesus did not answer.

[10]"Why won't you answer my question?" Pilate asked. "Don't you know that I have the power to let you go free or to nail you to a cross?"

[11]Jesus replied, "If God had not given you the power, you couldn't do anything at all to me. But the one who handed me over to you did something even worse."

[12]Then Pilate wanted to set Jesus free. But the crowd again yelled, "If you set this man free, you are no friend of the Emperor! Anyone who claims to be a king is an enemy of the Emperor."

[13]When Pilate heard this, he brought Jesus out. Then he sat down on the judge's bench at the place known as "The Stone Pavement." In Aramaic this pavement is called "Gabbatha." [14]It was about noon on the day before Passover, and Pilate said to the crowd, "Look at your king!"

[15]"Kill him! Kill him!" they yelled. "Nail him to a cross!"

"So you want me to nail your king to a cross?" Pilate asked.

The chief priests replied, "The Emperor is our king!" [16]Then Pilate handed Jesus over to be nailed to a cross.

Jesus Is Nailed to a Cross
(Matthew 27.32-44; Mark 15.21-32; Luke 23.26-43)

Jesus was taken away, [17]and he carried his cross to a place known as "The Skull."[i] In Aramaic this place is called "Golgotha." [18]There Jesus was nailed to the cross, and on each side of him a man was also nailed to a cross.

[19]Pilate ordered the charge against Jesus to be written on a board and put above the cross. It read, "Jesus of Nazareth, King of the Jews." [20]The words were written in Hebrew, Latin, and Greek.

The place where Jesus was taken wasn't far from the city, and many of the people read the charge against him. [21]So the chief priests went to Pilate and said, "Why did you write that he is King of the Jews? You should have written, 'He claimed to be King of the Jews.' "

[22]But Pilate told them, "What is written will not be changed!"

[23]After the soldiers had nailed Jesus to the cross, they divided up his clothes into four parts, one for each of them. But his outer garment was made from a single piece of cloth, and it did not have any seams. [24]The soldiers said to each other, "Let's not rip it apart. We will gamble to see who gets it." This happened so that the Scriptures would come true, which say,

"They divided up my clothes
and gambled
for my garments."

The soldiers then did what they had decided.

[25]Jesus' mother stood beside his cross with her sister and Mary the wife of Clopas. Mary Magdalene was standing there too.[j] [26]When Jesus saw his mother and his favorite disciple with her, he said to his mother, "This man is now your son." [27]Then he said to the disciple, "She is now your mother." From then on, that disciple took her into his own home.

The Death of Jesus
(Matthew 27.45-56; Mark 15.33-41; Luke 23.44-49)

[28]Jesus knew that he had now finished his work. And in order to make the Scriptures come true, he said, "I am thirsty!" [29]A jar of cheap wine was there. Someone then soaked a sponge with the wine and held it up to Jesus' mouth on the stem of a hyssop plant. [30]After Jesus drank the wine, he said, "Everything is done!" He bowed his head and died.

A Spear Is Stuck in Jesus' Side

[31]The next day would be both a Sabbath and the Passover. It was a special day for the Jewish people,[k] and they did not want the bodies to stay on the crosses during that day. So they asked

---

[i]**19.17** *The Skull*: The place was probably given this name because it was near a large rock in the shape of a human skull.   [j]**19.25** *Jesus' mother stood beside his cross with her sister and Mary the wife of Clopas. Mary Magdalene was standing there too*: The Greek text may also be understood to include only three women ("Jesus' mother stood beside the cross with her sister, Mary the mother of Clopas. Mary Magdalene was standing there too.") or merely two women ("Jesus' mother was standing there with her sister Mary of Clopas, that is, Mary Magdalene."). "Of Clopas" may mean "daughter of" or "mother of."   [k]**19.31** *a special day for the Jewish people*: Passover could be any day of the week. But according to the Gospel of John, Passover was on a Sabbath in the year that Jesus was nailed to a cross.

Pilate to break the men's legs[l] and take their bodies down. [32]The soldiers first broke the legs of the other two men who were nailed there. [33]But when they came to Jesus, they saw that he was already dead, and they did not break his legs.

[34]One of the soldiers stuck his spear into Jesus' side, and blood and water came out. [35]We know this is true, because it was told by someone who saw it happen. Now you can have faith too. [36]All this happened so that the Scriptures would come true, which say, "No bone of his body will be broken" [37]and, "They will see the one in whose side they stuck a spear."

Jesus Is Buried
(Matthew 27.57-61; Mark 15.42-47; Luke 23.50-56)

[38]Joseph from Arimathea was one of Jesus' disciples. He had kept it secret though, because he was afraid of the Jewish leaders. But now he asked Pilate to let him have Jesus' body. Pilate gave him permission, and Joseph took it down from the cross.

[39]Nicodemus also came with about seventy-five pounds of spices made from myrrh and aloes. This was the same Nicodemus who had visited Jesus one night.[m] [40]The two men wrapped the body in a linen cloth, together with the spices, which was how the Jewish people buried their dead. [41]In the place where Jesus had been nailed to a cross, there was a garden with a tomb that had never been used. [42]The tomb was nearby, and since it was the time to prepare for the Sabbath, they were in a hurry to put Jesus' body there.

Jesus Is Alive
(Matthew 28.1-10; Mark 16.1-8; Luke 24.1-12)

20 On Sunday morning while it was still dark, Mary Magdalene went to the tomb and saw that the stone had been rolled away from the entrance. [2]She ran to Simon Peter and to Jesus' favorite disciple and said, "They have taken the Lord from the tomb! We don't know where they have put him."

[3]Peter and the other disciple started for the tomb. [4]They ran side by side, until the other disciple ran faster than Peter and got there first. [5]He bent over and saw the strips of linen cloth lying inside the tomb, but he did not go in.

[6]When Simon Peter got there, he went into the tomb and saw the strips of cloth. [7]He also saw the piece of cloth that had been used to cover Jesus' face. It was rolled up and in a place by itself.

[8]The disciple who got there first then went into the tomb, and when he saw it, he believed. [9]At that time Peter and the other disciple did not know that the Scriptures said Jesus would rise to life. [10]So the two of them went back to the other disciples.

Jesus Appears to Mary Magdalene
(Mark 16.9-11)

[11]Mary Magdalene stood crying outside the tomb. She was still weeping, when she stooped down [12]and saw two angels inside. They were dressed in white and were sitting where Jesus' body had been. One was at the head and the other was at the foot. [13]The angels asked Mary, "Why are you crying?"

She answered, "They have taken away my Lord's body! I don't know where they have put him."

[14]As soon as Mary said this, she turned around and saw Jesus standing there. But she did not know who he was. [15]Jesus asked her, "Why are you crying? Who are you looking for?"

She thought he was the gardener and said, "Sir, if you have taken his body away, please tell me, so I can go and get him."

[16]Then Jesus said to her, "Mary!"

She turned and said to him, "Rabboni." The Aramaic word "Rabboni" means "Teacher."

[17]Jesus told her, "Don't hold on to me! I have not yet gone to the Father. But tell my disciples that I am going to the one who is my Father and my God, as well as your Father and your God." [18]Mary Magdalene then went and told the disciples that she had seen the Lord. She also told them what he had said to her.

Jesus Appears to His Disciples
(Matthew 28.16-20; Mark 16.14-18; Luke 24.36-49)

[19]The disciples were afraid of the Jewish leaders, and on the evening of that same Sunday they locked themselves in a room. Suddenly, Jesus appeared in the middle of the group. He greeted them [20]and showed them his hands and his side. When the disciples saw the Lord, they became very happy.

[21]After Jesus had greeted them again, he said, "I am sending you, just as the Father has sent me." [22]Then he breathed on them and said, "Receive the Holy Spirit. [23]If you forgive anyone's sins, they will be forgiven. But if you don't forgive their sins, they will not be forgiven."

---

[l]**19.31** *break the men's legs*: This was the way that the Romans sometimes speeded up the death of a person who had been nailed to a cross.   [m]**19.39** *Nicodemus who had visited Jesus one night*: See 3.1-21.

Jesus and Thomas

24Although Thomas the Twin was one of the twelve disciples, he wasn't with the others when Jesus appeared to them. 25So they told him, "We have seen the Lord!"

But Thomas said, "First, I must see the nail scars in his hands and touch them with my finger. I must put my hand where the spear went into his side. I won't believe unless I do this!"

26A week later the disciples were together again. This time, Thomas was with them. Jesus came in while the doors were still locked and stood in the middle of the group. He greeted his disciples 27and said to Thomas, "Put your finger here and look at my hands! Put your hand into my side. Stop doubting and have faith!"

28Thomas replied, "You are my Lord and my God!"

29Jesus said, "Thomas, do you have faith because you have seen me? The people who have faith in me without seeing me are the ones who are really blessed!"

Why John Wrote His Book

30Jesus worked many other miracles[n] for his disciples, and not all of them are written in this book. 31But these are written so that you will put your faith in Jesus as the Messiah and the Son of God. If you have faith in[o] him, you will have true life.

Jesus Appears to Seven Disciples

21 Jesus later appeared to his disciples along the shore of Lake Tiberias. 2Simon Peter, Thomas the Twin, Nathanael from Cana in Galilee, and the brothers James and John,[p] were there, together with two other disciples. 3Simon Peter said, "I'm going fishing!"

The others said, "We will go with you." They went out in their boat. But they didn't catch a thing that night.

4Early the next morning Jesus stood on the shore, but the disciples did not realize who he was. 5Jesus shouted, "Friends, have you caught anything?"

"No!" they answered.

6So he told them, "Let your net down on the right side of your boat, and you will catch some fish."

They did, and the net was so full of fish that they could not drag it up into the boat.

7Jesus' favorite disciple told Peter, "It's the Lord!" When Simon heard that it was the Lord, he put on the clothes that he had taken off while he was working. Then he jumped into the water. 8The boat was only about a hundred yards from shore. So the other disciples stayed in the boat and dragged in the net full of fish.

9When the disciples got out of the boat, they saw some bread and a charcoal fire with fish on it. 10Jesus told his disciples, "Bring some of the fish you just caught." 11Simon Peter got back into the boat and dragged the net to shore. In it were one hundred fifty-three large fish, but still the net did not rip.

12Jesus said, "Come and eat!" But none of the disciples dared ask who he was. They knew he was the Lord. 13Jesus took the bread in his hands and gave some of it to his disciples. He did the same with the fish. 14This was the third time that Jesus appeared to his disciples after he was raised from death.

Jesus and Peter

15When Jesus and his disciples had finished eating, he asked, "Simon son of John, do you love me more than the others do?"[q]

Simon Peter answered, "Yes, Lord, you know I do!"

"Then feed my lambs," Jesus said.

16Jesus asked a second time, "Simon son of John, do you love me?"

Peter answered, "Yes, Lord, you know I love you!"

"Then take care of my sheep," Jesus told him.

17Jesus asked a third time, "Simon son of John, do you love me?"

Peter was hurt because Jesus had asked him three times if he loved him. So he told Jesus, "Lord, you know everything. You know I love you."

Jesus replied, "Feed my sheep. 18I tell you for certain that when you were a young man, you dressed yourself and went wherever you wanted to go. But when you are old, you will hold out your hands. Then others will wrap your belt around you and lead you where you don't want to go."

19Jesus said this to tell how Peter would die and bring honor to God. Then he said to Peter, "Follow me!"

Jesus and His Favorite Disciple

20Peter turned and saw Jesus' favorite disciple following them. He was the same one who had sat next to Jesus at the meal and had asked, "Lord, who is going to betray you?" 21When Peter saw that disciple, he asked Jesus, "Lord, what about him?"

[n]20.30 miracles: See the note at 2.11. [o]20.31 put your faith in . . . have faith in: Some manuscripts have "keep on having faith in . . . keep on having faith in." [p]21.2 the brothers James and John: Greek "the two sons of Zebedee." [q]21.15 more than the others do?: Or "more than you love these things?"

[22]Jesus answered, "What is it to you, if I want him to live until I return? You must follow me." [23]So the rumor spread among the other disciples that this disciple would not die. But Jesus did not say he would not die. He simply said, "What is it to you, if I want him to live until I return?"

[24]This disciple is the one who told all of this. He wrote it, and we know he is telling the truth.

[25]Jesus did many other things. If they were all written in books, I don't suppose there would be room enough in the whole world for all the books.

ACTS

ABOUT THIS BOOK

This is the second book written by Luke. His first one is commonly known as the Gospel of Luke. In it he told "all that Jesus did and taught from the very first until he was taken up to heaven" (1.1, 2). In this book Luke continues the story by describing some of the struggles the disciples faced as they tried to obey the command of Jesus: "You will tell everyone about me in Jerusalem, in all Judea, in Samaria, and everywhere in the world" (1.8).

So many different countries are mentioned in Acts that the book may seem to have been written only to tell about the spread of the Christian message. But that is only part of the story. After Jesus was taken up to heaven, one of the big problems for his followers was deciding who could belong to God's people. And since Jesus and his first followers were Jews, it was only natural for many of them to think that his message was only for Jews. But in Acts, the Spirit is always present to show that Jesus came to save both Jews and Gentiles, and that God wants followers from every nation and race to be part of his people.

The first conflict between Christians and Jews took place when some of the Jewish religious leaders rejected the message about Jesus (4.1-31; 7.1-59). But the most serious problems for the early church happened because the disciples at first failed to understand that anyone could become a follower of Jesus without first becoming a Jew. This began to change when Philip dared to take the message to the Samaritans (8.7-25), and when Peter went to the home of Cornelius, a captain in the Roman army (10.1-48).

Finally, Peter reported to the church in Jerusalem (11.1-18) and a meeting was held there (15.3-35) to discuss the question of who could become followers of Christ. Before the meeting was over, everyone agreed that the Spirit of God was leading them to reach out to Gentiles as well as Jews with the good news of Jesus.

The one who did the most for the spread of the faith was a man named Paul, and much of the book tells about his preaching among the Gentiles. Finally, he took the message to Rome, the world's most important city at that time (28.16-31). One of Luke's main reasons for writing was to show that nothing could keep the Christian message from spreading everywhere:

For two years Paul stayed in a rented house and welcomed everyone who came to see him. He bravely preached about God's kingdom and taught about the Lord Jesus Christ, and no one tried to stop him. (28.30, 31)

A QUICK LOOK AT THIS BOOK

1 Theophilus, I first wrote to you[a] about all that Jesus did and <u>taught</u> from the very first [2]until he was taken up to heaven. But before he was taken up, he gave orders to the apostles he had chosen with the help of the Holy Spirit.

[3]For forty days after Jesus had suffered and died, he proved in many ways that he had been raised from death. He appeared to his apostles and spoke to them about God's kingdom. [4]While he was still with them, he said:

Don't leave Jerusalem yet. Wait here for the Father to give you the Holy Spirit, just as I told you he has promised to do. [5]John baptized with water, but in a few days you will be baptized with the Holy Spirit.

Jesus Is Taken to Heaven

[6]While the apostles were still with Jesus, they asked him, "Lord, are you now going to give Israel its own king again?"[b]

[7]Jesus said to them, "You don't need to know the time of those events that only the Father controls. [8]But the Holy Spirit will come upon you and give you power. Then you will tell everyone about me in Jerusalem, in all Judea, in Samaria, and everywhere in the world." [9]After Jesus had said this and while they were watching, he was taken up into a cloud. They could not see him, [10]but as he went up, they kept looking up into the sky.

Suddenly two men dressed in white clothes were standing there beside them. [11]They said, "Why are you men from Galilee standing here and looking up into the sky? Jesus has been taken to heaven. But he will come back in the same way that you have seen him go."

Someone To Take the Place of Judas

[12-13]The Mount of Olives was about half a mile from Jerusalem. The apostles who had gone there were Peter, John, James, Andrew, Philip, Thomas, Bartholomew, Matthew, James the son of Alphaeus, Simon, known as the Eager One,[c] and Judas the son of James.

After the apostles returned to the city, they went upstairs to the room where they had been staying.

[14]The apostles often met together and prayed with a single purpose in mind.[d] The women and Mary the mother of Je-

sus would meet with them, and so would his brothers. [15]One day there were about one hundred twenty of the Lord's followers meeting together, and Peter stood up to speak to them. [16-17]He said:

My friends, long ago by the power of the Holy Spirit, David said something about Judas, and what he said has now happened. Judas was one of us and had worked with us, but he brought the mob to arrest Jesus. [18]Then Judas bought some land with the money he <u>was</u> given for doing that evil thing. He fell headfirst into the field. His body burst open, and all his insides came out. [19]When the people of Jerusalem found out about this, they called the place Akeldama, which in the local language means "Field of Blood."

[20]In the book of Psalms it says,

"Leave his house empty,
and don't let anyone
    live there."

It also says,

"Let someone else
    have his job."

[21-22]So we need someone else to help us tell others that Jesus has been raised from death. He must also be one of the men who was with us from the very beginning. He must have been with us from the time the Lord Jesus was baptized by John until the day he was taken to heaven.

[23]Two men were suggested: One of them was Joseph Barsabbas, known as Justus, and the other was Matthias. [24]Then they all prayed, "Lord, you know what everyone is like! Show us the one you have chosen [25]to be an apostle and to serve in place of Judas, who got what he deserved." [26]They drew names, and Matthias was chosen to join the group of the eleven apostles.

The Coming of the Holy Spirit

2 On the day of Pentecost[e] all the Lord's followers were together in one place. [2]Suddenly there was a noise from heaven like the sound of a mighty wind! It filled the house where they were meeting. [3]Then they saw what looked like fiery tongues moving in all directions, and a tongue came and settled on each person there. [4]The Holy

---

[a]**1.1** *I first wrote to you*: The Gospel of Luke.   [b]**1.6** *are you now going to give Israel its own king again?*: Or "Are you now going to rule Israel as its king?"   [c]**1.12,13** *known as the Eager One*: The Greek text has "Zealot," a name later given to the members of a Jewish group that resisted and fought against the Romans.   [d]**1.14** *met together and prayed with a single purpose in mind*: Or "met together in a special place for prayer."   [e]**2.1** *Pentecost*: A Jewish festival that came fifty days after Passover and celebrated the wheat harvest. Jews later celebrated Pentecost as the time when they were given the Law of Moses.

Spirit took control of everyone, and they began speaking whatever languages the Spirit let them speak.

⁵Many religious Jews from every country in the world were living in Jerusalem. ⁶And when they heard this noise, a crowd gathered. But they were surprised, because they were hearing everything in their own languages. ⁷They were excited and amazed, and said:

Don't all these who are speaking come from Galilee? ⁸Then why do we hear them speaking our very own languages? ⁹Some of us are from Parthia, Media, and Elam. Others are from Mesopotamia, Judea, Cappadocia, Pontus, Asia, ¹⁰Phrygia, Pamphylia, Egypt, parts of Libya near Cyrene, Rome, ¹¹Crete, and Arabia. Some of us were born Jews, and others of us have chosen to be Jews. Yet we all hear them using our own languages to tell the wonderful things God has done.

¹²Everyone was excited and confused. Some of them even kept asking each other, "What does all this mean?"

¹³Others made fun of the Lord's followers and said, "They are drunk."

Peter Speaks to the Crowd

¹⁴Peter stood with the eleven apostles and spoke in a loud and clear voice to the crowd:

Friends and everyone else living in Jerusalem, listen carefully to what I have to say! ¹⁵You are wrong to think that these people are drunk. After all, it is only nine o'clock in the morning. ¹⁶But this is what God had the prophet Joel say,

¹⁷ "When the last days come,
   I will give my Spirit
      to everyone.
   Your sons and daughters
      will prophesy.
   Your young men
      will see visions,
   and your old men
      will have dreams.
¹⁸ In those days I will give
      my Spirit to my servants,
   both men and women,
      and they will prophesy.

¹⁹ I will work miracles
      in the sky above
   and wonders
      on the earth below.
   There will be blood and fire
      and clouds of smoke.
²⁰ The sun will turn dark,
   and the moon
      will be as red as blood

before the great
   and wonderful day
      of the Lord appears.
²¹ Then the Lord
   will save everyone
      who asks for his help."

²²Now, listen to what I have to say about Jesus from Nazareth. God proved that he sent Jesus to you by having him work miracles, wonders, and signs. All of you know this. ²³God had already planned and decided that Jesus would be handed over to you. So you took him and had evil men put him to death on a cross. ²⁴But God set him free from death and raised him to life. Death could not hold him in its power. ²⁵What David said are really the words of Jesus,

"I always see the Lord
      near me,
   and I will not be afraid
      with him at my right side.
²⁶ Because of this,
      my heart will be glad,
   my words will be joyful,
      and I will live in hope.
²⁷ The Lord won't leave me
      in the grave.
   I am his holy one,
   and he won't let
      my body decay.
²⁸ He has shown me
      the path to life,
   and he makes me glad
      by being near me."

²⁹My friends, it is right for me to speak to you about our ancestor David. He died and was buried, and his tomb is still here. ³⁰But David was a prophet, and he knew that God had made a promise he would not break. He had told David that someone from his own family would someday be king.

³¹David knew this would happen, and so he told us that Christ would be raised to life. He said that God would not leave him in the grave or let his body decay. ³²All of us can tell you that God has raised Jesus to life!

³³Jesus was taken up to sit at the right side^f of God, and he was given the Holy Spirit, just as the Father had promised. Jesus is also the one who has given the Spirit to us, and that is what you are now seeing and hearing.

³⁴David didn't go up to heaven. So he wasn't talking about himself when he said, "The Lord told my Lord to sit at his right side, ³⁵until he made my Lord's enemies into a foot-

---

ᶠ**2.33** *right side*: The place of honor and power.

stool for him." 36Everyone in Israel should then know for certain that God has made Jesus both Lord and Christ, even though you put him to death on a cross.

37When the people heard this, they were very upset. They asked Peter and the other apostles, "Friends, what shall we do?"

38Peter said, "Turn back to God! Be baptized in the name of Jesus Christ, so that your sins will be forgiven. Then you will be given the Holy Spirit. 39This promise is for you and your children. It is for everyone our Lord God will choose, no matter where they live."

40Peter told them many other things as well. Then he said, "I beg you to save yourselves from what will happen to all these evil people." 41On that day about three thousand believed his message and were baptized. 42They spent their time learning from the apostles, and they were like family to each other. They also broke bread*g* and prayed together.

Life among the Lord's Followers

43Everyone was amazed by the many miracles and wonders that the apostles worked. 44All the Lord's followers often met together, and they shared everything they had. 45They would sell their property and possessions and give the money to whoever needed it. 46Day after day they met together in the temple. They broke bread*g* together in different homes and shared their food happily and freely, 47while praising God. Everyone liked them, and each day the Lord added to their group others who were being saved.

Peter and John Heal a Lame Man

3 The time of prayer*h* was about three o'clock in the afternoon, and Peter and John were going into the temple. 2A man who had been born lame was being carried to the temple door. Each day he was placed beside this door, known as the Beautiful Gate. He sat there and begged from the people who were going in.

3The man saw Peter and John entering the temple, and he asked them for money. 4But they looked straight at him and said, "Look up at us!"

5The man stared at them and thought he was going to get something. 6But Peter said, "I don't have any silver or gold! But I will give you what I do have. In the name of Jesus Christ from Nazareth, get

up and start walking." 7Peter then took him by the right hand and helped him up.

At once the man's feet and ankles became strong, 8and he jumped up and started walking. He went with Peter and John into the temple, walking and jumping and praising God. 9Everyone saw him walking around and praising God. 10They knew that he was the beggar who had been lying beside the Beautiful Gate, and they were completely surprised. They could not imagine what had happened to the man.

Peter Speaks in the Temple

11While the man kept holding on to Peter and John, the whole crowd ran to them in amazement at the place known as Solomon's Porch.*i* 12Peter saw that a crowd had gathered, and he said:

Friends, why are you surprised at what has happened? Why are you staring at us? Do you think we have some power of our own? Do you think we were able to make this man walk because we are so religious? 13The God that Abraham, Isaac, Jacob, and our other ancestors worshiped has brought honor to his Servant*j* Jesus. He is the one you betrayed. You turned against him when he was being tried by Pilate, even though Pilate wanted to set him free.

14You rejected Jesus, who was holy and good. You asked for a murderer to be set free, 15and you killed the one who leads people to life. But God raised him from death, and all of us can tell you what he has done. 16You see this man, and you know him. He put his faith in the name of Jesus and was made strong. Faith in Jesus made this man completely well while everyone was watching.

17My friends, I am sure that you and your leaders didn't know what you were doing. 18But God had his prophets tell that his Messiah would suffer, and now he has kept that promise. 19So turn to God! Give up your sins, and you will be forgiven. 20Then that time will come when the Lord will give you fresh strength. He will send you Jesus, his chosen Messiah. 21But Jesus must stay in heaven until God makes all things new, just as his holy prophets promised long ago.

22Moses said, "The Lord your God will choose one of your own people

---

*g*2.42,46 *broke bread*: They ate together and celebrated the Lord's Supper.   *h*3.1 *The time of prayer*: Many of the Jewish people prayed in their homes at regular times each day (see Daniel 6.11), and on special occasions they prayed in the temple.   *i*3.11 *Solomon's Porch*: A public place with tall columns along the east side of the temple.   *j*3.13 *Servant*: Or "Son."

to be a prophet, just as he chose me. Listen to everything he tells you. ²³No one who disobeys that prophet will be one of God's people any longer."

²⁴Samuel and all the other prophets who came later also spoke about what is now happening. ²⁵You are really the ones God told his prophets to speak to. And you were given the promise that God made to your ancestors. He said to Abraham, "All nations on earth will be blessed because of someone from your family." ²⁶God sent his chosen Son*k* to you first, because God wanted to bless you and make each one of you turn away from your sins.

Peter and John Are Brought in Front of the Council

4 The apostles were still talking to the people, when some priests, the captain of the temple guard, and some Sadducees arrived. ²These men were angry because the apostles were teaching the people that the dead would be raised from death, just as Jesus had been raised from death. ³It was already late in the afternoon, and they arrested Peter and John and put them in jail for the night. ⁴But a lot of people who had heard the message believed it. So by now there were about five thousand followers of the Lord.

⁵The next morning the leaders, the elders, and the teachers of the Law of Moses met in Jerusalem. ⁶The high priest Annas was there, as well as Caiaphas, John, Alexander, and other members of the high priest's family. ⁷They brought in Peter and John and made them stand in the middle while they questioned them. They asked, "By what power and in whose name have you done this?"

⁸Peter was filled with the Holy Spirit and told the nation's leaders and the elders:

⁹You are questioning us today about a kind deed in which a crippled man was healed. ¹⁰But there is something we must tell you and everyone else in Israel. This man is standing here completely well because of the power of Jesus Christ from Nazareth. You put Jesus to death on a cross, but God raised him to life. ¹¹He is the stone that you builders thought was worthless, and now he is the most important stone of all. ¹²Only Jesus has the power to save! His name is the only one in all the world that can save anyone.

¹³The officials were amazed to see how brave Peter and John were, and they knew that these two apostles were only ordinary men and not well educated. The officials were certain that these men had been with Jesus. ¹⁴But they could not deny what had happened. The man who had been healed was standing there with the apostles.

¹⁵The officials commanded them to leave the council room. Then the officials said to each other, ¹⁶"What can we do with these men? Everyone in Jerusalem knows about this miracle, and we cannot say it didn't happen. ¹⁷But to keep this thing from spreading, we will warn them never again to speak to anyone about the name of Jesus." ¹⁸So they called the two apostles back in and told them that they must never, for any reason, teach anything about the name of Jesus.

¹⁹Peter and John answered, "Do you think God wants us to obey you or to obey him? ²⁰We cannot keep quiet about what we have seen and heard."

²¹⁻²²The officials could not find any reason to punish Peter and John. So they threatened them and let them go. The man who was healed by this miracle was more than forty years old, and everyone was praising God for what had happened.

Peter and Others Pray for Courage

²³As soon as Peter and John had been set free, they went back and told the others everything that the chief priests and the leaders had said to them. ²⁴When the rest of the Lord's followers heard this, they prayed together and said:

Master, you created heaven and earth, the sea, and everything in *ᴴᵖᵉᵍᴏᵏ* them. ²⁵And by the Holy Spirit you spoke to our ancestor David. He was your servant, and you told him to say:

"Why are all the Gentiles
    so furious?
Why do people
    make foolish plans?
²⁶ The kings of earth
    prepare for war,
  and the rulers
    join together
 against the Lord
    and his Messiah."

²⁷Here in Jerusalem, Herod*l* and Pontius Pilate got together with the Gentiles and the people of Israel. Then they turned against your holy Servant*m* Jesus, your chosen Mes-

---
*k***3.26** *Son:* Or "Servant."   *l***4.27** *Herod:* Herod Antipas, the son of Herod the Great.
*m***4.27,30** *Servant:* See the note at 3.13.

siah. [28]They did what you in your power and wisdom had already decided would happen.

[29]Lord, listen to their threats! We are your servants. So make us brave enough to speak your message. [30]Show your mighty power, as we heal people and work miracles and wonders in the name of your holy Servant[m] Jesus.

[31]After they had prayed, the meeting place shook. They were all filled with the Holy Spirit and bravely spoke God's message.

Sharing Possessions

[32]The group of followers all felt the same way about everything. None of them claimed that their possessions were their own, and they shared everything they had with each other. [33]In a powerful way the apostles told everyone that the Lord Jesus was now alive. God greatly blessed his followers,[n] [34]and no one went in need of anything. Everyone who owned land or houses would sell them and bring the money [35]to the apostles. Then they would give the money to anyone who needed it.

[36-37]Joseph was one of the followers who had sold a piece of property and brought the money to the apostles. He was a Levite from Cyprus, and the apostles called him Barnabas, which means "one who encourages others."

Peter Condemns Ananias and Sapphira

5 Ananias and his wife Sapphira also sold a piece of property. [2]But they agreed to cheat and keep some of the money for themselves.

So when Ananias took the rest of the money to the apostles, [3]Peter said, "Why has Satan made you keep back some of the money from the sale of the property? Why have you lied to the Holy Spirit? [4]The property was yours before you sold it, and even after you sold it, the money was still yours. What made you do such a thing? You didn't lie to people. You lied to God!"

[5]As soon as Ananias heard this, he dropped dead, and everyone who heard about it was frightened. [6]Some young men came in and wrapped up his body. Then they took it out and buried it.

[7]Three hours later Sapphira came in, but she did not know what had happened to her husband. [8]Peter asked her, "Tell me, did you sell the property for this amount?"

"Yes," she answered, "that's the amount."

[9]Then Peter said, "Why did the two of you agree to test the Lord's Spirit? The men who buried Ananias are by the door, and they will carry you out!" [10]At once she fell at Peter's feet and died.

When the young men came back in, they found Sapphira lying there dead. So they carried her out and buried her beside her husband. [11]The church members were afraid, and so was everyone else who heard what had happened.

Peter's Unusual Power

[12]The apostles worked many miracles and wonders among the people. All of the Lord's followers often met in the part of the temple known as Solomon's Porch.[o] [13]No one outside their group dared join them, even though everyone liked them very much.

[14]Many men and women started having faith in the Lord. [15]Then sick people were brought out to the road and placed on cots and mats. It was hoped that Peter would walk by, and his shadow would fall on them and heal them. [16]A lot of people living in the towns near Jerusalem brought those who were sick or troubled by evil spirits, and they were all healed.

Trouble for the Apostles

[17]The high priest and all the other Sadducees who were with him became jealous. [18]They arrested the apostles and put them in the city jail. [19]But that night an angel from the Lord opened the doors of the jail and led the apostles out. The angel said, [20]"Go to the temple and tell the people everything about this new life." [21]So they went into the temple before sunrise and started teaching.

The high priest and his men called together their council, which included all of Israel's leaders. Then they ordered the apostles to be brought to them from the jail. [22]The temple police who were sent to the jail did not find the apostles. They returned and said, [23]"We found the jail locked tight and the guards standing at the doors. But when we opened the doors and went in, we didn't find anyone there." [24]The captain of the temple police and the chief priests listened to their report, but they did not know what to think about it.

[25]Just then someone came in and said, "Right now those men you put in jail are in the temple, teaching the people!" [26]The captain went with some of the temple police and brought the apostles back. But they did not use force. They were afraid that the people might start throwing stones at them.

[m]**4.27,30** *Servant:* See the note at 3.13. "Everyone highly respected his followers." [n]**4.33** *God greatly blessed his followers:* Or [o]**5.12** *Solomon's Porch:* See the note at 3.11.

27When the apostles were brought before the council, the high priest said to them, 28"We told you plainly not to teach in the name of Jesus. But look what you have done! You have been teaching all over Jerusalem, and you are trying to blame us for his death."

29Peter and the apostles replied:

We don't obey people. We obey God. 30You killed Jesus by nailing him to a cross. But the God our ancestors worshiped raised him to life 31and made him our Leader and Savior. Then God gave him a place at his right side,*p* so that the people of Israel would turn back to him and be forgiven. 32We are here to tell you about all this, and so is the Holy Spirit, who is God's gift to everyone who obeys God.

33When the council members heard this, they became so angry that they wanted to kill the apostles. 34But one of the members was the Pharisee Gamaliel, a highly respected teacher. He ordered the apostles to be taken out of the room for a little while. 35Then he said to the council:

People of Israel, be careful what you do with these men. 36Not long ago Theudas claimed to be someone important, and about four hundred men joined him. But he was killed. All his followers were scattered, and that was the end of that.

37Later, when the people of our nation were being counted, Judas from Galilee showed up. A lot of people followed him, but he was killed, and all his followers were scattered.

38So I advise you to stay away from these men. Leave them alone. If what they are planning is something of their own doing, it will fail. 39But if God is behind it, you cannot stop it anyway, unless you want to fight against God.

The council members agreed with what he said, 40and they called the apostles back in. They had them beaten with a whip and warned them not to speak in the name of Jesus. Then they let them go.

41The apostles left the council and were happy, because God had considered them worthy to suffer for the sake of Jesus. 42Every day they spent time in the temple and in one home after another. They never stopped teaching and telling the good news that Jesus is the Messiah.

Seven Leaders for the Church

6 A lot of people were now becoming followers of the Lord. But some of the ones who spoke Greek started complaining about the ones who spoke Aramaic. They complained that the Greek-speaking widows were not given their share when the food supplies were handed out each day.

2The twelve apostles called the whole group of followers together and said, "We should not give up preaching God's message in order to serve at tables.*q* 3My friends, choose seven men who are respected and wise and filled with God's Spirit. We will put them in charge of these things. 4We can spend our time praying and serving God by preaching."

5This suggestion pleased everyone, and they began by choosing Stephen. He had great faith and was filled with the Holy Spirit. Then they chose Philip, Prochorus, Nicanor, Timon, Parmenas, and also Nicolaus, who worshiped with the Jewish people*r* in Antioch. 6These men were brought to the apostles. Then the apostles prayed and placed their hands on the men to show that they had been chosen to do this work. 7God's message spread, and many more people in Jerusalem became followers. Even a large number of priests put their faith in the Lord.

Stephen Is Arrested

8God gave Stephen the power to work great miracles and wonders among the people. 9But some Jews from Cyrene and Alexandria were members of a group who called themselves "Free Men."*s* They started arguing with Stephen. Some others from Cilicia and Asia also argued with him. 10But they were no match for Stephen, who spoke with the great wisdom that the Spirit gave him. 11So they talked some men into saying, "We heard Stephen say terrible things against Moses and God!"

12They turned the people and their leaders and the teachers of the Law of Moses against Stephen. Then they all grabbed Stephen and dragged him in front of the council.

13Some men agreed to tell lies about Stephen, and they said, "This man keeps on saying terrible things about this holy temple and the Law of Moses. 14We have heard him claim that Jesus from Nazareth will destroy this place and change the customs that Moses gave us." 15Then all the council members

---

*p***5.31** *right side*: See the note at 2.33.   *q***6.2** *to serve at tables*: This may mean either that they were in charge of handing out food to the widows or that they were in charge of the money, since the Greek word "table" may also mean "bank."   *r***6.5** *worshiped with the Jewish people*: This translates the Greek word "proselyte" that means a Gentile who had accepted the Jewish religion.   *s***6.9** *Free Men*: A group of Jewish men who had once been slaves, but had been freed.

stared at Stephen. They saw that his face looked like the face of an angel.

Stephen's Speech

7 The high priest asked Stephen, "Are they telling the truth about you?" ²Stephen answered:

Friends, listen to me. Our glorious God appeared to our ancestor Abraham while he was still in Mesopotamia, before he had moved to Haran. ³God told him, "Leave your country and your relatives and go to a land that I will show you." ⁴Then Abraham left the land of the Chaldeans and settled in Haran.

After his father died, Abraham came and settled in this land where you now live. ⁵God didn't give him any part of it, not even a square foot. But God did promise to give it to him and his family forever, even though Abraham didn't have any children. ⁶God said that Abraham's descendants would live for a while in a foreign land. There they would be slaves and would be mistreated four hundred years. ⁷But he also said, "I will punish the nation that makes them slaves. Then later they will come and worship me in this place."

⁸God said to Abraham, "Every son in each family must be circumcised to show that you have kept your agreement with me." So when Isaac was eight days old, Abraham circumcised him. Later, Isaac circumcised his son Jacob, and Jacob circumcised his twelve sons. ⁹ These men were our ancestors.

Joseph was also one of our famous ancestors. His brothers were jealous of him and sold him as a slave to be taken to Egypt. But God was with him ¹⁰and rescued him from all his troubles. God made him so wise that the Egyptian king Pharaohˣ thought highly of him. The king even made Joseph governor over Egypt and put him in charge of everything he owned.

¹¹Everywhere in Egypt and Canaan the grain crops failed. There was terrible suffering, and our ancestors could not find enough to eat. ¹²But when Jacob heard that there was grain in Egypt, he sent our ancestors there for the first time. ¹³It was on their second trip that Joseph told his brothers who he was, and Pharaoh learned about Joseph's family. ¹⁴Joseph sent for his father and his relatives. In all, there were seventy-five of them. ¹⁵His father went to Egypt and died there, just as our ancestors did. ¹⁵Later their bodies were taken back to Shechem and placed in the tomb that Abraham had bought from the sons of Hamor.

¹⁷Finally, the time came for God to do what he had promised Abraham. By then the number of our people in Egypt had greatly increased. ¹⁸Another king was ruling Egypt, and he didn't know anything about Joseph. ¹⁹He tricked our ancestors and was cruel to them. He even made them leave their babies outside, so they would die.

²⁰During this time Moses was born. He was a very beautiful child, and for three months his parents took care of him in their home. ²¹Then when they were forced to leave him outside, the king's daughter found him and raised him as her own son. ²²Moses was given the best education in Egypt. He was a strong man and a powerful speaker.

²³When Moses was forty years old, he wanted to help the Israelites because they were his own people. ²⁴One day he saw an Egyptian mistreating one of them. So he rescued the man and killed the Egyptian. ²⁵Moses thought the rest of his people would realize that God was going to use him to set them free. But they didn't understand.

²⁶The next day Moses saw two of his own people fighting, and he tried to make them stop. He said, "Men, you are both Israelites. Why are you so cruel to each other?"

²⁷But the man who had started the fight pushed Moses aside and asked, "Who made you our ruler and judge? ²⁸Are you going to kill me, just as you killed that Egyptian yesterday?" ²⁹When Moses heard this, he ran away to live in the country of Midian. His two sons were born there.

³⁰Forty years later, an angel appeared to Moses from a burning bush in the desert near Mount Sinai. ³¹Moses was surprised by what he saw. He went closer to get a better look, and the Lord said, ³²"I am the God who was worshiped by your ancestors, Abraham, Isaac, and Jacob." Moses started shaking all over and didn't dare to look at the bush.

³³The Lord said to him, "Take off your sandals. The place where you are standing is holy. ³⁴With my own eyes I have seen the suffering of my people in Egypt. I have heard their groans and have come down to rescue them. Now I am sending you back to Egypt."

³⁵This was the same Moses that the people rejected by saying, "Who

---

ˣ**7.10** *Pharaoh*: A Hebrew word sometimes used for the title of the King of Egypt.

made you our leader and judge?"
God's angel had spoken to Moses
from the bush. And God had even
sent the angel to help Moses rescue
the people and be their leader.
36In Egypt and at the Red Sea*t* and
in the desert, Moses rescued the people by working miracles and wonders for forty years. **37**Moses is the
one who told the people of Israel,
"God will choose one of your people
to be a prophet, just as he chose me."
38Moses brought our people together
in the desert, and the angel spoke to
him on Mount Sinai. There he was
given these life-giving words to pass
on to us. **39**But our ancestors refused
to obey Moses. They rejected him
and wanted to go back to Egypt.
40The people said to Aaron, "Make
some gods to lead us! Moses led us
out of Egypt, but we don't know
what's happened to him now."
41Then they made an idol in the
shape of a calf. They offered sacrifices to the idol and were pleased
with what they had done.

42God turned his back on his people and left them. Then they worshiped the stars in the sky, just as it
says in the Book of the Prophets,
"People of Israel, you didn't offer
sacrifices and offerings to me during
those forty years in the desert. **43**Instead, you carried the tent where the
god Molech is worshiped, and you
took along the star of your god
Rephan. You made those idols and
worshiped them. So now I will have
you carried off beyond Babylonia."

44The tent where our ancestors
worshiped God was with them in the
desert. This was the same tent that
God had commanded Moses to
make. And it was made like the
model that Moses had seen. **45**Later
it was given to our ancestors, and
they took it with them when they
went with Joshua. They carried the
tent along as they took over the land
from those people that God had
chased out for them. Our ancestors
used this tent until the time of King
David. **46** He pleased God and asked
him if he could build a house of worship for the people*u* of Israel. **47**And
it was finally King Solomon who
built a house for God.*v*
48But the Most High God doesn't

live in houses made by humans. It is
just as the prophet said, when he
spoke for the Lord,

49 "Heaven is my throne,
    and the earth
        is my footstool.
What kind of house
    will you build for me?
In what place will I rest?
50   I have made everything."

51You stubborn and hardheaded
people! You are always fighting
against the Holy Spirit, just as your
ancestors did. **52**Is there one prophet
that your ancestors didn't mistreat?
They killed the prophets who told
about the coming of the One Who
Obeys God.*w* And now you have
turned against him and killed him.
53Angels gave you God's Law, but
you still don't obey it.

Stephen Is Stoned to Death

54When the council members heard
Stephen's speech, they were angry and
furious. **55**But Stephen was filled with
the Holy Spirit. He looked toward
heaven, where he saw our glorious God
and Jesus standing at his right side.*x*
56Then Stephen said, "I see heaven open
and the Son of Man standing at the
right side of God!"

57The council members shouted and
covered their ears. At once they all attacked Stephen **58**and dragged him out
of the city. Then they started throwing
stones at him. The men who had
brought charges against him put their
coats at the feet of a young man named
Saul.*y*

59As Stephen was being stoned to
death, he called out, "Lord Jesus, please
welcome me!" **60**He knelt down and
shouted, "Lord, don't blame them for
what they have done." Then he died.

8 **1-2**Saul approved the stoning of
Stephen. Some faithful followers of
the Lord buried Stephen and mourned
very much for him.

Saul Makes Trouble for the Church

At that time the church in Jerusalem
suffered terribly. All of the Lord's followers, except the apostles, were scattered everywhere in Judea and Samaria.
3Saul started making a lot of trouble for
the church. He went from house to

---

*t*7.36 *Red Sea*: This name comes from the Bible of the early Christians, a translation made into
Greek about 200 B.C. It refers to the body of water that the Israelites crossed and was one of
the marshes or fresh water lakes near the eastern part of the Nile Delta, where they lived and
where the towns of Exodus 13.17—14.9 were located.   *u*7.46 *the people*: Some manuscripts
have "God."   *v*7.47 *God*: Or "the people."   *w*7.52 *One Who Obeys God*: That is, Jesus.
*x*7.55 *standing at his right side*: The "right side" is the place of honor and power. "Standing"
may mean that Jesus is welcoming Stephen (see verse 59).   *y*7.58 *Saul*: Better known as
Paul, who became a famous follower of Jesus.

house, arresting men and women and putting them in jail.

The Good News Is Preached in Samaria

⁴The Lord's followers who had been scattered went from place to place, telling the good news. ⁵Philip went to the city of Samaria and told the people about Christ. ⁶They crowded around Philip because they were eager to hear what he was saying and to see him work miracles. ⁷Many people with evil spirits were healed, and the spirits went out of them with a shout. A lot of crippled and lame people were also healed. ⁸Everyone in that city was very glad because of what was happening.

⁹For some time a man named Simon had lived in the city of Samaria and had amazed the people. He practiced witchcraft and claimed to be somebody great. ¹⁰Everyone, rich and poor, crowded around him. They said, "This man is the power of God called 'The Great Power.' " ¹¹For a long time, Simon had used witchcraft to amaze the people, and they kept crowding around him. ¹²But when they believed what Philip was saying about God's kingdom and about the name of Jesus Christ, they were all baptized. ¹³Even Simon believed and was baptized. He stayed close to Philip, because he marveled at all the miracles and wonders.

¹⁴The apostles in Jerusalem heard that some people in Samaria had accepted God's message, and they sent Peter and John. ¹⁵When the two apostles arrived, they prayed that the people would be given the Holy Spirit. ¹⁶Before this, the Holy Spirit had not been given to anyone in Samaria, though some of them had been baptized in the name of the Lord Jesus. ¹⁷Peter and John then placed their hands on everyone who had faith in the Lord, and they were given the Holy Spirit.

¹⁸Simon noticed that the Spirit was given only when the apostles placed their hands on the people. So he brought money ¹⁹and said to Peter and John, "Let me have this power too! Then anyone I place my hands on will also be given the Holy Spirit."

²⁰Peter said to him, "You and your money will both end up in hell if you think you can buy God's gift! ²¹You don't have any part in this, and God sees that your heart isn't right. ²²Get rid of these evil thoughts and ask God to forgive you. ²³I can see that you are jealous and bound by your evil ways."

²⁴Simon said, "Please pray to the

Lord, so that what you said won't happen to me."

²⁵After Peter and John had preached about the Lord, they returned to Jerusalem. On their way they told the good news in many villages of Samaria.

Philip and an Ethiopian Official

²⁶The Lord's angel said to Philip, "Go south[z] along the desert road that leads from Jerusalem to Gaza."[a] ²⁷So Philip left.

An important Ethiopian official happened to be going along that road in his chariot. He was the chief treasurer for Candace, the Queen of Ethiopia. The official had gone to Jerusalem to worship ²⁸and was now on his way home. He was sitting in his chariot, reading the book of the prophet Isaiah. ²⁹The Spirit told Philip to catch up with the chariot. ³⁰Philip ran up close and heard the man reading aloud from the book of Isaiah. Philip asked him, "Do you understand what you are reading?"

³¹The official answered, "How can I understand unless someone helps me?" He then invited Philip to come up and sit beside him.

³²The man was reading the passage that said,

"He was led like a sheep
on its way to be killed.
He was silent as a lamb
whose wool
is being cut off,
and he did not say
a word.
³³ He was treated like a nobody
and did not receive
a fair trial.
How can he have children,
if his life
is snatched away?"

³⁴The official said to Philip, "Tell me, was the prophet talking about himself or about someone else?" ³⁵So Philip began at this place in the Scriptures and explained the good news about Jesus.

³⁶⁻³⁷As they were going along the road, they came to a place where there was some water. The official said, "Look! Here is some water. Why can't I be baptized?"[b] ³⁸He ordered the chariot to stop. Then they both went down into the water, and Philip baptized him.

³⁹After they had come out of the water, the Lord's Spirit took Philip away. The official never saw him again, but he was very happy as he went on his way.

⁴⁰Philip later appeared in Azotus. He

---

[z]**8.26** *Go south*: Or "About noon go."   [a]**8.26** *the desert road that leads from Jerusalem to Gaza*: Or "the road that leads from Jerusalem to Gaza in the desert."   [b]**8.36,37** *Why can't I be baptized*: Some manuscripts add, "Philip replied, 'You can, if you believe with all your heart.' "The official answered, 'I believe that Jesus Christ is the Son of God.' "

went from town to town, all the way to Caesarea, telling people about Jesus.

Saul Becomes a Follower of the Lord
(Acts 22.6-16; 26.12-18)

9 Saul kept on threatening to kill the Lord's followers. He even went to the high priest ²and asked for letters to the Jewish leaders in Damascus. He did this because he wanted to arrest and take to Jerusalem any man or woman who had accepted the Lord's Way.*c* ³When Saul had almost reached Damascus, a bright light from heaven suddenly flashed around him. ⁴He fell to the ground and heard a voice that said, "Saul! Saul! Why are you so cruel to me?"

⁵"Who are you?" Saul asked.

"I am Jesus," the Lord answered. "I am the one you are so cruel to. ⁶Now get up and go into the city, where you will be told what to do."

⁷The men with Saul stood there speechless. They had heard the voice, but they had not seen anyone. ⁸Saul got up from the ground, and when he opened his eyes, he could not see a thing. Someone then led him by the hand to Damascus, ⁹and for three days he was blind and did not eat or drink.

¹⁰A follower named Ananias lived in Damascus, and the Lord spoke to him in a vision. Ananias answered, "Lord, here I am."

¹¹The Lord said to him, "Get up and go to the house of Judas on Straight Street. When you get there, you will find a man named Saul from the city of Tarsus. Saul is praying, ¹²and he has seen a vision. He saw a man named Ananias coming to him and putting his hands on him, so that he could see again."

¹³Ananias replied, "Lord, a lot of people have told me about the terrible things this man has done to your followers in Jerusalem. ¹⁴Now the chief priests have given him the power to come here and arrest anyone who worships in your name."

¹⁵The Lord said to Ananias, "Go! I have chosen him to tell foreigners, kings, and the people of Israel about me. ¹⁶I will show him how much he must suffer for worshiping in my name."

¹⁷Ananias left and went into the house where Saul was staying. Ananias placed his hands on him and said, "Saul, the Lord Jesus has sent me. He is the same one who appeared to you along the road. He wants you to be able to see and to be filled with the Holy Spirit."

¹⁸Suddenly something like fish scales fell from Saul's eyes, and he could see. He got up and was baptized. ¹⁹Then he ate and felt much better.

Saul Preaches in Damascus

For several days Saul stayed with the Lord's followers in Damascus. ²⁰Soon he went to the Jewish meeting places and started telling people that Jesus is the Son of God. ²¹Everyone who heard Saul was amazed and said, "Isn't this the man who caused so much trouble for those people in Jerusalem who worship in the name of Jesus? Didn't he come here to arrest them and take them to the chief priests?"

²²Saul preached with such power that he completely confused the Jewish people in Damascus, as he tried to show them that Jesus is the Messiah.

²³Later some of them made plans to kill Saul, ²⁴but he found out about it. He learned that they were guarding the gates of the city day and night in order to kill him. ²⁵Then one night his followers let him down over the city wall in a large basket.

Saul in Jerusalem

²⁶When Saul arrived in Jerusalem, he tried to join the followers. But they were all afraid of him, because they did not believe he was a true follower. ²⁷Then Barnabas helped him by taking him to the apostles. He explained how Saul had seen the Lord and how the Lord had spoken to him. Barnabas also said that when Saul was in Damascus, he had spoken bravely in the name of Jesus.

²⁸Saul moved about freely with the followers in Jerusalem and told everyone about the Lord. ²⁹He was always arguing with the Jews who spoke Greek, and so they tried to kill him. ³⁰But the followers found out about this and took Saul to Caesarea. From there they sent him to the city of Tarsus.

³¹The church in Judea, Galilee, and Samaria now had a time of peace and kept on worshiping the Lord. The church became stronger, as the Holy Spirit encouraged it and helped it grow.

Peter Heals Aeneas

³²While Peter was traveling from place to place, he visited the Lord's followers who lived in the town of Lydda. ³³There he met a man named Aeneas, who for eight years had been sick in bed and could not move. ³⁴Peter said to Aeneas, "Jesus Christ has healed you! Get up and make up your bed."*d* Right away he stood up.

³⁵Many people in the towns of Lydda and Sharon saw Aeneas and became followers of the Lord.

*c*9.2 *accepted the Lord's Way*: In the book of Acts, this means to become a follower of the Lord Jesus.   *d*9.34 *and make up your bed*: Or "and fix something to eat."

Peter Brings Dorcas Back to Life

³⁶In Joppa there was a follower named Tabitha. Her Greek name was Dorcas, which means "deer." She was always doing good things for people and had given much to the poor. ³⁷But she got sick and died, and her body was washed and placed in an upstairs room. ³⁸Joppa wasn't far from Lydda, and the followers heard that Peter was there. They sent two men to say to him, "Please come with us as quickly as you can!" ³⁹Right away, Peter went with them.

The men took Peter upstairs into the room. Many widows were there crying. They showed him the coats and clothes that Dorcas had made while she was still alive.

⁴⁰After Peter had sent everyone out of the room, he knelt down and prayed. Then he turned to the body of Dorcas and said, "Tabitha, get up!" The woman opened her eyes, and when she saw Peter, she sat up. ⁴¹He took her by the hand and helped her to her feet.

Peter called in the widows and the other followers and showed them that Dorcas had been raised from death. ⁴²Everyone in Joppa heard what had happened, and many of them put their faith in the Lord. ⁴³Peter stayed on for a while in Joppa in the house of a man named Simon, who made leather.

Peter and Cornelius

10 In Caesarea there was a man named Cornelius, who was the captain of a group of soldiers called "The Italian Unit." ²Cornelius was a very religious man. He worshiped God, and so did everyone else who lived in his house. He had given a lot of money to the poor and was always praying to God.

³One afternoon at about three o'clock,^e Cornelius had a vision. He saw an angel from God coming to him and calling him by name. ⁴Cornelius was surprised and stared at the angel. Then he asked, "What is this all about?"

The angel answered, "God has heard your prayers and knows about your gifts to the poor. ⁵Now send some men to Joppa for a man named Simon Peter. ⁶He is visiting with Simon the leather maker, who lives in a house near the sea." ⁷After saying this, the angel left.

Cornelius called in two of his servants and one of his soldiers who worshiped God. ⁸He explained everything to them and sent them off to Joppa.

⁹The next day about noon these men were coming near Joppa. Peter went up on the roof^f of the house to pray ¹⁰and became very hungry. While the food was being prepared, he fell sound asleep and had a vision. ¹¹He saw heaven open, and something came down like a huge sheet held up by its four corners. ¹²In it were all kinds of animals, snakes, and birds. ¹³A voice said to him, "Peter, get up! Kill these and eat them."

¹⁴But Peter said, "Lord, I can't do that! I've never eaten anything that is unclean and not fit to eat."^g

¹⁵The voice spoke to him again, "When God says that something can be used for food, don't say it isn't fit to eat."

¹⁶This happened three times before the sheet was suddenly taken back to heaven.

¹⁷Peter was still wondering what all of this meant, when the men sent by Cornelius came and stood at the gate. They had found their way to Simon's house ¹⁸and were asking if Simon Peter was staying there.

¹⁹While Peter was still thinking about the vision, the Holy Spirit said to him, "Three^h men are here looking for you. ²⁰Hurry down and go with them. Don't worry, I sent them."

²¹Peter went down and said to the men, "I am the one you are looking for. Why have you come?"

²²They answered, "Captain Cornelius sent us. He is a good man who worships God and is liked by the Jewish people. One of God's holy angels told Cornelius to send for you, so he could hear what you have to say." ²³Peter invited them to spend the night.

The next morning, Peter and some of the Lord's followers in Joppa left with the men who had come from Cornelius. ²⁴The next day they arrived in Caesarea where Cornelius was waiting for them. He had also invited his relatives and close friends.

²⁵When Peter arrived, Cornelius greeted him. Then he knelt at Peter's feet and started worshiping him. ²⁶But Peter took hold of him and said, "Stand up! I am nothing more than a human."

²⁷As Peter entered the house, he was still talking with Cornelius. Many people were there, ²⁸and Peter said to them, "You know that we Jews are not allowed to have anything to do with other people. But God has shown me that he doesn't think anyone is unclean or unfit. ²⁹I agreed to come here, but I want to know why you sent for me."

^e**10.3** *at about three o'clock*: Probably while he was praying (see 3.1 and the note there).   ^f**10.9** *roof*: In Palestine the houses usually had a flat roof. Stairs on the outside led up to the roof, which was made of beams and boards covered with packed earth.   ^g**10.14** *unclean and not fit to eat*: The Law of Moses taught that some foods were not fit to eat.   ^h**10.19** *Three*: One manuscript has "two;" some manuscripts have "some."

[30]Cornelius answered:

Four days ago at about three o'clock in the afternoon I was praying at home. Suddenly a man in bright clothes stood in front of me. [31]He said, "Cornelius, God has heard your prayers, and he knows about your gifts to the poor. [32]Now send to Joppa for Simon Peter. He is visiting in the home of Simon the leather maker, who lives near the sea."

[33]I sent for you right away, and you have been good enough to come. All of us are here in the presence of the Lord God, so that we can hear what he has to say.

[34]Peter then said:

Now I am certain that God treats all people alike. [35]God is pleased with everyone who worships him and does right, no matter what nation they come from. [36]This is the same message that God gave to the people of Israel, when he sent Jesus Christ, the Lord of all, to offer peace to them.

[37]You surely know what happened[i] everywhere in Judea. It all began in Galilee after John had told everyone to be baptized. [38]God gave the Holy Spirit and power to Jesus from Nazareth. He was with Jesus, as he went around doing good and healing everyone who was under the power of the devil. [39]We all saw what Jesus did both in Israel and in the city of Jerusalem.

Jesus was put to death on a cross. [40]But three days later, God raised him to life and let him be seen. [41]Not everyone saw him. He was seen only by us, who ate and drank with him after he was raised from death. We were the ones God chose to tell others about him.

[42]God told us to announce clearly to the people that Jesus is the one he has chosen to judge the living and the dead. [43]Every one of the prophets has said that all who have faith in Jesus will have their sins forgiven in his name.

[44]While Peter was still speaking, the Holy Spirit took control of everyone who was listening. [45]Some Jewish followers of the Lord had come with Peter, and they were surprised that the Holy Spirit had been given to Gentiles. [46]Now they were hearing Gentiles speaking unknown languages and praising God.

Peter said, [47]"These Gentiles have been given the Holy Spirit, just as we have! I am certain that no one would dare stop us from baptizing them." [48]Pe-ter ordered them to be baptized in the name of Jesus Christ, and they asked him to stay on for a few days.

Peter Reports to the Church in Jerusalem

11 The apostles and the followers in Judea heard that Gentiles had accepted God's message. [2]So when Peter came to Jerusalem, some of the Jewish followers started arguing with him. They wanted Gentile followers to be circumcised, and [3]they said, "You stayed in the homes of Gentiles, and you even ate with them!"

[4]Then Peter told them exactly what had happened:

[5]I was in the town of Joppa and was praying when I fell sound asleep and had a vision. I saw heaven open, and something like a huge sheet held by its four corners came down to me. [6]When I looked in it, I saw animals, wild beasts, snakes, and birds. [7]I heard a voice saying to me, "Peter, get up! Kill these and eat them."

[8]But I said, "Lord, I can't do that! I've never taken a bite of anything that is unclean and not fit to eat."[j]

[9]The voice from heaven spoke to me again, "When God says that something can be used for food, don't say it isn't fit to eat." [10]This happened three times before it was all taken back into heaven.

[11]Suddenly three men from Caesarea stood in front of the house where I was staying. [12]The Holy Spirit told me to go with them and not to worry. Then six of the Lord's followers went with me to the home of a man [13]who told us that an angel had appeared to him. The angel had ordered him to send to Joppa for someone named Simon Peter. [14]Then Peter would tell him how he and everyone in his house could be saved.

[15]After I started speaking, the Holy Spirit was given to them, just as the Spirit had been given to us at the beginning. [16]I remembered that the Lord had said, "John baptized with water, but you will be baptized with the Holy Spirit." [17]God gave those Gentiles the same gift that he gave us when we put our faith in the Lord Jesus Christ. So how could I have gone against God?

[18]When they heard Peter say this, they stopped arguing and started praising God. They said, "God has now let Gentiles turn to him, and he has given life to them!"

---

[i]**10.37** *what happened*: Or "the message that went." See the note at 10.14.

[j]**11.8** *unclean and not fit to eat*: See the note at 10.14.

The Church in Antioch oʻ gerous

¹⁹Some of the Lord's followers had been <u>scattered</u> because of the terrible trouble that started when Stephen was killed. They went as far as Phoenicia, Cyprus, and Antioch, but they told the message only to the Jews.

²⁰Some of the followers from Cyprus and Cyrene went to Antioch and started telling Gentiles[k] the good news about the Lord Jesus. ²¹The Lord's power was with them, and many people turned to the Lord and put their faith in him. ²²News of what was happening reached the church in Jerusalem. Then they sent Barnabas to Antioch.

²³When Barnabas got there and saw what God had been kind enough to do for them, he was very glad. So he begged them to remain faithful to the Lord with all their hearts. ²⁴Barnabas was a good man of great faith, and he was filled with the Holy Spirit. Many more people turned to the Lord.

²⁵Barnabas went to Tarsus to look for Saul. ²⁶He found Saul and brought him to Antioch, where they met with the church for a whole year and taught many of its people. There in Antioch the Lord's followers were first called Christians.

²⁷During this time some prophets from Jerusalem came to Antioch. ²⁸One of them was Agabus. Then with the help of the Spirit, he told that there would be a terrible famine everywhere in the world. And it happened when Claudius was Emperor.[l] ²⁹The followers in Antioch decided to send whatever help they could to the followers in Judea. ³⁰So they had Barnabas and Saul take their gifts to the church leaders in Jerusalem.

Herod Causes Trouble for the Church

12 At that time King Herod[m] caused terrible suffering for some members of the church. ²He ordered soldiers to cut off the head of James, the brother of John. ³When Herod saw that this pleased the Jewish people, he had Peter arrested during the Festival of Thin Bread. ⁴He put Peter in jail and ordered four squads of soldiers to guard him. Herod planned to put him on trial in public after the festival.

⁵While Peter was being kept in jail, the church never stopped praying to God for him.

Peter Is Rescued

⁶The night before Peter was to be put on trial, he was asleep and bound by two chains. A soldier was guarding him on each side, and two other soldiers were guarding the entrance to the jail. ⁷Suddenly an angel from the Lord appeared, and light flashed around in the cell. The angel poked Peter in the side and woke him up. Then he said, "Quick! Get up!"

The chains fell off his hands, ⁸and the angel said, "Get dressed and put on your sandals." Peter did what he was told. Then the angel said, "Now put on your coat and follow me." ⁹Peter left with the angel, but he thought everything was only a dream. ¹⁰They went past the two groups of soldiers, and when they came to the iron gate to the city, it opened by itself. They went out and were going along the street, when all at once the angel disappeared.

¹¹Peter now realized what had happened, and he said, "I am certain that the Lord sent his angel to rescue me from Herod and from everything the Jewish leaders planned to do to me." ¹²Then Peter went to the house of Mary the mother of John whose other name was Mark. Many of the Lord's followers had come together there and were praying.

¹³Peter knocked on the gate, and a servant named Rhoda came to answer. ¹⁴When she heard Peter's voice, she was too excited to open the gate. She ran back into the house and said that Peter was standing there.

¹⁵"You are crazy!" everyone told her. But she kept saying that it was Peter. Then they said, "It must be his angel."[n] ¹⁶But Peter kept on knocking, until finally they opened the gate. They saw him and were completely amazed.

¹⁷Peter motioned for them to keep quiet. Then he told how the Lord had led him out of jail. He also said, "Tell James[o] and the others what has happened." After that, he left and went somewhere else.

¹⁸The next morning the soldiers who had been on guard were terribly worried and wondered what had happened to Peter. ¹⁹Herod ordered his own soldiers to search for him, but they could not find him. Then he questioned the guards and had them put to death. After this, Herod left Judea to stay in Caesarea for a while.

---

[k]11.20 *Gentiles*: This translates a Greek word that may mean "people who speak Greek" or "people who live as Greeks do." Here the word seems to mean "people who are not Jews." Some manuscripts have "Greeks," which also seems to mean "people who are not Jews." [l]11.28 *when Claudius was Emperor*: A.D. 41-54. [m]12.1 *Herod*: Herod Agrippa I, the grandson of Herod the Great. [n]12.15 *his angel*: Probably meaning "his guardian angel." [o]12.17 *James*: The brother of the Lord.

Herod Dies

[20]Herod and the people of Tyre and Sidon were very angry with each other. But their country got its food supply from the region that he ruled. So a group of them went to see Blastus, who was one of Herod's high officials. They convinced Blastus that they wanted to make peace between their cities and Herod, [21]and a day was set for them to meet with him.

Herod came dressed in his royal robes. He sat down on his throne and made a speech. [22]The people shouted, "You speak more like a god than a man!" [23]At once an angel from the Lord struck him down because he took the honor that belonged to God. Later, Herod was eaten by worms and died.

[24]God's message kept spreading. [25]And after Barnabas and Saul had done the work they were sent to do, they went back to Jerusalem[p] with John, whose other name was Mark.

Barnabas and Saul Are Chosen and Sent

13 The church at Antioch had several prophets and teachers. They were Barnabas, Simeon, also called Niger, Lucius from Cyrene, Manaen, who was Herod's[q] close friend, and Saul. [2]While they were worshiping the Lord and going without eating,[r] the Holy Spirit told them, "Appoint Barnabas and Saul to do the work for which I have chosen them." [3]Everyone prayed and went without eating for a while longer. Next, they placed their hands on Barnabas and Saul to show that they had been appointed to do this work. Then everyone sent them on their way.

Barnabas and Saul in Cyprus

[4]After Barnabas and Saul had been sent by the Holy Spirit, they went to Seleucia. From there they sailed to the island of Cyprus. [5]They arrived at Salamis and began to preach God's message in the Jewish meeting places. They also had John[s] as a helper.

[6]Barnabas and Saul went all the way to the city of Paphos on the other end of the island, where they met a Jewish man named Bar-Jesus. He practiced witchcraft and was a false prophet. [7]He also worked for Sergius Paulus, who was very smart and was the governor of the island. Sergius Paulus wanted to hear God's message, and he sent for Barnabas and Saul. [8]But Bar-Jesus, whose other name was Elymas, was against them. He even tried to keep the governor from having faith in the Lord.

[9]Then Saul, better known as Paul, was filled with the Holy Spirit. He looked straight at Elymas [10]and said, "You son of the devil! You are a liar, a crook, and an enemy of everything that is right. When will you stop speaking against the true ways of the Lord? [11]The Lord is going to punish you by making you completely blind for a while."

Suddenly the man's eyes were covered by a dark mist, and he went around trying to get someone to lead him by the hand. [12]When the governor saw what had happened, he was amazed at this teaching about the Lord. So he put his faith in the Lord.

Paul and Barnabas in Antioch of Pisidia

[13]Paul and the others left Paphos and sailed to Perga in Pamphylia. But John[s] left them and went back to Jerusalem. [14]The rest of them went on from Perga to Antioch in Pisidia. Then on the Sabbath they went to the Jewish meeting place and sat down.

[15]After the reading of the Law and the Prophets,[t] the leaders sent someone over to tell Paul and Barnabas, "Friends, if you have anything to say that will help the people, please say it."

[16]Paul got up. He motioned with his hand and said:

People of Israel, and everyone else who worships God, listen! [17]The God of Israel chose our ancestors, and he let our people prosper while they were living in Egypt. Then with his mighty power he led them out, [18]and for about forty years he took care of[u] them in the desert. [19]He destroyed seven nations in the land of Canaan and gave their land to our people. [20]All this happened in about 450 years.

Then God gave our people judges until the time of the prophet Samuel, [21]but the people demanded a king. So for forty years God gave them King Saul, the son of Kish from the tribe of Benjamin. [22]Later, God removed Saul and let David rule in his place. God said about him, "David the son of Jesse is the kind of person who pleases me most! He does everything I want him to do."

[23]God promised that someone

---

[p]**12.25** *went back to Jerusalem*: Some manuscripts have "left Jerusalem," and others have "went to Antioch." [q]**13.1** *Herod's*: Herod Antipas, the son of Herod the Great.
[r]**13.2** *going without eating*: The Jews often went without eating as a way of showing how much they loved God. This is also called "fasting." [s]**13.5,13** *John*: Whose other name was Mark (see 12.12, 25). [t]**13.15** *the Law and the Prophets*: The Jewish Scriptures, that is, the Old Testament. [u]**13.18** *took care of*: Some manuscripts have "put up with."

from David's family would come to save the people of Israel, and that one is Jesus. [24]But before Jesus came, John was telling everyone in Israel to turn back to God and be baptized. [25]Then, when John's work was almost done, he said, "Who do you people think I am? Do you think I am the Promised One? He will come later, and I am not good enough to untie his sandals."

[26]Now listen, you descendants of Abraham! Pay attention, all of you Gentiles who are here to worship God! Listen to this message about how to be saved, because it is for everyone. [27]The people of Jerusalem and their leaders didn't realize who Jesus was. And they didn't understand the words of the prophets that they read each Sabbath. So they condemned Jesus just as the prophets had said.

[28-29]They did exactly what the Scriptures said they would. Even though they couldn't find any reason to put Jesus to death, they still asked Pilate to have him killed.

After Jesus had been put to death, he was taken down from the cross[v] and placed in a tomb. [30]But God raised him from death! [31]Then for many days Jesus appeared to his followers who had gone with him from Galilee to Jerusalem. Now they are telling our people about him.

[32]God made a promise to our ancestors. And we are here to tell you the good news [33]that he has kept this promise to us. It is just as the second Psalm says about Jesus,

"You are my son because today
I have become your Father."

[34]God raised Jesus from death and will never let his body decay. It is just as God said,

"I will make to you
the same holy promise
that I made to David."

[35]And in another psalm it says, "God will never let the body of his Holy One decay."

[36]When David was alive, he obeyed God. Then after he died, he was buried in the family grave, and his body decayed. [37]But God raised Jesus from death, and his body did not decay.

[38]My friends, the message is that Jesus can forgive your sins! The Law of Moses could not set you free from all your sins. [39]But everyone who has faith in Jesus is set free. [40]Make sure that what the prophets have said doesn't happen to you. They said,

[41] "Look, you people
who make fun of God!
Be amazed
and disappear.
I will do something today
that you won't believe,
even if someone
tells you about it!"

[42]As Paul and Barnabas were leaving the meeting, the people begged them to say more about these same things on the next Sabbath. [43]After the service, many Jews and a lot of Gentiles who worshiped God went with them. Paul and Barnabas begged them all to remain faithful to God, who had been so kind to them.

[44]The next Sabbath almost everyone in town came to hear the message about the Lord.[w] [45]When the Jewish people saw the crowds, they were very jealous. They insulted Paul and spoke against everything he said.

[46]But Paul and Barnabas bravely said:

We had to tell God's message to you before we told it to anyone else. But you rejected the message! This proves that you don't deserve eternal life. Now we are going to the Gentiles. [47]The Lord has given us this command,

"I have placed you here
as a light
for the Gentiles.
You are to take
the saving power of God
to people everywhere on earth."

[48]This message made the Gentiles glad, and they praised what they had heard about the Lord.[w] Everyone who had been chosen for eternal life then put their faith in the Lord.

[49]The message about the Lord spread all over that region. [50]But the Jewish leaders went to some of the important men in the town and to some respected women who were religious. They turned them against Paul and Barnabas and started making trouble for them. They even chased them out of that part of the country.

[51]Paul and Barnabas shook the dust from that place off their feet[x] and went on to the city of Iconium.

[52]But the Lord's followers in Antioch

were very happy and were filled with
the Holy Spirit.

Paul and Barnabas in Iconium

14 Paul and Barnabas spoke in the
Jewish meeting place in Iconium,
just as they had done at Antioch, and
many Jews and Gentiles[y] put their faith
in the Lord. [2]But the Jews who did not
have faith in him made the other Gentiles angry and turned them against the
Lord's followers.

[3]Paul and Barnabas stayed there for a
while, having faith in the Lord and
bravely speaking his message. The Lord
gave them the power to work miracles
and wonders, and he showed that their
message about his great kindness was
true.

[4]The people of Iconium did not know
what to think. Some of them believed
the Jewish group, and others believed
the apostles. [5]Finally, some Gentiles and
Jews, together with their leaders, decided to make trouble for Paul and
Barnabas and to stone them to death.

[6-7]But when the two apostles found
out what was happening, they escaped
to the region of Lycaonia. They
preached the good news there in the
towns of Lystra and Derbe and in the
nearby countryside.

Paul and Barnabas in Lystra

[8]In Lystra there was a man who had
been born with crippled feet and had
never been able to walk. [9]The man was
listening to Paul speak, when Paul saw
that he had faith in Jesus and could be
healed. So he looked straight at the man
[10]and shouted, "Stand up!" The man
jumped up and started walking around.
[11]When the crowd saw what Paul had
done, they yelled out in the language of
Lycaonia, "The gods have turned into
humans and have come down to us!"
[12]The people then gave Barnabas the
name Zeus, and they gave Paul the
name Hermes,[z] because he did the talking.
[13]The temple of Zeus was near the entrance to the city. Its priest and the
crowds wanted to offer a sacrifice to
Barnabas and Paul. So the priest
brought some bulls and flowers to the
city gates. [14]When the two apostles
found out about this, they tore their
clothes in horror and ran to the crowd,
shouting:

[15]Why are you doing this? We are
humans just like you. Please give up
all this foolishness. Turn to the living

God, who made the sky, the earth,
the sea, and everything in them. [16]In
times past, God let each nation go its
own way. [17]But he showed that he
was there by the good things he did.
God sends rain from heaven and
makes your crops grow. He gives
food to you and makes your hearts
glad.
[18]Even after Paul and Barnabas had
said all this, they could hardly keep the
people from offering a sacrifice to them.

[19]Some Jewish leaders from Antioch
and Iconium came and turned the
crowds against Paul. They hit him with
stones and dragged him out of the city,
thinking he was dead. [20]But when the
Lord's followers gathered around Paul,
he stood up and went back into the city.
The next day he and Barnabas went to
Derbe.

Paul and Barnabas Return to Antioch in Syria

[21]Paul and Barnabas preached the
good news in Derbe and won some people to the Lord. Then they went back to
Lystra, Iconium, and Antioch in Pisidia.
[22]They encouraged the followers and
begged them to remain faithful. They
told them, "We have to suffer a lot before we can get into God's kingdom."
[23]Paul and Barnabas chose some leaders
for each of the churches. Then they
went without eating[a] and prayed that
the Lord would take good care of these
leaders.

[24]Paul and Barnabas went on through
Pisidia to Pamphylia, [25]where they
preached in the town of Perga. Then
they went down to Attalia [26]and sailed
to Antioch in Syria. It was there that
they had been placed in God's care for
the work they had now completed.[b]
[27]After arriving in Antioch, they
called the church together. They told the
people what God had helped them do
and how he had made it possible for
the Gentiles to believe. [28]Then they
stayed there with the followers for a
long time.

15 Some people came from Judea
and started teaching the Lord's
followers that they could not be saved,
unless they were circumcised as Moses
had taught. [2]This caused trouble, and
Paul and Barnabas argued with them
about this teaching. So it was decided to
send Paul and Barnabas and a few others to Jerusalem to discuss this problem
with the apostles and the church leaders.

[y]**14.1** _Gentiles_: The Greek text has "Greeks," which probably means people who were not
Jews. But it may mean Gentiles who worshiped with the Jews.   [z]**14.12** _Hermes_: The Greeks
thought of Hermes as the messenger of the other gods, especially of Zeus, their chief god.
[a]**14.23** _went without eating_: See the note at 13.2.   [b]**14.26** _the work they had now
completed_: See 13.1-3.

The Church Leaders Meet in Jerusalem

³The men who were sent by the church went through Phoenicia and Samaria, telling how the Gentiles had turned to God. This news made the Lord's followers very happy. ⁴When the men arrived in Jerusalem, they were welcomed by the church, including the apostles and the leaders. They told them everything God had helped them do. ⁵But some Pharisees had become followers of the Lord. They stood up and said, "Gentiles who have faith in the Lord must be circumcised and told to obey the Law of Moses."

⁶The apostles and church leaders met to discuss this problem about Gentiles. ⁷They had talked it over for a long time, when Peter got up and said:

My friends, you know that God decided long ago to let me be the one from your group to preach the good news to the Gentiles. God did this so that they would hear and obey him. ⁸He knows what is in everyone's heart. And he showed that he had chosen the Gentiles, when he gave them the Holy Spirit, just as he had given his Spirit to us. ⁹God treated them in the same way that he treated us. They put their faith in him, and he made their hearts pure.

¹⁰Now why are you trying to make God angry by placing a heavy burden on these followers? This burden was too heavy for us or our ancestors. ¹¹But our Lord Jesus was kind to us, and we are saved by faith in him, just as the Gentiles are.

¹²Everyone kept quiet and listened as Barnabas and Paul told how God had given them the power to work a lot of miracles and wonders for the Gentiles.

¹³After they had finished speaking, James*c* said:

My friends, listen to me! ¹⁴Simon Peter*d* has told how God first came to the Gentiles and made some of them his own people. ¹⁵This agrees with what the prophets wrote,

¹⁶ "I, the Lord, will return
    and rebuild
        David's fallen house.
    I will build it from its ruins
        and set it up again.
¹⁷ Then other nations
    will turn to me
        and be my chosen ones.
    I, the Lord, say this.
¹⁸   I promised it long ago."

¹⁹And so, my friends, I don't think we should place burdens on the Gentiles who are turning to God. ²⁰We should simply write and tell them not to eat anything that has been offered to idols. They should be told not to eat the meat of any animal that has been strangled or that still has blood in it. They must also not commit any terrible sexual sins.*e*

²¹We must remember that the Law of Moses has been preached in city after city for many years, and every Sabbath it is read when we Jews meet.

A Letter to Gentiles Who Had Faith in the Lord

²²The apostles, the leaders, and all the church members decided to send some men to Antioch along with Paul and Barnabas. They chose Silas and Judas Barsabbas,*f* who were two leaders of the Lord's followers. ²³They wrote a letter that said:

We apostles and leaders send friendly greetings to all of you Gentiles who are followers of the Lord in Antioch, Syria, and Cilicia. ²⁴We have heard that some people from here have terribly upset you by what they said. But we did not send them! ²⁵So we met together and decided to choose some men and to send them to you along with our good friends Barnabas and Paul. ²⁶These men have risked their lives for our Lord Jesus Christ. ²⁷We are also sending Judas and Silas, who will tell you in person the same things that we are writing.

²⁸The Holy Spirit has shown us that we should not place any extra burden on you. ²⁹But you should not eat anything offered to idols. You should not eat any meat that still has the blood in it or any meat of any animal that has been strangled. You must also not commit any terrible sexual sins. If you follow these instructions, you will do well.

We send our best wishes.

³⁰The four men left Jerusalem and went to Antioch. Then they called the church members together and gave them the letter. ³¹When the letter was read, everyone was pleased and greatly encouraged. ³²Judas and Silas were prophets, and they spoke a long time, encouraging and helping the Lord's followers.

³³The men from Jerusalem stayed on

---

*c***15.13** *James:* The Lord's brother.   *d***15.14** *Simon Peter:* The Greek text has "Simeon," which is another form of the name "Simon." The apostle Peter is meant.   *e***15.20** *not commit any terrible sexual sins:* This probably refers to the laws about the wrong kind of marriages that are forbidden in Leviticus 18.6-18 or to some serious sexual sin.   *f***15.22** *Judas Barsabbas:* He may have been a brother of Joseph Barsabbas (see 1.23), but the name "Barsabbas" was often used by the Jewish people.

in Antioch for a while. And when they left to return to the ones who had sent them, the followers wished them well. 34-35But Paul and Barnabas stayed on in Antioch, where they and many others taught and preached about the Lord.g

Paul and Barnabas Go Their Separate Ways

36Sometime later Paul said to Barnabas, "Let's go back and visit the Lord's followers in the cities where we preached his message. Then we will know how they are doing." 37Barnabas wanted to take along John, whose other name was Mark. 38But Paul did not want to, because Mark had left them in Pamphylia and had stopped working with them.

39Paul and Barnabas argued, then each of them went his own way. Barnabas took Mark and sailed to Cyprus, 40but Paul took Silas and left after the followers had placed them in God's care. 41They traveled through Syria and Cilicia, encouraging the churches.

Timothy Works with Paul and Silas

16 Paul and Silas went back to Derbe and Lystra, where there was a follower named Timothy. His mother was also a follower. She was Jewish, and his father was Greek. 2The Lord's followers in Lystra and Iconium said good things about Timothy, 3and Paul wanted him to go with them. But Paul first had him circumcised, because all the Jewish people around there knew that Timothy's father was Greek.h

4As Paul and the others went from city to city, they told the followers what the apostles and leaders in Jerusalem had decided, and they urged them to follow these instructions. 5The churches became stronger in their faith, and each day more people put their faith in the Lord.

Paul's Vision in Troas

6Paul and his friends went through Phrygia and Galatia, but the Holy Spirit would not let them preach in Asia. 7After they arrived in Mysia, they tried to go into Bithynia, but the Spirit of Jesus would not let them. 8So they went on throughi Mysia until they came to Troas. 9During the night, Paul had a vision of someone from Macedonia who was standing there and begging him, "Come over to Macedonia and help us!" 10After Paul had seen the vision, we began looking for a way to go to Macedonia.

We were sure that God had called us to preach the good news there.

Lydia Becomes a Follower of the Lord

11We sailed straight from Troas to Samothrace, and the next day we arrived in Neapolis. 12From there we went to Philippi, which is a Roman colony in the first district of Macedonia.j

We spent several days in Philippi. 13Then on the Sabbath we went outside the city gate to a place by the river, where we thought there would be a Jewish meeting place for prayer. We sat down and talked with the women who came. 14One of them was Lydia, who was from the city of Thyatira and sold expensive purple cloth. She was a worshiper of the Lord God, and he made her willing to accept what Paul was saying. 15Then after she and her family were baptized, she kept on begging us, "If you think I really do have faith in the Lord, come stay in my home." Finally, we accepted her invitation.

Paul and Silas Are Put in Jail

16One day on our way to the place of prayer, we were met by a slave girl. She had a spirit in her that gave her the power to tell the future. By doing this she made a lot of money for her owners. 17The girl followed Paul and the rest of us and kept yelling, "These men are servants of the Most High God! They are telling you how to be saved."

18This went on for several days. Finally, Paul got so upset that he turned and said to the spirit, "In the name of Jesus Christ, I order you to leave this girl alone!" At once the evil spirit left her.

19When the girl's owners realized that they had lost all chances for making more money, they grabbed Paul and Silas and dragged them into court. 20They told the officials, "These Jews are upsetting our city! 21They are telling us to do things we Romans are not allowed to do."

22The crowd joined in the attack on Paul and Silas. Then the officials tore the clothes off the two men and ordered them to be beaten with a whip. 23After they had been badly beaten, they were put in jail, and the jailer was told to guard them carefully. 24The jailer did as he was told. He put them deep inside the jail and chained their feet to heavy blocks of wood.

25About midnight Paul and Silas were praying and singing praises to God, while the other prisoners listened.

g15.34,35 Verse 34, which says that Silas decided to stay on in Antioch, is not in some manuscripts.   h16.3 had him circumcised . . . Timothy's father was Greek: Timothy would not have been acceptable to the Jews unless he had been circumcised, and Greeks did not circumcise their sons.   i16.8 went on through: Or "passed by."   j16.12 in the first district of Macedonia: Some manuscripts have "and the leading city of Macedonia."

26Suddenly a strong earthquake shook the jail to its foundations. The doors opened, and the chains fell from all the prisoners.

27When the jailer woke up and saw that the doors were open, he thought that the prisoners had escaped. He pulled out his sword and was about to kill himself. 28But Paul shouted, "Don't harm yourself! No one has escaped."

29The jailer asked for a torch and went into the jail. He was shaking all over as he knelt down in front of Paul and Silas. 30After he had led them out of the jail, he asked, "What must I do to be saved?"

31They replied, "Have faith in the Lord Jesus and you will be saved! This is also true for everyone who lives in your home."

32Then Paul and Silas told him and everyone else in his house about the Lord. 33While it was still night, the jailer took them to a place where he could wash their cuts and bruises. Then he and everyone in his home were baptized. 34They were very glad that they had put their faith in God. After this, the jailer took Paul and Silas to his home and gave them something to eat.

35The next morning the officials sent some police with orders for the jailer to let Paul and Silas go. 36The jailer told Paul, "The officials have ordered me to set you free. Now you can leave in peace."

37But Paul told the police, "We are Roman citizens,*k* and the Roman officials had us beaten in public without giving us a trial. They threw us into jail. Now do they think they can secretly send us away? No, they cannot! They will have to come here themselves and let us out."

38When the police told the officials that Paul and Silas were Roman citizens, the officials were afraid. 39So they came and apologized. They led them out of the jail and asked them to please leave town. 40But Paul and Silas went straight to the home of Lydia, where they saw the Lord's followers and encouraged them. Then they left.

Trouble in Thessalonica

17 After Paul and his friends had traveled through Amphipolis and Apollonia, they went on to Thessalonica. A Jewish meeting place was in that city. 2So as usual, Paul went there to worship, and on three Sabbaths he spoke to the people. He used the Scriptures 3to show them that the Messiah

had to suffer, but that he would rise from death. Paul also told them that Jesus is the Messiah he was preaching about. 4Some of them believed what Paul had said, and they became followers with Paul and Silas. Some Gentiles*l* and many important women also believed the message.

5The Jewish leaders were jealous and got some worthless bums who hung around the marketplace to start a riot in the city. They wanted to drag Paul and Silas out to the mob, and so they went straight to Jason's home. 6But when they did not find them there, they dragged out Jason and some of the Lord's followers. They took them to the city authorities and shouted, "Paul and Silas have been upsetting things everywhere. Now they have come here, 7and Jason has welcomed them into his home. All of them break the laws of the Roman Emperor by claiming that someone named Jesus is king."

8The officials and the people were upset when they heard this. 9So they made Jason and the other followers pay bail before letting them go.

People in Berea Welcome the Message

10That same night the Lord's followers sent Paul and Silas on to Berea, and after they arrived, they went to the Jewish meeting place. 11The people in Berea were much nicer than those in Thessalonica, and they gladly accepted the message. Day after day they studied the Scriptures to see if these things were true. 12Many of them put their faith in the Lord, including some important Greek women and several men.

13When the Jewish leaders in Thessalonica heard that Paul had been preaching God's message in Berea, they went there and caused trouble by turning the crowds against Paul.

14Right away the followers sent Paul down to the coast, but Silas and Timothy stayed in Berea. 15Some men went with Paul as far as Athens, and then returned with instructions for Silas and Timothy to join him as soon as possible.

Paul in Athens

16While Paul was waiting in Athens, he was upset to see all the idols in the city. 17He went to the Jewish meeting place to speak to the Jews and to anyone who worshiped with them. Day after day he also spoke to everyone he met in the market. 18Some of them were Epicureans*m* and some were

---

*k***16.37** *Roman citizens:* Only a small number of the people living in the Roman Empire were citizens, and they had special rights and privileges.   *l***17.4** *Gentiles:* See the note at 14.1.   *m***17.18** *Epicureans:* People who followed the teaching of a man named Epicurus, who taught that happiness should be the main goal in life.

Stoics,[n] and they started arguing with him.

People were asking, "What is this know-it-all trying to say?"

Some even said, "Paul must be preaching about foreign gods! That's what he means when he talks about Jesus and about people rising from death."[o]

[19]They brought Paul before a council called the Areopagus, and said, "Tell us what your new teaching is all about. [20]We have heard you say some strange things, and we want to know what you mean."

[21]More than anything else the people of Athens and the foreigners living there loved to hear and to talk about anything new. [22]So Paul stood up in front of the council and said:

People of Athens, I see that you are very religious. [23]As I was going through your city and looking at the things you worship, I found an altar with the words, "To an Unknown God." You worship this God, but you don't really know him. So I want to tell you about him. [24]This God made the world and everything in it. He is Lord of heaven and earth, and he doesn't live in temples built by human hands. [25]He doesn't need help from anyone. He gives life, breath, and everything else to all people. [26]From one person God made all nations who live on earth, and he decided when and where every nation would be.

[27]God has done all this, so that we will look for him and reach out and find him. He isn't far from any of us, [28]and he gives us the power to live, to move, and to be who we are. "We are his children," just as some of your poets have said.

[29]Since we are God's children, we must not think that he is like an idol made out of gold or silver or stone. He isn't like anything that humans have thought up and made. [30]In the past, God forgave all this because people did not know what they were doing. But now he says that everyone everywhere must turn to him. [31]He has set a day when he will judge the world's people with fairness. And he has chosen the man Jesus to do the judging for him. God has given proof of this to all of us by raising Jesus from death.

[32]As soon as the people heard Paul say that a man had been raised from death, some of them started laughing. Others said, "We will hear you talk about this some other time." [33]When Paul left the council meeting, [34]some of the men put their faith in the Lord and went with Paul. One of them was a council member named Dionysius. A woman named Damaris and several others also put their faith in the Lord.

Paul in Corinth

18 Paul left Athens and went to Corinth, [2]where he met Aquila, a Jewish man from Pontus. Not long before this, Aquila had come from Italy with his wife Priscilla, because Emperor Claudius had ordered the Jewish people to leave Rome.[p] Paul went to see Aquila and Priscilla [3]and found out that they were tent makers. Paul was a tent maker too. So he stayed with them, and they worked together.

[4]Every Sabbath, Paul went to the Jewish meeting place. He spoke to Jews and Gentiles[q] and tried to win them over. [5]But after Silas and Timothy came from Macedonia, he spent all his time preaching to the Jews about Jesus the Messiah. [6]Finally, they turned against him and insulted him. So he shook the dust from his clothes[r] and told them, "Whatever happens to you will be your own fault! I am not to blame. From now on I am going to preach to the Gentiles."

[7]Paul then moved into the house of a man named Titius Justus, who worshiped God and lived next door to the Jewish meeting place. [8]Crispus was the leader of the meeting place. He and everyone in his family put their faith in the Lord. Many others in Corinth also heard the message, and all the people who had faith in the Lord were baptized.

[9]One night, Paul had a vision, and in it the Lord said, "Don't be afraid to keep on preaching. Don't stop! [10]I am with you, and you won't be harmed. Many people in this city belong to me." [11]Paul stayed on in Corinth for a year and a half, teaching God's message to the people.

[12]While Gallio was governor of Achaia, some of the Jewish leaders got together and grabbed Paul. They brought him into court [13]and said, "This man is trying to make our people worship God in a way that is against our Law!"

[14]Even before Paul could speak, Gallio said, "If you were charging this man

---

[n] **17.18** *Stoics:* Followers of a man named Zeno, who taught that people should learn self-control and be guided by their consciences. [o] **17.18** *people rising from death:* Or "a goddess named 'Rising from Death.'" [p] **18.2** *Emperor Claudius had ordered all the Jewish people to leave Rome:* Probably A.D. 49, though it may have been A.D. 41. [q] **18.4** *Gentiles:* Here the word is "Greeks." But see the note at 14.1. [r] **18.6** *shook the dust from his clothes:* This means the same as shaking dust from the feet (see the note at 13.51).

with a crime or some other wrong, I would have to listen to you. [15]But since this concerns only words, names, and your own law, you will have to take care of it. I refuse to judge such matters." [16]Then he sent them out of the court. [17]The crowd grabbed Sosthenes, the Jewish leader, and beat him up in front of the court. But none of this mattered to Gallio.

Paul Returns to Antioch in Syria

[18]After Paul had stayed for a while with the Lord's followers in Corinth, he told them good-by and sailed on to Syria with Aquila and Priscilla. But before he left, he had his head shaved[s] at Cenchreae because he had made a promise to God.

[19]The three of them arrived in Ephesus, where Paul left Priscilla and Aquila. He then went into the Jewish meeting place to talk with the people there. [20]They asked him to stay longer, but he refused. [21]He told them good-by and said, "If God lets me, I will come back."

[22]Paul sailed to Caesarea, where he greeted the church. Then he went on to Antioch. [23]After staying there for a while, he left and visited several places in Galatia and Phrygia. He helped the followers there to become stronger in their faith.

Apollos in Ephesus

[24]A Jewish man named Apollos came to Ephesus. Apollos had been born in the city of Alexandria. He was a very good speaker and knew a lot about the Scriptures. [25]He also knew much about the Lord's Way,[t] and he spoke about it with great excitement. What he taught about Jesus was right, but all he knew was John's message about baptism. [26]Apollos started speaking bravely in the Jewish meeting place. But when Priscilla and Aquila heard him, they took him to their home and helped him understand God's Way even better.

[27]Apollos decided to travel through Achaia. So the Lord's followers wrote letters, encouraging the followers there to welcome him. After Apollos arrived in Achaia, he was a great help to everyone who had put their faith in the Lord Jesus because of God's kindness. [28]He got into fierce arguments with the Jewish people, and in public he used the Scriptures to prove that Jesus is the Messiah.

Paul in Ephesus

19 While Apollos was in Corinth, Paul traveled across the hill country to Ephesus, where he met some of the Lord's followers. [2]He asked them, "When you put your faith in Jesus, were you given the Holy Spirit?"

"No!" they answered. "We have never even heard of the Holy Spirit."

[3]"Then why were you baptized?" Paul asked.

They answered, "Because of what John taught."[u]

[4]Paul replied, "John baptized people so that they would turn to God. But he also told them that someone else was coming, and that they should put their faith in him. Jesus is the one that John was talking about." [5]After the people heard Paul say this, they were baptized in the name of the Lord Jesus. [6]Then Paul placed his hands on them. The Holy Spirit was given to them, and they spoke unknown languages and prophesied. [7]There were about twelve men in this group.

[8]For three months Paul went to the Jewish meeting place and talked bravely with the people about God's kingdom. He tried to win them over, [9]but some of them were stubborn and refused to believe. In front of everyone they said terrible things about God's Way. Paul left and took the followers with him to the lecture hall of Tyrannus. He spoke there every day [10]for two years, until every Jew and Gentile[v] in Asia had heard the Lord's message.

The Sons of Sceva

[11]God gave Paul the power to work great miracles. [12]People even took handkerchiefs and aprons that had touched Paul's body, and they carried them to everyone who was sick. All of the sick people were healed, and the evil spirits went out.

[13]Some Jewish men started going around trying to force out evil spirits by using the name of the Lord Jesus. They said to the spirits, "Come out in the name of that same Jesus that Paul preaches about!"

[14]Seven sons of a Jewish high priest named Sceva were doing this, [15]when an evil spirit said to them, "I know Jesus! And I have heard about Paul. But who are you?" [16]Then the man with the evil spirit jumped on them and beat them up. They ran out of the house, naked and bruised.

---

[s]**18.18** *he had his head shaved*: Paul had promised to be a "Nazirite" for a while. This meant that for the time of the promise, he could not cut his hair or drink wine. When the time was over, he would have to cut his hair and offer a sacrifice to God.   [t]**18.25** *the Lord's Way*: See the note at 9.2.   [u]**19.3** *Then why were you baptized? . . . Because of what John taught*: Or "In whose name were you baptized? . . . We were baptized in John's name."
[v]**19.10,17** *Gentile(s)*: The text has "Greek(s)" (see the note at 14.1).

[17]When the Jews and Gentiles[v] in Ephesus heard about this, they were so frightened that they praised the name of the Lord Jesus. [18]Many who were followers now started telling everyone about the evil things they had been doing. [19]Some who had been practicing witchcraft even brought their books and burned them in public. These books were worth about fifty thousand silver coins. [20]So the Lord's message spread and became even more powerful.

The Riot in Ephesus

[21]After all of this had happened, Paul decided[w] to visit Macedonia and Achaia on his way to Jerusalem. Paul had said, "From there I will go on to Rome." [22]So he sent his two helpers, Timothy and Erastus, to Macedonia. But he stayed on in Asia for a while.

[23]At that time there was serious trouble because of the Lord's Way.[x] [24]A silversmith named Demetrius had a business that made silver models of the temple of the goddess Artemis. Those who worked for him earned a lot of money. [25]Demetrius brought together everyone who was in the same business and said:

Friends, you know that we make a good living at this. [26]But you have surely seen and heard how this man Paul is upsetting a lot of people, not only in Ephesus, but almost everywhere in Asia. He claims that the gods we humans make are not really gods at all. [27]Everyone will start saying terrible things about our business. They will stop respecting the temple of the goddess Artemis, who is worshiped in Asia and all over the world. Our great goddess will be forgotten!

[28]When the workers heard this, they got angry and started shouting, "Great is Artemis, the goddess of the Ephesians!" [29]Soon the whole city was in a riot, and some men grabbed Gaius and Aristarchus, who had come from Macedonia with Paul. Then everyone in the crowd rushed to the place where the town meetings were held.

[30]Paul wanted to go out and speak to the people, but the Lord's followers would not let him. [31]A few of the local officials were friendly to Paul, and they sent someone to warn him not to go.

[32]Some of the people in the meeting were shouting one thing, and others were shouting something else. Everyone was completely confused, and most of them did not even know why they were there.

[33]Several of the Jewish leaders pushed a man named Alexander to the front of the crowd and started telling him what to say. He motioned with his hand and tried to explain what was going on. [34]But when the crowd saw that he was Jewish, they all shouted for two hours, "Great is Artemis, the goddess of the Ephesians!"

[35]Finally, a town official made the crowd be quiet. Then he said:

People of Ephesus, who in the world doesn't know that our city is the center for worshiping the great goddess Artemis? Who doesn't know that her image which fell from heaven is right here? [36]No one can deny this, and so you should calm down and not do anything foolish. [37]You have brought men in here who have not robbed temples or spoken against our goddess.

[38]If Demetrius and his workers have a case against these men, we have courts and judges. Let them take their complaints there. [39]But if you want to do more than that, the matter will have to be brought before the city council. [40]We could easily be accused of starting a riot today. There is no excuse for it! We cannot even give a reason for this uproar.

[41]After saying this, he told the people to leave.

Paul Goes through Macedonia and Greece

20 When the riot was over, Paul sent for the followers and encouraged them. He then told them good-by and left for Macedonia. [2]As he traveled from place to place, he encouraged the followers with many messages. Finally, he went to Greece[y] [3]and stayed there for three months.

Paul was about to sail to Syria. But some of the Jewish leaders plotted against him, so he decided to return by way of Macedonia. [4]With him were Sopater, son of Pyrrhus from Berea, and Aristarchus and Secundus from Thessalonica. Gaius from Derbe was also with him, and so were Timothy and the two Asians, Tychicus and Trophimus. [5]They went on ahead to Troas and waited for us there. [6]After the Festival of Thin Bread, we sailed from Philippi. Five days later we met them in Troas and stayed there for a week.

---

[v]19.10,17 *Gentile(s)*: The text has "Greek(s)" (see the note at 14.1).   [w]19.21 *Paul decided*: Or "Paul was led by the Holy Spirit."   [x]19.23 *the Lord's Way*: See the note at 9.2.
[y]20.2 *Greece*: Probably Corinth.

Paul's Last Visit to Troas

[7]On the first day of the week[z] we met to break bread together.[a] Paul spoke to the people until midnight because he was leaving the next morning. [8]In the upstairs room where we were meeting, there were a lot of lamps. [9]A young man by the name of Eutychus was sitting on a window sill. While Paul was speaking, the young man got very sleepy. Finally, he went to sleep and fell three floors all the way down to the ground. When they picked him up, he was dead.

[10]Paul went down and bent over Eutychus. He took him in his arms and said, "Don't worry! He's alive." [11]After Paul had gone back upstairs, he broke bread, and ate with us. He then spoke until dawn and left. [12]Then the followers took the young man home alive and were very happy.

The Voyage from Troas to Miletus

[13]Paul decided to travel by land to Assos. The rest of us went on ahead by ship, and we were to take him aboard there. [14]When he met us in Assos, he came aboard, and we sailed on to Mitylene. [15]The next day we came to a place near Chios, and the following day we reached Samos. The day after that we sailed to Miletus. [16]Paul had decided to sail on past Ephesus, because he did not want to spend too much time in Asia. He was in a hurry and wanted to be in Jerusalem in time for Pentecost.[b]

Paul Says Good-By to the Church Leaders of Ephesus

[17]From Miletus, Paul sent a message for the church leaders at Ephesus to come and meet with him. [18]When they got there, he said:

You know everything I did during the time I was with you when I first came to Asia. [19]Some of the Jews plotted against me and caused me a lot of sorrow and trouble. But I served the Lord and was humble. [20]When I preached in public or taught in your homes, I didn't hold back from telling anything that would help you. [21]I told Jews and Gentiles to turn to God and have faith in our Lord Jesus.

[22]I don't know what will happen to me in Jerusalem, but I must obey God's Spirit and go there. [23]In every city I visit, I am told by the Holy Spirit that I will be put in jail and will be in trouble in Jerusalem. [24]But I don't care what happens to me, as long as I finish the work that the Lord Jesus gave me to do. And that work is to tell the good news about God's great kindness.

[25]I have gone from place to place, preaching to you about God's kingdom, but now I know that none of you will ever see me again. [26]I tell you today that I am no longer responsible for any of you! [27]I have told you everything God wants you to know. [28]Look after yourselves and everyone the Holy Spirit has placed in your care. Be like shepherds to God's church. It is the flock that he bought with the blood of his own Son.[c]

[29]I know that after I am gone, others will come like fierce wolves to attack you. [30]Some of your own people will tell lies to win over the Lord's followers. [31]Be on your guard! Remember how day and night for three years I kept warning you with tears in my eyes.

[32]I now place you in God's care. Remember the message about his great kindness! This message can help you and give you what belongs to you as God's people. [33]I have never wanted anyone's money or clothes. [34]You know how I have worked with my own hands to make a living for myself and my friends. [35]By everything I did, I showed how you should work to help everyone who is weak. Remember that our Lord Jesus said, "More blessings come from giving than from receiving."

[36]After Paul had finished speaking, he knelt down with all of them and prayed. [37]Everyone cried and hugged and kissed him. [38]They were especially sad because Paul had told them, "You will never see me again."

Then they went with him to the ship.

Paul Goes to Jerusalem

21 After saying good-by, we sailed straight to Cos. The next day we reached Rhodes and from there sailed on to Patara. [2]We found a ship going to Phoenicia, so we got on board and sailed off.

[3]We came within sight of Cyprus and then sailed south of it on to the port of Tyre in Syria, where the ship was going to unload its cargo. [4]We looked up the Lord's followers and stayed with them for a week. The Holy Spirit had told them to warn Paul not to go on to Jerusalem. [5]But when the week was

---

[z]**20.7** *On the first day of the week*: Since the Jewish day began at sunset, the meeting would have begun in the evening.   [a]**20.7** *break bread together*: See the note at 2.46.   [b]**20.16** *in time for Pentecost*: The Jewish people liked to be in Jerusalem for this festival (see the note at 2.1).   [c]**20.28** *the blood of his own Son*: Or "his own blood."

over, we started on our way again. All the men, together with their wives and children, walked with us from the town to the seashore. We knelt on the beach and prayed. ⁶Then after saying good-by to each other, we got into the ship, and they went back home.

⁷We sailed from Tyre to Ptolemais, where we greeted the followers and stayed with them for a day. ⁸The next day we went to Caesarea and stayed with Philip, the preacher. He was one of the seven men who helped the apostles, ⁹and he had four unmarried*d* daughters who prophesied.

¹⁰We had been in Caesarea for several days, when the prophet Agabus came to us from Judea. ¹¹He took Paul's belt, and with it he tied up his own hands and feet. Then he told us, "The Holy Spirit says that some of the Jewish leaders in Jerusalem will tie up the man who owns this belt. They will also hand him over to the Gentiles." ¹²After Agabus said this, we and the followers living there begged Paul not to go to Jerusalem.

¹³But Paul answered, "Why are you crying and breaking my heart? I am not only willing to be put in jail for the Lord Jesus. I am even willing to die for him in Jerusalem!"

¹⁴Since we could not get Paul to change his mind, we gave up and prayed, "Lord, please make us willing to do what you want."

¹⁵Then we got ready to go to Jerusalem. ¹⁶Some of the followers from Caesarea went with us and took us to stay in the home of Mnason. He was from Cyprus and had been a follower from the beginning.

Paul Visits James

¹⁷When we arrived in Jerusalem, the Lord's followers gladly welcomed us. ¹⁸Paul went with us to see James*e* the next day, and all the church leaders were present. ¹⁹Paul greeted them and told how God had used him to help the Gentiles. ²⁰Everyone who heard this praised God and said to Paul:

My friend, you can see how many tens of thousands of the Jewish people have become followers! And all of them are eager to obey the Law of Moses. ²¹But they have been told that you are teaching those who live among the Gentiles to disobey this Law. They claim that you are telling them not to circumcise their sons or to follow Jewish customs.

²²What should we do now that our people have heard that you are here? ²³Please do what we ask, because four of our men have made special promises to God. ²⁴Join with them and prepare yourself for the ceremony that goes with the promises. Pay the cost for their heads to be shaved. Then everyone will learn that the reports about you are not true. They will know that you do obey the Law of Moses.

²⁵Some while ago we told the Gentile followers what we think they should do. We instructed them not to eat anything offered to idols. They were told not to eat any meat with blood still in it or the meat of an animal that has been strangled. They were also told not to commit any terrible sexual sins.*f*

²⁶The next day Paul took the four men with him and got himself ready at the same time they did. Then he went into the temple and told when the final ceremony would take place and when an offering would be made for each of them.

Paul Is Arrested

²⁷When the period of seven days for the ceremony was almost over, some of the Jewish people from Asia saw Paul in the temple. They got a large crowd together and started attacking him. ²⁸They were shouting, "Friends, help us! This man goes around everywhere, saying bad things about our nation and about the Law of Moses and about this temple. He has even brought shame to this holy temple by bringing in Gentiles." ²⁹Some of them thought that Paul had brought Trophimus from Ephesus into the temple, because they had seen them together in the city.

³⁰The whole city was in an uproar, and the people turned into a mob. They grabbed Paul and dragged him out of the temple. Then suddenly the doors were shut. ³¹The people were about to kill Paul when the Roman army commander heard that all Jerusalem was starting to riot. ³²So he quickly took some soldiers and officers and ran to where the crowd had gathered.

As soon as the mob saw the commander and soldiers, they stopped beating Paul. ³³The army commander went over and arrested him and had him bound with two chains. Then he tried to find out who Paul was and what he had done. ³⁴Part of the crowd shouted one thing, and part of them shouted something else. But they were making so much noise that the commander could not find out a thing. Then he ordered Paul to be taken into the fortress. ³⁵As they reached the steps, the crowd became so wild that the soldiers had to lift Paul up and carry him. ³⁶The crowd fol-

---

*d*21.9 *unmarried:* Or "virgin."   *e*21.18 *James:* The Lord's brother.   *f*21.25 *not to commit any terrible sexual sins:* See the note at 15.20.

lowed and kept shouting, "Kill him! Kill him!"

Paul Speaks to the Crowd

[37]When Paul was about to be taken into the fortress, he asked the commander, "Can I say something to you?"

"How do you know Greek?" the commander asked. [38]"Aren't you that Egyptian who started a riot not long ago and led four thousand terrorists into the desert?"

[39]"No!" Paul replied. "I am a Jew from Tarsus, an important city in Cilicia. Please let me speak to the crowd."

[40]The commander told him he could speak, so Paul stood on the steps and motioned to the people. When they were quiet, he spoke to them in Aramaic:

22 "My friends and leaders of our nation, listen as I explain what happened!" [2]When the crowd heard Paul speak to them in Aramaic, they became even quieter. Then Paul said:

[3]I am a Jew, born and raised in the city of Tarsus in Cilicia. I was a student of Gamaliel and was taught to follow every single law of our ancestors. In fact, I was just as eager to obey God as any of you are today.

[4]I made trouble for everyone who followed the Lord's Way,[g] and I even had some of them killed. I had others arrested and put in jail. I didn't care if they were men or women. [5]The high priest and all the council members can tell you that this is true. They even gave me letters to the Jewish leaders in Damascus, so that I could arrest people there and bring them to Jerusalem to be punished.

[6]One day about noon I was getting close to Damascus, when a bright light from heaven suddenly flashed around me. [7]I fell to the ground and heard a voice asking, "Saul, Saul, why are you so cruel to me?"

[8]"Who are you?" I answered.

The Lord replied, "I am Jesus from Nazareth! I am the one you are so cruel to." [9]The men who were traveling with me saw the light, but did not hear the voice.

[10]I asked, "Lord, what do you want me to do?"

Then he told me, "Get up and go to Damascus. When you get there, you will be told what to do." [11]The light had been so bright that I couldn't see. And the other men had to lead me by the hand to Damascus.

[12]In that city there was a man named Ananias, who faithfully obeyed the Law of Moses and was well liked by all the Jewish people living there. [13]He came to me and said, "Saul, my friend, you can now see again!"

At once I could see. [14]Then Ananias told me, "The God that our ancestors worshiped has chosen you to know what he wants done. He has chosen you to see the One Who Obeys God[h] and to hear his voice. [15]You must tell everyone what you have seen and heard. [16]What are you waiting for? Get up! Be baptized, and wash away your sins by praying to the Lord."

[17]After this I returned to Jerusalem and went to the temple to pray. There I had a vision [18]of the Lord who said to me, "Hurry and leave Jerusalem! The people won't listen to what you say about me."

[19]I replied, "Lord, they know that in many of our meeting places I arrested and beat people who had faith in you. [20]Stephen was killed because he spoke for you, and I stood there and cheered them on. I even guarded the clothes of the men who murdered him."

[21]But the Lord told me to go, and he promised to send me far away to the Gentiles.

[22]The crowd listened until Paul said this. Then they started shouting, "Get rid of this man! He doesn't deserve to live." [23]They kept shouting. They waved their clothes around and threw dust into the air.

Paul and the Roman Army Commander

[24]The Roman commander ordered Paul to be taken into the fortress and beaten with a whip. He did this to find out why the people were screaming at Paul.

[25]While the soldiers were tying Paul up to be beaten, he asked the officer standing there, "Is it legal to beat a Roman citizen before he has been tried in court?"

[26]When the officer heard this, he went to the commander and said, "What are you doing? This man is a Roman citizen!"

[27]The commander went to Paul and asked, "Tell me, are you a Roman citizen?"

"Yes," Paul answered.

[28]The commander then said, "I paid a lot of money to become a Roman citizen."[i]

But Paul replied, "I was born a Roman citizen."

[29]The men who were about to beat and question Paul quickly backed off.

---

[g]22.4 *followed the Lord's Way*: See the note at 9.2.   [h]22.14 *One Who Obeys God*: See the note at 7.52.   [i]22.28 *Roman citizen*: See the note at 16.37.

And the commander himself was frightened when he realized that he had put a Roman citizen in chains.

Paul Is Tried by the Council

30The next day the commander wanted to know the real reason why the Jewish leaders had brought charges against Paul. So he had Paul's chains removed, and he ordered the chief priests and the whole council to meet. Then he had Paul led in and made him stand in front of them.

23 Paul looked straight at the council members and said, "My friends, to this day I have served God with a clear conscience!"

2Then Ananias the high priest ordered the men standing beside Paul to hit him on the mouth. 3Paul turned to the high priest and said, "You whitewashed wall!j God will hit you. You sit there to judge me by the Law of Moses. But at the same time you order men to break the Law by hitting me."

4The men standing beside Paul asked, "Don't you know you are insulting God's high priest?"

5Paul replied, "Oh! I didn't know he was the high priest. The Scriptures do tell us not to speak evil about a leader of our people."

6When Paul saw that some of the council members were Sadducees and others were Pharisees, he shouted, "My friends, I am a Pharisee and the son of a Pharisee. I am on trial simply because I believe that the dead will be raised to life."

7As soon as Paul said this, the Pharisees and the Sadducees got into a big argument, and the council members started taking sides. 8The Sadducees do not believe in angels or spirits or that the dead will rise to life. But the Pharisees believe in all of these, 9and so there was a lot of shouting. Some of the teachers of the Law of Moses were Pharisees. Finally, they became angry and said, "We don't find anything wrong with this man. Maybe a spirit or an angel really did speak to him."

10The argument became fierce, and the commander was afraid that Paul would be pulled apart. So he ordered the soldiers to go in and rescue Paul. Then they took him back into the fortress.

11That night the Lord stood beside Paul and said, "Don't worry! Just as you have told others about me in Jerusalem, you must also tell about me in Rome."

A Plot To Kill Paul

12-13The next morning more than forty Jewish men got together and vowed that they would not eat or drink anything until they had killed Paul. 14Then some of them went to the chief priests and the nation's leaders and said, "We have promised God that we would not eat a thing until we have killed Paul. 15You and everyone in the council must go to the commander and pretend that you want to find out more about the charges against Paul. Ask for him to be brought before your court. Meanwhile, we will be waiting to kill him before he gets there."

16When Paul's nephew heard about the plot, he went to the fortress and told Paul about it. 17So Paul said to one of the army officers, "Take this young man to the commander. He has something to tell him."

18The officer took him to the commander and said, "The prisoner named Paul asked me to bring this young man to you, because he has something to tell you."

19The commander took the young man aside and asked him in private, "What do you want to tell me?"

20He answered, "Some men are planning to ask you to bring Paul down to the Jewish council tomorrow. They will claim that they want to find out more about him. 21But please don't do what they say. More than forty men are going to attack Paul. They have made a vow not to eat or drink anything until they have killed him. Even now they are waiting to hear what you decide."

22The commander sent the young man away after saying to him, "Don't let anyone know that you told me this."

Paul Is Sent to Felix the Governor

23The commander called in two of his officers and told them, "By nine o'clock tonight have two hundred soldiers ready to go to Caesarea. Take along seventy men on horseback and two hundred foot soldiers with spears. 24Get a horse ready for Paul and make sure that he gets safely through to Felix the governor."

25The commander wrote a letter that said:

26Greetings from Claudius Lysias to the Honorable Governor Felix:

27Some Jews grabbed this man and were about to kill him. But when I found out that he was a Roman citizen, I took some soldiers and rescued him.

28I wanted to find out what they had against him. So I brought him before their council 29and learned that the charges concern only their religious laws. This man isn't guilty of anything for which he should die or even be put in jail.

---

j23.3 whitewashed wall: Someone who pretends to be good, but really isn't.

30As soon as I learned that there was a plot against him, I sent him to you and told their leaders to bring charges against him in your court. **31**The soldiers obeyed the commander's orders, and that same night they took Paul to the city of Antipatris. **32**The next day the foot soldiers returned to the fortress and let the soldiers on horseback take him the rest of the way. **33**When they came to Caesarea, they gave the letter to the governor and handed Paul over to him.

34The governor read the letter. Then he asked Paul and found out that he was from Cilicia. **35**The governor said, "I will listen to your case as soon as the people come to bring their charges against you." After saying this, he gave orders for Paul to be kept as a prisoner in Herod's palace.*k*

Paul Is Accused in the Court of Felix

24 Five days later Ananias the high priest, together with some of their leaders and a lawyer named Tertullus, went to the governor to present their case against Paul. **2**So Paul was called in, and Tertullus stated the case against him:*l*

Honorable Felix, you have brought our people a long period of peace, and because of your concern our nation is much better off. **3**All of us are always grateful for what you have done. **4**I don't want to bother you, but please be patient with us and listen to me for just a few minutes.

5This man has been found to be a real pest and troublemaker for Jews all over the world. He is also a leader of a group called Nazarenes. **6-8**When he tried to disgrace the temple, we arrested him.*m* If you question him, you will find out for yourself that our charges are true. **9**The Jewish crowd spoke up and agreed with what Tertullus had said.

Paul Defends Himself

10The governor motioned for Paul to speak, and he began:

I know that you have judged the people of our nation for many years, and I am glad to defend myself in your court. **11**It was no more than twelve days ago that I went to worship in Jerusalem. You can find this out easily enough. **12**Never once did the Jews find me arguing with anyone in the temple. I didn't cause trouble in the Jewish meeting places or in the city itself. **13**There is no way that they can prove these charges that they are now bringing against me.

14I admit that their leaders think that the Lord's Way*n* which I follow is based on wrong beliefs. But I still worship the same God that my ancestors worshiped. And I believe everything written in the Law of Moses and in the Prophets.*o* **15**I am just as sure as these people are that God will raise from death everyone who is good or evil. **16**And because I am sure, I try my best to have a clear conscience in whatever I do for God or for people.

17After being away for several years, I returned here to bring gifts for the poor people of my nation and to offer sacrifices. **18**This is what I was doing when I was found going through a ceremony in the temple. I wasn't with a crowd, and there was no uproar.

19Some Jews from Asia were there at that time, and if they have anything to say against me, they should be here now. **20**Or ask the ones who are here. They can tell you that they didn't find me guilty of anything when I was tried by their own council. **21**The only charge they can bring against me is what I shouted out in court, when I said, "I am on trial today because I believe that the dead will be raised to life!"

22Felix knew a lot about the Lord's Way.*p* But he brought the trial to an end and said, "I will make my decision after Lysias the commander arrives." **23**He then ordered the army officer to keep Paul under guard, but not to lock him up or to stop his friends from helping him.

Paul Is Kept under Guard

24Several days later Felix and his wife Drusilla, who was Jewish, went to the place where Paul was kept under guard. They sent for Paul and listened while he spoke to them about having faith in Christ Jesus. **25**But Felix was frightened when Paul started talking to them about doing right, about self-control, and about the coming judgment. So he said to Paul, "That's enough for now. You may go. But when I have time I will send

*k***23.35** *Herod's palace*: The palace built by Herod the Great and used by the Roman governors of Palestine.   *l***24.2** *Paul was called in, and Tertullus stated the case against him*: Or "Tertullus was called in and stated the case against Paul."   *m***24.6-8** *we arrested him*: Some manuscripts add, "We wanted to judge him by our own laws. But Lysias the commander took him away from us by force. Then Lysias ordered us to bring our charges against this man in your court."   *n***24.14** *the Lord's Way*: See the note at 9.2.   *o***24.14** *Law of Moses . . . the Prophets*: The Jewish Scriptures, that is, the Old Testament.   *p***24.22** *the Lord's Way*: See the note at 9.2.

for you." ²⁶After this, Felix often sent for Paul and talked with him, because he hoped that Paul would offer him a bribe.

²⁷Two years later Porcius Festus became governor in place of Felix. But since Felix wanted to do the Jewish leaders a favor, he kept Paul in jail.

Paul Asks To Be Tried
by the Roman Emperor

25 Three days after Festus had become governor, he went from Caesarea to Jerusalem. ²There the chief priests and some Jewish leaders told him about their charges against Paul. They also asked Festus ³if he would be willing to bring Paul to Jerusalem. They begged him to do this because they were planning to attack and kill Paul on the way. ⁴But Festus told them, "Paul will be kept in Caesarea, and I am soon going there myself. ⁵If he has done anything wrong, let your leaders go with me and bring charges against him there."

⁶Festus stayed in Jerusalem for eight or ten more days before going to Caesarea. Then the next day he took his place as judge and had Paul brought into court. ⁷As soon as Paul came in, the Jewish leaders from Jerusalem crowded around him and said he was guilty of many serious crimes. But they could not prove anything. ⁸Then Paul spoke in his own defense, "I have not broken the Law of my people. And I have not done anything against either the temple or the Emperor."

⁹Festus wanted to please the leaders. So he asked Paul, "Are you willing to go to Jerusalem and be tried by me on these charges?"

¹⁰Paul replied, "I am on trial in the Emperor's court, and that's where I should be tried. You know very well that I have not done anything to harm the Jewish nation. ¹¹If I had done something deserving death, I would not ask to escape the death penalty. But I am not guilty of any of these crimes, and no one has the right to hand me over to these people. I now ask to be tried by the Emperor himself."

¹²After Festus had talked this over with members of his council, he told Paul, "You have asked to be tried by the Emperor, and to the Emperor you will go!"

Paul Speaks to Agrippa and Bernice

¹³A few days later King Agrippa and Bernice came to Caesarea to visit Festus. ¹⁴They had been there for several days, when Festus told the king about the charges against Paul. He said:

Felix left a man here in jail, ¹⁵and when I went to Jerusalem, the chief priests and the Jewish leaders came and asked me to find him guilty. ¹⁶I told them that it isn't the Roman custom to hand a man over to people who are bringing charges against him. He must first have the chance to meet them face to face and to defend himself against their charges.

¹⁷So when they came here with me, I wasted no time. On the very next day I took my place on the judge's bench and ordered him to be brought in. ¹⁸But when the men stood up to make their charges against him, they did not accuse him of any of the crimes that I thought they would. ¹⁹Instead, they argued with him about some of their beliefs and about a dead man named Jesus, who Paul said was alive.

²⁰Since I did not know how to find out the truth about all this, I asked Paul if he would be willing to go to Jerusalem and be put on trial there. ²¹But Paul asked to be kept in jail until the Emperor could decide his case. So I ordered him to be kept here until I could send him to the Emperor.

²²Then Agrippa said to Festus, "I would also like to hear what this man has to say."

Festus answered, "You can hear him tomorrow."

²³The next day Agrippa and Bernice made a big show as they came into the meeting room. High ranking army officers and leading citizens of the town were also there. Festus then ordered Paul to be brought in ²⁴and said:

King Agrippa and other guests, look at this man! Every Jew from Jerusalem and Caesarea has come to me, demanding for him to be put to death. ²⁵I have not found him guilty of any crime deserving death. But because he has asked to be judged by the Emperor, I have decided to send him to Rome.

²⁶I have to write some facts about this man to the Emperor. So I have brought him before all of you, but especially before you, King Agrippa. After we have talked about his case, I will then have something to write. ²⁷It makes no sense to send a prisoner to the Emperor without stating the charges against him.

Paul's Defense before Agrippa

26 Agrippa told Paul, "You may now speak for yourself."
Paul stretched out his hand and said:

²King Agrippa, I am glad for this chance to defend myself before you today on all these charges that my own people have brought against

me. ³You know a lot about our religious customs and the beliefs that divide us. So I ask you to listen patiently to me.

⁴⁵All the Jews have known me since I was a child. They know what kind of life I have lived in my own country and in Jerusalem. And if they were willing, they could tell you that I was a Pharisee, a member of a group that is stricter than any other. ⁶Now I am on trial because I believe the promise God made to our people long ago.

⁷Day and night our twelve tribes have earnestly served God, waiting for his promised blessings. King Agrippa, because of this hope, the Jewish leaders have brought charges against me. ⁸Why should any of you doubt that God raises the dead to life?

⁹I once thought that I should do everything I could to oppose Jesus from Nazareth. ¹⁰I did this first in Jerusalem, and with the authority of the chief priests I put many of God's people in jail. I even voted for them to be killed. ¹¹I often had them punished in our meeting places, and I tried to make them give up their faith. In fact, I was so angry with them, that I went looking for them in foreign cities.

¹²King Agrippa, one day I was on my way to Damascus with the authority and permission of the chief priests. ¹³About noon I saw a light brighter than the sun. It flashed from heaven on me and on everyone traveling with me. ¹⁴We all fell to the ground. Then I heard a voice say to me in Aramaic, "Saul, Saul, why are you so cruel to me? It's foolish to fight against me!"

¹⁵"Who are you?" I asked.

Then the Lord answered, "I am Jesus! I am the one you are so cruel to. ¹⁶Now stand up. I have appeared to you, because I have chosen you to be my servant. You are to tell others what you have learned about me and what I will show you later."

¹⁷The Lord also said, "I will protect you from the Jews and from the Gentiles that I am sending you to. ¹⁸I want you to open their eyes, so that they will turn from darkness to light and from the power of Satan to God. Then their sins will be forgiven, and by faith in me they will become part of God's holy people."

¹⁹King Agrippa, I obeyed this vision from heaven. ²⁰First I preached to the people in Damascus, and then I went to Jerusalem and all over Judea. Finally, I went to the Gentiles

and said, "Stop sinning and turn to God! Then prove what you have done by the way you live."

²¹That is why some men grabbed me in the temple and tried to kill me. ²²But all this time God has helped me, and I have preached both to the rich and to the poor. I have told them only what the prophets and Moses said would happen. ²³I told them how the Messiah would suffer and be the first to be raised from death, so that he could bring light to his own people and to the Gentiles.

²⁴Before Paul finished defending himself, Festus shouted, "Paul, you're crazy! Too much learning has driven you out of your mind."

²⁵But Paul replied, "Honorable Festus, I am not crazy. What I am saying is true, and it makes sense. ²⁶None of these things happened off in a corner somewhere. I am sure that King Agrippa knows what I am talking about. That's why I can speak so plainly to him."

²⁷Then Paul said to Agrippa, "Do you believe what the prophets said? I know you do."

²⁸Agrippa asked Paul, "In such a short time do you think you can talk me into being a Christian?"

²⁹Paul answered, "Whether it takes a short time or a long time, I wish you and everyone else who hears me today would become just like me! Except, of course, for these chains."

³⁰Then King Agrippa, Governor Festus, Bernice, and everyone who was with them got up. ³¹But before they left, they said, "This man isn't guilty of anything. He doesn't deserve to die or to be put in jail."

³²Agrippa told Festus, "Paul could have been set free, if he had not asked to be tried by the Roman Emperor."

Paul Is Taken to Rome

27 When it was time for us to sail to Rome, Captain Julius from the Emperor's special troops was put in charge of Paul and the other prisoners. ²We went aboard a ship from Adramyttium that was about to sail to some ports along the coast of Asia. Aristarchus from Thessalonica in Macedonia sailed on the ship with us.

³The next day we came to shore at Sidon. Captain Julius was very kind to Paul. He even let him visit his friends, so they could give him whatever he needed. ⁴When we left Sidon, the winds were blowing against us, and we sailed close to the island of Cyprus to be safe from the wind. ⁵Then we sailed south of Cilicia and Pamphylia until we came to the port of Myra in Lycia. ⁶There the army captain found a ship

from Alexandria that was going to Italy. So he ordered us to board that ship.

⁷We sailed along slowly for several days and had a hard time reaching Cnidus. The wind would not let us go any farther in that direction, so we sailed past Cape Salmone, where the island of Crete would protect us from the wind. ⁸We went slowly along the coast and finally reached a place called Fair Havens, not far from the town of Lasea.

⁹By now we had already lost a lot of time, and sailing was no longer safe. In fact, even the Great Day of Forgiveness*a* was past. ¹⁰Then Paul spoke to the crew of the ship, "Men, listen to me! If we sail now, our ship and its cargo will be badly damaged, and many lives will be lost." ¹¹But Julius listened to the captain of the ship and its owner, rather than to Paul.

¹²The harbor at Fair Havens wasn't a good place to spend the winter. Because of this, almost everyone agreed that we should at least try to sail along the coast of Crete as far as Phoenix. It had a harbor that opened toward the southwest and northwest,*r* and we could spend the winter there.

The Storm at Sea

¹³When a gentle wind from the south started blowing, the men thought it was a good time to do what they had planned. So they pulled up the anchor, and we sailed along the coast of Crete. ¹⁴But soon a strong wind called "The Northeaster" blew against us from the island. ¹⁵The wind struck the ship, and we could not sail against it. So we let the wind carry the ship.

¹⁶We went along the island of Cauda on the side that was protected from the wind. We had a hard time holding the lifeboat in place, ¹⁷but finally we got it where it belonged. Then the sailors wrapped ropes around the ship to hold it together. They lowered the sail and let the ship drift along, because they were afraid it might hit the sandbanks in the gulf of Syrtis.

¹⁸The storm was so fierce that the next day they threw some of the ship's cargo overboard. ¹⁹Then on the third day, with their bare hands they threw overboard some of the ship's gear. ²⁰For several days we could not see either the sun or the stars. A strong wind kept blowing, and we finally gave up all hope of being saved.

²¹Since none of us had eaten anything for a long time, Paul stood up and told the men:

You should have listened to me! If you had stayed on in Crete, you would not have had this damage and loss. ²²But now I beg you to cheer up, because you will be safe. Only the ship will be lost.

²³I belong to God, and I worship him. Last night he sent an angel ²⁴to tell me, "Paul, don't be afraid! You will stand trial before the Emperor. And because of you, God will save the lives of everyone on the ship." ²⁵Cheer up! I am sure that God will do exactly what he promised. ²⁶But we will first be shipwrecked on some island.

²⁷For fourteen days and nights we had been blown around over the Mediterranean Sea. But about midnight the sailors realized that we were getting near land. ²⁸They measured and found that the water was about one hundred twenty feet deep. A little later they measured again and found it was only about ninety feet. ²⁹The sailors were afraid that we might hit some rocks, and they let down four anchors from the back of the ship. Then they prayed for daylight.

³⁰The sailors wanted to escape from the ship. So they lowered the lifeboat into the water, pretending that they were letting down an anchor from the front of the ship. ³¹But Paul said to Captain Julius and the soldiers, "If the sailors don't stay on the ship, you won't have any chance to save your lives." ³²The soldiers then cut the ropes that held the lifeboat and let it fall into the sea.

³³Just before daylight Paul begged the people to eat something. He told them, "For fourteen days you have been so worried that you haven't eaten a thing. ³⁴I beg you to eat something. Your lives depend on it. Do this and not one of you will be hurt."

³⁵After Paul had said this, he took a piece of bread and gave thanks to God. Then in front of everyone, he broke the bread and ate some. ³⁶They all felt encouraged, and each of them ate something. ³⁷There were 276 people on the ship, ³⁸and after everyone had eaten, they threw the cargo of wheat into the sea to make the ship lighter.

The Shipwreck

³⁹Morning came, and the ship's crew saw a coast that they did not recognize. But they did see a cove with a beach. So they decided to try to run the ship aground on the beach. ⁴⁰They cut the anchors loose and let them sink into the

---

*a***27.9** *Great Day of Forgiveness*: This Jewish festival took place near the end of September. The sailing season was dangerous after the middle of September, and it was stopped completely between the middle of November and the middle of March.   *r***27.12** *southwest and northwest*: Or "northeast and southeast."

sea. At the same time they untied the ropes that were holding the rudders. Next, they raised the sail at the front of the ship and let the wind carry the ship toward the beach. ⁴¹But it ran aground on a sandbank. The front of the ship stuck firmly in the sand, and the rear was being smashed by the force of the waves.

⁴²The soldiers decided to kill the prisoners to keep them from swimming away and escaping. ⁴³But Captain Julius wanted to save Paul's life, and he did not let the soldiers do what they had planned. Instead, he ordered everyone who could swim to dive into the water and head for shore. ⁴⁴Then he told the others to hold on to planks of wood or parts of the ship. At last, everyone safely reached shore.

On the Island of Malta

28 When we came ashore, we learned that the island was called Malta. ²The local people were very friendly, and they welcomed us by building a fire, because it was rainy and cold.

³After Paul had gathered some wood and had put it on the fire, the heat caused a snake to crawl out, and it bit him on the hand. ⁴When the local people saw the snake hanging from Paul's hand, they said to each other, "This man must be a murderer! He didn't drown in the sea, but the goddess of justice will kill him anyway."

⁵Paul shook the snake off into the fire and wasn't harmed. ⁶The people kept thinking that Paul would either swell up or suddenly drop dead. They watched him for a long time, and when nothing happened to him, they changed their minds and said, "This man is a god."

⁷The governor of the island was named Publius, and he owned some of the land around there. Publius was very friendly and welcomed us into his home for three days. ⁸His father was in bed, sick with fever and stomach trouble, and Paul went to visit him. Paul healed the man by praying and placing his hands on him.

⁹After this happened, everyone on the island brought their sick people to Paul, and they were all healed. ¹⁰The people were very respectful to us, and when we sailed, they gave us everything we needed.

From Malta to Rome

¹¹Three months later we sailed in a ship that had been docked at Malta for the winter. The ship was from Alexandria in Egypt and was known as "The Twin Gods."ˢ ¹²We arrived in Syracuse and stayed for three days. ¹³From there we sailed to Rhegium. The next day a south wind began to blow, and two days later we arrived in Puteoli. ¹⁴There we found some of the Lord's followers, who begged us to stay with them. A week later we left for the city of Rome.

¹⁵Some of the followers in Rome heard about us and came to meet us at the Market of Appius and at the Three Inns. When Paul saw them, he thanked God and was encouraged.

Paul in Rome

¹⁶We arrived in Rome, and Paul was allowed to live in a house by himself with a soldier to guard him.

¹⁷Three days after we got there, Paul called together some of the Jewish leaders and said:

My friends, I have never done anything to hurt our people, and I have never gone against the customs of our ancestors. But in Jerusalem I was handed over as a prisoner to the Romans. ¹⁸They looked into the charges against me and wanted to release me. They found that I had not done anything deserving death. ¹⁹The Jewish leaders disagreed, so I asked to be tried by the Emperor.

But I don't have anything to say against my own nation. ²⁰I am bound by these chains because of what we people of Israel hope for. That's why I have called you here to talk about this hope of ours.

²¹The leaders replied, "No one from Judea has written us a letter about you. And not one of them has come here to report on you or to say anything against you. ²²But we would like to hear what you have to say. We understand that people everywhere are against this new group."

²³They agreed on a time to meet with Paul, and many of them came to his house. From early morning until late in the afternoon, Paul talked to them about God's kingdom. He used the Law of Moses and the Books of the Prophetsᵗ to try to win them over to Jesus.

²⁴Some of the leaders agreed with what Paul said, but others did not. ²⁵Since they could not agree among themselves, they started leaving. But Paul said, "The Holy Spirit said the right thing when he sent Isaiah the prophet ²⁶to tell our ancestors,

'Go to these people
and tell them:

ˢ**28.11** *known as "The Twin Gods"*: Or "carried on its bow a wooden carving of the Twin Gods." These gods were Castor and Pollux, two of the favorite gods among sailors. ᵗ**28.23** *Law of Moses and the Books of the Prophets*: The Jewish Bible, that is, the Old Testament.

You will listen and listen,
   but never understand.
You will look and look,
   but never see.
²⁷ All of you
   have stubborn hearts.
Your ears are stopped up,
   and your eyes are covered.
You cannot see or hear
   or understand.
If you could,

you would turn to me,
   and I would heal you.' "

²⁸⁻²⁹Paul said, "You may be sure that God wants to save the Gentiles! And they will listen."^u

³⁰For two years Paul stayed in a rented house and welcomed everyone who came to see him. ³¹He bravely preached about God's kingdom and taught about the Lord Jesus Christ, and no one tried to stop him.

^u**28.28,29** _And they will listen_: Some manuscripts add, "After Paul said this, the people left, but they got into a fierce argument among themselves."

ROMANS

ABOUT THIS BOOK

Paul wrote this letter to introduce himself and his message to the church at Rome. He had never been to this important city, although he knew the names of many Christians there and hoped to visit them soon (15.22—16.21). Paul tells them that he is an apostle, chosen to preach the good news (1.1). And the message he proclaims "is God's powerful way of saving all people who have faith, whether they are Jews or Gentiles" (1.16).

Paul reminds his readers, "All of us have sinned and fallen short of God's glory" (3.23). But how can we be made acceptable to God? This is the main question that Paul answers in this letter. He begins by showing how everyone has failed to do what God requires. The Jews have not obeyed the Law of Moses, and the Gentiles have refused even to think about God, although God has spoken to them in many different ways (1.18—3.20).

Now we see how God does make us acceptable to him. . . . He accepts people only because they have faith in Jesus Christ . . . God treats us much better than we deserve, and because of Christ Jesus, he freely accepts us and sets us free from our sins.　　　　　　　　　　　　　　　　　　　　　　　　　*(3.21a-24)*

God gave Jesus to die for our sins, and he raised him to life, so that we would be made acceptable to God.　　　　　　　　　　　　　　　　　　　　　　　*(4.25)*

A QUICK LOOK AT THIS LETTER

Paul and His Message of Good News (1.1-17)
Everyone Is Guilty (1.18—3.20)
God's Way of Accepting People (3.21—4.25)
A New Life for God's People (5.1—8.39)
What about the People of Israel? (9.1—11.36)
How to Live the New Life of Love (12.1—15.13)
Paul's Plans and Personal Greetings (15.14—16.27)

---

1 From Paul, a servant of Christ Jesus.

God chose me to be an apostle, and he appointed me to preach the good news [2]that he promised long ago by what his prophets said in the holy Scriptures. [3-4]This good news is about his Son, our Lord Jesus Christ! As a human, he was from the family of David. But the Holy Spirit[a] proved that Jesus is the powerful Son of God,[b] because he was raised from death.

[5]Jesus was kind to me and chose me to be an apostle,[c] so that people of all nations would obey and have faith. [6]You are some of those people chosen by Jesus Christ.

[7]This letter is to all of you in Rome. God loves you and has chosen you to be his very own people.

I pray that God our Father and our Lord Jesus Christ will be kind to you and will bless you with peace!

---

[a]**1.4** *the Holy Spirit*: Or "his own spirit of holiness."　　　[b]**1.4** *proved that Jesus is the powerful Son of God*: Or "proved in a powerful way that Jesus is the Son of God."　　　[c]**1.5** *Jesus was kind to me and chose me to be an apostle*: Or "Jesus was kind to us and chose us to be his apostles."

A Prayer of Thanks

[8]First, I thank God in the name of Jesus Christ for all of you. I do this because people everywhere in the world are talking about your faith. [9]God has seen how I never stop praying for you, while I serve him with all my heart and tell the good news about his Son.

[10]In all my prayers, I ask God to make it possible for me to visit you. [11]I want to see you and share with you the same blessings that God's Spirit has given me. Then you will grow stronger in your faith. [12]What I am saying is that we can encourage each other by the faith that is ours.

[13]My friends, I want you to know that I have often planned to come for a visit. But something has always kept me from doing it. I want to win followers to Christ in Rome, as I have done in many other places. [14-15]It doesn't matter if people are civilized and educated, or if they are uncivilized and uneducated. I must tell the good news to everyone. That's why I am eager to visit all of you in Rome.

The Power of the Good News

[16]I am proud of the good news! It is God's powerful way of saving all people who have faith, whether they are Jews or Gentiles. [17]The good news tells how God accepts everyone who has faith, but only those who have faith.[d] It is just as the Scriptures say, "The people God accepts because of their faith will live."[e]

Everyone Is Guilty

[18]From heaven God shows how angry he is with all the wicked and evil things that sinful people do to crush the truth. [19]They know everything that can be known about God, because God has shown it all to them. [20]God's eternal power and character cannot be seen. But from the beginning of creation, God has shown what these are like by all he has made. That's why those people don't have any excuse. [21]They know about God, but they don't honor him or even thank him. Their thoughts are useless, and their stupid minds are in the dark. [22]They claim to be wise, but they are fools. [23]They don't worship the glorious and eternal God. Instead, they worship idols that are made to look like humans who cannot live forever, and like birds, animals, and reptiles.

[24]So God let these people go their own way. They did what they wanted to do, and their filthy thoughts made them do shameful things with their bodies.

[25]They gave up the truth about God for a lie, and they worshiped God's creation instead of God, who will be praised forever. Amen.

[26]God let them follow their own evil desires. Women no longer wanted to have sex in a natural way, and they did things with each other that were not natural. [27]Men behaved in the same way. They stopped wanting to have sex with women and had strong desires for sex with other men. They did shameful things with each other, and what has happened to them is punishment for their foolish deeds.

[28]Since these people refused even to think about God, he let their useless minds rule over them. That's why they do all sorts of indecent things. [29]They are evil, wicked, and greedy, as well as mean in every possible way. They want what others have, and they murder, argue, cheat, and are hard to get along with. They gossip, [30]say cruel things about others, and hate God. They are proud, conceited, and boastful, always thinking up new ways to do evil.

These people don't respect their parents. [31]They are stupid, unreliable, and don't have any love or pity for others. [32]They know God has said that anyone who acts this way deserves to die. But they keep on doing evil things, and they even encourage others to do them.

God's Judgment Is Fair

2 Some of you accuse others of doing wrong. But there is no excuse for what you do. When you judge others, you condemn yourselves, because you are guilty of doing the very same things. [2]We know that God is right to judge everyone who behaves in this way. [3]Do you really think God won't punish you, when you behave exactly like the people you accuse? [4]You surely don't think much of God's wonderful goodness or of his patience and willingness to put up with you. Don't you know that the reason God is good to you is because he wants you to turn to him?

[5]But you are stubborn and refuse to turn to God. So you are making things even worse for yourselves on that day when he will show how angry he is and will judge the world with fairness. [6]God will reward each of us for what we have done. [7]He will give eternal life to everyone who has patiently done what is good in the hope of receiving glory, honor, and life that lasts forever. [8]But he will show how angry and furious he can be with every selfish person who rejects the truth and wants to do evil. [9]All who

---

[d]**1.17** *but only those who have faith*: Or "and faith is all that matters."   [e]**1.17** *The people God accepts because of their faith will live*: Or "The people God accepts will live because of their faith."

are wicked will be punished with trouble and suffering. It doesn't matter if they are Jews or Gentiles. ¹⁰But all who do right will be rewarded with glory, honor, and peace, whether they are Jews or Gentiles. ¹¹God doesn't have any favorites!

¹²Those people who don't know about God's Law will still be punished for what they do wrong. And the Law will be used to judge everyone who knows what it says. ¹³God accepts those who obey his Law, but not those who simply hear it.

¹⁴Some people naturally obey the Law's commands, even though they don't have the Law. ¹⁵This proves that the conscience is like a law written in the human heart. And it will show whether we are forgiven or condemned, ¹⁶when God appoints Jesus Christ to judge everyone's secret thoughts, just as my message says.

The Jews and the Law

¹⁷Some of you call yourselves Jews. You trust in the Law and take pride in God. ¹⁸By reading the Scriptures you learn how God wants you to behave, and you discover what is right. ¹⁹You are sure that you are a guide for the blind and a light for all who are in the dark. ²⁰And since there is knowledge and truth in God's Law, you think you can instruct fools and teach young people.

²¹But how can you teach others when you refuse to learn? You preach that it is wrong to steal. But do you steal? ²²You say people should be faithful in marriage. But are you faithful? You hate idols, yet you rob their temples. ²³You take pride in the Law, but you disobey the Law and bring shame to God. ²⁴It is just as the Scriptures tell us, "You have made foreigners say insulting things about God."

²⁵Being circumcised is worthwhile, if you obey the Law. But if you don't obey the Law, you are no better off than people who are not circumcised. ²⁶In fact, if they obey the Law, they are as good as anyone who is circumcised. ²⁷So everyone who obeys the Law, but has never been circumcised, will condemn you. Even though you are circumcised and have the Law, you still don't obey its teachings.

²⁸Just because you live like a Jew and are circumcised doesn't make you a real Jew. ²⁹To be a real Jew you must obey the Law. True circumcision is something that happens deep in your heart, not something done to your body. And besides, you should want praise from God and not from humans.

3 What good is it to be a Jew? What good is it to be circumcised? ²It is good in a lot of ways! First of all, God's messages were spoken to the Jews. ³It is true that some of them did not believe the message. But does this mean that God cannot be trusted, just because they did not have faith? ⁴No, indeed! God tells the truth, even if everyone else is a liar. The Scriptures say about God,

"Your words
    will be proven true,
and in court
    you will win your case."

⁵If our evil deeds show how right God is, then what can we say? Is it wrong for God to become angry and punish us? What a foolish thing to ask. ⁶But the answer is, "No." Otherwise, how could God judge the world? ⁷Since your lies bring great honor to God by showing how truthful he is, you may ask why God still says you are a sinner. ⁸You might as well say, "Let's do something evil, so that something good will come of it!" Some people even claim that we are saying this. But God is fair and will judge them as well.

No One Is Good

⁹What does all this mean? Does it mean that we Jews are better off than the Gentiles? No, it doesn't! Jews, as well as Gentiles, are ruled by sin, just as I have said. ¹⁰The Scriptures tell us,

"No one is acceptable to God!
¹¹ Not one of them understands
    or even searches for God.
¹² They have all turned away
    and are worthless.
There isn't one person
    who does right.
¹³ Their words are like
    an open pit,
and their tongues are good
    only for telling lies.
Each word is as deadly
    as the fangs of a snake,
¹⁴ and they say nothing
    but bitter curses.
¹⁵ These people quickly
    become violent.
¹⁶ Wherever they go,
    they leave ruin
    and destruction.
¹⁷ They don't know how
    to live in peace.
¹⁸   They don't even fear God."

¹⁹We know that everything in the Law was written for those who are under its power. The Law says these things to stop anyone from making excuses and to let God show that the whole world is

ᶠ3.9 *better off:* Or "worse off."

guilty. [20]God doesn't accept people simply because they obey the Law. No, indeed! All the Law does is to point out our sin.

God's Way of Accepting People

[21]Now we see how God does make us acceptable to him. The Law and the Prophets[g] tell how we become acceptable, and it isn't by obeying the Law of Moses. [22]God treats everyone alike. He accepts people only because they have faith in Jesus Christ. [23]All of us have sinned and fallen short of God's glory. [24]But God treats us much better than we deserve,[h] and because of Christ Jesus, he freely accepts us and sets us free from our sins. [25-26]God sent Christ to be our sacrifice. Christ offered his life's blood, so that by faith in him we could come to God. And God did this to show that in the past he was right to be patient and forgive sinners. This also shows that God is right when he accepts people who have faith in Jesus.

[27]What is left for us to brag about? Not a thing! Is it because we obeyed some law? No! It is because of faith. [28]We see that people are acceptable to God because they have faith, and not because they obey the Law. [29]Does God belong only to the Jews? Isn't he also the God of the Gentiles? Yes, he is! [30]There is only one God, and he accepts Gentiles as well as Jews, simply because of their faith. [31]Do we destroy the Law by our faith? Not at all! We make it even more powerful.

The Example of Abraham

4 Well then, what can we say about our ancestor Abraham? [2]If he became acceptable to God because of what he did, then he would have something to brag about. But he would never be able to brag about it to God. [3]The Scriptures say, "God accepted Abraham because Abraham had faith in him."

[4]Money paid to workers isn't a gift. It is something they earn by working. [5]But you cannot make God accept you because of something you do. God accepts sinners only because they have faith in him. [6]In the Scriptures David talks about the blessings that come to people who are acceptable to God, even though they don't do anything to deserve these blessings. David says,

[7] "God blesses people
    whose sins are forgiven
and whose evil deeds
    are forgotten.

[8] The Lord blesses people
    whose sins are erased
    from his book."

[9]Are these blessings meant for circumcised people or for those who are not circumcised? Well, the Scriptures say that God accepted Abraham because Abraham had faith in him. [10]But when did this happen? Was it before or after Abraham was circumcised? Of course, it was before.

[11]Abraham let himself be circumcised to show that he had been accepted because of his faith even before he was circumcised. This makes Abraham the father of all who are acceptable to God because of their faith, even though they are not circumcised. [12]This also makes Abraham the father of everyone who is circumcised and has faith in God, as Abraham did before he was circumcised.

The Promise Is for All Who Have Faith

[13]God promised Abraham and his descendants that he would give them the world. This promise wasn't made because Abraham had obeyed a law, but because his faith in God made him acceptable. [14]If Abraham and his descendants were given this promise because they had obeyed a law, then faith would mean nothing, and the promise would be worthless.

[15]God becomes angry when his Law is broken. But where there isn't a law, it cannot be broken. [16]Everything depends on having faith in God, so that God's promise is assured by his great kindness. This promise isn't only for Abraham's descendants who have the Law. It is for all who are Abraham's descendants because they have faith, just as he did. Abraham is the ancestor of us all. [17]The Scriptures say that Abraham would become the ancestor of many nations. This promise was made to Abraham because he had faith in God, who raises the dead to life and creates new things.

[18]God promised Abraham a lot of descendants. And when it all seemed hopeless, Abraham still had faith in God and became the ancestor of many nations. [19]Abraham's faith never became weak, not even when he was nearly a hundred years old. He knew that he was almost dead and that his wife Sarah could not have children. [20]But Abraham never doubted or questioned God's promise. His faith made him strong, and he gave all the credit to God.

---

[g]3.21 *The Law and the Prophets*: The Jewish Scriptures, that is, the Old Testament.
[h]3.24 *treats us much better than we deserve*: The Greek word *charis*, traditionally rendered "grace," is translated here and other places in the CEV to express the overwhelming kindness of God.

²¹Abraham was certain that God could do what he had promised. ²²So God accepted him, ²³just as we read in the Scriptures. But these words were not written only for Abraham. ²⁴They were written for us, since we will also be accepted because of our faith in God, who raised our Lord Jesus to life. ²⁵God gave Jesus to die for our sins, and he raised him to life, so that we would be made acceptable to God.

What It Means To Be Acceptable to God

5 By faith we have been made acceptable to God. And now, because of our Lord Jesus Christ, we live at peace*ⁱ* with God. ²Christ has also introduced us*ʲ* to God's undeserved kindness on which we take our stand. So we are happy, as we look forward to sharing in the glory of God. ³But that's not all! We gladly suffer,*ᵏ* because we know that suffering helps us to endure. ⁴And endurance builds character, which gives us a hope ⁵that will never disappoint us. All of this happens because God has given us the Holy Spirit, who fills our hearts with his love.

⁶Christ died for us at a time when we were helpless and sinful. ⁷No one is really willing to die for an honest person, though someone might be willing to die for a truly good person. ⁸But God showed how much he loved us by having Christ die for us, even though we were sinful.

⁹But there is more! Now that God has accepted us because Christ sacrificed his life's blood, we will also be kept safe from God's anger. ¹⁰Even when we were God's enemies, he made peace with us, because his Son died for us. Yet something even greater than friendship is ours. Now that we are at peace with God, we will be saved by his Son's life. ¹¹And in addition to everything else, we are happy because God sent our Lord Jesus Christ to make peace with us.

Adam and Christ

¹²Adam sinned, and that sin brought death into the world. Now everyone has sinned, and so everyone must die. ¹³Sin was in the world before the Law came. But no record of sin was kept, because there was no Law. ¹⁴Yet death still had power over all who lived from the time of Adam to the time of Moses. This happened, though not everyone disobeyed a direct command from God, as Adam did.

In some ways Adam is like Christ who came later. ¹⁵But the gift that God was kind enough to give was very different from Adam's sin. That one sin brought death to many others. Yet in an even greater way, Jesus Christ alone brought God's gift of kindness to many people.

¹⁶There is a lot of difference between Adam's sin and God's gift. That one sin led to punishment. But God's gift made it possible for us to be acceptable to him, even though we have sinned many times. ¹⁷Death ruled like a king because Adam had sinned. But that cannot compare with what Jesus Christ has done. God has been so kind to us, and he has accepted us because of Jesus. And so we will live and rule like kings.

¹⁸Everyone was going to be punished because Adam sinned. But because of the good thing that Christ has done, God accepts us and gives us the gift of life. ¹⁹Adam disobeyed God and caused many others to be sinners. But Jesus obeyed him and will make many people acceptable to God.

²⁰The Law came, so that the full power of sin could be seen. Yet where sin was powerful, God's kindness was even more powerful. ²¹Sin ruled by means of death. But God's kindness now rules, and God has accepted us because of Jesus Christ our Lord. This means that we will have eternal life.

Dead to Sin but Alive because of Christ

6 What should we say? Should we keep on sinning, so that God's wonderful kindness will show up even better? ²No, we should not! If we are dead to sin, how can we go on sinning? ³Don't you know that all who share in Christ Jesus by being baptized also share in his death? ⁴When we were baptized, we died and were buried with Christ. We were baptized, so that we would live a new life, as Christ was raised to life by the glory of God the Father.

⁵If we shared in Jesus' death by being baptized, we will be raised to life with him. ⁶We know that the persons we used to be were nailed to the cross with Jesus. This was done, so that our sinful bodies would no longer be the slaves of sin. ⁷We know that sin doesn't have power over dead people.

⁸As surely as we died with Christ, we believe we will also live with him. ⁹We know that death no longer has any power over Christ. He died and was raised to life, never again to die. ¹⁰When Christ died, he died for sin once and for all. But now he is alive, and he lives only for God. ¹¹In the same way, you must think of yourselves as dead to the power of sin. But Christ Jesus has given life to you, and you live for God.

¹²Don't let sin rule your body. After all, your body is bound to die, so don't

---

*ⁱ***5.1** *we live at peace*: Some manuscripts have "let us live at peace."   *ʲ***5.2** *introduced us*: Some manuscripts add "by faith."   *ᵏ***5.3** *We gladly suffer*: Or "Let us gladly suffer."

obey its desires [13]or let any part of it become a slave of evil. Give yourselves to God, as people who have been raised from death to life. Make every part of your body a slave that pleases God. [14]Don't let sin keep ruling your lives. You are ruled by God's kindness and not by the Law.

Slaves Who Do What Pleases God

[15]What does all this mean? Does it mean we are free to sin, because we are ruled by God's wonderful kindness and not by the Law? Certainly not! [16]Don't you know that you are slaves of anyone you obey? You can be slaves of sin and die, or you can be obedient slaves of God and be acceptable to him. [17]You used to be slaves of sin. But I thank God that with all your heart you obeyed the teaching you received from me. [18]Now you are set free from sin and are slaves who please God.

[19]I am using these everyday examples, because in some ways you are still weak. You used to let the different parts of your body be slaves of your evil thoughts. But now you must make every part of your body serve God, so that you will belong completely to him.

[20]When you were slaves of sin, you didn't have to please God. [21]But what good did you receive from the things you did? All you have to show for them is your shame, and they lead to death. [22]Now you have been set free from sin, and you are God's slaves. This will make you holy and will lead you to eternal life. [23]Sin pays off with death. But God's gift is eternal life given by Jesus Christ our Lord.

An Example from Marriage

7 My friends, you surely understand enough about law to know that laws only have power over people who are alive. [2]For example, the Law says that a man's wife must remain his wife as long as he lives. But once her husband is dead, she is free [3]to marry someone else. However, if she goes off with another man while her husband is still alive, she is said to be unfaithful.

[4]That is how it is with you, my friends. You are now part of the body of Christ and are dead to the power of the Law. You are free to belong to Christ, who was raised to life so that we could serve God. [5]When we thought only of ourselves, the Law made us have sinful desires. It made every part of our bodies into slaves who are doomed to die. [6]But the Law no longer rules over us. We are like dead people, and it cannot have any power over us. Now we can serve God in a new way by obeying his Spirit, and

not in the old way by obeying the written Law.

The Battle with Sin

[7]Does this mean that the Law is sinful? Certainly not! But if it had not been for the Law, I would not have known what sin is really like. For example, I would not have known what it means to want something that belongs to someone else, unless the Law had told me not to do that. [8]It was sin that used this command as a way of making me have all kinds of desires. But without the Law, sin is dead.

[9]Before I knew about the Law, I was alive. But as soon as I heard that command, sin came to life, [10]and I died. The very command that was supposed to bring life to me, instead brought death. [11]Sin used this command to trick me, and because of it I died. [12]Still, the Law and its commands are holy and correct and good.

[13]Am I saying that something good caused my death? Certainly not! It was sin that killed me by using something good. Now we can see how terrible and evil sin really is. [14]We know that the Law is spiritual. But I am merely a human, and I have been sold as a slave to sin. [15]In fact, I don't understand why I act the way I do. I don't do what I know is right. I do the things I hate. [16]Although I don't do what I know is right, I agree that the Law is good. [17]So I am not the one doing these evil things. The sin that lives in me is what does them.

[18]I know that my selfish desires won't let me do anything that is good. Even when I want to do right, I cannot. [19]Instead of doing what I know is right, I do wrong. [20]And so, if I don't do what I know is right, I am no longer the one doing these evil things. The sin that lives in me is what does them.

[21]The Law has shown me that something in me keeps me from doing what I know is right. [22]With my whole heart I agree with the Law of God. [23]But in every part of me I discover something fighting against my mind, and it makes me a prisoner of sin that controls everything I do. [24]What a miserable person I am. Who will rescue me from this body that is doomed to die? [25]Thank God! Jesus Christ will rescue me.

So with my mind I serve the Law of God, although my selfish desires make me serve the law of sin.

Living by the Power of God's Spirit

8 If you belong to Christ Jesus, you won't be punished. [2]The Holy Spirit will give you life that comes from Christ Jesus and will set you[1] free from sin and

[1]8.2 _you:_ Some manuscripts have "me."

death. [3]The Law of Moses cannot do this, because our selfish desires make the Law weak. But God set you free when he sent his own Son to be like us sinners and to be a sacrifice for our sin. God used Christ's body to condemn sin. [4]He did this, so that we would do what the Law commands by obeying the Spirit instead of our own desires.

[5]People who are ruled by their desires think only of themselves. Everyone who is ruled by the Holy Spirit thinks about spiritual things. [6]If our minds are ruled by our desires, we will die. But if our minds are ruled by the Spirit, we will have life and peace. [7]Our desires fight against God, because they do not and cannot obey God's laws. [8]If we follow our desires, we cannot please God.

[9]You are no longer ruled by your desires, but by God's Spirit, who lives in you. People who don't have the Spirit of Christ in them don't belong to him. [10]But Christ lives in you. So you are alive because God has accepted you, even though your bodies must die because of your sins. [11]Yet God raised Jesus to life! God's Spirit now lives in you, and he will raise you to life by his Spirit.

[12]My dear friends, we must not live to satisfy our desires. [13]If you do, you will die. But you will live, if by the help of God's Spirit you say "No" to your desires. [14]Only those people who are led by God's Spirit are his children. [15]God's Spirit doesn't make us slaves who are afraid of him. Instead, we become his children and call him our Father.[m] [16]God's Spirit makes us sure that we are his children. [17]His Spirit lets us know that together with Christ we will be given what God has promised. We will also share in the glory of Christ, because we have suffered with him.

A Wonderful Future for God's People

[18]I am sure that what we are suffering now cannot compare with the glory that will be shown to us. [19]In fact, all creation is eagerly waiting for God to show who his children are. [20]Meanwhile, creation is confused, but not because it wants to be confused. God made it this way in the hope [21]that creation would be set free from decay and would share in the glorious freedom of his children. [22]We know that all creation is still groaning and is in pain, like a woman about to give birth.

[23]The Spirit makes us sure about what we will be in the future. But now we groan silently, while we wait for God to show that we are his children.[n] This means that our bodies will also be set free. [24]And this hope is what saves us. But if we already have what we hope for, there is no need to keep on hoping. [25]However, we hope for something we have not yet seen, and we patiently wait for it.

[26]In certain ways we are weak, but the Spirit is here to help us. For example, when we don't know what to pray for, the Spirit prays for us in ways that cannot be put into words. [27]All of our thoughts are known to God. He can understand what is in the mind of the Spirit, as the Spirit prays for God's people. [28]We know that God is always at work for the good of everyone who loves him.[o] They are the ones God has chosen for his purpose, [29]and he has always known who his chosen ones would be. He had decided to let them become like his own Son, so that his Son would be the first of many children. [30]God then accepted the people he had already decided to choose, and he has shared his glory with them.

God's Love

[31]What can we say about all this? If God is on our side, can anyone be against us? [32]God did not keep back his own Son, but he gave him for us. If God did this, won't he freely give us everything else? [33]If God says his chosen ones are acceptable to him, can anyone bring charges against them? [34]Or can anyone condemn them? No indeed! Christ died and was raised to life, and now he is at God's right side,[p] speaking to him for us. [35]Can anything separate us from the love of Christ? Can trouble, suffering, and hard times, or hunger and nakedness, or danger and death? [36]It is exactly as the Scriptures say,

"For you we face death
  all day long.
We are like sheep
  on their way
    to be butchered."

[37]In everything we have won more than a victory because of Christ who loves us. [38]I am sure that nothing can separate us from God's love—not life or death, not angels or spirits, not the present or the future, [39]and not powers above or powers below. Nothing in all creation

---

[m]**8.15** *our Father*: The Greek text uses the Aramaic word "Abba" (meaning "father"), which shows the close relation between the children and their father.   [n]**8.23** *to show that we are his children*: These words are not in some manuscripts. The translation of the remainder of the verse would then read, "while we wait for God to set our bodies free."   [o]**8.28** *God is always at work for the good of everyone who loves him*: Or "All things work for the good of everyone who loves God" or "God's Spirit always works for the good of everyone who loves God."
[p]**8.34** *right side*: The place of power and honor.

can separate us from God's love for us in Christ Jesus our Lord!

God's Choice of Israel

9 I am a follower of Christ, and the Holy Spirit is a witness to my conscience. So I tell the truth and I am not lying when I say [2]my heart is broken and I am in great sorrow. [3]I would gladly be placed under God's curse and be separated from Christ for the good of my own people. [4]They are the descendants of Israel, and they are also God's chosen people. God showed them his glory. He made agreements with them and gave them his Law. The temple is theirs and so are the promises that God made to them. [5]They have those famous ancestors, who were also the ancestors of Jesus Christ. I pray that God, who rules over all, will be praised forever![q] Amen.

[6]It cannot be said that God broke his promise. After all, not all of the people of Israel are the true people of God. [7-8]In fact, when God made the promise to Abraham, he meant only Abraham's descendants by his son Isaac. God was talking only about Isaac when he promised [9]Sarah, "At this time next year I will return, and you will already have a son."

[10]Don't forget what happened to the twin sons of Isaac and Rebekah. [11-12]Even before they were born or had done anything good or bad, the Lord told Rebekah that her older son would serve the younger one. The Lord said this to show that he makes his own choices and that it wasn't because of anything either of them had done. [13]That's why the Scriptures say that the Lord liked Jacob more than Esau.

[14]Are we saying that God is unfair? Certainly not! [15]The Lord told Moses that he has pity and mercy on anyone he wants to. [16]Everything then depends on God's mercy and not on what people want or do. [17]In the Scriptures the Lord says to the king of Egypt, "I let you become king, so that I could show you my power and be praised by all people on earth." [18]Everything depends on what God decides to do, and he can either have pity on people or make them stubborn.

God's Anger and Mercy

[19]Someone may ask, "How can God blame us, if he makes us behave in the way he wants us to?" [20]But, my friend, I ask, "Who do you think you are to question God? Does the clay have the right to ask the potter why he shaped it the way he did? [21]Doesn't a potter have the right to make a fancy bowl and a plain bowl out of the same lump of clay?"

[22]God wanted to show his anger and reveal his power against everyone who deserved to be destroyed. But instead, he patiently put up with them. [23]He did this by showing how glorious he is when he has pity on the people he has chosen to share in his glory. [24]Whether Jews or Gentiles, we are those chosen ones, [25]just as the Lord says in the book of Hosea,

"Although they are not
my people,
    I will make them my people.
I will treat with love
those nations
    that have never been loved.

[26] "Once they were told,
    'You are not my people.'
But in that very place
they will be called
    children of the living God."

[27]And this is what the prophet Isaiah said about the people of Israel,

"The people of Israel
    are as many
as the grains of sand
    along the beach.
But only a few who are left
    will be saved.
[28] The Lord will be quick
    and sure to do on earth
what he has warned
    he will do."

[29]Isaiah also said,

"If the Lord All-Powerful
had not spared some
    of our descendants,
we would have been destroyed
like the cities of Sodom
    and Gomorrah."[r]

Israel and the Good News

[30]What does all of this mean? It means that the Gentiles were not trying to be acceptable to God, but they found that he would accept them if they had faith. [31-32]It also means that the people of Israel were not acceptable to God. And why not? It was because they were trying[s] to be acceptable by obeying the Law instead of by having faith in God. The people of Israel fell over the stone that makes people stumble, [33]just as God says in the Scriptures,

---

[q]9.5 *Christ. I pray that God, who rules over all, will be praised forever*: Or "Christ, who rules over all. I pray that God will be praised forever" or "Christ. And I pray that Christ, who is God and rules over all, will be praised forever."   [r]9.29 *Sodom and Gomorrah*: During the time of Abraham the Lord destroyed these two cities because their people were so sinful.
[s]9.31 *because they were trying*: Or "while they were trying" or "even though they were trying."

"Look! I am placing in Zion
a stone to make people
stumble and fall.
But those who have faith
in that one will never
be disappointed."

10 Dear friends, my greatest wish and my prayer to God is for the people of Israel to be saved. [2]I know they love God, but they don't understand [3]what makes people acceptable to him. So they refuse to trust God, and they try to be acceptable by obeying the Law. [4]But Christ makes the Law no longer necessary[t] for those who become acceptable to God by faith.

Anyone Can Be Saved

[5]Moses said that a person could become acceptable to God by obeying the Law. He did this when he wrote, "If you want to live, you must do all that the Law commands."

[6]But people whose faith makes them acceptable to God will never ask, "Who will go up to heaven to bring Christ down?" [7]Neither will they ask, "Who will go down into the world of the dead to raise him to life?"

[8]All who are acceptable because of their faith simply say, "The message is as near as your mouth or your heart." And this is the same message we preach about faith. [9]So you will be saved, if you honestly say, "Jesus is Lord," and if you believe with all your heart that God raised him from death. [10]God will accept you and save you, if you truly believe this and tell it to others.

[11]The Scriptures say that no one who has faith will be disappointed, [12]no matter if that person is a Jew or a Gentile. There is only one Lord, and he is generous to everyone who asks for his help. [13]All who call out to the Lord will be saved.

[14]How can people have faith in the Lord and ask him to save them, if they have never heard about him? And how can they hear, unless someone tells them? [15]And how can anyone tell them without being sent by the Lord? The Scriptures say it is a beautiful sight to see even the feet of someone coming to preach the good news. [16]Yet not everyone has believed the message. For example, the prophet Isaiah asked, "Lord, has anyone believed what we said?"

[17]No one can have faith without hearing the message about Christ. [18]But am I saying that the people of Israel did not hear? No, I am not! The Scriptures say,

"The message was told
everywhere on earth.
It was announced
all over the world."

[19]Did the people of Israel understand or not? Moses answered this question when he told that the Lord had said,

"I will make Israel jealous
of people
who are a nation
of nobodies.
I will make them angry
at people
who don't understand
a thing."

[20]Isaiah was fearless enough to tell that the Lord had said,

"I was found by people
who were not looking
for me.
I appeared to the ones
who were not asking
about me."

[21]And Isaiah said about the people of Israel,

"All day long the Lord
has reached out
to people who are stubborn
and refuse to obey."

God Has Not Rejected His People

11 Am I saying that God has turned his back on his people? Certainly not! I am one of the people of Israel, and I myself am a descendant of Abraham from the tribe of Benjamin. [2]God did not turn his back on his chosen people. Don't you remember reading in the Scriptures how Elijah complained to God about the people of Israel? [3]He said, "Lord, they killed your prophets and destroyed your altars. I am the only one left, and now they want to kill me."

[4]But the Lord told Elijah, "I still have seven thousand followers who have not worshiped Baal." [5]It is the same way now. God was kind to the people of Israel, and so a few of them are still his followers. [6]This happened because of God's undeserved kindness and not because of anything they have done. It could not have happened except for God's kindness.

[7]This means that only a chosen few of the people of Israel found what all of them were searching for. And the rest of them were stubborn, [8]just as the Scriptures say,

"God made them so stupid
that their eyes are blind,
and their ears
are still deaf."

[9]Then David said,

---

[t]**10.4** *But Christ makes the Law no longer necessary*: Or "But Christ gives the full meaning to the Law."

"Turn their meals
  into bait for a trap,
so that they will stumble
and be given
  what they deserve.
10 Blindfold their eyes!
  Don't let them see.
Bend their backs
beneath a burden
  that will never be lifted."

Gentiles Will Be Saved

11Do I mean that the people of Israel fell, never to get up again? Certainly not! Their failure made it possible for the Gentiles to be saved, and this will make the people of Israel jealous. 12But if the rest of the world's people were helped so much by Israel's sin and loss, they will be helped even more by their full return.

13I am now speaking to you Gentiles, and as long as I am an apostle to you, I will take pride in my work. 14I hope in this way to make some of my own people jealous enough to be saved. 15When Israel rejected God,ᵘ the rest of the people in the world were able to turn to him. So when God makes friends with Israel, it will be like bringing the dead back to life. 16If part of a batch of dough is made holy by being offered to God, then all of the dough is holy. If the roots of a tree are holy, the rest of the tree is holy too.

17You Gentiles are like branches of a wild olive tree that were made to be part of a cultivated olive tree. You have taken the place of some branches that were cut away from it. And because of this, you enjoy the blessings that come from being part of that cultivated tree. 18But don't think you are better than the branches that were cut away. Just remember that you are not supporting the roots of that tree. Its roots are supporting you.

19Maybe you think those branches were cut away, so that you could be put in their place. 20That's true enough. But they were cut away because they did not have faith, and you are where you are because you do have faith. So don't be proud, but be afraid. 21If God cut away those natural branches, couldn't he do the same to you?

22Now you see both how kind and how hard God can be. He was hard on those who fell, but he was kind to you. And he will keep on being kind to you, if you keep on trusting in his kindness. Otherwise, you will be cut away too.

23If those other branches will start having faith, they will be made a part of that tree again. God has the power to put them back. 24After all, it wasn't natural for branches to be cut from a wild olive tree and to be made part of a cultivated olive tree. So it is much more likely that God will join the natural branches back to the cultivated olive tree.

The People of Israel
Will Be Brought Back

25My friends, I don't want you Gentiles to be too proud of yourselves. So I will explain the mystery of what has happened to the people of Israel. Some of them have become stubborn, and they will stay like that until the complete number of you Gentiles has come in. 26In this way all of Israel will be saved, as the Scriptures say,

"From Zion someone will come
  to rescue us.
Then Jacob's descendants
  will stop being evil.
27 This is what the Lord
  has promised to do
when he forgives their sins."

28The people of Israel are treated as God's enemies, so that the good news can come to you Gentiles. But they are still the chosen ones, and God loves them because of their famous ancestors. 29God doesn't take back the gifts he has given or forget about the people he has chosen.

30At one time you Gentiles rejected God. But now Israel has rejected God, and you have been shown mercy. 31And because of the mercy shown to you, they will also be shown mercy. 32All people have disobeyed God, and that's why he treats them as prisoners. But he does this, so that he can have mercy on all of them.

33Who can measure the wealth and wisdom and knowledge of God? Who can understand his decisions or explain what he does?

34 "Has anyone known
  the thoughts of the Lord
    or given him advice?
35 Has anyone loaned
  something to the Lord
    that must be repaid?"

36Everything comes from the Lord. All things were made because of him and will return to him. Praise the Lord forever! Amen.

Christ Brings New Life

12 Dear friends, God is good. So I beg you to offer your bodies to him as a living sacrifice, pure and pleasing. That's the most sensible way to serve God. 2Don't be like the people of this world, but let God change the way

---

ᵘ**11.15** _When Israel rejected God_: Or "When Israel was rejected."

you think. Then you will know how to do everything that is good and pleasing to him.

³I realize how kind God has been to me, and so I tell each of you not to think you are better than you really are. Use good sense and measure yourself by the amount of faith that God has given you. ⁴A body is made up of many parts, and each of them has its own use. ⁵That's how it is with us. There are many of us, but we each are part of the body of Christ, as well as part of one another.

⁶God has also given each of us different gifts to use. If we can prophesy, we should do it according to the amount of faith we have. ⁷If we can serve others, we should serve. If we can teach, we should teach. ⁸If we can encourage others, we should encourage them. If we can give, we should be generous. If we are leaders, we should do our best. If we are good to others, we should do it cheerfully.

Rules for Christian Living

⁹Be sincere in your love for others. Hate everything that is evil and hold tight to everything that is good. ¹⁰Love each other as brothers and sisters and honor others more than you do yourself. ¹¹Never give up. Eagerly follow the Holy Spirit and serve the Lord. ¹²Let your hope make you glad. Be patient in time of trouble and never stop praying. ¹³Take care of God's needy people and welcome strangers into your home.

¹⁴Ask God to bless everyone who mistreats you. Ask him to bless them and not to curse them. ¹⁵When others are happy, be happy with them, and when they are sad, be sad. ¹⁶Be friendly with everyone. Don't be proud and feel that you are smarter than others. Make friends with ordinary people.ᵛ ¹⁷Don't mistreat someone who has mistreated you. But try to earn the respect of others, ¹⁸and do your best to live at peace with everyone.

¹⁹Dear friends, don't try to get even. Let God take revenge. In the Scriptures the Lord says,

"I am the one to take revenge
    and pay them back."

²⁰The Scriptures also say,

"If your enemies are hungry,
    give them something to eat.
And if they are thirsty,
    give them something
        to drink.
This will be the same
    as piling burning coals
        on their heads."

²¹Don't let evil defeat you, but defeat evil with good.

Obey Rulers

13 Obey the rulers who have authority over you. Only God can give authority to anyone, and he puts these rulers in their places of power. ²People who oppose the authorities are opposing what God has done, and they will be punished. ³Rulers are a threat to evil people, not to good people. There is no need to be afraid of the authorities. Just do right, and they will praise you for it. ⁴After all, they are God's servants, and it is their duty to help you.

If you do something wrong, you ought to be afraid, because these rulers have the right to punish you. They are God's servants who punish criminals to show how angry God is. ⁵But you should obey the rulers because you know it is the right thing to do, and not just because of God's anger.

⁶You must also pay your taxes. The authorities are God's servants, and it is their duty to take care of these matters. ⁷Pay all that you owe, whether it is taxes and fees or respect and honor.

Love

⁸Let love be your only debt! If you love others, you have done all that the Law demands. ⁹In the Law there are many commands, such as, "Be faithful in marriage. Do not murder. Do not steal. Do not want what belongs to others." But all of these are summed up in the command that says, "Love others as much as you love yourself." ¹⁰No one who loves others will harm them. So love is all that the Law demands.

The Day When Christ Returns

¹¹You know what sort of times we live in, and so you should live properly. It is time to wake up. You know that the day when we will be saved is nearer now than when we first put our faith in the Lord. ¹²Night is almost over, and day will soon appear. We must stop behaving as people do in the dark and be ready to live in the light. ¹³So behave properly, as people do in the day. Don't go to wild parties or get drunk or be vulgar or indecent. Don't quarrel or be jealous. ¹⁴Let the Lord Jesus Christ be as near to you as the clothes you wear. Then you won't try to satisfy your selfish desires.

Don't Criticize Others

14 Welcome all the Lord's followers, even those whose faith is weak. Don't criticize them for having beliefs

---

ᵛ**12.16** *Make friends with ordinary people*: Or "Do ordinary jobs."

that are different from yours. ²Some think it is all right to eat anything, while those whose faith is weak will eat only vegetables. ³But you should not criticize others for eating or for not eating. After all, God welcomes everyone. ⁴What right do you have to criticize someone else's servants? Only their Lord can decide if they are doing right, and the Lord will make sure that they do right.

⁵Some of the Lord's followers think one day is more important than another. Others think all days are the same. But each of you should make up your own mind. ⁶Any followers who count one day more important than another day do it to honor their Lord. And any followers who eat meat give thanks to God, just like the ones who don't eat meat.

⁷Whether we live or die, it must be for God, rather than for ourselves. ⁸Whether we live or die, it must be for the Lord. Alive or dead, we still belong to the Lord. ⁹This is because Christ died and rose to life, so that he would be the Lord of the dead and of the living. ¹⁰Why do you criticize other followers of the Lord? Why do you look down on them? The day is coming when God will judge all of us. ¹¹In the Scriptures God says,

"I swear by my very life
that everyone will kneel down
    and praise my name!"

¹²And so, each of us must give an account to God for what we do.

Don't Cause Problems for Others

¹³We must stop judging others. We must also make up our minds not to upset anyone's faith. ¹⁴The Lord Jesus has made it clear to me that God considers all foods fit to eat. But if you think some foods are unfit to eat, then for you they are not fit.

¹⁵If you are hurting others by the foods you eat, you are not guided by love. Don't let your appetite destroy someone Christ died for. ¹⁶Don't let your right to eat bring shame to Christ. ¹⁷God's kingdom isn't about eating and drinking. It is about pleasing God, about living in peace, and about true happiness. All this comes from the Holy Spirit. ¹⁸If you serve Christ in this way, you will please God and be respected by people. ¹⁹We should try^w to live at peace and help each other have a strong faith.

²⁰Don't let your appetite destroy what God has done. All foods are fit to eat, but it is wrong to cause problems for others by what you eat. ²¹It is best not to eat meat or drink wine or do anything else that causes problems for other followers of the Lord. ²²What you believe about these things should be kept between you and God. You are fortunate, if your actions don't make you have doubts. ²³But if you do have doubts about what you eat, you are going against your beliefs. And you know that is wrong, because anything you do against your beliefs is sin.

Please Others and Not Yourself

15 If our faith is strong, we should be patient with the Lord's followers whose faith is weak. We should try to please them instead of ourselves. ²We should think of their good and try to help them by doing what pleases them. ³Even Christ did not try to please himself. But as the Scriptures say, "The people who insulted you also insulted me." ⁴And the Scriptures were written to teach and encourage us by giving us hope. ⁵God is the one who makes us patient and cheerful. I pray that he will help you live at peace with each other, as you follow Christ. ⁶Then all of you together will praise God, the Father of our Lord Jesus Christ.

The Good News Is for Jews and Gentiles

⁷Honor God by accepting each other, as Christ has accepted you. ⁸I tell you that Christ came as a servant of the Jews to show that God has kept the promises he made to their famous ancestors. Christ also came, ⁹so that the Gentiles would praise God for being kind to them. It is just as the Scriptures say,

"I will tell the nations
    about you,
and I will sing praises
    to your name."

¹⁰The Scriptures also say to the Gentiles, "Come and celebrate with God's people."
¹¹Again the Scriptures say,

"Praise the Lord,
    all you Gentiles.
All you nations, come
    and worship him."

¹²Isaiah says,

"Someone from David's family
    will come to power.
He will rule the nations,
and they will put their hope
    in him."

¹³I pray that God, who gives hope, will bless you with complete happiness and peace because of your faith. And may the power of the Holy Spirit fill you with hope.

---

^{w}**14.19** *We should try*: Some manuscripts have "We try."

Paul's Work as a Missionary

[14]My friends, I am sure that you are very good and that you have all the knowledge you need to teach each other. [15]But I have spoken to you plainly and have tried to remind you of some things. God was so kind to me! [16]He chose me to be a servant of Christ Jesus for the Gentiles and to do the work of a priest in the service of his good news. God did this so that the Holy Spirit could make the Gentiles into a holy offering, pleasing to him.

[17]Because of Christ Jesus, I can take pride in my service for God. [18]In fact, all I will talk about is how Christ let me speak and work, so that the Gentiles would obey him. [19]Indeed, I will tell how Christ worked miracles and wonders by the power of the Holy Spirit. I have preached the good news about him all the way from Jerusalem to Illyricum. [20]But I have always tried to preach where people have never heard about Christ. I am like a builder who doesn't build on anyone else's foundation. [21]It is just as the Scriptures say,

"All who haven't been told
about him
will see him,
and those who haven't heard
about him
will understand."

Paul's Plan To Visit Rome

[22]My work has always kept me from coming to see you. [23]Now there is nothing left for me to do in this part of the world, and for years I have wanted to visit you. [24]So I plan to stop off on my way to Spain. Then after a short, but refreshing, visit with you, I hope you will quickly send me on.

[25-26]I am now on my way to Jerusalem to deliver the money that the Lord's followers in Macedonia and Achaia collected for God's needy people. [27]This is something they really wanted to do. But sharing their money with the Jews was also like paying back a debt, because the Jews had already shared their spiritual blessings with the Gentiles. [28]After I have safely delivered this money, I will visit you and then go on to Spain. [29]And when I do arrive in Rome, I know it will be with the full blessings of Christ.

[30]My friends, by the power of the Lord Jesus Christ and by the love that comes from the Holy Spirit, I beg you to pray sincerely with me and for me. [31]Pray that God will protect me from the unbelievers in Judea, and that his people in Jerusalem will be pleased with what I am doing. [32]Ask God to let me come to you and have a pleasant and refreshing visit. [33]I pray that God, who gives peace, will be with all of you. Amen.

Personal Greetings

16 I have good things to say about Phoebe, who is a leader in the church at Cenchreae. [2]Welcome her in a way that is proper for someone who has faith in the Lord and is one of God's own people. Help her in any way you can. After all, she has proved to be a respected leader for many others, including me.

[3]Give my greetings to Priscilla and Aquila. They have not only served Christ Jesus together with me, [4]but they have even risked their lives for me. I am grateful for them and so are all the Gentile churches. [5]Greet the church that meets in their home.

Greet my dear friend Epaenetus, who was the first person in Asia to have faith in Christ.

[6]Greet Mary, who has worked so hard for you.

[7]Greet my relatives[x] Andronicus and Junias,[y] who were in jail with me. They are highly respected by the apostles and were followers of Christ before I was.

[8]Greet Ampliatus, my dear friend whose faith is in the Lord.

[9]Greet Urbanus, who serves Christ along with us.

Greet my dear friend Stachys.

[10]Greet Apelles, a faithful servant of Christ.

Greet Aristobulus and his family.

[11]Greet Herodion, who is a relative[z] of mine.

Greet Narcissus and the others in his family, who have faith in the Lord.

[12]Greet Tryphaena and Tryphosa, who work hard for the Lord.

Greet my dear friend Persis. She also works hard for the Lord.

[13]Greet Rufus, that special servant of the Lord, and greet his mother, who has been like a mother to me.

[14]Greet Asyncritus, Phlegon, Hermes, Patrobas, and Hermas, as well as our friends who are with them.

[15]Greet Philologus, Julia, Nereus and his sister, and Olympas, and all of God's people who are with them.

[16]Be sure to give each other a warm greeting.

All of Christ's churches greet you.

[17]My friends, I beg you to watch out for anyone who causes trouble and divides the church by refusing to do what all of you were taught. Stay away from them! [18]They want to serve themselves and not Christ the Lord. Their flattery and fancy talk fool people who don't know any better. [19]I am glad that

---

[x]**16.7** *relatives*: Or "Jewish friends."   [y]**16.7** *Junias*: Or Junia. Some manuscripts have *Julia*.
[z]**16.11, 21** *relative(s)*: See the note at verse 7.

everyone knows how well you obey the Lord. But still, I want you to understand what is good and not have anything to do with evil. [20]Then God, who gives peace, will soon crush Satan under your feet. I pray that our Lord Jesus will be kind to you.

[21]Timothy, who works with me, sends his greetings, and so do my relatives,[z] Lucius, Jason, and Sosipater.

[22]I, Tertius, also send my greetings. I am a follower of the Lord, and I wrote this letter.[a]

[23-24]Gaius welcomes me and the whole church into his home, and he sends his greetings.

Erastus, the city treasurer, and our dear friend Quartus send their greetings too.[b]

Paul's Closing Prayer

[25]Praise God! He can make you strong by means of my good news, which is the message about[c] Jesus Christ. For ages and ages this message was kept secret, [26]but now at last it has been told. The eternal God commanded his prophets to write about the good news, so that all nations would obey and have faith. [27]And now, because of Jesus Christ, we can praise the only wise God forever! Amen.[d]

[z]**16.11,21** *relative(s)*: See the note at verse 7.   [a]**16.22** *I wrote this letter*: Paul probably dictated this letter to Tertius.   [b]**16.23,24** *send their greetings too*: Some manuscripts add, "I pray that our Lord Jesus Christ will always be kind to you. Amen."   [c]**16.25** *about*: Or "from."   [d]**16.27** *Amen*: Some manuscripts have verses 25-27 after 14.23. Others have the verses here and after 14.23, and one manuscript has them after 15.33.

1 CORINTHIANS

ABOUT THIS LETTER

Although this letter is called the First Letter to the Corinthians, it is not really the first one that Paul wrote to this church. We know this because he mentions in this letter that he had written one before (5.9). The Christians in Corinth had also written to him (7.1), and part of First Corinthians contains Paul's answers to questions they had asked.

Corinth is a large port city in southern Greece. Paul began his work there in a Jewish meeting place, but he had to move next door to the home of a Gentile who had become a follower of Jesus (Acts 18.1-17). Most of the followers in Corinth were poor people (1 Corinthians 1.26-29), though some of them were wealthy (1 Corinthians 11.18-21), and one was even the city treasurer (Romans 16.23). While he was in Corinth, Paul worked as a tentmaker to earn a living (Acts 18.3; 1 Corinthians 4.12; 9.1-18).

Paul was especially concerned about the way the Corinthian Christians were always arguing and dividing themselves into groups (1.10—4.21) and about the way they treated one another (5.1—6.20). These are two of Paul's main concerns as he writes this letter. But he also wants to answer the questions they asked him about marriage (7.1-40) and food offered to idols (8.1-13). Paul encourages them to worship God the right way (10.1—14.40) and to be firm in their belief that God has given them victory over death (15.1-58).

Love, Paul tells them, is even more important than faith or hope. All of the problems in the church could be solved, if all the members would love one another, as Christians should:

> Love is kind and patient,
> never jealous, boastful,
>   proud, or rude.
> Love rejoices in the truth,
>   but not in evil.
> Love is always supportive,
> loyal, hopeful,
>   and trusting.
> Love never fails!
>   (13.4, 5a, 6-8a)

A QUICK LOOK AT THIS LETTER

Paul's Greeting and Prayer (1.1-9)
A Call for Unity (1.10—4.21)
Problems in Relationships (5.1—7.40)
Honoring God Instead of Idols (8.1—11.1)
Guidance for Worship and Church Life (11.2—14.40)
Christ's Victory Over Death (15.1-58)
An Offering for the Poor (16.1-4)
Paul's Travel Plans (16.5-12)
Personal Concerns and Greetings (16.13-24)

1 From Paul, chosen by God to be an apostle of Christ Jesus, and from Sosthenes, who is also a follower.

²To God's church in Corinth. Christ Jesus chose you to be his very own people, and you worship in his name, as we and all others do who call him Lord.

³My prayer is that God our Father and the Lord Jesus Christ will be kind to you and will bless you with peace!

⁴I never stop thanking my God for being kind enough to give you Christ Jesus, ⁵who helps you speak and understand so well. ⁶Now you are certain that everything we told you about our Lord Christ Jesus is true. ⁷You are not missing out on any blessings, as you wait for him to return. ⁸And until the day Christ does return, he will keep you completely innocent. ⁹God can be trusted, and he chose you to be partners with his Son, our Lord Jesus Christ.

Taking Sides

¹⁰My dear friends, as a follower of our Lord Jesus Christ, I beg you to get along with each other. Don't take sides. Always try to agree in what you think. ¹¹Several people from Chloe's family*a* have already reported to me that you keep arguing with each other. ¹²They have said that some of you claim to follow me, while others claim to follow Apollos or Peter*b* or Christ.

¹³Has Christ been divided up? Was I nailed to a cross for you? Were you baptized in my name? ¹⁴I thank God*c* that I didn't baptize any of you except Crispus and Gaius. ¹⁵Not one of you can say that you were baptized in my name. ¹⁶I did baptize the family*d* of Stephanas, but I don't remember if I baptized anyone else. ¹⁷Christ did not send me to baptize. He sent me to tell the good news without using big words that would make the cross of Christ lose its power.

Christ Is God's Power and Wisdom

¹⁸The message about the cross doesn't make any sense to lost people. But for those of us who are being saved, it is God's power at work. ¹⁹As God says in the Scriptures,

"I will destroy the wisdom
of all who claim
    to be wise.
I will confuse those
who think they know
    so much."

²⁰What happened to those wise people? What happened to those experts in the Scriptures? What happened to the ones who think they have all the answers? Didn't God show that the wisdom of this world is foolish? ²¹God was wise and decided not to let the people of this world use their wisdom to learn about him.

Instead, God chose to save only those who believe the foolish message we preach. ²²Jews ask for miracles, and Greeks want something that sounds wise. ²³But we preach that Christ was nailed to a cross. Most Jews have problems with this, and most Gentiles think it is foolish. ²⁴Our message is God's power and wisdom for the Jews and the Greeks that he has chosen. ²⁵Even when God is foolish, he is wiser than everyone else, and even when God is weak, he is stronger than everyone else.

²⁶My dear friends, remember what you were when God chose you. The people of this world didn't think that many of you were wise. Only a few of you were in places of power, and not many of you came from important families. ²⁷But God chose the foolish things of this world to put the wise to shame. He chose the weak things of this world to put the powerful to shame. ²⁸What the world thinks is worthless, useless, and nothing at all is what God has used to destroy what the world considers important. ²⁹God did all this to keep anyone from bragging to him. ³⁰You are God's children. He sent Christ Jesus to save us and to make us wise, acceptable, and holy. ³¹So if you want to brag, do what the Scriptures say and brag about the Lord.

Telling about Christ and the Cross

2 Friends, when I came and told you the mystery*e* that God had shared with us, I didn't use big words or try to sound wise. ²In fact, while I was with you, I made up my mind to speak only about Jesus Christ, who had been nailed to a cross.

³At first, I was weak and trembling with fear. ⁴When I talked with you or preached, I didn't try to prove anything by sounding wise. I simply let God's Spirit show his power. ⁵That way you would have faith because of God's power and not because of human wisdom.

⁶We do use wisdom when speaking to people who are mature in their faith. But it isn't the wisdom of this world or of its rulers, who will soon disappear. ⁷We speak of God's hidden and mysteri-

---

*a***1.11** *family*: Family members and possibly slaves and others who may have lived in the house. *b***1.12** *Peter*: The Greek text has "Cephas," which is an Aramaic name meaning "rock." Peter is the Greek name with the same meaning. *c***1.14** *I thank God*: Some manuscripts have "I thank my God." *d***1.16** *family*: See the note at 1.11. *e***2.1** *mystery*: Some manuscripts have "testimony."

ous wisdom that God decided to use for our glory long before the world began. [8]The rulers of this world didn't know anything about this wisdom. If they had known about it, they would not have nailed the glorious Lord to a cross. [9]But it is just as the Scriptures say,

"What God has planned
for people who love him
is more than eyes have seen
or ears have heard.
It has never even
entered our minds!"

[10]God's Spirit has shown you everything. His Spirit finds out everything, even what is deep in the mind of God. [11]You are the only one who knows what is in your own mind, and God's Spirit is the only one who knows what is in God's mind. [12]But God has given us his Spirit. That's why we don't think the same way that the people of this world think. That's also why we can recognize the blessings that God has given us.

[13]Every word we speak was taught to us by God's Spirit, not by human wisdom. And this same Spirit helps us teach spiritual things to spiritual people.[f] [14]That's why only someone who has God's Spirit can understand spiritual blessings. Anyone who doesn't have God's Spirit thinks these blessings are foolish. [15]People who are guided by the Spirit can make all kinds of judgments, but they cannot be judged by others. [16]The Scriptures ask,

"Has anyone ever known
the thoughts of the Lord
or given him advice?"

But we understand what Christ is thinking.[g]

Working Together for God

3 My friends, you are acting like the people of this world. That's why I could not speak to you as spiritual people. You are like babies as far as your faith in Christ is concerned. [2]So I had to treat you like babies and feed you milk. You could not take solid food, and you still cannot, [3]because you are not yet spiritual. You are jealous and argue with each other. This proves that you are not spiritual and that you are acting like the people of this world. [4]Some of you say that you follow me, and others claim to follow Apollos. Isn't that how ordinary people behave? [5]Apollos and I are merely servants who helped you to have faith. It was the Lord who made it all happen. [6]I planted the seeds, Apollos watered them, but God

made them sprout and grow. [7]What matters isn't those who planted or watered, but God who made the plants grow. [8]The one who plants is just as important as the one who waters. And each one will be paid for what they do. [9]Apollos and I work together for God, and you are God's garden and God's building.

Only One Foundation

[10]God was kind and let me become an expert builder. I laid a foundation on which others have built. But we must each be careful how we build, [11]because Christ is the only foundation. [12-13]Whatever we build on that foundation will be tested by fire on the day of judgment. Then everyone will find out if we have used gold, silver, and precious stones, or wood, hay, and straw. [14]We will be rewarded if our building is left standing. [15]But if it is destroyed by the fire, we will lose everything. Yet we ourselves will be saved, like someone escaping from flames.

[16]All of you surely know that you are God's temple and that his Spirit lives in you. [17]Together you are God's holy temple, and God will destroy anyone who destroys his temple.

[18]Don't fool yourselves! If any of you think you are wise in the things of this world, you will have to become foolish before you can be truly wise. [19]This is because God considers the wisdom of this world to be foolish. It is just as the Scriptures say, "God catches the wise when they try to outsmart him." [20]The Scriptures also say, "The Lord knows that the plans made by wise people are useless." [21-22]So stop bragging about what anyone has done. Paul and Apollos and Peter[h] all belong to you. In fact, everything is yours, including the world, life, death, the present, and the future. Everything belongs to you, [23]and you belong to Christ, and Christ belongs to God.

The Work of the Apostles

4 Think of us as servants of Christ who have been given the work of explaining God's mysterious ways. [2]And since our first duty is to be faithful to the one we work for, [3]it doesn't matter to me if I am judged by you or even by a court of law. In fact, I don't judge myself. [4]I don't know of anything against me, but that doesn't prove that I am right. The Lord is my judge. [5]So don't judge anyone until the Lord returns. He will show what is hidden in the dark and what is in everyone's heart. Then

[f]**2.13** *teach spiritual things to spiritual people*: Or "compare spiritual things with spiritual things." [g]**2.16** *we understand what Christ is thinking*: Or "we think as Christ does." [h]**3.21,22** *Peter*: See the note at 1.12.

God will be the one who praises each of us.

[6]Friends, I have used Apollos and myself as examples to teach you the meaning of the saying, "Follow the rules." I want you to stop saying that one of us is better than the other. [7]What is so special about you? What do you have that you were not given? And if it was given to you, how can you brag? [8]Are you already satisfied? Are you now rich? Have you become kings while we are still nobodies? I wish you were kings. Then we could have a share in your kingdom.

[9]It seems to me that God has put us apostles in the worst possible place. We are like prisoners on their way to death. Angels and the people of this world just laugh at us. [10]Because of Christ we are thought of as fools, but Christ has made you wise. We are weak and hated, but you are powerful and respected. [11]Even today we go hungry and thirsty and don't have anything to wear except rags. We are mistreated and don't have a place to live. [12]We work hard with our own hands, and when people abuse us, we wish them well. When we suffer, we are patient. [13]When someone curses us, we answer with kind words. Until now we are thought of as nothing more than the trash and garbage of this world.

[14]I am not writing to embarrass you. I want to help you, just as parents help their own dear children. [15]Ten thousand people may teach you about Christ, but I am your only father. You became my children when I told you about Christ Jesus, [16]and I want you to be like me. [17]That's why I sent Timothy to you. I love him like a son, and he is a faithful servant of the Lord. Timothy will tell you what I do to follow Christ and how it agrees with what I always teach about Christ in every church.

[18]Some of you think I am not coming for a visit, and so you are bragging. [19]But if the Lord lets me come, I will soon be there. Then I will find out if the ones who are doing all this bragging really have any power. [20]God's kingdom isn't just a lot of words. It is power. [21]What do you want me to do when I arrive? Do you want me to be hard on you or to be kind and gentle?

Immoral Followers

5 I have heard terrible things about some of you. In fact, you are behaving worse than the Gentiles. A man is even sleeping with his own stepmother.[i] [2]You are proud, when you ought to feel bad enough to chase away anyone who acts like that.

[3-4]I am with you only in my thoughts. But in the name of our Lord Jesus I have already judged this man, as though I were with you in person. So when you meet together and the power of the Lord Jesus is with you, I will be there too. [5]You must then hand that man over to Satan. His body will be destroyed, but his spirit will be saved when the Lord Jesus returns.

[6]Stop being proud! Don't you know how a little yeast can spread through the whole batch of dough? [7]Get rid of the old yeast! Then you will be like fresh bread made without yeast, and that is what you are. Our Passover lamb is Christ, who has already been sacrificed. [8]So don't celebrate the festival by being evil and sinful, which is like serving bread made with yeast. Be pure and truthful and celebrate by using bread made without yeast.

[9]In my other letter[j] I told you not to have anything to do with immoral people. [10]But I wasn't talking about the people of this world. You would have to leave this world to get away from everyone who is immoral or greedy or who cheats or worships idols. [11]I was talking about your own people who are immoral or greedy or worship idols or curse others or get drunk or cheat. Don't even eat with them! [12]Why should I judge outsiders? Aren't we supposed to judge only church members? [13]God judges everyone else. The Scriptures say, "Chase away any of your own people who are evil."

Taking Each Other to Court

6 When one of you has a complaint against another, do you take your complaint to a court of sinners? Or do you take it to God's people? [2]Don't you know that God's people will judge the world? And if you are going to judge the world, can't you settle small problems? [3]Don't you know that we will judge angels? And if that is so, we can surely judge everyday matters. [4]Why do you take everyday complaints to judges who are not respected by the church? [5]I say this to your shame. Aren't any of you wise enough to act as a judge between one follower and another? [6]Why should one of you take another to be tried by unbelievers?

[7]When one of you takes another to court, all of you lose. It would be better to let yourselves be cheated and robbed. [8]But instead, you cheat and rob other followers.

[9]Don't you know that evil people won't have a share in the blessings of

---

[i]*5.1 is even sleeping with his own stepmother*: Or "has even married his own stepmother."
[j]*5.9 other letter*: An unknown letter that Paul wrote to the Christians at Corinth before he wrote this one.

God's kingdom? Don't fool yourselves! No one who is immoral or worships idols or is unfaithful in marriage or is a pervert or behaves like a homosexual [10]will share in God's kingdom. Neither will any thief or greedy person or drunkard or anyone who curses and cheats others. [11]Some of you used to be like that. But now the name of our Lord Jesus Christ and the power of God's Spirit have washed you and made you holy and acceptable to God.

Honor God with Your Body

[12]Some of you say, "We can do anything we want to." But I tell you that not everything is good for us. So I refuse to let anything have power over me. [13]You also say, "Food is meant for our bodies, and our bodies are meant for food." But I tell you that God will destroy them both. We are not supposed to do indecent things with our bodies. We are to use them for the Lord who is in charge of our bodies. [14]God will raise us from death by the same power that he used when he raised our Lord to life.

[15]Don't you know that your bodies are part of the body of Christ? Is it right for me to join part of the body of Christ to a prostitute? No, it isn't! [16]Don't you know that a man who does that becomes part of her body? The Scriptures say, "The two of them will be one person." [17]But anyone who is joined to the Lord is one in spirit with him.

[18]Don't be immoral in matters of sex. That is a sin against your own body in a way that no other sin is. [19]You surely know that your body is a temple where the Holy Spirit lives. The Spirit is in you and is a gift from God. You are no longer your own. [20]God paid a great price for you. So use your body to honor God.

Questions about Marriage

7 Now I will answer the questions that you asked in your letter. You asked, "Is it best for people not to marry?"[k] [2]Well, having your own husband or wife should keep you from doing something immoral. [3]Husbands and wives should be fair with each other about having sex. [4]A wife belongs to her husband instead of to herself, and a husband belongs to his wife instead of to himself. [5]So don't refuse sex to each other, unless you agree not to have sex for a little while, in order to spend time in prayer. Then Satan won't be able to tempt you because of your lack of self-control. [6]In my opinion that is what should be done, though I don't know of anything the Lord said about this matter. [7]I wish that

all of you were like me, but God has given different gifts to each of us.

[8]Here is my advice for people who have never been married and for widows. You should stay single, just as I am. [9]But if you don't have enough self-control, then go ahead and get married. After all, it is better to marry than to burn with desire.[l]

[10]I instruct married couples to stay together, and this is exactly what the Lord himself taught. A wife who leaves her husband [11]should either stay single or go back to her husband. And a husband should not leave his wife.

[12]I don't know of anything else the Lord said about marriage. All I can do is to give you my own advice. If your wife isn't a follower of the Lord, but is willing to stay with you, don't divorce her. [13]If your husband isn't a follower, but is willing to stay with you, don't divorce him. [14]Your husband or wife who isn't a follower is made holy by having you as a mate. This also makes your children holy and keeps them from being unclean in God's sight.

[15]If your husband or wife isn't a follower of the Lord and decides to divorce you, then you should agree to it. You are no longer bound to that person. After all, God chose you and wants you to live at peace. [16]And besides, how do you know if you will be able to save your husband or wife who isn't a follower?

Obeying the Lord at All Times

[17]In every church I tell the people to stay as they were when the Lord Jesus chose them and God called them to be his own. Now I say the same thing to you. [18]If you are already circumcised, don't try to change it. If you are not circumcised, don't get circumcised. [19]Being circumcised or uncircumcised isn't really what matters. The important thing is to obey God's commands. [20]So don't try to change what you were when God chose you. [21]Are you a slave? Don't let that bother you. But if you can win your freedom, you should. [22]When the Lord chooses slaves, they become his free people. And when he chooses free people, they become slaves of Christ. [23]God paid a great price for you. So don't become slaves of anyone else. [24]Stay what you were when God chose you.

Unmarried People

[25]I don't know of anything that the Lord said about people who have never been married.[m] But I will tell you what I think. And you can trust me, because the Lord has treated me with kindness.

[k]**7.1** *people not to marry*: Or "married couples not to have sex."   [l]**7.9** *with desire*: Or "in the flames of hell."   [m]**7.25** *people who have never been married*: Or "virgins."

[26]We are now going through hard times, and I think it is best for you to stay as you are. [27]If you are married, stay married. If you are not married, don't try to get married. [28]It isn't wrong to marry, even if you have never been married before. But those who marry will have a lot of trouble, and I want to protect you from that.

[29]My friends, what I mean is that the Lord will soon come,[n] and it won't matter if you are married or not. [30]It will be all the same if you are crying or laughing, or if you are buying or are completely broke. [31]It won't make any difference how much good you are getting from this world or how much you like it. This world as we know it is now passing away.

[32]I want all of you to be free from worry. An unmarried man worries about how to please the Lord. [33]But a married man has more worries. He must worry about the things of this world, because he wants to please his wife. [34]So he is pulled in two directions. Unmarried women and women who have never been married[o] worry only about pleasing the Lord, and they keep their bodies and minds pure. But a married woman worries about the things of this world, because she wants to please her husband. [35]What I am saying is for your own good—it isn't to limit your freedom. I want to help you to live right and to love the Lord above all else.

[36]But suppose you are engaged to someone old enough to be married, and you want her so much that all you can think about is getting married. Then go ahead and marry.[p] There is nothing wrong with that. [37]But it is better to have self-control and to make up your mind not to marry. [38]It is perfectly all right to marry, but it is better not to get married at all.

[39]A wife should stay married to her husband until he dies. Then she is free to marry again, but only to a man who is a follower of the Lord. [40]However, I think I am obeying God's Spirit when I say she would be happier to stay single.

Food Offered to Idols

8 In your letter you asked me about food offered to idols. All of us know something about this subject. But knowledge makes us proud of ourselves, while love makes us helpful to others. [2]In fact, people who think they know so much don't know anything at all. [3]But God has no doubts about who loves him.

[4]Even though food is offered to idols, we know that none of the idols in this world are alive. After all, there is only one God. [5]Many things in heaven and on earth are called gods and lords, but none of them really are gods or lords. [6]We have only one God, and he is the Father. He created everything, and we live for him. Jesus Christ is our only Lord. Everything was made by him, and by him life was given to us.

[7]Not everyone knows these things. In fact, many people have grown up with the belief that idols have life in them. So when they eat meat offered to idols, they are bothered by a weak conscience. [8]But food doesn't bring us any closer to God. We are no worse off if we don't eat, and we are no better off if we do.

[9]Don't cause problems for someone with a weak conscience, just because you have the right to eat anything. [10]You know all this, and so it doesn't bother you to eat in the temple of an idol. But suppose a person with a weak conscience sees you and decides to eat food that has been offered to idols. [11]Then what you know has destroyed someone Christ died for. [12]When you sin by hurting a follower with a weak conscience, you sin against Christ. [13]So if I hurt one of the Lord's followers by what I eat, I will never eat meat as long as I live.

The Rights of an Apostle

9 I am free. I am an apostle. I have seen the Lord Jesus and have led you to have faith in him. [2]Others may think that I am not an apostle, but you are proof that I am an apostle to you.

[3]When people question me, I tell them [4]that Barnabas and I have the right to our food and drink. [5]We each have the right to marry one of the Lord's followers and to take her along with us, just as the other apostles and the Lord's brothers and Peter[q] do. [6]Are we the only ones who have to support ourselves by working at another job? [7]Do soldiers pay their own salaries? Don't people who raise grapes eat some of what they grow? Don't shepherds get milk from their own goats?

[8-9]I am not saying this on my own authority. The Law of Moses tells us not to muzzle an ox when it is grinding grain. But was God concerned only about an

[n]**7.29** _the Lord will soon come:_ Or "there's not much time left" or "the time for decision comes quickly." [o]**7.34** _women who have never been married:_ Or "virgins." [p]**7.36** _But suppose you are engaged . . . go ahead and marry:_ Verses 36-38 may also be translated: [36]"If you feel that you are not treating your grown daughter right by keeping her from getting married, then let her marry. You won't be doing anything wrong. [37]But it is better to have self-control and make up your mind not to let your daughter get married. [38]It is all right for you to let her marry. But it is better if you don't let her marry at all." [q]**9.5** _Peter:_ See the note at 1.12.

ox? [10]No, he wasn't! He was talking about us. This was written in the Scriptures so that all who plow and all who grind the grain will look forward to sharing in the harvest.

[11]When we told the message to you, it was like planting spiritual seed. So we have the right to accept material things as our harvest from you. [12]If others have the right to do this, we have an even greater right. But we haven't used this right of ours. We are willing to put up with anything to keep from causing trouble for the message about Christ.

[13]Don't you know that people who work in the temple make their living from what is brought to the temple? Don't you know that a person who serves at the altar is given part of what is offered? [14]In the same way, the Lord wants everyone who preaches the good news to make a living from preaching this message.

[15]But I have never used these privileges of mine, and I am not writing this because I want to start now. I would rather die than have someone rob me of the right to take pride in this. [16]I don't have any reason to brag about preaching the good news. Preaching is something God told me to do, and if I don't do it, I am doomed. [17]If I preach because I want to, I will be paid. But even if I don't want to, it is still something God has sent me to do. [18]What pay am I given? It is the chance to preach the good news free of charge and not to use the privileges that are mine because I am a preacher.

[19]I am not anyone's slave. But I have become a slave to everyone, so that I can win as many people as possible. [20]When I am with the Jews, I live like a Jew to win Jews. They are ruled by the Law of Moses, and I am not. But I live by the Law to win them. [21]And when I am with people who are not ruled by the Law, I forget about the Law to win them. Of course, I never really forget about the law of God. In fact, I am ruled by the law of Christ. [22]When I am with people whose faith is weak, I live as they do to win them. I do everything I can to win everyone I possibly can. [23]I do all this for the good news, because I want to share in its blessings.

A Race and a Fight

[24]You know that many runners enter a race, and only one of them wins the prize. So run to win! [25]Athletes work hard to win a crown that cannot last, but we do it for a crown that will last forever. [26]I don't run without a goal. And I don't box by beating my fists in the air. [27]I keep my body under control and

make it my slave, so I won't lose out after telling the good news to others.

Don't Worship Idols

10 Friends, I want to remind you that all of our ancestors walked under the cloud and went through the sea. [2]This was like being baptized and becoming followers of Moses. [3]All of them also ate the same spiritual food [4]and drank the same spiritual drink, which flowed from the spiritual rock that followed them. That rock was Christ. [5]But most of them did not please God. So they died, and their bodies were scattered all over the desert.

[6]What happened to them is a warning to keep us from wanting to do the same evil things. [7]They worshiped idols, just as the Scriptures say, "The people sat down to eat and drink. Then they got up to dance around." So don't worship idols. [8]Some of those people did shameful things, and in a single day about twenty-three thousand of them died. Don't do shameful things as they did. [9]And don't try to test Christ,[r] as some of them did and were later bitten by poisonous snakes. [10]Don't even grumble, as some of them did and were killed by the destroying angel. [11]These things happened to them as a warning to us. All this was written in the Scriptures to teach us who live in these last days.

[12]Even if you think you can stand up to temptation, be careful not to fall. [13]You are tempted in the same way that everyone else is tempted. But God can be trusted not to let you be tempted too much, and he will show you how to escape from your temptations.

[14]My friends, you must keep away from idols. [15]I am speaking to you as people who have enough sense to know what I am talking about. [16]When we drink from the cup that we ask God to bless, isn't that sharing in the blood of Christ? When we eat the bread that we break, isn't that sharing in the body of Christ? [17]By sharing in the same loaf of bread, we become one body, even though there are many of us.

[18]Aren't the people of Israel sharing in the worship when they gather around the altar and eat the sacrifices offered there? [19]Am I saying that either the idols or the food sacrificed to them is anything at all? [20]No, I am not! That food is really sacrificed to demons and not to God. I don't want you to have anything to do with demons. [21]You cannot drink from the cup of demons and still drink from the Lord's cup. You cannot eat at the table of demons and still eat at the Lord's table. [22]We would make

---

[r]**10.9** _Christ_: Some manuscripts have "the Lord."

the Lord jealous if we did that. And we are not stronger than the Lord.

Always Honor God

²³Some of you say, "We can do whatever we want to!" But I tell you that not everything may be good or helpful. ²⁴We should think about others and not about ourselves. ²⁵However, when you buy meat in the market, go ahead and eat it. Keep your conscience clear by not asking where the meat came from. ²⁶The Scriptures say, "The earth and everything in it belong to the Lord."

²⁷If an unbeliever invites you to dinner, and you want to go, then go. Eat whatever you are served. Don't cause a problem for someone's conscience by asking where the food came from. ²⁸⁻²⁹But if you are told that it has been sacrificed to idols, don't cause a problem by eating it. I don't mean a problem for yourself, but for the one who told you. Why should my freedom be limited by someone else's conscience? ³⁰If I give thanks for what I eat, why should anyone accuse me of doing wrong?

³¹When you eat or drink or do anything else, always do it to honor God. ³²Don't cause problems for Jews or Greeks or anyone else who belongs to God's church. ³³I always try to please others instead of myself, in the hope

11 that many of them will be saved. ¹You must follow my example, as I follow the example of Christ.

Rules for Worship

²I am proud of you, because you always remember me and obey the teachings I gave you. ³Now I want you to know that Christ is the head over all men, and a man is the head over a woman. But God is the head over Christ. ⁴This means that any man who prays or prophesies with something on his head brings shame to his head.

⁵But any woman who prays or prophesies without something on her head brings shame to her head. In fact, she may as well shave her head.ˢ ⁶A woman should wear something on her head. It is a disgrace for a woman to shave her head or cut her hair. But if she refuses to wear something on her head, let her cut off her hair.

⁷Men were created to be like God and to bring honor to God. This means that a man should not wear anything on his head. Women were created to bring honor to men. ⁸It was the woman who was made from a man, and not the man

who was made from a woman. ⁹He wasn't created for her. She was created for him. ¹⁰And so, because of this, and also because of the angels, a woman ought to wear something on her head, as a sign of her authority.ᵗ

¹¹As far as the Lord is concerned, men and women need each other. ¹²It is true that the first woman came from a man, but all other men have been given birth by women. Yet God is the one who created everything. ¹³Ask yourselves if it is proper for a woman to pray without something on her head. ¹⁴Isn't it unnatural and disgraceful for men to have long hair? ¹⁵But long hair is a beautiful way for a woman to cover her head. ¹⁶This is how things are done in all of God's churches,ᵘ and that's why none of you should argue about what I have said.

Rules for the Lord's Supper

¹⁷Your worship services do you more harm than good. I am certainly not going to praise you for this. ¹⁸I am told that you can't get along with each other when you worship, and I am sure that some of what I have heard is true. ¹⁹You are bound to argue with each other, but it is easy to see which of you have God's approval.

²⁰When you meet together, you don't really celebrate the Lord's Supper. ²¹You even start eating before everyone gets to the meeting, and some of you go hungry, while others get drunk. ²²Don't you have homes where you can eat and drink? Do you hate God's church? Do you want to embarrass people who don't have anything? What can I say to you? I certainly cannot praise you.

The Lord's Supper
(Matthew 26.26-29; Mark 14.22-25; Luke 22.14-20)

²³I have already told you what the Lord Jesus did on the night he was betrayed. And it came from the Lord himself.

He took some bread in his hands. ²⁴Then after he had given thanks, he broke it and said, "This is my body, which is given for you. Eat this and remember me."

²⁵After the meal, Jesus took a cup of wine in his hands and said, "This is my blood, and with it God makes his new agreement with you. Drink this and remember me."

²⁶The Lord meant that when you eat this bread and drink from this cup, you tell about his death until he comes.

ˢ**11.5** *she may as well shave her head*: A woman's hair was a mark of beauty, and it was shameful for a woman to cut her hair short or to shave her head, so that she looked like a man.
ᵗ**11.10** *as a sign of her authority*: Or "as a sign that she is under someone's authority."
ᵘ**11.16** *This is how things are done in all of God's churches*: Or "There is no set rule for this in any of God's churches."

²⁷But if you eat the bread and drink the wine in a way that isn't worthy of the Lord, you sin against his body and blood. ²⁸That's why you must examine the way you eat and drink. ²⁹If you fail to understand that you are the body of the Lord, you will condemn yourselves by the way you eat and drink. ³⁰That's why many of you are sick and weak and why a lot of others have died. ³¹If we carefully judge ourselves, we won't be punished. ³²But when the Lord judges and punishes us, he does it to keep us from being condemned with the rest of the world.

³³My dear friends, you should wait until everyone gets there before you start eating. ³⁴If you really are hungry, you can eat at home. Then you won't condemn yourselves when you meet together.

After I arrive, I will instruct you about the other matters.

Spiritual Gifts

12 My friends, you asked me about spiritual gifts. ²I want you to remember that before you became followers of the Lord, you were led in all the wrong ways by idols that cannot even talk. ³Now I want you to know that if you are led by God's Spirit, you will say that Jesus is Lord, and you will never curse Jesus.

⁴There are different kinds of spiritual gifts, but they all come from the same Spirit. ⁵There are different ways to serve the same Lord, ⁶and we can each do different things. Yet the same God works in all of us and helps us in everything we do.

⁷The Spirit has given each of us a special way of serving others. ⁸Some of us can speak with wisdom, while others can speak with knowledge, but these gifts come from the same Spirit. ⁹To others the Spirit has given great faith or the power to heal the sick ¹⁰or the power to work mighty miracles. Some of us are prophets, and some of us recognize when God's Spirit is present.ᵛ Others can speak different kinds of languages, and still others can tell what these languages mean. ¹¹But it is the Spirit who does all this and decides which gifts to give to each of us.

One Body with Many Parts

¹²The body of Christ has many different parts, just as any other body does. ¹³Some of us are Jews, and others are Gentiles. Some of us are slaves, and others are free. But God's Spirit baptized each of us and made us part of the body of Christ. Now we each drink from that same Spirit.ʷ

¹⁴Our bodies don't have just one part. They have many parts. ¹⁵Suppose a foot says, "I'm not a hand, and so I'm not part of the body." Wouldn't the foot still belong to the body? ¹⁶Or suppose an ear says, "I'm not an eye, and so I'm not part of the body." Wouldn't the ear still belong to the body? ¹⁷If our bodies were only an eye, we couldn't hear a thing. And if they were only an ear, we couldn't smell a thing. ¹⁸But God has put all parts of our body together in the way that he decided is best.

¹⁹A body isn't really a body, unless there is more than one part. ²⁰It takes many parts to make a single body. ²¹That's why the eyes cannot say they don't need the hands. That's also why the head cannot say it doesn't need the feet. ²²In fact, we cannot get along without the parts of the body that seem to be the weakest. ²³We take special care to dress up some parts of our bodies. We are modest about our personal parts, ²⁴but we don't have to be modest about other parts.

God put our bodies together in such a way that even the parts that seem the least important are valuable. ²⁵He did this to make all parts of the body work together smoothly, with each part caring about the others. ²⁶If one part of our body hurts, we hurt all over. If one part of our body is honored, the whole body will be happy.

²⁷Together you are the body of Christ. Each one of you is part of his body. ²⁸First, God chose some people to be apostles and prophets and teachers for the church. But he also chose some to work miracles or heal the sick or help others or be leaders or speak different kinds of languages. ²⁹Not everyone is an apostle. Not everyone is a prophet. Not everyone is a teacher. Not everyone can work miracles. ³⁰Not everyone can heal the sick. Not everyone can speak different kinds of languages. Not everyone can tell what these languages mean. ³¹I want you to desire the best gifts.ˣ So I will show you a much better way.

Love

13 What if I could speak all languages of humans and of angels?

ᵛ**12.10** *and some of us . . . present*: Or "and some of us recognize the difference between God's Spirit and other spirits." ʷ**12.13** *Some of us are Jews . . . that same Spirit*: Verse 13 may also be translated, "God's Spirit is inside each of us, and all around us as well. So it doesn't matter that some of us are Jews and others are Gentiles and that some are slaves and others are free. Together we are one body." ˣ**12.31** *I want you to desire the best gifts*: Or "You desire the best gifts."

If I did not love others,
    I would be nothing more
than a noisy gong
    or a clanging cymbal.
2 What if I could prophesy
and understand all secrets
    and all knowledge?
And what if I had faith
    that moved mountains?
I would be nothing,
    unless I loved others.
3 What if I gave away all
    that I owned
and let myself
    be burned alive?y
I would gain nothing,
    unless I loved others.
4 Love is kind and patient,
never jealous, boastful,
    proud, or 5rude.
Love isn't selfish
    or quick tempered.
It doesn't keep a record
    of wrongs that others do.
6 Love rejoices in the truth,
    but not in evil.
7 Love is always supportive,
loyal, hopeful,
    and trusting.
8 Love never fails!

Everyone who prophesies
    will stop,
and unknown languages
will no longer
    be spoken.
All that we know
    will be forgotten.
9 We don't know everything,
and our prophecies
    are not complete.
10 But what is perfect
    will someday appear,
and what isn't perfect
    will then disappear.

11 When we were children,
we thought and reasoned
    as children do.
But when we grew up,
    we quit our childish ways.
12 Now all we can see of God
    is like a cloudy picture
    in a mirror.
Later we will see him
    face to face.
We don't know everything,
    but then we will,
just as God completely
    understands us.
13 For now there are faith,
    hope, and love.
But of these three,
    the greatest is love.

Speaking Unknown Languages and Prophesying

14 Love should be your guide. Be eager to have the gifts that come from the Holy Spirit, especially the gift of prophecy. 2If you speak languages that others don't know, God will understand what you are saying, though no one else will know what you mean. You will be talking about mysteries that only the Spirit understands. 3But when you prophesy, you will be understood, and others will be helped. They will be encouraged and made to feel better.

4By speaking languages that others don't know, you help only yourself. But by prophesying you help everyone in the church. 5I am glad for you to speak unknown languages, although I had rather for you to prophesy. In fact, prophesying does much more good than speaking unknown languages, unless someone can help the church by explaining what you mean.

6My friends, what good would it do, if I came and spoke unknown languages to you and didn't explain what I meant? How would I help you, unless I told you what God had shown me or gave you some knowledge or prophecy or teaching? 7If all musical instruments sounded alike, how would you know the difference between a flute and a harp? 8If a bugle call isn't clear, how would you know to get ready for battle?

9That's how it is when you speak unknown languages. If no one can understand what you are talking about, you will only be talking to the wind. 10There are many different languages in this world, and all of them make sense. 11But if I don't understand the language that someone is using, we will be like foreigners to each other. 12If you really want spiritual gifts, choose the ones that will be most helpful to the church.

13When we speak languages that others don't know, we should pray for the power to explain what we mean. 14For example, if I use an unknown language in my prayers, my spirit prays but my mind is useless. 15Then what should I do? There are times when I should pray with my spirit, and times when I should pray with my mind. Sometimes I should sing with my spirit, and at other times I should sing with my mind.

16Suppose some strangers are in your worship service, when you are praising God with your spirit. If they don't understand you, how will they know to say, "Amen"? 17You may be worshiping God in a wonderful way, but no one else will be helped. 18I thank God that I

---

y13.3 *and let myself be burned alive*: Some manuscripts have "so that I could brag."

speak unknown languages more than any of you. 19But words that make sense can help the church. That's why in church I had rather speak five words that make sense than to speak ten thousand words in a language that others don't know.

20My friends, stop thinking like children. Think like mature people and be as innocent as tiny babies. 21In the Scriptures the Lord says,

"I will use strangers
who speak unknown languages
    to talk to my people.
They will speak to them
    in foreign languages,
but still my people
    won't listen to me."

22Languages that others don't know may mean something to unbelievers, but not to the Lord's followers. Prophecy, on the other hand, is for followers, not for unbelievers. 23Suppose everyone in your worship service started speaking unknown languages, and some outsiders or some unbelievers come in. Won't they think you are crazy? 24But suppose all of you are prophesying when those unbelievers and outsiders come in. They will realize that they are sinners, and they will want to change their ways because of what you are saying. 25They will tell what is hidden in their hearts. Then they will kneel down and say to God, "We are certain that you are with these people."

Worship Must Be Orderly

26My friends, when you meet to worship, you must do everything for the good of everyone there. That's how it should be when someone sings or teaches or tells what God has said or speaks an unknown language or explains what the language means. 27No more than two or three of you should speak unknown languages during the meeting. You must take turns, and someone should always be there to explain what you mean. 28If no one can explain, you must keep silent in church and speak only to yourself and to God.

29Two or three persons may prophesy, and everyone else must listen carefully. 30If someone sitting there receives a message from God, the speaker must stop and let the other person speak. 31Let only one person speak at a time, then all of you will learn something and be encouraged. 32A prophet should be willing to stop and let someone else speak. 33God wants everything to be done peacefully and in order.

When God's people meet in church,

34the women must not be allowed to speak. They must keep quiet and listen, as the Law of Moses teaches. 35If there is something they want to know, they can ask their husbands when they get home. It is disgraceful for women to speak in church. 36God's message did not start with you people, and you are not the only ones it has reached.

37If you think of yourself as a prophet or a spiritual person, you will know that I am writing only what the Lord has commanded. 38So don't pay attention to anyone who ignores what I am writing. 39My friends, be eager to prophesy and don't stop anyone from speaking languages that others don't know. 40But do everything properly and in order.

Christl Was Raised to Life

15 My friends, I want you to remember the message that I preached and that you believed and trusted. 2You will be saved by this message, if you hold firmly to it. But if you don't, your faith was all for nothing.

3I told you the most important part of the message exactly as it was told to me. That part is:

Christ died for our sins,
    as the Scriptures say.
4 He was buried,
    and three days later
he was raised to life,
    as the Scriptures say.
5 Christ appeared to Peter,z
    then to the twelve.
6 After this, he appeared
to more than five hundred
    other followers.
Most of them are still alive,
    but some have died.
7 He also appeared to James,
and then to all
    of the apostles.

8Finally, he appeared to me, even though I am like someone who was born at the wrong time.a

9I am the least important of all the apostles. In fact, I caused so much trouble for God's church that I don't even deserve to be called an apostle. 10But God was kind! He made me what I am, and his wonderful kindness wasn't wasted. I worked much harder than any of the other apostles, although it was really God's kindness at work and not me. 11But it doesn't matter if I preached or if they preached. All of you believed the message just the same.

God's People Will Be Raised to Life

12If we preach that Christ was raised from death, how can some of you say

---

z**15.5** *Peter*: See the note at 1.12.
these words in Greek is not clear.
a**15.8** *who was born at the wrong time*: The meaning of

that the dead will not be raised to life? 13If they won't be raised to life, Christ himself wasn't raised to life. 14And if Christ wasn't raised to life, our message is worthless, and so is your faith. 15If the dead won't be raised to life, we have told lies about God by saying that he raised Christ to life, when he really did not.

16So if the dead won't be raised to life, Christ wasn't raised to life. 17Unless Christ was raised to life, your faith is useless, and you are still living in your sins. 18And those people who died after putting their faith in him are completely lost. 19If our hope in Christ is good only for this life, we are worse off than anyone else.

20But Christ has been raised to life! And he makes us certain that others will also be raised to life. 21Just as we will die because of Adam, we will be raised to life because of Christ. 22Adam brought death to all of us, and Christ will bring life to all of us. 23But we must each wait our turn. Christ was the first to be raised to life, and his people will be raised to life when he returns. 24Then after Christ has destroyed all powers and forces, the end will come, and he will give the kingdom to God the Father.

25Christ will rule until he puts all his enemies under his power, 26and the last enemy he destroys will be death. 27When the Scriptures say that he will put everything under his power, they don't include God. It was God who put everything under the power of Christ. 28After everything is under the power of God's Son, he will put himself under the power of God, who put everything under his Son's power. Then God will mean everything to everyone.

29If the dead are not going to be raised to life, what will people do who are being baptized for them? Why are they being baptized for those dead people? 30And why do we always risk our lives 31and face death every day? The pride that I have in you because of Christ Jesus our Lord is what makes me say this. 32What do you think I gained by fighting wild animals in Ephesus? If the dead are not raised to life,

"Let's eat and drink.
    Tomorrow we die."

33Don't fool yourselves. Bad friends will destroy you. 34Be sensible and stop sinning. You should be embarrassed that some people still don't know about God.

What Our Bodies Will Be Like

35Some of you have asked, "How will the dead be raised to life? What kind of bodies will they have?" 36Don't be foolish. A seed must die before it can sprout from the ground. 37Wheat seeds and all other seeds look different from the sprouts that come up. 38This is because God gives everything the kind of body he wants it to have. 39People, animals, birds, and fish are each made of flesh, but none of them are alike. 40Everything in the heavens has a body, and so does everything on earth. But each one is very different from all the others. 41The sun isn't like the moon, the moon isn't like the stars, and each star is different.

42That's how it will be when our bodies are raised to life. These bodies will die, but the bodies that are raised will live forever. 43These ugly and weak bodies will become beautiful and strong. 44As surely as there are physical bodies, there are spiritual bodies. And our physical bodies will be changed into spiritual bodies.

45The first man was named Adam, and the Scriptures tell us that he was a living person. But Jesus, who may be called the last Adam, is a life-giving spirit. 46We see that the one with a spiritual body did not come first. He came after the one who had a physical body. 47The first man was made from the dust of the earth, but the second man came from heaven. 48Everyone on earth has a body like the body of the one who was made from the dust of the earth. And everyone in heaven has a body like the body of the one who came from heaven. 49Just as we are like the one who was made out of earth, we will be like the one who came from heaven.

50My friends, I want you to know that our bodies of flesh and blood will decay. This means that they cannot share in God's kingdom, which lasts forever. 51I will explain a mystery to you. Not every one of us will die, but we will all be changed. 52It will happen suddenly, quicker than the blink of an eye. At the sound of the last trumpet the dead will be raised. We will all be changed, so that we will never die again. 53Our dead and decaying bodies will be changed into bodies that won't die or decay. 54The bodies we now have are weak and can die. But they will be changed into bodies that are eternal. Then the Scriptures will come true,

"Death has lost the battle!
55 Where is its victory?
    Where is its sting?"

56Sin is what gives death its sting, and the Law is the power behind sin. 57But thank God for letting our Lord Jesus Christ give us the victory!

58My dear friends, stand firm and don't be shaken. Always keep busy working for the Lord. You know that everything you do for him is worthwhile.

A Collection for God's People

16 When you collect money for God's people, I want you to do exactly what I told the churches in Galatia to do. ²That is, each Sunday each of you must put aside part of what you have earned. If you do this, you won't have to take up a collection when I come. ³Choose some followers to take the money to Jerusalem. I will send them on with the money and with letters which show that you approve of them. ⁴If you think I should go along, they can go with me.

Paul's Travel Plans

⁵After I have gone through Macedonia, I hope to see you ⁶and visit with you for a while. I may even stay all winter, so that you can help me on my way to wherever I will be going next. ⁷If the Lord lets me, I would rather come later for a longer visit than to stop off now for only a short visit. ⁸I will stay in Ephesus until Pentecost, ⁹because there is a wonderful opportunity for me to do some work here. But there are also many people who are against me.

¹⁰When Timothy arrives, give him a friendly welcome. He is doing the Lord's work, just as I am. ¹¹Don't let anyone mistreat him. I am looking for him to return to me together with the other followers. So when he leaves, send him off with your blessings.

¹²I have tried hard to get our friend Apollos to visit you with the other followers. He doesn't want to come just now, but he will come when he can.

Personal Concerns and Greetings

¹³Keep alert. Be firm in your faith. Stay brave and strong. ¹⁴Show love in everything you do.

¹⁵You know that Stephanas and his family were the first in Achaia to have faith in the Lord. They have done all they can for God's people. My friends, I ask you ¹⁶to obey leaders like them and to do the same for all others who work hard with you.

¹⁷I was glad to see Stephanas and Fortunatus and Achaicus. Having them here was like having you. ¹⁸They made me feel much better, just as they made you feel better. You should appreciate people like them.

¹⁹Greetings from the churches in Asia. Aquila and Priscilla, together with the church that meets in their house, send greetings in the name of the Lord.

²⁰All of the Lord's followers send their greetings.

Give each other a warm greeting.

²¹I am signing this letter myself: PAUL.

²²I pray that God will put a curse on everyone who doesn't love the Lord. And may the Lord come soon.

²³I pray that the Lord Jesus will be kind to you.

²⁴I love everyone who belongs to Christ Jesus.

2 CORINTHIANS

ABOUT THIS LETTER

In the beginning of this letter Paul answers the concerns of the Christians in Corinth who accused him of not living up to his promise to visit them. Paul had changed his mind for a good reason. He had stayed away from Corinth so that he would not seem to be too hard and demanding (1.23). He also wanted to see if they would follow his instructions about forgiving and comforting people who had sinned (2.5-11).

Paul reminds the Corinthians that God is generous and wants them to be just as generous in their giving to help God's people in Jerusalem and Judea (8.1—9.15).

Paul is a servant of God's new agreement (3.1-17). He is faithful in trying to bring people to God, even if it means terrible suffering for himself (4.1—6.13; 10.1—12.10). And what has God done to make it possible for us to come to him?

> *God has done it all! He sent Christ to make peace between himself and us, and he has given us the work of making peace between himself and others.*
>
> *What we mean is that God was in Christ, offering peace and forgiveness to the people of this world. And he has given us the work of sharing his message about peace.* (5.18, 19)

A QUICK LOOK AT THIS LETTER

---

1 From Paul, chosen by God to be an apostle of Jesus Christ, and from Timothy, who is also a follower.

To God's church in Corinth and to all of God's people in Achaia.

²I pray that God our Father and the Lord Jesus Christ will be kind to you and will bless you with peace!

Paul Gives Thanks

³Praise God, the Father of our Lord Jesus Christ! The Father is a merciful God, who always gives us comfort. ⁴He comforts us when we are in trouble, so that we can share that same comfort with others in trouble. ⁵We share in the terrible sufferings of Christ, but also in the wonderful comfort he gives. ⁶We suffer in the hope that you will be comforted and saved. And because we are comforted, you will also be comforted, as you patiently endure suffering like ours. ⁷You never disappoint us. You suffered as much as we did, and we know that you will be comforted as we were.

⁸My friends, I want you to know what a hard time we had in Asia. Our sufferings were so horrible and so unbearable that death seemed certain. ⁹In fact, we felt sure that we were going to die. But this made us stop trusting in ourselves and start trusting God, who raises the dead to life. ¹⁰God saved us from the threat of death,ᵃ and we are sure that he will do it again and again. ¹¹Please help us by praying for us. Then many people will give thanks for the blessings we receive in answer to all these prayers.

ᵃ**1.10** *the threat of death*: Some manuscripts have "many threats of death."

Paul's Change of Plans

[12]We can be proud of our clear conscience. We have always lived honestly and sincerely, especially when we were with you. And we were guided by God's wonderful kindness instead of by the wisdom of this world. [13]I am not writing anything you cannot read and understand. I hope you will understand it completely, [14]just as you already partly understand us. Then when our Lord Jesus returns, you can be as proud of us as we are of you.

[15]I was so sure of your pride in us that I had planned to visit you first of all. In this way you would have the blessing of two visits from me. [16]Once on my way to Macedonia and again on my return from there. Then you could send me on to Judea. [17]Do you think I couldn't make up my mind about what to do? Or do I seem like someone who says "Yes" or "No" simply to please others? [18]God can be trusted, and so can I, when I say that our answer to you has always been "Yes" and never "No." [19]This is because Jesus Christ the Son of God is always "Yes" and never "No." And he is the one that Silas,[b] Timothy, and I told you about.

[20]Christ says "Yes" to all of God's promises. That's why we have Christ to say "Amen"[c] for us to the glory of God. [21]And so God makes it possible for you and us to stand firmly together with Christ. God is also the one who chose us [22]and put his Spirit in our hearts to show that we belong only to him.

[23]God is my witness that I stayed away from Corinth, just to keep from being hard on you. [24]We are not bosses who tell you what to believe. We are working with you to make you glad, because your faith is strong.

2 I have decided not to make my next visit with you so painful. [2]If I make you feel bad, who would be left to cheer me up, except the people I had made to feel bad? [3]The reason I want to be happy is to make you happy. I wrote as I did because I didn't want to visit you and be made to feel bad, when you should make me feel happy. [4]At the time I wrote, I was suffering terribly. My eyes were full of tears, and my heart was broken. But I didn't want to make you feel bad. I only wanted to let you know how much I cared for you.

Forgiveness

[5]I don't want to be hard on you. But if one of you has made someone feel bad, I am not really the one who has been made to feel bad. Some of you are the ones. [6]Most of you have already pointed out the wrong that person did, and that is punishment enough for what was done. [7]When people sin, you should forgive and comfort them, so they won't give up in despair. [8]You should make them sure of your love for them.

[9]I also wrote because I wanted to test you and find out if you would follow my instructions. [10]I will forgive anyone you forgive. Yes, for your sake and with Christ as my witness, I have forgiven whatever needed to be forgiven. [11]I have done this to keep Satan from getting the better of us. We all know what goes on in his mind.

[12]When I went to Troas to preach the good news about Christ, I found that the Lord had already prepared the way. [13]But I was worried when I didn't find my friend Titus there. So I left the other followers and went on to Macedonia.

[14]I am grateful that God always makes it possible for Christ to lead us to victory. God also helps us spread the knowledge about Christ everywhere, and this knowledge is like the smell of perfume. [15-16]In fact, God thinks of us as a perfume that brings Christ to everyone. For people who are being saved, this perfume has a sweet smell and leads them to a better life. But for people who are lost, it has a bad smell and leads them to a horrible death. No one really has what it takes to do this work. [17]A lot of people try to get rich from preaching God's message. But we are God's sincere messengers, and by the power of Christ we speak our message with God as our witness.

God's New Agreement

3 Are we once again bragging about ourselves? Do we need letters to you or from you to tell others about us? Some people do need letters that tell about them. [2]But you are our letter, and you are in our[d] hearts for everyone to read and understand. [3]You are like a letter written by Christ and delivered by us. But you are not written with pen and ink or on tablets made of stone. You are written in our hearts by the Spirit of the living God.

[4]We are sure about all this. Christ makes us sure in the very presence of God. [5]We don't have the right to claim that we have done anything on our own. God gives us what it takes to do all that we do. [6]He makes us worthy to be the servants of his new agreement that comes from the Holy Spirit and not from a written Law. After all, the Law brings death, but the Spirit brings life.

[b]1.19 *Silas:* The Greek text has "Silvanus," which is another form of the name Silas.
[c]1.20 *Amen:* The word "amen" is used here with the meaning of "yes."   [d]3.2 *our:* Some manuscripts have "your."

⁷The Law of Moses brought only the promise of death, even though it was carved on stones and given in a wonderful way. Still the Law made Moses' face shine so brightly that the people of Israel could not look at it, even though it was a fading glory. ⁸So won't the agreement that the Spirit brings to us be even more wonderful? ⁹If something that brings the death sentence is glorious, won't something that makes us acceptable to God be even more glorious? ¹⁰In fact, the new agreement is so wonderful that the Law is no longer glorious at all. ¹¹The Law was given with a glory that faded away. But the glory of the new agreement is much greater, because it will never fade away.

¹²This wonderful hope makes us feel like speaking freely. ¹³We are not like Moses. His face was shining, but he covered it to keep the people of Israel from seeing the brightness fade away. ¹⁴The people were stubborn, and something still keeps them from seeing the truth when the Law is read. Only Christ can take away the covering that keeps them from seeing.

¹⁵When the Law of Moses is read, they have their minds covered over ¹⁶with a covering that is removed only for those who turn to the Lord. ¹⁷The Lord and the Spirit are one and the same, and the Lord's Spirit sets us free. ¹⁸So our faces are not covered. They show the bright glory of the Lord, as the Lord's Spirit makes us more and more like our glorious Lord.

Treasure in Clay Jars

4 God has been kind enough to trust us with this work. That's why we never give up. ²We don't do shameful things that must be kept secret. And we don't try to fool anyone or twist God's message around. God is our witness that we speak only the truth, so others will be sure that we can be trusted. ³If there is anything hidden about our message, it is hidden only to someone who is lost.

⁴The god who rules this world has blinded the minds of unbelievers. They cannot see the light, which is the good news about our glorious Christ, who shows what God is like. ⁵We are not preaching about ourselves. Our message is that Jesus Christ is Lord. He also sent us to be your servants. ⁶The Scriptures say, "God commanded light to shine in the dark." Now God is shining in our hearts to let you know that his glory is seen in Jesus Christ.

⁷We are like clay jars in which this treasure is stored. The real power comes from God and not from us. ⁸We often suffer, but we are never crushed. Even when we don't know what to do, we never give up. ⁹In times of trouble, God is with us, and when we are knocked down, we get up again. ¹⁰⁻¹¹We face death every day because of Jesus. Our bodies show what his death was like, so that his life can also be seen in us. ¹²This means that death is working in us, but life is working in you.

¹³In the Scriptures it says, "I spoke because I had faith." We have that same kind of faith. So we speak ¹⁴because we know that God raised the Lord Jesus to life. And just as God raised Jesus, he will also raise us to life. Then he will bring us into his presence together with you. ¹⁵All of this has been done for you, so that more and more people will know how kind God is and will praise and honor him.

Faith in the Lord

¹⁶We never give up. Our bodies are gradually dying, but we ourselves are being made stronger each day. ¹⁷These little troubles are getting us ready for an eternal glory that will make all our troubles seem like nothing. ¹⁸Things that are seen don't last forever, but things that are not seen are eternal. That's why we keep our minds on the things that cannot be seen.

5 Our bodies are like tents that we live in here on earth. But when these tents are destroyed, we know that God will give each of us a place to live. These homes will not be buildings that someone has made, but they are in heaven and will last forever. ²While we are here on earth, we sigh because we want to live in that heavenly home. ³We want to put it on like clothes and not be naked.

⁴These tents we now live in are like a heavy burden, and we groan. But we don't do this just because we want to leave these bodies that will die. It is because we want to change them for bodies that will never die. ⁵God is the one who makes all of this possible. He has given us his Spirit to make us certain that he will do it. ⁶So always be cheerful!

As long as we are in these bodies, we are away from the Lord. ⁷But we live by faith, not by what we see. ⁸We should be cheerful, because we would rather leave these bodies and be at home with the Lord. ⁹But whether we are at home with the Lord or away from him, we still try our best to please him. ¹⁰After all, Christ will judge each of us for the good or the bad that we do while living in these bodies.

Bringing People to God

¹¹We know what it means to respect the Lord, and we encourage everyone to turn to him. God himself knows what

we are like, and I hope you also know what kind of people we are. [12]We are not trying once more to brag about ourselves. But we want you to be proud of us, when you are with those who are not sincere and brag about what others think of them.

[13]If we seem out of our minds, it is between God and us. But if we are in our right minds, it is for your good. [14]We are ruled by Christ's love for us. We are certain that if one person died for everyone else, then all of us have died. [15]And Christ did die for all of us. He died so we would no longer live for ourselves, but for the one who died and was raised to life for us.

[16]We are careful not to judge people by what they seem to be, though we once judged Christ in that way. [17]Anyone who belongs to Christ is a new person. The past is forgotten, and everything is new. [18]God has done it all! He sent Christ to make peace between himself and us, and he has given us the work of making peace between himself and others.

[19]What we mean is that God was in Christ, offering peace and forgiveness to the people of this world. And he has given us the work of sharing his message about peace. [20]We were sent to speak for Christ, and God is begging you to listen to our message. We speak for Christ and sincerely ask you to make peace with God. [21]Christ never sinned! But God treated him as a sinner, so that Christ could make us acceptable to God.

6 We work together with God, and we beg you to make good use of God's kindness to you. [2]In the Scriptures God says,

"When the time came,
    I listened to you,
and when you needed help,
    I came to save you."

That time has come. This is the day for you to be saved.

[3]We don't want anyone to find fault with our work, and so we try hard not to cause problems. [4]But in everything and in every way we show that we truly are God's servants. We have always been patient, though we have had a lot of trouble, suffering, and hard times. [5]We have been beaten, put in jail, and hurt in riots. We have worked hard and gone without sleep or food. [6]But we have kept ourselves pure and have been understanding, patient, and kind. The Holy Spirit has been with us, and our love has been real. [7]We have spoken the truth, and God's power has worked in us. In all our struggles we have said and done only what is right.

[8]Whether we were honored or dishonored or praised or cursed, we always told the truth about ourselves. But some people said we did not. [9]We are unknown to others, but well known to you. We seem to be dying, and yet we are still alive. We have been punished, but never killed, [10]and we are always happy, even in times of suffering. Although we are poor, we have made many people rich. And though we own nothing, everything is ours.

[11]Friends in Corinth, we are telling the truth when we say that there is room in our hearts for you. [12]We are not holding back on our love for you, but you are holding back on your love for us. [13]I speak to you as I would speak to my own children. Please make room in your hearts for us.

The Temple of the Living God

[14]Stay away from people who are not followers of the Lord! Can someone who is good get along with someone who is evil? Are light and darkness the same? [15]Is Christ a friend of Satan?[e] Can people who follow the Lord have anything in common with those who don't? [16]Do idols belong in the temple of God? We are the temple of the living God, as God himself says,

"I will live with these people
    and walk among them.
I will be their God,
and they will be
    my people."

[17]The Lord also says,

"Leave them and stay away!
Don't touch anything
    that isn't clean.
Then I will welcome you
[18]   and be your Father.
You will be my sons
    and my daughters,
as surely as I am God,
    the All-Powerful."

7 My friends, God has made us these promises. So we should stay away from everything that keeps our bodies and spirits from being clean. We should honor God and try to be completely like him.

The Church Makes Paul Happy

[2]Make a place for us in your hearts! We haven't mistreated or hurt anyone. We haven't cheated anyone. [3]I am not saying this to be hard on you. But, as I have said before, you will always be in our thoughts, whether we live or die.

---

[e]**6.15** *Satan*: The Greek text has "Beliar," which is another form of the Hebrew word "Belial," meaning "wicked" or "useless." The Jewish people sometimes used this as a name for Satan.

⁴I trust you completely.ᶠ I am always proud of you, and I am greatly encouraged. In all my trouble I am still very happy.

⁵After we came to Macedonia, we didn't have any chance to rest. We were faced with all kinds of problems. We were troubled by enemies and troubled by fears. ⁶But God cheers up people in need, and that is what he did when he sent Titus to us. ⁷Of course, we were glad to see Titus, but what really made us glad is the way you cheered him up. He told how sorry you were and how concerned you were about me. And this made me even happier.

⁸I don't feel bad anymore, even though my letterᵍ hurt your feelings. I did feel bad at first, but I don't now. I know that the letter hurt you for a while. ⁹Now I am happy, but not because I hurt your feelings. It is because God used your hurt feelings to make you turn back to him, and none of you were harmed by us. ¹⁰When God makes you feel sorry enough to turn to him and be saved, you don't have anything to feel bad about. But when this world makes you feel sorry, it can cause your death.

¹¹Just look what God has done by making you feel sorry! You sincerely want to prove that you are innocent. You are angry. You are shocked. You are eager to see that justice is done. You have proved that you were completely right in this matter. ¹²When I wrote you, it wasn't to accuse the one who was wrong or to take up for the one who was hurt. I wrote, so that God would show you how much you do care for us. ¹³And we were greatly encouraged.

Although we were encouraged, we felt even better when we saw how happy Titus was, because you had shown that he had nothing to worry about. ¹⁴We had told him how much we thought of you, and you did not disappoint us. Just as we have always told you the truth, so everything we told him about you has also proved to be true. ¹⁵Titus loves all of you very much, especially when he remembers how you obeyed him and how you trembled with fear when you welcomed him. ¹⁶It makes me really glad to know that I can depend on you.

Generous Giving

8 My friends, we want you to know that the churches in Macedoniaʰ have shown others how kind God is. ²Although they were going through hard times and were very poor, they were glad to give generously. ³They gave as much as they could afford and even more, simply because they wanted to. ⁴They even asked and begged us to let them have the joy of giving their money for God's people. ⁵And they did more than we had hoped. They gave themselves first to the Lord and then to us, just as God wanted them to do.

⁶Titus was the one who got you started doing this good thing, so we begged him to have you finish what you had begun. ⁷You do everything better than anyone else. You have stronger faith. You speak better and know more. You are eager to give, and you love us better.ⁱ Now you must give more generously than anyone else.

⁸I am not ordering you to do this. I am simply testing how real your love is by comparing it with the concern that others have shown. ⁹You know that our Lord Jesus Christ was kind enough to give up all his riches and become poor, so that you could become rich.

¹⁰A year ago you were the first ones to give, and you gave because you wanted to. So listen to my advice. ¹¹I think you should finish what you started. If you give according to what you have, you will prove that you are as eager to give as you were to think about giving. ¹²It doesn't matter how much you have. What matters is how much you are willing to give from what you have.

¹³I am not trying to make life easier for others by making life harder for you. But it is only fair ¹⁴for you to share with them when you have so much, and they have so little. Later, when they have more than enough, and you are in need, they can share with you. Then everyone will have a fair share, ¹⁵just as the Scriptures say,

"Those who gathered
too much
    had nothing left.
Those who gathered
only a little
    had all they needed."

Titus and His Friends

¹⁶I am grateful that God made Titus care as much about you as we do. ¹⁷When we begged Titus to visit you, he said he would. He wanted to because he cared so much for you. ¹⁸With Titus we are also sending one of the Lord's followers who is well known in every church for spreading the good news. ¹⁹The churches chose this follower to

---

ᶠ7.4 *I trust you completely*: Or "I have always spoken the truth to you" or "I can speak freely to you."   ᵍ7.8 *my letter*: There is no copy of this letter that Paul wrote to the church at Corinth.   ʰ8.1 *churches in Macedonia*: The churches that Paul had started in Philippi and Thessalonica. The church in Berea is probably also meant.   ⁱ8.7 *you love us better*: Some manuscripts have "we love you better."

travel with us while we carry this gift that will bring praise to the Lord and show how much we hope to help. [20]We don't want anyone to find fault with the way we handle your generous gift. [21]But we want to do what pleases the Lord and what people think is right.

[22]We are also sending someone else with Titus and the other follower. We approve of this man. In fact, he has already shown us many times that he wants to help. And now he wants to help even more than ever, because he trusts you so much. [23]Titus is my partner, who works with me to serve you. The other two followers are sent by the churches, and they bring honor to Christ. [24]Treat them in such a way that the churches will see your love and will know why we bragged about you.

The Money for God's People

9 I don't need to write you about the money you plan to give for God's people. [2]I know how eager you are to give. And I have proudly told the Lord's followers in Macedonia that you people in Achaia have been ready for a whole year. Now your desire to give has made them want to give. [3]That's why I am sending Titus and the two others to you. I want you to be ready, just as I promised. This will prove that we were not wrong to brag about you.

[4]Some followers from Macedonia may come with me, and I want them to find that you have the money ready. If you don't, I would be embarrassed for trusting you to do this. But you would be embarrassed even more. [5]So I have decided to ask Titus and the others to spend some time with you before I arrive. This way they can arrange to collect the money you have promised. Then you will have the chance to give because you want to, and not because you feel forced to.

[6]Remember this saying,

"A few seeds make
   a small harvest,
but a lot of seeds make
   a big harvest."

[7]Each of you must make up your own mind about how much to give. But don't feel sorry that you must give and don't feel that you are forced to give. God loves people who love to give. [8]God can bless you with everything you need, and you will always have more than enough to do all kinds of good things for others. [9]The Scriptures say,

"God freely gives his gifts
to the poor,
   and always does right."

[10]God gives seed to farmers and provides everyone with food. He will increase what you have, so that you can give even more to those in need. [11]You will be blessed in every way, and you will be able to keep on being generous. Then many people will thank God when we deliver your gift.

[12]What you are doing is much more than a service that supplies God's people with what they need. It is something that will make many others thank God. [13]The way in which you have proved yourselves by this service will bring honor and praise to God. You believed the message about Christ, and you obeyed it by sharing generously with God's people and with everyone else. [14]Now they are praying for you and want to see you, because God used you to bless them so very much. [15]Thank God for his gift that is too wonderful for words!

Paul Defends His Work for Christ

10 Do you think I am a coward when I am with you and brave when I am far away? Well, I ask you to listen, because Christ himself was humble and gentle. [2]Some people have said that we act like the people of this world. So when I arrive, I expect I will have to be firm and forceful in what I say to them. Please don't make me treat you that way. [3]We live in this world, but we don't act like its people [4]or fight our battles with the weapons of this world. Instead, we use God's power that can destroy fortresses. We destroy arguments [5]and every bit of pride that keeps anyone from knowing God. We capture people's thoughts and make them obey Christ. [6]And when you completely obey him, we will punish anyone who refuses to obey.

[7]You judge by appearances.[j] If any of you think you are the only ones who belong to Christ, then think again. We belong to Christ as much as you do. [8]Maybe I brag a little too much about the authority that the Lord gave me to help you and not to hurt you. Yet I am not embarrassed to brag. [9]And I am not trying to scare you with my letters. [10]Some of you are saying, "Paul's letters are harsh and powerful. But in person, he is a weakling and has nothing worth saying." [11]Those people had better understand that when I am with you, I will do exactly what I say in my letters.

[12]We won't dare compare ourselves with those who think so much of themselves. But they are foolish to compare themselves with themselves. [13]We won't brag about something we don't have a right to brag about. We will only brag

---

[j]**10.7** *You judge by appearances:* Or "Take a close look at yourselves."

about the work that God has sent us to do, and you are part of that work. ¹⁴We are not bragging more than we should. After all, we did bring the message about Christ to you.

¹⁵We don't brag about what others have done, as if we had done those things ourselves. But I hope that as you become stronger in your faith, we will be able to reach many more of the people around you.ᵏ That has always been our goal. ¹⁶Then we will be able to preach the good news in other lands where we cannot take credit for work someone else has already done. ¹⁷The Scriptures say, "If you want to brag, then brag about the Lord." ¹⁸You may brag about yourself, but the only approval that counts is the Lord's approval.

Paul and the False Apostles

11 Please put up with a little of my foolishness. ²I am as concerned about you as God is. You were like a virgin bride I had chosen only for Christ. ³But now I fear that you will be tricked, just as Eve was tricked by that lying snake. I am afraid that you might stop thinking about Christ in an honest and sincere way. ⁴We told you about Jesus, and you received the Holy Spirit and accepted our message. But you let some people tell you about another Jesus. Now you are ready to receive another spirit and accept a different message. ⁵I think I am as good as any of those super apostles. ⁶I may not speak as well as they do, but I know as much. And this has already been made perfectly clear to you.

⁷Was it wrong for me to lower myself and honor you by preaching God's message free of charge? ⁸I robbed other churches by taking money from them to serve you. ⁹Even when I was in need, I still didn't bother you. In fact, some of the Lord's followers from Macedonia brought me what I needed. I have not been a burden to you in the past, and I will never be a burden. ¹⁰As surely as I speak the truth about Christ, no one in Achaia can stop me from bragging about this. ¹¹And it isn't because I don't love you. God himself knows how much I do love you.

¹²I plan to go on doing just what I have always done. Then those people won't be able to brag about doing the same things we are doing. ¹³Anyway, they are no more than false apostles and dishonest workers. They only pretend to be apostles of Christ. ¹⁴And it is no wonder. Even Satan tries to make himself look like an angel of light. ¹⁵So why does it seem strange for Satan's servants to pretend to do what is right? Someday they will get exactly what they deserve.

Paul's Sufferings for Christ

¹⁶I don't want any of you to think that I am a fool. But if you do, then let me be a fool and brag a little. ¹⁷When I do all this bragging, I do it as a fool and not for the Lord. ¹⁸Yet if others want to brag about what they have done, so will I. ¹⁹And since you are so smart, you will gladly put up with a fool. ²⁰In fact, you let people make slaves of you and cheat you and steal from you. Why, you even let them strut around and slap you in the face. ²¹I am ashamed to say that we are too weak to behave in such a way.

If they can brag, so can I, but it is a foolish thing to do. ²²Are they Hebrews? So am I. Are they Jews? So am I. Are they from the family of Abraham? Well, so am I. ²³Are they servants of Christ? I am a fool to talk this way, but I serve him better than they do. I have worked harder and have been put in jail more times. I have been beaten with whips more and have been in danger of death more often.

²⁴Five times the Jews gave me thirty-nine lashes with a whip. ²⁵Three times the Romans beat me with a big stick, and once my enemies stoned me. I have been shipwrecked three times, and I even had to spend a night and a day in the sea. ²⁶During my many travels, I have been in danger from rivers, robbers, my own people, and foreigners. My life has been in danger in cities, in deserts, at sea, and with people who only pretended to be the Lord's followers.

²⁷I have worked and struggled and spent many sleepless nights. I have gone hungry and thirsty and often had nothing to eat. I have been cold from not having enough clothes to keep me warm. ²⁸Besides everything else, each day I am burdened down, worrying about all the churches. ²⁹When others are weak, I am weak too. When others are tricked into sin, I get angry.ˡ

³⁰If I have to brag, I will brag about how weak I am. ³¹God, the Father of our Lord Jesus, knows I am not lying. And God is to be praised forever! ³²The governor of Damascus at the time of King Aretas had the city gates guarded, so that he could capture me. ³³But I escaped by being let down in a basket through a window in the city wall.

ᵏ**10.15** *we will be able to reach many more of the people around you:* Or "you will praise us even more because of our work among you." ˡ**11.29** *When others are tricked into sin, I get angry:* Or "When others stumble into sin, I hurt for them."

Visions from the Lord

12 I have to brag. There is nothing to be gained by it, but I must brag about the visions and other things that the Lord has shown me. [2]I know about one of Christ's followers who was taken up into the third heaven fourteen years ago. I don't know if the man was still in his body when it happened, but God certainly knows.

[3]As I said, only God really knows if this man was in his body at the time. [4]But he was taken up into paradise,[m] where he heard things that are too wonderful to tell. [5]I will brag about that man, but not about myself, except to say how weak I am.

[6]Yet even if I did brag, I would not be foolish. I would simply be speaking the truth. But I will try not to say too much. That way, none of you will think more highly of me than you should because of what you have seen me do and say. [7]Of course, I am now referring to the wonderful things I saw. One of Satan's angels was sent to make me suffer terribly, so that I would not feel too proud.[n]

[8]Three times I begged the Lord to make this suffering go away. [9]But he replied, "My kindness is all you need. My power is strongest when you are weak." So if Christ keeps giving me his power, I will gladly brag about how weak I am. [10]Yes, I am glad to be weak or insulted or mistreated or to have troubles and sufferings, if it is for Christ. Because when I am weak, I am strong.

Paul's Concern for the Lord's Followers at Corinth

[11]I have been making a fool of myself. But you forced me to do it, when you should have been speaking up for me. I may be nothing at all, but I am as good as those super apostles. [12]When I was with you, I was patient and worked all the powerful miracles and signs and wonders of a true apostle. [13]You missed out on only one blessing that the other churches received. That is, you didn't have to support me. Forgive me for doing you wrong.

[14]I am planning to visit you for the third time. But I still won't make a burden of myself. What I really want is you, and not what you have. Children are not supposed to save up for their parents, but parents are supposed to take care of their children. [15]So I will gladly give all that I have and all that I am. Will you love me less for loving you too much?

[16]You agree that I wasn't a burden to you. Maybe that's because I was trying to catch you off guard and trick you. [17]Were you cheated by any of those I sent to you? [18]I urged Titus to visit you, and I sent another follower with him. But Titus didn't cheat you, and we felt and behaved the same way he did.

[19]Have you been thinking all along that we have been defending ourselves to you? Actually, we have been speaking to God as followers of Christ. But, my friends, we did it all for your good.

[20]I am afraid that when I come, we won't be pleased with each other. I fear that some of you may be arguing or jealous or angry or selfish or gossiping or insulting each other. I even fear that you may be proud and acting like a mob. [21]I am afraid God will make me ashamed when I visit you again. I will feel like crying because many of you have never given up your old sins. You are still doing things that are immoral, indecent, and shameful.

Final Warnings and Greetings

13 I am on my way to visit you for the third time. And as the Scriptures say, "Any charges must be proved true by at least two or three witnesses." [2]During my second visit I warned you that I would punish you and anyone else who doesn't stop sinning. I am far away from you now, but I give you the same warning. [3]This should prove to you that I am speaking for Christ. When he corrects you, he won't be weak. He will be powerful! [4]Although he was weak when he was nailed to the cross, he now lives by the power of God. We are weak, just as Christ was. But you will see that we will live by the power of God, just as Christ does.

[5]Test yourselves and find out if you really are true to your faith. If you pass the test, you will discover that Christ is living in you. But if Christ isn't living in you, you have failed. [6]I hope you will discover that we have not failed. [7]We pray that you will stop doing evil things. We don't pray like this to make ourselves look good, but to get you to do right, even if we are failures.

[8]All we can do is to follow the truth and not fight against it. [9]Even though we are weak, we are glad that you are strong, and we pray that you will do even better. [10]I am writing these things to you before I arrive. This way I won't have to be hard on you when I use the authority that the Lord has given me. I

---

[m]**12.4** *paradise:* In the Greek translation of the Old Testament, this word is used for the Garden of Eden. In New Testament times it was sometimes used for the place where God's people are happy and at rest, as they wait for the final judgment.   [n]**12.7** *Of course . . . too proud:* Or "Because of the wonderful things that I saw, one of Satan's angels was sent to make me suffer terribly, so that I would not feel too proud."

was given this authority, so that I could help you and not destroy you.

[11]Good-by, my friends. Do better and pay attention to what I have said. Try to get along and live peacefully with each other.

Now I pray that God, who gives love and peace, will be with you. [12]Give each other a warm greeting. All of God's people send their greetings.

[13]I pray that the Lord Jesus Christ will bless you and be kind to you! May God bless you with his love, and may the Holy Spirit join all your hearts together.

GALATIANS

ABOUT THIS LETTER

From the very beginning of this letter to the churches in the region of Galatia (in central Asia Minor), Paul makes two things clear to his readers: he is a true apostle, and his message is the only true message (1.1-10). These statements were very important, because some people claimed that Paul was a false apostle with a false message.

Paul was indeed a true apostle, and his mission to the Gentiles was given to him by the Lord and approved by the apostles in Jerusalem (1.18—2.10). Paul had even corrected the apostle Peter, when he had stopped eating with Gentile followers who were not obeying the Law of Moses (2.1-18).

Faith is the only way to be saved. Paul insists that this was true already for Abraham, who had received God's promise by faith. And Paul leaves no doubt about what his own faith means to him:

I have been nailed to the cross with Christ. I have died, but Christ lives in me. And I now live by faith in the Son of God, who loved me and gave his life for me.

(2.19b, 20)

A QUICK LOOK AT THIS LETTER

A True Apostle and the True Message (1.1-10)
God Chose Paul To Be an Apostle (1.11-24)
Paul Defends His Message (2.1-21)
Faith Is the Only Way To Be Saved (3.1—4.31)
Guided by the Spirit and Love (5.1—6.10)
Final Warnings (6.11-18)

---

1 ¹⁻²From the apostle Paul and from all the Lord's followers with me.

I was chosen to be an apostle by Jesus Christ and by God the Father, who raised him from death. No mere human chose or appointed me to this work.

To the churches in Galatia.

³I pray that God the Father and our Lord Jesus Christ will be kind to you and will bless you with peace! ⁴Christ obeyed God our Father and gave himself as a sacrifice to rescue us from this evil world. ⁵God will be given glory forever and ever. Amen.

The Only True Message

⁶I am shocked that you have so quickly turned from God, who chose you because of his wonderful kindness.ᵃ You have believed another message, ⁷when there is really only one true mes-sage. But some people are causing you trouble and want to make you turn away from the good news about Christ. ⁸I pray that God will punish anyone who preaches anything different from our message to you! It doesn't matter if that person is one of us or an angel from heaven. ⁹I have said it before, and I will say it again. I hope God will punish any-one who preaches anything different from what you have already believed.

¹⁰I am not trying to please people. I want to please God. Do you think I am trying to please people? If I were doing that, I would not be a servant of Christ.

How Paul Became an Apostle

¹¹My friends, I want you to know that no one made up the message I preach. ¹²It wasn't given or taught to me by some mere human. My message came

ᵃ**1.6** *his wonderful kindness*: Some manuscripts have "the wonderful kindness of Christ."

directly from Jesus Christ when he appeared to me.

[13]You know how I used to live as a Jew. I was cruel to God's church and even tried to destroy it. [14]I was a much better Jew than anyone else my own age, and I obeyed every law that our ancestors had given us. [15]But even before I was born, God had chosen me. He was kind and had decided [16]to show me his Son, so that I would announce his message to the Gentiles. I didn't talk this over with anyone. [17]I didn't say a word, not even to the men in Jerusalem who were apostles before I was. Instead, I went at once to Arabia, and afterwards I returned to Damascus.

[18]Three years later I went to visit Peter[b] in Jerusalem and stayed with him for fifteen days. [19]The only other apostle I saw was James, the Lord's brother. [20]And in the presence of God I swear I am telling the truth.

[21]Later, I went to the regions of Syria and Cilicia. [22]But no one who belonged to Christ's churches in Judea had ever seen me in person. [23]They had only heard that the one who had been cruel to them was now preaching the message that he had once tried to destroy. [24]And because of me, they praised God.

2 Fourteen years later I went to Jerusalem with Barnabas. I also took along Titus. [2]But I went there because God had told me to go, and I explained the good news that I had been preaching to the Gentiles. Then I met privately with the ones who seemed to be the most important leaders. I wanted to make sure that my work in the past and my future work would not be for nothing.

[3]Titus went to Jerusalem with me. He was a Greek, but still he wasn't forced to be circumcised. [4]We went there because of those who pretended to be followers and had sneaked in among us as spies. They had come to take away the freedom that Christ Jesus had given us, and they were trying to make us their slaves. [5]But we wanted you to have the true message. That's why we didn't give in to them, not even for a second.

[6]Some of them were supposed to be important leaders, but I didn't care who they were. God doesn't have any favorites! None of these so-called special leaders added anything to my message. [7]They realized that God had sent me with the good news for Gentiles, and that he had sent Peter with the same message for Jews. [8]God, who had sent Peter on a mission to the Jews, was now using me to preach to the Gentiles.

[9]James, Peter,[b] and John realized that God had given me the message about his undeserved kindness. And these men are supposed to be the backbone of the church. They even gave Barnabas and me a friendly handshake. This was to show that we would work with Gentiles and that they would work with Jews. [10]They only asked us to remember the poor, and that was something I had always been eager to do.

Paul Corrects Peter at Antioch

[11]When Peter came to Antioch, I told him face to face that he was wrong. [12]He used to eat with Gentile followers of the Lord, until James sent some Jewish followers. Peter was afraid of the Jews and soon stopped eating with Gentiles. [13]He and the other Jews hid their true feelings so well that even Barnabas was fooled. [14]But when I saw that they were not really obeying the truth that is in the good news, I corrected Peter in front of everyone and said:

Peter, you are a Jew, but you live like a Gentile. So how can you force Gentiles to live like Jews?

[15]We are Jews by birth and are not sinners like Gentiles. [16]But we know that God accepts only those who have faith in Jesus Christ. No one can please God by simply obeying the Law. So we put our faith in Christ Jesus, and God accepted us because of our faith.

[17]When we Jews started looking for a way to please God, we discovered that we are sinners too. Does this mean that Christ is the one who makes us sinners? No, it doesn't! [18]But if I tear down something and then build it again, I prove that I was wrong at first. [19]It was the Law itself that killed me and freed me from its power, so that I could live for God.

I have been nailed to the cross with Christ. [20]I have died, but Christ lives in me. And I now live by faith in the Son of God, who loved me and gave his life for me. [21]I don't turn my back on God's undeserved kindness. If we can be acceptable to God by obeying the Law, it was useless for Christ to die.

Faith Is the Only Way

3 You stupid Galatians! I told you exactly how Jesus Christ was nailed to a cross. Has someone now put an evil spell on you? [2]I want to know only one thing. How were you given God's Spirit? Was it by obeying the Law of Moses or by hearing about Christ and having

---

[b]**1.18;2.9** *Peter*: The Greek text has "Cephas," which is an Aramaic name meaning "rock." Peter is the Greek name with the same meaning.

faith in him? [3]How can you be so stupid? Do you think that by yourself you can complete what God's Spirit started in you? [4]Have you gone through all of this for nothing? Is it all really for nothing? [5]God gives you his Spirit and works miracles in you. But does he do this because you obey the Law of Moses or because you have heard about Christ and have faith in him?

[6]The Scriptures say that God accepted Abraham because Abraham had faith. [7]And so, you should understand that everyone who has faith is a child of Abraham.[c] [8]Long ago the Scriptures said that God would accept the Gentiles because of their faith. That's why God told Abraham the good news that all nations would be blessed because of him. [9]This means that everyone who has faith will share in the blessings that were given to Abraham because of his faith.

[10]Anyone who tries to please God by obeying the Law is under a curse. The Scriptures say, "Everyone who doesn't obey everything in the Law is under a curse." [11]No one can please God by obeying the Law. The Scriptures also say, "The people God accepts because of their faith will live."[d]

[12]The Law isn't based on faith. It promises life only to people who obey its commands. [13]But Christ rescued us from the Law's curse, when he became a curse in our place. This is because the Scriptures say that anyone who is nailed to a tree is under a curse. [14]And because of what Jesus Christ has done, the blessing that was promised to Abraham was taken to the Gentiles. This happened so that by faith we would be given the promised Holy Spirit.

The Law and the Promise

[15]My friends, I will use an everyday example to explain what I mean. Once someone agrees to something, no one else can change or cancel the agreement.[e] [16]That is how it is with the promises God made to Abraham and his descendant.[f] The promises were not made to many descendants, but only to one, and that one is Christ. [17]What I am saying is that the Law cannot change or cancel God's promise that was made 430 years before the Law was given. [18]If we have to obey the Law in order to receive God's blessings, those blessings don't really come to us because of God's promise. But God was kind to Abraham and made him a promise.

[19]What is the use of the Law? It was given later to show that we sin. But it was only supposed to last until the coming of that descendant[g] who was given the promise. In fact, angels gave the Law to Moses, and he gave it to the people. [20]There is only one God, and the Law did not come directly from him.

Slaves and Children

[21]Does the Law disagree with God's promises? No, it doesn't! If any law could give life to us, we could become acceptable to God by obeying that law. [22]But the Scriptures say that sin controls everyone, so that God's promises will be for anyone who has faith in Jesus Christ.

[23]The Law controlled us and kept us under its power until the time came when we would have faith. [24]In fact, the Law was our teacher. It was supposed to teach us until we had faith and were acceptable to God. [25]But once a person has learned to have faith, there is no more need to have the Law as a teacher.

[26]All of you are God's children because of your faith in Christ Jesus. [27]And when you were baptized, it was as though you had put on Christ in the same way you put on new clothes. [28]Faith in Christ Jesus is what makes each of you equal with each other, whether you are a Jew or a Greek, a slave or a free person, a man or a woman. [29]So if you belong to Christ, you are now part of Abraham's family,[h] and you will be given what God has promised. [1]Children who are under age are no better off than slaves, even though everything their parents own will someday be theirs. [2]This is because children are placed in the care of guardians and teachers until the time their parents have set. [3]That is how it was with us. We were like children ruled by the powers of this world.

[4]But when the time was right, God sent his Son, and a woman gave birth to him. His Son obeyed the Law, [5]so he could set us free from the Law, and we could become God's children. [6]Now that we are his children, God has sent the Spirit of his Son into our hearts. And his

---

[c]**3.7** *a child of Abraham*: God chose Abraham, and so it was believed that anyone who was a child of Abraham was also a child of God (see the note at 3.29).   [d]**3.11** *The people God accepts because of their faith will live*: Or "The people God accepts will live because of their faith."   [e]**3.15** *Once someone . . . cancel the agreement*: Or "Once a person makes out a will, no one can change or cancel it."   [f]**3.16** *descendant*: The Greek text has "seed," which may mean one or many descendants. In this verse Paul says it means Christ.   [g]**3.19** *that descendant*: Jesus.   [h]**3.29** *you are now part of Abraham's family*: Paul tells the Galatians that faith in Jesus Christ is what makes someone a true child of Abraham and of God (see the note at 3.7).

Spirit tells us that God is our Father. [7]You are no longer slaves. You are God's children, and you will be given what he has promised.

Paul's Concern for the Galatians

[8]Before you knew God, you were slaves of gods that are not real. [9]But now you know God, or better still, God knows you. How can you turn back and become the slaves of those weak and pitiful powers?[i] [10]You even celebrate certain days, months, seasons, and years. [11]I am afraid I have wasted my time working with you.

[12]My friends, I beg you to be like me, just as I once tried to be like you. Did you mistreat me [13]when I first preached to you? No you didn't, even though you knew I had come there because I was sick. [14]My illness must have caused you some trouble, but you didn't hate me or turn me away because of it. You welcomed me as though I were one of God's angels or even Christ Jesus himself. [15]Where is that good feeling now? I am sure that if it had been possible, you would have taken out your own eyes and given them to me. [16]Am I now your enemy, just because I told you the truth?

[17]Those people may be paying you a lot of attention, but it isn't for your good. They only want to keep you away from me, so you will pay them a lot of attention. [18]It is always good to give your attention to something worthwhile, even when I am not with you. [19]My children, I am in terrible pain until Christ may be seen living in you. [20]I wish I were with you now. Then I would not have to talk this way. You really have me puzzled.

Hagar and Sarah

[21]Some of you would like to be under the rule of the Law of Moses. But do you know what the Law says? [22]In the Scriptures we learn that Abraham had two sons. The mother of one of them was a slave, while the mother of the other one had always been free. [23]The son of the slave woman was born in the usual way. But the son of the free woman was born because of God's promise.

[24]All of this has another meaning as well. Each of the two women stands for one of the agreements God made with his people. Hagar, the slave woman, stands for the agreement that was made at Mount Sinai. Everyone born into her family is a slave. [25]Hagar also stands for Mount Sinai in Arabia[j] and for the pre-

sent city of Jerusalem. She[k] and her children are slaves. [26]But our mother is the city of Jerusalem in heaven above, and she isn't a slave. [27]The Scriptures say about her,

"You have never had children,
    but now you can be glad.
You have never given birth,
    but now you can shout.
Once you had no children,
    but now you will have
more children than a woman
who has been married
    for a long time."

[28]My friends, you were born because of this promise, just as Isaac was. [29]But the child who was born in the natural way made trouble for the child who was born because of the Spirit. The same thing is happening today. [30]The Scriptures say, "Get rid of the slave woman and her son! He won't be given anything. The son of the free woman will receive everything." [31]My friends, we are children of the free woman and not of the slave.

Christ Gives Freedom

5 Christ has set us free! This means we are really free. Now hold on to your freedom and don't ever become slaves of the Law again.

[2]I, Paul, promise you that Christ won't do you any good if you get circumcised. [3]If you do, you must obey the whole Law. [4]And if you try to please God by obeying the Law, you have cut yourself off from Christ and his wonderful kindness. [5]But the Spirit makes us sure that God will accept us because of our faith in Christ. [6]If you are a follower of Christ Jesus, it makes no difference whether you are circumcised or not. All that matters is your faith that makes you love others.

[7]You were doing so well until someone made you turn from the truth. [8]And that person was certainly not sent by the one who chose you. [9]A little yeast can change a whole batch of dough, [10]but you belong to the Lord. That makes me certain that you will do what I say, instead of what someone else tells you to do. Whoever is causing trouble for you will be punished.

[11]My friends, if I still preach that people need to be circumcised, why am I in so much trouble? The message about the cross would no longer be a problem, if I told people to be circumcised. [12]I wish that everyone who is upsetting you

---

[i]**4.9** _powers_: Spirits were thought to control human lives and were believed to be connected with the movements of the stars. [j]**4.25** _Hagar also stands for Mount Sinai in Arabia_: Some manuscripts have "Sinai is a mountain in Arabia." This sentence would then be translated: "Sinai is a mountain in Arabia, and Hagar stands for the present city of Jerusalem." [k]**4.25** _She_: "Hagar" or "Jerusalem."

would not only get circumcised, but would cut off much more!

¹³My friends, you were chosen to be free. So don't use your freedom as an excuse to do anything you want. Use it as an opportunity to serve each other with love. ¹⁴All that the Law says can be summed up in the command to love others as much as you love yourself. ¹⁵But if you keep attacking each other like wild animals, you had better watch out or you will destroy yourselves.

God's Spirit and Our Own Desires

¹⁶If you are guided by the Spirit, you won't obey your selfish desires. ¹⁷The Spirit and your desires are enemies of each other. They are always fighting each other and keeping you from doing what you feel you should. ¹⁸But if you obey the Spirit, the Law of Moses has no control over you.

¹⁹People's desires make them give in to immoral ways, filthy thoughts, and shameful deeds. ²⁰They worship idols, practice witchcraft, hate others, and are hard to get along with. People become jealous, angry, and selfish. They not only argue and cause trouble, but they are ²¹envious. They get drunk, carry on at wild parties, and do other evil things as well. I told you before, and I am telling you again: No one who does these things will share in the blessings of God's kingdom.

²²God's Spirit makes us loving, happy, peaceful, patient, kind, good, faithful, ²³gentle, and self-controlled. There is no law against behaving in any of these ways. ²⁴And because we belong to Christ Jesus, we have killed our selfish feelings and desires. ²⁵God's Spirit has given us life, and so we should follow the Spirit. ²⁶But don't be conceited or make others jealous by claiming to be better than they are.

Help Each Other

6 My friends, you are spiritual. So if someone is trapped in sin, you should gently lead that person back to the right path. But watch out, and don't be tempted yourself. ²You obey the law of Christ when you offer each other a helping hand.

³If you think you are better than others, when you really aren't, you are wrong. ⁴Do your own work well, and then you will have something to be proud of. But don't compare yourself with others. ⁵We each must carry our own load.

⁶Share every good thing you have with anyone who teaches you what God has said.

⁷You cannot fool God, so don't make a fool of yourself! You will harvest what you plant. ⁸If you follow your selfish desires, you will harvest destruction, but if you follow the Spirit, you will harvest eternal life. ⁹Don't get tired of helping others. You will be rewarded when the time is right, if you don't give up. ¹⁰We should help people whenever we can, especially if they are followers of the Lord.

Final Warnings

¹¹You can see what big letters I make when I write with my own hand. ¹²Those people who are telling you to get circumcised are only trying to show how important they are. And they don't want to get into trouble for preaching about the cross of Christ. ¹³They are circumcised, but they don't obey the Law of Moses. All they want is to brag about having you circumcised. ¹⁴But I will never brag about anything except the cross of our Lord Jesus Christ. Because of his cross, the world is dead as far as I am concerned, and I am dead as far as the world is concerned.

¹⁵It doesn't matter if you are circumcised or not. All that matters is that you are a new person.

¹⁶If you follow this rule, you will belong to God's true people. God will treat you with undeserved kindness and will bless you with peace.

¹⁷On my own body are scars that prove I belong to Christ Jesus. So I don't want anyone to bother me anymore.

¹⁸My friends, I pray that the Lord Jesus Christ will be kind to you! Amen.

EPHESIANS

ABOUT THIS LETTER

"Praise the God and Father of our Lord Jesus Christ for the spiritual blessings that Christ has brought us from heaven!" (1.3). Paul begins his letter to the Christians in Ephesus with a powerful reminder of the main theme of his message. Christ died on the cross to set us free (1.7, 8). But God raised Christ from death, and he now sits at God's right side in heaven, where he rules over this world. And he will rule over the future world as well (1.20, 21).

Christ brought Jews and Gentiles together by "breaking down the wall of hatred" that separated them (2.14) and he united them all as part of that holy temple where God's Spirit lives (2.22). This was according to God's eternal plan (3.11).

There is only one Lord, one Spirit of God, and one God, who is the Father of all people (4.4, 5). This means that Christians must let the Spirit keep their hearts united, so they can live at peace with each other (4.3). The idea of all Christians being one with Christ is so central to this letter that it occurs twenty times. There is one faith and one baptism by which believers become one body.

Ephesus was a port city on the western shore of Asia Minor (modern-day Turkey). In Paul's time this was the fourth largest city in the Roman Empire. It was also an ancient center of nature religion where the goddess Artemis was widely worshiped (Acts 19).

Paul lets the Ephesians know that much is expected of people who are called to a new life (4.17—5.20). Followers of the Lord are God's dear children, and they must do as God does (5.1). They used to live in the dark, but they must now live in the light and make their light shine (5.8, 9).

Paul then teaches husbands and wives, children and parents, and slaves and masters how to live as Christians (5.21—6.9).

Paul never forgets how kind God is:

God was merciful! We were dead because of our sins, but God loved us so much that he made us alive with Christ, and God's wonderful kindness is what saves you.

(2.4, 5)

You were saved by faith in God, who treats us much better than we deserve. This is God's gift to you, and not anything you have done on your own.

(2.8)

A QUICK LOOK AT THIS LETTER

Greetings (1.1, 2)
Christ Brings Spiritual Blessings (1.3—3.21)
A New Life in Unity with Christ (4.1—6.20)
Final Greetings (6.21-24)

---

1 From Paul, chosen by God to be an apostle of Christ Jesus.

To God's people who live in Ephesus and[a] are faithful followers of Christ Jesus.

²I pray that God our Father and our Lord Jesus Christ will be kind to you and will bless you with peace!

Christ Brings Spiritual Blessings

³Praise the God and Father of our Lord Jesus Christ for the spiritual bless-

---

[a]1.1 *live in Ephesus and*: Some manuscripts do not have these words.

ings that Christ has brought us from heaven! [4]Before the world was created, God had Christ choose us to live with him and to be his holy and innocent and loving people. [5]God was kind[b] and decided that Christ would choose us to be God's own adopted children. [6]God was very kind to us because of the Son he dearly loves, and so we should praise God.

[7-8]Christ sacrificed his life's blood to set us free, which means that our sins are now forgiven. Christ did this because God was so kind to us. God has great wisdom and understanding, [9]and by what Christ has done, God has shown us his own mysterious ways. [10]Then when the time is right, God will do all that he has planned, and Christ will bring together everything in heaven and on earth.

[11]God always does what he plans, and that's why he appointed Christ to choose us. [12]He did this so that we Jews would bring honor to him and be the first ones to have hope because of him. [13]Christ also brought you the truth, which is the good news about how you can be saved. You put your faith in Christ and were given the promised Holy Spirit to show that you belong to God. [14]The Spirit also makes us sure that we will be given what God has stored up for his people. Then we will be set free, and God will be honored and praised.

Paul's Prayer

[15]I have heard about your faith in the Lord Jesus and your love for all of God's people. [16]So I never stop being grateful for you, as I mention you in my prayers. [17]I ask the glorious Father and God of our Lord Jesus Christ to give you his Spirit. The Spirit will make you wise and let you understand what it means to know God. [18]My prayer is that light will flood your hearts and that you will understand the hope that was given to you when God chose you. Then you will discover the glorious blessings that will be yours together with all of God's people.

[19]I want you to know about the great and mighty power that God has for us followers. It is the same wonderful power he used [20]when he raised Christ from death and let him sit at his right side[c] in heaven. [21]There Christ rules over all forces, authorities, powers, and rulers. He rules over all beings in this world and will rule in the future world as well. [22]God has put all things under

the power of Christ, and for the good of the church he has made him the head of everything. [23]The church is Christ's body and is filled with Christ who completely fills everything.[d]

From Death to Life

2 In the past you were dead because you sinned and fought against God. [2]You followed the ways of this world and obeyed the devil. He rules the world, and his spirit has power over everyone who doesn't obey God. [3]Once we were also ruled by the selfish desires of our bodies and minds. We had made God angry, and we were going to be punished like everyone else.

[4-5]But God was merciful! We were dead because of our sins, but God loved us so much that he made us alive with Christ, and God's wonderful kindness is what saves you. [6]God raised us from death to life with Christ Jesus, and he has given us a place beside Christ in heaven. [7]God did this so that in the future world he could show how truly good and kind he is to us because of what Christ Jesus has done. [8]You were saved by faith in God, who treats us much better than we deserve.[e] This is God's gift to you, and not anything you have done on your own. [9]It isn't something you have earned, so there is nothing you can brag about. [10]God planned for us to do good things and to live as he has always wanted us to live. That's why he sent Christ to make us what we are.

United by Christ

[11]Don't forget that you are Gentiles. In fact, you used to be called "uncircumcised" by those who take pride in being circumcised. [12]At that time you did not know about Christ. You were foreigners to the people of Israel, and you had no part in the promises that God had made to them. You were living in this world without hope and without God, [13]and you were far from God. But Christ offered his life's blood as a sacrifice and brought you near God.

[14]Christ has made peace between Jews and Gentiles, and he has united us by breaking down the wall of hatred that separated us. Christ gave his own body [15]to destroy the Law of Moses with all its rules and commands. He even brought Jews and Gentiles together as though we were only one person, when he united us in peace. [16]On the cross

---

[b]**1.4,5** *holy and innocent and loving people.* [5]*God was kind*: Or "holy and innocent people. God was loving [5]and kind."   [c]**1.20** *right side*: The place of power and honor.   [d]**1.23** *and is filled with Christ who completely fills everything*: Or "which completely fills Christ and fully completes his work."   [e]**2.8** *treats us much better than we deserve*: The Greek word *charis*, traditionally rendered "grace," is translated here and other places in the CEV to express the overwhelming kindness of God.

Christ did away with our hatred for each other. He also made peace[f] between us and God by uniting Jews and Gentiles in one body. [17]Christ came and preached peace to you Gentiles, who were far from God, and peace to us Jews, who were near God. [18]And because of Christ, all of us can come to the Father by the same Spirit.

[19]You Gentiles are no longer strangers and foreigners. You are citizens with everyone else who belongs to the family of God. [20]You are like a building with the apostles and prophets as the foundation and with Christ as the most important stone. [21]Christ is the one who holds the building together and makes it grow into a holy temple for the Lord. [22]And you are part of that building Christ has built as a place for God's own Spirit to live.

Paul's Mission to the Gentiles

3 Christ Jesus made me his prisoner, so that I could help you Gentiles. [2]You have surely heard about God's kindness in choosing me to help you. [3]In fact, this letter tells you a little about how God has shown me his mysterious ways. [4]As you read the letter, you will also find out how well I really do understand the mystery about Christ. [5]No one knew about this mystery until God's Spirit told it to his holy apostles and prophets. [6]And the mystery is this: Because of Christ Jesus, the good news has given the Gentiles a share in the promises that God gave to the Jews. God has also let the Gentiles be part of the same body.

[7]God treated me with kindness. His power worked in me, and it became my job to spread the good news. [8]I am the least important of all God's people. But God was kind and chose me to tell the Gentiles that because of Christ there are blessings that cannot be measured. [9]God, who created everything, wanted me to help everyone understand the mysterious plan that had always been hidden in his mind. [10]Then God would use the church to show the powers and authorities in the spiritual world that he has many different kinds of wisdom.

[11]God did this according to his eternal plan. And he was able to do what he had planned because of all that Christ Jesus our Lord had done. [12]Christ now gives us courage and confidence, so that we can come to God by faith. [13]That's why you should not be discouraged when I suffer for you. After all, it will bring honor to you.

Christ's Love for Us

[14]I kneel in prayer to the Father. [15]All beings in heaven and on earth receive their life from him.[g] [16]God is wonderful and glorious. I pray that his Spirit will make you become strong followers [17]and that Christ will live in your hearts because of your faith. Stand firm and be deeply rooted in his love. [18]I pray that you and all of God's people will understand what is called wide or long or high or deep.[h] [19]I want you to know all about Christ's love, although it is too wonderful to be measured. Then your lives will be filled with all that God is.

[20-21]I pray that Christ Jesus and the church will forever bring praise to God. His power at work in us can do far more than we dare ask or imagine. Amen.

Unity with Christ

4 As a prisoner of the Lord, I beg you to live in a way that is worthy of the people God has chosen to be his own. [2]Always be humble and gentle. Patiently put up with each other and love each other. [3]Try your best to let God's Spirit keep your hearts united. Do this by living at peace. [4]All of you are part of the same body. There is only one Spirit of God, just as you were given one hope when you were chosen to be God's people. [5]We have only one Lord, one faith, and one baptism. [6]There is one God who is the Father of all people. Not only is God above all others, but he works by using all of us, and he lives in all of us.

[7]Christ has generously divided out his gifts to us. [8]As the Scriptures say,

"When he went up
    to the highest place,
he led away many prisoners
    and gave gifts to people."

[9]When it says, "he went up," it means that Christ had been deep in the earth. [10]This also means that the one who went deep into the earth is the same one who went into the highest heaven, so that he would fill the whole universe.

[11]Christ chose some of us to be apostles, prophets, missionaries, pastors, and teachers, [12]so that his people would learn to serve and his body would grow strong. [13]This will continue until we are united by our faith and by our understanding of the Son of God. Then we will be mature, just as Christ is, and we will be completely like him.[i]

[f]2.16 *He also made peace*: Or "The cross also made peace." [g]3.15 *receive their life from him*: Or "know who they really are because of him." [h]3.18 *what is called wide or long or high or deep*: This may refer to the heavenly Jerusalem or to God's love or wisdom or to the meaning of the cross. [i]4.13 *and we will be completely like him*: Or "and he is completely perfect."

[14]We must stop acting like children. We must not let deceitful people trick us by their false teachings, which are like winds that toss us around from place to place. [15]Love should always make us tell the truth. Then we will grow in every way and be more like Christ, the head [16]of the body. Christ holds it together and makes all of its parts work perfectly, as it grows and becomes strong because of love.

The Old Life and the New Life

[17]As a follower of the Lord, I order you to stop living like stupid, godless people. [18]Their minds are in the dark, and they are stubborn and ignorant and have missed out on the life that comes from God. They no longer have any feelings about what is right, [19]and they are so greedy that they do all kinds of indecent things.

[20-21]But that isn't what you were taught about Jesus Christ. He is the truth, and you heard about him and learned about him. [22]You were told that your foolish desires will destroy you and that you must give up your old way of life with all its bad habits. [23]Let the Spirit change your way of thinking [24]and make you into a new person. You were created to be like God, and so you must please him and be truly holy.

Rules for the New Life

[25]We are part of the same body. Stop lying and start telling each other the truth. [26]Don't get so angry that you sin. Don't go to bed angry [27]and don't give the devil a chance. [28]If you are a thief, quit stealing. Be honest and work hard, so you will have something to give to people in need. [29]Stop all your dirty talk. Say the right thing at the right time and help others by what you say. [30]Don't make God's Spirit sad. The Spirit makes you sure that someday you will be free from your sins. [31]Stop being bitter and angry and mad at others. Don't yell at one another or curse each other or ever be rude. [32]Instead, be kind and merciful, and forgive others, just as God forgave you because of Christ.

5 Do as God does. After all, you are his dear children. [2]Let love be your guide. Christ loved us[j] and offered his life for us as a sacrifice that pleases God.

[3]You are God's people, so don't let it be said that any of you are immoral or indecent or greedy. [4]Don't use dirty or foolish or filthy words. Instead, say how thankful you are. [5]Being greedy, inde-cent, or immoral is just another way of worshiping idols. You can be sure that people who behave in this way will never be part of the kingdom that belongs to Christ and to God.

Living as People of Light

[6]Don't let anyone trick you with foolish talk. God punishes everyone who disobeys him and says[k] foolish things. [7]So don't have anything to do with anyone like that.

[8]You used to be like people living in the dark, but now you are people of the light because you belong to the Lord. So act like people of the light [9]and make your light shine. Be good and honest and truthful, [10]as you try to please the Lord. [11]Don't take part in doing those worthless things that are done in the dark. Instead, show how wrong they are. [12]It is disgusting even to talk about what is done in the dark. [13]But the light will show what these things are really like. [14]Light shows up everything,[l] just as the Scriptures say,

"Wake up from your sleep
    and rise from death.
Then Christ will shine on you."

[15]Act like people with good sense and not like fools. [16]These are evil times, so make every minute count. [17]Don't be stupid. Instead, find out what the Lord wants you to do. [18]Don't destroy yourself by getting drunk, but let the Spirit fill your life. [19]When you meet together, sing psalms, hymns, and spiritual songs, as you praise the Lord with all your heart. [20]Always use the name of our Lord Jesus Christ to thank God the Father for everything.

Wives and Husbands

[21]Honor Christ and put others first. [22]A wife should put her husband first, as she does the Lord. [23]A husband is the head of his wife, as Christ is the head and the Savior of the church, which is his own body. [24]Wives should always put their husbands first, as the church puts Christ first.

[25]A husband should love his wife as much as Christ loved the church and gave his life for it. [26]He made the church holy by the power of his word, and he made it pure by washing it with water. [27]Christ did this, so that he would have a glorious and holy church, without faults or spots or wrinkles or any other flaws. [28]In the same way, a husband should love his wife as much as he loves himself. A husband who loves his wife shows that he loves himself. [29]None of us hate our own bodies. We provide for

---

[j]**5.2** *us:* Some manuscripts have "you."   [k]**5.6** *says:* Or "does."   [l]**5.14** *Light shows up everything:* Or "Everything that is seen in the light becomes light itself."

them and take good care of them, just as Christ does for the church, ³⁰because we are each part of his body. ³¹As the Scriptures say, "A man leaves his father and mother to get married, and he becomes like one person with his wife." ³²This is a great mystery, but I understand it to mean Christ and his church. ³³So each husband should love his wife as much as he loves himself, and each wife should respect her husband.

Children and Parents

6 Children, you belong to the Lord, and you do the right thing when you obey your parents. The first commandment with a promise says, ²"Obey your father and your mother, ³and you will have a long and happy life."

⁴Parents, don't be hard on your children. Raise them properly. Teach them and instruct them about the Lord.

Slaves and Masters

⁵Slaves, you must obey your earthly masters. Show them great respect and be as loyal to them as you are to Christ. ⁶Try to please them at all times, and not just when you think they are watching. You are slaves of Christ, so with your whole heart you must do what God wants you to do. ⁷Gladly serve your masters, as though they were the Lord himself, and not simply people. ⁸You know that you will be rewarded for any good things you do, whether you are slaves or free.

⁹Slave owners, you must treat your slaves with this same respect. Don't threaten them. They have the same Master in heaven that you do, and he doesn't have any favorites.

The Fight against Evil

¹⁰Finally, let the mighty strength of the Lord make you strong. ¹¹Put on all the armor that God gives, so you can defend yourself against the devil's tricks. ¹²We are not fighting against humans. We are fighting against forces and authorities and against rulers of darkness and powers in the spiritual world. ¹³So put on all the armor that God gives. Then when that evil day^m comes, you will be able to defend yourself. And when the battle is over, you will still be standing firm.

¹⁴Be ready! Let the truth be like a belt around your waist, and let God's justice protect you like armor. ¹⁵Your desire to tell the good news about peace should be like shoes on your feet. ¹⁶Let your faith be like a shield, and you will be able to stop all the flaming arrows of the evil one. ¹⁷Let God's saving power be like a helmet, and for a sword use God's message that comes from the Spirit.

¹⁸Never stop praying, especially for others. Always pray by the power of the Spirit. Stay alert and keep praying for God's people. ¹⁹Pray that I will be given the message to speak and that I may fearlessly explain the mystery about the good news. ²⁰I was sent to do this work, and that's the reason I am in jail. So pray that I will be brave and will speak as I should.

Final Greetings

²¹⁻²²I want you to know how I am getting along and what I am doing. That's why I am sending Tychicus to you. He is a dear friend, as well as a faithful servant of the Lord. He will tell you how I am doing, and he will cheer you up.

²³I pray that God the Father and the Lord Jesus Christ will give peace, love, and faith to every follower! ²⁴May God be kind to everyone who keeps on loving our Lord Jesus Christ.

---

^{m}**6.13** *that evil day*: Either the present (see 5.16) or "the day of death" or "the day of judgment."

PHILIPPIANS

ABOUT THIS LETTER

Paul wrote this letter from jail (1.7) to thank the Lord's followers at Philippi for helping him with their gifts and prayers (1.5; 4.10-19). He hopes to be set free, so that he can continue preaching the good news (3.17-19). But he knows that he might be put to death (1.21; 2.17; 3.10).

The city of Philippi is in the part of northern Greece known as Macedonia. It was at Philippi that Paul had entered Europe for the first time, and there he preached the good news and began a church (Acts 16). He now warns the Christians at Philippi that they may have to suffer, just as Christ suffered and Paul is now suffering. If this happens, the Philippians should count it a blessing that comes from having faith in Christ (1.28-30).

There were problems in the church at Philippi, because some of the members claimed that people must obey the law of Moses, or they could not be saved. But Paul has no patience with such members and warns the church, "Watch out for those people who behave like dogs!" (3.2-11). This letter is also filled with joy. Even in jail, Paul is happy because he has discovered how to make the best of a bad situation and because he remembers all the kindness shown to him by the people in the church at Philippi.

Paul reminds them that God's people are to live in harmony (2.2; 4.2, 3) and to think the same way that Christ Jesus did:

> Christ was truly God.
> But he did not try to remain
>   equal with God.
> He gave up everything
>   and became a slave,
> when he became
>   like one of us.   (2.6, 7)

A QUICK LOOK AT THIS LETTER

---

1 From Paul and Timothy, servants of Christ Jesus.

To all of God's people who belong to Christ Jesus at Philippi and to all of your church officials and officers.[a]

²I pray that God our Father and the Lord Jesus Christ will be kind to you and will bless you with peace!

Paul's Prayer for the Church in Philippi

³Every time I think of you, I thank my God. ⁴And whenever I mention you in my prayers, it makes me happy. ⁵This is because you have taken part with me in spreading the good news from the first day you heard about it. ⁶God is the one

---

[a]**1.1** *church officials and officers*: Or "bishops and deacons."

who began this good work in you, and I am certain that he won't stop before it is complete on the day that Christ Jesus returns.

⁷You have a special place in my heart. So it is only natural for me to feel the way I do. All of you have helped in the work that God has given me, as I defend the good news and tell about it here in jail. ⁸God himself knows how much I want to see you. He knows that I care for you in the same way that Christ Jesus does.

⁹I pray that your love will keep on growing and that you will fully know and understand ¹⁰how to make the right choices. Then you will still be pure and innocent when Christ returns. And until that day, ¹¹Jesus Christ will keep you busy doing good deeds that bring glory and praise to God.

What Life Means to Paul

¹²My dear friends, I want you to know that what has happened to me has helped to spread the good news. ¹³The Roman guards and all the others know that I am here in jail because I serve Christ. ¹⁴Now most of the Lord's followers have become brave and are fearlessly telling the message.[b]

¹⁵Some are preaching about Christ because they are jealous and envious of us. Others are preaching because they want to help. ¹⁶They love Christ and know that I am here to defend the good news about him. ¹⁷But the ones who are jealous of us are not sincere. They just want to cause trouble for me while I am in jail. ¹⁸But that doesn't matter. All that matters is that people are telling about Christ, whether they are sincere or not. That is what makes me glad.

I will keep on being glad, ¹⁹because I know that your prayers and the help that comes from the Spirit of Christ Jesus will keep me safe. ²⁰I honestly expect and hope that I will never do anything to be ashamed of. Whether I live or die, I always want to be as brave as I am now and bring honor to Christ.

²¹If I live, it will be for Christ, and if I die, I will gain even more. ²²I don't know what to choose. I could keep on living and doing something useful. ²³It is a hard choice to make. I want to die and be with Christ, because that would be much better. ²⁴⁻²⁵But I know that all of you still need me. That's why I am sure I will stay on to help you grow and be happy in your faith. ²⁶Then, when I visit you again, you will have good reason to

take great pride in Christ Jesus because of me.[c]

²⁷Above all else, you must live in a way that brings honor to the good news about Christ. Then, whether I visit you or not, I will hear that all of you think alike. I will know that you are working together and that you are struggling side by side to get others to believe the good news.

²⁸Be brave when you face your enemies. Your courage will show them that they are going to be destroyed, and it will show you that you will be saved. God will make all of this happen, ²⁹and he has blessed you. Not only do you have faith in Christ, but you suffer for him. ³⁰You saw me suffer, and you still hear about my troubles. Now you must suffer in the same way.

True Humility

2 Christ encourages you, and his love comforts you. God's Spirit unites you, and you are concerned for others. ²Now make me completely happy! Live in harmony by showing love for each other. Be united in what you think, as if you were only one person. ³Don't be jealous or proud, but be humble and consider others more important than yourselves. ⁴Care about them as much as you care about yourselves ⁵and think the same way that Christ Jesus thought:[d]

⁶ Christ was truly God.
But he did not try to remain[e]
    equal with God.
⁷ Instead he gave up everything[f]
    and became a slave,
when he became
    like one of us.

⁸ Christ was humble.
He obeyed God and even died
    on a cross.
⁹ Then God gave Christ
    the highest place
and honored his name
    above all others.

¹⁰ So at the name of Jesus
    everyone will bow down,
those in heaven, on earth,
    and under the earth.
¹¹ And to the glory
    of God the Father
everyone will openly agree,
    "Jesus Christ is Lord!"

Lights in the World

¹²My dear friends, you always obeyed when I was with you. Now that I am

---

[b]**1.14** _the message:_ Some manuscripts have "the Lord's message," and others have "God's message."   [c]**1.26** _take great pride in Christ Jesus because of me:_ Or "take great pride in me because of Christ Jesus."   [d]**2.5** _think the same way that Christ Jesus thought:_ Or "think the way you should because you belong to Christ Jesus."   [e]**2.6** _remain:_ Or "become."   [f]**2.7** _He gave up everything:_ Greek, "He emptied himself."

away, you should obey even more. So work with fear and trembling to discover what it really means to be saved. [13]God is working in you to make you willing and able to obey him.

[14]Do everything without grumbling or arguing. [15]Then you will be the pure and innocent children of God. You live among people who are crooked and evil, but you must not do anything that they can say is wrong. Try to shine as lights among the people of this world, [16]as you hold firmly to[g] the message that gives life. Then on the day when Christ returns, I can take pride in you. I can also know that my work and efforts were not useless.

[17]Your faith in the Lord and your service are like a sacrifice offered to him. And my own blood may have to be poured out with the sacrifice.[h] If this happens, I will be glad and rejoice with you. [18]In the same way, you should be glad and rejoice with me.

Timothy and Epaphroditus

[19]I want to be encouraged by news about you. So I hope the Lord Jesus will soon let me send Timothy to you. [20]I don't have anyone else who cares about you as much as he does. [21]The others think only about what interests them and not about what concerns Christ Jesus. [22]But you know what kind of person Timothy is. He has worked with me like a son in spreading the good news. [23]I hope to send him to you, as soon as I find out what is going to happen to me. [24]And I feel sure that the Lord will also let me come soon.

[25]I think I ought to send my dear friend Epaphroditus back to you. He is a follower and a worker and a soldier of the Lord, just as I am. You sent him to look after me, [26]but now he is eager to see you. He is worried, because you heard he was sick. [27]In fact, he was very sick and almost died. But God was kind to him, and also to me, and he kept me from being burdened down with sorrow. [28]Now I am more eager than ever to send Epaphroditus back again. You will be glad to see him, and I won't have to worry any longer. [29]Be sure to give him a cheerful welcome, just as people who serve the Lord deserve. [30]He almost died working for Christ, and he risked his own life to do for me what you could not.

Being Acceptable to God

3 Finally, my dear friends, be glad that you belong to the Lord. It doesn't bother me to write the same things to you that I have written before. In fact, it is for your own good.

[2]Watch out for those people who behave like dogs! They are evil and want to do more than just circumcise you. [3]But we are the ones who are truly circumcised, because we worship by the power of God's Spirit[i] and take pride in Christ Jesus. We don't brag about what we have done, [4]although I could. Others may brag about themselves, but I have more reason to brag than anyone else. [5]I was circumcised when I was eight days old,[j] and I am from the nation of Israel and the tribe of Benjamin. I am a true Hebrew. As a Pharisee, I strictly obeyed the Law of Moses. [6]And I was so eager that I even made trouble for the church. I did everything the Law demands in order to please God.

[7]But Christ has shown me that what I once thought was valuable is worthless. [8]Nothing is as wonderful as knowing Christ Jesus my Lord. I have given up everything else and count it all as garbage. All I want is Christ [9]and to know that I belong to him. I could not make myself acceptable to God by obeying the Law of Moses. God accepted me simply because of my faith in Christ. [10]All I want is to know Christ and the power that raised him to life. I want to suffer and die as he did, [11]so that somehow I also may be raised to life.

Running toward the Goal

[12]I have not yet reached my goal, and I am not perfect. But Christ has taken hold of me. So I keep on running and struggling to take hold of the prize. [13]My friends, I don't feel that I have already arrived. But I forget what is behind, and I struggle for what is ahead. [14]I run toward the goal, so that I can win the prize of being called to heaven. This is the prize that God offers because of what Christ Jesus has done. [15]All of us who are mature should think in this same way. And if any of you think differently, God will make it clear to you. [16]But we must keep going in the direction that we are now headed.

[17]My friends, I want you to follow my example and learn from others who closely follow the example we set for you. [18]I often warned you that many people are living as enemies of the cross of Christ. And now with tears in my eyes, I warn you again [19]that they are headed for hell! They worship their stomachs and brag about the disgusting things they do. All they can think about are the things of this world.

---

[g]**2.16** _hold firmly to:_ Or "offer them." [h]**2.17** _my own blood may have to be poured out with the sacrifice:_ Offerings of water or wine were sometimes poured out when animals were sacrificed on the altar. [i]**3.3** _by the power of God's Spirit:_ Some manuscripts have "sincerely." [j]**3.5** _when I was eight days old:_ Jewish boys are circumcised eight days after birth.

20But we are citizens of heaven and are eagerly waiting for our Savior to come from there. Our Lord Jesus Christ 21has power over everything, and he will make these poor bodies of ours like his own glorious body.

4 Dear friends, I love you and long to see you. Please keep on being faithful to the Lord. You are my pride and joy.

Paul Encourages the Lord's Followers

2Euodia and Syntyche, you belong to the Lord, so I beg you to stop arguing with each other. 3And, my true partner,[k] I ask you to help them. These women have worked together with me and with Clement and with the others in spreading the good news. Their names are now written in the book of life.[l]

4Always be glad because of the Lord! I will say it again: Be glad. 5Always be gentle with others. The Lord will soon be here. 6Don't worry about anything, but pray about everything. With thankful hearts offer up your prayers and requests to God. 7Then, because you belong to Christ Jesus, God will bless you with peace that no one can completely understand. And this peace will control the way you think and feel.

8Finally, my friends, keep your minds on whatever is true, pure, right, holy, friendly, and proper. Don't ever stop thinking about what is truly worthwhile and worthy of praise. 9You know the teachings I gave you, and you know what you heard me say and saw me do. So follow my example. And God, who gives peace, will be with you.

Paul Gives Thanks for the Gifts He Was Given

10The Lord has made me very grateful that at last you have thought about me once again. Actually, you were thinking about me all along, but you didn't have any chance to show it. 11I am not complaining about having too little. I have learned to be satisfied with[m] whatever I have. 12I know what it is to be poor or to have plenty, and I have lived under all kinds of conditions. I know what it means to be full or to be hungry, to have too much or too little. 13Christ gives me the strength to face anything.

14It was good of you to help me when I was having such a hard time. 15My friends at Philippi, you remember what it was like when I started preaching the good news in Macedonia.[n] After I left there, you were the only church that became my partner by giving blessings and by receiving them in return. 16Even when I was in Thessalonica, you helped me more than once. 17I am not trying to get something from you, but I want you to receive the blessings that come from giving.

18I have been paid back everything, and with interest. I am completely satisfied with the gifts that you had Epaphroditus bring me. They are like a sweet-smelling offering or like the right kind of sacrifice that pleases God. 19I pray that God will take care of all your needs with the wonderful blessings that come from Christ Jesus! 20May God our Father be praised forever and ever. Amen.

Final Greetings

21Give my greetings to all who are God's people because of Christ Jesus.

The Lord's followers here with me send you their greetings.

22All of God's people send their greetings, especially those in the service of the Emperor.

23I pray that our Lord Jesus Christ will be kind to you and will bless your life!

---

[k]**4.3** *partner*: Or "Syzygus," a person's name. names of God's people are written. [m]**4.11** *be satisfied with*: Or "get by on." [l]**4.3** *the book of life*: A book in which the [n]**4.15** *when I started preaching the good news in Macedonia*: Paul is talking about his first visit to Philippi (see Acts 16.12-40).

COLOSSIANS

ABOUT THIS LETTER

Colossae was an important city in western Asia Minor, about 100 miles east of the port city of Ephesus. Paul had never been to Colossae, but he was pleased to learn that the Christians there were strong in their faith (1.3-7; 2.6, 7). They had heard the good news from a man named Epaphras who had lived there (1.7; 4.12, 13), but was in jail with Paul (Philemon 23) at the time that Paul wrote this letter (1.14; 4.3, 10, 18).

Many of the church members in Colossae were Gentiles (1.27), and some of them were influenced by strange religious ideas and practices (2.16-23). They thought that to obey God fully they must give up certain physical desires and worship angels and other spiritual powers. But Paul wanted them to know that Christ was with God in heaven, ruling over all powers in the universe (3.1). And so, their worship should be directed to Christ.

Paul quotes a beautiful hymn that explains who Christ is:

> *Christ is exactly like God,*
> *who cannot be seen.*
> *He is the first-born Son,*
> *superior to all creation.*
>
> *God himself was pleased*
> *to live fully in his Son.*
> *And God was pleased*
> *for him to make peace*
> *by sacrificing his blood*
> *on the cross.*
> *(1.15, 19, 20a)*

A QUICK LOOK AT THIS LETTER

Greetings (1.1, 2)
A Prayer of Thanks (1.3-8)
The Person and Work of Christ (1.9—2.19)
New Life with Christ (2.20—4.6)
Final Greetings (4.7-18)

1 From Paul, chosen by God to be an apostle of Christ Jesus, and from Timothy, who is also a follower.

²To God's people who live in Colossae and are faithful followers of Christ.

I pray that God our Father will be kind to you and will bless you with peace!

A Prayer of Thanks

³Each time we pray for you, we thank God, the Father of our Lord Jesus Christ. ⁴We have heard of your faith in Christ and of your love for all of God's people, ⁵because what you hope for is kept safe for you in heaven. You first heard about this hope when you believed the true message, which is the good news.

⁶The good news is spreading all over the world with great success. It has spread in that same way among you, ever since the first day you learned the truth about God's wonderful kindness ⁷from our good friend Epaphras. He works together with us for Christ and is

a faithful worker for you.[a] [8]He is also the one who told us about the love that God's Spirit has given you.

The Person and Work of Christ

[9]We have not stopped praying for you since the first day we heard about you. In fact, we always pray that God will show you everything he wants you to do and that you may have all the wisdom and understanding that his Spirit gives. [10]Then you will live a life that honors the Lord, and you will always please him by doing good deeds. You will come to know God even better. [11]His glorious power will make you patient and strong enough to endure anything, and you will be truly happy.

[12]I pray that you will be grateful to God for letting you[a] have part in what he has promised his people in the kingdom of light. [13]God rescued us from the dark power of Satan and brought us into the kingdom of his dear Son, [14]who forgives our sins and sets us free.

[15] Christ is exactly like God,
     who cannot be seen.
     He is the first-born Son,
         superior to all creation.
[16] Everything was created by him,
     everything in heaven
         and on earth,
     everything seen and unseen,
     including all forces
         and powers,
     and all rulers
         and authorities.
     All things were created
         by God's Son,
     and everything was made
         for him.

[17] God's Son was before all else,
     and by him everything
         is held together.
[18] He is the head of his body,
     which is the church.
     He is the very beginning,
     the first to be raised
         from death,
     so that he would be
         above all others.

[19] God himself was pleased
     to live fully in his Son.
[20] And God was pleased
     for him to make peace
     by sacrificing his blood
         on the cross,
     so that all beings in heaven
         and on earth
     would be brought back to God.

[21]You used to be far from God. Your thoughts made you his enemies, and you did evil things. [22]But his Son became a human and died. So God made peace with you, and now he lets you stand in his presence as people who are holy and faultless and innocent. [23]But you must stay deeply rooted and firm in your faith. You must not give up the hope you received when you heard the good news. It was preached to everyone on earth, and I myself have become a servant of this message.

Paul's Service to the Church

[24]I am glad that I can suffer for you. I am pleased also that in my own body I can continue[b] the suffering of Christ for his body, the church. [25]God's plan was to make me a servant of his church and to send me to preach his complete message to you. [26]For ages and ages this message was kept secret from everyone, but now it has been explained to God's people. [27]God did this because he wanted you Gentiles to understand his wonderful and glorious mystery. And the mystery is that Christ lives in you, and he is your hope of sharing in God's glory. [28]We announce the message about Christ, and we use all our wisdom to warn and teach everyone, so that all of Christ's followers will grow and become mature. [29]That's why I work so hard and use the mighty power he gives me.

2 I want you to know what a struggle I am going through for you, for God's people at Laodicea, and for all of those followers who have never met me. [2]I do it to encourage them. Then as their hearts are joined together in love, they will be wonderfully blessed with complete understanding. And they will truly know Christ. Not only is he the key to God's mystery, [3]but all wisdom and knowledge are hidden away in him. [4]I tell you these things to keep you from being fooled by fancy talk. [5]Even though I am not with you, I keep thinking about you. I am glad to know that you are living as you should and that your faith in Christ is strong.

Christ Brings Real Life

[6]You have accepted Christ Jesus as your Lord. Now keep on following him. [7]Plant your roots in Christ and let him be the foundation for your life. Be strong in your faith, just as you were taught. And be grateful.

[8]Don't let anyone fool you by using senseless arguments. These arguments may sound wise, but they are only human teachings. They come from the

---

[a]**1.7,12** *you:* Some manuscripts have "us."   [b]**1.24** *continue:* Or "complete."

powers of this world[c] and not from Christ.

[9]God lives fully in Christ. [10]And you are fully grown because you belong to Christ, who is over every power and authority. [11]Christ has also taken away your selfish desires, just as circumcision removes flesh from the body. [12]And when you were baptized, it was the same as being buried with Christ. Then you were raised to life because you had faith in the power of God, who raised Christ from death. [13]You were dead, because you were sinful and were not God's people. But God let Christ make you[d] alive, when he forgave all our sins.

[14]God wiped out the charges that were against us for disobeying the Law of Moses. He took them away and nailed them to the cross. [15]There Christ defeated all powers and forces. He let the whole world see them being led away as prisoners when he celebrated his victory.

[16]Don't let anyone tell you what you must eat or drink. Don't let them say that you must celebrate the New Moon festival, the Sabbath, or any other festival. [17]These things are only a shadow of what was to come. But Christ is real!

[18]Don't be cheated by people who make a show of acting humble and who worship angels.[e] They brag about seeing visions. But it is all nonsense, because their minds are filled with selfish desires. [19]They are no longer part of Christ, who is the head of the whole body. Christ gives the body its strength, and he uses its joints and muscles to hold it together, as it grows by the power of God.

Christ Brings New Life

[20]You died with Christ. Now the forces of the universe[f] don't have any power over you. Why do you live as if you had to obey such rules as, [21]"Don't handle this. Don't taste that. Don't touch this."? [22]After these things are used, they are no longer good for anything. So why be bothered with the rules that humans have made up? [23]Obeying these rules may seem to be the smart thing to do. They appear to make you love God more and to be very humble and to have control over your body. But they don't really have any power over our desires.

3 You have been raised to life with Christ. Now set your heart on what is in heaven, where Christ rules at God's right side.[g] [2]Think about what is up there, not about what is here on earth. [3]You died, which means that your life is hidden with Christ, who sits beside God. [4]Christ gives meaning to your[h] life, and when he appears, you will also appear with him in glory.

[5]Don't be controlled by your body. Kill every desire for the wrong kind of sex. Don't be immoral or indecent or have evil thoughts. Don't be greedy, which is the same as worshiping idols. [6]God is angry with people who disobey him by doing[i] these things. [7]And that is exactly what you did, when you lived among people who behaved in this way. [8]But now you must stop doing such things. You must quit being angry, hateful, and evil. You must no longer say insulting or cruel things about others. [9]And stop lying to each other. You have given up your old way of life with its habits.

[10]Each of you is now a new person. You are becoming more and more like your Creator, and you will understand him better. [11]It doesn't matter if you are a Greek or a Jew, or if you are circumcised or not. You may even be a barbarian or a Scythian,[j] and you may be a slave or a free person. Yet Christ is all that matters, and he lives in all of us.

[12]God loves you and has chosen you as his own special people. So be gentle, kind, humble, meek, and patient. [13]Put up with each other, and forgive anyone who does you wrong, just as Christ has forgiven you. [14]Love is more important than anything else. It is what ties everything completely together.

[15]Each one of you is part of the body of Christ, and you were chosen to live together in peace. So let the peace that comes from Christ control your thoughts. And be grateful. [16]Let the message about Christ completely fill your lives, while you use all your wisdom to teach and instruct each other. With thankful hearts, sing psalms, hymns, and spiritual songs to God. [17]Whatever you say or do should be done in the name of the Lord Jesus, as you give thanks to God the Father because of him.

Some Rules for Christian Living

[18]A wife must put her husband first. This is her duty as a follower of the Lord.

---

[c]**2.8** *powers of this world*: Spirits and unseen forces were thought to control human lives and were believed to be connected with the movements of the stars.   [d]**2.13** *you*: See the note at 1.7.   [e]**2.18** *worship angels*: Or "worship with angels (in visions of heaven)."   [f]**2.20** *forces of the universe*: See the note at 2.8.   [g]**3.1** *right side*: The place of power and honor. [h]**3.4** *your*: Some manuscripts have "our."   [i]**3.6** *people who disobey him by doing*: Some manuscripts do not have these words.   [j]**3.11** *a barbarian or a Scythian*: Barbarians were people who could not speak Greek and would be in the lower class of society. Scythians were people who were known for their cruelty.

[19]A husband must love his wife and not abuse her.

[20]Children must always obey their parents. This pleases the Lord.

[21]Parents, don't be hard on your children. If you are, they might give up.

[22]Slaves, you must always obey your earthly masters. Try to please them at all times, and not just when you think they are watching. Honor the Lord and serve your masters with your whole heart. [23]Do your work willingly, as though you were serving the Lord himself, and not just your earthly master. [24]In fact, the Lord Christ is the one you are really serving, and you know that he will reward you. [25]But Christ has no favorites! He will punish evil people, just as they deserve.

4 Slave owners, be fair and honest with your slaves. Don't forget that you have a Master in heaven.

[2]Never give up praying. And when you pray, keep alert and be thankful. [3]Be sure to pray that God will make a way for us to spread his message and explain the mystery about Christ, even though I am in jail for doing this. [4]Please pray that I will make the message as clear as possible.

[5]When you are with unbelievers, always make good use of the time. [6]Be pleasant and hold their interest when you speak the message. Choose your words carefully and be ready to give answers to anyone who asks questions.

Final Greetings

[7]Tychicus is the dear friend, who faithfully works and serves the Lord with us, and he will give you the news about me. [8]I am sending him to cheer you up by telling you how we are getting along. [9]Onesimus, that dear and faithful follower from your own group, is coming with him. The two of them will tell you everything that has happened here.

[10]Aristarchus is in jail with me. He sends greetings to you, and so does Mark, the cousin of Barnabas. You have already been told to welcome Mark, if he visits you. [11]Jesus, who is known as Justus, sends his greetings. These three men are the only Jewish followers who have worked with me for the kingdom of God. They have given me much comfort.

[12]Your own Epaphras, who serves Christ Jesus, sends his greetings. He always prays hard that you may fully know what the Lord wants you to do and that you may do it completely. [13]I have seen how much trouble he has gone through for you and for the followers in Laodicea and Hierapolis.

[14]Our dear doctor Luke sends you his greetings, and so does Demas.

[15]Give my greetings to the followers at Laodicea, especially to Nympha and the church that meets in her home.

[16]After this letter has been read to your people, be sure to have it read in the church at Laodicea. And you should read the letter that I have sent to them.[k]

[17]Remind Archippus to do the work that the Lord has given him to do.

[18]I am signing this letter myself: PAUL.

Don't forget that I am in jail.

I pray that God will be kind to you.

[k]**4.16** *the letter that I have sent to them*: This is the only mention of the letter to the church at Laodicea.

1 THESSALONIANS

ABOUT THIS LETTER

Paul started the church in Thessalonica (2.13, 14), while working hard to support himself (2.9). In this important city of northern Greece, many of the followers had worshiped idols before becoming Christians (1.9). But they were faithful to the Lord, and because of them the Lord's message had spread everywhere in that region (1.8). This letter may have been the first one that Paul wrote, and maybe even the first of all the New Testament writings.

Some people in Thessalonica began to oppose Paul, and he had to escape to Athens. But he sent his young friend Timothy to find out how the Christians were doing (3.1-5). When Timothy returned, he gave Paul good reports of their faith and love (3.6-10).

The church itself had problems. Some of its members had quit working, since they thought that the Lord would soon return (4.11, 12). Others were worried because relatives and friends had already died before Christ's return. So Paul tried to explain to them more clearly what would happen when the Lord returns (4.13-15), and then told them how they should live in the meanwhile (5.1-11).

Paul's final instructions are well worth remembering:

Always be joyful and never stop praying. Whatever happens, keep thanking God because of Jesus Christ. This is what God wants you to do. (5.16-18)

A QUICK LOOK AT THIS LETTER

Greetings (1.1-3)
The Thessalonians' Faith and Example (1.4—3.13)
A Life That Pleases God (4.1-12)
What to Expect When the Lord Returns (4.13—5.11)
Final Instructions and Greetings (5.12-28)

1 From Paul, Silas,[a] and Timothy.
To the church in Thessalonica, the people of God the Father and of the Lord Jesus Christ.

I pray that God will be kind to you and will bless you with peace!

²We thank God for you and always mention you in our prayers. Each time we pray, ³we tell God our Father about your faith and loving work and about your firm hope in our Lord Jesus Christ.

The Thessalonians' Faith and Example

⁴My dear friends, God loves you, and we know he has chosen you to be his people. ⁵When we told you the good news, it was with the power and assurance that come from the Holy Spirit, and not simply with words. You knew what kind of people we were and how we helped you. ⁶So, when you accepted the message, you followed our example and the example of the Lord. You suffered, but the Holy Spirit made you glad.

⁷You became an example for all the Lord's followers in Macedonia and Achaia. ⁸And because of you, the Lord's message has spread everywhere in those regions. Now the news of your faith in God is known all over the world, and we don't have to say a thing about it. ⁹Everyone is talking about how you welcomed us and how you turned away from idols to serve the true and living God. ¹⁰They also tell how you are waiting for his Son Jesus to come from heaven. God raised him from death, and

a1.1 *Silas:* The Greek text has "Silvanus," another form of the name Silas.

on the day of judgment Jesus will save us from God's anger.

Paul's Work in Thessalonica

2 My friends, you know that our time with you wasn't wasted. ²As you remember, we had been mistreated and insulted at Philippi. But God gave us the courage to tell you the good news about him, even though many people caused us trouble. ³We didn't have any hidden motives when we won you over, and we didn't try to fool or trick anyone. ⁴God was pleased to trust us with his message. We didn't speak to please people, but to please God who knows our motives.

⁵You also know that we didn't try to flatter anyone. God himself knows that what we did wasn't a cover-up for greed. ⁶We were not trying to get you or anyone else to praise us. ⁷But as apostles, we could have demanded help from you. After all, Christ is the one who sent us. We chose to be like children or like a mother*ᵇ* nursing her baby. ⁸We cared so much for you, and you became so dear to us, that we were willing to give our lives for you when we gave you God's message.

⁹My dear friends, you surely haven't forgotten our hard work and hardships. You remember how night and day we struggled to make a living, so that we could tell you God's message without being a burden to anyone. ¹⁰Both you and God are witnesses that we were pure and honest and innocent in our dealings with you followers of the Lord. ¹¹You also know we did everything for you that parents would do for their own children. ¹²We begged, encouraged, and urged each of you to live in a way that would honor God. He is the one who chose you to share in his own kingdom and glory.

¹³We always thank God that you believed the message we preached. It came from him, and it isn't something made up by humans. You accepted it as God's message, and now he is working in you. ¹⁴My friends, you did just like God's churches in Judea and like the other followers of Christ Jesus there. And so, you were mistreated by your own people, in the same way they were mistreated by their people.

¹⁵Those Jews killed the Lord Jesus and the prophets, and they even chased us away. God doesn't like what they do and neither does anyone else. ¹⁶They keep us from speaking his message to the Gentiles and from leading them to be saved. The Jews have always gone too far with their sins. Now

God has finally become angry and will punish them.

Paul Wants To Visit the Church Again

¹⁷My friends, we were kept from coming to you for a while, but we never stopped thinking about you. We were eager to see you and tried our best to visit you in person. ¹⁸We really wanted to come. I myself tried several times, but Satan always stopped us. ¹⁹After all, when the Lord Jesus appears, who else but you will give us hope and joy and be like a glorious crown for us? ²⁰You alone are our glory and joy!

3 Finally, we couldn't stand it any longer. We decided to stay in Athens by ourselves ²and send our friend Timothy to you. He works with us as God's servant and preaches the good news about Christ. We wanted him to make you strong in your faith and to encourage you. ³We didn't want any of you to be discouraged by all these troubles. You knew we would have to suffer, ⁴because when we were with you, we told you this would happen. And we did suffer, as you well know. ⁵At last, when I could not wait any longer, I sent Timothy to find out about your faith. I hoped that Satan had not tempted you and made all our work useless.

⁶Timothy has come back from his visit with you and has told us about your faith and love. He also said that you always have happy memories of us and that you want to see us as much as we want to see you.

⁷My friends, even though we have a lot of trouble and suffering, your faith makes us feel better about you. ⁸Your strong faith in the Lord is like a breath of new life. ⁹How can we possibly thank God enough for all the happiness you have brought us? ¹⁰Day and night we sincerely pray that we will see you again and help you to have an even stronger faith.

¹¹We pray that God our Father and our Lord Jesus will let us visit you. ¹²May the Lord make your love for each other and for everyone else grow by leaps and bounds. That's how our love for you has grown. ¹³And when our Lord comes with all of his people, I pray that he will make your hearts pure and innocent in the sight of God the Father.

A Life That Pleases God

4 Finally, my dear friends, since you belong to the Lord Jesus, we beg and urge you to live as we taught you. Then you will please God. You are already living that way, but try even harder. ²Remember the instructions we

---

ᵇ2.7 like children or like a mother: Some manuscripts have "as gentle as a mother."

gave you as followers of the Lord Jesus. [3]God wants you to be holy, so don't be immoral in matters of sex. [4]Respect and honor your wife.[c] [5]Don't be a slave of your desires or live like people who don't know God. [6]You must not cheat any of the Lord's followers in matters of sex.[d] Remember, we warned you that he punishes everyone who does such things. [7]God didn't choose you to be filthy, but to be pure. [8]So if you don't obey these rules, you are not really disobeying us. You are disobeying God, who gives you his Holy Spirit.

[9]We don't have to write you about the need to love each other. God has taught you to do this, [10]and you already have shown your love for all of his people in Macedonia. But, my dear friends, we ask you to do even more. [11]Try your best to live quietly, to mind your own business, and to work hard, just as we taught you to do. [12]Then you will be respected by people who are not followers of the Lord, and you won't have to depend on anyone.

The Lord's Coming

[13]My friends, we want you to understand how it will be for those followers who have already died. Then you won't grieve over them and be like people who don't have any hope. [14]We believe that Jesus died and was raised to life. We also believe that when God brings Jesus back again, he will bring with him all who had faith in Jesus before they died. [15]Our Lord Jesus told us that when he comes, we won't go up to meet him ahead of his followers who have already died.

[16]With a loud command and with the shout of the chief angel and a blast of God's trumpet, the Lord will return from heaven. Then those who had faith in Christ before they died will be raised to life. [17]Next, all of us who are still alive will be taken up into the clouds together with them to meet the Lord in the sky. From that time on we will all be with the Lord forever. [18]Encourage each other with these words.

5 I don't need to write you about the time or date when all this will happen. [2]You surely know that the Lord's return[e] will be as a thief coming at night. [3]People will think they are safe and secure. But destruction will suddenly strike them like the pains of a woman about to give birth. And they won't escape.

[4]My dear friends, you don't live in darkness, and so that day won't surprise you like a thief. [5]You belong to the light and live in the day. We don't live in the night or belong to the dark. [6]Others may sleep, but we should stay awake and be alert. [7]People sleep during the night, and some even get drunk. [8]But we belong to the day. So we must stay sober and let our faith and love be like a suit of armor. Our firm hope that we will be saved is our helmet.

[9]God doesn't intend to punish us, but wants us to be saved by our Lord Jesus Christ. [10]Christ died for us, so that we could live with him, whether we are alive or dead when he comes. [11]That's why you must encourage and help each other, just as you are already doing.

Final Instructions and Greetings

[12]My friends, we ask you to be thoughtful of your leaders who work hard and tell you how to live for the Lord. [13]Show them great respect and love because of their work. Try to get along with each other. [14]My friends, we beg you to warn anyone who isn't living right. Encourage anyone who feels left out, help all who are weak, and be patient with everyone. [15]Don't be hateful to people, just because they are hateful to you. Rather, be good to each other and to everyone else.

[16]Always be joyful [17]and never stop praying. [18]Whatever happens, keep thanking God because of Jesus Christ. This is what God wants you to do.

[19]Don't turn away God's Spirit [20]or ignore prophecies. [21]Put everything to the test. Accept what is good [22]and don't have anything to do with evil.

[23]I pray that God, who gives peace, will make you completely holy. And may your spirit, soul, and body be kept healthy and faultless until our Lord Jesus Christ returns. [24]The one who chose you can be trusted, and he will do this.

[25]Friends, please pray for us.

[26]Give the Lord's followers a warm greeting.

[27]In the name of the Lord I beg you to read this letter to all his followers.

[28]I pray that our Lord Jesus Christ will be kind to you!

---

[c]**4.4** *your wife*: Or "your body."   [d]**4.6** *in matters of sex*: Or "in business."   [e]**5.2** *the Lord's return*: The Greek text has "the day of the Lord."

2 THESSALONIANS

ABOUT THIS LETTER

In this letter to the believers in Thessalonica, Paul begins by thanking God that their faith and love keep growing all the time (1.3). They were going through a lot of troubles, but Paul insists that this is God's way of testing their faith, not a way of punishing them (1.4, 5).

Someone in Thessalonica claimed to have a letter from Paul, saying that the Lord had already returned (2.2). But Paul warns the church not to be fooled! The Lord will not return until after the "wicked one" has appeared (2.3).

Paul also warns against laziness (3.6-10), and he tells the church to guard against any followers who refuse to obey what he has written in this letter.

The letter closes with a prayer:

I pray that the Lord, who gives peace, will always bless you with peace. May the
Lord be with all of you. (3.16)

A QUICK LOOK AT THIS LETTER

1 From Paul, Silas,[a] and Timothy. To the church in Thessalonica, the people of God our Father and of the Lord Jesus Christ.

²I pray that God our Father and the Lord Jesus Christ will be kind to you and will bless you with peace!

When Christ Returns

³My dear friends, we always have good reason to thank God for you, because your faith in God and your love for each other keep growing all the time. ⁴That's why we brag about you to all of God's churches. We tell them how patient you are and how you keep on having faith, even though you are going through a lot of trouble and suffering.

⁵All of this shows that God judges fairly and that he is making you fit to share in his kingdom for which you are suffering. ⁶It is only right for God to punish everyone who is causing you trouble, ⁷but he will give you relief from your troubles. He will do the same for us, when the Lord Jesus comes from heaven with his powerful angels ⁸and with a flaming fire.

Our Lord Jesus will punish anyone who doesn't know God and won't obey his message. ⁹Their punishment will be eternal destruction, and they will be kept far from the presence of our Lord and his glorious strength. ¹⁰This will happen on that day when the Lord returns to be praised and honored by all who have faith in him and belong to him. This includes you, because you believed what we said.

¹¹God chose you, and we keep praying that God will make you worthy of being his people. We pray for God's power to help you do all the good things that you hope to do and that your faith makes you want to do. ¹²Then, because God and our Lord Jesus Christ are so kind, you will bring honor to the name of our

Lord Jesus, and he will bring honor to you.

The Lord's Return

2 When our Lord Jesus returns, we will be gathered up to meet him. So I ask you, my friends, ²not to be easily upset or disturbed by people who claim that the Lord[b] has already come. They may say that they heard this directly from the Holy Spirit, or from someone else, or even that they read it in one of our letters. ³But don't be fooled! People will rebel against God. Then before the Lord returns, the wicked[c] one who is doomed to be destroyed will appear. ⁴He will brag and oppose everything that is holy or sacred. He will even sit in God's temple and claim to be God. ⁵Don't you remember that I told you this while I was still with you?

⁶You already know what is holding this wicked one back until it is time for him to come. ⁷His mysterious power is already at work, but someone is holding him back. And the wicked one won't appear until that someone is out of the way. ⁸Then he will appear, but the Lord Jesus will kill him simply by breathing on him. He will be completely destroyed by the Lord's glorious return.

⁹When the wicked one appears, Satan will pretend to work all kinds of miracles, wonders, and signs. ¹⁰Lost people will be fooled by his evil deeds. They could be saved, but they will refuse to love the truth and accept it. ¹¹So God will make sure that they are fooled into believing a lie. ¹²All of them will be punished, because they would rather do evil than believe the truth.

Be Faithful

¹³My friends, the Lord loves you, and it is only natural for us to thank God for you. God chose you to be the first ones to be saved.[d] His Spirit made you holy, and you put your faith in the truth. ¹⁴God used our preaching as his way of inviting you to share in the glory of our Lord Jesus Christ. ¹⁵My friends, that's why you must remain faithful and follow closely what we taught you in person and by our letters.

¹⁶God our Father loves us. He is kind and has given us eternal comfort and a wonderful hope. We pray that our Lord Jesus Christ and God our Father ¹⁷will encourage you and help you always to do and say the right thing.

Pray for Us

3 Finally, our friends, please pray for us. This will help the message about the Lord to spread quickly, and others will respect it, just as you do. ²Pray that we may be kept safe from worthless and evil people. After all, not everyone has faith. ³But the Lord can be trusted to make you strong and protect you from harm. ⁴He has made us sure that you are obeying what we taught you and that you will keep on obeying. ⁵I pray that the Lord will guide you to be as loving as God and as patient as Christ.

Warnings against Laziness

⁶My dear friends, in the name of[e] the Lord Jesus, I beg you not to have anything to do with any of your people who loaf around and refuse to obey the instructions we gave you. ⁷You surely know that you should follow our example. We didn't waste our time loafing, ⁸and we didn't accept food from anyone without paying for it. We didn't want to be a burden to any of you, so night and day we worked as hard as we could.

⁹We had the right not to work, but we wanted to set an example for you. ¹⁰We also gave you the rule that if you don't work, you don't eat. ¹¹Now we learn that some of you just loaf around and won't do any work, except the work of a busybody. ¹²So, for the sake of our Lord Jesus Christ, we ask and beg these people to settle down and start working for a living. ¹³Dear friends, you must never become tired of doing right.

¹⁴Be on your guard against any followers who refuse to obey what we have written in this letter. Put them to shame by not having anything to do with them. ¹⁵Don't consider them your enemies, but speak kindly to them as you would to any other follower.

Final Prayer

¹⁶I pray that the Lord, who gives peace, will always bless you with peace. May the Lord be with all of you.

¹⁷I always sign my letters as I am now doing: PAUL.

¹⁸I pray that our Lord Jesus Christ will be kind to all of you.

---

[b]**2.2** _Lord_: The Greek text has "day of the Lord." "sinful." [d]**2.13** _God chose you to be the first ones to be saved_: Some manuscripts have "From the beginning God chose you to be saved." [c]**2.3** _wicked_: Some manuscripts have [e]**3.6** _in the name of_: Or "as a follower of."

1 TIMOTHY

ABOUT THIS LETTER

Timothy traveled and worked with Paul (Romans 16.21; 1 Corinthians 16.10; Philippians 2.19), and because of their shared faith, Timothy was like a son to Paul (1.2). Timothy became one of Paul's most faithful co-workers, and Paul mentions Timothy in five of his letters.

Although this letter is addressed to Timothy personally, it actually addresses many of the concerns Paul had with the life of the entire church. Guidelines are given for choosing church officials (3.1-7), officers (3.8-13), and leaders (5.17-20).

Christians are to pray for everyone and to remember:

> *There is only one God,*
> *and Christ Jesus*
> *is the only one*
> *who can bring us*
> *to God.*   *(2.5)*

A QUICK LOOK AT THIS LETTER

Greetings (1.1, 2)
Instructions for Church Life (1.3—3.13)
The Mystery of Our Religion (3.14—4.5)
Paul's Advice to Timothy (4.6—6.21)

---

1 From Paul.
God our Savior and Christ Jesus commanded me to be an apostle of Christ Jesus, who gives us hope.

²Timothy, because of our faith, you are like a son to me. I pray that God our Father and our Lord Jesus Christ will be kind and merciful to you. May they bless you with peace!

Warning against False Teaching

³When I was leaving for Macedonia, I asked you to stay on in Ephesus and warn certain people there to stop spreading their false teachings. ⁴You needed to warn them to stop wasting their time on senseless stories and endless lists of ancestors. Such things only cause arguments. They don't help anyone to do God's work that can only be done by faith.

⁵You must teach people to have genuine love, as well as a good conscience and true faith. ⁶There are some who have given up these for nothing but empty talk. ⁷They want to be teachers of the Law of Moses. But they don't know what they are talking about, even though they think they do.

⁸We know that the Law is good, if it is used in the right way. ⁹We also understand that it wasn't given to control people who please God, but to control lawbreakers, criminals, godless people, and sinners. It is for wicked and evil people, and for murderers, who would even kill their own parents. ¹⁰The Law was written for people who are sexual perverts or who live as homosexuals or are kidnappers or liars or won't tell the truth in court. It is for anything else that opposes the correct teaching ¹¹of the good news that the glorious and wonderful God has given me.

Being Thankful for God's Kindness

¹²I thank Christ Jesus our Lord. He has given me the strength for my work because he knew that he could trust me. ¹³I used to say terrible and insulting

things about him, and I was cruel. But he had mercy on me because I didn't know what I was doing, and I had not yet put my faith in him. [14]Christ Jesus our Lord was very kind to me. He has greatly blessed my life with faith and love just like his own.

[15]"Christ Jesus came into the world to save sinners." This saying is true, and it can be trusted. I was the worst sinner of all! [16]But since I was worse than anyone else, God had mercy on me and let me be an example of the endless patience of Christ Jesus. He did this so that others would put their faith in Christ and have eternal life. [17]I pray that honor and glory will always be given to the only God, who lives forever and is the invisible and eternal King! Amen.

[18]Timothy, my son, the instructions I am giving you are based on what some prophets[a] once said about you. If you follow these instructions, you will fight like a good soldier. [19]You will be faithful and have a clear conscience. Some people have made a mess of their faith because they didn't listen to their consciences. [20]Two of them are Hymenaeus and Alexander. I have given these men over to the power of Satan, so they will learn not to oppose God.

How To Pray

2 First of all, I ask you to pray for everyone. Ask God to help and bless them all, and tell God how thankful you are for each of them. [2]Pray for kings and others in power, so that we may live quiet and peaceful lives as we worship and honor God. [3]This kind of prayer is good, and it pleases God our Savior. [4]God wants everyone to be saved and to know the whole truth, which is,

[5] There is only one God,
and Christ Jesus
is the only one
who can bring us
to God.
Jesus was truly human,
and he gave himself
to rescue all of us.
[6] God showed us this
at the right time.

[7]This is why God chose me to be a preacher and an apostle of the good news. I am telling the truth. I am not lying. God sent me to teach the Gentiles about faith and truth.

[8]I want everyone everywhere to lift innocent hands toward heaven and pray, without being angry or arguing with each other.

[9]I would like for women to wear modest and sensible clothes. They should not have fancy hairdos, or wear expensive clothes, or put on jewelry made of gold or pearls. [10]Women who claim to love God should do helpful things for others, [11]and they should learn by being quiet and paying attention. [12]They should be silent and not be allowed to teach or to tell men what to do. [13]After all, Adam was created before Eve, [14]and the man Adam wasn't the one who was fooled. It was the woman Eve who was completely fooled and sinned. [15]But women will be saved by having children,[b] if they stay faithful, loving, holy, and modest.

Church Officials

3 It is true that[c] anyone who desires to be a church official[d] wants to do something worthwhile. [2]That's why officials must have a good reputation and be faithful in marriage.[e] They must be self-controlled, sensible, well-behaved, friendly to strangers, and able to teach. [3]They must not be heavy drinkers or troublemakers. Instead, they must be kind and gentle and not love money.

[4]Church officials must be in control of their own families, and they must see that their children are obedient and always respectful. [5]If they don't know how to control their own families, how can they look after God's people?

[6]They must not be new followers of the Lord. If they are, they might become proud and be doomed along with the devil. [7]Finally, they must be well-respected by people who are not followers. Then they won't be trapped and disgraced by the devil.

Church Officers

[8]Church officers[f] should be serious. They must not be liars, heavy drinkers, or greedy for money. [9]And they must have a clear conscience and hold firmly to what God has shown us about our faith. [10]They must first prove themselves. Then if no one has anything against them, they can serve as officers. [11]Women[g] must also be serious. They must not gossip or be heavy drinkers,

---

[a]**1.18** *prophets*: Probably the Christian prophets referred to in 4.14.   [b]**2.15** *saved by having children*: Or "brought safely through childbirth" or "saved by the birth of a child" (that is, by the birth of Jesus) or "saved by being good mothers." And 3.1 would be translated, "Anyone who desires . . . something worthwhile."   [c]**3.1** *It is true that*: These words may be taken with 2.15. If so, that verse would be translated: "It is true that women will be saved . . . holy, and modest." And 3.1 would be translated, "Anyone who desires . . . something worthwhile."   [d]**3.1** *church official*: Or "bishop."   [e]**3.2** *be faithful in marriage*: Or "be the husband of only one wife" or "have never been divorced."   [f]**3.8** *Church officers*: Or "Deacons."   [g]**3.11** *Women*: Either church officers or the wives of church officers.

and they must be faithful in everything they do. [12]Church officers must be faithful in marriage.[h] They must be in full control of their children and everyone else in their home. [13]Those who serve well as officers will earn a good reputation and will be highly respected for their faith in Christ Jesus.

The Mystery of Our Religion

[14]I hope to visit you soon. But I am writing these instructions, [15]so that if I am delayed, you will know how everyone who belongs to God's family ought to behave. After all, the church of the living God is the strong foundation of truth.

[16]Here is the great mystery of our religion:

Christ[i] came as a human.
The Spirit proved
    that he pleased God,
and he was seen by angels.

Christ was preached
    to the nations.
People in this world
    put their faith in him,
and he was taken up to glory.

People Will Turn from Their Faith

4 God's Spirit clearly says that in the last days many people will turn from their faith. They will be fooled by evil spirits and by teachings that come from demons. [2]They will also be fooled by the false claims of liars whose consciences have lost all feeling. These liars [3]will forbid people to marry or to eat certain foods. But God created these foods to be eaten with thankful hearts by his followers who know the truth. [4]Everything God created is good. And if you give thanks, you may eat anything. [5]What God has said and your prayer will make it fit to eat.

Paul's Advice to Timothy

[6]If you teach these things to other followers, you will be a good servant of Christ Jesus. You will show that you have grown up on the teachings about our faith and on the good instructions you have obeyed. [7]Don't have anything to do with worthless, senseless stories. Work hard to be truly religious. [8-9]As the saying goes,

"Exercise is good
    for your body,

but religion helps you
    in every way.
It promises life
    now and forever."

These words are worthwhile and should not be forgotten. [10]We have put our hope in the living God, who is the Savior of everyone, but especially of those who have faith. That's why we work and struggle so hard.[j] [11]Teach these things and tell everyone to do what you say. [12]Don't let anyone make fun of you, just because you are young. Set an example for other followers by what you say and do, as well as by your love, faith, and purity. [13]Until I arrive, be sure to keep on reading the Scriptures in worship, and don't stop preaching and teaching. [14]Use the gift you were given when the prophets spoke and the group of church leaders[k] blessed you by placing their hands on you. [15]Remember these things and think about them, so everyone can see how well you are doing. [16]Be careful about the way you live and about what you teach. Keep on doing this, and you will save not only yourself, but the people who hear you.

How To Act toward Others

5 Don't correct an older man. Encourage him, as you would your own father. Treat younger men as you would your own brother, [2]and treat older women as you would your own mother. Show the same respect to younger women that you would to your sister.

[3]Take care of any widow who is really in need. [4]But if a widow has children or grandchildren, they should learn to serve God by taking care of her, as she once took care of them. This is what God wants them to do. [5]A widow who is really in need is one who doesn't have any relatives. She has faith in God, and she keeps praying to him night and day, asking for his help.

[6]A widow who thinks only about having a good time is already dead, even though she is still alive.

[7]Tell all of this to everyone, so they will do the right thing. [8]People who don't take care of their relatives, and especially their own families, have given up their faith. They are worse than someone who doesn't have faith in the Lord.

[9]For a widow to be put on the list of widows, she must be at least sixty years old, and she must have been faithful in

---

[h]**3.12** _be faithful in marriage_: See the note at 3.2.   [i]**3.16** _Christ_: The Greek text has "he," probably meaning "Christ." Some manuscripts have "God."   [j]**4.10** _struggle so hard_: Some manuscripts have "are treated so badly."   [k]**4.14** _group of church leaders_: Or "group of elders" or "group of presbyters" or "group of priests." This translates one Greek word, and it is related to the one used in 5.17, 19.

marriage.[l] 10She must also be well-known for doing all sorts of good things, such as raising children, giving food to strangers, welcoming God's people into her home,[m] helping people in need, and always making herself useful.

11Don't put young widows on the list. They may later have a strong desire to get married. Then they will turn away from Christ 12and become guilty of breaking their promise to him. 13Besides, they will become lazy and get into the habit of going from house to house. Next, they will start gossiping and become busybodies, talking about things that are none of their business.

14I would prefer that young widows get married, have children, and look after their families. Then the enemy won't have any reason to say insulting things about us. 15Look what's already happened to some of the young widows! They have turned away to follow Satan.

16If a woman who is a follower has any widows in her family, she[n] should help them. This will keep the church from having that burden, and then the church can help widows who are really in need.

Church Leaders

17Church leaders[o] who do their job well deserve to be paid[p] twice as much, especially if they work hard at preaching and teaching. 18It is just as the Scriptures say, "Don't muzzle an ox when you are using it to grind grain." You also know the saying, "Workers are worth their pay."

19Don't listen to any charge against a church leader, unless at least two or three people bring the same charges. 20But if any of the leaders should keep on sinning, they must be corrected in front of the whole group, as a warning to everyone else.

21In the presence of God and Christ Jesus and their chosen angels, I order you to follow my instructions! Be fair with everyone, and don't have any favorites.

22Don't be too quick to accept people into the service of the Lord[q] by placing your hands on them.

Don't sin because others do, but stay close to God.

23Stop drinking only water. Take a little wine to help your stomach trouble and the other illnesses you always have.

24Some people get caught in their sins right away, even before the time of judgment. But other people's sins don't show up until later. 25It is the same with good deeds. Some are easily seen, but none of them can be hidden.

6 If you are a slave, you should respect and honor your owner. This will keep people from saying bad things about God and about our teaching. 2If any of you slaves have owners who are followers, you should show them respect. After all, they are also followers of Christ, and he loves them. So you should serve and help them the best you can.

False Teaching and True Wealth

These are the things you must teach and tell the people to do. 3Anyone who teaches something different disagrees with the correct and godly teaching of our Lord Jesus Christ. 4Those people who disagree are proud of themselves, but they don't really know a thing. Their minds are sick, and they like to argue over words. They cause jealousy, disagreements, unkind words, evil suspicions, 5and nasty quarrels. They have wicked minds and have missed out on the truth.

These people think religion is supposed to make you rich. 6And religion does make your life rich, by making you content with what you have. 7We didn't bring anything into this world, and we won't[r] take anything with us when we leave. 8So we should be satisfied just to have food and clothes. 9People who want to be rich fall into all sorts of temptations and traps. They are caught by foolish and harmful desires that drag them down and destroy them. 10The love of money causes all kinds of trouble. Some people want money so much that they have given up their faith and caused themselves a lot of pain.

Fighting a Good Fight for the Faith

11Timothy, you belong to God, so keep away from all these evil things. Try your best to please God and to be like him. Be faithful, loving, dependable, and gentle. 12Fight a good fight for the faith and claim eternal life. God offered it to you when you clearly told about your faith,

[l]**5.9** *been faithful in marriage*: Or "been the wife of only one husband" or "never been divorced." [m]**5.10** *welcoming God's people into her home*: The Greek text has "washing the feet of God's people." In New Testament times most people either went barefoot or wore sandals, and a host would often wash the feet of special guests. [n]**5.16** *woman . . . she*: Some manuscripts have "man or woman . . . that person." [o]**5.17** *leaders*: Or "elders" or "presbyters" or "priests." [p]**5.17** *paid*: Or "honored" or "respected." [q]**5.22** *to accept people into the service of the Lord*: Or "to forgive people." [r]**6.7** *we won't*: Some manuscripts have "we surely won't."

while so many people listened. 13Now I
ask you to make a promise. Make it in
the presence of God, who gives life to
all, and in the presence of Jesus Christ,
who openly told Pontius Pilate about his
faith. 14Promise to obey completely and
fully all that you have been told until
our Lord Jesus Christ returns.

15 The glorious God
    is the only Ruler,
    the King of kings
    and Lord of lords.
At the time that God
    has already decided,
he will send Jesus Christ
    back again.

16 Only God lives forever!
And he lives in light
    that no one can come near.
No human has ever seen God
    or ever can see him.

God will be honored,
and his power
    will last forever. Amen.

17Warn the rich people of this world
not to be proud or to trust in wealth that
is easily lost. Tell them to have faith in
God, who is rich and blesses us with
everything we need to enjoy life. 18In-
struct them to do as many good deeds
as they can and to help everyone. Remind the rich to be generous and share
what they have. 19This will lay a solid
foundation for the future, so that they
will know what true life is like.

20Timothy, guard what God has placed
in your care! Don't pay any attention to
that godless and stupid talk that sounds
smart but really isn't. 21Some people
have even lost their faith by believing
this talk.

I pray that the Lord will be kind to all
of you!

2 TIMOTHY

ABOUT THIS LETTER

In his second letter to Timothy, Paul is more personal than in his first one. Timothy is like a "dear child" to Paul, and Paul always mentions him in his prayers (1.2, 3) because he wants Timothy to be a "good soldier" of Christ Jesus and to learn to endure suffering (2.1, 3). Paul mentions Timothy's mother and grandmother by name in this letter and reminds Timothy how he had placed his hands on him as a special sign that the Spirit was guiding his work.

Some who claimed to be followers of the Lord had already been trapped by the devil, and Paul warns Timothy to run from those temptations that often catch young people (2.20-26; 3.1-9). He tells Timothy to keep preaching God's message, even if it is not the popular thing to do (4.2). He should also beware of false teachers.

Paul knows that he will soon die for his faith, but he will be rewarded for his faithfulness (4.6-8), and he reminds Timothy of the true message:

> If we died with Christ,
> we will live with him.
> If we don't give up,
> we will rule with him.
> (2.11, 12a)

A QUICK LOOK AT THIS LETTER

Greetings and Prayer for Timothy (1.1, 2)
Do Not Be Ashamed of the Lord (1.3-18)
How To Be a Good Soldier of Christ (2.1-26)
What People Will Be Like in the Last Days (3.1-9)
Keep Being Faithful (3.10—4.8)
Personal Instructions and Final Greetings (4.9-22)

---

1 From Paul, an apostle of Christ Jesus.

God himself chose me to be an apostle, and he gave me the promised life that Jesus Christ makes possible.

²Timothy, you are like a dear child to me. I pray that God our Father and our Lord Christ Jesus will be kind and merciful to you and will bless you with peace!

Do Not Be Ashamed of the Lord

³Night and day I mention you in my prayers. I am always grateful for you, as I pray to the God my ancestors and I have served with a clear conscience. ⁴I remember how you cried, and I want to see you, because that will make me truly happy. ⁵I also remember the genuine faith of your mother Eunice. Your grandmother Lois had the same sort of faith, and I am sure that you have it as well. ⁶So I ask you to make full use of the gift that God gave you when I placed my hands on you.ᵃ Use it well. ⁷God's Spiritᵇ doesn't make cowards out of us. The Spirit gives us power, love, and self-control.

⁸Don't be ashamed to speak for our Lord. And don't be ashamed of me, just because I am in jail for serving him. Use the power that comes from God and join

---

ᵃ**1.6** *when I placed my hands on you*: Church leaders placed their hands on people who were being appointed to preach or teach (see 1 Timothy 4.14). ᵇ**1.7** *God's Spirit*: Or "God."

with me in suffering for telling the good news.

⁹ God saved us and chose us
   to be his holy people.
We did nothing
   to deserve this,
but God planned it
   because he is so kind.
Even before time began
God planned for Christ Jesus
   to show kindness to us.

¹⁰ Now Christ Jesus has come
   to show us the kindness
      of God.
Christ our Savior defeated death
and brought us
   the good news.
It shines like a light
and offers life
   that never ends.

¹¹My work is to be a preacher, an apostle, and a teacher.ᶜ ¹²That's why I am suffering now. But I am not ashamed! I know the one I have faith in, and I am sure that he can guard until the last day what he has trusted me with.ᵈ ¹³Now follow the example of the correct teaching I gave you, and let the faith and love of Christ Jesus be your model. ¹⁴You have been trusted with a wonderful treasure. Guard it with the help of the Holy Spirit, who lives within you.

¹⁵You know that everyone in Asia has turned against me, especially Phygelus and Hermogenes.

¹⁶I pray that the Lord will be kind to the family of Onesiphorus. He often cheered me up and wasn't ashamed of me when I was put in jail. ¹⁷Then after he arrived in Rome, he searched everywhere until he found me. ¹⁸I pray that the Lord Jesus will ask God to show mercy to Onesiphorus on the day of judgment. You know how much he helped me in Ephesus.

A Good Soldier of Christ Jesus

2 Timothy, my child, Christ Jesus is kind, and you must let him make you strong. ²You have often heard me teach. Now I want you to tell these same things to followers who can be trusted to tell others.

³As a good soldier of Christ Jesus you must endure your share of suffering. ⁴Soldiers on duty don't work at outside jobs. They try only to please their commanding officer. ⁵No one wins an athletic contest without obeying the rules. ⁶And farmers who work hard are the first to eat what grows in their field. ⁷If

you keep in mind what I have told you, the Lord will help you understand completely.

⁸Keep your mind on Jesus Christ! He was from the family of David and was raised from death, just as my good news says. ⁹And because of this message, I am locked up in jail and treated like a criminal. But God's good news isn't locked in jail, ¹⁰and so I am willing to put up with anything. Then God's special people will be saved. They will be given eternal glory because they belong to Christ Jesus. ¹¹Here is a true message:

   "If we died with Christ,
      we will live with him.
¹² If we don't give up,
      we will rule with him.
   If we deny
      that we know him,
   he will deny
      that he knows us.
¹³ If we are not faithful,
      he will still be faithful.
   Christ cannot deny
      who he is."

An Approved Worker

¹⁴Don't let anyone forget these things. And with Godᵉ as your witness, you must warn them not to argue about words. These arguments don't help anyone. In fact, they ruin everyone who listens to them. ¹⁵Do your best to win God's approval as a worker who doesn't need to be ashamed and who teaches only the true message.

¹⁶Keep away from worthless and useless talk. It only leads people farther away from God. ¹⁷That sort of talk is like a sore that won't heal. And Hymenaeus and Philetus have been talking this way ¹⁸by teaching that the dead have already been raised to life. This is far from the truth, and it is destroying the faith of some people.

¹⁹But the foundation that God has laid is solid. On it is written, "The Lord knows who his people are. So everyone who worships the Lord must turn away from evil."

²⁰In a large house some dishes are made of gold or silver, while others are made of wood or clay. Some of these are special, and others are not. ²¹That's also how it is with people. The ones who stop doing evil and make themselves pure will become special. Their lives will be holy and pleasing to their Master, and they will be able to do all kinds of good deeds.

²²Run from temptations that capture

ᶜ**1.11** _teacher_: Some manuscripts add "of the Gentiles." ᵈ**1.12** _what he has trusted me with_: Or "what I have trusted him with." ᵉ**2.14** _God_: Some manuscripts have "the Lord," and others have "Christ."

young people. Always do the right thing. Be faithful, loving, and easy to get along with. Worship with people whose hearts are pure. 23Stay away from stupid and senseless arguments. These only lead to trouble, 24and God's servants must not be troublemakers. They must be kind to everyone, and they must be good teachers and very patient.

25Be humble when you correct people who oppose you. Maybe God will lead them to turn to him and learn the truth. 26They have been trapped by the devil, and he makes them obey him, but God may help them escape.

What People Will Be Like in the Last Days

3 You can be certain that in the last days there will be some very hard times. 2People will love only themselves and money. They will be proud, stuck-up, rude, and disobedient to their parents. They will also be ungrateful, godless, 3heartless, and hateful. Their words will be cruel, and they will have no self-control or pity. These people will hate everything that is good. 4They will be sneaky, reckless, and puffed up with pride. Instead of loving God, they will love pleasure. 5Even though they will make a show of being religious, their religion won't be real. Don't have anything to do with such people.

6Some men fool whole families, just to get power over those women who are slaves of sin and are controlled by all sorts of desires. 7These women always want to learn something new, but they never can discover the truth. 8Just as Jannes and Jambres[f] opposed Moses, these people are enemies of the truth. Their minds are sick, and their faith isn't real. 9But they won't get very far with their foolishness. Soon everyone will know the truth about them, just as Jannes and Jambres were found out.

Paul's Last Instructions to Timothy

10Timothy, you know what I teach and how I live. You know what I want to do and what I believe. You have seen how patient and loving I am, and how in the past I put up with 11trouble and suffering in the cities of Antioch, Iconium, and Lystra. Yet the Lord rescued me from all those terrible troubles. 12Anyone who belongs to Christ Jesus and wants to live right will have trouble from others. 13But evil people who pretend to be what they are not will become worse

than ever, as they fool others and are fooled themselves.

14Keep on being faithful to what you were taught and to what you believed. After all, you know who taught you these things. 15Since childhood, you have known the Holy Scriptures that are able to make you wise enough to have faith in Christ Jesus and be saved. 16Everything in the Scriptures is God's Word. All of it is useful for teaching and helping people and for correcting them and showing them how to live. 17The Scriptures train God's servants to do all kinds of good deeds.

4 When Christ Jesus comes as king, he will be the judge of everyone, whether they are living or dead. So with God and Christ as witnesses, I command you 2to preach God's message. Do it willingly, even if it isn't the popular thing to do. You must correct people and point out their sins. But also cheer them up, and when you instruct them, always be patient. 3The time is coming when people won't listen to good teaching. Instead, they will look for teachers who will please them by telling them only what they are itching to hear. 4They will turn from the truth and eagerly listen to senseless stories. 5But you must stay calm and be willing to suffer. You must work hard to tell the good news and to do your job well.

6Now the time has come for me to die. My life is like a drink offering[g] being poured out on the altar. 7I have fought well. I have finished the race, and I have been faithful. 8So a crown will be given to me for pleasing the Lord. He judges fairly, and on the day of judgment he will give a crown to me and to everyone else who wants him to appear with power.

Personal Instructions

9Come to see me as soon as you can. 10Demas loves the things of this world so much that he left me and went to Thessalonica. Crescens has gone to Galatia, and Titus has gone to Dalmatia. 11Only Luke has stayed with me.

Mark can be very helpful to me, so please find him and bring him with you. 12I sent Tychicus to Ephesus.

13When you come, bring the coat I left at Troas with Carpus. Don't forget to bring the scrolls, especially the ones made of leather.[h]

14Alexander, the metalworker, has hurt me in many ways. But the Lord will

---

[f]3.8 *Jannes and Jambres*: These names are not found in the Old Testament. But many believe these were the names of the two Egyptian magicians who opposed Moses when he wanted to lead the people of Israel out of Egypt (see Exodus 7.11, 22).   [g]4.6 *drink offering*: Water or wine was sometimes poured out as an offering when an animal sacrifice was made.
[h]4.13 *the ones made of leather*: A scroll was a kind of rolled up book, and it could be made out of paper (called "papyrus") or leather (that is, animal skin) or even copper.

pay him back for what he has done. [15]Alexander opposes what we preach. You had better watch out for him.

[16]When I was first put on trial, no one helped me. In fact, everyone deserted me. I hope it won't be held against them. [17]But the Lord stood beside me. He gave me the strength to tell his full message, so that all Gentiles would hear it. And I was kept safe from hungry lions. [18]The Lord will always keep me from being harmed by evil, and he will bring me safely into his heavenly kingdom. Praise him forever and ever! Amen.

Final Greetings

[19]Give my greetings to Priscilla and Aquila and to the family of Onesiphorus.

[20]Erastus stayed at Corinth.

Trophimus was sick when I left him at Miletus.

[21]Do your best to come before winter.

Eubulus, Pudens, Linus, and Claudia send you their greetings, and so do the rest of the Lord's followers.

[22]I pray that the Lord will bless your life and will be kind to you.

TITUS

ABOUT THIS LETTER

Paul mentions Titus several times in his letters as someone who worked with him in Asia Minor and Greece (2 Corinthians 2.13; 7.6, 13; 8.6, 16, 23; 12.18; Galatians 2.3). He is told by Paul to appoint church leaders and officials in Crete.

Paul instructs Titus to make sure that church leaders and officials have good reputations (1.5-9) and that all of the Lord's followers keep themselves pure and avoid arguments (1.10—2.9).

Paul includes special instructions for the different groups within the church in Crete. He reminds Titus that a new way of life is possible because of what God has done by sending Jesus Christ: God has saved them, washed them by the power of the Holy Spirit, and given them a fresh start and the hope of eternal life.

Paul also tells how we are saved:

> God our Savior showed us
>   how good and kind he is.
> He saved us because
>   of his mercy,
> and not because
> of any good things
>   that we have done.
>
> *(3.4, 5)*

A QUICK LOOK AT THIS LETTER

---

1 From Paul, a servant of God and an apostle of Jesus Christ.

I encourage God's own people to have more faith and to understand the truth about religion. ²Then they will have the hope of eternal life that God promised long ago. And God never tells a lie! ³So, at the proper time, God our Savior gave this message and told me to announce what he had said.

⁴Titus, because of our faith, you are like a son to me. I pray that God our Father and Christ Jesus our Savior will be kind to you and will bless you with peace!

What Titus Was To Do in Crete

⁵I left you in Crete to do what had been left undone and to appoint leaders[a] for the churches in each town. As I told you, ⁶they must have a good reputation and be faithful in marriage.[b] Their children must be followers of the Lord and not have a reputation for being wild and disobedient.

⁷Church officials[c] are in charge of

---

[a]**1.5** *leaders*: Or "elders" or "presbyters" or "priests." [b]**1.6** *be faithful in marriage*: Or "be the husband of only one wife" or "have never been divorced." [c]**1.7** *Church officials*: Or "Bishops."

God's work, and so they must also have a good reputation. They must not be bossy, quick-tempered, heavy drinkers, bullies, or dishonest in business. [8]Instead, they must be friendly to strangers and enjoy doing good things. They must also be sensible, fair, pure, and self-controlled. [9]They must stick to the true message they were taught, so that their good teaching can help others and correct everyone who opposes it.

[10]There are many who don't respect authority, and they fool others by talking nonsense. This is especially true of some Jewish followers. [11]But you must make them be quiet. They are after money, and they upset whole families by teaching what they should not. [12]It is like one of their own prophets once said,

"The people of Crete
　　always tell lies.
They are greedy and lazy
　　like wild animals."

[13]That surely is a true saying. And you should be hard on such people, so you can help them grow stronger in their faith. [14]Don't pay any attention to any of those senseless Jewish stories and human commands. These are made up by people who won't obey the truth.

[15]Everything is pure for someone whose heart is pure. But nothing is pure for an unbeliever with a dirty mind. That person's mind and conscience are destroyed. [16]Such people claim to know God, but their actions prove that they really don't. They are disgusting. They won't obey God, and they are too worthless to do anything good.

Instructions for Different Groups of People

2 Titus, you must teach only what is correct. [2]Tell the older men to have self-control and to be serious and sensible. Their faith, love, and patience must never fail.

[3]Tell the older women to behave as those who love the Lord should. They must not gossip about others or be slaves of wine. They must teach what is proper, [4]so the younger women will be loving wives and mothers. [5]Each of the younger women must be sensible and kind, as well as a good homemaker, who puts her own husband first. Then no one can say insulting things about God's message.

[6]Tell the young men to have self-control in everything.

[7]Always set a good example for others. Be sincere and serious when you teach. [8]Use clean language that no one can criticize. Do this, and your enemies will be too ashamed to say anything against you.

[9]Tell slaves always to please their owners by obeying them in everything. Slaves must not talk back to their owners [10]or steal from them. They must be completely honest and trustworthy. Then everyone will show great respect for what is taught about God our Savior.

God's Kindness and the New Life

[11]God has shown us how kind he is by coming to save all people. [12]He taught us to give up our wicked ways and our worldly desires and to live decent and honest lives in this world. [13]We are filled with hope, as we wait for the glorious return of our great God and Savior Jesus Christ.[d] [14]He gave himself to rescue us from everything that is evil and to make our hearts pure. He wanted us to be his own people and to be eager to do right.

[15]Teach these things, as you use your full authority to encourage and correct people. Make sure you earn everyone's respect.

Doing Helpful Things

3 Remind your people to obey the rulers and authorities and not to be rebellious. They must always be ready to do something helpful [2]and not say cruel things or argue. They should be gentle and kind to everyone. [3]We used to be stupid, disobedient, and foolish, as well as slaves of all sorts of desires and pleasures. We were evil and jealous. Everyone hated us, and we hated everyone.

[4] God our Savior showed us
　　how good and kind he is.
[5] He saved us because
　　of his mercy,
　and not because
　of any good things
　　that we have done.

God washed us by the power
　　of the Holy Spirit.
He gave us new birth
　　and a fresh beginning.
[6] God sent Jesus Christ
　our Savior
　　to give us his Spirit.

[7] Jesus treated us much better
　　than we deserve.

---

[d]**2.13** _the glorious return of our great God and Savior Jesus Christ_: Or "the glorious return of our great God and our Savior Jesus Christ" or "the return of Jesus Christ, who is the glory of our great God and Savior."

He made us acceptable to God
and gave us the hope
of eternal life.

[8]This message is certainly true.

These teachings are useful and helpful for everyone. I want you to insist that the people follow them, so that all who have faith in God will be sure to do good deeds. [9]But don't have anything to do with stupid arguments about ancestors. And stay away from disagreements and quarrels about the Law of Moses. Such arguments are useless and senseless.

[10]Warn troublemakers once or twice. Then don't have anything else to do with them. [11]You know that their minds are twisted, and their own sins show how guilty they are.

Personal Instructions and Greetings

[12]I plan to send Artemas or Tychicus to you. After he arrives, please try your best to meet me at Nicopolis. I have decided to spend the winter there. [13]When Zenas the lawyer and Apollos get ready to leave, help them as much as you can, so they won't have need of anything.

[14]Our people should learn to spend their time doing something useful and worthwhile.

[15]Greetings to you from everyone here. Greet all of our friends who share in our faith.

I pray that the Lord will be kind to all of you!

PHILEMON

ABOUT THIS LETTER

Philemon was a wealthy man who owned slaves and who used his large house for church meetings (2). He probably lived in Colossae, since Paul's letter to the Colossians mentions Onesimus, a slave of Philemon, and Archippus (Colossians 4.9, 17).

Paul is writing from jail on behalf of Onesimus, a runaway slave owned by Philemon. Onesimus had become a follower of the Lord and a valuable friend to Paul, and Paul is writing to encourage Philemon to accept Onesimus also as a friend and follower of the Lord.

This letter is an excellent example of the art of letter-writing in the Roman world, and it is the most personal of all Paul's letters. The way the letter is written suggests that Paul and Philemon were close friends.

A QUICK LOOK AT THIS LETTER

Greetings to Philemon (1-3)
Paul Speaks to Philemon about Onesimus (4-22)
Final Greetings and a Prayer (23-25)

---

¹From Paul, who is in jail for serving Christ Jesus, and from Timothy, who is like a brother because of our faith.

Philemon, you work with us and are very dear to us. This letter is to you ²and to the church that meets in your home. It is also to our dear friend Apphia and to Archippus, who serves the Lord as we do.

³I pray that God our Father and our Lord Jesus Christ will be kind to you and will bless you with peace!

Philemon's Love and Faith

⁴Philemon, each time I mention you in my prayers, I thank God. ⁵I hear about your faith in our Lord Jesus and about your love for all of God's people. ⁶As you share your faith with others, I pray that they may come to know all the blessings Christ has given us. ⁷My friend, your love has made me happy and has greatly encouraged me. It has also cheered the hearts of God's people.

Paul Speaks to Philemon about Onesimus

⁸Christ gives me the courage to tell you what to do. ⁹But I would rather ask you to do it simply because of love. Yes, as someone*ᵃ* in jail for Christ, ¹⁰I beg you to help Onesimus!*ᵇ* He is like a son to me because I led him to Christ here in jail. ¹¹Before this, he was useless to you, but now he is useful both to you and to me.

¹²Sending Onesimus back to you makes me very sad. ¹³I would like to keep him here with me, where he could take your place in helping me while I am here in prison for preaching the good news. ¹⁴But I won't do anything unless you agree to it first. I want your act of kindness to come from your heart, and not be something you feel forced to do.

¹⁵Perhaps Onesimus was taken from you for a little while so that you could have him back for good, ¹⁶but not as a slave. Onesimus is much more than a slave. To me he is a dear friend, but to you he is even more, both as a person and as a follower of the Lord.

¹⁷If you consider me a friend because of Christ, then welcome Onesimus as you would welcome me. ¹⁸If he has cheated you or owes you anything, charge it to my account. ¹⁹With my own

---

ᵃ9 someone: Greek "a messenger" or "an old man."   *ᵇ10 Onesimus*: In Greek this name means "useful."

hand I write: I, PAUL, WILL PAY YOU BACK. But don't forget that you owe me your life. [20]My dear friend and follower of Christ our Lord, please cheer me up by doing this for me.

[21]I am sure you will do all I have asked, and even more. [22]Please get a room ready for me. I hope your pray-ers will be answered, and I can visit you.

[23]Epaphras is also here in jail for be-ing a follower of Christ Jesus. He sends his greetings, [24]and so do Mark, Aristarchus, Demas, and Luke, who work together with me.

[25]I pray that the Lord Jesus Christ will be kind to you!

HEBREWS

ABOUT THIS LETTER

Many religious people in the first century after Jesus' birth, both Jews and Gentiles, had questions about the religion of the early Christians. They were looking for evidence that this new faith was genuine. Jews had the miracle of crossing the Red Sea and the agreement made with God at Mount Sinai to support their faith. But what miracles did Christians have? Jews had beautiful worship ceremonies and a high priest who offered sacrifices in the temple so that the people would be forgiven. But what did Christians have? How could this new Christian faith, centered in Jesus, offer forgiveness of sins and friendship with God?

The letter to the Hebrews was written to answer exactly these kinds of questions. In it the author tells the readers how important Jesus really is. He is greater than any of God's angels (1.5-14), greater than any prophet, and greater even than Moses and Joshua (2.1—4.14). Jesus is the perfect high priest because he never sinned, and by offering his own life he has made the perfect sacrifice for sin once for all time (9.23—10.18). By his death and return from death he has opened the way for all people to come to God (4.14—5.10; 7.1—8.13).

This letter has much to say about the importance of faith. The writer points out that what Jesus offers comes only by faith. And this faith makes his followers sure of what they hope for and gives them proof of things that cannot be seen. The writer praises God's faithful people of the past (11.1-40) and encourages those who follow Jesus now to keep their eyes on him as they run the race (12.1-3).

What does it mean to have a high priest like Jesus?

Jesus understands every weakness of ours, because he was tempted in every way that we are. But he did not sin! So whenever we are in need, we should come bravely before the throne of our merciful God. There we will be treated with undeserved kindness, and we will find help. (4.15, 16)

A QUICK LOOK AT THIS LETTER

---

1 Long ago in many ways and at many times God's prophets spoke his message to our ancestors. ²But now at last, God sent his Son to bring his message to us. God created the universe by his Son, and everything will someday belong to the Son. ³God's Son has all the brightness of God's own glory and is like him in every way. By his own mighty word, he holds the universe together.

After the Son had washed away our

sins, he sat down at the right side*a* of the glorious God in heaven. [4]He had become much greater than the angels, and the name he was given is far greater than any of theirs.

God's Son Is Greater than Angels

[5] God has never said
    to any of the angels,
"You are my Son, because today
    I have become your Father!"
Neither has God said
    to any of them,
"I will be his Father,
    and he will be my Son!"

[6]When God brings his first-born Son*b* into the world, he commands all of his angels to worship him.
[7]And when God speaks about the angels, he says,

"I change my angels into wind
and my servants
    into flaming fire."

[8]But God says about his Son,

"You are God,
and you will rule
    as King forever!
Your*c* royal power
    brings about justice.
[9] You loved justice
    and hated evil,
and so I, your God,
    have chosen you.
I appointed you
and made you happier
    than any of your friends."

[10]The Scriptures also say,

"In the beginning, Lord,
    you were the one
who laid the foundation
of the earth
    and created the heavens.
[11] They will all disappear
and wear out like clothes,
    but you will last forever.
[12] You will roll them up
    like a robe
and change them
    like a garment.
But you are always the same,
    and you will live forever."

[13] God never said to any
    of the angels,
"Sit at my right side
until I make your enemies
    into a footstool for you!"

[14]Angels are merely spirits sent to serve people who are going to be saved.

This Great Way of Being Saved

2 We must give our full attention to what we were told, so that we won't drift away. [2]The message spoken by angels proved to be true, and all who disobeyed or rejected it were punished as they deserved. [3]So if we refuse this great way of being saved, how can we hope to escape? The Lord himself was the first to tell about it, and people who heard the message proved to us that it was true. [4]God himself showed that his message was true by working all kinds of powerful miracles and wonders. He also gave his Holy Spirit to anyone he chose to.

The One Who Leads Us To Be Saved

[5]We know that God did not put the future world under the power of angels. [6]Somewhere in the Scriptures someone says to God,

"What makes you care
    about us humans?
Why are you concerned
    for weaklings such as we?
[7] You made us lower
    than the angels
    for a while.
Yet you have crowned us
    with glory and honor.*d*
[8] And you have put everything
    under our power!"

God has put everything under our power and has not left anything out of our power. But we still don't see it all under our power. [9]What we do see is Jesus, who for a little while was made lower than the angels. Because of God's wonderful kindness, Jesus died for everyone. And now that Jesus has suffered and died, he is crowned with glory and honor!
[10]Everything belongs to God, and all things were created by his power. So God did the right thing when he made Jesus perfect by suffering, as Jesus led many of God's children to be saved and to share in his glory. [11]Jesus and the people he makes holy all belong to the same family. That is why he isn't ashamed to call them his brothers and sisters. [12]He even said to God,

"I will tell them your name
    and sing your praises
when they come together
    to worship."

[13]He also said,

"I will trust God."

Then he said,

---

*a***1.3** *right side*: The place of honor and power.   *b***1.6** *first-born Son*: The first son born into a family had certain privileges that the other children did not have. In 12.23 "first-born" refers to God's special people.   *c***1.8** *Your*: Some manuscripts have "His."   *d***2.7** *and honor*: Some manuscripts add "and you have placed us in charge of all you created."

"Here I am with the children
God has given me."

¹⁴We are people of flesh and blood.
That is why Jesus became one of us. He
died to destroy the devil, who had
power over death. ¹⁵But he also died to
rescue all of us who live each day in
fear of dying. ¹⁶Jesus clearly did not
come to help angels, but he did come to
help Abraham's descendants. ¹⁷He had
to be one of us, so that he could serve
God as our merciful and faithful high
priest and sacrifice himself for the forgiveness of our sins. ¹⁸And now that Jesus has suffered and was tempted, he
can help anyone else who is tempted.

Jesus Is Greater than Moses

3 My friends, God has chosen you to
be his holy people. So think about
Jesus, the one we call our apostle and
high priest! ²Jesus was faithful to God,
who appointed him, just as Moses was
faithful in serving all of*e* God's people.
³But Jesus deserves more honor than
Moses, just as the builder of a house deserves more honor than the house. ⁴Of
course, every house is built by someone,
and God is really the one who built
everything.
⁵Moses was a faithful servant and told
God's people what would be said in the
future. ⁶But Christ is the Son in charge
of God's people. And we are those people, if we keep on being brave and don't
lose hope.

A Rest for God's People

⁷It is just as the Holy Spirit says,

"If you hear God's voice today,
⁸   don't be stubborn!
Don't rebel like those people
who were tested
in the desert.
*⁹ For forty years your ancestors
tested God and saw
the things he did.

¹⁰ "Then God got tired of them
and said,
'You people never
show good sense,
and you don't understand
what I want you to do.'
¹¹ God became angry
and told the people,
'You will never enter
my place of rest!' "

¹²My friends, watch out! Don't let evil
thoughts or doubts make any of you
turn from the living God. ¹³You must encourage one another each day. And you
must keep on while there is still a time
that can be called "today." If you don't,
then sin may fool some of you and make

you stubborn. ¹⁴We were sure about
Christ when we first became his people.
So let's hold tightly to our faith until the
end. ¹⁵The Scriptures say,

"If you hear his voice today,
don't be stubborn
like those who rebelled."

¹⁶Who were those people that heard
God's voice and rebelled? Weren't they
the same ones that came out of Egypt
with Moses? ¹⁷Who were the people that
made God angry for forty years?
Weren't they the ones that sinned and
died in the desert? ¹⁸And who did God
say would never enter his place of rest?
Weren't they the ones that disobeyed
him? ¹⁹We see that those people did not
enter the place of rest because they did
not have faith.

4 The promise to enter the place of
rest is still good, and we must take
care that none of you miss out. ²We have
heard the message, just as they did. But
they failed to believe what they heard,
and the message did not do them any
good. ³Only people who have faith will
enter the place of rest. It is just as the
Scriptures say,

"God became angry
and told the people,
'You will never enter
my place of rest!' "

God said this, even though everything
has been ready from the time of creation. ⁴In fact, somewhere the Scriptures say that by the seventh day, God
had finished his work, and so he rested.
⁵We also read that he later said, "You
people will never enter my place of
rest!" ⁶This means that the promise to
enter is still good, because those who
first heard about it disobeyed and did
not enter. ⁷Much later God told David to
make the promise again, just as I have
already said,

"If you hear his voice today,
don't be stubborn!"

⁸If Joshua had really given the people
rest, there would not be any need for
God to talk about another day of rest.
⁹But God has promised us a Sabbath
when we will rest, even though it has
not yet come. ¹⁰On that day God's people will rest from their work, just as God
rested from his work.
¹¹We should do our best to enter that
place of rest, so that none of us will disobey and miss going there, as they did.
¹²What God has said isn't only alive and
active! It is sharper than any double-
edged sword. His word can cut through
our spirits and souls and through our
joints and marrow, until it discovers the

---

*e***3.2** *all of*: Some manuscripts do not have these words.

desires and thoughts of our hearts.
[13]Nothing is hidden from God! He sees
through everything, and we will have to
tell him the truth.

Jesus Is the Great High Priest

[14]We have a great high priest, who has
gone into heaven, and he is Jesus the
Son of God. That is why we must hold
on to what we have said about him. [15]Jesus understands every weakness of
ours, because he was tempted in every
way that we are. But he did not sin! [16]So
whenever we are in need, we should
come bravely before the throne of our
merciful God. There we will be treated
with undeserved kindness, and we will
find help.

5 Every high priest is appointed to
help others by offering gifts and
sacrifices to God because of their sins.
[2]A high priest has weaknesses of his
own, and he feels sorry for foolish and
sinful people. [3]That is why he must offer
sacrifices for his own sins and for the
sins of others. [4]But no one can have the
honor of being a high priest simply by
wanting to be one. Only God can choose
a priest, and God is the one who chose
Aaron.

[5]That is how it was with Christ. He became a high priest, but not just because
he wanted the honor of being one. It
was God who told him,

"You are my Son, because today
    I have become your Father!"

[6]In another place, God says,

"You are a priest forever
    just like Melchizedek."[f]

[7]God had the power to save Jesus
from death. And while Jesus was on
earth, he begged God with loud crying
and tears to save him. He truly worshiped God, and God listened to his
prayers. [8]Jesus is God's own Son, but
still he had to suffer before he could
learn what it really means to obey God.
[9]Suffering made Jesus perfect, and now
he can save forever all who obey him.
[10]This is because God chose him to be a
high priest like Melchizedek.

Warning against Turning Away

[11]Much more could be said about this
subject. But it is hard to explain, and all
of you are slow to understand. [12]By now
you should have been teachers, but once
again you need to be taught the simplest
things about what God has said. You
need milk instead of solid food. [13]People
who live on milk are like babies who
don't really know what is right. [14]Solid
food is for mature people who have
been trained to know right from wrong.

6 We must try to become mature and
start thinking about more than just
the basic things we were taught about
Christ. We shouldn't need to keep talking about why we ought to turn from
deeds that bring death and why we
ought to have faith in God. [2]And we
shouldn't need to keep teaching about
baptisms[g] or about the laying on of
hands[h] or about people being raised
from death and the future judgment.
[3]Let's grow up, if God is willing.

[4-6]But what about people who turn
away after they have already seen the
light and have received the gift from
heaven and have shared in the Holy
Spirit? What about those who turn away
after they have received the good message of God and the powers of the future world? There is no way to bring
them back. What they are doing is the
same as nailing the Son of God to a
cross and insulting him in public!

[7]A field is useful to farmers, if there is
enough rain to make good crops grow.
In fact, God will bless that field. [8]But
land that produces only thornbushes is
worthless. It is likely to fall under God's
curse, and in the end it will be set on
fire.

[9]My friends, we are talking this way.
But we are sure that you are doing those
really good things that people do when
they are being saved. [10]God is always
fair. He will remember how you helped
his people in the past and how you are
still helping them. You belong to God,
and he won't forget the love you have
shown his people. [11]We wish that each
of you would always be eager to show
how strong and lasting your hope really
is. [12]Then you would never be lazy. You
would be following the example of
those who had faith and were patient
until God kept his promise to them.

God's Promise Is Sure

[13]No one is greater than God. So he
made a promise in his own name when
he said to Abraham, [14]"I, the Lord, will
bless you with many descendants!"
[15]Then after Abraham had been very patient, he was given what God had
promised. [16]When anyone wants to settle an argument, they make a vow by using the name of someone or something
greater than themselves. [17]So when God
wanted to prove for certain that his

---

[f]**5.6** *Melchizedek*: When Melchizedek is mentioned in the Old Testament, he is described as a
priest who lived before Aaron. Nothing is said about his ancestors or his death (see 7.3 and
Genesis 14.17-20).   [g]**6.2** *baptisms*: Or "ceremonies of washing."   [h]**6.2** *laying on of hands*:
This was a ceremony in which church leaders and others put their hands on people to show
that those people were chosen to do some special kind of work.

promise to his people could not be broken, he made a vow. [18]God cannot tell lies! And so his promises and vows are two things that can never be changed.

We have run to God for safety. Now his promises should greatly encourage us to take hold of the hope that is right in front of us. [19]This hope is like a firm and steady anchor for our souls. In fact, hope reaches behind the curtain[i] and into the most holy place. [20]Jesus has gone there ahead of us, and he is our high priest forever, just like Melchizedek.[j]

The Priestly Family of Melchizedek

7 Melchizedek was both king of Salem and priest of God Most High. He was the one who went out and gave Abraham his blessing, when Abraham returned from killing the kings. [2]Then Abraham gave him a tenth of everything he had.

The meaning of the name Melchizedek is "King of Justice." But since Salem means "peace," he is also "King of Peace." [3]We are not told that he had a father or mother or ancestors or beginning or end. He is like the Son of God and will be a priest forever.[k]

[4]Notice how great Melchizedek is! Our famous ancestor Abraham gave him a tenth of what he had taken from his enemies. [5]The Law teaches that even Abraham's descendants must give a tenth of what they possess. And they are to give this to their own relatives, who are the descendants of Levi and are priests. [6]Although Melchizedek wasn't a descendant of Levi, Abraham gave him a tenth of what he had. Then Melchizedek blessed Abraham, who had been given God's promise. [7]Everyone agrees that a person who gives a blessing is greater than the one who receives the blessing.

[8]Priests are given a tenth of what people earn. But all priests die, except Melchizedek, and the Scriptures teach that he is alive. [9]Levi's descendants are now the ones who receive a tenth from people. We could even say that when Abraham gave Melchizedek a tenth, Levi also gave him a tenth. [10]This is because Levi was born later into the family of Abraham, who gave a tenth to Melchizedek.

[11]Even though the Law of Moses says that the priests must be descendants of Levi, those priests cannot make anyone perfect. So there needs to be a priest like Melchizedek, rather than one from the priestly family of Aaron.[l] [12]And when the rules for selecting a priest are changed, the Law must also be changed.

[13]The person we are talking about is our Lord, who came from a tribe that had never had anyone to serve as a priest at the altar. [14]Everyone knows he came from the tribe of Judah, and Moses never said that priests would come from that tribe.

[15]All of this becomes clearer, when someone who is like Melchizedek is appointed to be a priest. [16]That person wasn't appointed because of his ancestors, but because his life can never end. [17]The Scriptures say about him,

"You are a priest forever,
  just like Melchizedek."

[18]In this way a weak and useless command was put aside, [19]because the Law cannot make anything perfect. At the same time, we are given a much better hope, and it can bring us close to God.

[20-21]God himself made a promise when this priest was appointed. But he did not make a promise like this when the other priests were appointed. The promise he made is,

"I, the Lord, promise that you
  will be a priest forever!
And I will never
  change my mind!"

[22]This means that Jesus guarantees us a better agreement with God. [23]There have been a lot of other priests, and all of them have died. [24]But Jesus will never die, and so he will be a priest forever! [25]He is forever able to save[m] the people he leads to God, because he always lives to speak to God for them.

[26]Jesus is the high priest we need. He is holy and innocent and faultless, and not at all like us sinners. Jesus is honored above all beings in heaven, [27]and he is better than any other high priest. Jesus doesn't need to offer sacrifices each day for his own sins and then for the sins of the people. He offered a sacrifice once for all, when he gave himself. [28]The Law appoints priests who have weaknesses. But God's promise, which came later than the Law, appoints his Son. And he is the perfect high priest forever.

A Better Promise

8 What I mean is that we have a high priest who sits at the right side[n] of God's great throne in heaven. [2]He also

---

[i]**6.19** *behind the curtain:* In the tent that was used for worship, a curtain separated the "holy place" from the "most holy place," which only the high priest could enter.   [j]**6.20** *Melchizedek:* See the note at 5.6.   [k]**7.3** *will be a priest forever:* See the note at 5.6.   [l]**7.11** *descendants of Levi . . . from the priestly family of Aaron:* Levi was the ancestor of the tribe from which priests and their helpers (called "Levites") were chosen. Aaron was the first high priest. [m]**7.25** *forever able to save:* Or "able to save forever."   [n]**8.1** *right side:* See the note at 1.3.

serves as the priest in the most holy place[o] inside the real tent there in heaven. This tent of worship was set up by the Lord, not by humans.

[3]Since all priests must offer gifts and sacrifices, Christ also needed to have something to offer. [4]If he were here on earth, he would not be a priest at all, because here the Law appoints other priests to offer sacrifices. [5]But the tent where they serve is just a copy and a shadow of the real one in heaven. Before Moses made the tent, he was told, "Be sure to make it exactly like the pattern you were shown on the mountain!" [6]Now Christ has been appointed to serve as a priest in a much better way, and he has given us much assurance of a better agreement.

[7]If the first agreement with God had been all right, there would not have been any need for another one. [8]But the Lord found fault with it and said,

"I tell you the time will come,
when I will make
    a new agreement
with the people of Israel
    and the people of Judah.
[9] It won't be like the agreement
that I made
    with their ancestors,
when I took them by the hand
    and led them out of Egypt.
They broke their agreement
    with me,
and I stopped caring
    about them!

[10] "But now I tell the people
of Israel
    this is my new agreement:
'The time will come
    when I, the Lord,
will write my laws
    on their minds and hearts.
I will be their God,
and they will be
    my people.
[11] Not one of them
will have to teach another
    to know me, their Lord.'

"All of them will know me,
    no matter who they are.
[12] I will treat them with kindness,
even though they are wicked.
    I will forget their sins."

[13]When the Lord talks about a new agreement, he means that the first one is out of date. And anything that is old and useless will soon disappear.

The Tent in Heaven

9 The first promise that was made included rules for worship and a tent for worship here on earth. [2]The first part of the tent was called the holy place, and a lampstand, a table, and the sacred loaves of bread were kept there.

[3]Behind the curtain was the most holy place. [4]The gold altar that was used for burning incense was in this holy place. The gold-covered sacred chest was also there, and inside it were three things. First, there was a gold jar filled with manna.[p] Then there was Aaron's walking stick that sprouted.[q] Finally, there were the flat stones with the Ten Commandments written on them. [5]On top of the chest were the glorious creatures with wings[r] opened out above the place of mercy.[s]

Now isn't the time to go into detail about these things. [6]But this is how everything was when the priests went each day into the first part of the tent to do their duties. [7]However, only the high priest could go into the second part of the tent, and he went in only once a year. Each time he carried blood to offer for his sins and for any sins that the people had committed without meaning to.

[8]All of this is the Holy Spirit's way of saying that no one could enter the most holy place while the tent was still the place of worship. [9]This also has a meaning for today. It shows that we cannot make our consciences clear by offering gifts and sacrifices. [10]These rules are merely about such things as eating and drinking and ceremonies for washing ourselves. And rules about physical things will last only until the time comes to change them for something better.

[11]Christ came as the high priest of the good things that are now here.[t] He also went into a much better tent that wasn't made by humans and that doesn't belong to this world. [12]Then Christ went once for all into the most holy place and freed us from sin forever. He did this by offering his own blood instead of the blood of goats and bulls.

---

[o]**8.2** *most holy place*: See the note at 6.19.   [p]**9.4** *manna*: When the people of Israel were wandering through the desert, the Lord provided them with food that could be made into thin wafers. This food was called manna, which in Hebrew means "What is it?"   [q]**9.4** *Aaron's walking stick that sprouted*: According to Numbers 17.1-11, Aaron's walking stick sprouted and produced almonds to show that the Lord was pleased with him and Moses.
[r]**9.5** *glorious creatures with wings*: Two of these creatures (called "cherubim" in Hebrew and Greek) with outspread wings were on top of the sacred chest and were symbols of God's throne.   [s]**9.5** *place of mercy*: The lid of the sacred chest, which was thought to be God's throne on earth.   [t]**9.11** *that are now here*: Some manuscripts have "that were coming."

¹³According to the Law of Moses, those people who become unclean are not fit to worship God. Yet they will be considered clean, if they are sprinkled with the blood of goats and bulls and with the ashes of a sacrificed calf. ¹⁴But Christ was sinless, and he offered himself as an eternal and spiritual sacrifice to God. That's why his blood is much more powerful and makes our[u] consciences clear. Now we can serve the living God and no longer do things that lead to death.

¹⁵Christ died to rescue those who had sinned and broken the old agreement. Now he brings his chosen ones a new agreement with its guarantee of God's eternal blessings! ¹⁶In fact, making an agreement of this kind is like writing a will. This is because the one who makes the will must die before it is of any use. ¹⁷In other words, a will doesn't go into effect as long as the one who made it is still alive.

¹⁸Blood was also used[v] to put the first agreement into effect. ¹⁹Moses told the people all that the Law said they must do. Then he used red wool and a hyssop plant to sprinkle the people and the book of the Law with the blood of bulls and goats[w] and with water. ²⁰He told the people, "With this blood God makes his agreement with you." ²¹Moses also sprinkled blood on the tent and on everything else that was used in worship. ²²The Law says that almost everything must be sprinkled with blood, and no sins can be forgiven unless blood is offered.

Christ's Great Sacrifice

²³These things are only copies of what is in heaven, and so they had to be made holy by these ceremonies. But the real things in heaven must be made holy by something better. ²⁴This is why Christ did not go into a tent that had been made by humans and was only a copy of the real one. Instead, he went into heaven and is now there with God to help us.

²⁵Christ did not have to offer himself many times. He wasn't like a high priest who goes into the most holy place each year to offer the blood of an animal. ²⁶If he had offered himself every year, he would have suffered many times since the creation of the world. But instead, near the end of time he offered himself once and for all, so that he could be a sacrifice that does away with sin.

²⁷We die only once, and then we are judged. ²⁸So Christ died only once to take away the sins of many people. But when he comes again, it will not be to take away sin. He will come to save everyone who is waiting for him.

10 The Law of Moses is like a shadow of the good things to come. This shadow isn't the good things themselves, because it cannot free people from sin by the sacrifices that are offered year after year. ²If there were worshipers who already have their sins washed away and their consciences made clear, there would not be any need to go on offering sacrifices. ³⁻⁴But the blood of bulls and goats cannot take away sins. It only reminds people of their sins from one year to the next.

⁵When Christ came into the world, he said to God,

"Sacrifices and offerings
    are not what you want,
but you have given me
    my body.
⁶ No, you are not pleased
with animal sacrifices
    and offerings for sin."

⁷Then Christ said,

"And so, my God,
    I have come to do
what you want,
    as the Scriptures say."

⁸The Law teaches that offerings and sacrifices must be made because of sin. But why did Christ mention these things and say that God did not want them? ⁹Well, it was to do away with offerings and sacrifices and to replace them. That is what he meant by saying to God, "I have come to do what you want." ¹⁰So we are made holy because Christ obeyed God and offered himself once for all.

¹¹The priests do their work each day, and they keep on offering sacrifices that can never take away sins. ¹²But Christ offered himself as a sacrifice that is good forever. Now he is sitting at God's right side,[x] ¹³and he will stay there until his enemies are put under his power. ¹⁴By his one sacrifice he has forever set free from sin the people he brings to God.

¹⁵The Holy Spirit also speaks of this by telling us that the Lord said,

¹⁶ "When the time comes,
I will make an agreement
    with them.
I will write my laws
    on their minds and hearts.
¹⁷ Then I will forget
    about their sins
and no longer remember
    their evil deeds."

[u]**9.14** _our_: Some manuscripts have "your," and others have "their."   [v]**9.18** _Blood was also used_: Or "There also had to be a death."   [w]**9.19** _blood of bulls and goats_: Some manuscripts do not have "and goats."   [x]**10.12** _right side_: See the note at 1.3.

¹⁸When sins are forgiven, there is no more need to offer sacrifices.

Encouragement and Warning

¹⁹My friends, the blood of Jesus gives us courage to enter the most holy place ²⁰by a new way that leads to life! And this way takes us through the curtain that is Christ himself.

²¹We have a great high priest who is in charge of God's house. ²²So let's come near God with pure hearts and a confidence that comes from having faith. Let's keep our hearts pure, our consciences free from evil, and our bodies washed with clean water. ²³We must hold tightly to the hope that we say is ours. After all, we can trust the one who made the agreement with us. ²⁴We should keep on encouraging each other to be thoughtful and to do helpful things. ²⁵Some people have gotten out of the habit of meeting for worship, but we must not do that. We should keep on encouraging each other, especially since you know that the day of the Lord's coming is getting closer.

²⁶No sacrifices can be made for people who decide to sin after they find out about the truth. ²⁷They are God's enemies, and all they can look forward to is a terrible judgment and a furious fire. ²⁸If two or more witnesses accused someone of breaking the Law of Moses, that person could be put to death. ²⁹But it is much worse to dishonor God's Son and to disgrace the blood of the promise that made us holy. And it is just as bad to insult the Holy Spirit, who shows us mercy. ³⁰We know that God has said he will punish and take revenge. We also know that the Scriptures say the Lord will judge his people. ³¹It is a terrible thing to fall into the hands of the living God!

³²Don't forget all the hard times you went through when you first received the light. ³³Sometimes you were abused and mistreated in public, and at other times you shared in the sufferings of others. ³⁴You were kind to people in jail. And you gladly let your possessions be taken away, because you knew you had something better, something that would last forever.

³⁵Keep on being brave! It will bring you great rewards. ³⁶Learn to be patient, so that you will please God and be given what he has promised. ³⁷As the Scriptures say,

"God is coming soon!
    It won't be very long.
³⁸ The people God accepts
    will live because
        of their faith.ʸ

But he isn't pleased
    with anyone
        who turns back."

³⁹We are not like those people who turn back and get destroyed. We will keep on having faith until we are saved.

The Great Faith of God's People

11 Faith makes us sure of what we hope for and gives us proof of what we cannot see. ²It was their faith that made our ancestors pleasing to God.

³Because of our faith, we know that the world was made at God's command. We also know that what can be seen was made out of what cannot be seen.

⁴Because Abel had faith, he offered God a better sacrifice than Cain did. God was pleased with him and his gift, and even though Abel is now dead, his faith still speaks for him.

⁵Enoch had faith and did not die. He pleased God, and God took him up to heaven. That's why his body was never found. ⁶But without faith no one can please God. We must believe that God is real and that he rewards everyone who searches for him.

⁷Because Noah had faith, he was warned about something that had not yet happened. He obeyed and built a boat that saved him and his family. In this way the people of the world were judged, and Noah was given the blessings that come to everyone who pleases God.

⁸Abraham had faith and obeyed God. He was told to go to the land that God had said would be his, and he left for a country he had never seen. ⁹Because Abraham had faith, he lived as a stranger in the promised land. He lived there in a tent, and so did Isaac and Jacob, who were later given the same promise. ¹⁰Abraham did this, because he was waiting for the eternal city that God had planned and built.

¹¹Even when Sarah was too old to have children, she had faith that God would do what he had promised, and she had a son. ¹²Her husband Abraham was almost dead, but he became the ancestor of many people. In fact, there are as many of them as there are stars in the sky or grains of sand along the beach.

¹³Every one of those people died. But they still had faith, even though they had not received what they had been promised. They were glad just to see these things from far away, and they agreed that they were only strangers and foreigners on this earth. ¹⁴When

---

ʸ**10.38** *The people God accepts will live because of their faith*: Or "The people God accepts because of their faith will live."

people talk this way, it is clear that they are looking for a place to call their own. 15If they had been talking about the land where they had once lived, they could have gone back at any time. 16But they were looking forward to a better home in heaven. That's why God wasn't ashamed for them to call him their God. He even built a city for them.

17-18Abraham had been promised that Isaac, his only son,z would continue his family. But when Abraham was tested, he had faith and was willing to sacrifice Isaac, 19because he was sure that God could raise people to life. This was just like getting Isaac back from death.

20Isaac had faith, and he promised blessings to Jacob and Esau. 21Later, when Jacob was about to die, he leaned on his walking stick and worshiped. Then because of his faith he blessed each of Joseph's sons. 22And right before Joseph died, he had faith that God would lead the people of Israel out of Egypt. So he told them to take his bones with them.

23Because Moses' parents had faith, they kept him hidden until he was three months old. They saw that he was a beautiful child, and they were not afraid to disobey the king's orders.a 24Then after Moses grew up, his faith made him refuse to be called the king's grandson. 25He chose to be mistreated with God's people instead of having the good time that sin could bring for a little while. 26Moses knew that the treasures of Egypt were not as wonderful as what he would receive from suffering for the Messiah,b and he looked forward to his reward.

27Because of his faith, Moses left Egypt. Moses had seen the invisible God and wasn't afraid of the king's anger. 28His faith also made him celebrate Passover. He sprinkled the blood of animals on the doorposts, so that the firstborn sons of the people of Israel would not be killed by the destroying angel.

29Because of their faith, the people walked through the Red Seac on dry land. But when the Egyptians tried to do it, they were drowned.

30God's people had faith, and when they had walked around the city of Jericho for seven days, its walls fell down.

31Rahab had been a prostitute, but she had faith and welcomed the spies. So she wasn't killed with the people who disobeyed.

32What else can I say? There isn't enough time to tell about Gideon, Barak, Samson, Jephthah, David, Samuel, and the prophets. 33Their faith helped them conquer kingdoms, and because they did right, God made promises to them. They closed the jaws of lions 34and put out raging fires and escaped from the swords of their enemies. Although they were weak, they were given the strength and power to chase foreign armies away.

35Some women received their loved ones back from death. Many of these people were tortured, but they refused to be released. They were sure that they would get a better reward when the dead are raised to life. 36Others were made fun of and beaten with whips, and some were chained in jail. 37Still others were stoned to death or sawed in twod or killed with swords. Some had nothing but sheep skins or goat skins to wear. They were poor, mistreated, and tortured. 38The world did not deserve these good people, who had to wander in deserts and on mountains and had to live in caves and holes in the ground.

39All of them pleased God because of their faith! But still they died without being given what had been promised. 40This was because God had something better in store for us. And he did not want them to reach the goal of their faith without us.

A Large Crowd of Witnesses

12 Such a large crowd of witnesses is all around us! So we must get rid of everything that slows us down, especially the sin that just won't let go. And we must be determined to run the race that is ahead of us. 2We must keep our eyes on Jesus, who leads us and makes our faith complete. He endured the shame of being nailed to a cross, because he knew that later on he would be glad he did. Now he is seated at the right sidee of God's throne! 3So keep your mind on Jesus, who put up with many insults from sinners. Then you won't get discouraged and give up.

4None of you have yet been hurtf in your battle against sin. 5But you have

---

z11.17,18 _his only son_: Although Abraham had a son by a slave woman, his son Isaac was considered his only son, because he was born as a result of God's promise to Abraham. a11.23 _the king's orders_: The king of Egypt ordered all Israelite baby boys to be left outside of their homes, so they would die or be killed.   b11.26 _the Messiah_: Or "Christ." c11.29 _Red Sea_: This name comes from the Bible of the early Christians, a translation made into Greek about 200 B.C. It refers to the body of water that the Israelites crossed and was one of the marshes or fresh water lakes near the eastern part of the Nile Delta, where they lived and where the towns of Exodus 13.17—14.9 were located.   d11.37 _sawed in two_: Some manuscripts have "tested" or "tempted."   e12.2 _right side_: See the note at 1.3.   f12.4 _hurt_: Or "killed."

forgotten that the Scriptures say to God's children,

> "When the Lord punishes you,
>   don't make light of it,
> and when he corrects you,
>   don't be discouraged.
> 6 The Lord corrects the people
>   he loves
> and disciplines those
>   he calls his own."

[7]Be patient when you are being corrected. Don't all parents correct their children? [8]God corrects all of his children, and if he doesn't correct you, then you don't really belong to him. [9]Our earthly fathers correct us, and we still respect them. Isn't it even better to be given true life by letting our spiritual Father correct us?

[10]Our human fathers correct us for a short time, and they do it as they think best. But God corrects us for our own good, because he wants us to be holy, as he is. [11]It is never fun to be corrected. In fact, at the time it is always painful. But if we learn to obey by being corrected, we will do right and live at peace.

[12]Now stand up straight! Stop your knees from shaking [13]and walk a straight path. Then lame people will be healed, instead of getting worse.

Warning against Turning from God

[14]Try to live at peace with everyone! Live a clean life. If you don't, you will never see the Lord. [15]Make sure that no one misses out on God's wonderful kindness. Don't let anyone become bitter and cause trouble for the rest of you. [16]Watch out for immoral and ungodly people like Esau, who sold his future blessing[g] for only one meal. [17]You know how he later wanted it back. But there was nothing he could do to change things, even though he begged his father and cried.

[18]You have not come to a place like Mount Sinai[h] that can be seen and touched. There is no flaming fire or dark cloud or storm [19]or trumpet sound. The people of Israel heard a voice speak. But they begged it to stop, [20]because they could not obey its commands. They were even told to kill any animal that touched the mountain. [21]The sight was so frightening that Moses said he shook with fear.

[22]You have now come to Mount Zion and to the heavenly Jerusalem. This is the city of the living God, where thousands and thousands of angels have come to celebrate. [23]Here you will find all of God's dearest children,[i] whose names are written in heaven. And you will find God himself, who judges everyone. Here also are the spirits of those good people who have been made perfect. [24]And Jesus is here! He is the one who makes God's new agreement with us, and his sprinkled blood says much better things than the blood of Abel.[j]

[25]Make sure that you obey the one who speaks to you. The people did not escape, when they refused to obey the one who spoke to them at Mount Sinai. Do you think you can possibly escape, if you refuse to obey the one who speaks to you from heaven? [26]When God spoke the first time, his voice shook only the earth. This time he has promised to shake the earth once again, and heaven too.

[27]The words "once again" mean that these created things will someday be shaken and removed. Then what cannot be shaken will last. [28]We should be grateful that we were given a kingdom that cannot be shaken. And in this kingdom we please God by worshiping him and by showing him great honor and respect. [29]Our God is like a destructive fire!

Service That Pleases God

13 Keep being concerned about each other as the Lord's followers should.

[2]Be sure to welcome strangers into your home. By doing this, some people have welcomed angels as guests, without even knowing it.

[3]Remember the Lord's people who are in jail and be concerned for them. Don't forget those who are suffering, but imagine that you are there with them.

[4]Have respect for marriage. Always be faithful to your partner, because God will punish anyone who is immoral or unfaithful in marriage.

[5]Don't fall in love with money. Be satisfied with what you have. The Lord has promised that he will not leave us or desert us. [6]That should make you feel like saying,

> "The Lord helps me!
> Why should I be afraid
>   of what people
>   can do to me?"

[7]Don't forget about your leaders who taught you God's message. Remember

---

[g]**12.16** *sold his future blessing*: As the first-born son, Esau had certain privileges that were known as a "birthright." [h]**12.18** *a place like Mount Sinai*: The Greek text has "a place," but the writer is referring to the time that the Lord spoke to the people of Israel from Mount Sinai (see Exodus 19.16-25). [i]**12.23** *all of God's dearest children*: The Greek text has "the gathering of the first-born children" (see the note at 1.6). [j]**12.24** *blood of Abel*: Cain and Abel were the two sons of Adam and Eve. Cain murdered Abel (see Genesis 4.1-16).

what kind of lives they lived and try to have faith like theirs.

[8]Jesus Christ never changes! He is the same yesterday, today, and forever. [9]Don't be fooled by any kind of strange teachings. It is better to receive strength from God's undeserved kindness than to depend on certain foods. After all, these foods don't really help the people who eat them. [10]But we have an altar where even the priests who serve in the place of worship have no right to eat.

[11]After the high priest offers the blood of animals as a sin offering, the bodies of those animals are burned outside the camp. [12]Jesus himself suffered outside the city gate, so that his blood would make people holy. [13]That's why we should go outside the camp to Jesus and share in his disgrace. [14]On this earth we don't have a city that lasts forever, but we are waiting for such a city.

[15]Our sacrifice is to keep offering praise to God in the name of Jesus. [16]But don't forget to help others and to share your possessions with them. This too is like offering a sacrifice that pleases God.

[17]Obey your leaders and do what they say. They are watching over you, and they must answer to God. So don't make them sad as they do their work. Make them happy. Otherwise, they won't be able to help you at all.

[18]Pray for us. Our consciences are clear, and we always try to live right. [19]I especially want you to pray that I can visit you again soon.

Final Prayers and Greetings

[20]God gives peace, and he raised our Lord Jesus Christ from death. Now Jesus is like a Great Shepherd whose blood was used to make God's eternal agreement with his flock.[k] [21]I pray that God will make you ready to obey him and that you will always be eager to do right. May Jesus help you do what pleases God. To Jesus Christ be glory forever and ever! Amen.

[22]My friends, I have written only a short letter to encourage you, and I beg you to pay close attention to what I have said.

[23]By now you surely must know that our friend Timothy is out of jail. If he gets here in time, I will bring him with me when I come to visit you.

[24]Please give my greetings to your leaders and to the rest of the Lord's people.

His followers from Italy send you their greetings.

[25]I pray that God will be kind to all of you![l]

---

[k]**13.20** _whose blood was used to make God's eternal agreement with his flock_: See 9.18-22.
[l]**13.25** _to all of you!_: Some manuscripts add "Amen."

JAMES

ABOUT THIS LETTER

This is a good example of a general letter, because it is addressed to Christians scattered throughout the Roman Empire. Though written as a letter, it is more like a short book of instructions for daily living.

For James faith means action! In fact, the entire book is a series of examples that show faith in action in wise and practical ways.

His advice was clear and to the point: If you are poor, don't despair! Don't give up when your faith is being tested. Don't get angry quickly. Don't favor the rich over the poor. Do good things for others. Control your tongue and desires. Surrender to God and rely on his wisdom. Resist the devil. Don't brag about what you are going to do. If you are rich, use your money to help the poor. Be patient and kind, and pray for those who need God's help.

A QUICK LOOK AT THIS LETTER

Greetings (1.1)
A Life of Faith and Wisdom (1.2-18)
Hearing and Obeying God's Message (1.19-27)
Don't Favor the Rich and Powerful (2.1-13)
Faith and Works (2.14-26)
Wisdom and Words (3.1-18)
Warning against Friendship with the World (4.1—5.6)
Patience, Kindness, and Prayer (5.7-20)

---

1 From James, a servant of God and of our Lord Jesus Christ.
Greetings to the twelve tribes scattered all over the world.[a]

Faith and Wisdom

[2]My friends, be glad, even if you have a lot of trouble. [3]You know that you learn to endure by having your faith tested. [4]But you must learn to endure everything, so that you will be completely mature and not lacking in anything.

[5]If any of you need wisdom, you should ask God, and it will be given to you. God is generous and won't correct you for asking. [6]But when you ask for something, you must have faith and not doubt. Anyone who doubts is like an ocean wave tossed around in a storm. [7-8]If you are that kind of person, you can't make up your mind, and you surely can't be trusted. So don't expect the Lord to give you anything at all.

Poor People and Rich People

[9]Any of God's people who are poor should be glad that he thinks so highly of them. [10]But any who are rich should be glad when God makes them humble. Rich people will disappear like wild flowers [11]scorched by the burning heat of the sun. The flowers lose their blossoms, and their beauty is destroyed. That is how the rich will disappear, as they go about their business.

Trials and Temptations

[12]God will bless you, if you don't give up when your faith is being tested. He will reward you with a glorious life,[b] just as he rewards everyone who loves him.

[13]Don't blame God when you are

---

[a]1.1 *twelve tribes scattered all over the world*: James is saying that the Lord's followers are like the tribes of Israel that were scattered everywhere by their enemies.   [b]1.12 *a glorious life*: The Greek text has "the crown of life." In ancient times an athlete who had won a contest was rewarded with a crown of flowers as a sign of victory.

tempted! God cannot be tempted by evil, and he doesn't use evil to tempt others. [14]We are tempted by our own desires that drag us off and trap us. [15]Our desires make us sin, and when sin is finished with us, it leaves us dead.

[16]Don't be fooled, my dear friends. [17]Every good and perfect gift comes down from the Father who created all the lights in the heavens. He is always the same and never makes dark shadows by changing. [18]He wanted us to be his own special people,[c] and so he sent the true message to give us new birth.

Hearing and Obeying

[19]My dear friends, you should be quick to listen and slow to speak or to get angry. [20]If you are angry, you cannot do any of the good things that God wants done. [21]You must stop doing anything immoral or evil. Instead be humble and accept the message that is planted in you to save you.

[22]Obey God's message! Don't fool yourselves by just listening to it. [23]If you hear the message and don't obey it, you are like people who stare at themselves in a mirror [24]and forget what they look like as soon as they leave. [25]But you must never stop looking at the perfect law that sets you free. God will bless you in everything you do, if you listen and obey, and don't just hear and forget.

[26]If you think you are being religious, but can't control your tongue, you are fooling yourself, and everything you do is useless. [27]Religion that pleases God the Father must be pure and spotless. You must help needy orphans and widows and not let this world make you evil.

Warning against Having Favorites

2 My friends, if you have faith in our glorious Lord Jesus Christ, you won't treat some people better than others. [2]Suppose a rich person wearing fancy clothes and a gold ring comes to one of your meetings. And suppose a poor person dressed in worn-out clothes also comes. [3]You must not give the best seat to the one in fancy clothes and tell the one who is poor to stand at the side or sit on the floor. [4]That is the same as saying that some people are better than others, and you would be acting like a crooked judge.

[5]My dear friends, pay attention. God has given a lot of faith to the poor people in this world. He has also promised them a share in his kingdom that he will give to everyone who loves him. [6]You mistreat the poor. But isn't it the rich who boss you around and drag you off to court? [7]Aren't they the ones who make fun of your Lord?

[8]You will do all right, if you obey the most important law[d] in the Scriptures. It is the law that commands us to love others as much as we love ourselves. [9]But if you treat some people better than others, you have done wrong, and the Scriptures teach that you have sinned.

[10]If you obey every law except one, you are still guilty of breaking them all. [11]The same God who told us to be faithful in marriage also told us not to murder. So even if you are faithful in marriage, but murder someone, you still have broken God's Law.

[12]Speak and act like people who will be judged by the law that sets us free. [13]Do this, because on the day of judgment there will be no pity for those who have not had pity on others. But even in judgment, God is merciful![e]

Faith and Works

[14]My friends, what good is it to say you have faith, when you don't do anything to show that you really do have faith? Can that kind of faith save you? [15]If you know someone who doesn't have any clothes or food, [16]you shouldn't just say, "I hope all goes well for you. I hope you will be warm and have plenty to eat." What good is it to say this, unless you do something to help? [17]Faith that doesn't lead us to do good deeds is all alone and dead!

[18]Suppose someone disagrees and says, "It is possible to have faith without doing kind deeds."

I would answer, "Prove that you have faith without doing kind deeds, and I will prove that I have faith by doing them." [19]You surely believe there is only one God. That's fine. Even demons believe this, and it makes them shake with fear.

[20]Does some stupid person want proof that faith without deeds is useless? [21]Well, our ancestor Abraham pleased God by putting his son Isaac on the altar to sacrifice him. [22]Now you see how Abraham's faith and deeds worked together. He proved that his faith was real by what he did. [23]This is what the Scriptures mean by saying, "Abraham had faith in God, and God was pleased with him." That's how Abraham became God's friend.

[24]You can now see that we please God

---

[c]**1.18** _his own special people_: The Greek text has "the first of his creatures." The Law of Moses taught that the first-born of all animals and the first part of the harvest were special and belonged to the Lord.   [d]**2.8** _most important law_: The Greek text has "royal law," meaning the one given by the king (that is, God).   [e]**2.13** _But even in judgment, God is merciful!_: Or "So be merciful, and you will be shown mercy on the day of judgment."

by what we do and not only by what we believe. 25For example, Rahab had been a prostitute. But she pleased God when she welcomed the spies and sent them home by another way.

26Anyone who doesn't breathe is dead, and faith that doesn't do anything is just as dead!

The Tongue

3 My friends, we should not all try to become teachers. In fact, teachers will be judged more strictly than others. 2All of us do many wrong things. But if you can control your tongue, you are mature and able to control your whole body.

3By putting a bit into the mouth of a horse, we can turn the horse in different directions. 4It takes strong winds to move a large sailing ship, but the captain uses only a small rudder to make it go in any direction. 5Our tongues are small too, and yet they brag about big things.

It takes only a spark to start a forest fire! 6The tongue is like a spark. It is an evil power that dirties the rest of the body and sets a person's entire life on fire with flames that come from hell itself. 7All kinds of animals, birds, reptiles, and sea creatures can be tamed and have been tamed. 8But our tongues get out of control. They are restless and evil, and always spreading deadly poison.

9-10My dear friends, with our tongues we speak both praises and curses. We praise our Lord and Father, and we curse people who were created to be like God, and this isn't right. 11Can clean water and dirty water both flow from the same spring? 12Can a fig tree produce olives or a grapevine produce figs? Does fresh water come from a well full of salt water?

Wisdom from Above

13Are any of you wise or sensible? Then show it by living right and by being humble and wise in everything you do. 14But if your heart is full of bitter jealousy and selfishness, don't brag or lie to cover up the truth. 15That kind of wisdom doesn't come from above. It is earthly and selfish and comes from the devil himself. 16Whenever people are jealous or selfish, they cause trouble and do all sorts of cruel things. 17But the wisdom that comes from above leads us to be pure, friendly, gentle, sensible, kind, helpful, genuine, and sincere. 18When peacemakers plant seeds of peace, they will harvest justice.

Friendship with the World

4 Why do you fight and argue with each other? Isn't it because you are full of selfish desires that fight to control your body? 2You want something you don't have, and you will do anything to get it. You will even kill! But you still cannot get what you want, and you won't get it by fighting and arguing. You should pray for it. 3Yet even when you do pray, your prayers are not answered, because you pray just for selfish reasons.

4You people aren't faithful to God! Don't you know that if you love the world, you are God's enemies? And if you decide to be a friend of the world, you make yourself an enemy of God. 5Do you doubt the Scriptures that say, "God truly cares about the Spirit he has put in us"?f 6In fact, God treats us with even greater kindness, just as the Scriptures say,

"God opposes everyone
  who is proud,
but he is kind to everyone
  who is humble."

7Surrender to God! Resist the devil, and he will run from you. 8Come near to God, and he will come near to you. Clean up your lives, you sinners. Purify your hearts, you people who can't make up your mind. 9Be sad and sorry and weep. Stop laughing and start crying. Be gloomy instead of glad. 10Be humble in the Lord's presence, and he will honor you.

Saying Cruel Things about Others

11My friends, don't say cruel things about others! If you do, or if you condemn others, you are condemning God's Law. And if you condemn the Law, you put yourself above the Law and refuse to obey either it 12or God who gave it. God is our judge, and he can save or destroy us. What right do you have to condemn anyone?

Warning against Bragging

13You should know better than to say, "Today or tomorrow we will go to the city. We will do business there for a year and make a lot of money!" 14What do you know about tomorrow? How can you be so sure about your life? It is nothing more than mist that appears for only a little while before it disappears. 15You should say, "If the Lord lets us live, we will do these things." 16Yet you are stupid enough to brag, and it is wrong to be so proud. 17If you don't do what you know is right, you have sinned.

---

f4.5 *God truly cares about the Spirit he has put in us*: One possible meaning for the difficult Greek text; other translations are possible, such as, "the Spirit that God put in us truly cares."

Warning to the Rich

5 You rich people should cry and weep! Terrible things are going to happen to you. [2]Your treasures have already rotted, and moths have eaten your clothes. [3]Your money has rusted, and the rust will be evidence against you, as it burns your body like fire. Yet you keep on storing up wealth in these last days. [4]You refused to pay the people who worked in your fields, and now their unpaid wages are shouting out against you. The Lord All-Powerful has surely heard the cries of the workers who harvested your crops.

[5]While here on earth, you have thought only of filling your own stomachs and having a good time. But now you are like fat cattle on their way to be butchered. [6]You have condemned and murdered innocent people, who couldn't even fight back.

Be Patient and Kind

[7]My friends, be patient until the Lord returns. Think of farmers who wait patiently for the spring and summer rains to make their valuable crops grow. [8]Be patient like those farmers and don't give up. The Lord will soon be here! [9]Don't grumble about each other or you will be judged, and the judge is right outside the door.

[10]My friends, follow the example of the prophets who spoke for the Lord. They were patient, even when they had to suffer. [11]In fact, we praise the ones who endured the most. You remember how patient Job was and how the Lord finally helped him. The Lord did this because he is so merciful and kind.

[12]My friends, above all else, don't take an oath. You must not swear by heaven or by earth or by anything else. "Yes" or "No" is all you need to say. If you say anything more, you will be condemned.

[13]If you are having trouble, you should pray. And if you are feeling good, you should sing praises. [14]If you are sick, ask the church leaders[g] to come and pray for you. Ask them to put olive oil[h] on you in the name of the Lord. [15]If you have faith when you pray for sick people, they will get well. The Lord will heal them, and if they have sinned, he will forgive them.

[16]If you have sinned, you should tell each other what you have done. Then you can pray for one another and be healed. The prayer of an innocent person is powerful, and it can help a lot. [17]Elijah was just as human as we are, and for three and a half years his prayers kept the rain from falling. [18]But when he did pray for rain, it fell from the skies and made the crops grow.

[19]My friends, if any followers have wandered away from the truth, you should try to lead them back. [20]If you turn sinners from the wrong way, you will save them from death, and many of their sins will be forgiven.

---

[g]**5.14** *church leaders*: Or "elders" or "presbyters" or "priests."   [h]**5.14** *olive oil*: The Jewish people used olive oil for healing.

1 PETER

np. practice

ABOUT THIS LETTER

In this letter Peter has much to say about suffering. He shows how it can be a way of serving the Lord, of sharing the faith, and of being tested. The letter was written to Christians scattered all over the northern part of Asia Minor. In this part of the Roman Empire many Christians had already suffered unfair treatment from people who did not believe in Jesus. And they could expect to suffer even more.

Peter was quick to offer encouragement. His letter reminds the readers that some of the Lord's followers may have to go through times of hard testing. But this should make them glad, Peter declares, because it will strengthen their faith and bring them honor on the day when Jesus Christ returns (1.6, 7).

Peter reminds them that Christ suffered here on earth, and when his followers suffer for doing right they are sharing his sufferings (2.18-25; 4.12-17). In fact, Christians should expect to suffer for their faith (3.8—4.19).

But because of who God is and because of what God has done by raising Jesus Christ from death, Christians can have hope in the future. Just as Christ suffered before he received honor from God, so will Christians be tested by suffering before they receive honor when the Lord returns. Peter uses poetic language to remind his readers of what Christ has done:

> Christ died once for our sins.
> An *innocent* person died
>   for those who are guilty.
> Christ did this
>   to bring you to God,
> when his body
>   was put to death
> and his spirit
>   was made alive.   (3.18)

A QUICK LOOK AT THIS LETTER

---

1 From Peter, an apostle of Jesus Christ. To God's people who are scattered like foreigners in Pontus, Galatia, Cappadocia, Asia, and Bithynia.

²God the Father decided to choose you as his people, and his Spirit has made you holy. You have obeyed Jesus Christ and are sprinkled with his blood.*a*

a 1.2 *sprinkled with his blood*: According to Exodus 24.3-8 the people of Israel were sprinkled with the blood of cows to show they would keep their agreement with God. Peter says that it is the blood of Jesus that seals the agreement between God and his people (see Hebrews 9.18-21).

I pray that God will be kind to you and will keep on giving you peace!

A Real Reason for Hope

³Praise God, the Father of our Lord Jesus Christ. God is so good, and by raising Jesus from death, he has given us new life and a hope that lives on. ⁴God has something stored up for you in heaven, where it will never decay or be ruined or disappear.

⁵You have faith in God, whose power will protect you until the last day.[b] Then he will save you, just as he has always planned to do. ⁶On that day you will be glad, even if you have to go through many hard trials for a while. ⁷Your faith will be like gold that has been tested in a fire. And these trials will prove that your faith is worth much more than gold that can be destroyed. They will show that you will be given praise and honor and glory when Jesus Christ returns.

⁸You have never seen Jesus, and you don't see him now. But still you love him and have faith in him, and no words can tell how glad and happy ⁹you are to be saved. That's why you have faith.

¹⁰Some prophets told how kind God would be to you, and they searched hard to find out more about the way you would be saved. ¹¹The Spirit of Christ was in them and was telling them how Christ would suffer and would then be given great honor. So they searched to find out exactly who Christ would be and when this would happen. ¹²But they were told that they were serving you and not themselves. They preached to you by the power of the Holy Spirit, who was sent from heaven. And their message was only for you, even though angels would like to know more about it.

Chosen To Live a Holy Life

¹³Be alert and think straight. Put all your hope in how kind God will be to you when Jesus Christ appears. ¹⁴Behave like obedient children. Don't let your lives be controlled by your desires, as they used to be. ¹⁵Always live as God's holy people should, because God is the one who chose you, and he is holy. ¹⁶That's why the Scriptures say, "I am the holy God, and you must be holy too."

¹⁷You say that God is your Father, but God doesn't have favorites! He judges all people by what they do. So you must honor God while you live as strangers here on earth. ¹⁸You were rescued[c] from the useless way of life that you learned from your ancestors. But you know that you were not rescued by such things as silver or gold that don't last forever. ¹⁹You were rescued by the precious blood of Christ, that spotless and innocent lamb. ²⁰Christ was chosen even before the world was created, but because of you, he did not come until these last days. ²¹And when he did come, it was to lead you to have faith in God, who raised him from death and honored him in a glorious way. That's why you have put your faith and hope in God.

²²You obeyed the truth,[d] and your souls were made pure. Now you sincerely love each other. But you must keep on loving with all your heart. ²³Do this because God has given you new birth by his message that lives on forever. ²⁴The Scriptures say,

"Humans wither like grass,
and their glory fades
    like wild flowers.
Grass dries up,
and flowers fall
    to the ground.
²⁵ But what the Lord has said
    will stand forever."

Our good news to you is what the Lord has said.

A Living Stone and a Holy Nation

2 Stop being hateful! Quit trying to fool people, and start being sincere. Don't be jealous or say cruel things about others. ²Be like newborn babies who are thirsty for the pure spiritual milk that will help you grow and be saved. ³You have already found out how good the Lord really is.

⁴Come to Jesus Christ. He is the living stone that people have rejected, but which God has chosen and highly honored. ⁵And now you are living stones that are being used to build a spiritual house. You are also a group of holy priests, and with the help of Jesus Christ you will offer sacrifices that please God. ⁶It is just as God says in the Scriptures,

"Look! I am placing in Zion
a choice and precious
    cornerstone.
No one who has faith
in that one
    will be disappointed."

⁷You are followers of the Lord, and that stone is precious to you. But it isn't precious to those who refuse to follow

him. They are the builders who tossed aside the stone that turned out to be the most important one of all. [8]They disobeyed the message and stumbled and fell over that stone, because they were doomed.

[9]But you are God's chosen and special people. You are a group of royal priests and a holy nation. God has brought you out of darkness into his marvelous light. Now you must tell all the wonderful things that he has done. The Scriptures say,

[10] "Once you were nobody.
    Now you are God's people.
 At one time no one
    had pity on you.
 Now God has treated you
    with kindness.

Live as God's Servants Should

[11]Dear friends, you are foreigners and strangers on this earth. So I beg you not to surrender to those desires that fight against you. [12]Always let others see you behaving properly, even though they may still accuse you of doing wrong. Then on the day of judgment, they will honor God by telling the good things they saw you do.

[13]The Lord wants you to obey all human authorities, especially the Emperor, who rules over everyone. [14]You must also obey governors, because they are sent by the Emperor to punish criminals and to praise good citizens. [15]God wants you to silence stupid and ignorant people by doing right. [16]You are free, but still you are God's servants, and you must not use your freedom as an excuse for doing wrong. [17]Respect everyone and show special love for God's people. Honor God and respect the Emperor.

The Example of Christ's Suffering

[18]Servants, you must obey your masters and always show respect to them. Do this, not only to those who are kind and thoughtful, but also to those who are cruel. [19]God will bless you, even if others treat you unfairly for being loyal to him. [20]You don't gain anything by being punished for some wrong you have done. But God will bless you, if you have to suffer for doing something good. [21]After all, God chose you to suffer as you follow in the footsteps of Christ, who set an example by suffering for you.

[22] Christ did not sin
    or ever tell a lie.
[23] Although he was abused,
    he never tried to get even.
 And when he suffered,
    he made no threats.
 Instead, he had faith in God,
    who judges fairly.

[24] Christ carried the burden
    of our sins.
 He was nailed to the cross,
 so that we would stop sinning
    and start living right.
 By his cuts and bruises
    you are healed.
[25] You had wandered away
    like sheep.
 Now you have returned
    to the one
 who is your shepherd
    and protector.

Wives and Husbands

3 If you are a wife, you must put your husband first. Even if he opposes our message, you will win him over by what you do. No one else will have to say anything to him, [2]because he will see how you honor God and live a pure life. [3]Don't depend on things like fancy hairdos or gold jewelry or expensive clothes to make you look beautiful. [4]Be beautiful in your heart by being gentle and quiet. This kind of beauty will last, and God considers it very special.

[5]Long ago those women who worshiped God and put their hope in him made themselves beautiful by putting their husbands first. [6]For example, Sarah obeyed Abraham and called him her master. You are her true children, if you do right and don't let anything frighten you.

[7]If you are a husband, you should be thoughtful of your wife. Treat her with honor, because she isn't as strong as you are, and she shares with you in the gift of life. Then nothing will stand in the way of your prayers.

Suffering for Doing Right

[8]Finally, all of you should agree and have concern and love for each other. You should also be kind and humble. [9]Don't be hateful and insult people just because they are hateful and insult you. Instead, treat everyone with kindness. You are God's chosen ones, and he will bless you. The Scriptures say,

[10] "Do you really love life?
    Do you want to be happy?
 Then stop saying cruel things
    and quit telling lies.
[11] Give up your evil ways
    and do right,
 as you find and follow
 the road that leads
    to peace.
[12] The Lord watches over
    everyone who obeys him,
 and he listens
    to their prayers.
 But he opposes everyone
    who does evil."

¹³Can anyone really harm you for being eager to do good deeds? ¹⁴Even if you have to suffer for doing good things, God will bless you. So stop being afraid and don't worry about what people might do. ¹⁵Honor Christ and let him be the Lord of your life.

Always be ready to give an answer when someone asks you about your hope. ¹⁶Give a kind and respectful answer and keep your conscience clear. This way you will make people ashamed for saying bad things about your good conduct as a follower of Christ. ¹⁷You are better off to obey God and suffer for doing right than to suffer for doing wrong.

¹⁸ Christ died once for our sins.
An innocent person died
for those who are guilty.
Christ did this
to bring you to God,
when his body
was put to death
and his spirit
was made alive.

¹⁹Christ then preached to the spirits that were being kept in prison. ²⁰They had disobeyed God while Noah was building the boat, but God had been patient with them. Eight people went into that boat and were brought safely through the flood.

²¹Those flood waters were like baptism that now saves you. But baptism is more than just washing your body. It means turning to God with a clear conscience, because Jesus Christ was raised from death. ²²Christ is now in heaven, where he sits at the right side[e] of God. All angels, authorities, and powers are under his control.

Being Faithful to God

4 Christ suffered here on earth. Now you must be ready to suffer as he did, because suffering shows that you have stopped sinning. ²It means you have turned from your own desires and want to obey God for the rest of your life. ³You have already lived long enough like people who don't know God. You were immoral and followed your evil desires. You went around drinking and partying and carrying on. In fact, you even worshiped disgusting idols. ⁴Now your former friends wonder why you have stopped running around with them, and they curse you for it. ⁵But they will have to answer to God, who judges the living and the dead. ⁶The good news has even been preached to the dead,[f] so that after they have

been judged for what they have done in this life, their spirits will live with God.

⁷Everything will soon come to an end. So be serious and be sensible enough to pray.

⁸Most important of all, you must sincerely love each other, because love wipes away many sins.

⁹Welcome people into your home and don't grumble about it.

¹⁰Each of you has been blessed with one of God's many wonderful gifts to be used in the service of others. So use your gift well. ¹¹If you have the gift of speaking, preach God's message. If you have the gift of helping others, do it with the strength that God supplies. Everything should be done in a way that will bring honor to God because of Jesus Christ, who is glorious and powerful forever. Amen.

Suffering for Being a Christian

¹²Dear friends, don't be surprised or shocked that you are going through testing that is like walking through fire. ¹³Be glad for the chance to suffer as Christ suffered. It will prepare you for even greater happiness when he makes his glorious return.

¹⁴Count it a blessing when you suffer for being a Christian. This shows that God's glorious Spirit is with you. ¹⁵But you deserve to suffer if you are a murderer, a thief, a crook, or a busybody. ¹⁶Don't be ashamed to suffer for being a Christian. Praise God that you belong to him. ¹⁷God has already begun judging his own people. And if his judgment begins with us, imagine how terrible it will be for those who refuse to obey his message. The Scriptures say,

¹⁸ "If good people barely escape,
what will happen to sinners
and to others
who don't respect God?"

¹⁹If you suffer for obeying God, you must have complete faith in your faithful Creator and keep on doing right.

Helping Christian Leaders

5 Church leaders,[g] I am writing to encourage you. I too am a leader, as well as a witness to Christ's suffering, and I will share in his glory when it is shown to us.

²Just as shepherds watch over their sheep, you must watch over everyone God has placed in your care. Do it willingly in order to please God, and not simply because you think you must. Let it be something you want to do, instead of something you do merely to make

---

*e***3.22** *right side*: The place of honor and power. ᶠ**4.6** *the dead*: Either people who died after becoming followers of Christ or the people of Noah's day (see 3.19). ᵍ**5.1** *Church leaders*: Or "Elders" or "Presbyters" or "Priests."

money. [3]Don't be bossy to those people who are in your care, but set an example for them. [4]Then when Christ the Chief Shepherd returns, you will be given a crown that will never lose its glory.

[5]All of you young people should obey your elders. In fact, everyone should be humble toward everyone else. The Scriptures say,

"God opposes proud people,
but he helps everyone
    who is humble."

[6]Be humble in the presence of God's mighty power, and he will honor you when the time comes. [7]God cares for you, so turn all your worries over to him.

[8]Be on your guard and stay awake. Your enemy, the devil, is like a roaring lion, sneaking around to find someone to attack. [9]But you must resist the devil and stay strong in your faith. You know that all over the world the Lord's followers are suffering just as you are. [10]But God shows undeserved kindness to everyone. That's why he appointed Christ Jesus to choose you to share in his eternal glory. You will suffer for a while, but God will make you complete, steady, strong, and firm. [11]God will be in control forever! Amen.

Final Greetings

[12]Silvanus helped me write this short letter, and I consider him a faithful follower of the Lord. I wanted to encourage you and tell you how kind God really is, so that you will keep on having faith in him.

[13]Greetings from the Lord's followers in Babylon.[h] They are God's chosen ones.

Mark, who is like a son to me, sends his greetings too.

[14]Give each other a warm greeting. I pray that God will give peace to everyone who belongs to Christ.[i]

---

[h]**5.13** _Babylon_: This may be a secret name for the city of Rome.   [i]**5.14** Christ: Some manuscripts add "Amen."

2 PETER

ABOUT THIS LETTER

The writer of this letter wants the readers to know that Christians must live in a way that pleases God (1.3) and hold firmly to the truth they were given (1.12).

He warns them that false prophets and teachers had entered the Christian community and were trying to lead the Lord's followers away from the truth. But they will be punished for their evil deeds (2.1-22). When false teachers are at work, Christians must stick to their faith and be examples for others of right living. They must have understanding, self-control and patience, and they should show love for God and all people.

The readers must never forget that the Lord's return is certain, no matter what others may say (3.1-18):

Don't forget that for the Lord one day is the same as a thousand years, and a thousand years is the same as one day. The Lord isn't slow about keeping his promises, as some people think he is. In fact, God is patient, because he wants everyone to turn from sin and no one to be lost.
(3.8, 9)

A QUICK LOOK AT THIS LETTER

1 From Simon Peter, a servant and an apostle of Jesus Christ.

To everyone who shares with us in the privilege of believing that our God and Savior Jesus Christ will do what is just and fair.[a]

²I pray that God will be kind to you and will let you live in perfect peace! May you keep learning more and more about God and our Lord Jesus.

Living as the Lord's Followers

³We have everything we need to live a life that pleases God. It was all given to us by God's own power, when we learned that he had invited us to share in his wonderful goodness. ⁴God made great and marvelous promises, so that his nature would become part of us. Then we could escape our evil desires and the corrupt influences of this world.

⁵Do your best to improve your faith. You can do this by adding goodness, understanding, ⁶self-control, patience, devotion to God, ⁷concern for others, and love. ⁸If you keep growing in this way, it will show that what you know about our Lord Jesus Christ has made your lives useful and meaningful. ⁹But if you don't grow, you are like someone who is nearsighted or blind, and you have forgotten that your past sins are forgiven.

¹⁰My friends, you must do all you can to show that God has really chosen and selected you. If you keep on doing this, you won't stumble and fall. ¹¹Then our Lord and Savior Jesus Christ will give you a glorious welcome into his kingdom that will last forever.

¹²You are holding firmly to the truth

---

[a]**1.1** *To everyone who . . . just and fair*: Or "To everyone whose faith in the justice and fairness of our God and Savior Jesus Christ is as precious as our own faith."

that you were given. But I am still going to remind you of these things. [13]In fact, I think I should keep on reminding you until I leave this body. [14]And our Lord Jesus Christ has already told me that I will soon leave it behind. [15]That is why I am doing my best to make sure that each of you remembers all of this after I am gone.

The Message about the Glory of Christ

[16]When we told you about the power and the return of our Lord Jesus Christ, we were not telling clever stories that someone had made up. But with our own eyes we saw his true greatness. [17]God, our great and wonderful Father, truly honored him by saying, "This is my own dear Son, and I am pleased with him." [18]We were there with Jesus on the holy mountain and heard this voice speak from heaven.

[19]All of this makes us even more certain that what the prophets said is true. So you should pay close attention to their message, as you would to a lamp shining in some dark place. You must keep on paying attention until daylight comes and the morning star rises in your hearts. [20]But you need to realize that no one alone can understand any of the prophecies in the Scriptures. [21]The prophets did not think these things up on their own, but they were guided by the Spirit of God.

False Prophets and Teachers

2 Sometimes false prophets spoke to the people of Israel. False teachers will also sneak in and speak harmful lies to you. But these teachers don't really belong to the Master who paid a great price for them, and they will quickly destroy themselves. [2]Many people will follow their evil ways and cause others to tell lies about the true way. [3]They will be greedy and cheat you with smooth talk. But long ago God decided to punish them, and God doesn't sleep.

[4]God did not have pity on the angels that sinned. He had them tied up and thrown into the dark pits of hell until the time of judgment. [5]And during Noah's time, God did not have pity on the ungodly people of the world. He destroyed them with a flood, though he did save eight people, including Noah, who preached the truth.

[6]God punished the cities of Sodom and Gomorrah[b] by burning them to ashes, and this is a warning to anyone else who wants to sin.

[7-8]Lot lived right and was greatly troubled by the terrible way those wicked people were living. He was a good man, and day after day he suffered because of the evil things he saw and heard. So the Lord rescued him. [9]This shows that the Lord knows how to rescue godly people from their sufferings and to punish evil people while they wait for the day of judgment.

[10]The Lord is especially hard on people who disobey him and don't think of anything except their own filthy desires. They are reckless and proud and are not afraid of cursing the glorious beings in heaven. [11]Although angels are more powerful than these evil beings,[c] even the angels don't dare to accuse them to the Lord.

[12]These people are no better than senseless animals that live by their feelings and are born to be caught and killed. They speak evil of things they don't know anything about. But their own corrupt deeds will destroy them. [13]They have done evil, and they will be rewarded with evil.

They think it is fun to have wild parties during the day. They are immoral, and the meals they eat with you are spoiled by the shameful and selfish way they carry on.[d] [14]All they think about is having sex with someone else's husband or wife. There is no end to their wicked deeds. They trick people who are easily fooled, and their minds are filled with greedy thoughts. But they are headed for trouble!

[15]They have left the true road and have gone down the wrong path by following the example of the prophet Balaam. He was the son of Beor and loved what he got from being a crook. [16]But a donkey corrected him for this evil deed. It spoke to him with a human voice and made him stop his foolishness.

[17]These people are like dried up water holes and clouds blown by a windstorm. The darkest part of hell is waiting for them. [18]They brag out loud about their stupid nonsense. And by being vulgar and crude, they trap people who have barely escaped from living the wrong kind of life. [19]They promise freedom to everyone. But they are merely slaves of filthy living, because people are slaves of whatever controls them.

[20]When they learned about our Lord and Savior Jesus Christ, they escaped from the filthy things of this world. But they are again caught up and controlled by these filthy things, and now they are

---

[b]2.6 *Sodom and Gomorrah*: During the time of Abraham the Lord destroyed these cities because the people there were so evil (see Genesis 19.24).   [c]2.11 *evil beings*: Or "evil teachers."   [d]2.13 *and the meals they eat with you are spoiled by the shameful and selfish way they carry on*: Some manuscripts have "and the meals they eat with you are spoiled by the shameful way they carry on during your feasts of Christian love."

in worse shape than they were at first. [21]They would have been better off if they had never known about the right way. Even after they knew what was right, they turned their backs on the holy commandments that they were given. [22]What happened to them is just like the true saying,

"A dog will come back
to lick up its own vomit.
A pig that has been washed
will roll in the mud."

The Lord Will Return

3 My dear friends, this is the second letter I have written to encourage you to do some honest thinking. I don't want you to forget [2]what God's prophets said would happen. You must never forget what the holy prophets taught in the past. And you must remember what the apostles told you our Lord and Savior has commanded us to do.

[3]But first you must realize that in the last days some people won't think about anything except their own selfish desires. They will make fun of you [4]and say, "Didn't your Lord promise to come back? Yet the first leaders have already died, and the world hasn't changed a bit."

[5]They will say this because they want to forget that long ago the heavens and the earth were made at God's command. The earth came out of water and was made from water. [6]Later it was destroyed by the waters of a mighty flood. [7]But God has commanded the present heavens and earth to remain until the day of judgment. Then they will be set on fire, and ungodly people will be destroyed.

[8]Dear friends, don't forget that for the Lord one day is the same as a thousand years, and a thousand years is the same as one day. [9]The Lord isn't slow about keeping his promises, as some people think he is. In fact, God is patient, because he wants everyone to turn from sin and no one to be lost.

[10]The day of the Lord's return will surprise us like a thief. The heavens will disappear with a loud noise, and the heat will melt the whole universe.[e] Then the earth and everything on it will be seen for what they are.[f]

[11]Everything will be destroyed. So you should serve and honor God by the way you live. [12]You should look forward to the day when God judges everyone, and you should try to make it come soon.[g] On that day the heavens will be destroyed by fire, and everything else will melt in the heat. [13]But God has promised us a new heaven and a new earth, where justice will rule. We are really looking forward to that!

[14]My friends, while you are waiting, you should make certain that the Lord finds you pure, spotless, and living at peace. [15]Don't forget that the Lord is patient because he wants people to be saved. This is also what our dear friend Paul said when he wrote you with the wisdom that God had given him. [16]Paul talks about these same things in all his letters, but part of what he says is hard to understand. Some ignorant and unsteady people even destroy themselves by twisting what he said. They do the same thing with other Scriptures too.

[17]My dear friends, you have been warned ahead of time! So don't let the errors of evil people lead you down the wrong path and make you lose your balance. [18]Let the wonderful kindness and the understanding that come from our Lord and Savior Jesus Christ help you to keep on growing. Praise Jesus now and forever! Amen.[h]

[e]**3.10** _the whole universe_: Probably the sun, moon, and stars, or the elements that everything in the universe is made of. [f]**3.10** _will be seen for what they are_: Some manuscripts have "will go up in flames." [g]**3.12** _and you should try to make it come soon_: Or "and you should eagerly desire for that day to come." [h]**3.18** _Amen_: Some manuscripts do not have "Amen."

1 JOHN

ABOUT THIS LETTER

John wants Christian believers to know that when we tell God about our sins, God will forgive us and take them away (1.9).

The true test of faith is love for each other (3.11-24). Because God is love, his people must be like him (4.1-21). For a complete victory over sin, we must not only love others, but we must believe that Jesus, the Son of God, is truly Christ, and that his death for us was real (5.1-12).

Remember:

> *The Word that gives life*
> *was from the beginning,*
> *and this is the one*
> *our message is about.*
> *(1.1a)*

A QUICK LOOK AT THIS LETTER

1 The Word that gives life
     was from the beginning,
 and this is the one
     our message is about.

Our ears have heard,
     our own eyes have seen,
and our hands touched
     this Word.

²The one who gives life appeared! We saw it happen, and we are witnesses to what we have seen. Now we are telling you about this eternal life that was with the Father and appeared to us. ³We are telling you what we have seen and heard, so that you may share in this life with us. And we share in it with the Father and with his Son Jesus Christ. ⁴We are writing to tell you these things, because this makes us*ᵃ* truly happy.

God Is Light

⁵Jesus told us that God is light and doesn't have any darkness in him. Now we are telling you.

⁶If we say that we share in life with God and keep on living in the dark, we are lying and are not living by the truth. ⁷But if we live in the light, as God does, we share in life with each other. And the blood of his Son Jesus washes all our sins away. ⁸If we say that we have not sinned, we are fooling ourselves, and the truth isn't in our hearts. ⁹But if we confess our sins to God, he can always be trusted to forgive us and take our sins away.

ᵃ1.4 us: Some manuscripts have "you."

[10]If we say that we have not sinned, we make God a liar, and his message isn't in our hearts.[b]

Christ Helps Us

2 My children, I am writing this so that you won't sin. But if you do sin, Jesus Christ always does the right thing, and he will speak to the Father for us. [2]Christ is the sacrifice that takes away our sins and the sins of all the world's people.

[3]When we obey God, we are sure that we know him. [4]But if we claim to know him and don't obey him, we are lying and the truth isn't in our hearts. [5]We truly love God only when we obey him as we should, and then we know that we belong to him. [6]If we say we are his, we must follow the example of Christ.

The New Commandment

[7]My dear friends, I am not writing to give you a new commandment. It is the same one that you were first given, and it is the message you heard. [8]But it really is a new commandment, and you know its true meaning, just as Christ does. You can see the darkness fading away and the true light already shining. [9]If we claim to be in the light and hate someone, we are still in the dark. [10]But if we love others, we are in the light, and we don't cause problems for them.[c] [11]If we hate others, we are living and walking in the dark. We don't know where we are going, because we can't see in the dark.

[12] Children, I am writing you,
    because your sins
have been forgiven
    in the name of Christ.
[13] Parents, I am writing you,
    because you have known
the one who was there
    from the beginning.
Young people, I am writing you,
because you have defeated
    the evil one.
[14] Children, I am writing you,
because you have known
    the Father.

Parents, I am writing you,
    because you have known
the one who was there
    from the beginning.
Young people, I am writing you,
    because you are strong.
God's message is firm
    in your hearts,
and you have defeated
    the evil one.

[15]Don't love the world or anything that belongs to the world. If you love the world, you cannot love the Father. [16]Our foolish pride comes from this world, and so do our selfish desires and our desire to have everything we see. None of this comes from the Father. [17]The world and the desires it causes are disappearing. But if we obey God, we will live forever.

The Enemy of Christ

[18]Children, this is the last hour. You heard that the enemy of Christ would appear at this time, and many of Christ's enemies have already appeared. So we know that the last hour is here. [19]These people came from our own group, yet they were not part of us. If they had been part of us, they would have stayed with us. But they left, which proves that they did not belong to our group.

[20]Christ, the Holy One,[d] has blessed[e] you, and now all of you understand.[f] [21]I did not need to write you about the truth, since you already know it. You also know that liars do not belong to the truth. [22]And a liar is anyone who says that Jesus isn't truly Christ. Anyone who says this is an enemy of Christ and rejects both the Father and the Son. [23]If we reject the Son, we reject the Father. But if we say that we accept the Son, we have the Father. [24]Keep thinking about the message you first heard, and you will always be one in your heart with the Son and with the Father. [25]The Son[g] has promised us[h] eternal life.

[26]I am writing to warn you about those people who are misleading you. [27]But Christ has blessed you with the Holy Spirit.[i] Now the Spirit stays in you, and you don't need any teachers. The

---

[b]**1.10** *and his message isn't in our hearts*: Or "because we have not accepted his message."
[c]**2.10** *and we don't cause problems for them*: Or "and we can see anything that might make us fall." [d]**2.20** *Christ, the Holy One*: The Greek text has "the Holy One" which may refer either to Christ or to God the Father. [e]**2.20** *blessed*: This translates a word which means "to pour olive oil on (someone's head)." In Old Testament times it was the custom to pour olive oil on a person's head when that person was chosen to be a priest or a king. Here the meaning is not clear. It may refer to the ceremony of pouring olive oil on the followers of the Lord right before they were baptized or it may refer to the gift of the Holy Spirit which they were given at baptism (see verse 27). [f]**2.20** *now all of you understand*: Some manuscripts have "you understand all things." [g]**2.25** *The Son*: The Greek text has "he" and may refer to God the Father. [h]**2.25** *us*: Some manuscripts have "you." [i]**2.27** *Christ has blessed you with the Holy Spirit*: The Greek text has "You received a pouring on of olive oil from him" (see verse 20). The "pouring on of olive oil" is here taken to refer to the gift of the Holy Spirit, and "he" may refer either to Christ or to the Father.

Spirit is truthful and teaches you everything. So stay one in your heart with Christ, just as the Spirit has taught you to do.

Children of God

28Children, stay one in your hearts with Christ. Then when he returns, we will have confidence and won't have to hide in shame. 29You know that Christ always does right and that everyone who does right is a child of God.

3 Think how much the Father loves us. He loves us so much that he lets us be called his children, as we truly are. But since the people of this world did not know who Christ*ʲ* is, they don't know who we are. 2My dear friends, we are already God's children, though what we will be hasn't yet been seen. But we do know that when Christ returns, we will be like him, because we will see him as he truly is. 3This hope makes us keep ourselves holy, just as Christ*ᵏ* is holy.

4Everyone who sins breaks God's law, because sin is the same as breaking God's law. 5You know that Christ came to take away sins. He isn't sinful, 6and people who stay one in their hearts with him won't keep on sinning. If they do keep on sinning, they don't know Christ, and they have never seen him.

7Children, don't be fooled. Anyone who does right is good, just like Christ himself. 8Anyone who keeps on sinning belongs to the devil. He has sinned from the beginning, but the Son of God came to destroy all that he has done. 9God's children cannot keep on being sinful. His life-giving power*ˡ* lives in them and makes them his children, so that they cannot keep on sinning. 10You can tell God's children from the devil's children, because those who belong to the devil refuse to do right or to love each other.

Love Each Other

11From the beginning you were told that we must love each other. 12Don't be like Cain, who belonged to the devil and murdered his own brother. Why did he murder him? He did it because his brother was good, and he was evil. 13My friends, don't be surprised if the people of this world hate you. 14Our love for each other proves that we have gone from death to life. But if you don't love each other, you are still under the power of death.

15If you hate each other, you are murderers, and we know that murderers do not have eternal life. 16We know what love is because Jesus gave his life for us.

That's why we must give our lives for each other. 17If we have all we need and see one of our own people in need, we must have pity on that person, or else we cannot say we love God. 18Children, you show love for others by truly helping them, and not merely by talking about it.

19When we love others, we know that we belong to the truth, and we feel at ease in the presence of God. 20But even if we don't feel at ease, God is greater than our feelings, and he knows everything. 21Dear friends, if we feel at ease in the presence of God, we will have the courage to come near him. 22He will give us whatever we ask, because we obey him and do what pleases him. 23God wants us to have faith in his Son Jesus Christ and to love each other. This is also what Jesus taught us to do. 24If we obey God's commandments, we will stay one in our hearts with him, and he will stay one with us. The Spirit that he has given us is proof that we are one with him.

God Is Love

4 Dear friends, don't believe everyone who claims to have the Spirit of God. Test them all to find out if they really do come from God. Many false prophets have already gone out into the world, 2and you can know which ones come from God. His Spirit says that Jesus Christ had a truly human body. 3But when someone doesn't say this about Jesus, you know that person has a spirit that doesn't come from God and is the enemy of Christ. You knew that this enemy was coming into the world and now is already here.

4Children, you belong to God, and you have defeated these enemies. God's Spirit*ᵐ* is in you and is more powerful than the one that is in the world. 5These enemies belong to this world, and the world listens to them, because they speak its language. 6We belong to God, and everyone who knows God will listen to us. But the people who don't know God won't listen to us. That is how we can tell the Spirit that speaks the truth from the one that tells lies.

7My dear friends, we must love each other. Love comes from God, and when we love each other, it shows that we have been given new life. We are now God's children, and we know him. 8God is love, and anyone who doesn't love others has never known him. 9God showed his love for us when he sent his only Son into the world to give us life. 10Real love isn't our love for God, but

---

*ʲ***3.1** *Christ:* The Greek text has "he" and may refer to God.   *ᵏ***3.3** *Christ:* The Greek text has "that one" and may refer to God.   *ˡ***3.9** *His life-giving power:* The Greek text has "his seed."
*ᵐ***4.4** *God's Spirit:* The Greek text has "he" and may refer to the Spirit or to God or to Jesus.

his love for us. God sent his Son to be the sacrifice by which our sins are forgiven. [11]Dear friends, since God loved us this much, we must love each other.

[12]No one has ever seen God. But if we love each other, God lives in us, and his love is truly in our hearts.

[13]God has given us his Spirit. That is how we know that we are one with him, just as he is one with us. [14]God sent his Son to be the Savior of the world. We saw his Son and are now telling others about him. [15]God stays one with everyone who openly says that Jesus is the Son of God. That's how we stay one with God [16]and are sure that God loves us.

God is love. If we keep on loving others, we will stay one in our hearts with God, and he will stay one with us. [17]If we truly love others and live as Christ did in this world, we won't be worried about the day of judgment. [18]A real love for others will chase those worries away. The thought of being punished is what makes us afraid. It shows that we have not really learned to love.

[19]We love because God loved us first. [20]But if we say we love God and don't love each other, we are liars. We cannot see God. So how can we love God, if we don't love the people we can see? [21]The commandment that God has given us is: "Love God and love each other!"

Victory over the World

5 If we believe that Jesus is truly Christ, we are God's children. Everyone who loves the Father will also love his children. [2]If we love and obey God, we know that we will love his children. [3]We show our love for God by obeying his commandments, and they are not hard to follow.

[4]Every child of God can defeat the world, and our faith is what gives us this victory. [5]No one can defeat the world without having faith in Jesus as the Son of God.

Who Jesus Is

[6]Water and blood came out from the side of Jesus Christ. It wasn't just water, but water and blood.[n] The Spirit tells about this, because the Spirit is truthful. [7]In fact, there are three who tell about it. [8]They are the Spirit, the water, and the blood, and they all agree.

[9]We believe what people tell us. But we can trust what God says even more, and God is the one who has spoken about his Son. [10]If we have faith in God's Son, we have believed what God has said. But if we don't believe what God has said about his Son, it is the same as calling God a liar. [11]God has also said that he gave us eternal life and that this life comes to us from his Son. [12]And so, if we have God's Son, we have this life. But if we don't have the Son, we don't have this life.

Knowing about Eternal Life

[13]All of you have faith in the Son of God, and I have written to let you know that you have eternal life. [14]We are certain that God will hear our prayers when we ask for what pleases him. [15]And if we know that God listens when we pray, we are sure that our prayers have already been answered.

[16]Suppose you see one of our people commit a sin that isn't a deadly sin. You can pray, and that person will be given eternal life. But the sin must not be one that is deadly. [17]Everything that is wrong is sin, but not all sins are deadly.

[18]We are sure that God's children do not keep on sinning. God's own Son protects them, and the devil cannot harm them.

[19]We are certain that we come from God and that the rest of the world is under the power of the devil.

[20]We know that Jesus Christ the Son of God has come and has shown us the true God. And because of Jesus, we now belong to the true God who gives eternal life.

[21]Children, you must stay away from idols.

---

[n]**5.6** *Water and blood came out from the side of Jesus Christ. It wasn't just water, but water and blood*: See John 19.34. It is also possible to translate, "Jesus Christ came by the water of baptism and by the blood of his death! He was not only baptized, but he bled and died." The purpose of the verse is to tell that Jesus was truly human and that he really died.

2 JOHN

ABOUT THIS LETTER

John writes again about the importance of love in a Christian's life. He points out that truth and love must go together. We must also believe that Christ was truly human, and we must love each other.

A QUICK LOOK AT THIS LETTER

Greetings and Prayer (1-3)
Truth and Love (4-11)
Final Greetings (12, 13)

---

¹From the church leader.ᵃ

To a very special woman and her children.ᵇ I truly love all of you, and so does everyone else who knows the truth. ²We love you because the truth is now in our hearts, and it will be there forever.

³I pray that God the Father and Jesus Christ his Son will be kind and merciful to us! May they give us peace and truth and love.

Truth and Love

⁴I was very glad to learn that some of your children are obeying the truth, as the Father told us to do. ⁵Dear friend, I am not writing to tell you and your children to do something you have not done before. I am writing to tell you to love each other, which is the first thing you were told to do. ⁶Love means that we do what God tells us. And from the beginning, he told you to love him.

⁷Many liars have gone out into the world. These deceitful liars are saying that Jesus Christ did not have a truly human body. But they are liars and the enemies of Christ. ⁸So be sure not to lose what weᶜ have worked for. If you do, you won't be given your full reward. ⁹Don't keep changing what you were taught about Christ, or else God will no longer be with you. But if you hold firmly to what you were taught, both the Father and the Son will be with you. ¹⁰If people won't agree to this teaching, don't welcome them into your home or even greet them. ¹¹Greeting them is the same as taking part in their evil deeds.

Final Greetings

¹²I have much more to tell you, but I don't want to write it with pen and ink. I want to come and talk to you in person, because that will make usᵈ really happy.

¹³Greetings from the children of your very special sister.ᵉ

ᵃ1 *church leader*: Or "elder" or "presbyter" or "priest."   ᵇ1 *very special woman and her children*: A group of the Lord's followers who met together for worship. "The children of your . . . sister" (see verse 13) is another group of followers. "Very special" (here and verse 13) probably means "chosen (by the Lord)."   ᶜ8 *we*: Some manuscripts have "you."   ᵈ12 *us*: Some manuscripts have "you."   ᵉ13 *sister*: See the note at verse 1.

3 JOHN

ABOUT THIS LETTER

In this letter the writer reminds Christian readers that they should help support those who go to other parts of the world to tell others about the Lord. The letter is written to an important church member named Gaius, who had been very helpful to Christians who traveled around and preached the good news.

A QUICK LOOK AT THIS LETTER

Greetings to Gaius (1-4)
The Importance of Working Together (5-12)
Final Greetings (13-15)

---

¹From the church leader.ᵃ

To my dear friend Gaius.

I love you because we follow the truth, ²dear friend, and I pray that all goes well for you. I hope that you are as strong in body, as I know you are in spirit. ³It makes me very happy when the Lord's followers come by and speak openly of how you obey the truth. ⁴Nothing brings me greater happiness than to hear that my childrenᵇ are obeying the truth.

Working Together

⁵Dear friend, you have always been faithful in helping other followers of the Lord, even the ones you didn't know before. ⁶They have told the church about your love. They say you were good enough to welcome them and to send them on their mission in a way that God's servants deserve. ⁷When they left to tell others about the Lord, they decided not to accept help from anyone who wasn't a follower. ⁸We must support people like them, so that we can take part in what they are doing to spread the truth.

⁹I wrote to the church. But Diotrephes likes to be the number-one leader, and he won't pay any attention to us. ¹⁰So if I come, I will remind him of how he has been attacking us with gossip. Not only has he been doing this, but he refuses to welcome any of the Lord's followers who come by. And when other church members want to welcome them, he puts them out of the church.

¹¹Dear friend, don't copy the evil deeds of others! Follow the example of people who do kind deeds. They are God's children, but those who are always doing evil have never seen God.

¹²Everyone speaks well of Demetrius, and so does the true message that he teaches. I also speak well of him, and you know what I say is true.

Final Greetings

¹³I have much more to say to you, but I don't want to write it with pen and ink. ¹⁴I hope to see you soon, and then we can talk in person.

¹⁵I pray that God will bless you with peace!

Your friends send their greetings. Please give a personal greeting to each of our friends.

ᵃ1 *church leader*: Or "elder" or "presbyter" or "priest." the leader had led to be followers of the Lord. ᵇ4 *children*: Probably persons that

JUDE

ABOUT THIS LETTER

Jude has much to say about false teachers. They are evil! God will punish them, and Christians should not follow their teaching or imitate the way they live.

Jude ends with a beautiful prayer-like blessing:

> *Offer praise to God our Savior because of our Lord Jesus Christ! Only God can keep you from falling and make you pure and joyful in his glorious presence. Before time began and now and forevermore, God is worthy of glory, honor, power, and authority. Amen.*
> *(24, 25)*

A QUICK LOOK AT THIS LETTER

Greetings (1, 2)
Defending the Faith against False Teachers (3-23)
Final Prayer (24, 25)

---

pazhors paga, aspta,

¹From Jude, a servant of Jesus Christ and the brother of James.

To all who are chosen and loved by God the Father and are kept safe by Jesus Christ.

²I pray that God will greatly bless you with kindness, peace, and love!

False Teachers

³My dear friends, I really wanted to write you about God's saving power at work in our lives. But instead, I must write and ask you to defend the faith that God has once for all given to his people. ⁴Some godless people have sneaked in among us and are saying, "God treats us much better than we deserve, and so it is all right to be immoral." They even deny that we must obey Jesus Christ as our only Master and Lord. But long ago the Scriptures warned that these godless people were doomed.

⁵Don't forget what happened to those people that the Lord rescued from Egypt. Some of them did not have faith, and he later destroyed them. ⁶You also know about the angels*ᵃ* who didn't do their work and left their proper places. God chained them with everlasting chains and is now keeping them in dark pits until the great day of judgment. ⁷We should also be warned by what happened to the cities of Sodom and Gomorrah*ᵇ* and the nearby towns. Their people became immoral and did all sorts of sexual sins. Then God made an example of them and punished them with eternal fire.

⁸The people I am talking about are behaving just like those dreamers who destroyed their own bodies. They reject all authority and insult angels. ⁹Even Michael, the chief angel, didn't dare to insult the devil, when the two of them were arguing about the body of Moses.*ᶜ* All Michael said was, "The Lord will punish you!"

¹⁰But these people insult powers they don't know anything about. They are like senseless animals that end up

---

ᵃ6 angels: This may refer to the angels who liked the women on earth so much that they came down and married them (see Genesis 6.2).   *ᵇ7 Sodom and Gomorrah*: During the time of Abraham the Lord destroyed these cities because the people there were so evil.   *ᶜ9 Michael . . . the body of Moses*: This refers to what was said in an ancient Jewish book about Moses.

getting destroyed, because they live only by their feelings. [11]Now they are in for real trouble. They have followed Cain's example[d] and have made the same mistake that Balaam[e] did by caring only for money. They have also rebelled against God, just as Korah did.[f] Because of all this, they will be destroyed.

[12]These people are filthy minded, and by their shameful and selfish actions they spoil the meals you eat together. They are like clouds blown along by the wind, but never bringing any rain. They are like leafless trees, uprooted and dead, and unable to produce fruit. [13]Their shameful deeds show up like foam on wild ocean waves. They are like wandering stars forever doomed to the darkest pits of hell.

[14]Enoch was the seventh person after Adam, and he was talking about these people when he said:

Look! The Lord is coming with thousands and thousands of holy angels [15]to judge everyone. He will punish all those ungodly people for all the evil things they have done. The Lord will surely punish those ungodly sinners for every evil thing they have ever said about him.

[16]These people grumble and complain and live by their own selfish desires. They brag about themselves and flatter others to get what they want.

More Warnings

[17]My dear friends, remember the warning you were given by the apostles of our Lord Jesus Christ. [18]They told you that near the end of time, selfish and godless people would start making fun of God. [19]And now these people are already making you turn against each other. They think only about this life, and they don't have God's Spirit.

[20]Dear friends, keep building on the foundation of your most holy faith, as the Holy Spirit helps you to pray. [21]And keep in step with God's love, as you wait for our Lord Jesus Christ to show how kind he is by giving you eternal life. [22]Be helpful to[g] all who may have doubts. [23]Rescue any who need to be saved, as you would rescue someone from a fire. Then with fear in your own hearts, have mercy on everyone who needs it. But hate even the clothes of those who have been made dirty by their filthy deeds.

Final Prayer

[24-25]Offer praise to God our Savior because of our Lord Jesus Christ! Only God can keep you from falling and make you pure and joyful in his glorious presence. Before time began and now and forevermore, God is worthy of glory, honor, power, and authority. Amen.

---

[d]11 _Cain's example_: Cain murdered his brother Abel.   [e]11 _Balaam_: According to the biblical account, Balaam refused to curse the people of Israel for profit (see Numbers 22.18; 24.13), though he led them to be unfaithful to the Lord (see Numbers 25.1-3; 31.16). But by New Testament times, some Jewish teachers taught that Balaam was greedy and did accept money to curse them.   [f]11 _just as Korah did_: Together with Dathan and Abiram, Korah led a rebellion against Moses and Aaron (see Numbers 16.1-35; 26.9, 10).   [g]22 _Be helpful to_: Some manuscripts have "Correct."

REVELATION

ABOUT THIS BOOK

This book tells what John had seen in a vision about God's message and about what Jesus Christ had said and done (1.2). The message has three main parts: (1) There are evil forces at work in the world, and Christians may have to suffer and die; (2) Jesus is Lord, and he will conquer all people and powers who oppose God; and (3) God has wonderful rewards in store for his faithful people, who remain faithful to him, especially for those who lose their lives in his service.

This was a powerful message of hope for those early Christians who had to suffer or die for their faith. In this book they learned that, in spite of the cruel power of the Roman Empire, the Lamb of God would win the final victory. And this gave them the courage to be faithful.

Because this book is so full of visions that use ideas and word pictures from the Old Testament, it was like a book with secret messages for the early Christians. The book could be passed around and be understood by Christians, but an official of the Roman Empire would not be able to understand it. For example, when the fall of Babylon is described (chapter 18), the early Christians knew that this pointed to the fall of the Roman Empire. This knowledge gave them hope.

At the beginning of this book there are seven letters to seven churches. These letters show what different groups of the Lord's followers will do in times of persecution (2.1—3.22).

The author uses many powerful images to describe God's power and judgment. The vision of God's throne (4.1-11) and of the scroll and the Lamb (5.1-14) show that God and Christ are in control of all human and supernatural events. Opening seven seals (6.1—8.5), blowing the seven trumpets (8.6—11.19), and emptying the seven bowls (16.1-21) are among the visions that show God's fierce judgment on the world.

After the suffering has ended, God's faithful people will receive the greatest blessing of all:

God's home is now with his people. He will live with them, and they will be his own. Yes, God will make his home among his people. He will wipe all tears from their eyes, and there will be no more death, suffering, crying, or pain. These things of the past are gone forever.   *(21.3b, 4)*

A QUICK LOOK AT THIS BOOK

1 This is what God showed to Jesus Christ, so that he could tell his servants what must happen soon. Christ then sent his angel with the message to his servant John. [2]And John told everything that he had seen about God's message and about what Jesus Christ had said and done.

[3]God will bless everyone who reads this prophecy to others,[a] and he will bless everyone who hears and obeys it. The time is almost here.

[4]From John to the seven churches in Asia.[b]

I pray that you
      will be blessed
with kindness and peace
from God, who is and was
      and is coming.
May you receive
      kindness and peace
from the seven spirits
      before the throne of God.
[5] May kindness and peace
      be yours
from Jesus Christ,
      the faithful witness.

Jesus was the first
      to conquer death,
and he is the ruler
      of all earthly kings.
Christ loves us,
      and by his blood
he set us free
      from our sins.
[6] He lets us rule as kings
and serve God his Father
      as priests.
To him be glory and power
      forever and ever! Amen.
[7] Look! He is coming
      with the clouds.
Everyone will see him,
      even the ones who stuck
      a sword through him.
All people on earth
will weep because of him.
      Yes, it will happen! Amen.

[8]The Lord God says, "I am Alpha and Omega,[c] the one who is and was and is coming. I am God All-Powerful!"

A Vision of the Risen Lord

[9]I am John, a follower together with all of you. We suffer because Jesus is our king, but he gives us the strength to endure. I was sent to Patmos Island,[d] because I had preached God's message and had told about Jesus. [10]On the Lord's day the Spirit took control of me, and behind me I heard a loud voice that sounded like a trumpet. [11]The voice said, "Write in a book what you see. Then send it to the seven churches in Ephesus, Smyrna, Pergamum, Thyatira, Sardis, Philadelphia, and Laodicea."[e]

[12]When I turned to see who was speaking to me, I saw seven gold lampstands. [13]There with the lampstands was someone who seemed to be the Son of Man.[f] He was wearing a robe that reached down to his feet, and a gold cloth was wrapped around his chest. [14]His head and his hair were white as wool or snow, and his eyes looked like flames of fire. [15]His feet were glowing like bronze being heated in a furnace, and his voice sounded like the roar of a waterfall. [16]He held seven stars in his right hand, and a sharp double-edged sword was coming from his mouth. His face was shining as bright as the sun at noon.

[17]When I saw him, I fell at his feet like a dead person. But he put his right hand on me and said:

Don't be afraid! I am the first, the last, [18]and the living one. I died, but now I am alive forevermore, and I have the keys to death and the world of the dead.[g] [19]Write what you have seen and what is and what will happen after these things. [20]I will explain the mystery of the seven stars that you saw at my right side and the seven gold lampstands. The seven stars are the angels[h] of the seven churches, and the lampstands are the seven churches.

The Letter to Ephesus

2 This is what you must write to the angel of the church in Ephesus:
I am the one who holds the seven stars in my right hand, and I walk among the seven gold lampstands. Listen to what I say.
[2]I know everything you have done, including your hard work and how you have endured. I know you won't put up with anyone who is evil. When some people pretended to be apostles, you tested them and found out that they were liars. [3]You have

---

[a]**1.3** _who reads this prophecy to others_: A public reading, in a worship service.   [b]**1.4** _Asia_: The section 1.4—3.22 is in the form of a letter. Asia was in the eastern part of the Roman Empire and is present day Turkey.   [c]**1.8** _Alpha and Omega_: The first and last letters of the Greek alphabet, which sometimes mean "first" and "last."   [d]**1.9** _Patmos Island_: A small island where prisoners were sometimes kept by the Romans.   [e]**1.11** _Ephesus . . . Laodicea_: Ephesus was in the center with the six other cities forming a half-circle around it.
[f]**1.13** _Son of Man_: That is, Jesus.   [g]**1.18** _keys to death and the world of the dead_: That is, power over death and the world of the dead.   [h]**1.20** _angels_: Perhaps guardian angels that represent the churches, or they may be church leaders or messengers sent to the churches.

endured and gone through hard times because of me, and you have not given up.

⁴But I do have something against you! And it is this: You don't have as much love as you used to. ⁵Think about where you have fallen from, and then turn back and do as you did at first. If you don't turn back, I will come and take away your lampstand. ⁶But there is one thing you are doing right. You hate what the Nicolaitans[i] are doing, and so do I.

⁷If you have ears, listen to what the Spirit says to the churches. I will let everyone who wins the victory eat from the life-giving tree in God's wonderful garden.

The Letter to Smyrna

⁸This is what you must write to the angel of the church in Smyrna:

I am the first and the last. I died, but now I am alive! Listen to what I say.

⁹I know how much you suffer and how poor you are, but you are rich. I also know the cruel things being said about you by people who claim to be Jews. But they are not really Jews. They are a group that belongs to Satan.

¹⁰Don't worry about what you will suffer. The devil will throw some of you into jail, and you will be tested and made to suffer for ten days. But if you are faithful until you die, I will reward you with a glorious life.[j]

¹¹If you have ears, listen to what the Spirit says to the churches. Whoever wins the victory will not be hurt by the second death.[k]

The Letter to Pergamum

¹²This is what you must write to the angel of the church in Pergamum:

I am the one who has the sharp double-edged sword! Listen to what I say.

¹³I know that you live where Satan has his throne.[l] But you have kept true to my name. Right there where Satan lives, my faithful witness Antipas[m] was taken from you and put to death. Even then you did not give up your faith in me.

¹⁴I do have a few things against you. Some of you are following the teaching of Balaam.[n] Long ago he told Balak to teach the people of Israel to eat food that had been offered to idols and to be immoral. ¹⁵Now some of you are following the teaching of the Nicolaitans.[o] ¹⁶Turn back! If you don't, I will come quickly and fight against these people. And my words will cut like a sword.

¹⁷If you have ears, listen to what the Spirit says to the churches. To everyone who wins the victory, I will give some of the hidden food.[p] I will also give each one a white stone[q] with a new name[r] written on it. No one will know that name except the one who is given the stone.

The Letter to Thyatira

¹⁸This is what you must write to the angel of the church in Thyatira:

I am the Son of God! My eyes are like flames of fire, and my feet are like bronze. Listen to what I say.

¹⁹I know everything about you, including your love, your faith, your service, and how you have endured. I know that you are doing more now than you have ever done before. ²⁰But I still have something against you because of that woman Jezebel.[s] She calls herself a prophet, and you let her teach and mislead my servants to do immoral things and to eat food offered to idols. ²¹I gave her

---

[i]**2.6** *Nicolaitans*: Nothing else is known about these people, though it is possible that they claimed to be followers of Nicolaus from Antioch (see Acts 6.5). [j]**2.10** *a glorious life*: The Greek text has "a crown of life." In ancient times an athlete who had won a contest was rewarded with a crown of flowers as a sign of victory. [k]**2.11** *second death*: The first death is physical death, and the "second death" is eternal death. [l]**2.13** *where Satan has his throne*: The meaning is uncertain, but it may refer to the city as a center of pagan worship or of Emperor worship. [m]**2.13** *Antipas*: Nothing else is known about this man, who is mentioned only here in the New Testament. [n]**2.14** *Balaam*: According to Numbers 22–24, Balaam refused to disobey the Lord. But in other books of the Old Testament, he is spoken of as evil (see Deuteronomy 23.4, 5; Joshua 13.22; 24.9, 10; Nehemiah 13.2). [o]**2.15** *Nicolaitans*: See the note at 2.6. [p]**2.17** *hidden food*: When the people of Israel were going through the desert, the Lord provided a special food for them. Some of this was placed in a jar and stored in the sacred chest (see Exodus 16). According to later Jewish teaching, the prophet Jeremiah rescued the sacred chest when the temple was destroyed by the Babylonians. He hid the chest in a cave, where it would stay until God came to save his people. [q]**2.17** *white stone*: The meaning of this is uncertain, though it may be the same as a ticket that lets a person into God's banquet where the "hidden food" is eaten. Or it may be a symbol of victory. [r]**2.17** *a new name*: Either the name of Christ or God or the name of the follower who is given the stone. [s]**2.20** *Jezebel*: Nothing else is known about her. This may have been her real name or a name that was given to her because she was like Queen Jezebel, who opposed the Lord (see 1 Kings 19.1, 2; 21.1-26).

a chance to turn from her sins, but she did not want to stop doing these immoral things.

²²I am going to strike down Jezebel. Everyone who does these immoral things with her will also be punished, if they don't stop. ²³I will even kill her followers.ᵗ Then all the churches will see that I know everyone's thoughts and feelings. I will treat each of you as you deserve.

²⁴Some of you in Thyatira don't follow Jezebel's teaching. You don't know anything about what her followers call the "deep secrets of Satan." So I won't burden you down with any other commands. ²⁵But until I come, you must hold firmly to the teaching you have.

²⁶I will give power over the nations to everyone who wins the victory and keeps on obeying me until the end. ²⁷⁻²⁸I will give each of them the same power that my Father has given me. They will rule the nations with an iron rod and smash those nations to pieces like clay pots. I will also give them the morning star.ᵘ

²⁹If you have ears, listen to what the Spirit says to the churches.

The Letter to Sardis

3 This is what you must write to the angel of the church in Sardis:

I have the seven spirits of God and the seven stars. Listen to what I say.

I know what you are doing. Everyone may think you are alive, but you are dead. ²Wake up! You have only a little strength left, and it is almost gone. So try to become stronger. I have found that you are not completely obeying God. ³Remember the teaching that you were given and that you heard. Hold firmly to it and turn from your sins. If you don't wake up, I will come when you least expect it, just as a thief does.

⁴A few of you in Sardis haven't dirtied your clothes with sin. You will walk with me in white clothes, because you are worthy. ⁵Everyone who wins the victory will wear white clothes. Their names will not be erased from the book of life,ᵛ and I will tell my Father and his angels that they are my followers.

⁶If you have ears, listen to what the Spirit says to the churches.

The Letter to Philadelphia

⁷This is what you must write to the angel of the church in Philadelphia:

I am the one who is holy and true, and I have the keys that belonged to David.ʷ When I open a door, no one can close it. And when I close a door, no one can open it. Listen to what I say.

⁸I know everything you have done. And I have placed before you an open door that no one can close. You were not very strong, but you obeyed my message and did not deny that you are my followers.ˣ ⁹Now you will see what I will do with those people who belong to Satan's group. They claim to be Jews, but they are liars. I will make them come and kneel down at your feet. Then they will know that I love you.

¹⁰You obeyed my message and endured. So I will protect you from the time of testing that everyone in all the world must go through. ¹¹I am coming soon. So hold firmly to what you have, and no one will take away the crown that you will be given as your reward.

¹²Everyone who wins the victory will be made into a pillar in the temple of my God, and they will stay there forever. I will write on each of them the name of my God and the name of his city. It is the new Jerusalem that my God will send down from heaven. I will also write on them my own new name.

¹³If you have ears, listen to what the Spirit says to the churches.

The Letter to Laodicea

¹⁴This is what you must write to the angel of the church in Laodicea:

I am the one called Amen!ʸ I am the faithful and true witness and the sourceᶻ of God's creation. Listen to what I say.

¹⁵I know everything you have done, and you are not cold or hot. I wish you were either one or the other. ¹⁶But since you are lukewarm and neither cold nor hot, I will spit you out of my mouth. ¹⁷You claim to be rich and successful and to have everything you need. But you don't know how bad off you are. You are pitiful, poor, blind, and naked. ¹⁸Buy your gold from me. It has

---

ᵗ**2.23** *her followers:* Or "her children."   ᵘ**2.27,28** *the morning star:* Probably thought of as the star that signals the end of night and the beginning of day. In 22.16 Christ is called the "morning star."   ᵛ**3.5** *book of life:* The book in which the names of God's people are written. ʷ**3.7** *the keys that belonged to David:* The keys stand for authority over David's kingdom. ˣ**3.8** *did not deny that you are my followers:* Or "did not say evil things about me." ʸ**3.14** *Amen:* Meaning "Trustworthy."   ᶻ**3.14** *source:* Or "beginning."

been refined in a fire, and it will make you rich. Buy white clothes from me. Wear them and you can cover up your shameful nakedness. Buy medicine for your eyes, so that you will be able to see.

¹⁹I correct and punish everyone I love. So make up your minds to turn away from your sins. ²⁰Listen! I am standing and knocking at your door. If you hear my voice and open the door, I will come in and we will eat together. ²¹Everyone who wins the victory will sit with me on my throne, just as I won the victory and sat with my Father on his throne.

²²If you have ears, listen to what the Spirit says to the churches.

Worship in Heaven

4 After this, I looked and saw a door that opened into heaven. Then the voice that had spoken to me at first and that sounded like a trumpet said, "Come up here! I will show you what must happen next." ²Right then the Spirit took control of me, and there in heaven I saw a throne and someone sitting on it. ³The one who was sitting there sparkled like precious stones of jasper*ᵃ* and carnelian.*ᵇ* A rainbow that looked like an emerald*ᶜ* surrounded the throne.

⁴Twenty-four other thrones were in a circle around that throne. And on each of these thrones there was an elder dressed in white clothes and wearing a gold crown. ⁵Flashes of lightning and roars of thunder came out from the throne in the center of the circle. Seven torches, which are the seven spirits of God, were burning in front of the throne. ⁶Also in front of the throne was something that looked like a glass sea, clear as crystal.

Around the throne in the center were four living creatures covered front and back with eyes. ⁷The first creature was like a lion, the second one was like a bull, the third one had the face of a human, and the fourth was like a flying eagle. ⁸Each of the four living creatures had six wings, and their bodies were covered with eyes. Day and night they never stopped singing,

"Holy, holy, holy is the Lord,
 the all-powerful God,
who was and is
 and is coming!"

⁹The living creatures kept praising, honoring, and thanking the one who sits on the throne and who lives forever and ever. ¹⁰At the same time the twenty-four elders knelt down before the one sitting on the throne. And as they worshiped the one who lives forever, they placed their crowns in front of the throne and said,

¹¹ "Our Lord and God,
 you are worthy
to receive glory,
 honor, and power.
You created all things,
and by your decision they are
 and were created."

The Scroll and the Lamb

5 In the right hand of the one sitting on the throne I saw a scroll*ᵈ* that had writing on the inside and on the outside. And it was sealed in seven places. ²I saw a mighty angel ask with a loud voice, "Who is worthy to open the scroll and break its seals?" ³No one in heaven or on earth or under the earth was able to open the scroll or see inside it.

⁴I cried hard because no one was found worthy to open the scroll or see inside it. ⁵Then one of the elders said to me, "Stop crying and look! The one who is called both the 'Lion from the Tribe of Judah'*ᵉ* and 'King David's Great Descendant'*ᶠ* has won the victory. He will open the book and its seven seals."

⁶Then I looked and saw a Lamb standing in the center of the throne that was surrounded by the four living creatures and the elders. The Lamb looked as if it had once been killed. It had seven horns and seven eyes, which are the seven spirits*ᵍ* of God, sent out to all the earth.

⁷The Lamb went over and took the scroll from the right hand of the one who sat on the throne. ⁸After he had taken it, the four living creatures and the twenty-four elders knelt down before him. Each of them had a harp and a gold bowl full of incense,*ʰ* which are the prayers of God's people. ⁹Then they sang a new song,

"You are worthy
 to receive the scroll
and open its seals,
 because you were killed.
And with your own blood
 you bought for God

ᵃ4.3 jasper: Usually green or clear.   *ᵇ4.3 carnelian:* Usually deep-red or reddish-white. *ᶜ4.3 emerald:* A precious stone, usually green.   *ᵈ5.1 scroll:* A roll of paper or special leather used for writing on. Sometimes a scroll would be sealed on the outside with one or more pieces of wax.   *ᵉ5.5 'Lion from the Tribe of Judah':* In Genesis 49.9 the tribe of Judah is called a young lion, and King David was from Judah.   *ᶠ5.5 'King David's Great Descendant':* The Greek text has "the root of David" which is a title for the Messiah based on Isaiah 11.1, 10. *ᵍ5.6 the seven spirits:* Some manuscripts have "the spirits."   *ʰ5.8 incense:* A material that produces a sweet smell when burned. Sometimes it is a symbol for the prayers of God's people.

people from every tribe,
    language, nation, and race.
10 You let them become kings
    and serve God as priests,
and they will rule on earth."

11As I looked, I heard the voices of a lot of angels around the throne and the voices of the living creatures and of the elders. There were millions and millions of them, 12and they were saying in a loud voice,

"The Lamb who was killed
    is worthy to receive power,
riches, wisdom, strength,
    honor, glory, and praise."

13Then I heard all beings in heaven and on the earth and under the earth and in the sea offer praise. Together, all of them were saying,

"Praise, honor, glory,
and strength
    forever and ever
to the one who sits
on the throne
    and to the Lamb!"

14The four living creatures said "Amen," while the elders knelt down and worshiped.

Opening the Seven Seals

6 At the same time that I saw the Lamb open the first of the seven seals, I heard one of the four living creatures shout with a voice like thunder. It said, "Come out!" 2Then I saw a white horse. Its rider carried a bow and was given a crown. He had already won some victories, and he went out to win more.

3When the Lamb opened the second seal, I heard the second living creature say, "Come out!" 4Then another horse came out. It was fiery red. And its rider was given the power to take away all peace from the earth, so that people would slaughter one another. He was also given a big sword.

5When the Lamb opened the third seal, I heard the third living creature say, "Come out!" Then I saw a black horse, and its rider had a balance scale in one hand. 6I heard what sounded like a voice from somewhere among the four living creatures. It said, "A quart of wheat will cost you a whole day's wages! Three quarts of barley will cost you a day's wages too. But don't ruin the olive oil or the wine."

7When the Lamb opened the fourth seal, I heard the voice of the fourth living creature say, "Come out!" 8Then I saw a pale green horse. Its rider was

named Death, and Death's Kingdom followed behind. They were given power over one fourth of the earth, and they could kill its people with swords, famines, diseases, and wild animals.

9When the Lamb opened the fifth seal, I saw under the altar the souls of everyone who had been killed for speaking God's message and telling about their faith. 10They shouted, "Master, you are holy and faithful! How long will it be before you judge and punish the people of this earth who killed us?"

11Then each of those who had been killed was given a white robe and told to rest for a little while. They had to wait until the complete number of the Lord's other servants and followers would be killed.

12When I saw the Lamb open the sixth seal, I looked and saw a great earthquake. The sun turned as dark as sackcloth,i and the moon became as red as blood. 13The stars in the sky fell to earth, just like figs shaken loose by a windstorm. 14Then the sky was rolled up like a scroll,j and all mountains and islands were moved from their places.

15The kings of the earth, its famous people, and its military leaders hid in caves or behind rocks on the mountains. They hid there together with the rich and the powerful and with all the slaves and free people. 16Then they shouted to the mountains and the rocks, "Fall on us! Hide us from the one who sits on the throne and from the anger of the Lamb. 17That terrible day has come! God and the Lamb will show their anger, and who can face it?"

The 144,000 Are Marked for God

7 1-2After this I saw four angels. Each one was standing on one of the earth's four corners. The angels held back the four winds, so that no wind would blow on the earth or on the sea or on any tree. These angels had also been given the power to harm the earth and the sea. Then I saw another angel come up from where the sun rises in the east, and he was ready to put the mark of the living God on people. He shouted to the four angels, 3"Don't harm the earth or the sea or any tree! Wait until I have marked the foreheads of the servants of our God."

4Then I heard how many people had been marked on the forehead. There were one hundred forty-four thousand, and they came from every tribe of Israel:

5 12,000 from Judah,
  12,000 from Reuben,

---

i**6.12** *sackcloth:* A rough, dark-colored cloth made from goat or camel hair and used to make grain sacks. It was worn in times of trouble or sorrow.   j**6.14** *scroll:* See the note at 5.1.

12,000 from Gad,
[6] 12,000 from Asher,
12,000 from Naphtali,
12,000 from Manasseh,
[7] 12,000 from Simeon,
12,000 from Levi,
12,000 from Issachar,
[8] 12,000 from Zebulun,
12,000 from Joseph, and
12,000 from Benjamin.

People from Every Nation

[9]After this, I saw a large crowd with more people than could be counted. They were from every race, tribe, nation, and language, and they stood before the throne and before the Lamb. They wore white robes and held palm branches in their hands, [10]as they shouted,

"Our God, who sits
upon the throne,
has the power
to save his people,
and so does the Lamb."

[11]The angels who stood around the throne knelt in front of it with their faces to the ground. The elders and the four living creatures knelt there with them. Then they all worshiped God [12]and said,

"Amen! Praise, glory, wisdom,
thanks, honor, power,
and strength belong to our God
forever and ever! Amen!"

[13]One of the elders asked me, "Do you know who these people are that are dressed in white robes? Do you know where they come from?"

[14]"Sir," I answered, "you must know." Then he told me:

"These are the ones
who have gone through
the great suffering.
They have washed their robes
in the blood of the Lamb
and have made them white.
[15] And so they stand
before the throne of God
and worship him in his temple
day and night.
The one who sits on the throne
will spread his tent
over them.
[16] They will never hunger
or thirst again,
and they won't be troubled
by the sun
or any scorching heat.

[17] The Lamb in the center
of the throne
will be their shepherd.

He will lead them to streams
of life-giving water,
and God will wipe all tears
from their eyes."

The Seventh Seal Is Opened

8 When the Lamb opened the seventh seal, there was silence in heaven for about half an hour. [2]I noticed that the seven angels who stood before God were each given a trumpet.

[3]Another angel, who had a gold container for incense,[k] came and stood at the altar. This one was given a lot of incense to offer with the prayers of God's people on the gold altar in front of the throne. [4]Then the smoke of the incense, together with the prayers of God's people, went up to God from the hand of the angel.

[5]After this, the angel filled the incense container with fire from the altar and threw it on the earth. Thunder roared, lightning flashed, and the earth shook.

The Trumpets

[6]The seven angels now got ready to blow their trumpets.

[7]When the first angel blew his trumpet, hail and fire mixed with blood were thrown down on the earth. A third of the earth, a third of the trees, and a third of all green plants were burned.

[8]When the second angel blew his trumpet, something like a great fiery mountain was thrown into the sea. A third of the sea turned to blood, [9]a third of the living creatures in the sea died, and a third of the ships were destroyed.

[10]When the third angel blew his trumpet, a great star fell from heaven. It was burning like a torch, and it fell on a third of the rivers and on a third of the springs of water. [11]The name of the star was Bitter, and a third of the water turned bitter. Many people died because the water was so bitter.

[12]When the fourth angel blew his trumpet, a third of the sun, a third of the moon, and a third of the stars were struck. They each lost a third of their light. So during a third of the day there was no light, and a third of the night was also without light.

[13]Then I looked and saw a lone eagle flying across the sky. It was shouting, "Trouble, trouble, trouble to everyone who lives on earth! The other three angels are now going to blow their trumpets."

9 When the fifth angel blew his trumpet, I saw a star[l] fall from the sky to earth. It was given the key to the tunnel that leads down to the deep pit. [2]As it opened the tunnel, smoke poured out

---

[k]8.3 *incense*: See the note at 5.8.
as living beings, such as angels.

[l]9.1 *star*: In the ancient world, stars were often thought of

like the smoke of a great furnace. The sun and the air turned dark because of the smoke. [3]Locusts[m] came out of the smoke and covered the earth. They were given the same power that scorpions have.

[4]The locusts were told not to harm the grass on the earth or any plant or any tree. They were to punish only those people who did not have God's mark on their foreheads. [5]The locusts were allowed to make them suffer for five months, but not to kill them. The suffering they caused was like the sting of a scorpion. [6]In those days people will want to die, but they will not be able to. They will hope for death, but it will escape from them.

[7]These locusts looked like horses ready for battle. On their heads they wore something like gold crowns, and they had human faces. [8]Their hair was like a woman's long hair, and their teeth were like those of a lion. [9]On their chests they wore armor made of iron. Their wings roared like an army of horse-drawn chariots rushing into battle. [10]Their tails were like a scorpion's tail with a stinger that had the power to hurt someone for five months. [11]Their king was the angel in charge of the deep pit. In Hebrew his name was Abaddon, and in Greek it was Apollyon.[n]

[12]The first horrible thing has now happened! But wait. Two more horrible things will happen soon.

[13]Then the sixth angel blew his trumpet. I heard a voice speak from the four corners of the gold altar that stands in the presence of God. [14]The voice spoke to this angel and said, "Release the four angels who are tied up beside the great Euphrates River." [15]The four angels had been prepared for this very hour and day and month and year. Now they were set free to kill a third of all people. [16]By listening, I could tell there were more than two hundred million of these war horses. [17]In my vision their riders wore fiery-red, dark-blue, and yellow armor on their chests. The heads of the horses looked like lions, with fire and smoke and sulfur coming out of their mouths. [18]One-third of all people were killed by the three terrible troubles caused by the fire, the smoke, and the sulfur. [19]The horses had powerful mouths, and their tails were like poisonous snakes that bite and hurt.

[20]The people who lived through these terrible troubles did not turn away from the idols they had made, and they did not stop worshiping demons. They kept on worshiping idols that were made of gold, silver, bronze, stone, and wood. Not one of these idols could see, hear, or walk. [21]No one stopped murdering or practicing witchcraft or being immoral or stealing.

The Angel and the Little Scroll

10 I saw another powerful angel come down from heaven. This one was covered with a cloud, and a rainbow was over his head. His face was like the sun, his legs were like columns of fire, [2]and with his hand he held a little scroll[o] that had been unrolled. He stood there with his right foot on the sea and his left foot on the land. [3]Then he shouted with a voice that sounded like a growling lion. Thunder roared seven times.

[4]After the thunder stopped, I was about to write what it had said. But a voice from heaven shouted, "Keep it secret! Don't write these things."

[5]The angel I had seen standing on the sea and the land then held his right hand up toward heaven. [6]He made a promise in the name of God who lives forever and who created heaven, earth, the sea, and every living creature. The angel said, "You won't have to wait any longer. [7]God told his secret plans to his servants the prophets, and it will all happen by the time the seventh angel sounds his trumpet."

[8]Once again the voice from heaven spoke to me. It said, "Go and take the open scroll from the hand of the angel standing on the sea and the land."

[9]When I went over to ask the angel for the little scroll, the angel said, "Take the scroll and eat it! Your stomach will turn sour, but the taste in your mouth will be as sweet as honey." [10]I took the little scroll from the hand of the angel and ate it. The taste was as sweet as honey, but my stomach turned sour.

[11]Then some voices said, "Keep on telling what will happen to the people of many nations, races, and languages, and also to kings."

The Two Witnesses

11 An angel gave me a measuring stick and said:
Measure around God's temple. Be sure to include the altar and everyone worshiping there. [2]But don't measure the courtyard outside the temple building. Leave it out. It has been given to those people who don't know God, and they will trample all over the holy city for forty-two months. [3]My two witnesses will

---

[m]**9.3** *Locusts:* A type of grasshopper that comes in swarms and causes great damage to crops.
[n]**9.11** *Abaddon . . . Apollyon:* The Hebrew word "Abaddon" and the Greek word "Apollyon" each mean "destruction." [o]**10.2** *scroll:* See the note at 5.1.

wear sackcloth,[p] while I let them preach for one thousand two hundred sixty days.

[4]These two witnesses are the two olive trees and the two lampstands that stand in the presence of the Lord who rules the earth. [5]Any enemy who tries to harm them will be destroyed by the fire that comes out of their mouths. [6]They have the power to lock up the sky and to keep rain from falling while they are prophesying. And whenever they want to, they can turn water to blood and cause all kinds of terrible troubles on earth.

[7]After the two witnesses have finished preaching God's message, the beast that lives in the deep pit will come up and fight against them. It will win the battle and kill them. [8]Their bodies will be left lying in the streets of the same great city where their Lord was nailed to a cross. And that city is spiritually like the city of Sodom or the country of Egypt.

[9]For three and a half days the people of every nation, tribe, language, and race will stare at the bodies of these two witnesses and refuse to let them be buried. [10]Everyone on earth will celebrate and be happy. They will give gifts to each other, because of what happened to the two prophets who caused them so much trouble. [11]But three and a half days later, God will breathe life into their bodies. They will stand up, and everyone who sees them will be terrified.

[12]The witnesses then heard a loud voice from heaven, saying, "Come up here." And while their enemies were watching, they were taken up to heaven in a cloud. [13]At that same moment there was a terrible earthquake that destroyed a tenth of the city. Seven thousand people were killed, and the rest were frightened and praised the God who rules in heaven.

[14]The second horrible thing has now happened! But the third one will be here soon.

The Seventh Trumpet

[15]At the sound of the seventh trumpet, loud voices were heard in heaven. They said,

"Now the kingdom
of this world
belongs to our Lord
and to his Chosen One!
And he will rule
forever and ever!"

[16]Then the twenty-four elders, who were seated on thrones in God's presence, knelt down and worshiped him. [17]They said,

"Lord God All-Powerful,
you are and you were,
and we thank you.
You used your great power
and started ruling.
[18] When the nations got angry,
you became angry too!
Now the time has come
for the dead
to be judged.
It is time for you to reward
your servants the prophets
and all of your people
who honor your name,
no matter who they are.
It is time to destroy everyone
who has destroyed
the earth."

[19]The door to God's temple in heaven was then opened, and the sacred chest[q] could be seen inside the temple. I saw lightning and heard roars of thunder. The earth trembled and huge hailstones fell to the ground.

The Woman and the Dragon

12 Something important appeared in the sky. It was a woman whose clothes were the sun. The moon was under her feet, and a crown made of twelve stars was on her head. [2]She was about to give birth, and she was crying because of the great pain.

[3]Something else appeared in the sky. It was a huge red dragon with seven heads and ten horns, and a crown on each of its seven heads. [4]With its tail, it dragged a third of the stars from the sky and threw them down to the earth. Then the dragon turned toward the woman, because it wanted to eat her child as soon as it was born.

[5]The woman gave birth to a son, who would rule all nations with an iron rod. The boy was snatched away. He was taken to God and placed on his throne. [6]The woman ran into the desert to a place that God had prepared for her. There she would be taken care of for one thousand two hundred sixty days.

Michael Fights the Dragon

[7]A war broke out in heaven. Michael and his angels were fighting against the dragon and its angels. [8]But the dragon lost the battle. It and its angels were forced out of their places in heaven [9]and were thrown down to the earth. Yes, that old snake and his angels were thrown out of heaven! That snake, who fools everyone on earth, is known as the devil

and Satan. [10]Then I heard a voice from heaven shout,

"Our God has shown
his saving power,
and his kingdom has come!
God's own Chosen One
has shown his authority.
Satan accused our people
in the presence of God
day and night.
Now he has been thrown out!

[11] Our people defeated Satan
because of the blood[r]
of the Lamb
and the message of God.
They were willing
to give up their lives.

[12] The heavens should rejoice,
together with everyone
who lives there.
But pity the earth
and the sea,
because the devil
was thrown down
to the earth.
He knows his time is short,
and he is very angry."

[13]When the dragon realized that it had been thrown down to the earth, it tried to make trouble for the woman who had given birth to a son. [14]But the woman was given two wings like those of a huge eagle, so that she could fly into the desert. There she would escape from the snake and be taken care of for a time, two times, and half a time. [15]The snake then spewed out water like a river to sweep the woman away. [16]But the earth helped her and swallowed the water that had come from the dragon's mouth. [17]This made the dragon terribly angry with the woman. So it started a war against the rest of her children. They are the people who obey God and are faithful to what Jesus did and taught. [18]The dragon[s] stood on the beach beside the sea.

The Two Beasts

13 I looked and saw a beast coming up from the sea. This one had ten horns and seven heads, and a crown was on each of its ten horns. On each of its heads were names that were an insult to God. [2]The beast that I saw had the body of a leopard, the feet of a bear, and the mouth of a lion. The dragon handed over its own power and throne and great authority to this beast. [3]One of its heads seemed to have been fatally wounded, but now it was well. Everyone on earth marveled at this beast, [4]and they worshiped the dragon who had given its authority to the beast. They also worshiped the beast and said, "No one is like this beast! No one can fight against it."

[5]The beast was allowed to brag and claim to be God, and for forty-two months it was allowed to rule. [6]The beast cursed God, and it cursed the name of God. It even cursed the place where God lives, as well as everyone who lives in heaven with God. [7]It was allowed to fight against God's people and defeat them. It was also given authority over the people of every tribe, nation, language, and race. [8]The beast was worshiped by everyone whose name wasn't written before the time of creation in the book of the Lamb who was killed.[t]

[9] If you have ears,
then listen!
[10] If you are doomed
to be captured,
you will be captured.
If you are doomed
to be killed by a sword,
you will be killed
by a sword.

This means that God's people must learn to endure and be faithful!

[11]I now saw another beast. This one came out of the ground. It had two horns like a lamb, but spoke like a dragon. [12]It worked for the beast whose fatal wound had been healed. And it used all its authority to force the earth and its people to worship that beast. [13]It worked mighty miracles, and while people watched, it even made fire come down from the sky.

[14]This second beast fooled people on earth by working miracles for the first one. Then it talked them into making an idol in the form of the beast that did not die after being wounded by a sword. [15]It was allowed to put breath into the idol, so that it could speak. Everyone who refused to worship the idol of the beast was put to death. [16]All people were forced to put a mark on their right hand or forehead. Whether they were powerful or weak, rich or poor, free people or slaves, [17]they all had to have this mark, or else they could not buy or sell anything. This mark stood for the name of the beast and for the number of its name.

[18]You need wisdom to understand the number of the beast! But if you are smart enough, you can figure this out.

---

[r]12.11 *blood*: Or "death." [s]12.18 *The dragon*: The text has "he," and some manuscripts have "I." [t]13.8 *wasn't written . . . was killed*: Or "not written in the book of the Lamb who was killed before the time of creation."

Its number is six hundred sixty-six, and it stands for a person.

The Lamb and His 144,000 Followers

14 I looked and saw the Lamb standing on Mount Zion![u] With him were a hundred forty-four thousand, who had his name and his Father's name written on their foreheads. [2]Then I heard a sound from heaven that was like a roaring flood or loud thunder or even like the music of harps. [3]And a new song was being sung in front of God's throne and in front of the four living creatures and the elders. No one could learn that song, except the one hundred forty-four thousand who had been rescued from the earth. [4]All of these are pure virgins, and they follow the Lamb wherever he leads. They have been rescued to be presented to God and the Lamb as the most precious people[v] on earth. [5]They never tell lies, and they are innocent.

The Messages of the Three Angels

[6]I saw another angel. This one was flying across the sky and had the eternal good news to announce to the people of every race, tribe, language, and nation on earth. [7]The angel shouted, "Worship and honor God! The time has come for him to judge everyone. Kneel down before the one who created heaven and earth, the oceans, and every stream."

[8]A second angel followed and said, "The great city of Babylon has fallen! This is the city that made all nations drunk and immoral. Now God is angry, and Babylon has fallen."

[9]Finally, a third angel came and shouted:

Here is what will happen if you worship the beast and the idol and have the mark of the beast on your hand or forehead. [10]You will have to drink the wine that God gives to everyone who makes him angry. You will feel his mighty anger, and you will be tortured with fire and burning sulfur, while the holy angels and the Lamb look on. [11]If you worship the beast and the idol and accept the mark of its name, you will be tortured day and night. The smoke from your torture will go up forever and ever, and you will never be able to rest. [12]God's people must learn to endure.

They must also obey his commands and have faith in Jesus.

[13]Then I heard a voice from heaven say, "Put this in writing. From now on, the Lord will bless everyone who has faith in him when they die."

The Spirit answered, "Yes, they will rest from their hard work, and they will be rewarded for what they have done."

The Earth Is Harvested

[14]I looked and saw a bright cloud, and someone who seemed to be the Son of Man[w] was sitting on the cloud. He wore a gold crown on his head and held a sharp sickle[x] in his hand. [15]An angel came out of the temple and shouted, "Start cutting with your sickle! Harvest season is here, and all crops on earth are ripe." [16]The one on the cloud swung his sickle and harvested the crops.

[17]Another angel with a sharp sickle then came out of the temple in heaven. [18]After this, an angel with power over fire came from the altar and shouted to the angel who had the sickle. He said, "All grapes on earth are ripe! Harvest them with your sharp sickle." [19]The angel swung his sickle on earth and cut off its grapes. He threw them into a pit[y] where they were trampled on as a sign of God's anger. [20]The pit was outside the city, and when the grapes were mashed, blood flowed out. The blood turned into a river that was about two hundred miles long and almost deep enough to cover a horse.

The Last of the Terrible Troubles

15 After this, I looked at the sky and saw something else that was strange and important. Seven angels were bringing the last seven terrible troubles. When these are ended, God will no longer be angry.

[2]Then I saw something that looked like a glass sea mixed with fire, and people were standing on it. They were the ones who had defeated the beast and the idol and the number that tells the name of the beast. God had given them harps, [3]and they were singing the song that his servant Moses and the Lamb had sung. They were singing,

"Lord God All-Powerful,
 you have done great
    and marvelous things.
You are the ruler
    of all nations,

---

[u]14.1 *Mount Zion*: Another name for Jerusalem.   [v]14.4 *the most precious people*: The Greek text has "the first people." The Law of Moses taught that the first-born of all animals and the first part of the harvest were special and belonged to the Lord.   [w]14.14 *Son of Man*: See the note at 1.13.   [x]14.14 *sickle*: A knife with a long curved blade, used to cut grain and other crops.   [y]14.19 *pit*: It was the custom to put grapes in a pit (called a wine press) and stomp on them to make juice that would later turn into wine.

and you do what is
   right and fair.
4 Lord, who doesn't honor
   and praise your name?
You alone are holy,
and all nations will come
   and worship you,
because you have shown
that you judge
   with fairness."

5After this, I noticed something else in heaven. The sacred tent used for a temple was open. 6And the seven angels who were bringing the terrible troubles were coming out of it. They were dressed in robes of pure white linen and wore belts made of pure gold. 7One of the four living creatures gave each of the seven angels a bowl made of gold. These bowls were filled with the anger of God who lives forever and ever. 8The temple quickly filled with smoke from the glory and power of God. No one could enter it until the seven angels had finished pouring out the seven last troubles.

The Bowls of God's Anger

16 From the temple I heard a voice shout to the seven angels, "Go and empty the seven bowls of God's anger on the earth."

2The first angel emptied his bowl on the earth. At once ugly and painful sores broke out on everyone who had the mark of the beast and worshiped the idol.

3The second angel emptied his bowl on the sea. Right away the sea turned into blood like that of a dead person, and every living thing in the sea died.

4The third angel emptied his bowl into the rivers and streams. At once they turned to blood. 5Then I heard the angel, who has power over water, say,

"You have always been,
and you always will be
   the holy God.
You had the right
   to judge in this way.
6 They poured out the blood[z]
   of your people
   and your prophets.
So you gave them blood
   to drink, as they deserve!"
7 After this, I heard
   the altar shout,
"Yes, Lord God All-Powerful,
your judgments are honest
   and fair."

8The fourth angel emptied his bowl on the sun, and it began to scorch people like fire. 9Everyone was scorched by its great heat, and all of them cursed the name of God who had power over these terrible troubles. But no one turned to God and praised him.

10The fifth angel emptied his bowl on the throne of the beast. At once darkness covered its kingdom, and its people began biting their tongues in pain. 11And because of their painful sores, they cursed the God who rules in heaven. But still they did not stop doing evil things.

12The sixth angel emptied his bowl on the great Euphrates River, and it completely dried up to make a road for the kings from the east. 13An evil spirit that looked like a frog came out of the mouth of the dragon. One also came out of the mouth of the beast, and another out of the mouth of the false prophet. 14These evil spirits had the power to work miracles. They went to every king on earth, to bring them together for a war against God All-Powerful. But that will be the day of God's great victory.

15Remember that Christ says, "When I come, it will surprise you like a thief! But God will bless you, if you are awake and ready. Then you won't have to walk around naked and be ashamed."

16Those armies came together in a place that in Hebrew is called Armagedon.[a]

17As soon as the seventh angel emptied his bowl in the air, a loud voice from the throne in the temple shouted, "It's done!" 18There were flashes of lightning, roars of thunder, and the worst earthquake in all history. 19The great city of Babylon split into three parts, and the cities of other nations fell. So God made Babylon drink from the wine cup that was filled with his anger. 20Every island ran away, and the mountains disappeared. 21Hailstones, weighing about a hundred pounds each, fell from the sky on people. Finally, the people cursed God, because the hail was so terrible.

The Prostitute and the Beast

17 One of the seven angels who had emptied the bowls came over and said to me, "Come on! I will show you how God will punish that shameless prostitute who sits on many oceans. 2Every king on earth has slept with her, and her shameless ways are like wine that has made everyone on earth drunk."

3With the help of the Spirit, the angel took me into the desert, where I saw a woman sitting on a red beast. The beast

---

[z]16.6 *They poured out the blood*: A way of saying, "They murdered." [a]16.16 *Armagedon*: The Hebrew form of the name would be "Har Megiddo," meaning "Hill of Megiddo," where many battles were fought in ancient times (see Judges 5.19; 2 Kings 23.29, 30).

was covered with names that were an insult to God, and it had seven heads and ten horns. [4]The woman was dressed in purple and scarlet robes, and she wore jewelry made of gold, precious stones, and pearls. In her hand she held a gold cup filled with the filthy and nasty things she had done. [5]On her forehead a mysterious name was written:

I AM THE GREAT CITY OF BABYLON, THE MOTHER OF EVERY IMMORAL AND FILTHY THING ON EARTH.

[6]I could tell that the woman was drunk on the blood of God's people who had given their lives for Jesus. This surprising sight amazed me, [7]and the angel said:

Why are you so amazed? I will explain the mystery about this woman and about the beast she is sitting on, with its seven heads and ten horns. [8]The beast you saw is one that used to be and no longer is. It will come back from the deep pit, but only to be destroyed. Everyone on earth whose names were not written in the book of life[b] before the time of creation will be amazed. They will see this beast that used to be and no longer is, but will be once more.

[9]Anyone with wisdom can figure this out. The seven heads that the woman is sitting on stand for seven hills. These heads are also seven kings. [10]Five of the kings are dead. One is ruling now, and the other one has not yet come. But when he does, he will rule for only a little while. [11]You also saw a beast that used to be and no longer is. That beast is one of the seven kings who will return as the eighth king, but only to be destroyed.

[12]The ten horns that you saw are ten more kings, who have not yet come into power, and they will rule with the beast for only a short time. [13]They all think alike and will give their power and authority to the beast. [14]These kings will go to war against the Lamb. But he will defeat them, because he is Lord over all lords and King over all kings. His followers are chosen and special and faithful.

[15]The oceans that you saw the prostitute sitting on are crowds of people from all races and languages. [16]The ten horns and the beast will start hating the shameless woman. They will strip off her clothes and leave her naked. Then they will eat

her flesh and throw the rest of her body into a fire. [17]God is the one who made these kings all think alike and decide to give their power to the beast. And they will do this until what God has said comes true.

[18]The woman you saw is the great city that rules over all kings on earth.

The Fall of Babylon

18 I saw another angel come from heaven. This one had great power, and the earth was bright because of his glory. [2]The angel shouted,

"Fallen! Powerful Babylon
  has fallen
and is now the home
  of demons.
It is the den
  of every filthy spirit
and of all unclean birds,
  and every dirty
  and hated animal.
[3] Babylon's evil and immoral wine
  has made all nations drunk.
Every king on earth
  has slept with her,
and every merchant on earth
is rich because of
  her evil desires."

[4] Then I heard another voice
  from heaven shout,
"My people, you must escape
  from Babylon.
Don't take part in her sins
  and share her punishment.
[5] Her sins are piled
  as high as heaven.
God has remembered the evil
  she has done.
[6] Treat her as she
  has treated others.
Make her pay double
  for what she has done.
Make her drink twice as much
of what she mixed
  for others.
[7] That woman honored herself
  with a life of luxury.
Reward her now
  with suffering and pain.

"Deep in her heart
Babylon said,
  'I am the queen!
Never will I be a widow
or know what it means
  to be sad.'
[8] And so, in a single day
she will suffer the pain
  of sorrow, hunger, and death.
Fire will destroy
  her dead body,

[b]**17.8** *book of life*: See the note at 3.5.

because her judge
is the powerful Lord God."

9Every king on earth who slept with her and shared in her luxury will mourn. They will weep, when they see the smoke from that fire. **10**Her sufferings will frighten them, and they will stand at a distance and say,

"Pity that great
and powerful city!
Pity Babylon!
In a single hour
her judgment has come."

11Every merchant on earth will mourn, because there is no one to buy their goods. **12**There won't be anyone to buy their gold, silver, jewels, pearls, fine linen, purple cloth, silk, scarlet cloth, sweet-smelling wood, fancy carvings of ivory and wood, as well as things made of bronze, iron, or marble. **13**No one will buy their cinnamon, spices, incense, myrrh, frankincense,ᶜ wine, olive oil, fine flour, wheat, cattle, sheep, horses, chariots, slaves, and other humans.

14 Babylon, the things
your heart desired
have all escaped
from you.
Every luxury
and all your glory
will be lost forever.
You will never
get them back.

15The merchants had become rich because of her. But when they saw her sufferings, they were terrified. They stood at a distance, crying and mourning. **16**Then they shouted,

"Pity the great city
of Babylon!
She dressed in fine linen
and wore purple
and scarlet cloth.
She had jewelry
made of gold
and precious stones
and pearls.
17 Yet in a single hour
her riches disappeared."

Every ship captain and passenger and sailor stood at a distance, together with everyone who does business by traveling on the sea. **18**When they saw the smoke from her fire, they shouted, "This was the greatest city ever!"
19They cried loudly, and in their sorrow they threw dust on their heads, as they said,

"Pity the great city
of Babylon!

Everyone who sailed the seas
became rich
from her treasures.
But in a single hour
the city was destroyed.
20 The heavens should be happy
with God's people
and apostles and prophets.
God has punished her
for them."

21A powerful angel then picked up a huge stone and threw it into the sea. The angel said,

"This is how the great city
of Babylon
will be thrown down,
never to rise again.
22 The music of harps and singers
and of flutes and trumpets
will no longer be heard.
No workers will ever
set up shop in that city,
and the sound
of grinding grain
will be silenced forever.
23 Lamps will no longer shine
anywhere in Babylon,
and couples will never again
say wedding vows there.
Her merchants ruled
the earth,
and by her witchcraft
she fooled all nations.
24 On the streets of Babylon
is found the blood
of God's people
and of his prophets,
and everyone else."

19 After this, I heard what sounded like a lot of voices in heaven, and they were shouting,

"Praise the Lord!
To our God belongs
the glorious power to save,
2 because his judgments
are honest and fair.
That filthy prostitute
ruined the earth
with shameful deeds.
But God has judged her
and made her pay
the price for murdering
his servants."

3Then the crowd shouted,

"Praise the Lord!
Smoke will never stop rising
from her burning body."

4After this, the twenty-four elders and the four living creatures all knelt before the throne of God and worshiped him. They said, "Amen! Praise the Lord!"

ᶜ **18.13** *myrrh, frankincense*: Myrrh was a valuable sweet-smelling powder often used in perfume. Frankincense was a valuable powder that was burned to make a sweet smell.

The Marriage Supper of the Lamb

⁵From the throne a voice said,

"If you worship
and fear our God,
give praise to him,
no matter who you are."

⁶Then I heard what seemed to be a large crowd that sounded like a roaring flood and loud thunder all mixed together. They were saying,

"Praise the Lord!
Our Lord God All-Powerful
now rules as king.
⁷ So we will be glad and happy
and give him praise.
The wedding day of the Lamb
is here,
and his bride is ready.
⁸ She will be given
a wedding dress
made of pure
and shining linen.
This linen stands for
the good things
God's people have done."

⁹Then the angel told me, "Put this in writing. God will bless everyone who is invited to the wedding feast of the Lamb." The angel also said, "These things that God has said are true."

¹⁰I knelt at the feet of the angel and began to worship him. But the angel said, "Don't do that! I am a servant, just like you and everyone else who tells about Jesus. Don't worship anyone but God. Everyone who tells about Jesus does it by the power of the Spirit."

The Rider on the White Horse

¹¹I looked and saw that heaven was open, and a white horse was there. Its rider was called Faithful and True, and he is always fair when he judges or goes to war. ¹²He had eyes like flames of fire, and he was wearing a lot of crowns. His name was written on him, but he was the only one who knew what the name meant.

¹³The rider wore a robe that was covered with[d] blood, and he was known as "The Word of God." ¹⁴He was followed by armies from heaven that rode on horses and were dressed in pure white linen. ¹⁵From his mouth a sharp sword went out to attack the nations. He will rule them with an iron rod and will show the fierce anger of God All-Powerful by trampling the grapes in the pit where wine is made. ¹⁶On the part of the robe that covered his thigh was written, "KING OF KINGS AND LORD OF LORDS."

¹⁷I then saw an angel standing on the sun, and he shouted to all the birds flying in the sky, "Come and join in God's great feast! ¹⁸You can eat the flesh of kings, rulers, leaders, horses, riders, free people, slaves, important people, and everyone else."

¹⁹I also saw the beast and all kings of the earth come together. They fought against the rider on the white horse and against his army. ²⁰But the beast was captured and so was the false prophet. This is the same prophet who had worked miracles for the beast, so that he could fool everyone who had the mark of the beast and worshiped the idol. The beast and the false prophet were thrown alive into a lake of burning sulfur. ²¹But the rest of their army was killed by the sword that came from the mouth of the rider on the horse. Then birds stuffed themselves on the dead bodies.

The Thousand Years

20 I saw an angel come down from heaven, carrying the key to the deep pit and a big chain. ²He chained the dragon for a thousand years. It is that old snake, who is also known as the devil and Satan. ³Then the angel threw the dragon into the pit. He locked and sealed it, so that a thousand years would go by before the dragon could fool the nations again. But after that, it would have to be set free for a little while.

⁴I saw thrones, and sitting on those thrones were the ones who had been given the right to judge. I also saw the souls of the people who had their heads cut off because they had told about Jesus and preached God's message. They were the same ones who had not worshiped the beast or the idol, and they had refused to let its mark be put on their hands or foreheads. They will come to life and rule with Christ for a thousand years.

⁵⁻⁶These people are the first to be raised to life, and they are especially blessed and holy. The second death[e] has no power over them. They will be priests for God and Christ and will rule with them for a thousand years.

No other dead people were raised to life until a thousand years later.

Satan Is Defeated

⁷At the end of the thousand years, Satan will be set free. ⁸He will fool the countries of Gog and Magog, which are at the far ends of the earth, and their people will follow him into battle. They will have as many followers as there are

---

[d]**19.13** *covered with*: Some manuscripts have "sprinkled with."   [e]**20.5,6** *second death*: See the note at 2.11.

grains of sand along the beach, [9]and they will march all the way across the earth. They will surround the camp of God's people and the city that his people love. But fire will come down from heaven and destroy the whole army. [10]Then the devil who fooled them will be thrown into the lake of fire and burning sulfur. He will be there with the beast and the false prophet, and they will be in pain day and night forever and ever.

The Judgment at the Great White Throne

[11]I saw a great white throne with someone sitting on it. Earth and heaven tried to run away, but there was no place for them to go. [12]I also saw all the dead people standing in front of that throne. Every one of them was there, no matter who they had once been. Several books were opened, and then the book of life[f] was opened. The dead were judged by what those books said they had done.

[13]The sea gave up the dead people who were in it, and death and its kingdom also gave up their dead. Then everyone was judged by what they had done. [14]Afterwards, death and its kingdom were thrown into the lake of fire. This is the second death.[g] [15]Anyone whose name wasn't written in the book of life was thrown into the lake of fire.

The New Heaven and the New Earth

21 I saw a new heaven and a new earth. The first heaven and the first earth had disappeared, and so had the sea. [2]Then I saw New Jerusalem, that holy city, coming down from God in heaven. It was like a bride dressed in her wedding gown and ready to meet her husband.

[3]I heard a loud voice shout from the throne:

God's home is now with his people. He will live with them, and they will be his own. Yes, God will make his home among his people. [4]He will wipe all tears from their eyes, and there will be no more death, suffering, crying, or pain. These things of the past are gone forever.

[5]Then the one sitting on the throne said:

I am making everything new. Write down what I have said. My words are true and can be trusted. [6]Everything is finished! I am Alpha and Omega,[h] the beginning and the

end. I will freely give water from the life-giving fountain to everyone who is thirsty. [7]All who win the victory will be given these blessings. I will be their God, and they will be my people.

[8]But I will tell you what will happen to cowards and to everyone who is unfaithful or dirty-minded or who murders or is sexually immoral or uses witchcraft or worships idols or tells lies. They will be thrown into that lake of fire and burning sulfur. This is the second death.[i]

The New Jerusalem

[9]I saw one of the seven angels who had the bowls filled with the seven last terrible troubles. The angel came to me and said, "Come on! I will show you the one who will be the bride and wife of the Lamb." [10]Then with the help of the Spirit, he took me to the top of a very high mountain. There he showed me the holy city of Jerusalem coming down from God in heaven.

[11]The glory of God made the city bright. It was dazzling and crystal clear like a precious jasper stone. [12]The city had a high and thick wall with twelve gates, and each one of them was guarded by an angel. On each of the gates was written the name of one of the twelve tribes of Israel. [13]Three of these gates were on the east, three were on the north, three more were on the south, and the other three were on the west. [14]The city was built on twelve foundation stones. On each of the stones was written the name of one of the Lamb's twelve apostles.

[15]The angel who spoke to me had a gold measuring stick to measure the city and its gates and its walls. [16]The city was shaped like a cube, because it was just as high as it was wide. When the angel measured the city, it was about fifteen hundred miles high and fifteen hundred miles wide. [17]Then the angel measured the wall, and by our measurements it was about two hundred sixteen feet high.

[18]The wall was built of jasper, and the city was made of pure gold, clear as crystal. [19]Each of the twelve foundations was a precious stone. The first was jasper,[j] the second was sapphire, the third was agate, the fourth was emerald, [20]the fifth was onyx, the sixth was carnelian, the seventh was chrysolite, the

---

[f]**20.12** *book of life*: See the note at 3.5.   [g]**20.14** *second death*: See the note at 2.11.
[h]**21.6** *Alpha and Omega*: See the note at 1.8.   [i]**21.8** *second death*: See the note at 2.11.
[j]**21.19** *jasper*: The precious and semi-precious stones mentioned in verses 19, 20 are of different colors. *Jasper* is usually green or clear; *sapphire* is blue; *agate* has circles of brown and white; *emerald* is green; *onyx* has different bands of color; *carnelian* is deep-red or reddish-white; *chrysolite* is olive-green; *beryl* is green or bluish-green; *topaz* is yellow; *chrysoprase* is apple-green; *jacinth* is reddish-orange; and *amethyst* is deep purple.

eighth was beryl, the ninth was topaz, the tenth was chrysoprase, the eleventh was jacinth, and the twelfth was amethyst. ²¹Each of the twelve gates was a solid pearl. The streets of the city were made of pure gold, clear as crystal.

²²I did not see a temple there. The Lord God All-Powerful and the Lamb were its temple. ²³And the city did not need the sun or the moon. The glory of God was shining on it, and the Lamb was its light.

²⁴Nations will walk by the light of that city, and kings will bring their riches there. ²⁵Its gates are always open during the day, and night never comes. ²⁶The glorious treasures of nations will be brought into the city. ²⁷But nothing unworthy will be allowed to enter. No one who is dirty-minded or who tells lies will be there. Only those whose names are written in the Lamb's book of life*ᵏ* will be in the city.

22 The angel showed me a river that was crystal clear, and its waters gave life. The river came from the throne where God and the Lamb were seated. ²Then it flowed down the middle of the city's main street. On each side of the river are trees*ˡ* that grow a different kind of fruit each month of the year. The fruit gives life, and the leaves are used as medicine to heal the nations.

³God's curse will no longer be on the people of that city. He and the Lamb will be seated there on their thrones, and its people will worship God ⁴and will see him face to face. God's name will be written on the foreheads of the people. ⁵Never again will night appear, and no one who lives there will ever need a lamp or the sun. The Lord God will be their light, and they will rule forever.

The Coming of Christ

⁶Then I was told:

These words are true and can be trusted. The Lord God controls the spirits of his prophets, and he is the one who sent his angel to show his servants what must happen right away. ⁷Remember, I am coming soon! God will bless everyone who pays attention to the message of this book.

⁸My name is John, and I am the one who heard and saw these things. Then after I had heard and seen all this, I knelt down and began to worship at the feet of the angel who had shown it to me.

⁹But the angel said,

Don't do that! I am a servant, just like you. I am the same as a follower or a prophet or anyone else who obeys what is written in this book. God is the one you should worship.

¹⁰Don't keep the prophecies in this book a secret. These things will happen soon. ¹¹Evil people will keep on being evil, and everyone who is dirty-minded will still be dirty-minded. But good people will keep on doing right, and God's people will always be holy.

¹²Then I was told:

I am coming soon! And when I come, I will reward everyone for what they have done. ¹³I am Alpha and Omega,*ᵐ* the first and the last, the beginning and the end.

¹⁴God will bless all who have washed their robes. They will each have the right to eat fruit from the tree that gives life, and they can enter the gates of the city. ¹⁵But outside the city will be dogs, witches, immoral people, murderers, idol worshipers, and everyone who loves to tell lies and do wrong.

¹⁶I am Jesus! And I am the one who sent my angel to tell all of you these things for the churches. I am David's Great Descendant,*ⁿ* and I am also the bright morning star.*ᵒ*

¹⁷The Spirit and the bride say, "Come!"

Everyone who hears this*ᵖ* should say, "Come!"

If you are thirsty, come! If you want life-giving water, come and take it. It's free!

¹⁸Here is my warning for everyone who hears the prophecies in this book:

If you add anything to them, God will make you suffer all the terrible troubles written in this book. ¹⁹If you take anything away from these prophecies, God will not let you have part in the life-giving tree and in the holy city described in this book.

²⁰The one who has spoken these things says, "I am coming soon!"

So, Lord Jesus, please come soon! ²¹I pray that the Lord Jesus will be kind to all of you.

---

*ᵏ*21.27 *book of life*: See the note at 3.5. *ˡ*22.2 *trees*: The Greek has "tree," which is used in a collective sense of trees on both sides of the heavenly river. *ᵐ*22.13 *Alpha and Omega*: See the note at 1.8. *ⁿ*22.16 *David's Great Descendant*: See the note at 5.5. *ᵒ*22.16 *the bright morning star*: Probably thought of as the brightest star (see 2.27, 28). *ᵖ*22.17 *who hears this*: The reading of the book of Revelation in a service of worship.

PSALMS

ABOUT THIS BOOK

The book of Psalms is the longest book in the Bible. Psalms are poems that can either be sung as songs or spoken as prayers by individuals or groups. There are 150 psalms in this book, and many of them list King David as their author. They were collected over a long period of time and became a very important part of the worship of the people of Israel.

Some of the psalms tell the music leader what instruments should be used and what tunes should be followed. For example, look at Psalm 4 and Psalm 45.

Many of the Bible's main ideas are echoed in the Psalms: praise, thankfulness, faith, hope, sorrow for sin, God's loyalty and help. And at the heart of all the psalms there is a deep trust in God. The writers of the psalms always express their true feelings, whether they are praising God for his blessings or complaining in times of trouble.

In ancient Israel the psalms were used in several different ways: (1) to praise God, as in Psalm 105; (2) to express sorrow, as in Psalm 13; (3) to teach, as in Psalm 1; (4) to honor Israel's king and pray for fairness in his rule, as in Psalm 72; (5) to tell of God's power over all creation, as in Psalm 47; (6) to show love for Jerusalem, as in Psalm 122; and (7) to celebrate festivals, as in Psalm 126. Of course, many of the psalms could be used for more than one purpose.

Jesus used the psalms when he preached and taught, and they were often quoted by the writers of the New Testament. The earliest Christians also used the psalms in worship, teaching, and telling others the good news about what God has done through Jesus Christ. A verse from Psalm 118, for example, is directly referred to six times in the New Testament:

> *The stone that the builders*
> *tossed aside*
> *has now become*
> *the most important stone.*
> *(118.22)*

A QUICK LOOK AT THIS BOOK

The book of Psalms is divided into five sections or "books." Most of the psalms in Books I and II were written by David, while many in Book III were written by either Asaph or the people of Korah. Psalms 120–134 are all "celebration psalms." The five sections of the book of Psalms are:

Book I (1–41)
Book II (42–72)
Book III (73–89)
Book IV (90–106)
Book V (107–150)

BOOK I

(Psalms 1–41)

Psalm 1

The Way to Happiness

¹ God blesses those people
  who refuse evil advice
and won't follow sinners
  or join in sneering at God.
² Instead, the Law of the LORD
  makes them happy,
and they think about it
  day and night.
³ They are like trees
  growing beside a stream,

trees that produce
fruit in season
and always have leaves.
Those people succeed
in everything they do.

⁴ That isn't true of those
who are evil,
because they are like straw
blown by the wind.
⁵ Sinners won't have an excuse
on the day of judgment,
and they won't have a place
with the people of God.
⁶ The LORD protects everyone
who follows him,
but the wicked follow a road
that leads to ruin.

Psalm 2

The LORD's Chosen King

¹ Why do the nations plot,ᵃ
and why do their people
make useless plans?ᵇ
² The kings of this earth
have all joined together
to turn against the LORD
and his chosen one.
³ They say, "Let's cut the ropes
and set ourselves free!"

⁴ In heaven the LORD laughs
as he sits on his throne,
making fun of the nations.
⁵ The LORD becomes furious
and threatens them.
His anger terrifies them
as he says,
⁶ "I've put my king on Zion,
my sacred hill."

⁷ I will tell the promise
that the LORD made to me:
"You are my son, because today
I have become your father.
⁸ Ask me for the nations,
and every nation on earth
will belong to you.
⁹ You will smash them
with an iron rod
and shatter them
like dishes of clay."

¹⁰ Be smart, all you rulers,
and pay close attention.
¹¹ Serve and honor the LORD;
be glad and tremble.
¹² Show respect to his son
because if you don't,
the LORD might become furious
and suddenly destroy you.ᶜ

But he blesses and protects
everyone who runs to him.

Psalm 3

*[Written by David when he was
running from his son Absalom.]*

An Early Morning Prayer

¹ I have a lot of enemies, LORD.
Many fight against ²me and say,
"God won't rescue you!"

³ But you are my shield,
and you give me victory
and great honor.
⁴ I pray to you, and you answer
from your sacred hill.

⁵ I sleep and wake up refreshed
because you, LORD,
protect me.
⁶ Ten thousand enemies attack
from every side,
but I am not afraid.

⁷ Come and save me, LORD God!
Break my enemies' jaws
and shatter their teeth,
⁸ because you protect
and bless your people.

Psalm 4

*[A psalm by David for the music leader.
Use stringed instruments.]*

An Evening Prayer

¹ You are my God and protector.
Please answer my prayer.
I was in terrible distress,
but you set me free.
Now have pity and listen
as I pray.

² How long will you people
refuse to respect me?ᵈ
You love foolish things,
and you run after
what is worthless.ᵉ

³ The LORD has chosen
everyone who is faithful
to be his very own,ᶠ
and he answers my prayers.
⁴ But each of you
had better tremble
and turn from your sins.
Silently search your heart
as you lie in bed.
⁵ Offer the proper sacrifices
and trust the LORD.

ᵃ**2.1** *Why . . . plot?*: Or "Why are the nations restless?"   ᵇ**2.1** *make useless plans*: Or
"grumble uselessly."   ᶜ**2.11,12** *Serve . . . you*: One possible meaning for the difficult Hebrew
text of verses 11, 12.   ᵈ**4.2** *me*: Or "my God."   ᵉ**4.2** *foolish . . . worthless*: This may refer
to idols and false gods.   ᶠ**4.3** *has chosen . . . very own*: Some Hebrew manuscripts have
"work miracles for his faithful people."

6 There are some who ask,
  "Who will be good to us?"
Let your kindness, LORD,
  shine brightly on us.
7 You brought me more happiness
than a rich harvest
  of grain and grapes.
8 I can lie down
  and sleep soundly
because you, LORD,
  will keep me safe.

Psalm 5
[*A psalm by David
for the music leader. Use flutes.*]

A Prayer for Help

1 Listen, LORD, as I pray!
  Pay attention when I groan.*g*
2 You are my King and my God.
Answer my cry for help
  because I pray to you.
3 Each morning you listen
  to my prayer,
as I bring my requests*h* to you
  and wait for your reply.

4 You are not the kind of God
who is pleased with evil.
  Sinners can't stay with you.
5 No one who boasts can stand
in your presence, LORD,
  and you hate evil people.
6 You destroy every liar,
and you despise violence
  and deceit.

7 Because of your great mercy,
  I come to your house, LORD,
and I am filled with wonder
as I bow down to worship
  at your holy temple.
8 You do what is right,
  and I ask you to guide me.
Make your teaching clear
  because of my enemies.

9 Nothing they say is true!
  They just want to destroy.
Their words are deceitful
  like a hidden pit,
and their tongues are good
  only for telling lies.
10 Punish them, God,
  and let their own plans
  bring their downfall.
Get rid of them!
They keep committing crimes
  and turning against you.

11 Let all who run to you
  for protection

always sing joyful songs.
Provide shelter for those
who truly love you
  and let them rejoice.
12 Our LORD, you bless those
  who live right,
and you shield them
  with your kindness.

Psalm 6
[*A psalm by David for the music leader.
Use stringed instruments.*i]

A Prayer in Time of Trouble

1 Don't punish me, LORD,
or even correct me
  when you are angry!
2 Have pity on me and heal
  my feeble body.
My bones tremble with fear,
3 and I am in deep distress.
  How long will it be?

4 Turn and come to my rescue.
Show your wonderful love
  and save me, LORD.
5 If I die, I cannot praise you
  or even remember you.
6 My groaning has worn me out.
At night my bed and pillow
  are soaked with tears.
7 Sorrow has made my eyes dim,
and my sight has failed
  because of my enemies.

8 You, LORD, heard my crying,
and those hateful people
  had better leave me alone.
9 You have answered my prayer
  and my plea for mercy.
10 My enemies will be ashamed
  and terrified,
as they quickly run away
  in complete disgrace.

Psalm 7
[*Written by David.j He sang this to the LORD
because of Cush from the tribe of Benjamin.*]

The LORD Always Does Right

1 You, LORD God,
  are my protector.
Rescue me and keep me safe
  from all who chase me.
2 Or else they will rip me apart
like lions attacking a victim,
  and no one will save me.

3 I am innocent, LORD God!
4 I have not betrayed a friend
  or had pity on an enemy*k*
  who attacks for no reason.

---

*g***5.1** *when I groan*: Or "to my thoughts" or "to my words."   *h***5.3** *requests*: Or "sacrifices."
*i***Psalm 6** *instruments*: The Hebrew text adds "according to the sheminith," which may refer to
a musical instrument with eight strings.   *j***Psalm 7** *Written by David*: The Hebrew text has
"a shiggaion by David," which may refer to a psalm of mourning.   *k***7.4** *had pity on an
enemy*: Or "failed to have pity on an enemy."

5 If I have done any of this,
then let my enemies
chase and capture me.
Let them stomp me to death
and leave me in the dirt.

6 Get angry, LORD God!
Do something!
Attack my furious enemies.
See that justice is done.
7 Make the nations come to you,
as you sit on your throne[l]
above them all.

8 Our LORD, judge the nations!
Judge me and show that I
am honest and innocent.
9 You know every heart and mind,
and you always do right.
Now make violent people stop,
but protect all of us
who obey you.

10 You, God, are my shield,
the protector of everyone
whose heart is right.
11 You see that justice is done,
and each day
you take revenge.
12 Whenever your enemies refuse
to change their ways,
you sharpen your sword
and string your bow.
13 Your deadly arrows are ready
with flaming tips.

14 An evil person is like a woman
about to give birth
to a hateful, deceitful,
and rebellious child.
15 Such people dig a deep hole,
then fall in it themselves.
16 The trouble they cause
comes back on them,
and their heads are crushed
by their own evil deeds.

17 I will praise you, LORD!
You always do right.
I will sing about you,
the LORD Most High.

Psalm 8
[_A psalm by David for the music leader._[m]]

The Wonderful Name of the LORD

1 Our LORD and Ruler,
your name is wonderful
everywhere on earth!
You let your glory be seen[n]
in the heavens above.
2 With praises from children

and from tiny infants,
you have built a fortress.
It makes your enemies silent,
and all who turn against you
are left speechless.

3 I often think of the heavens
your hands have made,
and of the moon and stars
you put in place.
4 Then I ask, "Why do you care
about us humans?
Why are you concerned
for us weaklings?"
5 You made us a little lower
than you yourself,[o]
and you have crowned us
with glory and honor.

6 You let us rule everything
your hands have made.
And you put all of it
under our power—
7 the sheep and the cattle,
and every wild animal,
8 the birds in the sky,
the fish in the sea,
and all ocean creatures.

9 Our LORD and Ruler,
your name is wonderful
everywhere on earth!

Psalm 9
[_A psalm by David for the music leader.
To the tune "The Death of the Son."_]

Sing Praises to the LORD

1 I will praise you, LORD,
with all my heart
and tell about the wonders
you have worked.
2 God Most High, I will rejoice;
I will celebrate and sing
because of you.

3 When my enemies face you,
they run away and stumble
and are destroyed.
4 You take your seat as judge,
and your fair decisions prove
that I was in the right.
5 You warn the nations
and destroy evil people;
you wipe out their names
forever and ever.
6 Our enemies are destroyed
completely for all time.
Their cities are torn down,
and they will never
be remembered again.

---

[l]7.7 _sit . . . throne_: Or "return to your place."   [m]**Psalm 8** _leader_: The Hebrew text adds
"according to the gittith," which may refer to either a musical instrument or a tune.
[n]8.1 _You . . . seen_: Or "I will worship your glory."   [o]8.5 _you yourself_: Or "the angels" or "the
beings in heaven."

7 You rule forever, LORD,
and you are on your throne,
ready for judgment.
8 You judge the world fairly
and treat all nations
with justice.
9 The poor can run to you
because you are a fortress
in times of trouble.
10 Everyone who honors your name
can trust you,
because you are faithful
to all who depend on you.

11 You rule from Zion, LORD,
and we sing about you
to let the nations know
everything you have done.
12 You did not forget
to punish the guilty
or listen to the cries
of those in need.

13 Please have mercy, LORD!
My enemies mistreat me.
Keep me from the gates
that lead to death,
14 and I will sing about you
at the gate to Zion.
I will be happy there
because you rescued me.

15 Our LORD, the nations fell
into their own pits,
and their feet were caught
in their own traps.
16 You showed what you are like,
and you made certain
that justice is done,
but evil people are trapped
by their own evil deeds.
17 The wicked will go down
to the world of the dead
to be with those nations
that forgot about you.

18 The poor and the homeless
won't always be forgotten
and without hope.

19 Do something, LORD!
Don't let the nations win.
Make them stand trial
in your court of law.
20 Make the nations afraid
and let them all discover
just how weak they are.

Psalm 10

A Prayer for Help

1 Why are you far away, LORD?
Why do you hide yourself
when I am in trouble?
2 Proud and brutal people
hunt down the poor.

But let them get caught
by their own evil plans!
3 The wicked brag about
their deepest desires.
Those greedy people hate
and curse you, LORD.
4 The wicked are too proud
to turn to you
or even think about you.
5 They are always successful,
though they can't understand
your teachings,
and they keep sneering
at their enemies.

6 In their hearts they say,
"Nothing can hurt us!
We'll always be happy
and free from trouble."
7 They curse and tell lies,
and all they talk about
is how to be cruel
or how to do wrong.

8 They hide outside villages,
waiting to strike and murder
some innocent victim.
9 They are hungry lions
hiding in the bushes,
hoping to catch
some helpless passerby.
They trap the poor in nets
and drag them away.
10 They crouch down and wait
to grab a victim.
11 They say, "God can't see!
He's got on a blindfold."

12 Do something, LORD God,
and use your powerful arm
to help those in need.
13 The wicked don't respect you.
In their hearts they say,
"God won't punish us!"

14 But you see the trouble
and the distress,
and you will do something.
The poor can count on you,
and so can orphans.
15 Now break the arms
of all merciless people.
Punish them for doing wrong
and make them stop.

16 Our LORD, you will always rule,
but nations will vanish
from the earth.
17 You listen to the longings
of those who suffer.
You offer them hope,
and you pay attention
to their cries for help.
18 You defend orphans
and everyone else in need,
so that no one on earth
can terrify others again.

Psalm 11
[A psalm by David for the music leader.]

Trusting the LORD

1 The LORD is my fortress!
   Don't say to me,
   "Escape like a bird
      to the mountains!"
2 You tell me, "Watch out!
   Those evil people have put
      their arrows on their bows,
   and they are standing
   in the shadows,
      aiming at good people.
3 What can an honest person do
      when everything crumbles?"

4 The LORD is sitting
   in his sacred temple
      on his throne in heaven.
   He knows everything we do
      because he sees us all.
5 The LORD tests honest people,
   but despises those
      who are cruel
      and love violence.
6 He will send fiery coals[p]
   and flaming sulfur
      down on the wicked,
   and they will drink nothing
      but a scorching wind.

7 The LORD always does right
      and wants justice done.
   Everyone who does right
      will see his face.

Psalm 12
[A psalm by David for the music leader.[q]]

A Prayer for Help

1 Please help me, LORD!
   All who were faithful
   and all who were loyal
      have disappeared.
2 Everyone tells lies,
      and no one is sincere.
3 Won't you chop off
   all flattering tongues
      that brag so loudly?
4 They say to themselves,
   "We are great speakers.
      No one else has a chance."

5 But you, LORD, tell them,
   "I will do something!
   The poor are mistreated
   and helpless people moan.
   I'll rescue all who suffer."

6 Our LORD, you are true
      to your promises,

and your word is like silver
heated seven times
   in a fiery furnace.[r]
7 You will protect us
   and always keep us safe
      from those people.
8 But all who are wicked
      will keep on strutting,
   while everyone praises
      their shameless deeds.[s]

Psalm 13
[A psalm by David for the music leader.]

A Prayer for the LORD's Help

1 How much longer, LORD,
      will you forget about me?
   Will it be forever?
      How long will you hide?
2 How long must I be confused
      and miserable all day?
   How long will my enemies
      keep beating me down?

3 Please listen, LORD God,
      and answer my prayers.
   Make my eyes sparkle again,
   or else I will fall
      into the sleep of death.
4 My enemies will say,
      "Now we've won!"
   They will be greatly pleased
      when I am defeated.

5 I trust your love,
   and I feel like celebrating
      because you rescued me.
6 You have been good to me, LORD,
      and I will sing about you.

Psalm 14
[A psalm by David for the music leader.]

No One Can Ignore the LORD

1 Only a fool would say,
      "There is no God!"
   People like that are worthless;
   they are heartless and cruel
      and never do right.

2 From heaven the LORD
      looks down to see
   if anyone is wise enough
      to search for him.
3 But all of them are corrupt;
      no one does right.

4 Won't you evil people learn?
      You refuse to pray,
   and you gobble down
      the LORD's people.

---

[p]**11.6** *fiery coals*: Or "trouble, fire."   [q]**Psalm 12** *leader*: The Hebrew text adds "according to the sheminith," which may be a musical instrument with eight strings.   [r]**12.6** *in a fiery furnace*: The Hebrew text has "in a furnace to the ground," which may describe part of a process for refining silver in Old Testament times.   [s]**12.8** *while . . . deeds*: One possible meaning for the difficult Hebrew text.

⁵ But you will be frightened,
  because God is on the side
    of every good person.
⁶ You may spoil the plans
  of the poor,
    but the LORD protects them.

⁷ I long for someone from Zion
    to come and save Israel!
  Our LORD, when you bless
    your people again,
  Jacob's family will be glad,
    and Israel will celebrate.

Psalm 15
[*A psalm by David.*]

Who May Worship the LORD?

¹ Who may stay in God's temple
  or live on the holy mountain
    of the LORD?

² Only those who obey God
    and do as they should.
  They speak the truth
³   and don't spread gossip;
  they treat others fairly
    and don't say cruel things.

⁴ They hate worthless people,
  but show respect for all
    who worship the LORD.
  And they keep their promises,
    no matter what the cost.
⁵ They lend their money
    without charging interest,
  and they don't take bribes
    to hurt the innocent.

  Those who do these things
    will always stand firm.

Psalm 16
[*A special psalm by David.*]

The Best Choice

¹ Protect me, LORD God!
    I run to you for safety,
² and I have said,
    "Only you are my Lord!
  Every good thing I have
    is a gift from you."

³ Your people are wonderful,
    and they make me happy,ᵗ
⁴ but worshipers of other gods
    will have much sorrow.ᵘ
  I refuse to offer sacrifices
  of blood to those gods
    or worship in their name.

⁵ You, LORD, are all I want!
  You are my choice,
    and you keep me safe.

⁶ You make my life pleasant,
    and my future is bright.

⁷ I praise you, LORD,
    for being my guide.
  Even in the darkest night,
    your teachings fill my mind.
⁸ I will always look to you,
    as you stand beside me
    and protect me from fear.
⁹ With all my heart,
  I will celebrate,
    and I can safely rest.

¹⁰ I am your chosen one.
  You won't leave me in the grave
    or let my body decay.
¹¹ You have shown me
    the path to life,
  and you make me glad
    by being near to me.
  Sitting at your right side,ᵛ
    I will always be joyful.

Psalm 17
[*A prayer by David.*]

The Prayer of an Innocent Person

¹ I am innocent, LORD!
  Won't you listen as I pray
    and beg for help?
  I am honest!
    Please hear my prayer.
² Only you can say
    that I am innocent,
  because only your eyes
    can see the truth.

³ You know my heart,
    and even during the night
  you have tested me
    and found me innocent.
  I have made up my mind
    never to tell a lie.
⁴ I don't do like others.
  I obey your teachings
    and am not cruel.
⁵ I have followed you,
    without ever stumbling.

⁶ I pray to you, God,
    because you will help me.
  Listen and answer my prayer!
⁷   Show your wonderful love.
  Your mighty arm protects those
  who run to you for safety
    from their enemies.
⁸ Protect me as you would
    your very own eyes;
  hide me in the shadow
    of your wings.

ᵗ**16.3** *Your people . . . happy*: Or "I was happy worshiping gods I thought were powerful."
ᵘ**16.4** *but . . . sorrow*: One possible meaning for the difficult Hebrew text.   ᵛ**16.11** *right side*:
The place of power and honor.

⁹ Don't let my brutal enemies
attack from all sides
and kill me.
¹⁰ They refuse to show mercy,
and they keep bragging.

¹¹ They have caught up with me!
My enemies are everywhere,
eagerly hoping to smear me
in the dirt.
¹² They are like hungry lions
hunting for food,
or like young lions
hiding in ambush.

¹³ Do something, LORD!
Attack and defeat them.
Take your sword and save me
from those evil people.
¹⁴ Use your powerful arm
and rescue me
from the hands of mere humans
whose world won't last.ʷ

You provide food
for those you love.
Their children have plenty,
and their grandchildren
will have more than enough.

¹⁵ I am innocent, LORD,
and I will see your face!
When I awake, all I want
is to see you as you are.

Psalm 18

_[For the music leader. A psalm by David, the
LORD's servant. David sang this to the LORD
after the LORD had rescued him from his
enemies, but especially from Saul.]_

David's Song of Thanks

¹ I love you, LORD God,
and you make me strong.
² You are my mighty rock,ˣ
my fortress, my protector,
the rock where I am safe,
my shield, my powerful weapon,ʸ
and my place of shelter.

³ I praise you, LORD!
I prayed, and you rescued me
from my enemies.
⁴ Death had wrapped
its ropes around me,
and I was almost swallowed
by its flooding waters.

⁵ Ropes from the world
of the dead
had coiled around me,
and death had set a trap
in my path.

⁶ I was in terrible trouble
when I called out to you,
but from your temple
you heard me
and answered my prayer.
⁷ The earth shook and shivered,
and the mountains trembled
down to their roots.
You were angry
⁸   and breathed out smoke.
Scorching heat and fiery flames
spewed from your mouth.

⁹ You opened the heavens
like curtains,
and you came down
with storm clouds
under your feet.
¹⁰ You rode on the backs
of flying creatures
and swooped down
with the wind as wings.
¹¹ Darkness was your robe;
thunderclouds filled the sky,
hiding you from sight.
¹² Hailstones and fiery coals
lit up the sky
in front of you.

¹³ LORD Most High, your voice
thundered from the heavens,
as hailstones and fiery coals
poured down like rain.
¹⁴ You scattered your enemies
with arrows of lightning.
¹⁵ You roared at the sea,
and its deepest channels
could be seen.
You snorted,
and the earth shook
to its foundations.

¹⁶ You reached down from heaven,
and you lifted me
from deep in the ocean.
¹⁷ You rescued me from enemies,
who were hateful
and too powerful for me.
¹⁸ On the day disaster struck,
they came and attacked,
but you defended me.
¹⁹ When I was fenced in,
you freed and rescued me
because you love me.

²⁰ You are good to me, LORD,
because I do right,
and you reward me
because I am innocent.
²¹ I do what you want
and never turn to do evil.

ʷ**17.14** _last:_ One possible meaning for the difficult Hebrew text of verse 14.   ˣ**18.2** _mighty
rock:_ The Hebrew text has "rock," which is sometimes used in poetry to compare the Lord to a
mountain where his people can run for protection from their enemies.   ʸ**18.2** _my powerful
weapon:_ The Hebrew text has "the horn," which refers to the horn of a bull, one of the most
powerful animals in ancient Palestine.

22 I keep your laws in mind
and never look away
from your teachings.
23 I obey you completely
and guard against sin.
24 You have been good to me
because I do right;
you have rewarded me
for being innocent
by your standards.

25 You are always loyal
to your loyal people,
and you are faithful
to the faithful.
26 With all who are sincere,
you are sincere,
but you treat the unfaithful
as their deeds deserve.
27 You rescue the humble,
but you put down all
who are proud.

28 You, the LORD God,
keep my lamp burning
and turn darkness to light.
29 You help me defeat armies
and capture cities.

30 Your way is perfect, LORD,
and your word is correct.
You are a shield for those
who run to you for help.
31 You alone are God!
Only you are a mighty rock. z
32 You give me strength
and guide me right.
33 You make my feet run as fast
as those of a deer,
and you help me stand
on the mountains.

34 You teach my hands to fight
and my arms to use
a bow of bronze.
35 You alone are my shield.
Your right hand supports me,
and by coming to help me,
you have made me famous.
36 You clear the way for me,
and now I won't stumble.

37 I kept chasing my enemies,
until I caught them
and destroyed them.
38 I stuck my sword
through my enemies,
and they were crushed
under my feet.
39 You helped me win victories,
and you forced my attackers
to fall victim to me.

40 You made my enemies run,
and I killed them.

41 They cried out for help,
but no one saved them;
they called out to you,
but there was no answer.
42 I ground them to dust
blown by the wind,
and I poured them out
like mud in the streets.

43 You rescued me
from stubborn people,
and you made me the leader
of foreign nations,
who are now my slaves.
44 They obey and come crawling.
45   They have lost all courage,
and from their fortresses,
they come trembling.

46 You are the living LORD!
I will praise you.
You are a mighty rock. z
I will honor you
for keeping me safe.
47 You took revenge for me,
and you put nations
in my power.
48 You protected me
from violent enemies
and made me much greater
than all of them.

49 I will praise you, LORD,
and I will honor you
among the nations.
50 You give glorious victories
to your chosen king.
Your faithful love for David
and for his descendants
will never end.

Psalm 19
[*A psalm by David for the music leader.*]

The Wonders of God and the
Goodness of His Law

1 The heavens keep telling
the wonders of God,
and the skies declare
what he has done.
2 Each day informs
the following day;
each night announces
to the next.
3 They don't speak a word,
and there is never
the sound of a voice.
4 Yet their message reaches
all the earth,
and it travels
around the world.

In the heavens a tent
is set up for the sun.
5 It rises like a bridegroom

---

z **18.31** *mighty rock*: See the note at 18.2.   z **18.46** *mighty rock*: See the note at 18.2.

and gets ready like a hero
  eager to run a race.
⁶ It travels all the way
across the sky.
  Nothing hides from its heat.

⁷ The Law of the LORD is perfect;
  it gives us new life.
His teachings last forever,
and they give wisdom
  to ordinary people.
⁸ The LORD's instruction is right;
  it makes our hearts glad.
His commands shine brightly,
  and they give us light.

⁹ Worshiping the LORD is sacred;
  he will always be worshiped.
All of his decisions
  are correct and fair.
¹⁰ They are worth more
  than the finest gold
and are sweeter than honey
  from a honeycomb.

¹¹ By your teachings, Lord,
  I am warned;
by obeying them,
  I am greatly rewarded.
¹² None of us know our faults.
Forgive me when I sin
  without knowing it.
¹³ Don't let me do wrong
  on purpose, Lord,
or let sin have control
  over my life.
Then I will be innocent,
and not guilty
  of some terrible fault.

¹⁴ Let my words and my thoughts
  be pleasing to you, LORD,
because you are my mighty rock ᶻ
  and my protector.

Psalm 20
[*A psalm by David for the music leader.*]

A Prayer for Victory

¹ I pray that the LORD
will listen when you
  are in trouble,
and that the God of Jacob
  will keep you safe.
² May the LORD send help
  from his temple
and come to your rescue
  from Mount Zion.
³ May he remember your gifts
and be pleased
  with what you bring.

⁴ May God do what you want most
  and let all go well for you.

⁵ Then you will win victories,
  and we will celebrate,
while raising our banners
  in the name of our God.
May the LORD answer
  all of your prayers!

⁶ I am certain, LORD,
that you will help
  your chosen king.
You will answer my prayers
from your holy place
  in heaven,
and you will save me
  with your mighty arm.

⁷ Some people trust the power
of chariots or horses,
  but we trust you, LORD God.
⁸ Others will stumble and fall,
but we will be strong
  and stand firm.

⁹ Give the king victory, LORD,
  and answer our prayers. ᵃ

Psalm 21
[*A psalm by David for the music leader.*]

Thanking the LORD for Victory

¹ Our LORD, your mighty power
  makes the king glad,
and he celebrates victories
  that you have given him.
² You did what he wanted most
  and never told him "No."
³ You truly blessed the king,
and you placed on him
  a crown of finest gold.
⁴ He asked to live a long time,
and you promised him life
  that never ends.

⁵ The king is highly honored.
You have let him win victories
  that have made him famous.
⁶ You have given him blessings
  that will last forever,
and you have made him glad
  by being so near to him.
⁷ LORD Most High,
  the king trusts you,
and your kindness
  keeps him from defeat.

⁸ With your mighty arm, LORD,
you will strike down all
  of your hateful enemies.
⁹ They will be destroyed by fire
  once you are here,
and because of your anger,
  flames will swallow them.
¹⁰ You will wipe their families
  from the earth,
  and they will disappear.

ᶻ **19.14** *mighty rock*: See the note at 18.2.

ᵃ **20.9** *victory . . . prayers*: Or "victory. He (God or the king) answers us."

11 All their plans to harm you
   will come to nothing.
12 You will make them run away
   by shooting your arrows
   at their faces.

13 Show your strength, LORD,
   so that we may sing
   and praise your power.

Psalm 22

[*A psalm by David for the music leader.
To the tune "A Deer at Dawn."*]

Suffering and Praise

1 My God, my God, why have you
   deserted me?
Why are you so far away?
Won't you listen to my groans
   and come to my rescue?
2 I cry out day and night,
   but you don't answer,
   and I can never rest.

3 Yet you are the holy God,
   ruling from your throne
   and praised by Israel.
4 Our ancestors trusted you,
   and you rescued them.
5 When they cried out for help,
   you saved them,
   and you did not let them down
   when they depended on you.

6 But I am merely a worm,
   far less than human,
   and I am hated and rejected
   by people everywhere.
7 Everyone who sees me
   makes fun and sneers.
They shake their heads,
8   and say, "Trust the LORD!
If you are his favorite,
   let him protect you
   and keep you safe."

9 You, LORD, brought me
   safely through birth,
   and you protected me
   when I was a baby
   at my mother's breast.
10 From the day I was born,
   I have been in your care,
   and from the time of my birth,
   you have been my God.

11 Don't stay far off
   when I am in trouble
   with no one to help me.
12 Enemies are all around
   like a herd of wild bulls.
Powerful bulls from Bashan*b*
   are everywhere.

13 My enemies are like lions
   roaring and attacking
   with jaws open wide.

14 I have no more strength
   than a few drops of water.
All my bones are out of joint;
   my heart is like melted wax.
15 My strength has dried up
   like a broken clay pot,
and my tongue sticks
   to the roof of my mouth.
You, God, have left me
   to die in the dirt.

16 Brutal enemies attack me
   like a pack of dogs,
   tearing at*c* my hands
   and my feet.
17 I can count all my bones,
   and my enemies just stare
   and sneer at me.
18 They took my clothes
   and gambled for them.

19 Don't stay far away, LORD!
My strength comes from you,
   so hurry and help.
20 Rescue me from enemy swords
   and save me from those dogs.
21   Don't let lions eat me.

You rescued me from the horns
   of wild bulls,
22 and when your people meet,
   I will praise you, LORD.

23 All who worship the LORD,
   now praise him!
You belong to Jacob's family
   and to the people of Israel,
   so fear and honor the LORD!
24 The LORD doesn't hate
   or despise the helpless
   in all of their troubles.
When I cried out, he listened
   and did not turn away.

25 When your people meet,
   you will fill my heart
   with your praises, LORD,
and everyone will see me
   keep my promises to you.
26 The poor will eat and be full,
   and all who worship you
   will be thankful
   and live in hope.

27 Everyone on this earth
   will remember you, LORD.
People all over the world
   will turn and worship you,
28 because you are in control,
   the ruler of all nations.

*b***22.12** *Bashan:* A land east of the Jordan River, where there were pastures suitable for raising
fine cattle.   *c***22.16** *tearing at:* One possible meaning for the difficult Hebrew text.

²⁹ All who are rich
and have more than enough
will bow down to you, Lord.
Even those who are dying
and almost in the grave
will come and bow down.
³⁰ In the future, everyone
will worship and learn
about you, our Lord.
³¹ People not yet born
will be told,
"The Lord has saved us!"

Psalm 23
[*A psalm by David.*]

The Good Shepherd

¹ You, LORD, are my shepherd.
I will never be in need.
² You let me rest in fields
of green grass.
You lead me to streams
of peaceful water,
³   and you refresh my life.

You are true to your name,
and you lead me
along the right paths.
⁴ I may walk through valleys
as dark as death,
but I won't be afraid.
You are with me,
and your shepherd's rod^d
makes me feel safe.

⁵ You treat me to a feast,
while my enemies watch.
You honor me as your guest,
and you fill my cup
until it overflows.

⁶ Your kindness and love
will always be with me
each day of my life,
and I will live forever
in your house, LORD.

Psalm 24
[*A psalm by David.*]

Who Can Enter the LORD's Temple?

¹ The earth and everything on it
belong to the LORD.
The world and its people
belong to him.
² The LORD placed it all
on the oceans and rivers.

³ Who may climb the LORD's hill^e
or stand in his holy temple?
⁴ Only those who do right
for the right reasons,

and don't worship idols
or tell lies under oath.
⁵ The LORD God, who saves them,
will bless and reward them,
⁶ because they worship and serve
the God of Jacob.^f
⁷ Open the ancient gates,
so that the glorious king
may come in.

⁸ Who is this glorious king?
He is our LORD, a strong
and mighty warrior.

⁹ Open the ancient gates,
so that the glorious king
may come in.

¹⁰ Who is this glorious king?
He is our LORD,
the All-Powerful!

Psalm 25
[*By David.*]

A Prayer for Guidance and Help

¹ I offer you my heart, LORD God,
²   and I trust you.
Don't make me ashamed
or let enemies defeat me.
³ Don't disappoint any
of your worshipers,
but disappoint all
deceitful liars.
⁴ Show me your paths
and teach me to follow;
⁵ guide me by your truth
and instruct me.
You keep me safe,
and I always trust you.

⁶ Please, LORD, remember,
you have always
been patient and kind.
⁷ Forget each wrong I did
when I was young.
Show how truly kind you are
and remember me.
⁸ You are honest and merciful,
and you teach sinners
how to follow your path.

⁹ You lead humble people
to do what is right
and to stay on your path.
¹⁰ In everything you do,
you are kind and faithful
to everyone who keeps
our agreement with you.

¹¹ Be true to your name, LORD,
by forgiving each one
of my terrible sins.

---

^d**23.4** *shepherd's rod:* The Hebrew text mentions two objects carried by the shepherd: a club to defend against wild animals and a long pole to guide and control the sheep.   ^e**24.3** *the* LORD's *hill:* The hill in Jerusalem where the temple was built.   ^f**24.6** *worship . . . Jacob:* Two ancient translations; Hebrew "worship God and serve the descendants of Jacob."

¹² You will show the right path
to all who worship you.
¹³ They will have plenty,
and then their children
will receive the land.

¹⁴ Our LORD, you are the friend
of your worshipers,
and you make an agreement
with all of us.
¹⁵ I always look to you,
because you rescue me
from every trap.
¹⁶ I am lonely and troubled.
Show that you care
and have pity on me.
¹⁷ My awful worries keep growing.
Rescue me from sadness.
¹⁸ See my troubles and misery
and forgive my sins.

¹⁹ Look at all my enemies!
See how much they hate me.
²⁰ I come to you for shelter.
Protect me, keep me safe,
and don't disappoint me.
²¹ I obey you with all my heart,
and I trust you, knowing
that you will save me.

²² Our God, please save Israel
from all of its troubles.

Psalm 26
[By David.]

The Prayer of an Innocent Person

¹ Show that I am right, LORD!
I stay true to myself,
and I have trusted you
without doubting.
² Test my thoughts and find out
what I am like.
³ I never forget your kindness,
and I am always faithful
to you.ᵍ
⁴ I don't spend my time
with worthless liars
⁵   or go with evil crowds.

⁶ I wash my hands, LORD,
to show my innocence,
and I worship at your altar,
⁷ while gratefully singing
about your wonders.
⁸ I love the temple
where you live, and where
your glory shines.
⁹ Don't sweep me away,
as you do sinners.
Don't punish me with death
as you do those people
who are brutal
¹⁰   or full of meanness
or who bribe others.

¹¹ I stay true to myself.
Be kind and rescue me.

¹² Now I stand on solid ground!
And when your people meet,
I will praise you, LORD.

Psalm 27
[By David.]

A Prayer of Praise

¹ You, LORD, are the light
that keeps me safe.
I am not afraid of anyone.
You protect me,
and I have no fears.
² Brutal people may attack
and try to kill me,
but they will stumble.
Fierce enemies may attack,
but they will fall.
³ Armies may surround me,
but I won't be afraid;
war may break out,
but I will trust you.

⁴ I ask only one thing, LORD:
Let me live in your house
every day of my life
to see how wonderful you are
and to pray in your temple.

⁵ In times of trouble,
you will protect me.
You will hide me in your tent
and keep me safe
on top of a mighty rock.ʰ
⁶ You will let me defeat
all of my enemies.
Then I will celebrate,
as I enter your tent
with animal sacrifices
and songs of praise.

⁷ Please listen when I pray!
Have pity. Answer my prayer.
⁸ My heart tells me to pray.
I am eager to see your face,
⁹   so don't hide from me.
I am your servant,
and you have helped me.
Don't turn from me in anger.
You alone keep me safe.
Don't reject or desert me.
¹⁰ Even if my father and mother
should desert me,
you will take care of me.

¹¹ Teach me to follow, LORD,
and lead me on the right path
because of my enemies.
¹² Don't let them do to me
what they want.
People tell lies about me
and make terrible threats,

ᵍ**26.3** *I am . . . to you*: Or "I trust your faithfulness."   ʰ**27.5** *mighty rock*: See the note at 18.2.

13 but I know I will live
   to see how kind you are.

14 Trust the LORD!
   Be brave and strong
      and trust the LORD.

Psalm 28
[*By David.*]

A Prayer for Help

1 Only you, LORD,
   are a mighty rock!*h*
Don't refuse to help me
   when I pray.
If you don't answer me,
   I will soon be dead.
2 Please listen to my prayer
      and my cry for help,
as I lift my hands
   toward your holy temple.

3 Don't drag me away, LORD,
      with those cruel people,
who speak kind words,
   while planning trouble.
4 Treat them as they deserve!
   Punish them for their sins.
5 They don't pay any attention
   to your wonderful deeds.
Now you will destroy them
   and leave them in ruin.

6 I praise you, LORD,
   for answering my prayers.
7 You are my strong shield,
   and I trust you completely.
You have helped me,
and I will celebrate
   and thank you in song.

8 You give strength
   to your people, LORD,
and you save and protect
   your chosen ones.
9 Come save us and bless us.
Be our shepherd and always
   carry us in your arms.

Psalm 29
[*A psalm by David.*]

The Voice of the LORD in a Storm

1 All of you angels*i* in heaven,
   honor the glory and power
   of the LORD!
2 Honor the wonderful name
   of the LORD,
and worship the LORD
   most holy and glorious.*j*

3 The voice of the LORD
   echoes over the oceans.
The glorious LORD God
   thunders above the roar
   of the raging sea,
4 and his voice is mighty
   and marvelous.
5 The voice of the LORD
   destroys the cedar trees;
the LORD shatters cedars
   on Mount Lebanon.
6 God makes Mount Lebanon
   skip like a calf
and Mount Hermon
   jump like a wild ox.

7 The voice of the LORD
   makes lightning flash
8   and the desert tremble.
And because of the LORD,
the desert near Kadesh
   shivers and shakes.

9 The voice of the LORD
   makes deer give birth
   before their time.*k*
Forests are stripped of leaves,
and the temple is filled
   with shouts of praise.

10 The LORD rules on his throne,
   king of the flood*l* forever.
11 Pray that our LORD
   will make us strong
      and give us peace.

Psalm 30
[*A psalm by David for the
dedication of the temple.*]

A Prayer of Thanks

1 I will praise you, LORD!
   You saved me from the grave
and kept my enemies
   from celebrating my death.
2 I prayed to you, LORD God,
   and you healed me,
3 saving me from death
   and the grave.

4 Your faithful people, LORD,
   will praise you with songs
      and honor your holy name.
5 Your anger lasts a little while,
but your kindness lasts
   for a lifetime.
At night we may cry,
but when morning comes
   we will celebrate.

6 I was carefree and thought,
   "I'll never be shaken!"

---

*h*28.1 *mighty rock*: See the note at 18.2.   *i*29.1 *angels*: Or "supernatural beings" or "gods."
*j*29.2 *most . . . glorious*: Or "in his holy place" or "and wear your glorious clothes."
*k*29.9 *makes . . . time*: Or "twists the oak trees around."   *l*29.10 *king of the flood*: In ancient
times the people of Israel believed that a mighty ocean surrounded all of creation, and that God
could release the water to flood the earth.

7 You, LORD, were my friend,
and you made me strong
as a mighty mountain.
But when you hid your face,
I was crushed.

8 I prayed to you, LORD,
and in my prayer I said,
9 "What good will it do you
if I am in the grave?
Once I have turned to dust,
how can I praise you
or tell how loyal you are?
10   Have pity, LORD! Help!"

11 You have turned my sorrow
into joyful dancing.
No longer am I sad
and wearing sackcloth.*m*
12 I thank you from my heart,
and I will never stop
singing your praises,
my LORD and my God.

Psalm 31
[*A psalm by David for the music leader.*]

A Prayer for Protection

1 I come to you, LORD,
for protection.
Don't let me be ashamed.
Do as you have promised
and rescue me.
2 Listen to my prayer
and hurry to save me.
Be my mighty rock*n*
and the fortress
where I am safe.

3 You, LORD God,
are my mighty rock
and my fortress.
Lead me and guide me,
so that your name
will be honored.
4 Protect me from hidden traps
and keep me safe.
5 You are faithful,
and I trust you
because you rescued me.

6 I hate the worshipers
of worthless idols,
but I trust you, LORD.
7 I celebrate and shout
because you are kind.
You saw all my suffering,
and you cared for me.
8 You kept me from the hands
of my enemies,
and you set me free.

9 Have pity, LORD!
I am hurting and almost blind.
My whole body aches.

10 I have known only sorrow
all my life long, and I suffer
year after year.
I am weak from sin,
and my bones are limp.

11 My enemies insult me.
Neighbors are even worse,
and I disgust my friends.
People meet me on the street,
and they turn and run.
12 I am completely forgotten
like someone dead.
I am merely a broken dish.
13 I hear the crowds whisper,
"Everyone is afraid!"
They are plotting and scheming
to murder me.

14 But I trust you, LORD,
and I claim you as my God.
15 My life is in your hands.
Save me from enemies
who hunt me down.
16 Smile on me, your servant.
Have pity and rescue me.

17 I pray only to you.
Don't disappoint me.
Disappoint my cruel enemies
until they lie silent
in their graves.
18 Silence those proud liars!
Make them stop bragging
and insulting your people.

19 You are wonderful,
and while everyone watches,
you store up blessings for all
who honor and trust you.
20 You are their shelter
from harmful plots,
and you are their protection
from vicious gossip.

21 I will praise you, LORD,
for showing great kindness
when I was like a city
under attack.
22 I was terrified and thought,
"They've chased me
far away from you!"
But you answered my prayer
when I shouted for help.

23 All who belong to the LORD,
show how you love him.
The LORD protects the faithful,
but he severely punishes
everyone who is proud.
24 All who trust the LORD,
be cheerful and strong.

*m*30.11 *sackcloth*: A rough, dark-colored cloth made from goat or camel hair and used to make grain sacks. It was worn in times of trouble or sorrow.   *n*31.2 *mighty rock*: See the note at 18.2.

Psalm 32

[A special psalm by David.]

The Joy of Forgiveness

1 Our God, you bless everyone
  whose sins you forgive
    and wipe away.
2 You bless them by saying,
  "You told me your sins,
without trying to hide them,
    and now I forgive you."

3 Before I confessed my sins,
  my bones felt limp,
    and I groaned all day long.
4 Night and day your hand
    weighed heavily on me,
and my strength was gone
    as in the summer heat.

5 So I confessed my sins
    and told them all to you.
I said, "I'll tell the LORD
    each one of my sins."
Then you forgave me
    and took away my guilt.

6 We worship you, Lord,
    and we should always pray
whenever we find out
    that we have sinned.°
Then we won't be swept away
    by a raging flood.
7 You are my hiding place!
    You protect me from trouble,
and you put songs in my heart
    because you have saved me.

8 You said to me,
  "I will point out the road
    that you should follow.
I will be your teacher
    and watch over you.
9 Don't be stupid
    like horses and mules
that must be led with ropes
    to make them obey."

10 All kinds of troubles
    will strike the wicked,
but your kindness shields those
    who trust you, LORD.
11 And so your good people
    should celebrate and shout.

Psalm 33

Sing Praises to the LORD

1 You are the LORD's people.
  Obey him and celebrate!
  He deserves your praise.
2 Praise the LORD with harps!
  Use harps with ten strings
    to make music for him.
3 Sing a new song. Shout!
  Play beautiful music.

4 The LORD is truthful;
  he can be trusted.
5 He loves justice and fairness,
  and he is kind to everyone
    everywhere on earth.

6 The LORD made the heavens
  and everything in them
    by his word.
7 He scooped up the ocean
  and stored the water.
8 Everyone in this world
  should worship and honor
    the LORD!
9 As soon as he spoke
    the world was created;
at his command,
    the earth was formed.

10 The LORD destroys the plans
  and spoils the schemes
    of the nations.
11 But what the LORD has planned
  will stand forever.
    His thoughts never change.
12 The LORD blesses each nation
  that worships only him.
    He blesses his chosen ones.
13 The LORD looks at the world
14 from his throne in heaven,
    and he watches us all.
15 The LORD gave us each a mind,
  and nothing we do
    can be hidden from him.

16 Mighty armies alone
    cannot win wars for a king;
great strength by itself
    cannot keep a soldier safe.
17 In war the strength of a horse
  cannot be trusted
    to take you to safety.
18 But the LORD watches over
  all who honor him
    and trust his kindness.
19 He protects them from death
  and starvation.

20 We depend on you, LORD,
  to help and protect us.
21 You make our hearts glad
  because we trust you,
    the only God.
22 Be kind and bless us!
  We depend on you.

Psalm 34

*[Written by David when he pretended to
be crazy in front of Abimelech, so that
Abimelech would send him away, and
David could leave.]*

Honor the LORD

1 I will always praise the LORD.
2 With all my heart,
  I will praise the LORD.

°**32.6** *whenever . . . sinned*: Hebrew "at a time of finding only."

Let all who are helpless,
 listen and be glad.
³ Honor the LORD with me!
 Celebrate his great name.

⁴ I asked the LORD for help,
 and he saved me
 from all my fears.
⁵ Keep your eyes on the LORD!
 You will shine like the sun
 and never blush with shame.
⁶ I was a nobody, but I prayed,
 and the LORD saved me
 from all my troubles.

⁷ If you honor the LORD,
 his angel will protect you.
⁸ Discover for yourself
 that the LORD is kind.
 Come to him for protection,
 and you will be glad.

⁹ Honor the LORD!
 You are his special people.
 No one who honors the LORD
 will ever be in need.
¹⁰ Young lions*p* may go hungry
 or even starve,
 but if you trust the LORD,
 you will never miss out
 on anything good.

¹¹ Come, my children, listen
 as I teach you
 to respect the LORD.
¹² Do you want to live
 and enjoy a long life?
¹³ Then don't say cruel things
 and don't tell lies.
¹⁴ Do good instead of evil
 and try to live at peace.

¹⁵ If you obey the LORD,
 he will watch over you
 and answer your prayers.
¹⁶ But God despises evil people,
 and he will wipe them all
 from the earth,
 till they are forgotten.
¹⁷ When his people pray for help,
 he listens and rescues them
 from their troubles.
¹⁸ The LORD is there to rescue
 all who are discouraged
 and have given up hope.

¹⁹ The LORD's people
 may suffer a lot,
 but he will always
 bring them safely through.
²⁰ Not one of their bones
 will ever be broken.

²¹ Wicked people are killed
 by their own evil deeds,
 and if you hate God's people
 you will be punished.
²² The LORD saves the lives
 of his servants.
 Run to him for protection,
 and you won't be punished.

Psalm 35
[A psalm by David.]

A Prayer for Protection from Enemies

¹ Fight my enemies, LORD!
 Attack my attackers!
² Shield me and help me.
³ Aim your spear at everyone
 who hunts me down,
 but promise to save me.

⁴ Let all who want to kill me
 be disappointed
 and disgraced.
 Chase away and confuse
 all who plan to harm me.
⁵ Send your angel after them
 and let them be like straw
 in the wind.
⁶ Make them run in the dark
 on a slippery road,
 as your angel chases them.
⁷ I did them no harm,
 but they hid a net
 to trap me,
 and they dug a deep pit
 to catch and kill me.
⁸ Surprise them with disaster!
 Trap them in their own nets
 and let them fall and rot
 in the pits they have dug.

⁹ I will celebrate and be joyful
 because you, LORD,
 have saved me.
¹⁰ Every bone in my body
 will shout:
 "No one is like the LORD!"
 You protect the helpless
 from those in power;
 you save the poor and needy
 from those who hurt them.

¹¹ Liars accuse me of crimes
 I know nothing about.
¹² They repay evil for good,
 and I feel all alone.
¹³ When they were sick,
 I wore sackcloth*q*
 and went without food.*r*
 I truly prayed for them,*s*
¹⁴ as I would for a friend
 or a relative.

---

*p***34.10** *Young lions*: In the Psalms wild animals often stand for God's enemies.
*q***35.13** *sackcloth*: See the note at 30.11.   *r***35.13** *went without food*: People sometimes went
without food (called "fasting") to show sorrow.   *s***35.13** *I . . . them*: Or "My prayer wasn't
answered, but I prayed."

I was in sorrow and mourned,
    as I would for my mother.

15 I have stumbled,
    and worthless liars
I don't even know
    surround me and sneer.
16 Worthless people make fun[t]
    and never stop laughing.
17 But all you do is watch!
    When will you do something?
Save me from the attack
    of those vicious lions.
18 And when your people meet,
    I will praise you
and thank you, Lord,
    in front of them all.

19 Don't let my brutal enemies
    be glad because of me.
They hate me for no reason.
Don't let them wink
    behind my back.
20 They say hurtful things,
    and they lie to people
    who want to live in peace.
21 They are quick to accuse me.
They say, "You did it!
    We saw you ourselves."

22 You see everything, LORD!
Please don't keep silent
    or stay so far away.
23 Fight to defend me, Lord God,
24 and prove that I am right
    by your standards.
Don't let them laugh at me
25   or say to each other,
"Now we've got what we want!
    We'll gobble him down!"

26 Disappoint and confuse
    all who are glad
    to see me in trouble,
but disgrace and embarrass
my proud enemies who say to me,
    "You are nothing!"

27 Let all who want me to win
    be happy and joyful.
From now on let them say,
    "The LORD is wonderful!
God is glad when all goes well
    for his servant."
28 Then I will shout all day,
    "Praise the LORD God!
    He did what was right."

Psalm 36
[For the music leader by David,
the LORD's servant.]

Human Sin and God's Goodness

1 Sinners don't respect God;
    sin is all they think about.

2 They like themselves too much
    to hate their own sins
    or even to see them.
3 They tell deceitful lies,
    and they don't have the sense
    to live right.
4 Those people stay awake,
    thinking up mischief,
and they follow the wrong road,
    refusing to turn from sin.

5 Your love is faithful, LORD,
    and even the clouds in the sky
    can depend on you.
6 Your decisions are always fair.
They are firm like mountains,
    deep like the sea,
and all people and animals
    are under your care.

7 Your love is a treasure,
    and everyone finds shelter
    in the shadow of your wings.
8 You give your guests a feast
    in your house,
and you serve a tasty drink
    that flows like a river.
9 The life-giving fountain
    belongs to you,
and your light gives light
    to each of us.

10 Our LORD, keep showing love
    to everyone who knows you,
and use your power to save all
    whose thoughts please you.
11 Don't let those proud
    and merciless people
kick me around
    or chase me away.

12 Look at those wicked people!
They are knocked down,
    never to get up again.

Psalm 37
[By David.]

Trust the LORD

1 Don't be annoyed by anyone
who does wrong,
    and don't envy them.
2 They will soon disappear
    like grass without rain.

3 Trust the LORD and live right!
The land will be yours,
    and you will be safe.
4 Do what the LORD wants,
    and he will give you
    your heart's desire.

5 Let the LORD lead you
    and trust him to help.
6 Then it will be as clear

[t]35.16 Worthless . . . fun: One possible meaning for the difficult Hebrew text.

as the noonday sun
  that you were right.

7 Be patient and trust the LORD.
  Don't let it bother you
when all goes well for those
  who do sinful things.
8 Don't be angry or furious.
  Anger can lead to sin.
9 All sinners will disappear,
but if you trust the LORD,
  the land will be yours.

10 Sinners will soon disappear,
  never to be found,
11 but the poor will take the land
  and enjoy a big harvest.

12 Merciless people make plots
against good people
  and snarl like animals,
13 but the Lord laughs and knows
  their time is coming soon.
14 The wicked kill with swords
and shoot arrows to murder
  the poor and the needy
  and all who do right.
15 But they will be killed
  by their own swords,
and their arrows
  will be broken.

16 It is better to live right
and be poor
  than to be sinful and rich.
17 The wicked will lose all
  of their power,
but the LORD gives strength
  to everyone who is good.

18 Those who obey the LORD
  are daily in his care,
and what he has given them
  will be theirs forever.
19 They won't be in trouble
  when times are bad,
and they will have plenty
  when food is scarce.

20 Wicked people are enemies
  of the LORD
and will vanish like smoke
  from a field on fire.

21 An evil person borrows
  and never pays back;
a good person is generous
  and never stops giving.
22 Everyone the LORD blesses
  will receive the land;
everyone the LORD curses
  will be destroyed.

23 If you do what the LORD wants,
he will make certain
  each step you take is sure.

24 The LORD will hold your hand,
and if you stumble,
  you still won't fall.

25 As long as I can remember,
good people have never
  been left helpless,
and their children have never
  gone begging for food.
26 They gladly give and lend,
and their children
  turn out good.

27 If you stop sinning
  and start doing right,
you will keep living
  and be secure forever.
28 The LORD loves justice,
and he won't ever desert
  his faithful people.
He always protects them,
but destroys the children
  of the wicked.
29 God's people will own the land
  and live here forever.

30 Words of wisdom come
  when good people speak
  for justice.
31 They remember God's teachings,
  and they never take
  a wrong step.

32 The wicked try to trap
  and kill good people,
33 but the LORD is on their side,
and he will defend them
  when they are on trial.

34 Trust the LORD and follow him.
  He will give you the land,
and you will see
  the wicked destroyed.

35 I have seen brutal people
  abuse others and grow strong
  like trees in rich soil.[u]
36 Suddenly they disappeared!
I looked, but they were gone
  and no longer there.

37 Think of the bright future
waiting for all the families
  of honest and innocent
  and peace-loving people.
38 But not a trace will be left
of the wicked
  or their families.

39 The LORD protects his people,
and they can come to him
  in times of trouble.
40 The LORD helps them

---

[u] **37.35** *like . . . soil:* One possible meaning for the difficult Hebrew text.

and saves them from the wicked
because they run to him.

Psalm 38
[*A psalm by David to be used
when an offering is made.*]

A Prayer in Times of Trouble

1 When you are angry, LORD,
please don't punish me
or even correct me.
2 You shot me with your arrows,
and you struck me
with your hand.

3 My body hurts all over
because of your anger.
Even my bones are in pain,
and my sins 4are so heavy
that I am crushed.

5 Because of my foolishness,
I am covered with sores
that stink and spread.
6 My body is twisted and bent,
and I groan all day long.
7 Fever has my back in flames,
and I hurt all over.
8 I am worn out and weak,
moaning and in distress.

9 You, Lord, know every one
of my deepest desires,
and my noisy groans
are no secret to you.
10 My heart is beating fast.
I feel weak all over,
and my eyes are red.

11 Because of my sickness,
no friends or neighbors
will come near me.
12 All who want me dead
set traps to catch me,
and those who want
to harm and destroy me
plan and plot all day.

13 I am not able to hear
or speak a word;
14 I am completely deaf
and can't make a sound.

15 I trust you, LORD God,
and you will do something.
16 I said, "Don't let them laugh
or brag because I slip."

17 I am about to collapse
from constant pain.
18 I told you my sins,
and I am sorry for them.
19 Many deadly and powerful
enemies hate me,

20 and they repay evil for good
because I try to do right.

21 You are the LORD God!
Stay nearby
and don't desert me.
22 You are the one who saves me.
Please hurry and help.

Psalm 39
[*A psalm by David
for Jeduthun, the music leader.*]

A Prayer for Forgiveness

1 I told myself, "I'll be careful
not to sin by what I say,
and I'll muzzle my mouth
when evil people are near."
2 I kept completely silent,
but it did no good,^{v}
and I hurt even worse.

3 I felt a fire burning inside,
and the more I thought,
the more it burned,
until at last I said:
4 "Please, LORD,
show me my future.
Will I soon be gone?
5 You made my life short,
so brief that the time
means nothing to you.

"Human life is but a breath,
6 and it disappears
like a shadow.
Our struggles are senseless;
we store up more and more,
without ever knowing
who will get it all.

7 "What am I waiting for?
I depend on you, Lord!
8 Save me from my sins.
Don't let fools sneer at me.
9 You treated me like this,
and I kept silent,
not saying a word.

10 "Won't you stop punishing me?
You have worn me down.
11 You punish us severely
because of our sins.
Like a moth, you destroy
what we treasure most.
We are as frail as a breath.

12 "Listen, LORD, to my prayer!
My eyes are flooded with tears,
as I pray to you.
I am merely a stranger
visiting in your home
as my ancestors did.
13 Stop being angry with me

^{v}**39.2** *but . . . good*: One possible meaning for the difficult Hebrew text.

and let me smile again
   before I am dead and gone."

Psalm 40
[A psalm by David for the music leader.]

A Prayer for Help

¹ I patiently waited, LORD,
   for you to hear my prayer.
You listened ²and pulled me
from a lonely pit
   full of mud and mire.
You let me stand on a rock
   with my feet firm,
³ and you gave me a new song,
   a song of praise to you.
Many will see this,
and they will honor and trust
   you, the LORD God.

⁴ You bless all of those
   who trust you, LORD,
and refuse to worship idols
   or follow false gods.
⁵ You, LORD God, have done
   many wonderful things,
and you have planned
   marvelous things for us.
No one is like you!
I would never be able to tell
   all you have done.

⁶ Sacrifices and offerings
   are not what please you;
gifts and payment for sin
   are not what you demand.
But you made me willing
   to listen and obey.
⁷ And so, I said, "I am here
   to do what is written
about me in the book,
   where it says,
⁸ 'I enjoy pleasing you.
   Your Law is in my heart.' "

⁹ When your people worshiped,
   you know I told them,
   "Our LORD always helps!"
¹⁰ When all your people met,
   I did not keep silent.
I said, "Our LORD is kind.
He is faithful and caring,
   and he saves us."

¹¹ You, LORD, never fail
   to have pity on me;
your love and faithfulness
   always keep me secure.

¹² I have more troubles
   than I can count.
My sins are all around me,
   and I can't find my way.
My sins outnumber
the hairs on my head,
   and I feel weak.
¹³ Please show that you care

and come to my rescue.
   Hurry and help me!

¹⁴ Disappoint and confuse
   all who want me dead;
turn away and disgrace
   all who want to hurt me.
¹⁵ Embarrass and shame
   all of those who say,
   "Just look at you now!"
¹⁶ Our LORD, let your worshipers
   rejoice and be glad.
They love you for saving them,
so let them always say,
   "The LORD is wonderful!"

¹⁷ I am poor and needy,
but, LORD God,
   you care about me,
and you come to my rescue.
   Please hurry and help.

Psalm 41
[A psalm by David for the music leader.]

A Prayer in Time of Sickness

¹ You, LORD God, bless everyone
   who cares for the poor,
and you rescue those people
   in times of trouble.
² You protect them
   and keep them alive.
You make them happy here
   in this land,
and you don't hand them over
   to their enemies.
³ You always heal them
and restore their strength
   when they are sick.
⁴ I prayed, "Have pity, LORD!
Heal me, though I have sinned
   against you."

⁵ My vicious enemies ask me,
   "When will you die
   and be forgotten?"
⁶ When visitors come,
   all they ever bring
   are worthless words,
and when they leave,
   they spread gossip.

⁷ My enemies whisper about me.
   They think the worst,
⁸   and they say,
   "You have some fatal disease!
   You'll never get well."
⁹ My most trusted friend
has turned against me,
   though he ate at my table.

¹⁰ Have pity, LORD! Heal me,
   so I can pay them back.
¹¹ Then my enemies
   won't defeat me,
and I will know
   that you really care.

¹² You have helped me
  because I am innocent,
and you will always
  be close to my side.

¹³ You, the LORD God of Israel,
  will be praised forever!
  Amen and amen.

BOOK II

(Psalms 42–72)

Psalm 42

[*A special psalm for the people of Korah
and for the music leader.*]

Longing for God

¹ As a deer gets thirsty
  for streams of water,
I truly am thirsty
  for you, my God.
² In my heart, I am thirsty
for you, the living God.
  When will I see your face?
³ Day and night my tears
  are my only food,
as everyone keeps asking,
  "Where is your God?"

⁴ Sorrow floods my heart,
  when I remember
leading the worshipers
  to your house.^w
I can still hear them shout
  their joyful praises.
⁵ Why am I discouraged?
Why am I restless?
  I trust you!
And I will praise you again
because you help me,
⁶   and you are my God.

I am deeply discouraged
  as I think about you
from where the Jordan begins
at Mount Hermon
  and from Mount Mizar.^x
⁷ Your vicious waves
  have swept over me
like an angry ocean
  or a roaring waterfall.

⁸ Every day, you are kind,
  and at night
you give me a song
as my prayer to you,
  the living LORD God.

⁹ You are my mighty rock.^y
  Why have you forgotten me?
Why must enemies mistreat me
  and make me sad?

¹⁰ Even my bones are in pain,
  while all day long
my enemies sneer and ask,
  "Where is your God?"

¹¹ Why am I discouraged?
Why am I restless?
  I trust you!
And I will praise you again
because you help me,
  and you are my God.

Psalm 43

A Prayer in Times of Trouble

¹ Show that I am right, God!
Defend me against everyone
  who doesn't know you;
rescue me from each
  of those deceitful liars.
² I run to you
  for protection.
Why have you turned me away?
Why must enemies mistreat me
  and make me sad?

³ Send your light and your truth
  to guide me.
Let them lead me to your house
  on your sacred mountain.
⁴ Then I will worship
at your altar because you
  make me joyful.
You are my God,
  and I will praise you.
Yes, I will praise you
  as I play my harp.

⁵ Why am I discouraged?
Why am I restless?
  I trust you!
And I will praise you again
because you help me,
  and you are my God.

Psalm 44

[*A special psalm for the people of Korah
and for the music leader.*]

A Prayer for Help

¹ Our God, our ancestors told us
what wonders you worked
  and we listened carefully.
² You chased off the nations
by causing them trouble
  with your powerful arm.
Then you let our ancestors
  take over their land.
³ Their strength and weapons
were not what won the land
  and gave them victory!
You loved them and fought
with your powerful arm
  and your shining glory.

^w**42.4** *leading . . . house*: One possible meaning for the difficult Hebrew text.   ^x**42.6** *Mount
Mizar*: The location is not known.   ^y**42.9** *mighty rock*: See the note at 18.2.

⁴ You are my God and King,
  and you give victory ᶻ
    to the people of Jacob.
⁵ By your great power,
  we knocked our enemies down
    and stomped on them.
⁶ I don't depend on my arrows
    or my sword to save me.
⁷ But you saved us
  from our hateful enemies,
    and you put them to shame.
⁸ We boast about you, our God,
    and we are always grateful.

⁹ But now you have rejected us;
  you don't lead us into battle,
    and we look foolish.
¹⁰ You made us retreat,
  and our enemies have taken
    everything we own.
¹¹ You let us be slaughtered
    like sheep,
  and you scattered us
    among the nations.
¹² You sold your people
  for little or nothing,
    and you earned no profit.

¹³ You made us look foolish
    to our neighbors,
  and people who live nearby
    insult us and sneer.
¹⁴ Foreigners joke about us
    and shake their heads.
¹⁵ I am embarrassed every day,
    and I blush with shame.
¹⁶ But others mock and sneer,
  as they watch my enemies
    take revenge on me.

¹⁷ All of this has happened to us,
  though we didn't forget you
    or break our agreement.
¹⁸ We always kept you in mind
    and followed your teaching.
¹⁹ But you crushed us,
    and you covered us
  with deepest darkness
    where wild animals live.

²⁰ We did not forget you
  or lift our hands in prayer
    to foreign gods.
²¹ You would have known it
  because you discover
    every secret thought.
²² We face death all day for you.
  We are like sheep on their way
    to be slaughtered.

²³ Wake up! Do something, Lord!
  Why are you sleeping?
    Don't desert us forever.

²⁴ Why do you keep looking away?
  Don't forget our sufferings
    and all of our troubles.
²⁵ We are flat on the ground,
    holding on to the dust.
²⁶ Do something! Help us!
  Show how kind you are
    and come to our rescue.

Psalm 45

*[A special psalm for the people
of Korah and for the music leader.
To the tune "Lilies." A love song.]*

For a Royal Wedding

¹ My thoughts are filled
with beautiful words
    for the king,
and I will use my voice
as a writer would use
    pen and ink.

² No one is as handsome as you!
    Your words are always kind.
That is why God
    will always bless you.
³ Mighty king, glorious ruler,
strap on your sword
⁴   and ride out in splendor!
Win victories for truth
    and mercy and justice.
Do fearsome things
    with your powerful arm.
⁵ Send your sharp arrows
    through enemy hearts
and make all nations fall
    at your feet.

⁶ You are God, and you will rule
    forever as king. ᵃ
Your royal power
    brings about justice.
⁷ You love justice and hate evil.
    And so, your God chose you
and made you happier
    than any of your friends.
⁸ The sweet aroma of the spices
  myrrh, aloes, and cassia,
    covers your royal robes.
You enjoy the music of harps
in palaces decorated
    with ivory.
⁹ Daughters of kings are here,
  and your bride stands
    at your right side,
wearing a wedding gown
    trimmed with pure gold. ᵇ

¹⁰ Bride of the king,
    listen carefully to me.
Forget your own people
    and your father's family.

ᶻ**44.4** *and . . . victory*: One ancient translation; Hebrew "please give victory."   ᵃ**45.6** *You . . . king*: Or "God has made you king, and you will rule forever."   ᵇ**45.9** *trimmed with pure gold*: Hebrew has "with gold from Ophir," which may have been in Africa or India. Gold from there was considered the very best.

11 The king is your husband,
   so do what he desires.
12 All of the richest people
   from the city of Tyre
   will try to influence you
13   with precious treasures.

Your bride, my king,
   has inward beauty,[c]
and her wedding gown is woven
   with threads of gold.
14 Wearing the finest garments,
   she is brought to you,
followed by her young friends,
   the bridesmaids.
15 Everyone is excited,
   as they follow you
   to the royal palace.

16 Your sons and your grandsons
   will also be kings
   as your ancestors were.
You will make them the rulers
   everywhere on earth.

17 I will make your name famous
   from now on,
and you will be praised
   forever and ever.

Psalm 46
[_A special song for the people of Korah
and for the music leader._]

God Is Our Mighty Fortress

1 God is our mighty fortress,
   always ready to help
   in times of trouble.
2 And so, we won't be afraid!
   Let the earth tremble
and the mountains tumble
   into the deepest sea.
3 Let the ocean roar and foam,
   and its raging waves
   shake the mountains.

4 A river and its streams
   bring joy to the city,
which is the sacred home
   of God Most High.
5 God is in that city,
   and it won't be shaken.
   He will help it at dawn.

6 Nations rage! Kingdoms fall!
   But at the voice of God
   the earth itself melts.
7 The LORD All-Powerful
   is with us.
The God of Jacob
   is our fortress.

8 Come! See the fearsome things
   the LORD has done on earth.

9 God brings wars to an end
   all over the world.
He breaks the arrows,
   shatters the spears,
   and burns the shields.[d]
10 Our God says, "Calm down,
   and learn that I am God!
All nations on earth
   will honor me."

11 The LORD All-Powerful
   is with us.
The God of Jacob
   is our fortress.

Psalm 47
[_A psalm for the people of Korah
and for the music leader._]

God Rules the Nations

1 All of you nations,
   clap your hands and shout
   joyful praises to God.
2 The LORD Most High is fearsome,
   the ruler of all the earth.
3 God has put every nation
   under our power,
4 and he chose for us the land
   that was the pride of Jacob,
   his favorite.

5 God goes up to his throne,
   as people shout
   and trumpets blast.
6 Sing praises to God our King,
7 the ruler of all the earth!
   Praise God with songs.

8 God rules the nations
   from his sacred throne.
9 Their leaders come together
   and are now the people
   of Abraham's God.
All rulers on earth
   surrender their weapons,
   and God is greatly praised!

Psalm 48
[_A song and a psalm for the people of Korah._]

The City of God

1 The LORD God is wonderful!
   He deserves all praise
   in the city where he lives.
His holy mountain,
2 beautiful and majestic,
   brings joy to all on earth.
Mount Zion, truly sacred,
   is home for the Great King.
3 God is there to defend it
   and has proved to be
   its protector.

4 Kings joined forces
   to attack the city,
5 but when they saw it,

---

[c]**45.13** _has inward beauty_: Or "is dressed in her room."   [d]**46.9** _shields_: Or "chariots."

they were terrified
and ran away.
6 They trembled all over
like women giving birth
7 or like seagoing ships*e*
wrecked by eastern winds.
8 We had heard about it,
and now we have seen it
in the city of our God,
the LORD All-Powerful.
This is the city that God
will let stand forever.

9 Our God, here in your temple
we think about your love.
10 You are famous and praised
everywhere on earth,
as you win victories
with your powerful arm.
11 Mount Zion will celebrate,
and all Judah will be glad,
because you bring justice.

12 Let's walk around Zion
and count its towers.
13 We will see its strong walls
and visit each fortress.
Then you can say
to future generations,
14 "Our God is like this forever
and will always*f* guide us."

Psalm 49
*[A psalm for the people of Korah
and for the music leader.]*

Don't Depend on Wealth

1 Everyone on this earth,
now listen to what I say!
2 Listen, no matter who you are,
rich or poor.
3 I speak words of wisdom,
and my thoughts make sense.
4 I have in mind a mystery
that I will explain
while playing my harp.

5 Why should I be afraid
in times of trouble,
when I am surrounded
by vicious enemies?
6 They trust in their riches
and brag about
all of their wealth.
7 You cannot buy back your life
or pay off God!
8 It costs far too much
to buy back your life.
You can never pay God enough
9 to stay alive forever
and safe from death.

10 We see that wise people die,
and so do stupid fools.
Then their money is left
for someone else.
11 The grave*g* will be their home
forever and ever,
although they once had land
of their own.
12 Our human glory disappears,
and, like animals, we die.

13 Here is what happens to fools
and to those who trust
the words of fools:
14 They are like sheep
with death as their shepherd,
leading them to the grave.*h*
In the morning God's people
will walk all over them,
as their bodies lie rotting
in their home, the grave.
15 But God will rescue me
from the power of death.

16 Don't let it bother you
when others get rich
and live in luxury.
17 Soon they will die
and all of their wealth
will be left behind.

18 We humans are praised
when we do well,
and all of us are glad
to be alive.
19 But we each will go down
to our ancestors,
never again to see
the light of day.
20 Our human glory disappears,
and, like animals, we die.

Psalm 50
[A psalm by Asaph.]

What Pleases God

1 From east to west,
the powerful LORD God
has been calling together
everyone on earth.
2 God shines brightly from Zion,
the most beautiful city.

3 Our God approaches,
but not silently;
a flaming fire comes first,
and a storm surrounds him.
4 God comes to judge his people.
He shouts to the heavens
and to the earth,
5 "Call my followers together!
They offered me a sacrifice,
and we made an agreement."

---

*e*48.7 *seagoing ships*: The Hebrew text has "ships of Tarshish," which probably means large, seagoing ships.   *f*48.14 *always*: One possible meaning for the difficult Hebrew text.
*g*49.11 *The grave*: Some ancient translations; Hebrew "Their inward thoughts."   *h*49.14 *as their . . . grave*: One possible meaning for the difficult Hebrew text.

6 The heavens announce,
   "God is the judge,
      and he is always honest."

7 My people, I am God!
   Israel, I am your God.
   Listen to my charges
      against you.
8 Although you offer sacrifices
      and always bring gifts,
9 I won't accept your offerings
      of bulls and goats.

10 Every animal in the forest
      belongs to me,
   and so do the cattle
      on a thousand hills.
11 I know all the birds
      in the mountains,
   and every wild creature
      is in my care.

12 If I were hungry,
      I wouldn't tell you,
   because I own the world
      and everything in it.
13 I don't eat the meat of bulls
      or drink the blood of goats.
14 I am God Most High!
      The only sacrifice I want
   is for you to be thankful
      and to keep your word.
15 Pray to me in time of trouble.
   I will rescue you,
      and you will honor me.

16 But to the wicked I say:
      "You don't have the right
   to mention my laws or claim
      to keep our agreement!
17 You refused correction
      and rejected my commands.
18 You made friends
      with every crook you met,
   and you liked people who break
      their wedding vows.
19 You talked only about violence
      and told nothing but lies;
20 you sat around gossiping,
      ruining the reputation
      of your own relatives."

21 When you did all of this,
   I didn't say a word,
      and you thought,
   "God is just like us!"
      But now I will accuse you.
22 You have ignored me!
      So pay close attention
   or I will tear you apart,
      and no one can help you.

23 The sacrifice that honors me
   is a thankful heart.

Obey me,[i] and I, your God,
   will show my power to save.

Psalm 51

[*For the music leader. A psalm by David
when the prophet Nathan came to him
after David had been with Bathsheba.*]

A Prayer for Forgiveness

1 You are kind, God!
      Please have pity on me.
   You are always merciful!
      Please wipe away my sins.
2 Wash me clean from all
      of my sin and guilt.
3 I know about my sins,
   and I cannot forget
      my terrible guilt.
4 You are really the one
      I have sinned against;
   I have disobeyed you
      and have done wrong.
   So it is right and fair for you
      to correct and punish me.

5 I have sinned and done wrong
      since the day I was born.
6 But you want complete honesty,
      so teach me true wisdom.
7 Wash me with hyssop[j]
   until I am clean
      and whiter than snow.
8 Let me be happy and joyful!
   You crushed my bones,
      now let them celebrate.
9 Turn your eyes from my sin
      and cover my guilt.
10 Create pure thoughts in me
      and make me faithful again.
11 Don't chase me away from you
   or take your Holy Spirit
      away from me.

12 Make me as happy as you did
   when you saved me;
      make me want to obey!
13 I will teach sinners your Law,
      and they will return to you.
14 Keep me from any deadly sin.
      Only you can save me!
   Then I will shout and sing
      about your power to save.

15 Help me to speak,
      and I will praise you, Lord.
16 Offerings and sacrifices
      are not what you want.
17 The way to please you
   is to feel sorrow
      deep in our hearts.
   This is the kind of sacrifice
      you won't refuse.

[i]50.23 *Obey me*: One possible meaning for the difficult Hebrew text.   [j]51.7 *hyssop*: A small
bush with bunches of small, white flowers. It was sometimes used as a symbol for making a
person clean from sin.

18 Please be willing, Lord,
 to help the city of Zion
  and to rebuild its walls.
19 Then you will be pleased
  with the proper sacrifices,
 and we will offer bulls
  on your altar once again.

Psalm 52
*[A special psalm by David for the music
leader. He wrote this when Doeg from Edom
went to Saul and said, "David has gone to
Ahimelech's house."]*

God Is in Control

1 You people may be strong
 and brag about your sins,
 but God can be trusted
  day after day.
2 You plan brutal crimes,
 and your lying words cut
  like a sharp razor.
3 You would rather do evil
 than good, and tell lies
  than speak the truth.
4 You love to say cruel things,
 and your words are a trap.

5 God will destroy you forever!
 He will grab you and drag you
  from your homes.
 You will be uprooted
  and left to die.
6 When good people see
  this fearsome sight,
 they will laugh and say,
7   "Just look at them now!
 Instead of trusting God,
 they trusted their wealth
  and their cruelty."

8 But I am like an olive tree
  growing in God's house,
 and I can count on his love
  forever and ever.
9 I will always thank God
  for what he has done;
 I will praise his good name
  when his people meet.

Psalm 53
*[A special psalm by David for the music
leader. To the tune "Mahalath."*[k]*]*

No One Can Ignore God

1 Only a fool would say,
 "There is no God!"
 People like that are worthless!
 They are heartless and cruel
  and never do right.

2 From heaven God
  looks down to see
 if anyone is wise enough
  to search for him.

3 But all of them
  are crooked and corrupt.
  Not one of them does right.

4 Won't you lawbreakers learn?
  You refuse to pray,
 and you gobble down
  the people of God.
5 But you will be terrified
  worse than ever before.
 God will scatter the bones
  of his enemies,
 and you will be ashamed
  when God rejects you.

6 I long for someone from Zion
  to come and save Israel!
 Our God, when you bless
  your people again,
 Jacob's family will be glad,
  and Israel will celebrate.

Psalm 54
*[For the music leader. Use with stringed
instruments. A special psalm that David
wrote when the people of Ziph went to Saul
and said, "David is hiding here with us."]*

Trusting God in Times of Trouble

1 Save me, God, by your power
  and prove that I am right.
2 Listen to my prayer
  and hear what I say.
3 Cruel strangers have attacked
  and want me dead.
 Not one of them cares
  about you.

4 You will help me, Lord God,
  and keep me from falling;
5 you will punish my enemies
  for their evil deeds.
 Be my faithful friend
  and destroy them.

6 I will bring a gift
 and offer a sacrifice
  to you, LORD.
 I will praise your name
  because you are good.
7 You have rescued me
  from all of my troubles,
 and my own eyes have seen
  my enemies fall.

Psalm 55
*[A special psalm by David for the music
leader. Use with stringed instruments.]*

Betrayed by a Friend

1 Listen, God, to my prayer!
  Don't reject my request.
2 Please listen and help me.

_____

*[k]***Psalm 53** *Mahalath:* Or "For flutes," one possible meaning for the difficult Hebrew text.

My thoughts are troubled,
  and I keep groaning
3 because my loud enemies
  shout and attack.
They treat me terribly
  and hold angry grudges.
4 My heart is racing fast,
  and I am afraid of dying.
5 I am trembling with fear,
  completely terrified.

6 I wish I had wings
  like a dove,
so I could fly far away
  and be at peace.
7 I would go and live
  in some distant desert.
8 I would quickly find shelter
  from howling winds
  and raging storms.

9 Confuse my enemies, Lord!
  Upset their plans.
Cruelty and violence
  are all I see in the city,
10 and they are like guards
  on patrol day and night.
The city is full of trouble,
  evil, 11and corruption.
Troublemakers and liars
  freely roam the streets.

12 My enemies are not the ones
  who sneer and make fun.
I could put up with that
  or even hide from them.
13 But it was my closest friend,
  the one I trusted most.
14 We enjoyed being together,
  and we went with others
  to your house, our God.

15 All who hate me are controlled
  by the power of evil.
Sentence them to death
and send them down alive
  to the world of the dead.

16 I ask for your help, LORD God,
  and you will keep me safe.
17 Morning, noon, and night
you hear my concerns
  and my complaints.
18 I am attacked from all sides,
but you will rescue me
  unharmed by the battle.
19 You have always ruled,
  and you will hear me.
You will defeat my enemies
because they won't turn
  and worship you.

20 My friend turned against me
  and broke his promise.
21 His words were smoother

than butter, and softer
  than olive oil.
But hatred filled his heart,
and he was ready to attack
  with a sword.

22 Our LORD, we belong to you.
We tell you what worries us,
  and you won't let us fall.
23 But what about those people
  who are cruel and brutal?
You will throw them down
  into the deepest pit
long before their time.
  I trust you, LORD!

Psalm 56

[*For the music leader. To the tune
"A Silent Dove in the Distance."l
A special psalm by David when the
Philistines captured him in Gath.*]

A Prayer of Trust in God

1 Have pity, God Most High!
  My enemies chase me all day.
2 Many of them are pursuing
  and attacking me,
3 but even when I am afraid,
  I keep on trusting you.
4 I praise your promises!
I trust you and am not afraid.
  No one can harm me.

5 Enemies spend the whole day
  finding fault with me;
all they think about
  is how to do me harm.
6 They attack from ambush,
watching my every step
  and hoping to kill me.
7 They won't get awaym
  with these crimes, God,
because when you get angry,
  you destroy people.

8 You have kept record
  of my days of wandering.
You have stored my tears
  in your bottle
  and counted each of them.

9 When I pray, LORD God,
  my enemies will retreat,
because I know for certain
  that you are with me.
10 I praise your promises!
11 I trust you and am not afraid.
  No one can harm me.

12 I will keep my promises
to you, my God,
  and bring you gifts.
13 You protected me from death
  and kept me from stumbling,

lPsalm 56 *A Silent . . . Distance*: One possible meaning for the difficult Hebrew text.
m56.7 *They . . . away*: One possible meaning for the difficult Hebrew text.

so that I would please you
and follow the light
that leads to life.

Psalm 57

[*For the music leader. To the tune "Don't Destroy."*[n] *A special psalm by David when he was in the cave while running from Saul.*]

Praise and Trust in Times of Trouble

[1] God Most High, have pity on me!
Have mercy. I run to you
for safety.
In the shadow of your wings,
I seek protection
till danger dies down.
[2] I pray to you, my protector.
[3] You will send help from heaven
and save me,
but you will bring trouble
on my attackers.
You are faithful,
and you can be trusted.

[4] I live among lions,
who gobble down people!
They have spears and arrows
instead of teeth,
and they have sharp swords
instead of tongues.

[5] May you, my God, be honored
above the heavens;
may your glory be seen
everywhere on earth.

[6] Enemies set traps for my feet
and struck me down.
They dug a pit in my path,
but fell in it themselves.
[7] I am faithful to you,
and you can trust me.
I will sing and play music
for you, my God.
[8] I feel wide awake!
I will wake up my harp
and wake up the sun.
[9] I will praise you, Lord,
for everyone to hear,
and I will sing hymns to you
in every nation.
[10] Your love reaches higher
than the heavens;
your loyalty extends
beyond the clouds.

[11] May you, my God, be honored
above the heavens;
may your glory be seen
everywhere on earth.

Psalm 58

[*A special psalm by David for the music leader. To the tune "Don't Destroy."*[n]]

A Prayer When All Goes Wrong

[1] Do you mighty people[o] talk
only to oppose justice?[p]
Don't you ever judge fairly?
[2] You are always planning evil,
and you are brutal.
[3] You have done wrong and lied
from the day you were born.
[4] Your words spread poison
like the bite of a cobra
[5] that refuses to listen
to the snake charmer.

[6] My enemies are fierce
as lions, LORD God!
Shatter their teeth.
Snatch out their fangs.
[7] Make them disappear
like leaking water,
and make their arrows miss.
[8] Let them dry up like snails
or be like a child that dies
before seeing the sun.
[9] Wipe them out quicker
than a pot can be heated
by setting thorns on fire.[q]

[10] Good people will be glad
when they see the wicked
getting what they deserve,
and they will wash their feet
in their enemies' blood.
[11] Everyone will say, "It's true!
Good people are rewarded.
God does rule the earth
with justice."

Psalm 59

[*For the music leader. To the tune "Don't Destroy."*[r] *A special psalm by David when Saul had David's house watched so that he could kill him.*]

A Prayer for Protection

[1] Save me, God! Protect me
from enemy attacks!
[2] Keep me safe from brutal people
who want to kill me.

[3] Merciless enemies, LORD,
are hiding and plotting,
hoping to kill me.
I have not hurt them
in any way at all.
[4] But they are ready to attack.
Do something! Help me!
Look at what's happening.

---

[n]**Psalm 57** *Don't Destroy:* One possible meaning for the difficult Hebrew text.
[n]**Psalm 58** *Don't Destroy:* One possible meaning for the difficult Hebrew text.   [o]**58.1** *mighty people:* Or "mighty rulers" or "mighty gods."   [p]**58.1** *Do . . . justice:* One possible meaning for the difficult Hebrew text.   [q]**58.9** *Wipe . . . fire:* See the note at Psalm 57.
[r]**Psalm 59** *Don't Destroy:* See the note at Psalm 57.

5 LORD God All-Powerful,
   you are the God of Israel.
Punish the other nations
and don't pity those terrible
   and rebellious people.

6 My enemies return at evening,
   growling like dogs
      roaming the city.
7 They curse and their words
      cut like swords,
   as they say to themselves,
   "No one can hear us!"

8 You, LORD, laugh at them
   and sneer at the nations.
9 You are my mighty fortress,
   and I depend on you.
10 You love me and will let me
   see my enemies defeated.
11 Don't kill them,
   or everyone may forget!
Just use your mighty power
   to make them tremble
      and fall.

You are a shield
   for your people.
12 My enemies are liars!
So let them be trapped
   by their boastful lies.
13 Get angry and destroy them.
   Leave them in ruin.
Then all the nations will know
   that you rule in Israel.

14 Those liars return at evening,
   growling like dogs
      roaming the city.
15 They search for scraps of food,
   and they snarl
      until they are stuffed.

16 But I will sing about
   your strength, my God,
and I will celebrate
   because of your love.
You are my fortress,
my place of protection
   in times of trouble.
17 I will sing your praises!
You are my mighty fortress,
   and you love me.

Psalm 60

[*For the music leader. To the tune "Lily of the Promise." A special psalm by David for teaching. He wrote it during his wars with the Arameans of northern Syria, s when Joab came back and killed twelve thousand Edomites t in Salt Valley.*]

You Can Depend on God

1 You, God, are angry with us!
We are rejected and crushed.
   Make us strong again!

2 You made the earth shake
   and split wide open;
now heal its wounds
   and stop its trembling.
3 You brought hard times
   on your people,
and you gave us wine
   that made us stagger.

4 You gave a signal to those
   who worship you,
so they could escape
   from enemy arrows. u
5 Answer our prayers!
Use your powerful arm
   and give us victory.
Then the people you love
   will be safe.

6 Our God, you solemnly promised,
"I would gladly divide up
   the city of Shechem
and give away Succoth Valley
   piece by piece.
7 The lands of Gilead
   and Manasseh are mine.
Ephraim is my war helmet,
and Judah is the symbol
   of my royal power.
8 Moab is merely my washbasin.
   Edom belongs to me,
and I shout in triumph
   over the Philistines."

9 Our God, who will bring me
   to the fortress,
   or lead me to Edom?
10 Have you rejected us
   and deserted our armies?
11 Help us defeat our enemies!
   No one else can rescue us.
12 You will give us victory
   and crush our enemies.

Psalm 61

[*A psalm by David for the music leader. Use with stringed instruments.*]

Under the Protection of God

1 Please listen, God,
   and answer my prayer!
2 I feel hopeless,
and I cry out to you
   from a faraway land.

Lead me to the mighty rock v
   high above me.
3 You are a strong tower,
where I am safe
   from my enemies.

---

s**Psalm 60** *wars . . . Syria*: See 2 Samuel 8.3-8; 10.16-18; 1 Chronicles 18.3-11; 19.6-19.
t**Psalm 60** *killed . . . Edomites*: See 2 Samuel 8.13; 1 Chronicles 18.12.   u**60.4** *so . . . arrows*:
Some ancient translations and one possible meaning for the difficult Hebrew text.
v**61.2** *mighty rock*: See the note at 18.2.

⁴ Let me live with you forever
and find protection
under your wings, my God.
⁵ You heard my promises,
and you have blessed me,
just as you bless everyone
who worships you.

⁶ Let the king have a long
and healthy life.
⁷ May he always rule
with you, God, at his side;
may your love and loyalty
watch over him.

⁸ I will sing your praises
forever and will always
keep my promises.

Psalm 62

[*A psalm by David
for Jeduthun, the music leader.*]

God Is Powerful and Kind

¹ Only God can save me,
and I calmly wait for[w] him.
² God alone is the mighty rock[x]
that keeps me safe
and the fortress
where I am secure.

³ I feel like a shaky fence
or a sagging wall.
How long will all of you
attack and assault me?
⁴ You want to bring me down
from my place of honor.
You love to tell lies,
and when your words are kind,
hatred hides in your heart.
⁵ Only God gives inward peace,
and I depend on him.
⁶ God alone is the mighty rock
that keeps me safe,
and he is the fortress
where I feel secure.
⁷ God saves me and honors me.
He is that mighty rock
where I find safety.

⁸ Trust God, my friends,
and always tell him
each one of your concerns.
God is our place of safety.

⁹ We humans are only a breath;
none of us are truly great.
All of us together weigh less
than a puff of air.
¹⁰ Don't trust in violence
or depend on dishonesty
or rely on great wealth.

¹¹ I heard God say two things:
"I am powerful,

¹² and I am very kind."
The Lord rewards each of us
according to what we do.

Psalm 63

[*A psalm by David
when he was in the desert of Judah.*]

God's Love Means More than Life

¹ You are my God. I worship you.
In my heart, I long for you,
as I would long for a stream
in a scorching desert.

² I have seen your power
and your glory
in the place of worship.
³ Your love means more
than life to me,
and I praise you.
⁴ As long as I live,
I will pray to you.
⁵ I will sing joyful praises
and be filled with excitement
like a guest at a banquet.

⁶ I think about you
before I go to sleep,
and my thoughts turn to you
during the night.
⁷ You have helped me,
and I sing happy songs
in the shadow of your wings.
⁸ I stay close to you,
and your powerful arm
supports me.

⁹ All who want to kill me
will end up in the ground.
¹⁰ Swords will run them through,
and wild dogs will eat them.

¹¹ Because of you, our God,
the king will celebrate
with your faithful followers,
but liars will be silent.

Psalm 64

[*A psalm by David for the music leader.*]

Celebrate because of the Lord

¹ Listen to my concerns, God,
and protect me
from my terrible enemies.
² Keep me safe from secret plots
of corrupt and evil gangs.
³ Their words cut like swords,
and their cruel remarks
sting like sharp arrows.
⁴ They fearlessly ambush
and shoot innocent people.

⁵ They are determined to do evil,
and they tell themselves,

---

[w]**62.1** *calmly wait for*: Or "am at peace with."   [x]**62.2** *mighty rock*: See the note at 18.2.

"Let's set traps!
No one can see us."[y]
[6] They make evil plans and say,
"We'll commit a perfect crime.
No one knows our thoughts."[z]

[7] But God will shoot his arrows
and quickly wound them.
[8] They will be destroyed
by their own words,
and everyone who sees them
will tremble with fear.[a]
[9] They will be afraid and say,
"Look at what God has done
and keep it all in mind."

[10] May the LORD bless his people
with peace and happiness
and let them celebrate.

Psalm 65
*[A psalm by David
and a song for the music leader.]*

God Answers Prayer

[1] Our God, you deserve[b] praise
in Zion, where we keep
our promises to you.
[2] Everyone will come to you
because you answer prayer.
[3] Our terrible sins get us down,
but you forgive us.
[4] You bless your chosen ones,
and you invite them
to live near you
in your temple.
We will enjoy your house,
the sacred temple.

[5] Our God, you save us,
and your fearsome deeds answer
our prayers for justice!
You give hope to people
everywhere on earth,
even those across the sea.
[6] You are strong,
and your mighty power
put the mountains in place.
[7] You silence the roaring waves
and the noisy shouts
of the nations.
[8] People far away marvel
at your fearsome deeds,
and all who live under the sun
celebrate and sing
because of you.

[9] You take care of the earth
and send rain to help the soil
grow all kinds of crops.
Your rivers never run dry,
and you prepare the earth
to produce much grain.

[10] You water all of its fields
and level the lumpy ground.
You send showers of rain
to soften the soil
and help the plants sprout.
[11] Wherever your footsteps
touch the earth,
a rich harvest is gathered.
[12] Desert pastures blossom,
and mountains celebrate.
[13] Meadows are filled
with sheep and goats;
valleys overflow with grain
and echo with joyful songs.

Psalm 66
[A song and a psalm for the music leader.]

Shout Praises to God

[1] Tell everyone on this earth
to shout praises to God!
[2] Sing about his glorious name.
Honor him with praises.
[3] Say to God, "Everything you do
is fearsome,
and your mighty power makes
your enemies come crawling.
[4] You are worshiped by everyone!
We all sing praises to you."

[5] Come and see the fearsome things
our God has done!
[6] When God made the sea dry up,
our people walked across,
and because of him,
we celebrated there.
[7] His mighty power rules forever,
and nothing the nations do
can be hidden from him.
So don't turn against God.

[8] All of you people,
come praise our God!
Let his praises be heard.
[9] God protects us from death
and keeps us steady.

[10] Our God, you tested us,
just as silver is tested.
[11] You trapped us in a net
and gave us heavy burdens.
[12] You sent war chariots
to crush our skulls.
We traveled through fire
and through floods,
but you brought us
to a land of plenty.

[13] I will bring sacrifices
into your house, my God,
and I will do what I promised
[14] when I was in trouble.
[15] I will sacrifice my best sheep

---

[y]*64.5 us*: One ancient translation; Hebrew "them."   [z]*64.6 thoughts*: One possible meaning
for the difficult Hebrew text of verse 6.   [a]*64.8 tremble with fear*: Or "turn and run."
[b]*65.1 deserve*: One possible meaning for the difficult Hebrew text.

and offer bulls and goats
on your altar.

16 All who worship God,
come here and listen;
I will tell you everything
God has done for me.
17 I prayed to the Lord,
and I praised him.
18 If my thoughts had been sinful,
he would have refused
to hear me.
19 But God did listen
and answered my prayer.
20 Let's praise God!
He listened when I prayed,
and he is always kind.

Psalm 67

[*A psalm and a song for the music leader.
Use with stringed instruments.*]

Tell the Nations To Praise God

1 Our God, be kind and bless us!
Be pleased and smile.
2 Then everyone on earth
will learn to follow you,
and all nations will see
your power to save us.

3 Make everyone praise you
and shout your praises.
4 Let the nations celebrate
with joyful songs,
because you judge fairly
and guide all nations.
5 Make everyone praise you
and shout your praises.

6 Our God has blessed the earth
with a wonderful harvest!
7 Pray for his blessings
to continue
and for everyone on earth
to worship our God.

Psalm 68

[*A psalm and a song by David
for the music leader.*]

God Will Win the Battle

1 Do something, God!
Scatter your hateful enemies.
Make them turn and run.
2 Scatter them like smoke!
When you come near,
make them melt
like wax in a fire.
3 But let your people be happy
and celebrate because of you.

4 Our God, you are the one
who rides on the clouds,
and we praise you.

Your name is the LORD,
and we celebrate
as we worship you.

5 Our God, from your sacred home
you take care of orphans
and protect widows.
6 You find families
for those who are lonely.
You set prisoners free
and let them prosper,[c]
but all who rebel will live
in a scorching desert.

7 You set your people free,
and you led them
through the desert.
8 God of Israel,
the earth trembled,
and rain poured down.
You alone are the God
who rules from Mount Sinai.
9 When your land was thirsty,
you sent showers
to refresh it.
10 Your people settled there,
and you were generous
to everyone in need.

11 You gave the command,
and a chorus of women told
what had happened:
12 "Kings and their armies
retreated and ran,
and everything they left
is now being divided.
13 And for those who stayed back
to guard the sheep,
there are metal doves
with silver-coated wings
and shiny gold feathers."

14 God All-Powerful, you scattered
the kings like snow falling
on Mount Zalmon.[d]

15 Our LORD and our God,
Bashan is a mighty mountain
covered with peaks.
16 Why is it jealous of Zion,
the mountain you chose
as your home forever?

17 When you, LORD God, appeared
to your people[e] at Sinai,
you came with thousands
of mighty chariots.
18 When you climbed
the high mountain,
you took prisoners with you
and were given gifts.
Your enemies didn't want you

---

[c]**68.6** *and let them prosper*: Or "and give them a song."   [d]**68.14** *Mount Zalmon*: The location of this mountain is not known.   [e]**68.17** *to your people*: Or "in all your holiness" or "in your holy place."

to live there,
but they gave you gifts.

19 We praise you, Lord God!
You treat us with kindness
day after day,
and you rescue us.
20 You always protect us
and save us from death.

21 Our Lord and our God,
your terrible enemies
are ready for war,*f*
but you will crush
their skulls.
22 You promised to bring them
from Bashan
and from the deepest sea.
23 Then we could stomp
on their blood,
and our dogs could chew
on their bones.

24 We have seen crowds marching
to your place of worship,
our God and King.
25 The singers come first,
and then the musicians,
surrounded by young women
playing tambourines.
26 They come shouting,
"People of Israel,
praise the LORD God!"
27 The small tribe of Benjamin
leads the way,
followed by the leaders
from Judah.
Then come the leaders
from Zebulun and Naphtali.

28 Our God, show your strength!
Show us once again.
29 Then kings will bring gifts
to your temple
in Jerusalem.*g*

30 Punish that animal
that lives in the swamp!*h*
Punish that nation
whose leaders and people
are like wild bulls.
Make them come crawling
with gifts of silver.
Scatter those nations
that enjoy making war.*i*
31 Force the Egyptians to bring
gifts of bronze;
make the Ethiopians*j* hurry
to offer presents.*k*

32 Now sing praises to God!
Every kingdom on earth,
sing to the Lord!
33 Praise the one who rides
across the ancient skies;
listen as he speaks
with a mighty voice.

34 Tell about God's power!
He is honored in Israel,
and he rules the skies.
35 The God of Israel is fearsome
in his temple,
and he makes us strong.
Let's praise our God!

Psalm 69
[*By David for the music leader.
To the tune "Lilies."*]

God Can Be Trusted

1 Save me, God!
I am about to drown.
2 I am sinking deep in the mud,
and my feet are slipping.
I am about to be swept under
by a mighty flood.
3 I am worn out from crying,
and my throat is dry.
I have waited for you
till my eyes are blurred.

4 There are more people
who hate me for no reason
than there are hairs
on my head.
Many terrible enemies
want to destroy me, God.
Am I supposed to give back
something I didn't steal?
5 You know my foolish sins.
Not one is hidden from you.

6 LORD God All-Powerful,
ruler of Israel,
don't let me embarrass anyone
who trusts and worships you.
7 It is for your sake alone
that I am insulted
and blush with shame.
8 I am like a stranger
to my relatives
and like a foreigner
to my own family.

9 My love for your house
burns in me like a fire,
and when others insulted you,
they insulted me as well.

---

*f***68.21** *are ready for war*: The Hebrew text has "have long hair," which probably refers to the ancient custom of wearing long hair on special occasions, such as a "holy war."
*g***68.28,29** *Our God . . . Jerusalem*: One possible meaning for the difficult Hebrew text of verses 28, 29.   *h***68.30** *animal . . . swamp*: Probably Egypt.   *i***68.30** *war*: One possible meaning for the difficult Hebrew text of verse 30.   *j***68.31** *the Ethiopians*: The Hebrew text has "the people of Cush," which was a region south of Egypt that included parts of the present countries of Ethiopia and Sudan.   *k***68.31** *presents*: One possible meaning for the difficult Hebrew text of verse 31.

¹⁰ I cried and went without food,^l
    but they still insulted me.
¹¹ They sneered at me
  for wearing sackcloth^m
    to show my sorrow.
¹² Rulers and judges gossip
    about me,
  and drunkards make up songs
    to mock me.

¹³ But I pray to you, LORD.
    So when the time is right,
  answer me and help me
    with your wonderful love.
¹⁴ Don't let me sink in the mud,
  but save me from my enemies
    and from the deep water.
¹⁵ Don't let me be
    swept away by a flood
    or drowned in the ocean
    or swallowed by death.

¹⁶ Answer me, LORD!
    You are kind and good.
  Pay attention to me!
    You are truly merciful.
¹⁷ Don't turn away from me.
  I am your servant,
    and I am in trouble.
  Please hurry and help!
¹⁸ Come and save me
    from my enemies.

¹⁹ You know how I am insulted,
    mocked, and disgraced;
  you know every one
    of my enemies.
²⁰ I am crushed by insults,
    and I feel sick.
  I had hoped for mercy and pity,
    but there was none.
²¹ Enemies poisoned my food,
  and when I was thirsty,
    they gave me vinegar.

²² Make their table a trap
    for them and their friends.
²³ Blind them with darkness
    and make them tremble.
²⁴ Show them how angry you are!
    Be furious and catch them.
²⁵ Destroy their camp
  and don't let anyone live
    in their tents.

²⁶ They cause trouble for people
    you have already punished;
  their gossip hurts those
    you have wounded.
²⁷ Make them guiltier than ever
    and don't forgive them.
²⁸ Wipe their names from the book
    of the living;
  remove them from the list
    of the innocent.
²⁹ I am mistreated and in pain.

Protect me, God,
    and keep me safe!

³⁰ I will praise the LORD God
  with a song
    and a thankful heart.
³¹ This will please the LORD
  better than offering an ox
    or a full-grown bull.
³² When those in need see this,
    they will be happy,
  and the LORD's worshipers
    will be encouraged.
³³ The LORD will listen
    when the homeless cry out,
  and he will never forget
    his people in prison.

³⁴ Heaven and earth
    will praise our God,
  and so will the oceans
    and everything in them.
³⁵ God will rescue Jerusalem,
  and he will rebuild
    the towns of Judah.
  His people will live there
    on their own land,
³⁶ and when the time comes,
    their children will inherit
    the land.
  Then everyone who loves God
    will also settle there.

Psalm 70

*[By David for the music leader.
To be used when an offering is made.]*

God Is Wonderful

¹ Save me, LORD God!
    Hurry and help.
² Disappoint and confuse
    all who want to kill me.
  Turn away and disgrace
    all who want to hurt me.
³ Embarrass and shame those
    who say, "We told you so!"

⁴ Let your worshipers celebrate
    and be glad because of you.
  They love your saving power,
  so let them always say,
    "God is wonderful!"
⁵ I am poor and needy,
  but you, the LORD God,
    care about me.

You are the one who saves me.
  Please hurry and help!

Psalm 71

A Prayer for God's Protection

¹ I run to you, LORD,
  for protection.
    Don't disappoint me.

^l**69.10** *went without food:* See the note at 35.13.   ^m**69.11** *sackcloth:* See the note at 30.11.

2 You do what is right,
   so come to my rescue.
Listen to my prayer
   and keep me safe.
3 Be my mighty rock,[n] the place
   where I can always run
      for protection.
Save me by your command!
You are my mighty rock
   and my fortress.

4 Come and save me, LORD God,
   from vicious and cruel
      and brutal enemies!
5 I depend on you,
   and I have trusted you
      since I was young.
6 I have relied on you[o]
   from the day I was born.
You brought me safely
   through birth,
      and I always praise you.

7 Many people think of me
   as something evil.
But you are my mighty protector,
8 and I praise and honor you
   all day long.
9 Don't throw me aside
   when I am old;
don't desert me
   when my strength is gone.
10 My enemies are plotting
   because they want me dead.
11 They say, "Now we'll catch you!
God has deserted you,
   and no one can save you."
12 Come closer, God!
   Please hurry and help.
13 Embarrass and destroy
   all who want me dead;
disgrace and confuse
   all who want to hurt me.
14 I will never give up hope
   or stop praising you.
15 All day long I will tell
   the wonderful things you do
      to save your people.
But you have done much more
   than I could possibly know.
16 I will praise you, LORD God,
   for your mighty deeds
      and your power to save.

17 You have taught me
   since I was a child,
and I never stop telling about
   your marvelous deeds.
18 Don't leave me when I am old
   and my hair turns gray.
Let me tell future generations
   about your mighty power.
19 Your deeds of kindness

are known in the heavens.
   No one is like you!

20 You made me suffer a lot,
   but you will bring me
back from this deep pit
   and give me new life.
21 You will make me truly great
   and take my sorrow away.

22 I will praise you, God,
   the Holy One of Israel.
      You are faithful.
I will play the harp
   and sing your praises.
23 You have rescued me!
   I will celebrate and shout,
singing praises to you
   with all my heart.
24 All day long I will announce
   your power to save.
I will tell how you disgraced
and disappointed those
   who wanted to hurt me.

Psalm 72
[*By Solomon.*]

A Prayer for God To Guide
and Help the King

1 Please help the king
   to be honest and fair
      just like you, our God.
2 Let him be honest and fair
with all your people,
   especially the poor.
3 Let peace and justice rule
   every mountain and hill.
4 Let the king defend the poor,
rescue the homeless, and crush
   everyone who hurts them.
5 Let the king live[p] forever
   like the sun and the moon.
6 Let him be as helpful as rain
   that refreshes the meadows
      and the ground.
7 Let the king be fair
   with everyone,
and let there be peace
until the moon
   falls from the sky.

8 Let his kingdom reach
   from sea to sea,
from the Euphrates River
   across all the earth.
9 Force the desert tribes
   to accept his rule,
and make his enemies
   crawl in the dirt.
10 Force the rulers of Tarshish[q]
and of the islands
   to pay taxes to him.

---

[n]**71.3** *mighty rock*: See the note at 18.2.   [o]**71.6** *I . . . you*: One possible meaning for the difficult Hebrew text.   [p]**72.5** *Let the king live*: One ancient translation: Hebrew "Let them worship you."   [q]**72.10** *Tarshish*: Possibly a city in Spain.

Make the kings of Sheba
and of Seba[r] bring gifts.
11 Make other rulers bow down
and all nations serve him.

12 Do this because the king
rescues the homeless
when they cry out,
and he helps everyone
who is poor and in need.
13 The king has pity
on the weak and the helpless
and protects those in need.
14 He cares when they hurt,
and he saves them from cruel
and violent deaths.

15 Long live the king!
Give him gold from Sheba.
Always pray for the king
and praise him each day.
16 Let cities overflow with food
and hills be covered with grain,
just like Mount Lebanon.
Let the people in the cities
prosper like wild flowers.
17 May the glory of the king
shine brightly forever
like the sun in the sky.
Let him make nations prosper
and learn to praise him.

18 LORD God of Israel,
we praise you.
Only you can work miracles.
19 We will always praise
your glorious name.
Let your glory be seen
everywhere on earth.
Amen and amen.

20 This ends the prayers
of David, the son of Jesse.

BOOK III

(Psalms 73–89)

Psalm 73

[A psalm by Asaph.]

God Is Good

1 God is truly good to Israel,[s]
especially to everyone
with a pure heart.
2 But I almost stumbled and fell,
3 because it made me jealous
to see proud and evil people
and to watch them prosper.
4 They never have to suffer,[t]
they stay healthy,
5 and they don't have troubles
like everyone else.

6 Their pride is like a necklace,
and they commit sin more often
than they dress themselves.
7 Their eyes poke out with fat,
and their minds are flooded
with foolish thoughts.
8 They sneer and say cruel things,
and because of their pride,
they make violent threats.
9 They dare to speak against God
and to order others around.

10 God will bring his people back,
and they will drink the water
he so freely gives.[u]

11 Only evil people would say,
"God Most High cannot
know everything!"
12 Yet all goes well for them,
and they live in peace.
13 What good did it do me
to keep my thoughts pure
and refuse to do wrong?
14 I am sick all day,
and I am punished
each morning.
15 If I had said evil things,
I would not have been loyal
to your people.

16 It was hard for me
to understand all this!
17 Then I went to your temple,
and there I understood
what will happen
to my enemies.
18 You will make them stumble,
never to get up again.
19 They will be terrified,
suddenly swept away
and no longer there.
20 They will disappear, Lord,
despised like a bad dream
the morning after.

21 Once I was bitter
and brokenhearted.
22 I was stupid and ignorant,
and I treated you
as a wild animal would.
23 But I never really left you,
and you hold my right hand.
24 Your advice has been my guide,
and later you will welcome me
in glory.[v]
25 In heaven I have only you,
and on this earth
you are all I want.
26 My body and mind may fail,
but you are my strength
and my choice forever.

[r]*72.10 Sheba . . . Seba:* Sheba may have been a place in what is now southwest Arabia, and Seba may have been in southern Arabia.   [s]*73.1 to Israel:* Or "to those who do right."   [t]*73.4 They . . . suffer:* Or "They die a painless death."   [u]*73.10 gives:* One possible meaning for the difficult Hebrew text of verse 10.   [v]*73.24 in glory:* Or "with honor."

²⁷ Powerful LORD God,
    all who stay far from you
        will be lost,
    and you will destroy those
        who are unfaithful.
²⁸ It is good for me
    to be near you.
    I choose you as my protector,
    and I will tell about
        your wonderful deeds.

Psalm 74
[_A special psalm by Asaph._]

A Prayer for the Nation
in Times of Trouble

¹ Our God, why have you
        completely rejected us?
    Why are you so angry
        with the ones you care for?
² Remember the people
        you rescued long ago,
    the tribe you chose
        to be your very own.
    Think of Mount Zion,
        your home;
³ walk over to the temple
    left in ruins forever
        by those who hate us.

⁴ Your enemies roared like lions
        in your holy temple,
    and they have placed
        their banners there.
⁵ It looks like a forest
        chopped to pieces.ʷ
⁶ They used axes and hatchets
        to smash the carvings.
⁷ They burned down your temple
        and badly disgraced it.
⁸ They said to themselves,
        "We'll crush them!"
    Then they burned every one
        of your meeting places
        all over the country.
⁹ There are no more miracles
        and no more prophets.
    Who knows how long
        it will be like this?

¹⁰ Our God, how much longer
        will our enemies sneer?
    Won't they ever stop
        insulting you?
¹¹ Why don't you punish them?
        Why are you holding back?

¹² Our God and King,
        you have ruled
        since ancient times;
    you have won victories
        everywhere on this earth.

¹³ By your power you made a path
        through the sea,
    and you smashed the heads
        of sea monsters.
¹⁴ You crushed the heads
        of the monster Leviathan,ˣ
    then fed him to wild creatures
        in the desert.
¹⁵ You opened the ground
        for streams and springs
        and dried up mighty rivers.
¹⁶ You rule the day and the night,
    and you put the moon
        and the sun in place.
¹⁷ You made summer and winter
        and gave them to the earth.ʸ

¹⁸ Remember your enemies, LORD!
    They foolishly sneer
        and won't respect you.
¹⁹ You treat us like pet doves,
        but they mistreat us.
    Don't keep forgetting us
    and letting us be fed
        to those wild animals.
²⁰ Remember the agreement
        you made with us.
    Violent enemies are hiding
    in every dark corner
        of the earth.
²¹ Don't disappoint those in need
        or make them turn from you,
    but help the poor and homeless
        to shout your praises.
²² Do something, God!
        Defend yourself.
    Remember how those fools
        sneer at you all day long.
²³ Don't forget the loud shouts
        of your enemies.

Psalm 75
[_A psalm and a song by Asaph for the music
    leader. To the tune "Don't Destroy."ᶻ_]

Praise God for All He Has Done

¹ Our God, we thank you
        for being so near to us!
    Everyone celebrates
        your wonderful deeds.

² You have set a time
        to judge with fairness.
³ The earth trembles,
        and its people shake;
    you alone keep
        its foundations firm.
⁴ You tell every bragger,
        "Stop bragging!"
    And to the wicked you say,
        "Don't boast of your power!

ʷ**74.5** _pieces_: One meaning for the difficult Hebrew text of verse 5.   ˣ**74.14** _Leviathan_:
God's victory over this monster sometimes stands for his power over all creation and
sometimes for his defeat of Egypt.   ʸ**74.17** _gave . . . earth_: Or "made boundaries for the
earth."   ᶻ**Psalm 75** _Don't Destroy_: See the note at Psalm 57.

⁵ Stop bragging! Quit telling me
how great you are."

⁶ Our LORD and our God,
victory doesn't come
from the east or the west
or from the desert.
⁷ You are the one who judges.
You can take away power
and give it to others.
⁸ You hold in your hand
a cup filled with wine,ᵃ
strong and foaming.
You will pour out some
for every sinful person
on this earth,
and they will have to drink
until it is gone.
⁹ But I will always tell about
you, the God of Jacob,
and I will sing your praise.

¹⁰ Our Lord, you will destroy
the power of evil people,
but you will give strength
to those who are good.

Psalm 76
[A song and a psalm for the music leader.
Use stringed instruments.]

God Always Wins

¹ You, our God,
are famous in Judah
and honored in Israel.
² Your home is on Mount Zion
in the city of peace.
³ There you destroyed
fiery arrows, shields, swords,
and all the other weapons.

⁴ You are more glorious than
the eternal mountains.ᵇ
⁵ Brave warriors were robbed
of what they had taken,
and now they lie dead,
unable to lift an arm.
⁶ God of Jacob, when you roar,
enemy chariots and horses
drop dead in their tracks.

⁷ Our God, you are fearsome,
and no one can oppose you
when you are angry.
⁸ From heaven you announced
your decisions as judge!
And all who live on this earth
were terrified and silent
⁹ when you took over as judge,
ready to rescue
everyone in need.
¹⁰ Even the most angry people

will praise you
when you are furious.ᶜ

¹¹ Everyone, make your promises
to the LORD your God
and do what you promise.
The LORD is fearsome,
and all of his servants
should bring him gifts.
¹² God destroys the courage
of rulers and kings
and makes cowards of them.

Psalm 77
[A psalm by Asaph
for Jeduthun, the music leader.]

In Times of Trouble
God Is with His People

¹ I pray to you, Lord God,
and I beg you to listen.
² In days filled with trouble,
I search for you.
And at night I tirelessly
lift my hands in prayer,
refusing comfort.
³ When I think of you,
I feel restless and weak.

⁴ Because of you, Lord God,
I can't sleep.
I am restless
and can't even talk.
⁵ I think of times gone by,
of those years long ago.
⁶ Each night my mind
is flooded with questions:ᵈ
⁷ "Have you rejected me forever?
Won't you be kind again?
⁸ Is this the end of your love
and your promises?
⁹ Have you forgotten
how to have pity?
Do you refuse to show mercy
because of your anger?"
¹⁰ Then I said, "God Most High,
what hurts me most
is that you no longer help us
with your mighty arm."

¹¹ Our LORD, I will remember
the things you have done,
your miracles of long ago.
¹² I will think about each one
of your mighty deeds.
¹³ Everything you do is right,
and no other god
compares with you.
¹⁴ You alone work miracles,
and you have let nations
see your mighty power.
¹⁵ With your own arm you rescued

ᵃ**75.8** *a cup . . . wine*: In the Old Testament "a cup filled with wine" sometimes stands for God's anger.   ᵇ**76.4** *the eternal mountains*: One ancient translation; Hebrew "the mountains of victims (of wild animals)."   ᶜ**76.10** *furious*: One possible meaning for the difficult Hebrew text of verse 10.   ᵈ**77.6** *my mind . . . questions*: One ancient translation; Hebrew "I remember my music."

your people, the descendants
of Jacob and Joseph.

16 The ocean looked at you, God,
and it trembled deep down
with fear.
17 Water flowed from the clouds.
Thunder was heard above
as your arrows of lightning
flashed about.
18 Your thunder roared
like chariot wheels.
The world was made bright
by lightning,
and all the earth trembled.

19 You walked through the water
of the mighty sea,
but your footprints
were never seen.
20 You guided your people
like a flock of sheep,
and you chose Moses and Aaron
to be their leaders.

Psalm 78
[*A special psalm by Asaph.*]

What God Has Done for His People

1 My friends, I beg you
to listen as I teach.
2 I will give instruction
and explain the mystery
of what happened long ago.
3 These are things we learned
from our ancestors,
4 and we will tell them
to the next generation.
We won't keep secret
the glorious deeds
and the mighty miracles
of the LORD.

5 God gave his Law
to Jacob's descendants,
the people of Israel.
And he told our ancestors
to teach their children,
6 so that each new generation
would know his Law
and tell it to the next.
7 Then they would trust God
and obey his teachings,
without forgetting anything
God had done.
8 They would be different
from their ancestors,
who were stubborn, rebellious,
and unfaithful to God.

9 The warriors from Ephraim
were armed with arrows,
but they ran away
when the battle began.

10 They broke their agreement
with God,
and they turned their backs
on his teaching.
11 They forgot all he had done,
even the mighty miracles
12 he did for their ancestors
near Zoan*e* in Egypt.

13 God made a path in the sea
and piled up the water
as he led them across.
14 He guided them during the day
with a cloud,
and each night he led them
with a flaming fire.
15 God made water flow
from rocks he split open
in the desert,
and his people drank freely,
as though from a lake.
16 He made streams gush out
like rivers from rocks.

17 But in the desert,
the people of God Most High
kept sinning and rebelling.
18 They stubbornly tested God
and demanded from him
what they wanted to eat.
19 They challenged God by saying,
"Can God provide food
out here in the desert?
20 It's true God struck the rock
and water gushed out
like a river,
but can he give his people
bread and meat?"

21 When the LORD heard this,
he was angry and furious
with Jacob's descendants,
the people of Israel.
22 They had refused to trust him,
and they had doubted
his saving power.

23 But God gave a command
to the clouds,
and he opened the doors
in the skies.
24 From heaven he sent grain
that they called manna.*f*
25 He gave them more than enough,
and each one of them ate
this special food.

26 God's mighty power
brought a strong wind
from the southeast,
27 and it brought birds
that covered the ground,
like sand on the beach.

*e*78.12 *Zoan:* A city in the eastern part of the Nile Delta.   *f*78.24 *manna:* When the people of
Israel were wandering through the desert, the Lord gave them a special kind of food to eat. It
tasted like a wafer and was called "manna," which in Hebrew means, "What is this?"

28 Then God made the birds fall
in the camp of his people
near their tents.

29 God gave his people
all they wanted,
and each of them ate
until they were full.
30 But before they had swallowed
the last bite,
31 God became angry and killed
the strongest and best
from the families of Israel.

32 But the rest kept on sinning
and would not trust
God's miracles.
33 So he cut their lives short
and made them terrified.
34 After he killed some of them,
the others turned to him
with all their hearts.
35 They remembered God Most High,
the mighty rock[g]
that kept them safe.
36 But they tried to flatter God,
and they told him lies;
37 they were unfaithful
and broke their promises.

38 Yet God was kind.
He kept forgiving their sins
and didn't destroy them.
He often became angry,
but never lost his temper.
39 God remembered that they
were made of flesh
and were like a wind
that blows once
and then dies down.

40 While they were in the desert,
they often rebelled
and made God sad.
41 They kept testing him
and caused terrible pain
for the Holy One of Israel.
42 They forgot about his power
and how he had rescued them
from their enemies.
43 God showed them all kinds
of wonderful miracles
near Zoan[h] in Egypt.
44 He turned the rivers of Egypt
into blood,
and no one could drink
from the streams.
45 He sent swarms of flies
to pester the Egyptians,
and he sent frogs
to cause them trouble.

46 God let worms and grasshoppers
eat their crops.

47 He destroyed their grapevines
and their fig trees
with hail and floods.[i]
48 Then he killed their cattle
with hail
and their other animals
with lightning.

49 God was so angry and furious
that he went into a rage
and caused them great trouble
by sending swarms
of destroying angels.
50 God gave in to his anger
and slaughtered them
in a terrible way.
51 He killed the first-born son
of each Egyptian family.

52 Then God led his people
out of Egypt
and guided them in the desert
like a flock of sheep.
53 He led them safely along,
and they were not afraid,
but their enemies drowned
in the sea.

54 God brought his people
to the sacred mountain
that he had taken
by his own power.
55 He made nations run
from the tribes of Israel,
and he let the tribes
take over their land.

56 But the people tested
God Most High,
and they refused
to obey his laws.
57 They were as unfaithful
as their ancestors,
and they were as crooked
as a twisted arrow.
58 God demanded all their love,
but they made him angry
by worshiping idols.

59 So God became furious
and completely rejected
the people of Israel.
60 Then he deserted his home
at Shiloh, where he lived
here on earth.
61 He let enemies capture
the sacred chest[j]
and let them dishonor him.

62 God took out his anger
on his chosen ones
and let them be killed
by enemy swords.
63 Fire destroyed the young men,

<hr>

[g]**78.35** *mighty rock*: See the note at 18.2.   [h]**78.43** *Zoan*: See the note at 78.12.
[i]**78.47** *floods*: Or "frost."   [j]**78.61** *sacred chest*: The Hebrew text has "his power," which refers to the sacred chest. In Psalm 132.8 it is called "powerful."

and the young women were left
with no one to marry.
⁶⁴ Priests died violent deaths,
but their widows
were not allowed to mourn.

⁶⁵ Finally the Lord woke up,
and he shouted
like a drunken soldier.
⁶⁶ God scattered his enemies
and made them ashamed
forever.

⁶⁷ Then the Lord decided
not to make his home
with Joseph's descendants
in Ephraim.*ᵏ*
⁶⁸ Instead he chose the tribe
of Judah,
and he chose Mount Zion,
the place he loves.
⁶⁹ There he built his temple
as lofty as the mountains
and as solid as the earth
that he had made
to last forever.

⁷⁰ The Lord God chose David
to be his servant and took him
from tending sheep
⁷¹ and from caring for lambs.
Then God made him the leader
of Israel, his own nation.
⁷² David treated the people fairly
and guided them with wisdom.

Psalm 79
[*A psalm by Asaph.*]

Have Pity on Jerusalem

¹ Our God, foreign nations
have taken your land,
disgraced your temple,
and left Jerusalem in ruins.
² They have fed the bodies
of your servants
to flesh-eating birds;
your loyal people are food
for savage animals.
³ All Jerusalem is covered
with their blood,
and there is no one left
to bury them.
⁴ Every nation around us
sneers and makes fun.

⁵ Our LORD, will you keep on
being angry?
Will your angry feelings
keep flaming up like fire?
⁶ Get angry with those nations

that don't know you
and won't worship you!
⁷ They have gobbled down
Jacob's descendants
and left the land in ruins.

⁸ Don't make us pay for the sins
of our ancestors.
Have pity and come quickly!
We are completely helpless.
⁹ Our God, you keep us safe.
Now help us! Rescue us.
Forgive our sins
and bring honor to yourself.

¹⁰ Why should nations ask us,
"Where is your God?"
Let us and the other nations
see you take revenge
for your servants who died
a violent death.

¹¹ Listen to the prisoners groan!
Let your mighty power save all
who are sentenced to die.
¹² Each of those nations sneered
at you, our Lord.
Now let others sneer at them,
seven times as much.
¹³ Then we, your people,
will always thank you.
We are like sheep
with you as our shepherd,
and all generations
will hear us praise you.

Psalm 80
[*A psalm by Asaph for the music leader.
To the tune "Lilies of the Agreement."*]

Help Our Nation

¹ Shepherd of Israel, you lead
the descendants of Joseph,
and you sit on your throne
above the winged creatures.*ˡ*
Listen to our prayer
and let your light shine
² for the tribes of Ephraim,
Benjamin, and Manasseh.
Save us by your power.

³ Our God, make us strong again!
Smile on us and save us.

⁴ LORD God All-Powerful,
how much longer
will the prayers of your people
make you angry?
⁵ You gave us tears for food,
and you made us drink them
by the bowlful.

ᵏ**78.67** *with . . . Ephraim*: Ephraim was Joseph's youngest son. One of the twelve tribes was named after him, and sometimes the northern kingdom of Israel was also known as Ephraim. The town of Shiloh was in the territory of Ephraim, but the place where God was worshiped was moved from there to Zion (Jerusalem) in the territory of Judah.   ˡ**80.1** *winged creatures*: Two winged creatures made of gold were on the top of the sacred chest and were symbols of the Lords's throne on earth (see Exodus 25.18).

6 Because of you,
our enemies who live nearby
laugh and joke about us.
7 But if you smile on us,
we will be saved.

8 We were like a grapevine
you brought out of Egypt.
You chased other nations away
and planted us here.
9 Then you cleared the ground,
and we put our roots deep,
spreading over the land.
10 Shade from this vine covered
the mountains.
Its branches climbed
the mighty cedars
11 and stretched to the sea;
its new growth reached
to the river.*m*

12 Our Lord, why have you
torn down the wall
from around the vineyard?
You let everyone who walks by
pick the grapes.
13 Now the vine is gobbled down
by pigs from the forest
and other wild animals.

14 God All-Powerful,
please do something!
Look down from heaven
and see what's happening
to this vine.
15 With your own hands
you planted its roots,
and you raised it
as your very own.

16 Enemies chopped the vine down
and set it on fire.
Now show your anger
and destroy them.
17 But help the one who sits
at your right side,*n*
the one you raised
to be your own.
18 Then we will never turn away.
Put new life into us,
and we will worship you.

19 LORD God All-Powerful,
make us strong again!
Smile on us and save us.

Psalm 81

*[By Asaph for the music leader.*o*]*

God Makes Us Strong

1 Be happy and shout to God
who makes us strong!
Shout praises to the God
of Jacob.
2 Sing as you play tambourines
and the lovely sounding
stringed instruments.
3 Sound the trumpets and start
the New Moon Festival.*p*
We must also celebrate
when the moon is full.
4 This is the law in Israel,
and it was given to us
by the God of Jacob.
5 The descendants of Joseph
were told to obey it,
when God led them out
from the land of Egypt.

In a language unknown to me,
I heard someone say:
6 "I lifted the burden
from your shoulder
and took the heavy basket
from your hands.
7 When you were in trouble,
I rescued you,
and from the thunderclouds,
I answered your prayers.
Later I tested you
at Meribah Spring.*q*

8 "Listen, my people,
while I, the Lord,
correct you!
Israel, if you would only
pay attention to me!
9 Don't worship foreign gods
or bow down to gods
you know nothing about.
10 I am the LORD your God.
I rescued you from Egypt.
Just ask, and I will give you
whatever you need.

11 "But, my people, Israel,
you refused to listen,
and you would have nothing
to do with me!
12 So I let you be stubborn
and keep on following
your own advice.

*m*80.11 *the sea . . . the river*: The Mediterranean Sea and the Euphrates River were part of the ideal boundaries for Israel. *n*80.17 *right side*: See the note at 16.11. *o*Psalm 81 *leader*: See the note at Psalm 8. *p*81.3 *New Moon Festival*: Celebrated on the first day of each new moon, which was the beginning of the month. But this may refer to either the New Year celebration or the Harvest Festival. "The moon is full" suggests a festival in the middle of the month. *q*81.7 *Meribah Spring*: When the people of Israel complained to Moses about the need for water, God commanded Moses to strike a rock with his walking stick, and water came out. The place was then named Massah ("test") and Meribah ("complaining").

¹³ "My people, Israel,
if only you would listen
and do as I say!
¹⁴ I, the LORD, would quickly
defeat your enemies
with my mighty power.
¹⁵ Everyone who hates me
would come crawling,
and that would be the end
of them.
¹⁶ But I would feed you
with the finest bread
and with the best honey ʳ
until you were full."

Psalm 82
[A psalm by Asaph.]

Please Do Something, God!

¹ When all of the other gods ˢ
have come together,
the Lord God judges them
and says:
² "How long will you
keep judging unfairly
and favoring evil people?
³ Be fair to the poor
and to orphans.
Defend the helpless
and everyone in need.
⁴ Rescue the weak and homeless
from the powerful hands
of heartless people.

⁵ "None of you know
or understand a thing.
You live in darkness,
while the foundations
of the earth tremble. ᵗ

⁶ "I, the Most High God, say
that all of you are gods ᵘ
and also my own children.
⁷ But you will die,
just like everyone else,
including powerful rulers."

⁸ Do something, God!
Judge the nations of the earth;
they belong to you.

Psalm 83
[A song and a psalm by Asaph.]

God Rules All the Earth

¹ Our God, don't just sit there,
silently doing nothing!
² Your hateful enemies

are turning against you
and rebelling.
³ They are sly, and they plot
against those you treasure.
⁴ They say, "Let's wipe out
the nation of Israel
and make sure that no one
remembers its name!"

⁵ All of them fully agree
in their plans against you,
and among them are
⁶ Edom and the Ishmaelites;
Moab and the Hagrites;
⁷ Gebal, Ammon, and Amalek;
Philistia and Phoenicia. ᵛ
⁸ Even Assyria has joined forces
with Moab and Ammon. ʷ

⁹ Our Lord, punish all of them
as you punished Midian.
Destroy them, as you destroyed
Sisera and Jabin
at Kishon Creek ¹⁰near Endor,
and let their bodies rot.
¹¹ Treat their leaders as you did
Oreb and Zeeb,
Zebah and Zalmunna.
¹² All of them said, "We'll take
God's valuable land!"

¹³ Our God, scatter them around
like dust in a whirlwind.
¹⁴ Just as flames destroy forests
on the mountains,
¹⁵ pursue and terrify them
with storms of your own.
¹⁶ Make them blush with shame,
until they turn and worship
you, our LORD.
¹⁷ Let them be forever ashamed
and confused.
Let them die in disgrace.
¹⁸ Make them realize that you
are the LORD Most High,
the only ruler of earth!

Psalm 84
[For the music leader. ˣ
A psalm for the people of Korah.]

The Joy of Worship

¹ LORD God All-Powerful,
your temple is so lovely!
² Deep in my heart I long
for your temple,
and with all that I am
I sing joyful songs to you.

ʳ**81.16** *the best honey*: The Hebrew text has "honey from rocks," referring to honey taken from beehives in holes or cracks in large rocks.   ˢ**82.1** *the other gods*: This probably refers to the gods of the nations that God defeated, but it could refer to God's servants (angels) in heaven or even to human rulers.   ᵗ**82.5** *foundations . . . tremble*: In ancient times it was believed that the earth was flat and supported by columns.   ᵘ**82.6** *all of you are gods*: See the note at 82.1.
ᵛ**83.7** *Phoenicia*: The Hebrew text has "Tyre," the main city in Phoenicia.   ʷ**83.8** *Moab and Ammon*: The Hebrew text has "the descendants of Lot," whose older daughter was the mother of the Moabites and whose younger daughter was the mother of the Ammonites (see Genesis 19.30-38).   ˣ**Psalm 84** *leader*: See the note at Psalm 8.

3 LORD God All-Powerful,
my King and my God,
sparrows find a home
near your altars;
swallows build nests there
to raise their young.

4 You bless everyone
who lives in your house,
and they sing your praises.
5 You bless all who depend
on you for their strength
and all who deeply desire
to visit your temple.
6 When they reach Dry Valley,[y]
springs start flowing,
and the autumn rain fills it
with pools of water.[z]
7 Your people grow stronger,
and you, the God of gods,
will be seen in Zion.

8 LORD God All-Powerful,
the God of Jacob,
please answer my prayer!
9 You are the shield
that protects your people,
and I am your chosen one.
Won't you smile on me?

10 One day in your temple
is better than a thousand
anywhere else.
I would rather serve
in your house,
than live in the homes
of the wicked.

11 Our LORD and our God,
you are like the sun
and also like a shield.
You treat us with kindness
and with honor,
never denying any good thing
to those who live right.

12 LORD God All-Powerful,
you bless everyone
who trusts you.

Psalm 85

[*A psalm by the people of Korah
for the music leader.*]

A Prayer for Peace

1 Our LORD, you have blessed
your land
and made all go well
for Jacob's descendants.
2 You have forgiven the sin
and taken away the guilt
of your people.
3 Your fierce anger is no longer
aimed at us.

4 Our LORD and our God,
you save us!
Please bring us back home
and don't be angry.
5 Will you always be angry
with us and our families?
6 Won't you give us fresh life
and let your people be glad
because of you?
7 Show us your love
and save us!

8 I will listen to you, LORD God,
because you promise peace
to those who are faithful
and no longer foolish.
9 You are ready to rescue
everyone who worships you,
so that you will live with us
in all of your glory.

10 Love and loyalty
will come together;
goodness and peace
will unite.
11 Loyalty will sprout
from the ground;
justice will look down
from the sky above.

12 Our LORD, you will bless us;
our land will produce
wonderful crops.
13 Justice will march in front,
making a path
for you to follow.

Psalm 86

[*A prayer by David.*]

A Prayer for Help

1 Please listen, LORD,
and answer my prayer!
I am poor and helpless.
2 Protect me and save me
because you are my God.
I am your faithful servant,
and I trust you.
3 Be kind to me!
I pray to you all day.
4 Make my heart glad!
I serve you,
and my prayer is sincere.
5 You willingly forgive,
and your love is always there
for those who pray to you.
6 Please listen, LORD!
Answer my prayer for help.
7 When I am in trouble, I pray,
knowing you will listen.

8 No other gods are like you;
only you work miracles.
9 You created each nation,

---

[y]**84.6** *Dry Valley*: Or "Balsam Tree Valley." The exact location is not known.   [z]**84.6** *and . . .
water*: One possible meaning for the difficult Hebrew text.

and they will all bow down
to worship and honor you.
10 You perform great wonders
because you alone are God.

11 Teach me to follow you,
and I will obey your truth.
Always keep me faithful.
12 With all my heart I thank you.
I praise you, LORD God.
13 Your love for me is so great
that you protected me
from death and the grave.

14 Proud and violent enemies,
who don't care about you,
have ganged up to attack
and kill me.
15 But you, the Lord God,
are kind and merciful.
You don't easily get angry,
and your love
can always be trusted.
16 I serve you, LORD,
and I am the child
of one of your servants.
Look on me with kindness.
Make me strong and save me.
17 Show that you approve of me!
Then my hateful enemies
will feel like fools,
because you have helped
and comforted me.

Psalm 87

[*A psalm and a song by the people of Korah.*]

The Glory of Mount Zion

1 Zion was built by the LORD
on the holy mountain,
2 and he loves that city
more than any other place
in all of Israel.
3 Zion, you are the city of God,
and wonderful things
are told about you.

4 Egypt,*a* Babylonia, Philistia,
Phoenicia,*b* and Ethiopia*c*
are some of those nations
that know you,
and their people all say,
"I was born in Zion."

5 God Most High will strengthen
the city of Zion.
Then everyone will say,
"We were born here too."
6 The LORD will make a list
of his people,
and all who were born here
will be included.

7 All who sing or dance will say,
"I too am from Zion."

Psalm 88

[*A song and a psalm by the people of Korah
for the music leader. To the tune "Mahalath
Leannoth."*d *A special psalm by Heman the
Ezrahite.*]

A Prayer When You Can't Find the Way

1 You keep me safe, LORD God.
So when I pray at night,
2   please listen carefully
to each of my concerns.

3 I am deeply troubled
and close to death;
4 I am as good as dead
and completely helpless.
5 I am no better off
than those in the grave,
those you have forgotten
and no longer help.

6 You have put me in the deepest
and darkest grave;
7 your anger rolls over me
like ocean waves.
8 You have made my friends turn
in horror from me.
I am a prisoner
who cannot escape,
9 and I am almost blind
because of my sorrow.

Each day I lift my hands
in prayer to you, LORD.
10 Do you work miracles
for the dead?
Do they stand up
and praise you?
11 Are your love and loyalty
announced in the world
of the dead?
12 Do they know of your miracles
or your saving power
in the dark world below
where all is forgotten?

13 Each morning I pray
to you, LORD.
14 Why do you reject me?
Why do you turn from me?
15 Ever since I was a child,
I have been sick
and close to death.
You have terrified me
and made me helpless.*e*

16 Your anger is like a flood!
And I am shattered
by your furious attacks

---

*a*87.4 *Egypt*: The Hebrew text has "Rahab," the name of a monster that stands for Egypt (see
Isaiah 30.7).   *b*87.4 *Phoenicia*: See the note at 83.7.   *c*87.4 *Ethiopia*: See the note at 68.31.
*d***Psalm 88** *To . . . Leannoth*: Or "For the flutes," one possible meaning for the difficult Hebrew
text.   *e***88.15** *and made me helpless*: One possible meaning for the difficult Hebrew text.

17 that strike each day
   and from every side.
18 My friends and neighbors
   have turned against me
      because of you,
   and now darkness
      is my only companion.

Psalm 89
[*A special psalm by Ethan the Ezrahite.*]

The LORD's Agreement with David

1 Our LORD, I will sing
      of your love forever.
   Everyone yet to be born
   will hear me praise
      your faithfulness.
2 I will tell them, "God's love
      can always be trusted,
   and his faithfulness lasts
      as long as the heavens."

3 You said, "David, my servant,
      is my chosen one,
   and this is the agreement
      I made with him:
4 David, one of your descendants
      will always be king."

5 Our LORD, let the heavens
      now praise your miracles,
   and let all of your angels
      praise your faithfulness.

6 None who live in the heavens
      can compare with you.
7 You are the most fearsome
      of all who live in heaven;
   all the others fear
      and greatly honor you.
8 You are LORD God All-Powerful!
   No one is as loving
      and faithful as you are.
9 You rule the roaring sea
      and calm its waves.
10 You crushed the monster Rahab,*f*
   and with your powerful arm
      you scattered your enemies.
11 The heavens and the earth
      belong to you.
   And so does the world
      with all its people
   because you created them
12   and everything else.*g*

   Mount Tabor and Mount Hermon
      gladly praise you.
13 You are strong and mighty!
14 Your kingdom is ruled
      by justice and fairness
   with love and faithfulness
      leading the way.

15 Our LORD, you bless those
      who join in the festival
   and walk in the brightness
      of your presence.
16 We are happy all day
      because of you,
   and your saving power
      brings honor to us.
17 Your own glorious power
      makes us strong,
   and because of your kindness,
      our strength increases.
18 Our LORD and our King,
   the Holy One of Israel,
      you are truly our shield.

19 In a vision, you once said
      to your faithful followers:
   "I have helped a mighty hero.
   I chose him from my people
      and made him famous.
20 David, my servant, is the one
      I chose to be king,
21 and I will always be there
      to help and strengthen him.

22 "No enemy will outsmart David,
      and he won't be defeated
      by any hateful people.
23 I will strike down and crush
      his troublesome enemies.
24 He will always be able
      to depend on my love,
   and I will make him strong
      with my own power.
25 I will let him rule the lands
      across the rivers and seas.
26 He will say to me,
   'You are my Father
      and my God,
   as well as the mighty rock*h*
      where I am safe.'

27 "I have chosen David
      as my first-born son,
   and he will be the ruler
      of all kings on earth.
28 My love for him will last,
   and my agreement with him
      will never be broken.

29 "One of David's descendants
      will always be king,
   and his family will rule
      until the sky disappears.
30 Suppose some of his children
      should reject my Law
      and refuse my instructions.
31 Or suppose they should disobey
      all of my teachings.
32 Then I will correct

---

*f*89.10 *Rahab:* Many people in the ancient world thought that the world was controlled by this sea monster that the Lord destroyed at the time of creation (see Isaiah 51.9).   *g*89.12 *and everything else:* The Hebrew text has "Zaphon and Yamin," which may either be the names of mountains or refer to the directions "north and south," with the meaning "everything from north to south."   *h*89.26 *mighty rock:* See the note at 18.2.

and punish them
because of their sins.
³³ But I will always love David
and faithfully keep all
of my promises to him.

³⁴ "I won't break my agreement
or go back on my word.
³⁵ I have sworn once and for all
by my own holy name,
and I won't lie to David.
³⁶ His family will always rule.
I will let his kingdom last
as long as the sun ³⁷and moon
appear in the sky."

³⁸ You are now angry, God,
and you have turned your back
on your chosen king.
³⁹ You broke off your agreement
with your servant, the king,
and you completely destroyed
his kingdom.
⁴⁰ The walls of his city
have been broken through,
and every fortress
now lies in ruin.
⁴¹ All who pass by
take what they want,
and nations everywhere
joke about the king.

⁴² You made his enemies powerful
and let them celebrate.
⁴³ But you forced him to retreat
because you did not fight
on his side.
⁴⁴ You took his crownⁱ
and threw his throne
in the dirt.
⁴⁵ You made an old man of him
and put him to shame.

⁴⁶ How much longer, LORD?
Will you hide forever?
How long will your anger
keep burning like fire?
⁴⁷ Remember, life is short!ʲ
Why did you empty our lives
of all meaning?
⁴⁸ No one can escape the power
of death and the grave.

⁴⁹ Our Lord, where is the love
you have always shown
and that you promised
so faithfully to David?
⁵⁰ Remember your servant, Lord!
People make jokes about me,
and I suffer many insults.
⁵¹ I am your chosen one,
but your enemies chase
and make fun of me.

⁵² Our LORD, we praise you
forever. Amen and amen.

BOOK IV

(Psalms 90–106)

Psalm 90
[*A prayer by Moses, the man of God.*]

God Is Eternal

¹ Our Lord, in all generations
you have been our home.
² You have always been God—
long before the birth
of the mountains,
even before you created
the earth and the world.

³ At your command we die
and turn back to dust,
⁴ but a thousand years
mean nothing to you!
They are merely a day gone by
or a few hours in the night.

⁵ You bring our lives to an end
just like a dream.
We are merely tender grass
⁶   that sprouts and grows
in the morning,
but dries up by evening.
⁷ Your furious anger frightens
and destroys us,
⁸ and you know all of our sins,
even those we do in secret.

⁹ Your anger is a burden
each day we live,
then life ends like a sigh.
¹⁰ We can expect seventy years,
or maybe eighty,
if we are healthy,
but even our best years
bring trouble and sorrow.
Suddenly our time is up,
and we disappear.
¹¹ No one knows the full power
of your furious anger,
but it is as great as the fear
that we owe to you.
¹² Teach us to use wisely
all the time we have.

¹³ Help us, LORD! Don't wait!
Pity your servants.
¹⁴ When morning comes,
let your love satisfy
all our needs.
Then we can celebrate
and be glad for what time
we have left.
¹⁵ Make us happy for as long
as you caused us trouble
and sorrow.

ⁱ89.44 *You took . . . crown*: One possible meaning for the difficult Hebrew text.
ʲ89.47 *Remember . . . short*: One possible meaning for the difficult Hebrew text.

16 Do wonderful things for us,
   your servants,
and show your mighty power
   to our children.
17 Our Lord and our God,
   treat us with kindness
and let all go well for us.
   Please let all go well!

Psalm 91

The LORD Is My Fortress

1 Live under the protection
   of God Most High
and stay in the shadow
   of God All-Powerful.
2 Then you will say to the LORD,
"You are my fortress,
   my place of safety;
you are my God,
   and I trust you."

3 The Lord will keep you safe
from secret traps
   and deadly diseases.
4 He will spread his wings
over you
   and keep you secure.
His faithfulness is like
   a shield or a city wall.*k*

5 You won't need to worry
about dangers at night
   or arrows during the day.
6 And you won't fear diseases
that strike in the dark
   or sudden disaster at noon.

7 You will not be harmed,
though thousands fall
   all around you.
8 And with your own eyes
you will see the punishment
   of the wicked.
9 The LORD Most High
   is your fortress.
Run to him for safety,
10 and no terrible disasters
   will strike you
   or your home.

11 God will command his angels
to protect you
   wherever you go.
12 They will carry you
in their arms,
and you won't hurt your feet
   on the stones.
13 You will overpower
the strongest lions
   and the most deadly snakes.

14 The Lord says, "If you love me
   and truly know who I am,

I will rescue you
   and keep you safe.
15 When you are in trouble,
   call out to me.
I will answer and be there
   to protect and honor you.
16 You will live a long life
   and see my saving power."

Psalm 92

[*A psalm and a song for the Sabbath.*]

Sing Praises to the LORD

1 It is wonderful to be grateful
and to sing your praises,
   LORD Most High!
2 It is wonderful each morning
to tell about your love
and at night to announce
   how faithful you are.
3 I enjoy praising your name
   to the music of harps,
4 because everything you do
makes me happy,
   and I sing joyful songs.

5 You do great things, LORD.
   Your thoughts are too deep
6 for an ignorant fool
   to know or understand.
7 Though the wicked sprout
   and spread like grass,
they will be pulled up
   by their roots.
8 But you will rule
   over all of us forever,
9 and your hateful enemies
will be scattered
   and then destroyed.

10 You have given me
   the strength of a wild ox,
and you have chosen me
   to be your very own.
11 My eyes have seen,
   and my ears have heard
the doom and destruction
   of my terrible enemies.

12 Good people will prosper
   like palm trees,
and they will grow strong
   like the cedars of Lebanon.
13 They will take root
in your house, LORD God,
   and they will do well.
14 They will be like trees
that stay healthy and fruitful,
   even when they are old.
15 And they will say about you,
"The LORD always does right!
   God is our mighty rock."*l*

---

*k*91.4 *city wall:* One possible meaning for a difficult Hebrew word; it may possibly mean some
kind of shield or weapon.   *l*92.15 *mighty rock:* See the note at 18.2.

Psalm 93

The LORD Is King

1 Our LORD, you are King!
Majesty and power
   are your royal robes.
You put the world in place,
   and it will never be moved.
2 You have always ruled,
   and you are eternal.

3 The ocean is roaring, LORD!
   The sea is pounding hard.
4 Its mighty waves are majestic,
but you are more majestic,
   and you rule over all.
5 Your decisions are firm,
and your temple will always
   be beautiful and holy.

Psalm 94

The LORD Punishes the Guilty

1 LORD God, you punish
   the guilty.
Show what you are like
   and punish them now.
2 You judge the earth.
   Come and help us!
Pay back those proud people
   for what they have done.
3 How long will the wicked
   celebrate and be glad?

4 All of those cruel people
   strut and boast,
5 and they crush and wound
   your chosen nation, LORD.
6 They murder widows,
   foreigners, and orphans.
7 Then they say,
"The LORD God of Jacob
   doesn't see or know."

8 Can't you fools see?
   Won't you ever learn?
9 God gave us ears and eyes!
   Can't he hear and see?
10 God instructs the nations
and gives knowledge to us all.
   Won't he also correct us?
11 The LORD knows how useless
   our plans really are.

12 Our LORD, you bless everyone
that you instruct and teach
   by using your Law.
13 You give them rest
   from their troubles,
until a pit can be dug
   for the wicked.
14 You won't turn your back
   on your chosen nation.

15 Justice and fairness
   will go hand in hand,
and all who do right
   will follow along.

16 Who will stand up for me
   against those cruel people?
17 If you had not helped me, LORD,
I would soon have gone
   to the land of silence.[m]
18 When I felt my feet slipping,
you came with your love
   and kept me steady.
19 And when I was burdened
   with worries,
you comforted me
   and made me feel secure.
20 But you are opposed
   to dishonest lawmakers
21 who gang up to murder
   innocent victims.

22 You, LORD God, are my fortress,
that mighty rock[n]
   where I am safe.
23 You will pay back my enemies,
and you will wipe them out
   for the evil they did.

Psalm 95

Worship and Obey the LORD

1 Sing joyful songs to the LORD!
Praise the mighty rock[n]
   where we are safe.
2 Come to worship him
with thankful hearts
   and songs of praise.

3 The LORD is the greatest God,
   king over all other gods.
4 He holds the deepest part
   of the earth in his hands,
and the mountain peaks
   belong to him.
5 The ocean is the Lord's
   because he made it,
and with his own hands
   he formed the dry land.

6 Bow down and worship
   the LORD our Creator!
7 The LORD is our God,
   and we are his people,
the sheep he takes care of
   in his own pasture.

Listen to God's voice today!
8 Don't be stubborn and rebel
   as your ancestors did
at Meribah and Massah[o]
   out in the desert.
9 For forty years

---

[m]94.17 *land of silence*: The grave or the world of the dead.   [n]94.22 *mighty rock*: See the note at 18.2.   [n]95.1 *mighty rock*: See the note at 18.2.   [o]95.8 *Meribah and Massah*: See the note at 81.7.

they tested God and saw
the things he did.
¹⁰ Then God got tired of them
and said,
"You never show good sense,
and you don't understand
what I want you to do."
¹¹ In his anger, God told them,
"You people will never enter
my place of rest."

Psalm 96

Sing a New Song to the LORD

¹ Sing a new song to the LORD!
Everyone on this earth,
sing praises to the LORD,
² sing and praise his name.

Day after day announce,
"The LORD has saved us!"
³ Tell every nation on earth,
"The LORD is wonderful
and does marvelous things!
⁴ The LORD is great and deserves
our greatest praise!
He is the only God
worthy of our worship.
⁵ Other nations worship idols,
but the LORD created
the heavens.
⁶ Give honor and praise
to the LORD,
whose power and beauty
fill his holy temple."

⁷ Tell everyone of every nation,
"Praise the glorious power
of the LORD.
⁸ He is wonderful! Praise him
and bring an offering
into his temple.
⁹ Everyone on earth, now tremble
and worship the LORD,
majestic and holy."

¹⁰ Announce to the nations,
"The LORD is King!
The world stands firm,
never to be shaken,
and he will judge its people
with fairness."

¹¹ Tell the heavens and the earth
to be glad and celebrate!
Command the ocean to roar
with all of its creatures
¹² and the fields to rejoice
with all of their crops.
Then every tree in the forest
will sing joyful songs
¹³ to the LORD.
He is coming to judge
all people on earth
with fairness and truth.

Psalm 97

The LORD Brings Justice

¹ The LORD is King!
Tell the earth to celebrate
and all islands to shout.
² Dark clouds surround him,
and his throne is supported
by justice and fairness.
³ Fire leaps from his throne,
destroying his enemies,
⁴ and his lightning is so bright
that the earth sees it
and trembles.
⁵ Mountains melt away like wax
in the presence of the LORD
of all the earth.

⁶ The heavens announce,
"The LORD brings justice!"
Everyone sees God's glory.
⁷ Those who brag about
the useless idols they worship
are terribly ashamed,
and all the false gods
bow down to the LORD.

⁸ When the people of Zion
and of the towns of Judah
hear that God brings justice,
they will celebrate.
⁹ The LORD rules the whole earth,
and he is more glorious
than all the false gods.

¹⁰ Love the LORD
and hate evil!
God protects his loyal people
and rescues them
from violence.
¹¹ If you obey and do right,
a light will show you the way
and fill you with happiness.
¹² You are the LORD's people!
So celebrate and praise
the only God.

Psalm 98

The LORD Works Miracles

¹ Sing a new song to the LORD!
He has worked miracles,
and with his own powerful arm,
he has won the victory.
² The LORD has shown the nations
that he has the power to save
and to bring justice.
³ God has been faithful
in his love for Israel,
and his saving power is seen
everywhere on earth.

⁴ Tell everyone on this earth
to sing happy songs
in praise of the LORD.
⁵ Make music for him on harps.
Play beautiful melodies!

6 Sound the trumpets and horns
and celebrate with joyful songs
for our LORD and King!

7 Command the ocean to roar
with all of its creatures,
and the earth to shout
with all of its people.
8 Order the rivers
to clap their hands,
and all of the hills
to sing together.
9 Let them worship the LORD!
He is coming to judge
everyone on the earth,
and he will be honest
and fair.

Psalm 99

Our LORD Is King

1 Our LORD, you are King!
You rule from your throne
above the winged creatures,[p]
as people tremble
and the earth shakes.
2 You are praised in Zion,
and you control all nations.
3 Only you are God!
And your power alone,
so great and fearsome,
is worthy of praise.
4 You are our mighty King,[q]
a lover of fairness,
who sees that justice is done
everywhere in Israel.
5 Our LORD and our God,
we praise you
and kneel down to worship you,
the God of holiness!

6 Moses and Aaron were two
of your priests.
Samuel was also one of those
who prayed in your name,
and you, our LORD,
answered their prayers.
7 You spoke to them
from a thick cloud,
and they obeyed your laws.

8 Our LORD and our God,
you answered their prayers
and forgave their sins,
but when they did wrong,
you punished them.
9 We praise you, LORD God,
and we worship you
at your sacred mountain.
Only you are God!

Psalm 100

[A psalm of praise.]

The LORD Is God

1 Shout praises to the LORD,
everyone on this earth.
2 Be joyful and sing
as you come in
to worship the LORD!

3 You know the LORD is God!
He created us,
and we belong to him;
we are his people,
the sheep in his pasture.

4 Be thankful and praise the LORD
as you enter his temple.
5 The LORD is good!
His love and faithfulness
will last forever.

Psalm 101

[A psalm by David.]

A King and His Promises

1 I will sing to you, LORD!
I will celebrate your kindness
and your justice.
2 Please help me learn
to do the right thing,
and I will be honest and fair
in my own kingdom.
3 I refuse to be corrupt
or to take part
in anything crooked,
4 and I won't be dishonest
or deceitful.

5 Anyone who spreads gossip
will be silenced,
and no one who is conceited
will be my friend.

6 I will find trustworthy people
to serve as my advisors,
and only an honest person
will serve as an official.

7 No one who cheats or lies
will have a position
in my royal court.
8 Each morning I will silence
any lawbreakers I find
in the countryside
or in the city of the LORD.

Psalm 102

[A prayer for someone who hurts and needs to ask the LORD for help.]

A Prayer in Time of Trouble

1 I pray to you, LORD!
Please listen.

[p] **99.1** *winged creatures*: See the note at 80.1.

[q] **99.4** *You . . . King*: One possible meaning for the difficult Hebrew text.

2 Don't hide from me
in my time of trouble.
Pay attention to my prayer
and quickly give an answer.

3 My days disappear like smoke,
and my bones are burning
as though in a furnace.
4 I am wasting away like grass,
and my appetite is gone.
5 My groaning never stops,
and my bones can be seen
through my skin.
6 I am like a lonely owl
in the desert
7 or a restless sparrow
alone on a roof.

8 My enemies insult me all day,
and they use my name
for a curse word.
9 Instead of food,
I have ashes to eat
and tears to drink,
10 because you are furious
and have thrown me aside.
11 My life fades like a shadow
at the end of day
and withers like grass.

12 Our LORD, you are King forever
and will always be famous.
13 You will show pity to Zion
because the time has come.
14 We, your servants,
love each stone in the city,
and we are sad to see them
lying in the dirt.

15 Our LORD, the nations
will honor you,
and all kings on earth
will praise your glory.
16 You will rebuild
the city of Zion.
Your glory will be seen,
17 and the prayers of the homeless
will be answered.

18 Future generations must also
praise the LORD,
so write this for them:
19 "From his holy temple,
the LORD looked down
at the earth.
20 He listened to the groans
of prisoners,
and he rescued everyone
who was doomed to die."

21 All Jerusalem should praise
you, our LORD,
22 when people from every nation
meet to worship you.

23 I should still be strong,
but you, LORD, have made
an old person of me.
24 You will live forever!
Years mean nothing to you.
Don't cut my life in half!

25 In the beginning, LORD,
you laid the earth's foundation
and created the heavens.
26 They will all disappear
and wear out like clothes.
You change them,
as you would a coat,
but you last forever.
27 You are always the same.
Years cannot change you.
28 Every generation of those
who serve you
will live in your presence.

Psalm 103
[*By David.*]

The LORD's Wonderful Love

1 With all my heart
I praise the LORD,
and with all that I am
I praise his holy name!
2 With all my heart
I praise the LORD!
I will never forget
how kind he has been.

3 The LORD forgives our sins,
heals us when we are sick,
4   and protects us from death.
His kindness and love
are a crown on our heads.
5 Each day that we live,[r]
he provides for our needs
and gives us the strength
of a young eagle.

6 For all who are mistreated,
the LORD brings justice.
7 He taught his Law to Moses
and showed all Israel
what he could do.

8 The LORD is merciful!
He is kind and patient,
and his love never fails.
9 The LORD won't always be angry
and point out our sins;
10 he doesn't punish us
as our sins deserve.

11 How great is God's love for all
who worship him?
Greater than the distance
between heaven and earth!
12 How far has the LORD taken
our sins from us?

[r]**103.5** *Each . . . live*: One possible meaning for the difficult Hebrew text.

Farther than the distance
from east to west!

13 Just as parents are kind
to their children,
the LORD is kind
to all who worship him,
14 because he knows
we are made of dust.
15 We humans are like grass
or wild flowers
that quickly bloom.
16 But a scorching wind blows,
and they quickly wither
to be forever forgotten.

17 The LORD is always kind
to those who worship him,
and he keeps his promises
to their descendants
18   who faithfully obey him.

19 God has set up his kingdom
in heaven, and he rules
the whole creation.
20 All of you mighty angels,
who obey God's commands,
come and praise your LORD!
21 All of you thousands
who serve and obey God,
come and praise your LORD!
22 All of God's creation
and all that he rules,
come and praise your LORD!
With all my heart
I praise the LORD!

Psalm 104

The LORD Takes Care of His Creation

1 I praise you, LORD God,
with all my heart.
You are glorious and majestic,
dressed in royal robes
2   and surrounded by light.
You spread out the sky
like a tent,
3 and you built your home
over the mighty ocean.
The clouds are your chariot
with the wind as its wings.
4 The winds are your messengers,
and flames of fire
are your servants.

5 You built foundations
for the earth, and it
will never be shaken.
6 You covered the earth
with the ocean that rose
above the mountains.
7 Then your voice thundered!
And the water flowed
8   down the mountains
and through the valleys
to the place you prepared.

9 Now you have set boundaries,
so that the water will never
flood the earth again.

10 You provide streams of water
in the hills and valleys,
11 so that the donkeys
and other wild animals
can satisfy their thirst.
12 Birds build their nests nearby
and sing in the trees.
13 From your home above
you send rain on the hills
and water the earth.
14 You let the earth produce
grass for cattle,
plants for our food,
15   wine to cheer us up,
olive oil for our skin,
and grain for our health.

16 Our LORD, your trees
always have water,
and so do the cedars
you planted in Lebanon.
17 Birds nest in those trees,
and storks make their home
in the fir trees.
18 Wild goats find a home
in the tall mountains,
and small animals can hide
between the rocks.

19 You created the moon
to tell us the seasons.
The sun knows when to set,
20   and you made the darkness,
so the animals in the forest
could come out at night.
21 Lions roar as they hunt
for the food you provide.
22 But when morning comes,
they return to their dens,
23 then we go out to work
until the end of day.

24 Our LORD, by your wisdom
you made so many things;
the whole earth is covered
with your living creatures.
25 But what about the ocean
so big and wide?
It is alive with creatures,
large and small.
26 And there are the ships,
as well as Leviathan, [s]
the monster you created
to splash in the sea.

27 All of these depend on you
to provide them with food,
28 and you feed each one
with your own hand,
until they are full.
29 But when you turn away,
they are terrified;

[s] **104.26** _Leviathan:_ See the note at 74.14.

when you end their life,
they die and rot.
30 You created all of them
by your Spirit,
and you give new life
to the earth.

31 Our LORD, we pray
that your glory
will last forever
and that you will be pleased
with what you have done.
32 You look at the earth,
and it trembles.
You touch the mountains,
and smoke goes up.
33 As long as I live,
I will sing and praise you,
the LORD God.
34 I hope my thoughts
will please you,
because you are the one
who makes me glad.

35 Destroy all wicked sinners
from the earth
once and for all.
With all my heart
I praise you, LORD!
I praise you!

Psalm 105

The LORD Can Be Trusted

1 Praise the LORD
and pray in his name!
Tell everyone
what he has done.
2 Sing praises to the LORD!
Tell about his miracles.
3 Celebrate and worship
his holy name
with all your heart.

4 Trust the LORD
and his mighty power.
5 Remember his miracles
and all his wonders
and his fair decisions.
6 You belong to the family
of Abraham, his servant;
you are his chosen ones,
the descendants of Jacob.

7 The LORD is our God,
bringing justice
everywhere on earth.
8 He will never forget
his agreement or his promises,
not in thousands of years.
*9 God made an eternal promise
10   to Abraham, Isaac, and Jacob,
11 when he said, "I'll give you
the land of Canaan."

12 At the time there were
only a few of us,
and we were homeless.

13 We wandered from nation
to nation, from one country
to another.
14 God did not let anyone
mistreat our people.
Instead he protected us
by punishing rulers
15 and telling them,
"Don't touch my chosen leaders
or harm my prophets!"

16 God kept crops from growing
until food was scarce
everywhere in the land.
17 But he had already sent Joseph,
sold as a slave into Egypt,
18 with chains of iron
around his legs and neck.

19 Joseph remained a slave
until his own words
had come true,
and the LORD had finished
testing him.
20 Then the king of Egypt
set Joseph free
21 and put him in charge
of everything he owned.
22 Joseph was in command
of the officials,
and he taught the leaders
how to use wisdom.

23 Jacob and his family
came and settled in Egypt
as foreigners.
24 They were the LORD's people,
so he let them grow stronger
than their enemies.
25 They served the LORD,
and he made the Egyptians plan
hateful things against them.
26 God sent his servant Moses.
He also chose and sent Aaron
27   to his people in Egypt,
and they worked miracles
and wonders there.
28 Moses and Aaron obeyed God,
and he sent darkness
to cover Egypt.
29 God turned their rivers
into streams of blood,
and the fish all died.
30 Frogs were everywhere,
even in the royal palace.
31 When God gave the command,
flies and gnats
swarmed all around.

32 In place of rain,
God sent hailstones
and flashes of lightning.
33 He destroyed their grapevines
and their fig trees,
and he made splinters
of all the other trees.

34 God gave the command,
   and more grasshoppers came
      than could be counted.
35 They ate every green plant
   and all the crops that grew
      in the land of Egypt.
36 Then God took the life
   of every first-born son.

37 When God led Israel from Egypt,
   they took silver and gold,
      and no one was left behind.
38 The Egyptians were afraid
   and gladly let them go.
39 God hid them under a cloud
   and guided them by fire
      during the night.

40 When they asked for food,
   he sent more birds
      than they could eat.
41 God even split open a rock,
   and streams of water
      gushed into the desert.
42 God never forgot
   his sacred promise
      to his servant Abraham.

43 When the Lord rescued
   his chosen people from Egypt,
      they celebrated with songs.
44 The Lord gave them the land
   and everything else
      the nations had worked for.
45 He did this so that his people
   would obey all of his laws.
      Shout praises to the LORD!

Psalm 106

A Nation Asks for Forgiveness

1 We will celebrate
   and praise you, LORD!
   You are good to us,
   and your love never fails.
2 No one can praise you enough
   for all of the mighty things
      you have done.
3 You bless those people
   who are honest and fair
      in everything they do.

4 Remember me, LORD,
   when you show kindness
      by saving your people.

5 Let me prosper with the rest
   of your chosen ones,
   as they celebrate with pride
      because they belong to you.

6 We and our ancestors
   have sinned terribly.
7 When they were in Egypt,
   they paid no attention
   to your marvelous deeds
      or your wonderful love.
   And they turned against you
      at the Red Sea. *t*

8 But you were true to your name,
   and you rescued them to prove
      how mighty you are.
9 You said to the Red Sea, *t*
   "Dry up!"
   Then you led your people across
      on land as dry as a desert.
10 You saved all of them
11 and drowned every one
   of their enemies.
12 Then your people trusted you
   and sang your praises.

13 But they soon forgot
   what you had done
      and rejected your advice.
14 They became greedy for food
   and tested you there
      in the desert.
15 So you gave them
   what they wanted,
   but later you destroyed them
      with a horrible disease.

16 Everyone in camp was jealous
   of Moses and of Aaron,
      your chosen priest.
17 Dathan and Abiram rebelled,
   and the earth opened up
      and swallowed them.
18 Then fire broke out
   and destroyed all
      of their followers.

19 At Horeb your people
   made and worshiped the statue
20   of a bull, instead of you,
      their glorious God.
21 You worked powerful miracles
   to save them from Egypt,
   but they forgot about you
22 and the fearsome things
   you did at the Red Sea. *t*

t **106.7** *Red Sea*: Hebrew *yam suph* "Sea of Reeds," one of the marshes or fresh water lakes near the eastern part of the Nile Delta. This identification is based on Exodus 13.17—14.9, which lists the towns on the route of the Israelites before crossing the sea. In the Greek translation of the Scriptures made about 200 B.C., the "Sea of Reeds" was named "Red Sea."
t **106.9** *Red Sea*: Hebrew *yam suph* "Sea of Reeds," one of the marshes or fresh water lakes near the eastern part of the Nile Delta. This identification is based on Exodus 13.17—14.9, which lists the towns on the route of the Israelites before crossing the sea. In the Greek translation of the Scriptures made about 200 B.C., the "Sea of Reeds" was named "Red Sea."
t **106.22** *Red Sea*: Hebrew *yam suph* "Sea of Reeds," one of the marshes or fresh water lakes near the eastern part of the Nile Delta. This identification is based on Exodus 13.17—14.9, which lists the towns on the route of the Israelites before crossing the sea. In the Greek translation of the Scriptures made about 200 B.C., the "Sea of Reeds" was named "Red Sea."

23 You were angry and started
to destroy them,
but Moses, your chosen leader,
begged you not to do it.

24 They would not trust
you, LORD,
and they did not like
the promised land.
25 They would not obey you,
and they grumbled
in their tents.
26 So you threatened them
by saying, "I'll kill you
out here in the desert!
27 I'll scatter your children
everywhere in the world."

28 Your people became followers
of a god named Baal Peor,
and they ate sacrifices
offered to the dead. *u*
29 They did such terrible things
that you punished them
with a deadly disease.
30 But Phinehas *v* helped them,
and the sickness stopped.
31 Now he will always
be highly honored.

32 At Meribah Spring *w*
they turned against you
and made you furious.
33 Then Moses got into trouble
for speaking in anger.

34 Our LORD, they disobeyed you
by refusing to destroy
the nations.
35 Instead they were friendly
with those foreigners
and followed their customs.
36 Then they fell into the trap
of worshiping idols.
37 They sacrificed their sons
and their daughters to demons
38 and to the gods of Canaan.
Then they poured out the blood
of these innocent children
and made the land filthy.
39 By doing such gruesome things,
they also became filthy.

40 Finally, LORD, you were angry
and terribly disgusted
with your people.
41 So you put them in the power
of nations that hated them.
42 They were mistreated and abused
by their enemies,
43 but you saved them
time after time.
They were determined to rebel,

and their sins caused
their downfall.

44 You answered their prayers
when they were in trouble.
45 You kept your agreement
and were so merciful
46 that their enemies
had pity on them.

47 Save us, LORD God!
Bring us back
from among the nations.
Let us celebrate and shout
in praise of your holy name.

48 LORD God of Israel,
you deserve to be praised
forever and ever.
Let everyone say, "Amen!
Shout praises to the LORD!"

BOOK V

(Psalms 107–150)

Psalm 107

The LORD Is Good to His People

1 Shout praises to the LORD!
He is good to us,
and his love never fails.
2 Everyone the LORD has rescued
from trouble
should praise him,
3 everyone he has brought
from the east and the west,
the north and the south. *x*

4 Some of you were lost
in the scorching desert,
far from a town.
5 You were hungry and thirsty
and about to give up.
6 You were in serious trouble,
but you prayed to the LORD,
and he rescued you.
7 Right away he brought you
to a town.
8 You should praise the LORD
for his love
and for the wonderful things
he does for all of us.
9 To everyone who is thirsty,
he gives something to drink;
to everyone who is hungry,
he gives good things to eat.

10 Some of you were prisoners
suffering in deepest darkness
and bound by chains,
11 because you had rebelled

___

u **106.28** *the dead:* Or "lifeless idols."   *v* **106.30** *Phinehas:* The grandson of Aaron, who put
two people to death and kept the Lord from being angry with the rest of his people (see
Numbers 25.1-13).   *w* **106.32** *Meribah Spring:* See the note at 81.7.   *x* **107.3** *south:* The
Hebrew text has "sea," probably referring to the Mediterranean Sea.

against God Most High
and refused his advice.
12 You were worn out
from working like slaves,
and no one came to help.
13 You were in serious trouble,
but you prayed to the LORD,
and he rescued you.
14 He brought you out
of the deepest darkness
and broke your chains.

15 You should praise the LORD
for his love
and for the wonderful things
he does for all of us.
16 He breaks down bronze gates
and shatters iron locks.

17 Some of you had foolishly
committed a lot of sins
and were in terrible pain.
18 The very thought of food
was disgusting to you,
and you were almost dead.
19 You were in serious trouble,
but you prayed to the LORD,
and he rescued you.
20 By the power of his own word,
he healed you and saved you
from destruction.

21 You should praise the LORD
for his love
and for the wonderful things
he does for all of us.
22 You should celebrate
by offering sacrifices
and singing joyful songs
to tell what he has done.

23 Some of you made a living
by sailing the mighty sea,
24 and you saw the miracles
the LORD performed there.
25 At his command a storm arose,
and waves covered the sea.
26 You were tossed to the sky
and to the ocean depths,
until things looked so bad
that you lost your courage.
27 You staggered like drunkards
and gave up all hope.
28 You were in serious trouble,
but you prayed to the LORD,
and he rescued you.
29 He made the storm stop
and the sea be quiet.
30 You were happy because of this,
and he brought you to the port
where you wanted to go.

31 You should praise the LORD
for his love
and for the wonderful things
he does for all of us.
32 Honor the LORD

when you and your leaders
meet to worship.

33 If you start doing wrong,
the LORD will turn rivers
into deserts,
34 flowing streams
into scorched land,
and fruitful fields
into beds of salt.

35 But the LORD can also turn
deserts into lakes
and scorched land
into flowing streams.
36 If you are hungry,
you can settle there
and build a town.
37 You can plant fields
and vineyards that produce
a good harvest.
38 The LORD will bless you
with many children
and with herds of cattle.

39 Sometimes you may be crushed
by troubles and sorrows,
until only a few of you
are left to survive.
40 But the LORD will take revenge
on those who conquer you,
and he will make them wander
across desert sands.
41 When you are suffering
and in need,
he will come to your rescue,
and your families will grow
as fast as a herd of sheep.
42 You will see this because
you obey the LORD,
but everyone who is wicked
will be silenced.

43 Be wise! Remember this
and think about the kindness
of the LORD.

Psalm 108

[*A song and a psalm by David.*]

With God on Our Side

1 Our God, I am faithful to you
with all my heart,
and you can trust me.
I will sing
and play music for you
with all that I am.
2 I will start playing my harps
before the sun rises.
3 I will praise you, LORD,
for everyone to hear;
I will sing hymns to you
in every nation.
4 Your love reaches higher
than the heavens,
and your loyalty extends
beyond the clouds.

5 Our God, may you be honored
    above the heavens;
may your glory be seen
    everywhere on earth.
6 Answer my prayers
    and use your powerful arm
        to give us victory.
Then the people you love
    will be safe.

7 Our God, from your holy place
    you made this promise:
"I will gladly divide up
    the city of Shechem
and give away Succoth Valley
    piece by piece.
8 The lands of Gilead
    and Manasseh are mine.
Ephraim is my war helmet,
    and Judah is my symbol
        of royal power.
9 Moab is merely my washbasin,
    and Edom belongs to me.
I shout with victory
    over the Philistines."

10 Our God, who will bring me
    to the fortress
        or lead me to Edom?
11 Have you rejected us?
    You don't lead our armies.
12 Help us defeat our enemies!
    No one else can rescue us.
13 You are the one
    who gives us victory
        and crushes our enemies.

Psalm 109
[A psalm by David for the music leader.]

A Prayer for the LORD's Help

1 I praise you, God!
    Don't keep silent.
2 Destructive and deceitful lies
    are told about me,
3 and hateful things are said
    for no reason.
4 I had pity and prayed[y]
    for my enemies,
but their words to me
    were harsh and cruel.
5 For being friendly and kind,
    they paid me back
        with meanness and hatred.
6 My enemies said,
    "Find some worthless fools
        to accuse him of a crime.
7 Try him and find him guilty!
    Consider his prayers a lie.
8 Cut his life short
    and let someone else
        have his job.
9 Make orphans of his children
    and a widow of his wife;

10 make his children beg for food
    and live in the slums.
11 "Let the people he owes
    take everything he owns.
        Give it all to strangers.
12 Don't let anyone be kind to him
    or have pity on the children
        he leaves behind.
13 Bring an end to his family,
    and from now on let him be
        a forgotten man.

14 "Don't let the LORD forgive
    the sins of his parents
        and his ancestors.
15 Don't let the LORD forget
    the sins of his family,
or let anyone remember
    his family ever lived.
16 He was so cruel to the poor,
    homeless, and discouraged
        that they died young.

17 "He cursed others.
    Now place a curse on him!
He never wished others well.
    Wish only trouble for him!
18 He cursed others more often
    than he dressed himself.
Let his curses strike him deep,
    just as water and olive oil
        soak through to our bones.
19 Let his curses surround him,
    just like the clothes
        he wears each day."

20 Those are the cruel things
    my enemies wish for me.
        Let it all happen to them!
21 Be true to your name, LORD God!
    Show your great kindness
        and rescue me.

22 I am poor and helpless,
    and I have lost all hope.
23 I am fading away
    like an evening shadow;
I am tossed aside
    like a crawling insect.
24 I have gone without eating,[z]
    until my knees are weak,
        and my body is bony.
25 When my enemies see me,
    they say cruel things
        and shake their heads.

26 Please help me, LORD God!
    Come and save me
        because of your love.
27 Let others know that you alone
    have saved me.
28 I don't care if they curse me,
    as long as you bless me.

y 109.4 *and prayed*: One possible meaning for the difficult Hebrew text.   z 109.24 *without eating*: See the note at 35.13.

You will make my enemies fail
 when they attack,
and you will make me glad
 to be your servant.
29 You will cover them with shame,
 just as their bodies
 are covered with clothes.

30 I will sing your praises
 and thank you, LORD,
 when your people meet.
31 You help everyone in need,
 and you defend them
 when they are on trial.

Psalm 110

[*A psalm by David.*]

The LORD Gives Victory

1 The LORD said to my Lord,
 "Sit at my right side,*a*
until I make your enemies
 into a footstool for you."

2 The LORD will let your power
 reach out from Zion,
and you will rule
 over your enemies.
3 Your glorious power
will be seen on the day
 you begin to rule.
You will wear the sacred robes
and shine like the morning sun
 in all of your strength.*b*
4 The LORD has made a promise
 that will never be broken:
"You will be a priest forever,
 just like Melchizedek."

5 My Lord is at your right side,
 and when he gets angry
he will crush
 the other kings.
6 He will judge the nations
 and crack their skulls,
leaving piles of dead bodies
 all over the earth.
7 He will drink from any stream
that he chooses, while winning
 victory after victory.*c*

Psalm 111

Praise the LORD for All He Has Done

1 Shout praises to the LORD!
 With all my heart
I will thank the LORD
 when his people meet.
2 The LORD has done
 many wonderful things!
Everyone who is pleased
with God's marvelous deeds
 will keep them in mind.

3 Everything the LORD does
 is glorious and majestic,
and his power to bring justice
 will never end.

4 The LORD God is famous
 for his wonderful deeds,
 and he is kind and merciful.
5 He gives food to his worshipers
 and always keeps his agreement
 with them.
6 He has shown his mighty power
 to his people
and has given them the lands
 of other nations.

7 God is always honest and fair,
 and his laws can be trusted.
8 They are true and right
 and will stand forever.
9 God rescued his people,
 and he will never break
his agreement with them.
 He is fearsome and holy.

10 Respect and obey the LORD!
This is the first step
 to wisdom and good sense.*d*
God will always be respected.

Psalm 112

God Blesses His Worshipers

1 Shout praises to the LORD!
 The LORD blesses everyone
who worships him and gladly
 obeys his teachings.
2 Their descendants will have
 great power in the land,
because the LORD blesses
 all who do right.
3 They will get rich and prosper
and will always be remembered
 for their fairness.
4 They will be so kind
 and merciful and good,
that they will be a light
in the dark for others
 who do the right thing.

5 Life will go well for those
who freely lend
 and are honest in business.
6 They won't ever be troubled,
and the kind things they do
 will never be forgotten.
7 Bad news won't bother them;
they have decided
 to trust the LORD.
8 They are dependable
 and not afraid,
and they will live to see
 their enemies defeated.

---

*a*110.1 *right side*: See the note at 16.11.   *b*110.3 *You will . . . strength*: One possible meaning
for the difficult Hebrew text.   *c*110.7 *while . . . victory*: Or "God will give him victory after
victory."   *d*111.10 *This . . . sense*: Or "This is what wisdom and good sense are all about."

9 They will always be remembered
and greatly praised,
because they were kind
and freely gave to the poor.
10 When evil people see this,
they angrily bite their tongues
and disappear.
They will never get
what they really want.

Psalm 113

The LORD Helps People in Need

1 Shout praises to the LORD!
Everyone who serves him,
come and praise his name.

2 Let the name of the LORD
be praised now and forever.
3 From dawn until sunset
the name of the LORD
deserves to be praised.
4 The LORD is far above
all of the nations;
he is more glorious
than the heavens.

5 No one can compare
with the LORD our God.
His throne is high above,
6 and he looks down to see
the heavens and the earth.
7 God lifts the poor and needy
from dust and ashes,
8 and he lets them take part
in ruling his people.
9 When a wife has no children,
he blesses her with some,
and she is happy.
Shout praises to the LORD!

Psalm 114

The LORD Works Wonders

1 God brought his people
out of Egypt, that land
with a strange language.
2 He made Judah his holy place
and ruled over Israel.

3 When the sea looked at God,
it ran away,
and the Jordan River
flowed upstream.
4 The mountains and the hills
skipped around like goats.

5 Ask the sea why it ran away
or ask the Jordan
why it flowed upstream.
6 Ask the mountains and the hills
why they skipped like goats!

7 Earth, you will tremble,
when the Lord God of Jacob
comes near,

8 because he turns solid rock
into flowing streams
and pools of water.

Psalm 115

The LORD Deserves To Be Praised

1 We don't deserve praise!
The LORD alone deserves
all of the praise,
because of his love
and faithfulness.
2 Why should the nations ask,
"Where is your God?"

3 Our God is in the heavens,
doing as he chooses.
4 The idols of the nations
are made of silver and gold.
5 They have a mouth and eyes,
but they can't speak or see.
6 Their ears can't hear,
and their noses can't smell.
7 Their hands have no feeling,
their legs don't move,
and they can't make a sound.
8 Everyone who made the idols
and all who trust them
are just as helpless
as those useless gods.

9 People of Israel,
you must trust the LORD
to help and protect you.
10 Family of Aaron the priest,
you must trust the LORD
to help and protect you.
11 All of you worship the LORD,
so you must trust him
to help and protect you.

12 The LORD will not forget
to give us his blessing;
he will bless all of Israel
and the family of Aaron.
13 All who worship the LORD,
no matter who they are,
will receive his blessing.

14 I pray that the LORD
will let your family
and your descendants
always grow strong.
15 May the LORD who created
the heavens and the earth
give you his blessing.

16 The LORD has kept the heavens
for himself,
but he has given the earth
to us humans.
17 The dead are silent
and cannot praise the LORD,
18 but we will praise him
now and forevermore.
Shout praises to the LORD!

Psalm 116

When the LORD Saves You from Death

[1] I love you, LORD!
  You answered my prayers.
[2] You paid attention to me,
  and so I will pray to you
    as long as I live.
[3] Death attacked from all sides,
  and I was captured
    by its painful chains.
  But when I was really hurting,
[4] I prayed and said, "LORD,
    please don't let me die!"

[5] You are kind, LORD,
  so good and merciful.
[6] You protect ordinary people,
  and when I was helpless,
    you saved me
[7] and treated me so kindly
  that I don't need
    to worry anymore.

[8] You, LORD, have saved
    my life from death,
  my eyes from tears,
  my feet from stumbling.
[9] Now I will walk at your side
  in this land of the living.
[10] I was faithful to you
    when I was suffering,
[11] though in my confusion I said,
  "I can't trust anyone!"

[12] What must I give you, LORD,
    for being so good to me?
[13] I will pour out an offering
    of wine to you,
  and I will pray in your name
  because you
    have saved me.
[14] I will keep my promise to you
    when your people meet.
[15] You are deeply concerned
  when one of your loyal people
    faces death.

[16] I worship you, LORD,
    just as my mother did,
  and you have rescued me
    from the chains of death.
[17] I will offer you a sacrifice
  to show how grateful I am,
    and I will pray.
[18] I will keep my promise to you
    when your people
[19] gather at your temple
  in Jerusalem.
    Shout praises to the LORD!

Psalm 117

Come Praise the LORD

[1] All of you nations,
  come praise the LORD!
    Let everyone praise him.
[2] His love for us is wonderful;

his faithfulness never ends.
  Shout praises to the LORD!

Psalm 118

The LORD Is Always Merciful

[1] Tell the LORD
    how thankful you are,
  because he is kind
    and always merciful.

[2] Let Israel shout,
  "God is always merciful!"
[3] Let the family of Aaron
  the priest shout,
    "God is always merciful!"
[4] Let every true worshiper
  of the LORD shout,
    "God is always merciful!"

[5] When I was really hurting,
    I prayed to the LORD.
  He answered my prayer,
    and took my worries away.
[6] The LORD is on my side,
  and I am not afraid
    of what others can do to me.
[7] With the LORD on my side,
  I will defeat all
    of my hateful enemies.
[8] It is better to trust the LORD
    for protection
  than to trust anyone else,
[9]   including strong leaders.
[10] Nations surrounded me,
  but I got rid of them
    by the power of the LORD.
[11] They attacked from all sides,
  but I got rid of them
    by the power of the LORD.
[12] They swarmed around like bees,
  but by the power of the LORD,
    I got rid of them
    and their fiery sting.
[13] Their attacks were so fierce
  that I nearly fell,
    but the LORD helped me.
[14] My power and my strength
  come from the LORD,
    and he has saved me.

[15] From the tents of God's people
  come shouts of victory:
    "The LORD is powerful!
[16] With his mighty arm
  the LORD wins victories!
    The LORD is powerful!"

[17] And so my life is safe,
  and I will live to tell
    what the LORD has done.
[18] He punished me terribly,
  but he did not let death
    lay its hands on me.
[19] Open the gates of justice!
  I will enter and tell the LORD
    how thankful I am.

20 Here is the gate of the LORD!
Everyone who does right
may enter this gate.

21 I praise the LORD
for answering my prayers
and saving me.
22 The stone that the builders
tossed aside
has now become
the most important stone.

23 The LORD has done this,
and it is amazing to us.
24 This day belongs to the LORD!
Let's celebrate
and be glad today.
25 We'll ask the LORD to save us!
We'll sincerely ask the LORD
to let us win.

26 God bless the one who comes
in the name of the LORD!
We praise you from here
in the house of the LORD.

27 The LORD is our God,
and he has given us light!
Start the celebration!
March with palm branches
all the way to the altar.*e*

28 The LORD is my God!
I will praise him and tell him
how thankful I am.

29 Tell the LORD
how thankful you are,
because he is kind
and always merciful.

Psalm 119

In Praise of the Law of the LORD

1 Our LORD, you bless everyone
who lives right
and obeys your Law.
2 You bless all of those
who follow your commands
from deep in their hearts
3 and who never do wrong
or turn from you.
4 You have ordered us always
to obey your teachings;
5 I don't ever want to stray
from your laws.
6 Thinking about your commands
will keep me from doing
some foolish thing.
7 I will do right and praise you
by learning to respect
your perfect laws.
8 I will obey all of them!
Don't turn your back on me.

9 Young people can live
a clean life
by obeying your word.
10 I worship you
with all my heart.
Don't let me walk away
from your commands.
11 I treasure your word
above all else;
it keeps me from sinning
against you.
12 I praise you, LORD!
Teach me your laws.
13 With my own mouth,
I tell others the laws
that you have spoken.
14 Obeying your instructions
brings as much happiness
as being rich.
15 I will study your teachings
and follow your footsteps.
16 I will take pleasure
in your laws
and remember your words.

17 Treat me with kindness, LORD,
so that I may live
and do what you say.
18 Open my mind
and let me discover
the wonders of your Law.
19 I live here as a stranger.
Don't keep me from knowing
your commands.
20 What I want most of all
and at all times
is to honor your laws.
21 You punish those boastful,
worthless nobodies who turn
from your commands.
22 Don't let them sneer
and insult me
for following you.
23 I keep thinking about
your teachings, LORD,
even if rulers plot
against me.
24 Your laws are my greatest joy!
I follow their advice.

25 I am at the point of death.
Let your teachings
breathe new life into me.
26 When I told you my troubles,
you answered my prayers.
Now teach me your laws.
27 Help me to understand
your teachings,
and I will think about
your marvelous deeds.
28 I am overcome with sorrow.
Encourage me,
as you have promised to do.
29 Keep me from being deceitful,
and be kind enough
to teach me your Law.

*e*118.27 *Start . . . altar*: One possible meaning for the difficult Hebrew text.

³⁰ I am determined to be faithful
 and to respect your laws.
³¹ I follow your rules, LORD.
 Don't let me be ashamed.
³² I am eager to learn all
 that you want me to do;
help me to understand
 more and more.

³³ Point out your rules to me,
 and I won't disobey
 even one of them.
³⁴ Help me to understand your Law;
 I promise to obey it
 with all my heart.
³⁵ Direct me by your commands!
 I love to do what you say.
³⁶ Make me want to obey you,
 rather than to be rich.
³⁷ Take away my foolish desires,
 and let me find life
 by walking with you.
³⁸ I am your servant!
 Do for me what you promised
 to those who worship you.
³⁹ Your wonderful teachings
 protect me from the insults
 that I hate so much.
⁴⁰ I long for your teachings.
 Be true to yourself
 and let me live.

⁴¹ Show me your love
 and save me, LORD,
 as you have promised.
⁴² Then I will have an answer
 for everyone who insults me
 for trusting your word.
⁴³ I rely on your laws!
 Don't take away my chance
 to speak your truth.
⁴⁴ I will keep obeying your Law
 forever and ever.
⁴⁵ I have gained perfect freedom
 by following your teachings,
⁴⁶ and I trust them so much
 that I tell them to kings.
⁴⁷ I love your commands!
 They bring me happiness.
⁴⁸ I love and respect them
 and will keep them in mind.

⁴⁹ Don't forget your promise
 to me, your servant.
 I depend on it.
⁵⁰ When I am hurting,
 I find comfort in your promise
 that leads to life.
⁵¹ Conceited people sneer at me,
 but I obey your Law.
⁵² I find true comfort, LORD,
 because your laws have stood
 the test of time.
⁵³ I get furious when evil people
 turn against your Law.
⁵⁴ No matter where I am,
 your teachings
 fill me with songs.

⁵⁵ Even in the night
 I think about you, LORD,
 and I obey your Law.
⁵⁶ You have blessed me
 because I have always followed
 your teachings.

⁵⁷ You, LORD, are my choice,
 and I will obey you.
⁵⁸ With all my heart
 I beg you to be kind to me,
 just as you have promised.
⁵⁹ I pay careful attention
 as you lead me,
 and I follow closely.
⁶⁰ As soon as you command,
 I do what you say.
⁶¹ Evil people may set a trap,
 but I obey your Law.
⁶² Your laws are so fair
 that I wake up and praise you
 in the middle of the night.
⁶³ I choose as my friends
 everyone who worships you
 and follows your teachings.
⁶⁴ Our LORD, your love is seen
 all over the world.
 Teach me your laws.

⁶⁵ I am your servant, LORD,
 and you have kept your promise
 to treat me with kindness.
⁶⁶ Give me wisdom and good sense.
 I trust your commands.
⁶⁷ Once you corrected me
 for not obeying you,
 but now I obey.
⁶⁸ You are kindhearted,
 and you do good things,
 so teach me your laws.
⁶⁹ My reputation is being ruined
 by conceited liars,
but with all my heart
 I follow your teachings.
⁷⁰ Those liars have no sense,
 but I find happiness
 in your Law.
⁷¹ When you corrected me,
 it did me good
because it taught me
 to study your laws.
⁷² I would rather obey you
 than to have a thousand pieces
 of silver and gold.

⁷³ You created me
 and put me together.
Make me wise enough to learn
 what you have commanded.
⁷⁴ Your worshipers will see me,
 and they will be glad
 that I trust your word.
⁷⁵ Your decisions are correct,
 and you were right
 to punish me.
⁷⁶ I serve you, LORD.
 Comfort me with your love,
 just as you have promised.

⁷⁷ I love to obey your Law!
   Have mercy and let me live.
⁷⁸ Put down those proud people
      who hurt me with their lies,
   because I have chosen
      to study your teachings.
⁷⁹ Let your worshipers come to me,
   so they will learn
      to obey your rules.
⁸⁰ Let me truly respect your laws,
      so I won't be ashamed.

⁸¹ I long for you to rescue me!
      Your word is my only hope.
⁸² I am worn out from waiting
      for you to keep your word.
   When will you have mercy?
⁸³ My life is wasting away
      like a dried-up wineskin,ᶠ
   but I have not forgotten
      your teachings.
⁸⁴ I am your servant!
      How long must I suffer?
   When will you punish
      those troublemakers?
⁸⁵ Those proud people reject
      your teachings,
   and they dig pits
      for me to fall in.
⁸⁶ Your laws can be trusted!
      Protect me from cruel liars.
⁸⁷ They have almost killed me,
   but I have been faithful
      to your teachings.
⁸⁸ Show that you love me
      and let me live,
   so that I may obey all
      of your commands.

⁸⁹ Our LORD, you are eternal!
   Your word will last as long
      as the heavens.ᵍ
⁹⁰ You remain faithful
      in every generation,
   and the earth you created
      will keep standing firm.
⁹¹ All things are your servants,
   and the laws you made
      are still in effect today.
⁹² If I had not found happiness
      in obeying your Law,
   I would have died in misery.
⁹³ I won't ever forget
      your teachings,
   because you give me new life
      by following them.
⁹⁴ I belong to you,
   and I have respected your laws,
      so keep me safe.
⁹⁵ Brutal enemies are waiting
      to ambush and destroy me,
   but I obey your rules.

⁹⁶ Nothing is completely perfect,
      except your teachings.

⁹⁷ I deeply love your Law!
      I think about it all day.
⁹⁸ Your laws never leave my mind,
   and they make me much wiser
      than my enemies.
⁹⁹ Thinking about your teachings
   gives me better understanding
      than my teachers,
¹⁰⁰ and obeying your laws
   makes me wiser than those
      who have lived a long time.
¹⁰¹ I obey your word
   instead of following a way
      that leads to trouble.
¹⁰² You have been my teacher,
   and I won't reject
      your instructions.
¹⁰³ Your teachings are sweeter
      than honey.
¹⁰⁴ They give me understanding
      and make me hate all lies.

¹⁰⁵ Your word is a lamp
      that gives light
         wherever I walk.
¹⁰⁶ Your laws are fair,
   and I have given my word
      to respect them all.
¹⁰⁷ I am in terrible pain!
   Save me, LORD,
      as you said you would.
¹⁰⁸ Accept my offerings of praise
      and teach me your laws.
¹⁰⁹ I never forget your teachings,
   although my life is always
      in danger.
¹¹⁰ Some merciless people
      are trying to trap me,
   but I never turn my back
      on your teachings.
¹¹¹ They will always be
   my most prized possession
      and my source of joy.
¹¹² I have made up my mind
   to obey your laws forever,
      no matter what.

¹¹³ I hate anyone
   whose loyalty is divided,
      but I love your Law.
¹¹⁴ You are my place of safety
   and my shield.
      Your word is my only hope.

¹¹⁵ All of you worthless people,
      get away from me!
   I am determined to obey
      the commands of my God.

ᶠ**119.83** *a dried-up wineskin:* The Hebrew text has "a wineskin in the smoke." In ancient times bags were made from animal skins to hold wine, but when the bags dried up they cracked and could no longer be used.   ᵍ**119.89** *Our . . . heavens:* Or "Our LORD, your word is eternal. It will last as long as the heavens."

116 Be true to your word, LORD.
　Keep me alive and strong;
　don't let me be ashamed
　because of my hope.
117 Keep me safe and secure,
　so that I will always
　respect your laws.
118 You reject all deceitful liars
　because they refuse
　your teachings.
119 As far as you are concerned,
　all evil people are[h] garbage,
　and so I follow your rules.
120 I tremble all over
　when I think of you
　and the way you judge.

121 I did what was fair and right!
　Don't hand me over to those
　who want to mistreat me.
122 Take good care of me,
　your servant,
　and don't let me be harmed
　by those conceited people.
123 My eyes are weary from waiting
　to see you keep your promise
　to come and save me.
124 Show your love for me,
　your servant,
　and teach me your laws.
125 I serve you,
　so let me understand
　your teachings.
126 Do something, LORD!
　They have broken your Law.
127 Your laws mean more to me
　than the finest gold.
128 I follow all of your commands,[i]
　but I hate anyone
　who leads me astray.

129 Your teachings are wonderful,
　and I respect them all.
130 Understanding your word
　brings light to the minds
　of ordinary people.
131 I honestly want to know
　everything you teach.
132 Think about me and be kind,
　just as you are to everyone
　who loves your name.
133 Keep your promise
　and don't let me stumble
　or let sin control my life.
134 Protect me from abuse,
　so I can obey your laws.
135 Smile on me, your servant,
　and teach me your laws.
136 When anyone disobeys you,
　my eyes overflow with tears.

137 Our LORD, you always do right,
　and your decisions are fair.

138 All of your teachings are true
　and trustworthy.
139 It upsets me greatly
　when my enemies neglect
　your teachings.
140 Your word to me, your servant,
　is like pure gold;
　I treasure what you say.
141 Everyone calls me a nobody,
　but I remember your laws.
142 You will always do right,
　and your teachings are true.
143 I am in deep distress,
　but I love your teachings.
144 Your rules are always fair.
　Help me to understand them
　and live.

145 I pray to you, LORD!
　Please answer me.
　I promise to obey your laws.
146 I beg you to save me,
　so I can follow your rules.
147 Even before sunrise,
　I pray for your help,
　and I put my hope
　in what you have said.
148 I lie awake at night,
　thinking of your promises.
149 Show that you love me, LORD,
　and answer my prayer.
　Please do the right thing
　and save my life.
150 People who disobey your Law
　have made evil plans
　and want to hurt me,
151 but you are with me,
　and all of your commands
　can be trusted.
152 From studying your laws,
　I found out long ago
　that you made them
　to last forever.

153 I have not forgotten your Law!
　Look at the trouble I am in,
　and rescue me.
154 Be my defender and protector!
　Keep your promise
　and save my life.
155 Evil people won't obey you,
　and so they have no hope
　of being saved.
156 You are merciful, LORD!
　Please do the right thing
　and save my life.
157 I have a lot of brutal enemies,
　but still I never turn
　from your laws.
158 All of those unfaithful people
　who refuse to obey you
　are disgusting to me.
159 Remember how I love your laws,

h 119.119 As far as . . . are: A few Hebrew manuscripts and ancient translations. Most Hebrew manuscripts have "You get rid of evil people as if they were."　i 119.128 I . . . commands: One possible meaning for the difficult Hebrew text.

and show your love for me
   by keeping me safe.
160 All you say can be trusted;
   your teachings are true
   and will last forever.

161 Rulers are cruel to me
   for no reason.
But with all my heart
   I respect your words,
162 because they bring happiness
   like treasures taken in war.
163 I can't stand liars,
   but I love your Law.
164 I praise you seven times a day
   because your laws are fair.
165 You give peace of mind
   to all who love your Law.
   Nothing can make them fall.
166 You are my only hope
   for being saved, LORD,
   and I do all you command.
167 I love and obey your laws
   with all my heart.
168 You know everything I do.
   You know I respect every law
   you have given.

169 Please, LORD, hear my prayer
   and give me the understanding
   that comes from your word.
170 Listen to my concerns
   and keep me safe,
   just as you have promised.
171 If you will teach me your laws,
   I will praise you 172and sing
   about your promise,
   because all of your teachings
   are what they ought to be.
173 Be ready to protect me
   because I have chosen
   to obey your laws.
174 I am waiting for you
   to save me, LORD.
   Your Law makes me happy.
175 Keep me alive,
   so I can praise you,
   and let me find help
   in your teachings.
176 I am your servant,
   but I have wandered away
   like a lost sheep.
   Please come after me,
   because I have not forgotten
   your teachings.

Psalm 120
[A song for worship.]

A Prayer for the LORD's Help

1 When I am in trouble, I pray,
2 "Come and save me, LORD,
   from deceitful liars!"

3 What punishment is fitting
   for you deceitful liars?
4 Your reward should be
   sharp and flaming arrows!

5 But I must live as a foreigner
   among the people of Meshech
   and in the tents of Kedar.j
6 I have spent too much time
   living among people
   who hate peace.
7 I am in favor of peace,
but when I speak of it,
   all they want is war.

Psalm 121
[A song for worship.]

The LORD Will Protect His People

1 I look to the hills!
   Where will I find help?
2 It will come from the LORD,
who created the heavens
   and the earth.

3 The LORD is your protector,
   and he won't go to sleep
   or let you stumble.
4 The protector of Israel
doesn't doze
   or ever get drowsy.

5 The LORD is your protector,
there at your right side
   to shade you from the sun.
6 You won't be harmed
by the sun during the day
   or by the moonk at night.

7 The LORD will protect you
   and keep you safe
   from all dangers.
8 The LORD will protect you
now and always
   wherever you go.

Psalm 122
[A song by David for worship.]

A Song of Praise

1 It made me glad
   to hear them say,
"Let's go to the house
   of the LORD!"
2 Jerusalem, we are standing
   inside your gates.

3 Jerusalem, what a strong
   and beautiful city you are!
4 Every tribe of the LORD
obeys him and comes to you
   to praise his name.

j120.5 *Meshech . . . Kedar*: Meshech was a country near the Black Sea, and Kedar was a tribe of the Syrian desert.   k121.6 *harmed . . . sun . . . moon*: In ancient times people saw the harmful effects of the rays of the sun, and they thought that certain illnesses (especially mental disorders) were also caused by the rays of the moon.

5 David's royal throne is here
    where justice rules.

6 Jerusalem, we pray
    that you will have peace,
and that all will go well
    for those who love you.
7 May there be peace
inside your city walls
    and in your palaces.
8 Because of my friends
and my relatives,
    I will pray for peace.
9 And because of the house
of the LORD our God,
    I will work for your good.

Psalm 123
[*A song for worship.*]

A Prayer for Mercy

1 Our LORD and our God,
I turn my eyes to you,
    on your throne in heaven.
2 Servants look to their master,
but we will look to you,
    until you have mercy on us.

3 Please have mercy, LORD!
We have been insulted
    more than we can stand,
4 and we can't take more abuse
from those proud,
    conceited people.

Psalm 124
[*A song by David for worship.*]

Thanking the LORD for Victory

1 The LORD was on our side!
Let everyone in Israel say:
2   "The LORD was on our side!
Otherwise, the enemy attack
3 would have killed us all,
    because it was furious.
4 We would have been swept away
in a violent flood
5   of high and roaring waves."

6 Let's praise the LORD!
He protected us from enemies
    who were like wild animals,
7 and we escaped like birds
    from a hunter's torn net.

8 The LORD made heaven and earth,
and he is the one
    who sends us help.

Psalm 125
[*A song for worship.*]

The LORD's People Are Safe

1 Everyone who trusts the LORD
is like Mount Zion

that cannot be shaken
    and will stand forever.
2 Just as Jerusalem is protected
    by mountains on every side,
the LORD protects his people
by holding them in his arms
    now and forever.
3 He won't let the wicked
rule his people
    or lead them to do wrong.
4 Let's ask the LORD to be kind
to everyone who is good
    and completely obeys him.

5 When the LORD punishes
    the wicked,
he will punish everyone else
who lives a crooked life.
    Pray for peace in Israel!

Psalm 126
[*A song for worship.*]

Celebrating the Harvest

1 It seemed like a dream
when the LORD brought us back
    to the city of Zion.[l]
2 We celebrated with laughter
    and joyful songs.
In foreign nations it was said,
"The LORD has worked miracles
    for his people."
3 And so we celebrated
because the LORD had indeed
    worked miracles for us.

4 Our LORD, we ask you to bless
    our people again,
and let us be like streams
    in the Southern Desert.
5 We cried as we went out
    to plant our seeds.
Now let us celebrate
    as we bring in the crops.
6 We cried on the way
    to plant our seeds,
but we will celebrate and shout
    as we bring in the crops.

Psalm 127
[*A song by Solomon for worship.*]

Only the LORD Can Bless a Home

1 Without the help of the LORD
it is useless to build a home
    or to guard a city.
2 It is useless to get up early
and stay up late
    in order to earn a living.
God takes care of his own,
    even while they sleep.[m]

3 Children are a blessing
    and a gift from the LORD.

---

[l] 126.1 *brought . . . Zion:* Or "made the city of Zion prosperous again."   [m] 127.2 *God . . . sleep:* One possible meaning for the difficult Hebrew text.

4 Having a lot of children
   to take care of you
      in your old age
   is like a warrior
      with a lot of arrows.
5 The more you have,
      the better off you will be,
   because they will protect you
   when your enemies attack
      with arguments.

Psalm 128
[A song for worship.]

The Lord Rewards
His Faithful People

1 The Lord will bless you
   if you respect him
      and obey his laws.
2 Your fields will produce,
   and you will be happy
      and all will go well.
3 Your wife will be as fruitful
      as a grapevine,
   and just as an olive tree
      is rich with olives,
   your home will be rich
      with healthy children.
4 That is how the Lord will bless
      everyone who respects him.

5 I pray that the Lord
      will bless you from Zion
   and let Jerusalem prosper
      as long as you live.
6 May you live long enough
      to see your grandchildren.
   Let's pray for peace in Israel!

Psalm 129
[A song for worship.]

A Prayer for Protection

1 Since the time I was young,
      enemies have often attacked!
   Let everyone in Israel say:
2 "Since the time I was young,
      enemies have often attacked!
   But they have not defeated me,
3 though my back is like a field
      that has just been plowed."

4 The Lord always does right,
      and he has set me free
   from the ropes
      of those cruel people.
5 I pray that all who hate
      the city of Zion
   will be made ashamed
      and forced to turn and run.
6 May they be like grass
      on the flat roof of a house,
   grass that dries up
      as soon as it sprouts.
7 Don't let them be like wheat
      gathered in bundles.

8 And don't let anyone
   who passes by say to them,
      "The Lord bless you!
   I give you my blessing
      in the name of the Lord."

Psalm 130
[A song for worship.]

Trusting the Lord
in Times of Trouble

1 From a sea of troubles
      I call out to you, Lord.
2 Won't you please listen
      as I beg for mercy?

3 If you kept record of our sins,
      no one could last long.
4 But you forgive us,
      and so we will worship you.

5 With all my heart,
   I am waiting, Lord, for you!
      I trust your promises.
6 I wait for you more eagerly
      than a soldier on guard duty
         waits for the dawn.
   Yes, I wait more eagerly
      than a soldier on guard duty
         waits for the dawn.

7 Israel, trust the Lord!
      He is always merciful,
   and he has the power
      to save you.
8 Israel, the Lord will save you
      from all of your sins.

Psalm 131
[A song by David for worship.]

Trust the Lord!

1 I am not conceited, Lord,
   and I don't waste my time
      on impossible schemes.
2 But I have learned to feel safe
      and satisfied,
   just like a young child
      on its mother's lap.

3 People of Israel,
   you must trust the Lord
      now and forever.

Psalm 132
[A song for worship.]

The Lord Is Always with His People

1 Our Lord, don't forget David
      and how he suffered.
2 Mighty God of Jacob,
      remember how he promised:
3 "I won't go home
   or crawl into bed
4   or close my eyelids,

5 until I find a home for you,
the mighty LORD God of Jacob."

6 When we were in Ephrath,
we heard that the sacred chest
was somewhere near Jaar.
7 Then we said, "Let's go
to the throne of the LORD
and worship at his feet."

8 Come to your new home, LORD,
you and the sacred chest
with all of its power.
9 Let victory be like robes
for the priests;
let your faithful people
celebrate and shout.
10 David is your chosen one,
so don't reject him.
11 You made a solemn promise
to David, when you said,
"I, the LORD, promise
that someone in your family
will always be king.
12 If they keep our agreement
and follow my teachings,
then someone in your family
will rule forever."

13 You have gladly chosen Zion
as your home, our LORD.
14 You said, "This is my home!
I will live here forever.
15 I will bless Zion with food,
and even the poor will eat
until they are full.
16 Victory will be like robes
for the priests,
and its faithful people
will celebrate and shout.
17 I will give mighty power
to the kingdom of David.
Each one of my chosen kings
will shine like a lamp
18 and wear a sparkling crown.
But I will disgrace
their enemies."

Psalm 133
[*A song for worship.*]

Living Together in Peace

1 It is truly wonderful
when relatives live together
in peace.
2 It is as beautiful as olive oil
poured on Aaron's head[n]
and running down his beard
and the collar of his robe.
3 It is like the dew
from Mount Hermon,
falling on Zion's mountains,
where the LORD has promised
to bless his people
with life forevermore.

Psalm 134
[*A song for worship.*]

Praising the LORD at Night

1 Everyone who serves the LORD,
come and offer praises.
Everyone who has gathered
in his temple tonight,
2 lift your hands in prayer
toward his holy place
and praise the LORD.

3 The LORD is the Creator
of heaven and earth,
and I pray that the LORD
will bless you from Zion.

Psalm 135

In Praise of the LORD's Kindness

1 Shout praises to the LORD!
You are his servants,
so praise his name.
2 All who serve in the temple
of the LORD our God,
3 come and shout praises.
Praise the name of the LORD!
He is kind and good.
4 He chose the family of Jacob
and the people of Israel
for his very own.

5 The LORD is much greater
than any other god.
6 He does as he chooses
in heaven and on earth
and deep in the sea.
7 The LORD makes the clouds rise
from far across the earth,
and he makes lightning
to go with the rain.
Then from his secret place
he sends out the wind.

8 The LORD killed the first-born
of people and animals
in the land of Egypt.
9 God used miracles and wonders
to fight the king of Egypt
and all of his officials.
10 He destroyed many nations
and killed powerful kings,
11 including King Sihon
of the Amorites
and King Og of Bashan.
He conquered every kingdom
in the land of Canaan
12 and gave their property
to his people Israel.

13 The name of the LORD
will be remembered forever,
and he will be famous
for all time to come.
14 The LORD will bring justice
and show mercy to all
who serve him.

n 133.2 *head*: Olive oil was poured on Aaron's head to show that God had chosen him to be the high priest.

15 Idols of silver and gold
  are made and worshiped
    in other nations.
16 They have a mouth and eyes,
  but they can't speak or see.
17 They are completely deaf,
  and they can't breathe.
18 Everyone who makes idols
  and all who trust them
will end up as helpless
  as their idols.

19 Everyone in Israel,
  come praise the LORD!
All the family of Aaron
20 and all the tribe of Levi,o
  come praise the LORD!
All of his worshipers,
  come praise the LORD.
21 Praise the LORD from Zion!
He lives here in Jerusalem.
  Shout praises to the LORD!

Psalm 136

God's Love Never Fails

1 Praise the LORD! He is good.
  God's love never fails.
2 Praise the God of all gods.
  God's love never fails.
3 Praise the Lord of lords.
  God's love never fails.

4 Only God works great miracles.p
  God's love never fails.
5 With wisdom he made the sky.
  God's love never fails.
6 The Lord stretched the earth
  over the ocean.
  God's love never fails.
7 He made the bright lights
  in the sky.
  God's love never fails.
8 He lets the sun rule each day.
  God's love never fails.
9 He lets the moon and the stars
rule each night.
  God's love never fails.

10 God struck down the first-born
  in every Egyptian family.
  God's love never fails.
11 He rescued Israel from Egypt.
  God's love never fails.
12 God used his great strength
  and his powerful arm.
  God's love never fails.
13 He split the Red Seaq apart.
  God's love never fails.

14 The Lord brought Israel safely
  through the sea.
  God's love never fails.

15 He destroyed the Egyptian king
  and his army there.
  God's love never fails.
16 The Lord led his people
  through the desert.
  God's love never fails.

17 Our God defeated mighty kings.
  God's love never fails.
18 And he killed famous kings.
  God's love never fails.
19 One of them was Sihon,
  king of the Amorites.
  God's love never fails.
20 Another was King Og of Bashan.
  God's love never fails.
21 God took away their land.
  God's love never fails.
22 He gave their land to Israel,
  the people who serve him.
  God's love never fails.

23 God saw the trouble we were in.
  God's love never fails.
24 He rescued us from our enemies.
  God's love never fails.
25 He gives food to all who live.
  God's love never fails.

26 Praise God in heaven!
  God's love never fails.

Psalm 137

A Prayer for Revenge

1 Beside the rivers of Babylon
we thought about Jerusalem,
  and we sat down and cried.
2 We hung our small harps
  on the willowr trees.
3 Our enemies had brought us here
  as their prisoners,
and now they wanted us to sing
  and entertain them.
They insulted us and shouted,
  "Sing about Zion!"

4 Here in a foreign land,
how can we sing
  about the LORD?
5 Jerusalem, if I forget you,
  let my right hand go limp.
6 Let my tongue stick
  to the roof of my mouth,
if I don't think about you
  above all else.

7 Our LORD, punish the Edomites!
Because the day Jerusalem fell,
  they shouted,
"Completely destroy the city!
  Tear down every building!"

o135.19,20 Aaron . . . Levi: Aaron was from the tribe of Levi, and all priests were from his family. The temple helpers, singers, and musicians were also from the tribe of Levi.
p136.4 great miracles: One Hebrew manuscript and one ancient translation have "miracles."
q136.13 Red Sea: See the note at 106.7.   r137.2 willow: Or "poplar."

8 Babylon, you are doomed!
  I pray the Lord's blessings
on anyone who punishes you
  for what you did to us.
9 May the Lord bless everyone
who beats your children
  against the rocks!

Psalm 138
[*By David.*]

Praise the Lord with All Your Heart

1 With all my heart
  I praise you, Lord.
In the presence of angels[s]
  I sing your praises.
2 I worship at your holy temple
and praise you for your love
  and your faithfulness.
You were true to your word
and made yourself more famous
  than ever before.[t]
3 When I asked for your help,
you answered my prayer
  and gave me courage.[u]

4 All kings on this earth
have heard your promises, Lord,
  and they will praise you.
5 You are so famous
that they will sing about
  the things you have done.
6 Though you are above us all,
  you care for humble people,
and you keep a close watch
  on everyone who is proud.

7 I am surrounded by trouble,
but you protect me
  against my angry enemies.
With your own powerful arm
  you keep me safe.

8 You, Lord, will always
treat me with kindness.
Your love never fails.
You have made us what we are.
  Don't give up on us now![v]

Psalm 139
[*A psalm by David for the music leader.*]

The Lord Is Always Near

1 You have looked deep
into my heart, Lord,
  and you know all about me.
2 You know when I am resting
or when I am working,
and from heaven
  you discover my thoughts.

3 You notice everything I do
  and everywhere I go.

·4 Before I even speak a word,
  you know what I will say,
5 and with your powerful arm
you protect me
  from every side.
6 I can't understand all of this!
Such wonderful knowledge
  is far above me.

7 Where could I go to escape
from your Spirit
  or from your sight?
8 If I were to climb up
to the highest heavens,
  you would be there.
If I were to dig down
to the world of the dead
  you would also be there.

9 Suppose I had wings
like the dawning day
  and flew across the ocean.
10 Even then your powerful arm
  would guide and protect me.
11 Or suppose I said, "I'll hide
in the dark until night comes
  to cover me over."
12 But you see in the dark
because daylight and dark
  are all the same to you.

13 You are the one
who put me together
  inside my mother's body,
14 and I praise you because of
the wonderful way
  you created me.
Everything you do is marvelous!
  Of this I have no doubt.

15 Nothing about me
  is hidden from you!
I was secretly woven together
  deep in the earth below,
16 but with your own eyes you saw
  my body being formed.
Even before I was born,
you had written in your book
  everything I would do.

17 Your thoughts are far beyond
  my understanding,
much more than I
  could ever imagine.
18 I try to count your thoughts,
but they outnumber the grains
  of sand on the beach.
And when I awake,
  I will find you nearby.

19 How I wish that you would kill
all cruel and heartless people
  and protect me from them!

---

[s]**138.1** *angels*: Or "gods" or "supernatural beings" who worship and serve God in heaven or "rulers" or "leaders."   [t]**138.2** *You were . . . before*: One possible meaning for the difficult Hebrew text.   [u]**138.3** *and gave me courage*: One possible meaning for the difficult Hebrew text.   [v]**138.8** *You have . . . now*: Or "Please don't desert your people."

20 They are always rebelling
and speaking evil of you.ʷ
21 You know I hate anyone
who hates you, LORD,
and refuses to obey.
22 They are my enemies too,
and I truly hate them.

23 Look deep into my heart, God,
and find out everything
I am thinking.
24 Don't let me follow evil ways,
but lead me in the way
that time has proven true.

Psalm 140
[A psalm by David for the music leader.]

A Prayer for the LORD's Help

1 Rescue me from cruel
and violent enemies, LORD!
2 They think up evil plans
and always cause trouble.
3 Their words bite deep
like the poisonous fangs
of a snake.

4 Protect me, LORD, from cruel
and brutal enemies,
who want to destroy me.
5 Those proud people have hidden
traps and nets
to catch me as I walk.

6 You, LORD, are my God!
Please listen to my prayer.
7 You have the power to save me,
and you keep me safe
in every battle.

8 Don't let the wicked succeed
in doing what they want,
or else they might never
stop planning evil.
9 They have me surrounded,
but make them the victims
of their own vicious lies.ˣ
10 Dump flaming coals on them
and throw them into pits
where they can't climb out.
11 Chase those cruel liars away!
Let trouble hunt them down.

12 Our LORD, I know that you
defend the homeless
and see that the poor
are given justice.
13 Your people will praise you
and will live with you
because they do right.

Psalm 141
[A psalm by David.]

A Prayer for the LORD's Protection

1 I pray to you, LORD!
Please listen when I pray
and hurry to help me.
2 Think of my prayer
as sweet-smelling incense,
and think of my lifted hands
as an evening sacrifice.

3 Help me to guard my words
whenever I say something.
4 Don't let me want to do evil
or waste my time doing wrong
with wicked people.
Don't let me even taste
the good things they offer.

5 Let your faithful people
correct and punish me.
My prayers condemn the deeds
of those who do wrong,
so don't let me be friends
with any of them.
6 Everyone will admit
that I was right
when their rulers are thrown
down a rocky cliff,
7 and their bones lie scattered
like broken rocks
on top of a grave.ʸ

8 You are my LORD and God,
and I look to you for safety.
Don't let me be harmed.
9 Protect me from the traps
of those violent people,
10 and make them fall
into their own traps
while you help me escape.

Psalm 142
[A special psalm and a prayer by David
when he was in the cave.]

A Prayer for Help

1 I pray to you, LORD.
I beg for mercy.
2 I tell you all of my worries
and my troubles,
3 and whenever I feel low,
you are there to guide me.

A trap has been hidden
along my pathway.
4 Even if you look,
you won't see anyone
who cares enough
to walk beside me.
There is no place to hide,
and no one who really cares.

ʷ**139.20** *you:* One possible meaning for the difficult Hebrew text of verse 20.   ˣ**140.8,9** *or else . . . lies:* One possible meaning for the difficult Hebrew text.   ʸ**141.5-7** *Let . . . grave:* One possible meaning for the difficult Hebrew text of verses 5-7.

⁵ I pray to you, LORD!
　　You are my place of safety,
　and you are my choice
　　in the land of the living.
　Please answer my prayer.
　　I am completely helpless.

⁶ Help! They are chasing me,
　　and they are too strong.
⁷ Rescue me from this prison,
　　so I can praise your name.
　And when your people notice
　your wonderful kindness to me,
　　they will rush to my side.

Psalm 143
[A psalm by David.]
A Prayer in Time of Danger

¹ Listen, LORD, as I pray!
　You are faithful and honest
　　and will answer my prayer.
² I am your servant.
　　Don't try me in your court,
　because no one is innocent
　　by your standards.
³ My enemies are chasing me,
　　crushing me in the ground.
　I am in total darkness,
　　like someone long dead.
⁴ I have given up all hope,
　　and I feel numb all over.

⁵ I remember to think about
　the many things you did
　　in years gone by.
⁶ Then I lift my hands in prayer,
　because my soul is a desert,
　　thirsty for water from you.

⁷ Please hurry, LORD,
　and answer my prayer.
　　I feel hopeless.
　Don't turn away
　　and leave me here to die.
⁸ Each morning let me learn
　more about your love
　　because I trust you.
　I come to you in prayer,
　　asking for your guidance.

⁹ Please rescue me
　from my enemies, LORD!
　　I come to you for safety.ᶻ
¹⁰ You are my God. Show me
　　what you want me to do,
　and let your gentle Spirit
　　lead me in the right path.

¹¹ Be true to your name, LORD,
　and keep my life safe.
　Use your saving power
　　to protect me from trouble.

¹² I am your servant.
　Show how much you love me
　　by destroying my enemies.

Psalm 144
[By David.]
A Prayer for the Nation

¹ I praise you, LORD!
　　You are my mighty rock,ᵃ
　and you teach me
　　how to fight my battles.
² You are my friend,
　and you are my fortress
　　where I am safe.
　You are my shield,
　and you made me the ruler
　　of our people.ᵇ

³ Why do we humans mean anything
　to you, our LORD?
　　Why do you care about us?
⁴ We disappear like a breath;
　we last no longer
　　than a faint shadow.

⁵ Open the heavens like a curtain
　　and come down, LORD.
　Touch the mountains
　　and make them send up smoke.
⁶ Use your lightning as arrows
　to scatter my enemies
　　and make them run away.
⁷ Reach down from heaven
　　and set me free.
　Save me from the mighty flood
⁸ of those lying foreigners
　　who can't tell the truth.

⁹ In praise of you, our God,
　I will sing a new song,
　　while playing my harp.
¹⁰ By your power, kings win wars,
　and your servant David is saved
　　from deadly swords.
¹¹ Won't you keep me safe
　from those lying foreigners
　　who can't tell the truth?

¹² Let's pray that our young sons
　　will grow like strong plants
　and that our daughters
　will be as lovely as columns
　　in the corner of a palace.
¹³ May our barns be filled
　　with all kinds of crops.
　May our fields be covered
　with sheep by the thousands,
¹⁴　　and every cow have calves.ᶜ
　Don't let our city be captured
　　or any of us be taken away,
　and don't let cries of sorrow
　　be heard in our streets.

ᶻ **143.9** *I . . . safety*: Or "You are my hiding place."　　ᵃ **144.1** *mighty rock*: See the note at 18.2.
ᵇ **144.2** *of our people*: Some Hebrew manuscripts and ancient translations have "of the nations."
ᶜ **144.14** *have calves*: Or "grow fat."

15 Our LORD and our God,
   you give these blessings
         to all who worship you.

Psalm 145
[*By David for praise.*]

The LORD Is Kind and Merciful

1 I will praise you,
   my God and King,
         and always honor your name.
2 I will praise you each day
   and always honor your name.
3 You are wonderful, LORD,
   and you deserve all praise,
         because you are much greater
         than anyone can understand.

4 Each generation will announce
   to the next your wonderful
         and powerful deeds.
5 I will keep thinking about
   your marvelous glory
         and your mighty miracles.*d*
6 Everyone will talk about
   your fearsome deeds,
         and I will tell all nations
         how great you are.
7 They will celebrate and sing
   about your matchless mercy
         and your power to save.

8 You are merciful, LORD!
   You are kind and patient
         and always loving.
9 You are good to everyone,
   and you take care
         of all your creation.

10 All creation will thank you,
    and your loyal people
          will praise you.
11 They will tell about
    your marvelous kingdom
          and your power.
12 Then everyone will know about
    the mighty things you do
          and your glorious kingdom.
13 Your kingdom will never end,
    and you will rule forever.

   Our LORD, you keep your word
    and do everything you say.*e*
14 When someone stumbles or falls,
    you give a helping hand.
15 Everyone depends on you,
    and when the time is right,
          you provide them with food.
16 By your own hand you satisfy
    the desires of all who live.

17 Our LORD, everything you do
    is kind and thoughtful,

18 and you are near to everyone
    whose prayers are sincere.
19 You satisfy the desires
    of all your worshipers,
    and you come to save them
          when they ask for help.
20 You take care of everyone
    who loves you,
          but you destroy the wicked.

21 I will praise you, LORD,
    and everyone will respect
          your holy name forever.

Psalm 146

Shout Praises to the LORD

1 Shout praises to the LORD!
   With all that I am,
         I will shout his praises.
2 I will sing and praise
   the LORD God
         for as long as I live.

3 You can't depend on anyone,
   not even a great leader.
4 Once they die and are buried,
   that will be the end
         of all their plans.

5 The LORD God of Jacob blesses
   everyone who trusts him
         and depends on him.
6 God made heaven and earth;
   he created the sea
         and everything else.
   God always keeps his word.
7 He gives justice to the poor
   and food to the hungry.

   The LORD sets prisoners free
8   and heals blind eyes.
   He gives a helping hand
      to everyone who falls.
   The LORD loves good people
9   and looks after strangers.
   He defends the rights
   of orphans and widows,
         but destroys the wicked.

10 The LORD God of Zion
    will rule forever!
          Shout praises to the LORD!

Psalm 147

Sing and Praise the LORD

1 Shout praises to the LORD!
   Our God is kind,
   and it is right and good
         to sing praises to him.
2 The LORD rebuilds Jerusalem

---

*d*145.5 *and . . . miracles:* One Hebrew manuscript and two ancient translations have "as others
tell about your mighty miracles." *e*145.13 *Our . . . say:* These words are found in one
Hebrew manuscript and two ancient translations.

and brings the people of Israel
back home again.
³ He renews our hopes
and heals our bodies.
⁴ He decided how many stars
there would be in the sky
and gave each one a name.
⁵ Our LORD is great and powerful!
He understands everything.
⁶ The LORD helps the poor,
but he smears the wicked
in the dirt.

⁷ Celebrate and sing!
Play your harps
for the LORD our God.
⁸ He fills the sky with clouds
and sends rain to the earth,
so that the hills
will be green with grass.
⁹ He provides food for cattle
and for the young ravens,
when they cry out.
¹⁰ The LORD doesn't care about
the strength of horses
or powerful armies.
¹¹ The LORD is pleased only
with those who worship him
and trust his love.

¹² Everyone in Jerusalem,
come and praise
the LORD your God!
¹³ He makes your city gates strong
and blesses your people
by giving them children.
¹⁴ God lets you live in peace,
and he gives you
the very best wheat.
¹⁵ As soon as God speaks,
the earth obeys.
¹⁶ He covers the ground with snow
like a blanket of wool,
and he scatters frost
like ashes on the ground.
¹⁷ God sends down hailstones
like chips of rocks.
Who can stand the cold?
¹⁸ At his command the ice melts,
the wind blows,
and streams begin to flow.

¹⁹ God gave his laws and teachings
to the descendants of Jacob,
the nation of Israel.
²⁰ But he has not given his laws
to any other nation.
Shout praises to the LORD!

Psalm 148

Come Praise the LORD

¹ Shout praises to the LORD!
Shout the LORD's praises
in the highest heavens.

² All of you angels,
and all who serve him above,
come and offer praise.

³ Sun and moon,
and all of you bright stars,
come and offer praise.
⁴ Highest heavens, and the water
above the highest heavens,[f]
come and offer praise.

⁵ Let all things praise
the name of the LORD,
because they were created
at his command.
⁶ He made them to last forever,
and nothing can change
what he has done.[g]

⁷ All creatures on earth,
you obey his commands,
so come praise the LORD!

⁸ Sea monsters and the deep sea,
fire and hail, snow and frost,
and every stormy wind,
come praise the LORD!

⁹ All mountains and hills,
fruit trees and cedars,
¹⁰ every wild and tame animal,
all reptiles and birds,
come praise the LORD!
¹¹ Every king and every ruler,
all nations on earth,
¹² every man and every woman,
young people and old,
come praise the LORD!

¹³ All creation, come praise
the name of the LORD.
Praise his name alone.
The glory of God is greater
than heaven and earth.

¹⁴ Like a bull with mighty horns,
the LORD protects
his faithful nation Israel,
because they belong to him.
Shout praises to the LORD!

Psalm 149

A New Song of Praise

¹ Shout praises to the LORD!
Sing him a new song of praise
when his loyal people meet.
² People of Israel, rejoice
because of your Creator.
People of Zion, celebrate
because of your King.

---

[f]**148.4** *the water . . . heavens:* It was believed that the earth and the heavens were surrounded
by water.   [g]**148.6** *nothing . . . done:* Or "his laws will never change."

3 Praise his name by dancing
and playing music on harps
and tambourines.
4 The LORD is pleased
with his people,
and he gives victory
to those who are humble.
5 All of you faithful people,
praise our glorious Lord!
Celebrate and worship.
6 Praise God with songs
on your lips
and a sword in your hand.
7 Take revenge and punish
the nations.
8 Put chains of iron
on their kings and rulers.
9 Punish them as they deserve;
this is the privilege
of God's faithful people.
Shout praises to the LORD!

Psalm 150
The LORD Is Good to His People

1 Shout praises to the LORD!
Praise God in his temple.
Praise him in heaven,
his mighty fortress.
2 Praise our God!
His deeds are wonderful,
too marvelous to describe.

3 Praise God with trumpets
and all kinds of harps.
4 Praise him with tambourines
and dancing,
with stringed instruments
and woodwinds.
5 Praise God with cymbals,
with clashing cymbals.
6 Let every living creature
praise the LORD.
Shout praises to the LORD!

PROVERBS

ABOUT THIS BOOK

The book of Proverbs is a collection of sayings that were used in ancient Israel to teach God's people how to live right. For the most part, these sayings go back to Solomon, but others are traced back to Agur (30.1) and King Lemuel (31.1).

Like the psalms, all the proverbs are written in poetic form. A typical proverb takes the form of a short verse in which the first half states the theme and the second half echoes it. What makes the Bible's proverbs so popular is that they make such powerful statements with very few words. This makes them easy to memorize and apply to daily life.

One of the main teachings in Proverbs is that all wisdom is a gift from God. This wisdom supplies practical advice for everyday living, in the home, in society, in politics, at school and at work. The book of Proverbs also teaches the importance of fairness, humility, loyalty and concern for the poor and needy.

Because most proverbs are so brief, and make their point in one verse, many are often not connected to those around them. In some parts of the book, however, a common theme can be found. How not to be a fool is the theme of chapter 26.1-12, for example. In chapters 8-9, Wisdom is pictured as a woman who advises people to turn from their foolish ways and to live wisely.

A QUICK LOOK AT THIS BOOK

How Proverbs Can Be Used

1 These are the proverbs
of King Solomon of Israel,
    the son of David.
² Proverbs will teach you
    wisdom and self-control
and how to understand
    sayings with deep meanings.
³ You will learn what is right
    and honest and fair.
⁴ From these, an ordinary person
    can learn to be smart,
and young people can gain
    knowledge and good sense.

⁵ If you are already wise,
    you will become even wiser.
And if you are smart,
you will learn to understand
⁶   proverbs and sayings,
as well as words of wisdom
    and all kinds of riddles.
⁷ Respect and obey the LORD!
This is the beginning
    of knowledge.ᵃ
Only a fool rejects wisdom
    and good advice.

Warnings against Bad Friends

⁸ My child, obey the teachings
    of your parents,
⁹ and wear their teachings
as you would a lovely hat
    or a pretty necklace.

ᵃ**1.7** *the beginning of knowledge*: Or "what knowledge is all about."

[10] Don't be tempted by sinners
or listen [11]when they say,
"Come on! Let's gang up
and kill somebody,
just for the fun of it!
[12] They're well and healthy now,
but we'll finish them off
once and for all.
[13] We'll take their valuables
and fill our homes
with stolen goods.
[14] If you join our gang,
you'll get your share."

[15] Don't follow anyone like that
or do what they do.
[16] They are in a big hurry
to commit some crime,
perhaps even murder.
[17] They are like a bird
that sees the bait,
but ignores the trap.[b]
[18] They gang up to murder someone,
but they are the victims.
[19] The wealth you get from crime
robs you of your life.

Wisdom Speaks

[20] Wisdom[c] shouts in the streets
wherever crowds gather.
[21] She shouts in the marketplaces
and near the city gates
as she says to the people,
[22] "How much longer
will you enjoy
being stupid fools?
Won't you ever stop sneering
and laughing at knowledge?
[23] Listen as I correct you
and tell you what I think.
[24] You completely ignored me
and refused to listen;
[25] you rejected my advice
and paid no attention
when I warned you.

[26] "So when you are struck
by some terrible disaster,
[27] or when trouble and distress
surround you like a whirlwind,
I will laugh and make fun.
[28] You will ask for my help,
but I won't listen;
you will search,
but you won't find me.
[29] No, you would not learn,
and you refused
to respect the LORD.
[30] You rejected my advice
and paid no attention
when I warned you.

[31] "Now you will eat the fruit
of what you have done,

until you are stuffed full
with your own schemes.
[32] Sin and self-satisfaction
bring destruction and death
to stupid fools.
[33] But if you listen to me,
you will be safe and secure
without fear of disaster."

Wisdom and Bad Friends

2 My child, you must follow
and treasure my teachings
and my instructions.
[2] Keep in tune with wisdom
and think what it means
to have common sense.
[3] Beg as loud as you can
for good common sense.
[4] Search for wisdom
as you would search for silver
or hidden treasure.
[5] Then you will understand
what it means to respect
and to know the LORD God.

[6] All wisdom comes from the LORD,
and so do common sense
and understanding.
[7] God gives helpful advice[d]
to everyone who obeys him
and protects all of those
who live as they should.
[8] God sees that justice is done,
and he watches over everyone
who is faithful to him.
[9] With wisdom you will learn
what is right
and honest and fair.

[10] Wisdom will control your mind,
and you will be pleased
with knowledge.
[11] Sound judgment and good sense
will watch over you.
[12] Wisdom will protect you
from evil schemes
and from those liars
[13] who turned from doing good
to live in the darkness.
[14] Most of all they enjoy
being mean and deceitful.
[15] They are dishonest themselves,
and all they do is crooked.

Wisdom and Sexual Purity

[16] Wisdom will protect you
from the smooth talk
of a sinful woman,
[17] who breaks her wedding vows
and leaves the man she married
when she was young.
[18] The road to her house leads

---

[b]1.17 *They are . . . trap*: Or "Be like a bird that won't go for the bait, if it sees the trap."
[c]1.20 *Wisdom*: In the book of Proverbs the word "wisdom" is sometimes used as though wisdom were a supernatural being who was with God at the time of creation. [d]2.7 *helpful advice*: Or "wisdom."

down to the dark world
    of the dead.
¹⁹ Visit her, and you will never
    find the road to life again.

²⁰ Follow the example
    of good people
    and live an honest life.
²¹ If you are honest and innocent,
    you will keep your land;
²² if you do wrong
    and can never be trusted,
        you will be rooted out.

Trust God

3 My child, remember
    my teachings and instructions
        and obey them completely.
² They will help you live
    a long and prosperous life.
³ Let love and loyalty
    always show like a necklace,
        and write them in your mind.
⁴ God and people will like you
    and consider you a success.

⁵ With all your heart
    you must trust the LORD
        and not your own judgment.
⁶ Always let him lead you,
    and he will clear the road
        for you to follow.
⁷ Don't ever think that you
    are wise enough,
but respect the LORD
    and stay away from evil.
⁸ This will make you healthy,
    and you will feel strong.
⁹ Honor the LORD by giving him
    your money and the first part
        of all your crops.
¹⁰ Then you will have
    more grain and grapes
        than you will ever need.

¹¹ My child, don't turn away
    or become bitter
        when the LORD corrects you.
¹² The LORD corrects
    everyone he loves,
just as parents correct
    their favorite child.

The Value of Wisdom

¹³ God blesses everyone
    who has wisdom
        and common sense.
¹⁴ Wisdom is worth more
    than silver;
it makes you much richer
    than gold.
¹⁵ Wisdom is more valuable
    than precious jewels;
nothing you want
    compares with her.

¹⁶ In her right hand
    Wisdom holds a long life,

and in her left hand
    are wealth and honor.
¹⁷ Wisdom makes life pleasant
    and leads us safely along.
¹⁸ Wisdom is a life-giving tree,
    the source of happiness
        for all who hold on to her.

¹⁹ By his wisdom and knowledge
    the LORD created
        heaven and earth.
²⁰ By his understanding
    he let the ocean break loose
        and clouds release the rain.
²¹ My child, use common sense
    and sound judgment!
        Always keep them in mind.
²² They will help you to live
    a long and beautiful life.
²³ You will walk safely
    and never stumble;
²⁴ you will rest without a worry
    and sleep soundly.
²⁵ So don't be afraid
    of sudden disasters
or storms that strike
    those who are evil.
²⁶ You can be sure that the LORD
    will protect you from harm.

²⁷ Do all you can for everyone
    who deserves your help.
²⁸ Don't tell your neighbor
    to come back tomorrow,
        if you can help today.
²⁹ Don't try to be mean
    to neighbors who trust you.
³⁰ Don't argue just to be arguing,
    when you haven't been hurt.
³¹ Don't be jealous
    of cruel people
        or follow their example.

³² The LORD doesn't like
    anyone who is dishonest,
but he lets good people
    be his friends.
³³ He places a curse on the home
    of everyone who is evil,
but he blesses the home
    of every good person.
³⁴ The LORD sneers at those
    who sneer at him,
but he is kind to everyone
    who is humble.
³⁵ You will be praised
    if you are wise,
but you will be disgraced
    if you are a stubborn fool.

Advice to Young People

4 My child, listen closely
    to my teachings
        and learn common sense.
² My advice is useful,
    so don't turn away.
³ When I was still very young
    and my mother's favorite child,

my father ⁴said to me:
"If you follow my teachings
and keep them in mind,
  you will live.
⁵ Be wise and learn good sense;
remember my teachings
  and do what I say.

⁶ If you love Wisdom
and don't reject her,
  she will watch over you.
⁷ The best thing about Wisdom
is Wisdom herself;
good sense is more important
  than anything else.
⁸ If you value Wisdom
and hold tightly to her,
  great honors will be yours.
⁹ It will be like wearing
a glorious crown
  of beautiful flowers.

The Right Way and the Wrong Way

¹⁰ My child, if you listen
and obey my teachings,
  you will live a long time.
¹¹ I have shown you the way
that makes sense;
I have guided you
  along the right path.
¹² Your road won't be blocked,
and you won't stumble
  when you run.
¹³ Hold firmly to my teaching
and never let go.
  It will mean life for you.
¹⁴ Don't follow the bad example
  of cruel and evil people.
¹⁵ Turn aside and keep going.
  Stay away from them.
¹⁶ They can't sleep or rest
until they do wrong or harm
  some innocent victim.
¹⁷ Their food and drink
  are violence and cruelty.

¹⁸ The lifestyle of good people
is like sunlight at dawn
that keeps getting brighter
  until broad daylight.
¹⁹ The lifestyle of the wicked
is like total darkness,
and they will never know
  what makes them stumble.

²⁰ My child, listen carefully
  to everything I say.
²¹ Don't forget a single word,
  but think about it all.
²² Knowing these teachings
will mean true life
  and good health for you.
²³ Carefully guard your thoughts
because they are the source
  of true life.
²⁴ Never tell lies or be deceitful

in what you say.
²⁵ Keep looking straight ahead,
  without turning aside.
²⁶ Know where you are headed,
and you will stay
  on solid ground.
²⁷ Don't make a mistake by turning
  to the right or the left.

Be Faithful to Your Wife

5 My son, if you listen closely
  to my wisdom and good sense,
² you will have sound judgment,
and you will always know
  the right thing to say.
³ The words of an immoral woman
may be as sweet as honey
  and as smooth as olive oil.
⁴ But all that you really get
from being with her
  is bitter poison and pain.
⁵ If you follow her,
she will lead you down
  to the world of the dead.
⁶ She has missed the path
that leads to life
  and doesn't even know it.

⁷ My son, listen to me
  and do everything I say.
⁸ Stay away from a bad woman!
Don't even go near the door
  of her house.
⁹ You will lose your self-respect
and end up in debt
to some cruel person
  for the rest of your life.
¹⁰ Strangers will get your money
and everything else
  you have worked for.
¹¹ When it's all over,
your body will waste away,
  as you groan ¹²and shout,
"I hated advice and correction!
¹³ I paid no attention
  to my teachers,
¹⁴ and now I am disgraced
  in front of everyone."

¹⁵ You should be faithful
  to your wife,
just as you take water
  from your own well.ᵉ
¹⁶ And don't be like a stream
from which just any woman
  may take a drink.
¹⁷ Save yourself for your wife
and don't have sex
  with other women.
¹⁸ Be happy with the wife
you married
  when you were young.
¹⁹ She is beautiful and graceful,
  just like a deer;
you should be attracted to her
  and stay deeply in love.

ᵉ**5.15** *own well*: In biblical times water was scarce and wells were carefully guarded.

20 Don't go crazy over a woman
who is unfaithful
to her own husband!
21 The LORD sees everything,
and he watches us closely.
22 Sinners are trapped and caught
by their own evil deeds.
23 They get lost and die
because of their foolishness
and lack of self-control.

Don't Be Foolish

6 My child, suppose you agree
to pay the debt of someone,
who cannot repay a loan.
2 Then you are trapped
by your own words,
3 and you are now in the power
of someone else.
Here is what you should do:
Go and beg for permission
to call off the agreement.
4 Do this before you fall asleep
or even get sleepy.
5 Save yourself, just as a deer
or a bird tries to escape
from a hunter.

6 You lazy people can learn
by watching an anthill.
7 Ants don't have leaders,
8 but they store up food
during harvest season.
9 How long will you lie there
doing nothing at all?
When are you going to get up
and stop sleeping?
10 Sleep a little. Doze a little.
Fold your hands
and twiddle your thumbs.
11 Suddenly, everything is gone,
as though it had been taken
by an armed robber.

12 Worthless liars go around
13 winking and giving signals
to deceive others.
14 They are always thinking up
something cruel and evil,
and they stir up trouble.
15 But they will be struck
by sudden disaster
and left without a hope.

16 There are six or seven
kinds of people
the LORD doesn't like:
17 Those who are too proud
or tell lies or murder,
18 those who make evil plans
or are quick to do wrong,
19 those who tell lies in court
or stir up trouble
in a family.

20 Obey the teaching
of your parents—
21 always keep it in mind
and never forget it.
22 Their teaching will guide you
when you walk,
protect you when you sleep,
and talk to you
when you are awake.

23 The Law of the Lord is a lamp,
and its teachings
shine brightly.
Correction and self-control
will lead you through life.
24 They will protect you
from the flattering words
of someone else's wife.*f*
25 Don't let yourself be attracted
by the charm and lovely eyes
of someone like that.
26 A woman who sells her love
can be bought for as little
as the price of a meal.
But making love
to another man's wife
will cost you everything.
27 If you carry burning coals,
you burn your clothes;
28 if you step on hot coals,
you burn your feet.
29 And if you go to bed
with another man's wife,
you pay the price.

30 We don't put up with thieves,
not even*g* with one who steals
for something to eat.
31 And thieves who get caught
must pay back
seven times what was stolen
and lose everything.
32 But if you go to bed
with another man's wife,
you will destroy yourself
by your own stupidity.
33 You will be beaten
and forever disgraced,
34 because a jealous husband
can be furious and merciless
when he takes revenge.
35 He won't let you pay him off,
no matter what you offer.

The Foolishness of Unfaithfulness

7 My son, pay close attention
and don't forget
what I tell you to do.
2 Obey me, and you will live!
Let my instructions be
your greatest treasure.
3 Keep them at your fingertips
and write them
in your mind.
4 Let wisdom be your sister

---

*f*6.24 *someone else's wife:* Or "an evil woman."   *g*6.30 *not even:* Or "except."

and make common sense
    your closest friend.
5 They will protect you
  from the flattering words
    of someone else's wife.

6 From the window of my house,
  I once happened to see
7   some foolish young men.
8 It was late in the evening,
    sometime after dark.
9 One of these young men
    turned the corner
  and was walking by the house
    of an unfaithful wife.
10 She was dressed fancy
  like a woman of the street
    with only one thing in mind.
11 She was one of those women
  who are loud and restless
    and never stay at home,
12 who walk street after street,
    waiting to trap a man.

13 She grabbed him and kissed him,
  and with no sense of shame,
    she said:
14 "I had to offer a sacrifice,
  and there is enough meat
    left over for a feast.
15 So I came looking for you,
    and here you are!
16 The sheets on my bed
  are bright-colored cloth
    from Egypt.
17 And I have covered it
  with perfume made of myrrh,
    aloes, and cinnamon.

18 "Let's go there
    and make love all night.
19 My husband is traveling,
    and he's far away.
20 He took a lot of money along,
  and he won't be back home
  before the middle
    of the month."

21 And so, she tricked him
  with all of her sweet talk
    and her flattery.
22 Right away he followed her
  like an ox on the way
    to be slaughtered,
  or like a fool on the way
  to be punished[h]
23   and killed with arrows.
  He was no more than a bird
    rushing into a trap,
  without knowing
    it would cost him his life.

24 My son, pay close attention
    to what I have said.
25 Don't even think about

that kind of woman
  or let yourself be misled
    by someone like her.
26 Such a woman has caused
  the downfall and destruction
    of a lot of men.
27 Her house is a one-way street
  leading straight down
    to the world of the dead.

In Praise of Wisdom

8 With great understanding,
    Wisdom[i] is calling out
2 as she stands at the crossroads
    and on every hill.
3 She stands by the city gate
  where everyone enters the city,
    and she shouts:
4 "I am calling out
    to each one of you!
5 Good sense and sound judgment
    can be yours.
6 Listen, because what I say
    is worthwhile and right.
7 I always speak the truth
    and refuse to tell a lie.
8 Every word I speak is honest,
  not one is misleading
    or deceptive.

9 "If you have understanding,
  you will see that my words
    are just what you need.
10 Let instruction and knowledge
  mean more to you than silver
    or the finest gold.
11 Wisdom is worth much more
  than precious jewels
    or anything else you desire."

Wisdom Speaks

12 I am Wisdom[i]—Common Sense
    is my closest friend;
  I possess knowledge
    and sound judgment.
13 If you respect the LORD,
    you will hate evil.
  I hate pride and conceit
    and deceitful lies.
14 I am strong, and I offer
  sensible advice
    and sound judgment.
15 By my power kings govern,
  and rulers make laws
    that are fair.
16 Every honest leader rules
    with help from me.

17 I love everyone who loves me,
  and I will be found by all
    who honestly search.
18 I can make you rich and famous,
    important and successful.

---

[h]**7.22** *a fool . . . punished*: One possible meaning for the difficult Hebrew text.   [i]**8.1** *Wisdom*:
See the note at 1.20.   [i]**8.12** *Wisdom*: See the note at 1.20.

19 What you receive from me
    is more valuable
than even the finest gold
    or the purest silver.
20 I always do what is right,
21 and I give great riches
    to everyone who loves me.

22 From the beginning,
    I was with the LORD.^j
I was there before he began
23   to create the earth.
At the very first,
    the LORD gave life to^k me.
24 When I was born,
    there were no oceans
    or springs of water.
25 My birth was before
    mountains were formed
    or hills were put in place.
26 It happened long before God
    had made the earth
or any of its fields
    or even the dust.

27 I was there when the LORD
    put the heavens in place
and stretched the sky
    over the surface of the sea.
28 I was with him when he placed
    the clouds in the sky
and created the springs
    that fill the ocean.
29 I was there when he set
    boundaries for the sea
to make it obey him,
and when he laid foundations
    to support the earth.

30 I was right beside the LORD,
    helping him plan and build.^l
I made him happy each day,
    and I was happy at his side.
31 I was pleased with his world
    and pleased with its people.

32 Pay attention, my children!
Follow my advice,
    and you will be happy.
33 Listen carefully
to my instructions,
    and you will be wise.

34 Come to my home each day
and listen to me.
    You will find happiness.
35 By finding me, you find life,
    and the LORD will be pleased
    with you.
36 But if you don't find me,
    you hurt only yourself,
and if you hate me,
    you are in love with death.

Wisdom Gives a Feast

9 Wisdom has built her house
    with its seven columns.
2 She has prepared the meat
and set out the wine.
    Her feast is ready.

3 She has sent her servant women
    to announce her invitation
    from the highest hills:
4 "Everyone who is ignorant
    or foolish is invited!
5 All of you are welcome
    to my meat and wine.
6 If you want to live,
    give up your foolishness
and let understanding
    guide your steps."

True Wisdom

7 Correct a worthless bragger,
    and all you will get
    are insults and injuries.
8 Any bragger you correct
    will only hate you.
But if you correct someone
who has common sense,
    you will be loved.
9 If you have good sense,
instruction will help you
    to have even better sense.
And if you live right,
education will help you
    to know even more.

10 Respect and obey the LORD!
This is the beginning
    of wisdom.^m
To have understanding,
    you must know the Holy God.
11 I am Wisdom. If you follow me,
    you will live a long time.
12 Good sense is good for you,
but if you brag,
    you hurt yourself.

A Foolish Invitation

13 Stupidity^n is reckless,
    senseless, and foolish.
14 She sits in front of her house
and on the highest hills
    in the town.
15 She shouts to everyone
    who passes by,
16 "If you are stupid,
    come on inside!"
And to every fool she says,
17   "Stolen water tastes best,
    and the food you eat in secret
    tastes best of all."
18 None who listen to Stupidity
    understand that her guests
    are as good as dead.

---

^j**8.22** *From the beginning . . . with the* LORD: Or "In the very beginning, the LORD created me."
^k**8.23** *gave life to:* Or "formed." ^l**8.30** *helping . . . build:* Or "like his own child."
^m**9.10** *the beginning of wisdom:* Or "what wisdom is all about." ^n**9.13** *Stupidity:* Or "A foolish woman."

Solomon's Wise Sayings

10 Here are some proverbs
of Solomon:
Children with good sense
make their parents happy,
but foolish children
make them sad.
2 What you gain by doing evil
won't help you at all,
but being good[o]
can save you from death.

3 If you obey the LORD,
you won't go hungry;
if you are wicked,
God won't let you have
what you want.
4 Laziness leads to poverty;
hard work makes you rich.
5 At harvest season
it's smart to work hard,
but stupid to sleep.

6 Everyone praises good people,
but evil hides behind
the words of the wicked.
7 Good people are remembered
long after they are gone,
but the wicked
are soon forgotten.

8 If you have good sense,
you will listen and obey;
if all you do is talk,
you will destroy yourself.
9 You will be safe,
if you always do right,
but you will get caught,
if you are dishonest.
10 Deceit causes trouble,
and foolish talk
will bring you to ruin.[p]
11 The words of good people
are a source of life,
but evil hides behind
the words of the wicked.

12 Hatred stirs up trouble;
love overlooks the wrongs
that others do.
13 If you have good sense,
it will show when you speak.
But if you are stupid,
you will be beaten
with a stick.
14 If you have good sense,
you will learn all you can,
but foolish talk
will soon destroy you.

15 Great wealth can be a fortress,
but poverty
is no protection at all.

16 If you live right,
the reward is a good life;
if you are evil,
all you have is sin.

17 Accept correction,
and you will find life;
reject correction,
and you will miss the road.
18 You can hide your hatred
by telling lies,
but you are a fool
to spread lies.
19 You will say the wrong thing
if you talk too much—
so be sensible and watch
what you say.
20 The words of a good person
are like pure silver,
but the thoughts
of an evil person
are almost worthless.
21 Many are helped
by useful instruction,
but fools are killed
by their own stupidity.

22 When the LORD blesses you
with riches,
you have nothing to regret.[q]
23 Fools enjoy doing wrong,
but anyone with good sense
enjoys acting wisely.
24 What evil people dread most
will happen to them,
but good people will get
what they want most.
25 Those crooks will disappear
when a storm strikes,
but God will keep safe
all who obey him.
26 Having a lazy person on the job
is like a mouth full of vinegar
or smoke in your eyes.

27 If you respect the LORD,
you will live longer;
if you keep doing wrong,
your life will be cut short.
28 If you obey the Lord,
you will be happy,
but there is no future
for the wicked.
29 The LORD protects everyone
who lives right,
but he destroys anyone
who does wrong.
30 Good people will stand firm,
but the wicked
will lose their land.
31 Honest people speak sensibly,
but deceitful liars
will be silenced.

---

[o]10.2 *good*: Or "generous." 　[p]10.10 *and foolish . . . ruin*: One ancient translation "but you can help people by correcting them." 　[q]10.22 *When . . . regret*: Or "No matter how hard you work, your riches really come from the Lord."

³² If you obey the Lord,
you will always know
the right thing to say.
But no one will trust you
if you tell lies.

Watch What You Say and Do

11 The Lord hates anyone
who cheats,
but he likes everyone
who is honest.
² Too much pride
can put you to shame.
It's wiser to be humble.
³ If you do the right thing,
honesty will be your guide.
But if you are crooked,
you will be trapped
by your own dishonesty.

⁴ When God is angry,
money won't help you.
Obeying God is the only way
to be saved from death.
⁵ If you are truly good,
you will do right;
if you are wicked,
you will be destroyed
by your own sin.
⁶ Honesty can keep you safe,
but if you can't be trusted,
you trap yourself.
⁷ When the wicked die,
their hopes die with them.
⁸ Trouble goes right past
the Lord's people
and strikes the wicked.

⁹ Dishonest people use gossip
to destroy their neighbors;
good people are protected
by their own good sense.
¹⁰ When honest people prosper
and the wicked disappear,
the whole city celebrates.
¹¹ When God blesses his people,
their city prospers,
but deceitful liars
can destroy a city.

¹² It's stupid to say bad things
about your neighbors.
If you are sensible,
you will keep quiet.
¹³ A gossip tells everything,
but a true friend
will keep a secret.
¹⁴ A city without wise leaders
will end up in ruin;
a city with many wise leaders
will be kept safe.

¹⁵ It's a dangerous thing
to guarantee payment
for someone's debts.
Don't do it!
¹⁶ A gracious woman
will be respected,
but a man must work hard
to get rich.ʳ
¹⁷ Kindness is rewarded—
but if you are cruel,
you hurt yourself.
¹⁸ Meanness gets you nowhere,
but goodness is rewarded.
¹⁹ Always do the right thing,
and you will live;
keep on doing wrong,
and you will die.

²⁰ The Lord hates sneaky people,
but he likes everyone
who lives right.
²¹ You can be sure of this:
All crooks will be punished,
but God's people won't.
²² A beautiful woman
who acts foolishly
is like a gold ring
on the snout of a pig.
²³ Good people want what is best,
but troublemakers
hope to stir up trouble.ˢ

²⁴ Sometimes you can become rich
by being generous
or poor by being greedy.
²⁵ Generosity will be rewarded:
Give a cup of water,
and you will receive
a cup of water in return.
²⁶ Charge too much for grain,
and you will be cursed;
sell it at a fair price,
and you will be praised.
²⁷ Try hard to do right,
and you will win friends;
go looking for trouble,
and you will find it.
²⁸ Trust in your wealth,
and you will be a failure,
but God's people will prosper
like healthy plants.

²⁹ Fools who cause trouble
in the family
won't inherit a thing.
They will end up as slaves
of someone with good sense.
³⁰ Live right, and you will eat
from the life-giving tree.
And if you act wisely,
others will follow.ᵗ
³¹ If good people are rewardedᵘ
here on this earth,

ʳ**11.16** *but . . . rich*: Or "a ruthless man will only get rich." ˢ**11.23** *Good people . . . trouble*:
Or "Good people do what is best, but troublemakers just stir up trouble." ᵗ**11.30** *act . . .
follow*: Hebrew; one ancient translation "but violence leads to death." ᵘ**11.31** *rewarded*: Or
"punished."

all who are cruel and mean
will surely be punished.

You Can't Hide behind Evil

12 To accept correction is wise,
to reject it is stupid.
2 The LORD likes everyone
who lives right,
but he punishes everyone
who makes evil plans.
3 Sin cannot offer security!
But if you live right,
you will be as secure
as a tree with deep roots.
4 A helpful wife is a jewel
for her husband,
but a shameless wife
will make his bones rot.

5 Good people have kind thoughts,
but you should never trust
the advice of someone evil.
6 Bad advice is a deadly trap,
but good advice
is like a shield.
7 Once the wicked are defeated,
they are gone forever,
but no one who obeys God
will ever be thrown down.
8 Good sense is worthy of praise,
but stupidity is a curse.
9 It's better to be ordinary
and have only one servant[v]
than to think you are somebody
and starve to death.
10 Good people are kind
to their animals,
but a mean person is cruel.

11 Hard working farmers have more
than enough food;
daydreamers are nothing more
than stupid fools.
12 An evil person tries to hide
behind evil;[w]
good people are like trees
with deep roots.
13 We trap ourselves
by telling lies,
but we stay out of trouble
by living right.
14 We are rewarded or punished
for what we say and do.
15 Fools think they know
what is best,
but a sensible person
listens to advice.

16 Losing your temper is foolish;
ignoring an insult is smart.
17 An honest person
tells the truth in court,
but a dishonest person

tells nothing but lies.
18 Sharp words cut like a sword,
but words of wisdom heal.
19 Truth will last forever;
lies are soon found out.
20 An evil mind is deceitful,
but gentle thoughts
bring happiness.
21 Good people never have trouble,
but troublemakers
have more than enough.
22 The LORD hates every liar,
but he is the friend of all
who can be trusted.
23 Be sensible and don't tell
everything you know—
only fools spread
foolishness everywhere.

24 Work hard, and you
will be a leader;
be lazy, and you
will end up a slave.
25 Worry is a heavy burden,
but a kind word
always brings cheer.
26 You are better off to do right,
than to lose your way
by doing wrong.[x]
27 Anyone too lazy to cook
will starve,
but a hard worker
is a valuable treasure.[y]
28 Follow the road to life,
and you won't be bothered
by death.

Wise Friends Make You Wise

13 Children with good sense
accept correction
from their parents,
but stubborn children
ignore it completely.
2 You will be well rewarded
for saying something kind,
but all some people think about
is how to be cruel and mean.
3 Keep what you know to yourself,
and you will be safe;
talk too much,
and you are done for.
4 No matter how much you want,
laziness won't help a bit,
but hard work will reward you
with more than enough.
5 A good person hates deceit,
but those who are evil
cause shame and disgrace.
6 Live right, and you are safe!
But sin will destroy you.

7 Some who have nothing
may pretend to be rich,

---

[v]**12.9** *It's . . . servant*: Or "It is better just to have an ordinary job."   [w]**12.12** *An evil . . . evil*:
Or "Evil people love what they get from being evil."   [x]**12.26** *wrong*: One possible meaning
for the difficult Hebrew text of verse 26.   [y]**12.27** *but . . . treasure*: One possible meaning for
the difficult Hebrew text.

and some who have everything
may pretend to be poor.
8 The rich may have
to pay a ransom,
but the poor don't have
that problem.
9 The lamp of a good person
keeps on shining;
the lamp of an evil person
soon goes out.
10 Too much pride causes trouble.
Be sensible and take advice.

11 Money wrongly gotten
will disappear bit by bit;
money earned little by little
will grow and grow.
12 Not getting what you want
can make you feel sick,
but a wish that comes true
is a life-giving tree.
13 If you reject God's teaching,
you will pay the price;
if you obey his commands,
you will be rewarded.

14 Sensible instruction
is a life-giving fountain
that helps you escape
all deadly traps.
15 Sound judgment is praised,
but people without good sense
are on the way to disaster.ᶻ
16 If you have good sense,
you will act sensibly,
but fools act like fools.
17 Whoever delivers your message
can make things better
or worse for you.

18 All who refuse correction
will be poor and disgraced;
all who accept correction
will be praised.
19 It's a good feeling
to get what you want,
but only a stupid fool
hates to turn from evil.
20 Wise friends make you wise,
but you hurt yourself
by going around with fools.
21 You are in for trouble
if you sin,
but you will be rewarded
if you live right.
22 If you obey God,
you will have something
to leave your grandchildren.
If you don't obey God,
those who live right
will get what you leave.

23 Even when the land of the poor
produces good crops,

they get cheated
out of what they grow.ᵃ
24 If you love your children,
you will correct them;
if you don't love them,
you won't correct them.
25 If you live right,
you will have plenty to eat;
if you don't live right,
you will go away empty.

Wisdom Makes Good Sense

14 A woman's family
is held together
by her wisdom,
but it can be destroyed
by her foolishness.
2 By living right, you show
that you respect the LORD;
by being deceitful, you show
that you despise him.
3 Proud fools are punished
for their stupid talk,
but sensible talk
can save your life.
4 Without the help of an ox
there can be no crop,
but with a strong ox
a big crop is possible.
5 An honest witness
tells the truth;
a dishonest witness
tells nothing but lies.

6 Make fun of wisdom,
and you will never find it.
But if you have understanding,
knowledge comes easily.
7 Stay away from fools,
or you won't learn a thing.
8 Wise people have enough sense
to find their way,
but stupid fools get lost.
9 Fools don't care
if they are wrong,ᵇ
but God is pleased
when people do right.

10 No one else can really know
how sad or happy you are.
11 The tent of a good person
stands longer than the house
of someone evil.
12 You may think you are
on the right road
and still end up dead.
13 Sorrow may hide
behind laughter,
and happiness may end
in sorrow.
14 You harvest what you plant,
whether good or bad.

15 Don't be stupid
and believe all you hear;

ᶻ **13.15** *people . . . disaster*: One possible meaning for the difficult Hebrew text.
ᵃ **13.23** *grow*: One possible meaning for the difficult Hebrew text of verse 23.   ᵇ **14.9** *Fools
. . . wrong*: One possible meaning for the difficult Hebrew text.

be smart and know
    where you are headed.
¹⁶ Only a stupid fool
    is never cautious—
so be extra careful
    and stay out of trouble.
¹⁷ Fools have quick tempers,
    and no one likes you
        if you can't be trusted.
¹⁸ Stupidity leads to foolishness;
    be smart and learn.

¹⁹ The wicked will come crawling
    to those who obey God.
²⁰ You have no friends
    if you are poor,
but you have lots of friends
    if you are rich.
²¹ It's wrong to hate others,
    but God blesses everyone
        who is kind to the poor.
²² It's a mistake
    to make evil plans,
but you will have loyal friends
    if you want to do right.
²³ Hard work is worthwhile,
    but empty talk
        will make you poor.
²⁴ Wisdom can make you rich,
    but foolishness leads
        to more foolishness.
²⁵   An honest witness
can save your life,
    but liars can't be trusted.

²⁶ If you respect the LORD,
you and your children
    have a strong fortress
²⁷ and a life-giving fountain
that keeps you safe
    from deadly traps.

²⁸ Rulers of powerful nations
    are held in honor;
rulers of weak nations
    are nothing at all.
²⁹ It's smart to be patient,
    but it's stupid
        to lose your temper.
³⁰ It's healthy to be content,
    but envy can eat you up.
³¹ If you mistreat the poor,
    you insult your Creator;
if you are kind to them,
    you show him respect.
³² In times of trouble
    the wicked are destroyed,
but even at death
    the innocent have faith.ᶜ

³³ Wisdom is found in the minds
of people with good sense,
    but fools don't know it.ᵈ
³⁴ Doing right brings honor

to a nation,
    but sin brings disgrace.
³⁵ Kings reward servants
    who act wisely,
but they punish those
    who act foolishly.

The LORD Sees Everything

15 A kind answer
    soothes angry feelings,
but harsh words
    stir them up.
² Words of wisdom
come from the wise,
    but fools speak foolishness.

³ The LORD sees everything,
    whether good or bad.
⁴ Kind words are good medicine,
    but deceitful words
        can really hurt.
⁵ Don't be a fool
and disobey your parents.
    Be smart! Accept correction.
⁶ Good people become wealthy,
    but those who are evil
        will lose what they have.
⁷ Words of wisdom
    make good sense;
the thoughts of a fool
    make no sense at all.

⁸ The LORD is disgusted
    by gifts from the wicked,
but it makes him happy
    when his people pray.
⁹ The LORD is disgusted
    with all who do wrong,
but he loves everyone
    who does right.
¹⁰ If you turn from the right way,
    you will be punished;
if you refuse correction,
    you will die.

¹¹ If the LORD can see everything
    in the world of the dead,
he can see in our hearts.
¹² Those who sneer at others
    don't like to be corrected,
and they won't ask help
    from someone with sense.
¹³ Happiness makes you smile;
    sorrow can crush you.
¹⁴ Anyone with good sense
    is eager to learn more,
but fools are hungry
    for foolishness.

¹⁵ The poor have a hard life,
    but being content is as good
        as an endless feast.
¹⁶ It's better to obey the LORD
    and have only a little,

ᶜ**14.32** *but even . . . faith*: One possible meaning for the difficult Hebrew text. Some ancient translations "but good people trust their innocence."   ᵈ**14.33** *but . . . it*: One possible meaning for the difficult Hebrew text; some ancient translations "but not in the mind of a fool."

than to be very rich
and terribly confused.

¹⁷ A simple meal with love
is better than a feast
where there is hatred.

¹⁸ Losing your temper
causes a lot of trouble,
but staying calm
settles arguments.
¹⁹ Being lazy is like walking
in a thorn patch,
but everyone who does right
walks on a smooth road.
²⁰ Children with good sense
make their parents happy,
but foolish children
are hateful to them.
²¹ Stupidity brings happiness
to senseless fools,
but everyone with good sense
follows the straight path.

²² Without good advice
everything goes wrong—
it takes careful planning
for things to go right.
²³ Giving the right answer
at the right time
makes everyone happy.
²⁴ All who are wise follow a road
that leads upward to life
and away from death.

²⁵ The LORD destroys the homes
of those who are proud,
but he protects the property
of widows.
²⁶ The LORD hates evil thoughts,
but kind words please him.
²⁷ Being greedy causes trouble
for your family,
but you protect yourself
by refusing bribes.
²⁸ Good people think
before they answer,
but the wicked speak evil
without ever thinking.

²⁹ The LORD never even hears
the prayers of the wicked,
but he answers the prayers
of all who obey him.
³⁰ A friendly smile
makes you happy,
and good news
makes you feel strong.
³¹ Healthy correction is good,
and if you accept it,
you will be wise.
³² You hurt only yourself
by rejecting instruction,
but it makes good sense
to accept it.
³³ Showing respect to the LORD
will make you wise,

and being humble
will bring honor to you.

The LORD Has the Final Word

16 We humans make plans,
but the LORD
has the final word.
² We may think we know
what is right,
but the LORD is the judge
of our motives.
³ Share your plans with the LORD,
and you will succeed.

⁴ The LORD has a reason
for everything he does,
and he lets evil people live
only to be punished.
⁵ The LORD doesn't like
anyone who is conceited—
you can be sure
they will be punished.
⁶ If we truly love God,
our sins will be forgiven;
if we show him respect,
we will keep away from sin.
⁷ When we please the LORD,
even our enemies
make friends with us.
⁸ It's better to be honest
and poor
than to be dishonest
and rich.

⁹ We make our own plans,
but the LORD decides
where we will go.
¹⁰ Rulers speak with authority
and are never wrong.
¹¹ The LORD doesn't like it
when we cheat in business.
¹² Justice makes rulers powerful.
They should hate evil
¹³ and like honesty and truth.
¹⁴ An angry ruler
can put you to death.
So be wise!
Don't make one angry.
¹⁵ When a ruler is happy
and pleased with you,
it's like refreshing rain,
and you will live.

¹⁶ It's much better to be wise
and sensible
than to be rich.
¹⁷ God's people avoid evil ways,
and they protect themselves
by watching where they go.
¹⁸ Too much pride
will destroy you.
¹⁹ You are better off
to be humble and poor
than to get rich
from what you take by force.
²⁰ If you know what you're doing,ᵉ

ᵉ**16.20** *know what . . . doing*: Or "do what you're taught."

you will prosper.
God blesses everyone
who trusts him.
²¹ Good judgment proves
that you are wise,
and if you speak kindly,
you can teach others.
²² Good sense is a fountain
that gives life,
but fools are punished
by their foolishness.
²³ You can persuade others
if you are wise
and speak sensibly.

²⁴ Kind words are like honey—
they cheer you up
and make you feel strong.
²⁵ Sometimes what seems right
is really a road to death.
²⁶ The hungrier you are,
the harder you work.
²⁷ Worthless people plan trouble.
Even their words burn
like a flaming fire.
²⁸ Gossip is no good!
It causes hard feelings
and comes between friends.

²⁹ Don't trust violent people.
They will mislead you
to do the wrong thing.
³⁰ When someone winks
or grins behind your back,
trouble is on the way.
³¹ Gray hair is a glorious crown
worn by those
who have lived right.
³² Controlling your temper
is better than being a hero
who captures a city.
³³ We make our own decisions,
but the LORD alone
determines what happens.

Our Thoughts Are Tested by the LORD

17 A dry crust of bread eaten
in peace and quiet
is better than a feast eaten
where everyone argues.
² A hard-working slave
will be placed in charge
of a no-good child,
and that slave will be given
the same inheritance
that each child receives.
³ Silver and gold are tested
by flames of fire;
our thoughts are tested
by the LORD.
⁴ Troublemakers listen
to troublemakers,
and liars listen to liars.
⁵ By insulting the poor,
you insult your Creator.
You will be punished
if you make fun
of someone in trouble.

⁶ Grandparents are proud
of their grandchildren,
and children should be proud
of their parents.

⁷ It sounds strange for a fool
to talk sensibly,
but it's even worse
for a ruler to tell lies.
⁸ A bribe works miracles
like a magic charm
that brings good luck.
⁹ You will keep your friends
if you forgive them,
but you will lose your friends
if you keep talking about
what they did wrong.
¹⁰ A sensible person
accepts correction,
but you can't beat sense
into a fool.

¹¹ Cruel people want to rebel,
and so vicious attackers
will be sent against them.
¹² A bear robbed of her cubs
is far less dangerous
than a stubborn fool.
¹³ You will always have trouble
if you are mean to those
who are good to you.
¹⁴ The start of an argument
is like a water leak—
so stop it before
real trouble breaks out.
¹⁵ The LORD doesn't like those
who defend the guilty
or condemn the innocent.
¹⁶ Why should fools have money
for an education
when they refuse to learn?

¹⁷ A friend is always a friend,
and relatives are born
to share our troubles.
¹⁸ It's stupid to guarantee
someone else's loan.
¹⁹ The wicked and the proud
love trouble and keep begging
to be hurt.
²⁰ Dishonesty does you no good,
and telling lies
will get you in trouble.
²¹ It's never pleasant
to be the parent of a fool
and have nothing but pain.
²² If you are cheerful,
you feel good;
if you are sad,
you hurt all over.

²³ Crooks accept secret bribes
to keep justice
from being done.
²⁴ Anyone with wisdom knows
what makes good sense,
but fools can never
make up their minds.

25 Foolish children bring sorrow
  to their father
    and pain to their mother.
26 It isn't fair
  to punish the innocent
    and those who do right.
27 It makes a lot of sense
  to be a person of few words
    and to stay calm.
28 Even fools seem smart
  when they are quiet.

It's Wrong to Favor the Guilty

18 It's selfish and stupid
    to think only of yourself
  and to sneer at people
    who have sense.*f*
2 Fools have no desire to learn;
  they would much rather
    give their own opinion.
3 Wrongdoing leads to shame
  and disgrace.
4 Words of wisdom
  are a stream that flows
    from a deep fountain.
5 It's wrong to favor the guilty
  and keep the innocent
    from getting justice.

6 Foolish talk will get you
  into a lot of trouble.
7 Saying foolish things
  is like setting a trap
    to destroy yourself.
8 There's nothing so delicious
  as the taste of gossip!
    It melts in your mouth.
9 Being lazy is no different
  from being a troublemaker.

10 The LORD is a mighty tower
  where his people can run
    for safety—
11 the rich think their money
  is a wall of protection.

12 Pride leads to destruction;
  humility leads to honor.
13 It's stupid and embarrassing
  to give an answer
    before you listen.
14 Being cheerful helps
  when we are sick,
  but nothing helps
    when we give up.
15 Everyone with good sense
  wants to learn.
16 A gift will get you in
  to see anyone.
17 You may think you have won
  your case in court,
    until your opponent speaks.
18 Drawing straws is one way

to settle a difficult case.
19 Making up with a friend
  you have offended*g*
  is harder than breaking
    through a city wall.

20 Make your words good—
  you will be glad you did.
21 Words can bring death or life!
  Talk too much, and you will eat
    everything you say.
22 A man's greatest treasure
  is his wife—
    she is a gift from the LORD.
23 The poor must beg for help,
  but the rich can give
    a harsh reply.
24 Some friends don't help,*h*
  but a true friend is closer
    than your own family.

It's Wise To Be Patient

19 It's better to be poor
    and live right
      than to be a stupid liar.
2 Willingness and stupidity
  don't go well together.
  If you are too eager,
    you will miss the road.
3 We are ruined
  by our own stupidity,
    though we blame the LORD.

4 The rich have many friends;
  the poor have none.
5 Dishonest witnesses and liars
  won't escape punishment.
6 Everyone tries to be friends
  of those who can help them.
7 If you are poor,
  your own relatives reject you,
    and your friends are worse.
  When you really need them,
    they are not there.*i*

8 Do yourself a favor
  by having good sense—
    you will be glad you did.
9 Dishonest witnesses and liars
  will be destroyed.
10 It isn't right for a fool
  to live in luxury
  or for a slave to rule
    in place of a king.
11 It's wise to be patient
  and show what you are like
    by forgiving others.
12 An angry king roars
  like a lion,
  but when a king is pleased,
    it's like dew on the crops.

13 A foolish son brings disgrace
  to his father.

*f*18.1 *sense*: One possible meaning for the difficult Hebrew text of verse 1.   *g*18.19 *Making
. . . offended*: One possible meaning for the difficult Hebrew text.   *h*18.24 *Some . . . help*:
One possible meaning for the difficult Hebrew text.   *i*19.7 *When . . . there*: One possible
meaning for the difficult Hebrew text.

A nagging wife goes on and on
like the drip, drip, drip
    of the rain.
14 You may inherit all you own
    from your parents,
but a sensible wife
    is a gift from the LORD.
15 If you are lazy
and sleep your time away,
    you will starve.

16 Obey the Lord's teachings
and you will live—
    disobey and you will die.
17 Caring for the poor
is lending to the LORD,
    and you will be well repaid.
18 Correct your children
    before it's too late;
if you don't punish them,
    you are destroying them.
19 People with bad tempers
    are always in trouble,
and they need help
    over and over again.*j*
20 Pay attention to advice
and accept correction,
    so you can live sensibly.

21 We may make a lot of plans,
    but the LORD will do
    what he has decided.
22 What matters most is loyalty.
It's better to be poor
    than to be a liar.
23 Showing respect to the LORD
    brings true life—
if you do it, you can relax
    without fear of danger.

24 Some people are too lazy
    to lift a hand
    to feed themselves.
25 Stupid fools learn good sense
    by seeing others punished;
a sensible person learns
    by being corrected.
26 Children who bring disgrace
    rob their father
    and chase their mother away.
27 If you stop learning,
you will forget
    what you already know.
28 A lying witness makes fun
    of the court system,
and criminals think crime
    is really delicious.
29 Every stupid fool
is just waiting
    to be punished.

Words of Wisdom Are Better than Gold

20 It isn't smart to get drunk!
Drinking makes a fool of you
    and leads to fights.

2 An angry ruler
    is like a roaring lion—
make either one angry,
    and you are dead.
3 It makes you look good
when you avoid a fight—
    only fools love to quarrel.
4 If you are too lazy to plow,
    don't expect a harvest.
5 Someone's thoughts may be
    as deep as the ocean,
but if you are smart,
    you will discover them.

6 There are many who say,
"You can trust me!"
    But can they be trusted?
7 Good people live right,
and God blesses the children
    who follow their example.
8 When rulers decide cases,
    they weigh the evidence.
9 Can any of us really say,
"My thoughts are pure,
    and my sins are gone"?

10 Two things the LORD hates
    are dishonest scales
    and dishonest measures.
11 The good or bad
    that children do
    shows what they are like.
12 Hearing and seeing
    are gifts from the LORD.
13 If you sleep all the time,
    you will starve;
if you get up and work,
    you will have enough food.
14 Everyone likes to brag
    about getting a bargain.
15 Sensible words are better
    than gold or jewels.

16 You deserve to lose your coat
    if you loan it to someone
to guarantee payment
    for the debt of a stranger.
17 The food you get by cheating
    may taste delicious,
    but it turns to gravel.
18 Be sure you have sound advice
    before making plans
    or starting a war.
19 Stay away from gossips—
    they tell everything.
20 Children who curse their parents
    will go to the land of darkness
    long before their time.
21 Getting rich quick*k*
    may turn out to be a curse.
22 Don't try to get even.
Trust the LORD,
    and he will help you.

23 The LORD hates dishonest scales
    and dishonest weights.

---

j **19.19** *and they . . . again:* One possible meaning for the difficult Hebrew text.
k **20.21** *quick:* Or "the wrong way."

So don't cheat!
²⁴ How can we know
what will happen to us
when the LORD alone decides?
²⁵ Don't fall into the trap
of making promises to God
before you think!
²⁶ A wise ruler severely punishes
every criminal.
²⁷ Our inner thoughts are a lamp
from the LORD,
and they search our hearts.
²⁸ Rulers are protected
by God's mercy and loyalty,
but[l] they must be merciful
for their kingdoms to last.
²⁹ Young people take pride
in their strength,
but the gray hairs of wisdom
are even more beautiful.
³⁰ A severe beating can knock all
of the evil out of you!

The LORD Is In Charge

21 The LORD controls rulers,
just as he determines
the course of rivers.
² We may think we are doing
the right thing,
but the LORD always knows
what is in our hearts.
³ Doing what is right and fair
pleases the LORD
more than an offering.
⁴ Evil people are proud
and arrogant,
but sin is the only crop
they produce.[m]
⁵ If you plan and work hard,
you will have plenty;
if you get in a hurry,
you will end up poor.

⁶ Cheating to get rich
is a foolish dream
and no less than suicide.[n]
⁷ You destroy yourself
by being cruel and violent
and refusing to live right.
⁸ All crooks are liars,
but anyone who is innocent
will do right.
⁹ It's better to stay outside
on the roof of your house
than to live inside
with a nagging wife.
¹⁰ Evil people want to do wrong,
even to their friends.
¹¹ An ignorant fool learns
by seeing others punished;
a sensible person learns
by being instructed.

¹² God is always fair!
He knows what the wicked do
and will punish them.
¹³ If you won't help the poor,
don't expect to be heard
when you cry out for help.
¹⁴ A secret bribe will save you
from someone's fierce anger.
¹⁵ When justice is done,
good citizens are glad
and crooks are terrified.
¹⁶ If you stop using good sense,
you will find yourself
in the grave.
¹⁷ Heavy drinkers and others
who live only for pleasure
will lose all they have.

¹⁸ God's people will escape,
but all who are wicked
will pay the price.
¹⁹ It's better out in the desert
than at home with a nagging,
complaining wife.
²⁰ Be sensible and store up
precious treasures—
don't waste them
like a fool.
²¹ If you try to be kind and good,
you will be blessed with life
and goodness and honor.
²² One wise person can defeat
a city full of soldiers
and capture their fortress.
²³ Watching what you say
can save you
a lot of trouble.
²⁴ If you are proud and conceited,
everyone will say,
"You're a snob!"

²⁵ If you want too much
and are too lazy to work,
it could be fatal.
²⁶ But people who obey God
are always generous.

²⁷ The Lord despises the offerings
of wicked people
with evil motives.
²⁸ If you tell lies in court,
you are done for;
only a reliable witness
can do the job.
²⁹ Wicked people bluff their way,
but God's people think
before they take a step.

³⁰ No matter how much you know
or what plans you make,
you can't defeat the LORD.
³¹ Even if your army has horses
ready for battle,
the LORD will always win.

---

[l]**20.28** *by God's mercy . . . but*: Or "by their mercy . . . and."   [m]**21.4** *but sin . . . produce*: Or "but sin is the only light they ever follow."   [n]**21.6** *and . . . suicide*: One possible meaning for the difficult Hebrew text.

The Value of a Good Reputation

22 A good reputation and respect are worth much more
than silver and gold.

2 The rich and the poor
are all created
by the LORD.

3 When you see trouble coming,
don't be stupid
and walk right into it—
be smart and hide.

4 Respect and serve the LORD!
Your reward will be wealth,
a long life, and honor.

5 Crooks walk down a road
full of thorny traps.
Stay away from there!

6 Teach your children
right from wrong,
and when they are grown
they will still do right.

7 The poor are ruled by the rich,
and those who borrow
are slaves of moneylenders.

8 Troublemakers get in trouble,
and their terrible anger
will get them nowhere.

9 The LORD blesses everyone
who freely gives food
to the poor.

10 Arguments and fights
will come to an end,
if you chase away those
who insult others.

11 The king is the friend of all
who are sincere
and speak with kindness.

12 The LORD watches over everyone
who shows good sense,
but he frustrates the plans
of deceitful liars.

13 Don't be so lazy that you say,
"If I go to work,
a lion will eat me!"

14 The words of a bad woman
are like a deep pit;
if you make the LORD angry,
you will fall right in.

15 All children are foolish,
but firm correction
will make them change.

16 Cheat the poor to make profit
or give gifts to the rich—
either way you lose.

Thirty Wise Sayings

17 Here are some sayings
of people with wisdom,
so listen carefully
as I teach.

18 You will be glad

that you know these sayings
and can recite them.

19 I am teaching them today,
so that you
may trust the LORD.

20 I have written thirty sayings
filled with sound advice.

21 You can trust them completely
to give you the right words
for those in charge of you.

– 1 –

22 Don't take advantage
of the poor
or cheat them in court.

23 The LORD is their defender,
and what you do to them,
he will do to you.

– 2 –

24 Don't make friends with anyone
who has a bad temper.

25 You might turn out like them
and get caught in a trap.

– 3 –

26 Don't guarantee to pay
someone else's debt.

27 If you don't have the money,
you might lose your bed.

– 4 –

28 Don't move a boundary marker *o*
set up by your ancestors.

– 5 –

29 If you do your job well,
you will work for a ruler
and never be a slave.

– 6 –

23 When you are invited
to eat with a king,
use your best manners.

2 Don't go and stuff yourself!
That would be just the same
as cutting your throat.

3 Don't be greedy for all
of that fancy food!
It may not be so tasty.

– 7 –

4 Give up trying so hard
to get rich.

5 Your money flies away
before you know it,
just like an eagle
suddenly taking off.

– 8 –

6 Don't accept an invitation
to eat a selfish person's food,
no matter how good it is.

7 People like that take note

*o*22.28 *marker*: In ancient Israel boundary lines were sacred because all property was a gift from the Lord (see Deuteronomy 19.14).

of how much you eat.^p
They say, "Take all you want!"
But they don't mean it.
⁸ Each bite will come back up,
and all your kind words
will be wasted.

– 9 –

⁹ Don't talk to fools—-
they will just make fun.

– 10 –

¹⁰ Don't move a boundary marker ^q
or take the land
that belongs to orphans.
¹¹ God All-Powerful is there
to defend them against you.

– 11 –

¹² Listen to instruction
and do your best to learn.

– 12 –

¹³ Don't fail to correct
your children.
You won't kill them
by being firm,
¹⁴ and it may even
save their lives.

– 13 –

¹⁵ My children,
if you show good sense,
I will be happy,
¹⁶ and if you are truthful,
I will really be glad.

– 14 –

¹⁷ Don't be jealous of sinners,
but always honor the LORD.
¹⁸ Then you will truly have hope
for the future.

– 15 –

¹⁹ Listen to me, my children!
Be wise and have enough sense
to follow the right path.
²⁰ Don't be a heavy drinker
or stuff yourself with food.
²¹ It will make you feel drowsy,
and you will end up poor
with only rags to wear.

– 16 –

²² Pay attention to your father,
and don't neglect your mother
when she grows old.
²³ Invest in truth and wisdom,
discipline and good sense,
and don't part with them.
²⁴ Make your father truly happy
by living right and showing
sound judgment.
²⁵ Make your parents proud,
especially your mother.

– 17 –

²⁶ My son, pay close attention,
and gladly follow
my example.
²⁷ Bad women and unfaithful wives
are like a deep pit—
²⁸ they are waiting to attack you
like a gang of robbers
with victim after victim.

– 18 –

²⁹ Who is always in trouble?
Who argues and fights?
Who has cuts and bruises?
Whose eyes are red?
³⁰ Everyone who stays up late,
having just one more drink.
³¹ Don't even look
at that colorful stuff
bubbling up in the glass!
It goes down so easily,
³² but later it bites
like a poisonous snake.
³³ You will see weird things,
and your mind
will play tricks on you.
³⁴ You will feel tossed about
like someone trying to sleep
on a ship in a storm.
³⁵ You will be bruised all over,
without even remembering
how it all happened.
And you will lie awake asking,
"When will morning come,
so I can drink some more?"

– 19 –

24 Don't be jealous of crooks
or want to be their friends.
² All they think about
and talk about
is violence and cruelty.

– 20 –

³ Use wisdom and understanding
to establish your home;
⁴ let good sense fill the rooms
with priceless treasures.

– 21 –

⁵ Wisdom brings strength,
and knowledge gives power.
⁶ Battles are won
by listening to advice
and making a lot of plans.

– 22 –

⁷ Wisdom is too much for fools!
Their advice is no good.

– 23 –

⁸ No one but troublemakers
think up trouble.
⁹ Everyone hates senseless fools
who think up ways to sin.

^p**23.7** *People . . . eat*: One possible meaning for the difficult Hebrew text.   ^q**23.10** *marker*:
See the note at 22.28.

– 24 –

¹⁰ Don't give up and be helpless
in times of trouble.

– 25 –

¹¹ Don't fail to rescue those
who are doomed to die.
¹² Don't say, "I didn't know it!"
God can read your mind.
He watches each of us
and knows our thoughts.
And God will pay us back
for what we do.

– 26 –

¹³ Honey is good for you,
my children,
and it tastes sweet.
¹⁴ Wisdom is like honey
for your life—
if you find it,
your future is bright.

– 27 –

¹⁵ Don't be a cruel person
who attacks good people
and hurts their families.
¹⁶ Even if good people
fall seven times,
they will get back up.
But when trouble strikes
the wicked,
that's the end of them.

– 28 –

¹⁷ Don't be happy
to see your enemies trip
and fall down.
¹⁸ The LORD will find out
and be unhappy.
Then he will stop
being angry with them.

– 29 –

¹⁹ Don't let evil people
worry you
or make you jealous.
²⁰ They will soon be gone
like the flame of a lamp
that burns out.

– 30 –

²¹ My children, you must respect
the LORD and the king,
and you must not make friends
with anyone who rebels
against either of them.
²² Who knows what sudden disaster
the LORD or a ruler
might bring?

More Sayings That Make Good Sense

²³ Here are some more sayings
that make good sense:
When you judge,
you must be fair.

²⁴ If you let the guilty
go free,
people of all nations
will hate and curse you.
²⁵ But if you punish the guilty,
things will go well for you,
and you will prosper.
²⁶ Giving an honest answer
is a sign
of true friendship.
²⁷ Get your fields ready
and plant your crops
before starting a home.
²⁸ Don't accuse anyone
who isn't guilty.
Don't ever tell a lie
²⁹ or say to someone,
"I'll get even with you!"

³⁰ I once walked by the field
and the vineyard
of a lazy fool.
³¹ Thorns and weeds
were everywhere,
and the stone wall
had fallen down.
³² When I saw this,
it taught me a lesson:
³³ Sleep a little. Doze a little.
Fold your hands
and twiddle your thumbs.
³⁴ Suddenly poverty hits you
and everything is gone!

More of Solomon's Wise Sayings

25 Here are more
of Solomon's proverbs.
They were copied by the officials
of King Hezekiah of Judah.
² God is praised
for being mysterious;
rulers are praised
for explaining mysteries.
³ Who can fully understand
the thoughts of a ruler?
They reach beyond the sky
and go deep in the earth.

⁴ Silver must be purified
before it can be used
to make something of value.
⁵ Evil people must be removed
before anyone can rule
with justice.

⁶ Don't try to seem important
in the court of a ruler.
⁷ It's better for the ruler
to give you a high position
than for you to be embarrassed
in front of royal officials.
Be sure you are right
⁸ before you sue someone,
or you might lose your case
and be embarrassed.

⁹ When you and someone else
can't get along,

don't gossip about it.[r]
10 Others will find out,
and your reputation
will then be ruined.

11 The right word
at the right time
is like precious gold
set in silver.
12 Listening to good advice
is worth much more
than jewelry made of gold.
13 A messenger you can trust
is just as refreshing
as cool water in summer.
14 Broken promises
are worse than rain clouds
that don't bring rain.
15 Patience and gentle talk
can convince a ruler
and overcome any problem.

16 Eating too much honey
can make you sick.
17 Don't visit friends too often,
or they will get tired of it
and start hating you.
18 Telling lies about friends
is like attacking them
with clubs and swords
and sharp arrows.
19 A friend you can't trust
in times of trouble
is like having a toothache
or a sore foot.
20 Singing to someone
in deep sorrow
is like pouring vinegar
in an open cut.[s]

21 If your enemies are hungry,
give them something to eat.
And if they are thirsty,
give them something
to drink.
22 This will be the same
as piling burning coals
on their heads.
And the LORD
will reward you.
23 As surely as rain blows in
from the north,
anger is caused
by cruel words.
24 It's better to stay outside
on the roof of your house
than to live inside
with a nagging wife.

25 Good news from far away
refreshes like cold water
when you are thirsty.

26 When a good person gives in
to the wicked,
it's like dumping garbage
in a stream of clear water.
27 Don't eat too much honey
or always want praise.[t]
28 Losing self-control
leaves you as helpless
as a city without a wall.

Don't Be a Fool

26 Expecting snow in summer
and rain in the dry season
makes more sense
than honoring a fool.
2 A curse you don't deserve
will take wings and fly away
like a sparrow or a swallow.
3 Horses and donkeys
must be beaten and bridled—
and so must fools.
4 Don't make a fool of yourself
by answering a fool.
5 But if you answer any fools,
show how foolish they are,
so they won't feel smart.

6 Sending a message by a fool
is like chopping off your foot
and drinking poison.
7 A fool with words of wisdom
is like an athlete
with legs that can't move.[u]
8 Are you going to honor a fool?
Why not shoot a slingshot
with the rock tied tight?
9 A thornbush waved around
in the hand of a drunkard
is no worse than a proverb
in the mouth of a fool.

10 It's no smarter to shoot arrows
at every passerby
than it is to hire a bunch
of worthless nobodies.[v]
11 Dogs return to eat their vomit,
just as fools repeat
their foolishness.
12 There is more hope for a fool
than for someone who says,
"I'm really smart!"

13 Don't be lazy and keep saying,
"There's a lion outside!"
14 A door turns on its hinges,
but a lazy person
just turns over in bed.
15 Some of us are so lazy
that we won't lift a hand
to feed ourselves.
16 A lazy person says,

"I am smarter
   than everyone else."

17 It's better to take hold
   of a mad dog by the ears
than to take part
   in someone else's argument.
18 It's no crazier to shoot
   sharp and flaming arrows
19 than to cheat someone and say,
   "I was only fooling!"

20 Where there is no fuel
   a fire goes out;
where there is no gossip
   arguments come to an end.
21 Troublemakers start trouble,
just as sparks and fuel
   start a fire.
22 There is nothing so delicious
as the taste of gossip!
   It melts in your mouth.

23 Hiding hateful thoughts
   behind smooth*w* talk
is like coating a clay pot
   with a cheap glaze.
24 The pleasant talk
   of an enemy
hides more evil plans
25 than can be counted—
   so don't believe a word!
26 Everyone will see through
   those evil plans.
27 If you dig a pit,
   you will fall in;
if you start a stone rolling,
   it will roll back on you.
28 Watch out for anyone
who tells lies and flatters—
   they are out to get you.

Don't Brag about Tomorrow

27 Don't brag about tomorrow!
Each day brings
   its own surprises.
2 Don't brag about yourself—
   let others praise you.
3 Stones and sand are heavy,
but trouble caused by a fool
   is a much heavier load.
4 An angry person is dangerous,
but a jealous person
   is even worse.

5 A truly good friend
   will openly correct you.
6 You can trust a friend
   who corrects you,
but kisses from an enemy
   are nothing but lies.
7 If you have had enough to eat,
   honey doesn't taste good,
but if you are really hungry,
   you will eat anything.

8 When you are far from home,
   you feel like a bird
   without a nest.
9 The sweet smell of incense
   can make you feel good,
but true friendship
   is better still.*x*
10 Don't desert an old friend
   of your family
or visit your relatives
   when you are in trouble.
A friend nearby is better
   than relatives far away.

11 My child, show good sense!
   Then I will be happy
and able to answer anyone
   who criticizes me.
12 Be cautious and hide
   when you see danger—
don't be stupid and walk
   right into trouble.
13 Don't loan money to a stranger
unless you are given something
   to guarantee payment.
14 A loud greeting
   early in the morning
   is the same as a curse.
15 The steady dripping of rain
   and the nagging of a wife
   are one and the same.
16 It's easier to catch the wind
   or hold olive oil in your hand
   than to stop a nagging wife.

17 Just as iron sharpens iron,
   friends sharpen the minds
   of each other.
18 Take care of a tree,
   and you will eat its fruit;
look after your master,
   and you will be praised.
19 You see your face in a mirror
   and your thoughts
   in the minds of others.
20 Death and the grave
   are never satisfied,
   and neither are we.
21 Gold and silver are tested
   in a red-hot furnace,
but we are tested by praise.
22 No matter how hard
   you beat a fool,
you can't pound out
   the foolishness.

23 You should take good care
   of your sheep and goats,
24 because wealth and honor
   don't last forever.
25 After the hay is cut
   and the new growth appears
   and the harvest is over,
26 you can sell lambs and goats
   to buy clothes and land.

---

*w***26.23** *smooth:* One ancient translation; Hebrew "hateful."   *x***27.9** *still:* One possible meaning for the difficult Hebrew text of verse 9.

²⁷ From the milk of the goats,
you can make enough cheese
to feed your family
and all your servants.

The Law of God Makes Sense

28 Wicked people run away
when no one chases them,
but those who live right
are as brave as lions.

² In time of civil war
there are many leaders,
but a sensible leader
restores law and order.^y

³ When someone poor takes over
and mistreats the poor,
it's like a heavy rain
destroying the crops.

⁴ Lawbreakers praise criminals,
but law-abiding citizens
always oppose them.

⁵ Criminals don't know
what justice means,
but all who respect the LORD
understand it completely.

⁶ It's better to be poor
and live right,
than to be rich
and dishonest.

⁷ It makes good sense
to obey the Law of God,
but you disgrace your parents
if you make friends
with worthless nobodies.

⁸ If you make money by charging
high interest rates,
you will lose it all to someone
who cares for the poor.

⁹ God cannot stand the prayers
of anyone who disobeys
his Law.

¹⁰ By leading good people to sin,
you dig a pit for yourself,
but all who live right
will have a bright future.

¹¹ The rich think highly
of themselves,
but anyone poor and sensible
sees right through them.

¹² When an honest person wins,
it's time to celebrate;
when crooks are in control,
it's best to hide.

¹³ If you don't confess your sins,
you will be a failure.
But God will be merciful
if you confess your sins
and give them up.

¹⁴ The LORD blesses everyone
who is afraid to do evil,
but if you are cruel,
you will end up in trouble.

¹⁵ A ruler who mistreats the poor
is like a roaring lion
or a bear hunting for food.

¹⁶ A heartless leader is a fool,
but anyone who refuses
to get rich by cheating others
will live a long time.

¹⁷ Don't give help to murderers!
Make them stay on the run
for as long as they live.^z

¹⁸ Honesty will keep you safe,
but everyone who is crooked
will suddenly fall.

¹⁹ Work hard, and you will have
a lot of food;
waste time, and you will have
a lot of trouble.

²⁰ God blesses his loyal people,
but punishes all who want
to get rich quick.

²¹ It isn't right to be unfair,
but some people can be bribed
with only a piece of bread.

²² Don't be selfish
and eager to get rich—
you will end up worse off
than you can imagine.

²³ Honest correction
is appreciated
more than flattery.

²⁴ If you cheat your parents
and don't think it's wrong,
you are a common thief.

²⁵ Selfish people cause trouble,
but you will live a full life
if you trust the LORD.

²⁶ Only fools would trust
what they alone think,
but if you live by wisdom,
you will do all right.

²⁷ Giving to the poor
will keep you from poverty,
but if you close your eyes
to their needs,
everyone will curse you.

²⁸ When crooks are in control,
everyone tries to hide,
but when they lose power,
good people are everywhere.

Use Good Sense

29 If you keep being stubborn
after many warnings,
you will suddenly discover
you have gone too far.

² When justice rules a nation,
everyone is glad;
when injustice rules,
everyone groans.

³ If you love wisdom
your parents will be glad,

^y**28.2** *but . . . order*: One possible meaning for the difficult Hebrew text.   ^z**28.17** *live*: One
possible meaning for the difficult Hebrew text of verse 17.

but chasing after bad women
   will cost you everything.
4 An honest ruler
   makes the nation strong;
a ruler who takes bribes
   will bring it to ruin.

5 Flattery is nothing less
   than setting a trap.
6 Your sins will catch you,
   but everyone who lives right
   will sing and celebrate.
7 The wicked don't care
   about the rights of the poor,
   but good people do.
8 Sneering at others is a spark
   that sets a city on fire;
using good sense can put out
   the flames of anger.

9 Be wise and don't sue a fool.
   You won't get satisfaction,
because all the fool will do
   is sneer and shout.
10 A murderer hates everyone
who is honest
   and lives right.*a*
11 Don't be a fool
and quickly lose your temper—
   be sensible and patient.

12 A ruler who listens to lies
   will have corrupt officials.
13 The poor and all who abuse them
   must each depend on God
   for light.
14 Kings who are fair to the poor
   will rule forever.

15 Correct your children,
   and they will be wise;
children out of control
   disgrace their mothers.
16 Crime increases
   when crooks are in power,
but law-abiding citizens
   will see them fall.
17 If you correct your children,
they will bring you peace
   and happiness.

18 Without guidance from God
   law and order disappear,
but God blesses everyone
   who obeys his Law.
19 Even when servants are smart,
it takes more than words
   to make them obey.
20 There is more hope for a fool
than for someone who speaks
   without thinking.
21 Slaves that you treat kindly
   from their childhood

will cause you sorrow.*b*
22 A person with a quick temper
stirs up arguments
   and commits a lot of sins.

23 Too much pride brings disgrace;
   humility leads to honor.
24 If you take part in a crime
   you are your worst enemy,
because even under oath
   you can't tell the truth.
25 Don't fall into the trap
   of being a coward—
trust the LORD,
   and you will be safe.
26 Many try to make friends
   with a ruler,
but justice comes
   from the LORD.
27 Good people and criminals
   can't stand each other.

The Sayings of Agur

30 These are the sayings
      and the message
   of Agur son of Jakeh.
Someone cries out to God,
"I am completely worn out!
   How can I last?"*c*
2 I am far too stupid
   to be considered human.
3 I never was wise,
and I don't understand
   what God is like."

4 Has anyone gone up to heaven
   and come back down?
Has anyone grabbed hold
   of the wind?
Has anyone wrapped up the sea
   or marked out boundaries
   for the earth?
If you know of any
   who have done such things,
then tell me their names
   and their children's names.

5 Everything God says is true—
   and it's a shield for all
   who come to him for safety.
6 Don't change what God has said!
   He will correct you and show
   that you are a liar.

7 There are two things, Lord,
   I want you to do for me
   before I die:
8 Make me absolutely honest
   and don't let me be too poor
   or too rich.
Give me just what I need.
9 If I have too much to eat,
   I might forget about you;
if I don't have enough,

---

*a*29.10 *and lives right:* Or "and those who live right are friends of honest people."
*b*29.21 *will . . . sorrow:* One possible meaning for the difficult Hebrew text.   *c*30.1 *last:* One
possible meaning for the difficult Hebrew text of verse 1.

I might steal
and disgrace your name.

10 Don't tell a slave owner
something bad about one
of the slaves.
That slave will curse you,
and you will be in trouble.

11 Some people curse their father
and even their mother;
12 others think they are perfect,
but they are stained by sin.
13 Some people are stuck-up
and act like snobs;
14 others are so greedy
that they gobble down
the poor and homeless.

15 Greed*d* has twins,
each named "Give me!"
There are three or four things
that are never satisfied:
16 The world of the dead
and a childless wife,
the thirsty earth
and a flaming fire.

17 Don't make fun of your father
or disobey your mother—
crows will peck out your eyes,
and buzzards will eat
the rest of you.

18 There are three or four things
I cannot understand:
19 How eagles fly so high
or snakes crawl on rocks,
how ships sail the ocean
or people fall in love.

20 An unfaithful wife says,
"Sleeping with another man
is as natural as eating."

21 There are three or four things
that make the earth tremble
and are unbearable:
22 A slave who becomes king,
a fool who eats too much,
23 a hateful woman
who finds a husband,
and a slave who takes the place
of the woman who owns her.

24 On this earth four things
are small but very wise:
25 Ants, who seem to be feeble,
but store up food
all summer long;
26 badgers, who seem to be weak,
but live among the rocks;
27 locusts, who have no king,
but march like an army;
28 lizards,*e* which can be caught

in your hand,
but sneak into palaces.

29 Three or four creatures
really strut around:
30 Those fearless lions
who rule the jungle,
31 those proud roosters,
those mountain goats,
and those rulers
who have no enemies.*f*

32 If you are foolishly bragging
or planning something evil,
then stop it now!
33 If you churn milk
you get butter;
if you pound on your nose,
you get blood—
and if you stay angry,
you get in trouble.

What King Lemuel's Mother Taught Him

31 These are the sayings
that King Lemuel of Massa
was taught by his mother.
2 My son Lemuel, you were born
in answer to my prayers,
so listen carefully.
3 Don't waste your life
chasing after women!
This has ruined many kings.

4 Kings and leaders
should not get drunk
or even want to drink.
5 Drinking makes you forget
your responsibilities,
and you mistreat the poor.
6 Beer and wine are only
for the dying or for those
who have lost all hope.
7 Let them drink and forget
how poor and miserable
they feel.
8 But you must defend
those who are helpless
and have no hope.
9 Be fair and give justice
to the poor and homeless.

In Praise of a Good Wife

10 A truly good wife
is the most precious treasure
a man can find!
11 Her husband depends on her,
and she never
lets him down.
12 She is good to him
every day of her life,
13 and with her own hands
she gladly makes clothes.

14 She is like a sailing ship
that brings food

---

*d*30.15 *Greed:* Or "A leech."   *e*30.28 *lizards:* Or "spiders."   *f*30.31 *enemies:* One possible
meaning for the difficult Hebrew text of verse 31.

from across the sea.
15 She gets up before daylight
to prepare food for her family
and for her servants.*g*
16 She knows how to buy land
and how to plant a vineyard,
17   and she always works hard.
18 She knows when to buy or sell,
and she stays busy
until late at night.
19 She spins her own cloth,
20 and she helps the poor
and the needy.
21 Her family has warm clothing,
and so she doesn't worry
when it snows.
22 She does her own sewing,
and everything she wears
is beautiful.

23 Her husband is a well-known
and respected leader
in the city.
24 She makes clothes to sell

to the shop owners.
25 She is strong and graceful,*h*
as well as cheerful
about the future.
26 Her words are sensible,
and her advice
is thoughtful.
27 She takes good care
of her family
and is never lazy.
28 Her children praise her,
and with great pride
her husband says,
29 "There are many good women,
but you are the best!"

30 Charm can be deceiving,
and beauty fades away,
but a woman
who honors the LORD
deserves to be praised.
31 Show her respect—
praise her in public
for what she has done.

*g***31.15** *and . . . servants*: Or "and to tell her servants what to do." *h***31.25** *She . . . graceful*:
Or "The clothes she makes are attractive and of good quality."

WORD LIST

Word List

Aaron The brother of Moses. Only he and his descendants were to serve as priests and offer sacrifices for the people of Israel.

Abel The second son of Adam and Eve and the younger brother of Cain, who killed him, after God accepted Abel's offering and refused Cain's.

Abijah A descendant of Aaron. King David divided the priests into twenty-four groups, and Abijah was head of the eighth group.

Abimelech The Philistine king of Gath when David escaped from there by pretending to be crazy. See the title of Psalm 34. He is called Achish in 1 Samuel 21.10—22.1.

Abraham The first great ancestor of the people of Israel. He was the husband of Sarah and the father of Isaac. Abraham put his faith in God, and God promised to bless everyone on earth because of Abraham.

Adam The first man and the husband of Eve.

Agrippa (1) Herod Agrippa was king of Judea A.D. 41–44 and mistreated Christians (Acts 12.1–5). (2) Agrippa II was the son of Herod Agrippa and ruled Judea A.D. 44–53. He and his sister Bernice listened to Paul defend himself (Acts 25.13–26, 32).

Agur, Son of Jakeh A wise man, otherwise unknown. Agur wrote some of the proverbs. See Proberbs 30.1.

Ahimelech A priest at Nob who gave food and a sword to David when he fled from Saul. See the title of Psalm 52.

aloes A sweet-smelling spice that was mixed with myrrh and used as a perfume.

altar A raised structure where sacrifices and offerings were presented to God or gods. Altars could be made of rocks, packed earth, metal or pottery.

amen A Hebrew word used after a prayer or a blessing and meaning, "Let it be that way."

ancestor Someone born one or more generations earlier in a family line, such as a grandparent or great-grandparent.

angel A supernatural being who tells God's messages or protects God's people.

Antipas The father of Herod the Great and ruler of Judea 55–43 B.C. He was also known as Antipater.

apostle A person chosen by Christ to take his message to others.

Aram-naharaim A territory in northern Mesopotamia. The name means Arameans from the land of the Two Rivers. See the title of Psalm 60.

Aram-zobah An Aramean kingdom north of Damascus. See the title of Psalm 60 and 2 Samuel 8.3–13.

Aramaic A language closely related to Hebrew. It was spoken by many Jews including Jesus during New Testament times.

Asaph One of David's musicians. He wrote many psalms and also sang at the dedication of Solomon's temple. See the titles of Psalms 50 and 73–83.

Asia A Roman province in what is today modern Turkey.

Augustus This is the title meaning "honored" that the Romans gave to Octavian when he began ruling the Roman world in 27 B.C. He was Emperor when Jesus was born (Luke 2.1).

Babylon A large city in south-central Mesopotamia, the capital of the kingdom of Babylonia. The Babylonians defeated the southern kingdom of Judah in the sixth century B.C. and forced many of its people to live in Babylonia.

barley A grain something like wheat and used to make bread.

Bashan Flatlands and wooded hills in southern Syria, northeast of Lake Galilee. It was known for its fat cattle and fine grain. See Psalm 68.15, 16.

Benjamin One of the tribes of Israel. It occupied land between Bethel and Jerusalem. The people of this tribe descended from Benjamin, the younger of Jacob and

Rachel's two sons. When the ten northern tribes of Israel broke away following the death of Solomon, only the tribes of Benjamin and Judah were left to form the southern kingdom.

Cain The first son of Adam and Eve and the brother of Abel.

Christ A Greek word meaning "the Chosen One" and used to translate the Hebrew word "Messiah." It is used in the New Testament both as a title and a name for Jesus.

circumcise To cut off the foreskin from the male organ. This is done for Jewish boys as part of a religious ceremony eight days after they are born to show that they belong to God's people. God's command to Abraham (Genesis 17.9–14) was to circumcise all males on the eighth day. Jesus' circumcision on the eighth day is reported in Luke 2.21.

citizen A person who is given special rights and privileges by a nation or state. In return, a citizen was expected to be loyal to that nation or state.

commandments God's rules for his people to live by.

council A leading group of Jewish men who were allowed by the Roman government to meet and make certain decisions for their people.

cumin A plant with small seeds used for seasoning food.

David The most famous ancestor of the Jewish people and the most powerful king Israel ever had. They hoped that one of his descendants would always be their king.

Day of Atonement The one day each year (the tenth day after the Jewish new year's day in the fall) when the high priest went into the most holy part of the temple and sprinkled some of the blood of a sacrificed bull on the sacred chest. This was done so that the people's sins would be forgiven. This holy day is called Yom Kippur in Hebrew.

demons and *evil spirits* Supernatural beings that do harmful things to people and sometimes cause them to do bad things. In the New Testament they are sometimes called "unclean spirits," because people under their power were thought to be unclean and unfit to worship God.

descendant Someone born one or more generations later in a family line, such as a grandchild or great-grandchild.

devil The chief of the demons and evil spirits, also known as "Satan."

disciple Someone who was a follower of Jesus and learned from him.

Doeg of Edom An Edomite who worked for King Saul as the head of his shepherds. He was known to be ruthless and conniving. See the title of Psalm 52 and 1 Samuel 21–22.

Edom A kingdom south of the Dead Sea as far as the Gulf of Aqaba. The Edomites descended from Esau, the twin brother of Jacob.

Elijah A prophet who spoke for God in the ninth century B.C. Many Jews in later centuries thought Elijah would return to get things ready for the coming of the Lord.

elders Men whose age and wisdom made them respected leaders.

Emperor The ruler who lived in the city of Rome and governed all the land around the Mediterranean Sea.

Ephraim One of the most important tribes of northern Israel. It occupied the land north of Benjamin and south of Manasseh. The people of this tribe descended from Ephraim, Joseph's second son.

Epicureans People who followed the teachings of a man named Epicurus, who taught that happiness should be a person's main goal in life.

eternal life Life that is the gift of God and never ends.

Ethan the Ezrahite One of David's musicians. See the title of Psalm 89.

Ethiopia The extensive territory south of Egypt called Cush in Hebrew, traditionally translated as Ethiopia. In Bible times it included within its borders most of modern Sudan and present day Ethiopia.

evil spirits See "demons."

exile The time in Jewish history (597–539 B.C.) when the Babylonians took away most of the people of Jerusalem and Judah as prisoners of war and made them live in Babylonia.

Feast of Thin Bread The days after Passover when Jews eat a kind of thin, flat bread made without yeast to remember how God freed the people of Israel from slavery in Egypt and give them a fresh start.

Felix The Roman governor of Judea A.D. 52–60, who listened to Paul speak and kept him in jail.

Festival of Shelters This festival celebrates the period of forty years when the people of Israel walked through the desert and lived in small shelters. This happy celebration takes place each year in connection with the fall harvest season. Its name in Hebrew is Sukkoth.

Festus The Roman governor after Felix, who sent Paul to stand trial in Rome.

Gath One of the five major Philistine towns on the coastal plain of southern Palestine.

Generation One way of describing a group of people who live during the same period of time. The time of one generation is often understood to be about forty years. See Psalm 95.10.

Gentile Someone who is not a Jew.

Glory The magnificence of God's presence that inspires awe and worship.

God's kingdom God's rule over people, both in this life and in the next.

God's Law God's rules for his people to live by. They are found in the Old Testament, especially in the first five books.

God's Tent The tent where the people of Israel worshiped God before the temple was built.

Greek The language in which the New Testament was written.

Hagar A personal servant of Sarah, the wife of Abraham. When Sarah could not have any children, she followed the ancient custom of letting her husband have a child by Hagar, her servant woman. The boy's name was Ishmael.

Hebrew The language used by the people of Israel and for the writing of most of the Old Testament.

Heman the Ezrahite One of David's musicians. See the title of Psalm 88.

Hermes The Greek god of skillful speaking and the messenger of the other Greek gods.

Herod (1) Herod the Great was the king of all Palestine 37–4 B.C. He ruled Judea at the time Jesus was born. (2) Herod Antipas was the son of Herod the Great and the ruler of Galilee 4 B.C.–A.D. 39, during the time of John the Baptist and Jesus. (3) Herod Agrippa I, the grandson of Herod the Great, ruled Palestine A.D. 41–44.

Hezekiah King of Judah during the Assyrian attack on Jerusalem in 701 B.C., known for his loyalty to the LORD.

high priest See "priest."

Holy One A name for the Savior that God had promised to send. See "Savior."

hyssop A bush with bunches of small, white flowers. A bunch of hyssop was used for sprinkling blood and water in religious ceremonies. These ceremonies made people rightly prepared to worship God after having a bad skin disease. In a similar way, Psalm 51.7 mentions using hyssop in making a person rightly prepared to worship God by taking away sin.

incense A material that makes a sweet smell when burned and is used in the worship of God.

Isaac The second of the three great ancestors of the people of Israel. He was the son of Abraham and father of Jacob.

Isaiah A prophet from Jerusalem, who lived during the eighth century B.C. He served as a prophet during the rule of four different kings of Judah, between the years 740–700 B.C.

Israel See Jacob/Israel.

Jacob/Israel The third great ancestor of the people of Israel. He was the son of Isaac. His name was changed to Israel when he struggled with God at the Jabbok River.

Jeduthun One of David's musicians. See the titles of Psalms 39, 62, 77.

Joab The commander of David's army during most of his reign. See the title of Psalm 60.

Joseph The older son of Jacob and Rachel. He was the father of Ephraim and Manasseh, whose descendants formed two of the most important northern tribes.

Judah One of the tribes of Israel. It occupied the hill country between the Dead Sea and the coastal flatlands. The people of this tribe descended from Judah, the fourth son of Jacob and Leah. When the ten northern tribes of Israel broke away following the death of Solomon, only the tribes of Judah and Benjamin were left to form the southern kingdom.

judges   Leaders chosen by the Lord for the people of Israel after the time of Joshua and before the time of the kings.

Kadesh   A town in the desert of Paran southwest of the Dead Sea, also known as Kadesh-Barnea. It was near the southern border of Israel and the western border of Edom.

King Lemuel of Massa   King of Massa, a country possibly located in northern Arabia. King Lemuel wrote a few of the proverbs. See Proverbs 31.1.

Korah   A Levite family of the clan of Kohath whose people formed one of the major groups of temple singers. The Korahites were also known as temple gatekeepers (1 Chronicles 9.19) and temple bakers (1 Chronicles 9.31).

Law and the Prophets   The sacred writings of the Jews in Jesus' day (the first two of the three sections of the Old Testament).

Law of Moses and **Law of the Lord**   Usually refers to the first five books of the Old Testament, but sometimes to the entire Old Testament.

Leviathan   A legendary sea monster representing revolt and evil, also known from Canaanite writings. Psalm 74.14 celebrates its defeat by God.

Levite   A member of the tribe of Levi, from which priests were chosen. Men from this tribe who were not priests helped with the work in the temple.

Lord   The word "Lord" in capital letters stands for the Hebrew consonants YHWH, the personal names of God. The word "Lord" represents the Hebrew term *Adonai*, the general word for "Lord." By late Old Testament times Jews considered God's personal name too holy to be pronounced. So they said *Adonai*, "Lord," whenever they read the Hebrew consonants YHWH. When the Jewish scribes first translated the Hebrew Scriptures into ancient Greek, they translated the personal name of God as *Kurios*, "Lord." Since then most translations, including the *Contemporary English Version*, have followed the Jewish example and avoided using the personal name of God.

Manasseh   One of the most important tribes of northern Israel. It occupied two areas of land. One was east of the Jordan River, from the Jabbok River north to include all of Bashan. The other was on the west side of the Jordan River and went all the way to the Mediterranean Sea. Its northern boundary began a few miles south of Lake Galilee and went as far south as the border with Ephraim. The people of this tribe descended from Manasseh, Joseph's first son.

Messiah   A Hebrew word meaning "the Chosen One." See "Christ."

mint   A garden plant used for seasoning and medicine.

Moab   A country east of the Dead Sea. Its people descended from Moab, the son of Lot, who was Abraham's nephew.

Moses   The leader of the people of Israel when God rescued them from Egypt.

Mt. Hermon   One of the highest mountains in the Near East, with an elevation of 9,230 feet. Located about 45 miles north of Lake Galilee, its three peaks tower over the upper Jordan River valley. In Hebrew the name means "sacred" or "forbidden."

Mt. Lebanon   A mountain range that stretches about 100 miles north and south along the coast of Phoenicia. In Hebrew the name means "white," and it was known for its white peaks and cedar forests.

Mt. Mizar   Probably a name for one of the lesser peaks of Mt. Hermon. Possibly a way of referring to the small size of Mt. Zion. In Hebrew the name means "small." See Psalm 42.6.

myrrh   A valuable sweet-smelling powder used in perfume.

Naphtali   One of the tribes of Israel. Its people descended from Naphtali, the second son of Jacob and Bilhah. The tribe occupied land north and west of Lake Galilee.

Nazarenes   A name that was sometimes used for the followers of Jesus, who came from the small town of Nazareth.

Noah   When God destroyed the world by a flood, Noah and his family were kept safe in a big boat that God had told him to build.

paradise   The place where God's people go when they die, often understood as another name for heaven.

Passover   A day each year in the spring when Jews celebrate the time God rescued them from slavery in Egypt.

Pentecost   A Jewish festival fifty days

after Passover to celebrate the wheat harvest.

Pharisees A large group of Jews who thought they could best serve God by strictly obeying the laws of the Old Testament as well as their own teachings.

Philistia The fertile strip of land along the Mediterranean coast controlled by the Philistine people. This land began at the Brook of Egypt, below Gaza in the south, and ended at the town of Joppa in the north. Philistia was often at war with Israel.

Phoenicia The territory along the Mediterranean Sea controlled by the cities of Tyre, Sidon, Arvad and Byblos. The coast of modern Lebanon covers about the same area.

pit or *deep pit* The place of punishment for demons and evil spirits.

priest A man who led the worship in the temple and offered sacrifices. Some of the more important priests were called "chief priests," and the most important priest was called the "high priest."

Promised One A title for the Savior that God promised to send. See "Savior."

prophesy See "prophet."

Prophet A person who delivers a message from God to another person or to a group. Often a prophet's message tells what will happen in the future. To speak as a prophet is thus to "prophesy."

Proverb A wise saying that is short and easy to remember.

Psalm A Hebrew poem that could be used as a song or a prayer. Psalms could be prayed by individuals or sung by groups in worship of God. Some of the psalms thank and praise God. Others ask God to take away sins or to give protection, comfort, vengeance or mercy.

rue A garden plant used for seasoning and medicine.

Sabbath The seventh day of the week when Jews worship and do not work, in obedience to the commandment.

Sacrifice/Offering Gifts to God of certain animals, grains, fruits, and sweet-smelling spices. Israelites offered sacrifices to give thanks to God, to beg for forgiveness, to make a payment for a wrong, or to ask for God's blessing. Some sacrifices were completely burned on the altar. In other sacrifices, a portion was offered to the

Lord and the remaining portions were eaten by the priests or ordinary people.

Sadducees A small and powerful group of Jews who were closely connected with the high priests and who accepted only the first five books of the Old Testament as their Bible. They also did not believe in life after death.

Samaria A district between Judea and Galilee. The people of Samaria, called Samaritans, worshiped God differently from the Jews and did not get along with them.

Sarah The wife of Abraham and the mother of Isaac. When she was very old, God promised her that she would have a son.

Satan See "devil."

save To rescue people from the power of evil, to give them new life, and to place them under God's care. See "Savior."

Savior The one who rescues people from the power of evil, gives them new life, and places them under God's care. See "save."

Scriptures The sacred writings known as the Old Testament. These were first written in Hebrew and Aramaic, then translated into Greek about two centuries before the birth of Jesus. This Greek translation, known as the Septuagint, was used both by Jews and Christians in the first century.

Sin Turning away from God and disobeying the teachings of God.

Solomon One of King David's sons. After David's death, Solomon took his place as king and became widely known for his wisdom. He wrote many of the proverbs and two of the psalms. See Proverbs 10.1 and 25.1; Psalms 72 and 127.

Son of Man A name often used by Jesus to refer to himself. It is also found in the book of Daniel and refers to the one to whom God has given the power to rule.

Stoics Followers of a man named Zeno, who believed that nature was controlled by the gods and who taught that people should learn self-control.

taxes and *tax collectors* Special fees collected by rulers, usually part of the value of a citizen's crop, property, or income. There were also market taxes to be paid, and customs taxes were collected at ports and border crossings. The wealthy Zacchaeus (Luke 19.1–10) was a tax collector who collected taxes at a border crossing near Jericho. Jews hired by the Roman government to collect taxes from other Jews were hated by their own people.

temple A building used as a place of worship. The Jewish temple was in Jerusalem.

Temple Festival In 165 B.C. the Jewish people recaptured the Jerusalem temple from their enemies and made it fit for worship again. They celebrate this event in December of each year by a festival which they call "dedication" (Hanukkah). In the New Testament it is mentioned only in John 10.22.

Theophilus The name means "someone God loves" and is found only in Luke 1.3 and Acts 1.1. Nothing else is known about him.

Way In the book of Acts the Christian religion is sometimes called "the Way" or "the Way of the Lord" or "God's Way."

Wisdom The cleverness, common sense, and practical skill needed to solve the everyday problems of life. Wisdom is sometimes pictured as a wise woman who invites people to use good judgment. In Proverbs 8, Wisdom is pictured as helping God plan and build the universe.

Zebulun One of the tribes of Israel. It occupied land that was north of Manasseh and that stretched from the eastern end of Mt. Carmel to Mt. Tabor. The people of this tribe descended from Zebulun, the sixth son of Jacob and Leah.

Zeus The chief god of the Greeks.

Zion Another name for Jerusalem. It can also refer to the hill in Jerusalem where the temple was built.

Ziph A town in the hill country of southern Judah where David hid while running away from King Saul. See the title of Psalm 54 and 1 Samuel 23.19; 26.1.

Who is this JESUS?

By Dr. Bill Bright

Who, in your opinion, is the most outstanding personality of all time? The greatest leader? The greatest teacher?

Who has done the most good for humankind and lived the most holy life of anyone who has ever lived?

Visit any part of the world today, and talk to people of any religion. No matter how committed to their particular religion they may be, if they know anything of the facts, they will have to acknowledge that there has never been a man like Jesus of Nazareth. He is the unique personality of all time.

Jesus changed the course of history. Even the date on your morning newspaper gives witness to the fact that Jesus of Nazareth lived on earth nearly 2,000 years ago.

HIS COMING FORETOLD

Hundreds of years before Jesus' birth, Scripture recorded the words of the great prophets of Israel foretelling his coming. The Old Testament, written by many individuals over a period of 1,500 years, contains more than 300 prophecies detailing his coming, all of which came true exactly as predicted during Jesus' life, death, and resurrection.

The life Jesus led, the miracles he performed, the words he spoke, his death on the cross, his resurrection, his ascent to heaven—these all point to the fact that he was not merely human but more than human. Jesus claimed, "I am one with the Father" (John 10.30), "If you have seen me, you have seen the Father" (John 14.9a) and "Without me, no one can go to the Father." (John 14.6b)

HIS MESSAGE EFFECTS CHANGE

Trace the life and influence of Jesus Christ, and you will observe that his message always effects great change in the lives of people and nations. Wherever his message has gone, the sacredness of marriage, women's rights and suffrage have been acknowledged; institutions of higher learning have been established, child labor laws have been enacted; slavery has been abolished and a multitude of other changes have been made for the good of humankind.

ATHEIST'S LIFE TRANSFORMED

Lew Wallace, a famous general and literary genius, was an avowed atheist. For two years, Mr. Wallace studied in the leading libraries of Europe and America, seeking information to write a book that would forever destroy Christianity. While writing the second chapter of his book, he suddenly found himself on his knees crying out to Jesus, "My Lord and my God."

Because of solid irrefutable evidence, he could no longer deny that Jesus Christ was the Son of God. Later Lew Wallace wrote *Ben Hur*, one of the greatest novels ever written concerning the time of Christ.

Similarly, the late C. S. Lewis, professor at Oxford University, was an agnostic who denied the deity of Christ for years. But he, too, in intellectual honesty, submitted to Jesus as his God and Savior after studying the overwhelming evidence for Jesus' deity.

LORD, LIAR OR LUNATIC?

In his famous book *Mere Christianity*, Lewis makes this statement:

"A man who was merely a man and said the sort of things Jesus said would not be a great moral teacher. He would either be a lunatic – on the level with the man who says he is a poached egg – or else he would be the devil of hell. You must take your choice. Either this was, and is the Son of God; or else a madman or something worse. You can shut Him up for a fool...or you can fall at His feet and call Him Lord and God. But let us not come with any patronizing nonsense about His being a great human teacher. He has not left that open to us."

> *Either this was, and is the Son of God; or else a madman or something worse.*

Who is Jesus of Nazareth to you? Your life on this earth and for all eternity is affected by your answer to this question.

Take Buddha out of Buddhism, Mohammed out of Islam and, in like manner, the founder of various other religions out of their religions, and little would change. But take Jesus Christ out of Christianity, and there would be nothing left, for Christianity is not a philosophy or ethic but a personal relationship with a living, risen Savior.

A RISEN FOUNDER

No other religion claims that its founder has been raised from the dead; Christianity is unique in this regard. Any argument for its validity stands or falls on the proof of the resurrection of Jesus of Nazareth.

Many great scholars have believed, and do believe, in his resurrection. After examining the evidence for the resurrection given by the gospel writers, the late Simon Greenleaf, an authority in jurisprudence at Harvard Law School, concluded, "It was therefore impossible that they could have persisted in affirming the truths they have narrated, had not Jesus actually risen from the dead, and had they not known this fact as certainly as they knew any other fact."

John Singleton Copely, recognized as one of the greatest legal minds in British history, comments: "I know pretty well what evidence is: and I tell you, such evidence as that for the resurrection has never broken down yet."

I have yet to meet anyone who, after honestly considering the overwhelming evidence concerning Jesus of Nazareth, does not admit that he is the Son of God. While some do not believe, they are honest in confessing, "I have not taken the time to read the Bible or consider the historical facts concerning Jesus."

THE VISIBLE EXPRESSION OF THE INVISIBLE GOD

Consider these passages concerning Jesus, taken from the Bible: "Christ is exactly like God, who cannot be seen. He is the first-born Son, superior to all creation. Everything was created by him, everything in heaven and on earth, everything seen and unseen, including all forces and powers, and all rulers and authorities. All things were created by God's Son, and everything was made for him." (Colossians 1.15,16)

"God has told us his secret reason for sending Christ, a plan He decided on in mercy long ago; And this was His purpose: that when the time is ripe He will gather us all together from wherever we are – in heaven or on earth – to be with Him in Christ forever." (Ephesians 1.9, 10 Living Bible)

A LIVING LORD

Because of Jesus' resurrection, His followers do not merely comply with the ethical code of a dead founder, but rather can have vital contact with a living Lord. Jesus Christ lives today and anxiously waits to work in the lives of those who will trust and obey him. Blaise Pascal, a French physicist and philosopher, spoke of everyone's need for Jesus when he said, "There is a God-shaped vacuum in the heart of every man, which only God can fill through His Son, Jesus Christ."

Would you like to know Jesus Christ personally? You can! As presumptuous as it may sound, Jesus is so eager to establish a personal, loving relationship with you that he has already made all the arrangements. The major barrier that prevents us from enjoying this relationship is ignorance of who Jesus is and what he has done for us.

JESUS *investigative*
BIBLE STUDY

I. Jesus   His Beginnings

In this study we will see:

- *How Luke's Gospel fits into history.*

- *That Jesus is "the Son of God."*

- *What Jesus said he came to do.*

Background to the New Testament

The New Testament is made up of several short books and letters. Our English Bibles are translations of what the early Christians actually wrote. The experts tell us that we can be sure that the text on which these translations are based has very few mistakes in it. How can we be sure?

In the days of the first Christians, there were many writings about the life of Jesus. But some had a special quality – they had been written by Jesus' followers or their close friends. These gospels and letters were carefully copied by hand. Over the years, archaeologists have found thousands of manuscripts of bits of the New Testament and even some complete copies. By comparing these, we can get very close to what the New Testament writers originally wrote. Some of these copies are dated less than one hundred years after the original gospel or letter was written.

For an idea of how good this evidence is, compare the New Testament with other writings that are about as old as the New Testament. For example, Julius Caesar wrote a book called *The Gallic War* about fifty years before Christ was born. We obviously do not have the original copy. Yet, we do have nine or ten copies, and the earliest of these was made about nine hundred years after the original. This is a normal gap for ancient writings.

> *...we have good reason to believe that we know almost exactly what Luke, Paul and the others wrote.*

When we examine the historical evidence relating to the Bible, we learn that there are thousands of manuscripts of the New Testament books. Therefore, we have good reason to believe that we know almost exactly what Luke, Paul and the others wrote.

About the Author

The author of Luke also wrote another book in the New Testament, Acts. He was the only New Testament writer who was not Jewish. Luke was a doctor, and independent evidence confirms that he was a very careful and accurate historian.

A. Luke's Gospel: fact or fiction?

Read Luke 1.1-4

1. Where did Luke get his information? (1.2) _____

2. How did he write it? (1.3) _____

3. Why do you think Luke wrote this introduction? _____

B. Where did Jesus come from?

Luke gives details of the unique origin of Jesus, and the following passage explains how Jesus' birth was foretold.

Read Luke 1.26-38

1. What would the future hold for Mary's child? (1.32,33) _____

2. How would Jesus be conceived? (1.35-37) _____

3. Jesus is said to be the Son of God. What do these verses say about Jesus' "double origin"?_____

C. Jesus explains his purpose

Jesus was born in Bethlehem in Judea, in the south of Palestine. He grew up in a very ordinary town, named Nazareth, located in Galilee which was in northern Palestine. Jesus was a carpenter, but at the age of thirty, he became a religious teacher, moving from town to town.

In Luke 4.14-22, we read what happened when Jesus began teaching. He went to the synagogue, which was the local place of worship. Although he probably had no more religious education than the average Jewish man, people wanted to hear him. He was asked to speak at the synagogue in Nazareth.

Read Luke 4.14-22

1. What kind of people had Jesus come to help? (4.18) _____

Who do you think this means? _____

2. What was he going to announce? (4.19) _____

What does this mean? _____

3. What do you think the people in the synagogue understood when he said the words in verse 21? _____

To think about

Jesus came to help the "poor", the "captive", the "blind", and the "oppressed". In what ways are people today poor, captive, blind or oppressed?

_____

_____

_____

II. Jesus   *The Healer*

In the first study, we saw that Jesus was not just an unusual person; he was God's Son. He came into the world in order to meet the deepest needs of men and women.

In this study, we will look at how Jesus met the needs of two particular people. Everywhere Jesus went, he came across needy people. Often, the people he met had incurable diseases, but he was able to change their lives completely by healing them.

He healed Simon's mother-in-law, a Roman officer's servant, a man with a paralyzed hand, a crippled woman, a paralyzed man, people suffering from spiritual and mental disorders, people with skin diseases, blind people, and he even raised the dead. "After the sun had set, people with all kinds of diseases were brought to Jesus. He put his hands on each one of them and healed them" (Luke 4.40).

A. Jesus Heals a Blind Beggar
> Read Luke 18.35-43

1. What do you think life was like for this blind man? _____

2. Why do you think he kept calling for Jesus? _____

3. What did Jesus do and say once he had heard the man? (18.40-42) _____

4. In what way did the man show he believed in Jesus? _____

5. If you had seen this miracle, what would you have thought of Jesus? _____

This was a blind man to whom Jesus gave "sight" (see Luke 4.18). He healed many people of different physical illnesses. But he also healed people in other ways.

B. Jesus and Zacchaeus
The Romans gave the job of collecting taxes to the highest bidder. Tax collectors did not get any wages for their work. They collected as much money as they could so there would be plenty left over for themselves after paying the government. Zacchaeus was one of these tax collectors – a greedy and unpopular man.

> Read Luke 19.1-10

1. What was Zacchaeus' attitude toward Jesus? (19.3,4,6) _____

2. Many people grumbled about Jesus talking to such a man. What was Jesus' attitude toward Zacchaeus? (19.5,9,10) _____

3. How did Zacchaeus change after meeting Jesus? (19.8) _____

4. What do you think Jesus meant by "the lost"? (19.10) _____

5. What does this incident show about Jesus? _____

To think about
Zacchaeus was captive to his own greed. Jesus gave him freedom. Jesus said that he had come "to look for and to save people who are lost" (19.10). People changed when they met Jesus. How do you think meeting Jesus would affect your life?

III. Jesus   *The Teacher*

In the last study, we looked at Jesus the Healer. But people didn't come just to be healed by him; they also wanted to listen to him. Large crowds from all over the country would come to hear what he had to say. He talked about God's Kingdom, prayer, wise and foolish lifestyles, love and forgiveness, and also himself.

Not everyone liked Jesus' teaching. He was outspoken against the religious leaders who were hypocrites. He had enemies who tried to trick him with questions, but he always managed to give wise answers. Even when the religious leaders wanted to kill Jesus, they found it hard because the crowds were "eager to listen to him." (Luke 19.48)

In this study, we will discuss two of the best-known parables (stories which teach biblical truth) that Jesus told.

A. The Good Samaritan
Read Luke 10.25-37

1. What would you say are the most important things in life? _____

Many people went to Jesus with their important questions. For one man, his concern focused on what would happen to him after his death. He asked Jesus what he must do "to have eternal life."

Jesus got the man to answer it himself, from the Scriptures. (Luke 10.27)

_____

Read Luke 10.25-28

2. What did the man say were the two most important things in life? (10.27) _____
What do you think of these answers? _____

Jesus was then asked, "Who are my neighbors?" He answered by telling the story of the good Samaritan.

3. What did the priest and Levite do that was wrong? (10.31,32) _____
Did they break the Law? _____
Did they disobey the principle "I never do anyone any harm"? _____

4. Due to their religions and cultural upbringing, Jews looked upon the Samaritans with contempt. How did the Samaritan in this parable show love?

_____

5. How would you answer the question, "Who is my neighbor?" _____

Jesus acts as a good Samaritan toward us. He sees our needs and failures, and instead of passing by, He reaches out to help.

B. The Lost Son
This is a simple story, yet one of the greatest in the world of literature. It uses the problems that often arise between people to illustrate how men and women react toward God.

Read Luke 15.11-32

1. What do you think the younger son was thinking as he left home? (15.12,13)

_____

Where did he go? (15.13) _____

How do you think the father felt when his son had gone? _____

2. Things went fine for a while. What happened when things got bad? (15.14-16)

_____

3. The son changed his mind. Why? (15.17) _____

How did he show that his attitude had changed? (15.18-20) _____

4. What was the father's attitude? (15.20, 22-24)_____

5. In what ways do you think this story is a picture of our relationship with God?

_____

This story shows us that God still offers his love in spite of our willful selfishness. It also shows us that we can come back to God, no matter how far we have wandered from him.

To think about

What do you identify with more: the attitude of the son as he left home or his attitude when he decided to return? _____

Can you believe that God would accept you as completely as the father accepted his son? _____

You may be at a point in your life where you know that you need God, and want to return to him. Perhaps you would like to pray:

Dear Father, I have wandered away from you, and I have sinned against you. I have not loved you or other people as I should. I want to come back to you now, just as the lost son came back to his father. Please forgive me, and come into my life, so that I can be the person you want me to be. Amen.

The next study will explain what Jesus did to make our return to God possible.

IV. Jesus   *The Redeemer*

At the trial of Jesus it seemed that both the weak-willed Roman governor, Pilate, and the shouts of the crowd sent Jesus to death. In fact, the Bible tells us that these events amazingly formed part of God's purpose.

Jesus took the twelve disciples aside and said to them, "We are now on our way to Jerusalem. Everything that the prophets wrote about the Son of Man will happen there. He will be handed over to foreigners, who will make fun of him, mistreat him, and spit on him. They will beat him and kill him, but three days later he will rise to life." The apostles did not understand what Jesus was talking about. (Luke 18.31-34a)

(See the section at the end of this lesson for background notes on unfamiliar terms.)

A. The Passover

On the last night of his life, Jesus ate a meal with His disciples.

> *Read Luke 22.7-20*

1. What do you think the atmosphere was like during that meal?

_____

2. What did Jesus say about the bread and cup of wine? (22.19,20)

_____

3. What do you think Jesus meant when he said his body was "given for you," and his blood was "poured out for you"?

_____

B. The Council

After the Passover meal Jesus was arrested in the Garden of Gethsemane. He was taken before the Jewish ruling council.

> *Read Luke 22.66-71*

1. What did the Jewish leaders want to find out from Jesus?

_____

2. What did Jesus tell them?

_____

3. How did the Jewish leaders respond? (22.71) _____

C. The Cross

Jesus was not condemned to death for anything he had done. He was condemned for who he claimed to be.

> *Read Luke 23.26-49*

1. What did the following groups say about Jesus:

(23.35) Jewish leaders? _____

(23.36) soldiers? _____

(23.37) the criminal? _____

2. How was the second criminal's reply different from that of the first? (23.39-42)

_____

What did he recognize about Jesus? _____

3. What did the army officer say when Jesus died? (23.47)_____

4. What do you think Jesus' attitude was while he was being crucified? (23.34,43,46)

_____

This study is called "Jesus the Redeemer." To redeem means to buy something back, to recover something by payment. Jesus' death was for the sake of other people, to bring them back to God.

To think about

As the criminal faced his own death, he asked Jesus to remember him in his future kingdom. Jesus promised that the robber would be with him that day in paradise.

In what ways can we have the same hope as that criminal did after hearing Jesus' words? _____

Background notes

Passover (Luke 22.7 and following)

The Passover is an annual religious festival when the Jewish people recall how God rescued their nation from slavery in Egypt. They remember particularly how the angel of death killed the first-born of all Egyptians, yet "passed over" all the Jewish families. God told them they would be protected by sprinkling lamb's blood on their doorposts. It was after this event that the Egyptians finally allowed the Jews to leave Egypt. An important part of the Passover festival was the killing and eating of the Passover lamb.

New covenant (Luke 22.20)

God had promised in the Old Testament (Jeremiah 31.31-34) that he would bring in a new era. This promise became known as the new covenant. In the New Testament Jesus says that this era is now beginning and that his death would confirm it. This is the guarantee that God gives to us that he will forgive us and that we will have a special relationship with him.

Messiah (Luke 22.67)

The Hebrew word "Messiah" means "anointed one." (To anoint someone with olive oil was to honor him or to appoint him to do some special work.) In Greek, the language of the New Testament, "Messiah" is translated "Christ." The Jewish people hoped that the promised Messiah would come as king, to deliver the nation from foreign rule and to set up a righteous, divine kingdom in Israel. There are many verses in the Old Testament that speak of this anointed one who was to come. Although Jesus claimed to be the Messiah, he did not do what the Jewish people expected. Instead he came as a servant and as one who would suffer. His Kingdom was to be established, not in a palace, but in the hearts of men and women. Yet in the end all things were to be brought under his rule.

Son of Man (Luke 22.69)

To describe Himself Jesus used "Son of Man" most often. In Luke 22.69 He refers to an Old Testament passage (Daniel 7.13,14) about a son of a man (human being) who was given an everlasting kingdom. The Jewish people have understood Daniel to be referring to the promised Messiah.

V. Jesus   The Life-Giver

The last chapter of Luke gives a clear account of the fantastic miracle of the resurrection. After Jesus' crucifixion his disciples were afraid of the Jewish leaders. While they continued to meet, they did so in secret. Suddenly, Jesus came to them.

C.S. Lewis, a famous writer and Christian, wrote: "The New Testament writers speak as if Christ's achievement in rising from the dead was the first event of its kind in the whole history of the universe. He has forced open a door that has been locked since the death of the first man. He has met, fought and beaten the king of death."

A. Jesus Is Alive

Read Luke 24.1-53

1. How do you think the disciples felt after seeing Jesus crucified?

_____

News began to reach them that Jesus was alive again. The disciples' reaction shows that they did not expect this. They thought the story was nonsense (24.11). The two on the road said that they were surprised by the news. (24.22) and Jesus himself confirmed that they had doubts in their minds (24.38). Nevertheless, various people became convinced that Jesus had risen from the dead.

2. What convinced the women? (24.5-8) _____

3. What convinced the two people on the road? (24.25-32)

_____

4. What convinced the group of disciples? (24.36-43)

_____

5. How did the disciples' attitude toward Jesus change? (24.52,53)

_____

The resurrection of Jesus Christ was the climax of his life's work. Jesus rose from the dead as he said he would. This challenges us to believe that the other things he said about himself are also true. The resurrection demands a response from us, one way or another.

B. Responding to Jesus

Let's look at one particular woman about whom Luke wrote, and see how she responded to Jesus.

Read Luke 7.36-50

This woman had a bad past. Her behavior toward Jesus was very different from the stiff and starchy response of Simon the Pharisee.

1. Why do you think the woman acted as she did? (7.37,38)

_____

2. Jesus told Simon a story to explain the woman's actions. (7.40-43) Why do you think he did that?

_____

3. How were the woman's sins cleared before God? (7.48) _____

4. What does "faith" mean? (7.50)

_____

5. What did "God give you peace" mean to this woman? (7.50)

_____

She could be sure that she was at peace with God. Jesus had welcomed, accepted and forgiven her because of his love and mercy. Nothing she had done could have earned his response. But she was now free to live as a new person.

We can be sure in this same way. We can never pay God the debt we owe him for our sinful behavior. But, if we come to Jesus as this woman did, we can know that he forgives and accepts us completely. In the last session we discussed how this happens through Jesus' death on our behalf.

C. Becoming a Christian

The sinful woman came to Jesus and recognized her sin. She trusted Jesus to forgive her and, by her actions, thanked him for the new life he offered her. We must do the same if we want to be at peace with God, both now and eternally.

You could pray something like this:

Jesus, I realize that I have been running my own life and have rebelled against you. Thank you for dying for my sins. I open my life to you and ask you to be my Savior and Lord. Make me the kind of person you want me to be. Amen.

D. Growing as a Christian

These five studies have shown us who Jesus is and why he came.

Luke 6.46-49 teaches that we must not only hear what Jesus said, but put it into practice.

Read Luke 6.46-49

A decision to become a Christian is just the beginning of a lifetime of getting to know God better.

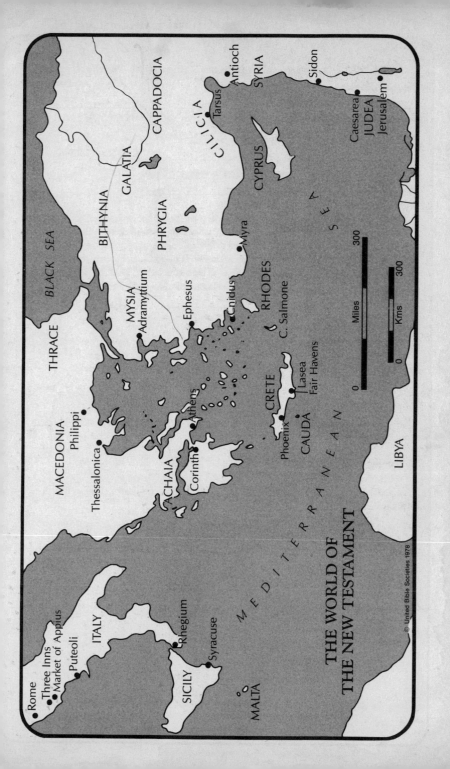

THE WORLD OF
THE NEW TESTAMENT

© United Bible Societies 1978

PALESTINE IN THE TIME OF JESUS

Miles 0 — 40
Kms 0 — 40

MEDITERRANEAN

SEA

Abila
ABILENE
Damascus
Sidon
Zarephath
SYRIA
MT. HERMON
PHOENICIA
LEBANON MTS.
Tyre
Caesarea Philippi
Ptolemais
GALILEE
Chorazin
Capernaum
Bethsaida
MT. CARMEL
Magadan
Lake
Cana
Tiberias
Galilee
Nazareth
MT. TABOR
Nain
Gadara
Caesarea
DECAPOLIS
Salim
SAMARIA
Aenon
Samaria
Gerasa
MT. EBAL
MT. GERIZIM
Sychar
Joppa
Jordan River
Arimathea?
PEREA
Ephraim
Jericho
Emmaus
Bethany
Jerusalem
Azotus
Qumran
Ascalon
JUDEA
Bethlehem
Gaza
Hebron
Dead
Sea
IDUMEA
NABATEA

© United Bible Societies, 1976